Patterns for College Writing

A Rhetorical Reader
and Guide

TENTH EDITION

Patterns for College Writing

A Rhetorical Reader and Guide

LAURIE G. KIRSZNER
UNIVERSITY OF THE SCIENCES IN PHILADELPHIA

STEPHEN R. MANDELL
DREXEL UNIVERSITY

BEDFORD / ST. MARTIN'S

Boston ◆ New York

For Bedford/St. Martin's

Developmental Editor: Joelle Hann
Senior Production Editor: Harold Chester
Production Supervisor: Jennifer Wetzel
Marketing Manager: Karita dos Santos
Art Director: Lucy Krikorian
Text Design: Anne Carter
Copy Editor: Kay Kaylor
Photo Research: Robin Raffer
Cover Design: Donna Dennison
Cover Photo: Photo courtesy of Workbookstock
Composition: Pine Tree Composition, Inc.
Printing and Binding: R.R. Donnelley & Sons Company

President: Joan E. Feinberg
Editorial Director: Denise B. Wydra
Editor in Chief: Nancy Perry
Director of Marketing: Karen Melton Soeltz
Director of Editing, Design, and Production: Marcia Cohen
Managing Editor: Erica T. Appel

Library of Congress Control Number: 2005934865

Manufactured in the United States of America.

2 1 0 9 8 7

f e d c

For information, write: Bedford/St. Martin's, 75 Arlington Street, Boston, MA 02116   (617-399-4000)

ISBN: 0-312-44586-5 (paperback)
       0-312-45460-0 (hardcover)
EAN: 978-0-312-44586-7 (paperback)
       978-0-312-45460-9 (hardcover)

Acknowledgments

For Peter Phelps (1936–1990), with thanks

Preface

Since it was first published, *Patterns for College Writing* has been adopted at over a thousand colleges and universities. We have been delighted by the overwhelmingly positive response to the first nine editions of *Patterns,* and we continue to be gratified by the many instructors who find *Patterns* to be the most accessible and the most pedagogically sound rhetoric-reader they have ever used. In preparing this tenth edition, we have worked hard to fine-tune the features that have made *Patterns* the most popular composition reader available today, and we have tried to develop new features to enhance the book's usefulness for both instructors and students.

What Instructors and Students Like about *Patterns for College Writing*

An Emphasis on Critical Reading

Chapter 1, "Reading to Write: How to Use This Book," prepares students to become analytical readers and writers by showing them how to apply critical reading strategies to a typical selection and by providing sample responses to various kinds of writing prompts. Not only does this chapter introduce students to the book's features, but it also prepares them for reading and writing assignments in other courses.

Extensive Coverage of the Writing Process

Part One, "The Writing Process" (Chapters 2 through 5), is a "mini-rhetoric," offering students advice on drafting, writing, revising, and editing as it introduces them to activities such as freewriting, brainstorming, clustering, and journal writing. These chapters also include some twenty writing exercises to give students opportunities for immediate practice.

Detailed Coverage of the Patterns of Development

In Part Two, "Readings for Writers," Chapters 6 through 14 explain and illustrate the patterns of development that students typically use in their college writing assignments: narration, description, exemplification, process, cause and effect, comparison and contrast, classification and division, definition, and argumentation. Each chapter begins with a comprehensive introduction that presents a definition and a paragraph-length example of the pattern to be discussed and then explains the particular writing strategies and applications associated with it. Next, each chapter analyzes one or two annotated student papers to show how the pattern can be used in particular college writing situations. Chapter 15, "Combining the Patterns," illustrates how the various patterns of development discussed in Chapters 6 through 14 can work together in an essay.

A Diverse and Popular Selection of Readings

Varied in subject, style, and cultural perspective, the seventy-one professional selections engage students while providing them with outstanding models for writing. We have tried to achieve a balance between classic authors (George Orwell, Jessica Mitford, E. B. White, Martin Luther King Jr.) and contemporary voices (Deborah Tannen, Scott Russell Sanders, Amy Tan, Robin Tolmach Lakoff) so that instructors have a broad range to choose from.

More Student Essays Than Any Competing Text

To provide students with realistic models for improving their own writing, we include sixteen sample student essays (two new to this edition). These essays are also available as transparency masters so that instructors can use them more effectively in the classroom. The transparency masters can be obtained as a printed package or as files downloadable from the *Patterns for College Writing* companion Web site, **bedfordstmartins.com/patterns**.

Helpful Coverage of Grammar Issues

Grammar in Context boxes in chapter introductions offer specific advice on how to identify and correct the grammar, mechanics, and punctuation problems that students are likely to encounter when they use particular patterns of development. Practice exercises for mastering these grammar skills are available on *Exercise Central*, a comprehensive online exercise collection accessible at *Patterns'* companion Web site.

Apparatus Designed to Help Students Learn

Each professional essay is followed by four types of questions. These questions are designed to help students assess their understanding of the essay's content and the writer's purpose and audience; to recognize the stylistic and structural techniques used to shape the essay; and to become sensitive to the nuances of language. Each essay is also accompanied by a Journal Entry prompt, Writing Workshop topics (suggestions for the full-length writing assignments), and Thematic Connections that identify related readings in the text. Also following each essay is a Combining the Patterns feature that focuses on different patterns used in the essay and possible alternatives to those patterns. Each chapter ends with a list of Writing Assignments, a Collaborative Activity, and an Internet Assignment. Many of these assignments and activities have been updated to reflect the most current topics as well as the most up-to-date trends and sites available on the Web.

Extensive Cultural and Historical Background for All Readings

In addition to a biographical headnote, each reading is accompanied by a headnote containing essential cultural and historical background information to help students make connections between the reading and the historical, social, and economic forces that shaped it.

An Introduction to Visual Texts

Every rhetorical chapter includes a visual text—such as a photograph, a piece of fine art, or panels from a comic strip—that provides an accessible introduction to each rhetorical pattern. Apparatus that helps students discuss the pattern in its visual form follows each visual.

Thorough Coverage of Writing Research Papers

The appendix, "Using Research in Your Writing," which includes a student research paper that uses MLA format, takes students through the process of writing a research paper—from choosing a topic and finding reliable sources to avoiding plagiarism and documenting both print and online sources. This appendix includes examples of MLA documentation style that follow the guidelines set forth in the *MLA Handbook for Writers of Research Papers,* sixth edition (2003).

What's New in This Edition

Engaging New Readings

The nineteen compelling new professional essays treat topics of current interest—from post-9/11 America to blogs to the history of Monopoly—and represent such writers as comic-book author Gerard Jones, noted playwright Arthur Miller, and novelist Isabel Allende. Readings have been carefully selected for their effectiveness as teachable models for student writing. In addition, with more argumentative and informative essays than in previous editions, *Patterns* now offers students even more models for critical thinking and writing.

A New Chapter on Recognizing Sentence-Level Problems

A new chapter has been added to Part One, "The Writing Process." Chapter 5, "Editing and Proofreading," offers specific advice on how to identify and address the grammar, punctuation, and mechanics problems common in many student essays. Checklists give students quick reference guides to essential skills, while cross-references to Grammar in Context boxes and to *Exercise Central* provide them with additional explanations, examples, and practice.

Two New Debates in the Argumentation Chapter

The argumentation chapter has been thoroughly revised and updated to include two new paired arguments — one on the controversy surrounding Wal-Mart superstores and one on recent proposals to bring back the military draft.

More Support for Peer Editing

Peer editing worksheets now appear in the introduction to each rhetorical chapter to help students develop writing, revising, and editing skills with the support of their classmates. These worksheets are also downloadable from the *Patterns* companion Web site.

More Advice on Analyzing Visual Texts

Because today's students need to interpret visuals as well as written texts, *Patterns* now provides more guidance — and more examples — for analyzing visuals and for incorporating them effectively into student essays. (Two of the student essays now include visuals.)

Expanded Coverage of Using Sources

To help students identify and use reliable sources, the research appendix offers expanded coverage of how to find appropriate sources in the library and on the Internet, as well as how to paraphrase, summarize, and quote source material and integrate it into papers.

New Color Design

Color throughout the book now highlights popular features — such as checklists, Grammar in Context boxes, and annotated student essays — and facilitates reading. Professional essays, headnotes, and apparatus have been redesigned to further enhance comprehension.

Extensive Support for Students and Instructors

Support for Student Writers

Four CD-ROMs, each packageable for free upon request, offer students extra practice with writing and editing skills, analyzing visual texts, making arguments, and documenting sources.

- *Exercise Central to Go* contains hundreds of practice items to help students build their writing and editing skills. Drawn from the popular *Exercise Central* Web site, the practices have been extensively class tested and provide instant feedback. No Internet connection is necessary.

- *ix: visual exercises* offers a new way for students to focus on visual rhetoric, with nine exercises that give them a vocabulary to use as they read and write about different kinds of texts.

- *i-claim: visualizing argument* offers a new way for students to see argument, with six tutorials, an illustrated glossary, and more than seventy multimedia arguments.

- *i-cite: visualizing sources* allows students to practice working with all types of sources, from Web sites to audio and video clips.

Support for Instructors

The extensive ancillary package available to instructors who adopt *Patterns* includes the following items:

- An *Instructor's Edition,* incorporating *Resources for Instructors,* gives instructors guidance in teaching from the text and provides sample answers to the questions that follow each reading. (*Resources for Instructors* is also available as a separate booklet.)

- *Transparency Masters* feature ten peer editing worksheets, ten Grammar in Context boxes, and sixteen sample student essays (available as a printed package and as files downloadable from the *Patterns for College Writing* companion Web site).

Patterns for College Writing Companion Web Site

For students who need more practice in mastering specific grammatical skills, the companion Web site at **bedfordstmartins.com/patterns** includes *Exercise Central*—a unique online collection of more than 8,000 exercise items conveniently arranged by topic that enable students to practice essential grammar skills and get immediate feedback on their progress. In addition, the companion site now offers access to a free online collection of Web resources for the writing class at *Re:Writing*, including plagiarism tutorials, model documents, research guides, bibliography tools, and much more.

For instructors, the companion Web site offers a downloadable version of *Resources for Instructors to Accompany* PATTERNS FOR COLLEGE WRITING; downloadable files of the transparency masters and peer editing worksheets; access to Reading Quizzes and grade book for each reading in the book; access to TopLinks, a database that guides students to the best links available on the most commonly chosen writing topics; and access to further debate topics, Internet assignments, and author research.

Acknowledgments

As always, friends, colleagues, students, and family all helped this project along. Of particular value were the responses to questionnaires sent to users of the ninth edition, and we thank each of the instructors who responded so frankly and helpfully: Marilyn Bauer, Leeward Community College; April Childress, Greenville Technical College; Jennifer Clay, Okaloosa-Walton College; Christine A. Colón, Wheaton College; Jeff Cox, Seminole State College; Nancy Durham, Wharton County Junior College; Muriel Fuqua, Daytona Beach Community College; Melita Gardner, Okaloosa-Walton College; Scott Grunow, University of Illinois at Chicago; John Hare, Montgomery College—Germantown Campus; Francesca Hitchcock, Bessemer State Technical College; Thomasita Homan, Benedictine College; Vickie Hunt, Okaloosa-Walton College; Alyson Indrunas, Everett Community College; Stephen Lambert, Hillsborough Community College; Alice Longaker, University of Northern Colorado; John Lusk, St. Clair County Community College; David Luther, Middle Georgia College; J. D. Marshall, North Country Community College; Jim Martin, Mount Ida College; Michael McAllister, Iowa Western Community College; Trish Mercer, Southern Virginia University; Rebecca Mills, Hillsborough Community College; Deborah Nester, Okaloosa-Walton College; Sean Nighbert, St. Philip's College; Mary Peterson, Carl Sandburg College; Michael Powell, Shawnee State University; Lynette Shaw-Smith, Springfield College in Illinois; Phil Snider, Casper College; Rosie Soy, Hudson County Community College; Marie Stokes, Stark State College of Technology; Philip Stucky, Harold Washington College; Basak Tarkan-Blanco, Miami Dade College—Kendall Campus; Edward Washington, Mansfield University of Pennsylvania; Pamela Watkins, Los Angeles Harbor College; Patrice Williams, Okaloosa-Walton College; Maggie Wood, Klamath Community College.

Special thanks go to Mark Gallaher, a true professional and a valued friend, for revising the headnotes and the *Resources for Instructors* for this edition.

Through ten editions of *Patterns for College Writing,* we have enjoyed a wonderful working relationship with Bedford/St. Martin's. We have always found the editorial and production staff to be efficient, cooperative, and generous with their time and advice. As always, we appreciate the encouragement and advice of our longtime friend, editor in chief Nancy Perry. In addition, we thank Joan Feinberg, president of Bedford/St. Martin's, for her support for this project and for her trust in us. During our work on this edition, we have benefited from our productive relationship with Joelle Hann, development editor, who worked long hours to help us make this edition of *Patterns* the best it could be. We are also grateful to Harold Chester, senior project editor, and to Jennifer Wetzel, production supervisor, for their work overseeing the production of this edition; to Lucy Krikorian and Donna Dennison, art directors, for the attractive new cover and design; to New Media editor Coleen O'Hanley, for her work on the *Patterns for College Writing* Web site; and to editorial assistant Robin Butterhof for her invaluable help with tasks large and small.

We are fortunate to have enjoyed our more than twenty-five years of collaboration; we know how rare a successful partnership like ours is. We also know how lucky we are to have our families — Mark, Adam, and Rebecca Kirszner and Demi, David, and Sarah Mandell — to help keep us in touch with the things that really matter.

Laurie G. Kirszner
Stephen R. Mandell

Contents

Preface   *vii*

Thematic Guide to the Contents   *xxxvii*

1 Reading to Write: How to Use This Book   *1*

READING CRITICALLY   *1*

READING ACTIVELY   *2*
  Before You Read   *2*
  As You Read   *2*
  ✔ CHECKLIST: READING ACTIVELY   *2*

HIGHLIGHTING AND ANNOTATING   *3*

READING THE ESSAYS IN THIS BOOK   *4*

HENRY LOUIS GATES JR., *"What's in a Name?"*   *5*

RESPONDING TO AN ESSAY   *7*

PART ONE: THE WRITING PROCESS   *13*

2 Invention   *15*

UNDERSTANDING YOUR ASSIGNMENT   *15*

SETTING LIMITS   *16*
  Length   *16*
  Purpose   *16*

Audience   *17*
Occasion   *18*
Knowledge   *18*

✔ **CHECKLIST: SETTING LIMITS**   *19*

MOVING FROM SUBJECT TO TOPIC   *20*
Questions for Probing   *21*

✔ **CHECKLIST: QUESTIONS FOR PROBING**   *21*
Freewriting   *23*

➤ **A STUDENT WRITER: FREEWRITING**   *24*

FINDING SOMETHING TO SAY   *25*
Brainstorming   *25*

➤ **A STUDENT WRITER: BRAINSTORMING**   *25*
Journal Writing   *27*

➤ **A STUDENT WRITER: JOURNAL WRITING**   *27*

GROUPING IDEAS   *28*
Clustering   *28*

➤ **A STUDENT WRITER: CLUSTERING**   *28*
Making an Informal Outline   *29*

➤ **A STUDENT WRITER: MAKING AN INFORMAL OUTLINE**   *29*

UNDERSTANDING THESIS AND SUPPORT   *30*

FORMULATING A THESIS   *30*
Defining the Thesis Statement   *30*
Deciding on a Thesis   *31*
Stating Your Thesis   *32*
Implying a Thesis   *33*

➤ **A STUDENT WRITER: FORMULATING A THESIS**   *33*

3 Arrangement   *37*

RECOGNIZING A PATTERN   *37*

✔ **CHECKLIST: RECOGNIZING A PATTERN**   *38*

UNDERSTANDING THE PARTS OF THE ESSAY   *38*
The Introduction   *39*
The Body Paragraphs   *41*

✔ **CHECKLIST: EFFECTIVE SUPPORT**   *44*
The Conclusion   *46*

CONSTRUCTING A FORMAL OUTLINE   *47*

✔ **CHECKLIST: CONSTRUCTING A FORMAL OUTLINE**   *48*

➤ **A STUDENT WRITER: CONSTRUCTING A FORMAL OUTLINE**   *48*

4 Drafting and Revising   *51*

WRITING YOUR FIRST DRAFT   *51*

✔ **CHECKLIST: DRAFTING**   *51*

➤ **A STUDENT WRITER: WRITING A FIRST DRAFT**   *52*

REVISING YOUR ESSAY   *53*

    Revising with a Checklist   *54*

✔ **CHECKLIST: REVISING**   *54*

    Revising with an Outline   *55*

    Revising with a Peer Critique   *55*

✔ **CHECKLIST: GUIDELINES FOR PEER CRITIQUES**   *56*

    Revising with Your Instructor's Comments   *56*

➤ **A STUDENT WRITER: REVISING A FIRST DRAFT**   *57*

POINTS FOR SPECIAL ATTENTION: FIRST DRAFT   *58*

    The Introduction   *58*

    The Body Paragraphs   *59*

    The Conclusion   *59*

➤ **A STUDENT WRITER: REVISING A SECOND DRAFT**   *59*

POINTS FOR SPECIAL ATTENTION: SECOND DRAFT   *61*

    The Introduction   *61*

    The Body Paragraphs   *61*

    The Conclusion   *62*

    The Title   *62*

➤ **A STUDENT WRITER: PREPARING A FINAL DRAFT**   *62*

➤ **SAMPLE STUDENT ESSAY: LAURA BOBNAK, *THE PRICE OF SILENCE***   *62*

5 Editing and Proofreading   *67*

EDITING FOR GRAMMAR   *67*

    Be Sure Subjects and Verbs Agree   *67*

    Be Sure Verb Tenses Are Accurate and Consistent   *68*

    Be Sure Pronoun References Are Clear   *68*

    Be Sure Sentences Are Complete   *69*

    Be Careful Not to Run Sentences Together without Proper
      Punctuation   *69*

    Be Careful to Avoid Misplaced and Dangling Modifiers   *70*

    Be Sure Sentence Elements Are Parallel   *70*

✔ **CHECKLIST: EDITING FOR GRAMMAR**   *71*

EDITING FOR PUNCTUATION   *71*

    Learn When to Use Commas—and When Not to Use Them   *71*

Learn When to Use Semicolons   *72*
Learn When to Use Quotation Marks   *72*
Learn When to Use Dashes and Colons   *73*

✔ **CHECKLIST: EDITING FOR PUNCTUATION**   *73*

EDITING FOR SENTENCE STYLE AND WORD CHOICE   *74*
Eliminate Awkward Phrasing   *74*
Be Sure Your Sentences Are Concise   *75*
Be Sure Your Sentences Are Varied   *75*
Choose Your Words Carefully   *76*

✔ **CHECKLIST: EDITING FOR SENTENCE STYLE AND WORD CHOICE**   *76*

PROOFREADING YOUR ESSAY   *76*
Check for Commonly Confused Words   *76*
Check for Misspellings and Faulty Capitalization   *77*
Check for Correct Use of Underlining and Italics   *77*
Check for Typos   *77*

✔ **CHECKLIST: PROOFREADING**   *77*

CHECKING MANUSCRIPT FORMAT   *78*

✔ **CHECKLIST: CHECKING MANUSCRIPT FORMAT**   *78*

PART TWO: READINGS FOR WRITERS   *81*

6 NARRATION   *83*

WHAT IS NARRATION?   *83*

USING NARRATION   *83*

PLANNING A NARRATIVE ESSAY   *84*
Including Enough Detail   *84*
Varying Sentence Structure   *85*
Maintaining Clear Narrative Order   *85*

STRUCTURING A NARRATIVE ESSAY   *86*

REVISING A NARRATIVE ESSAY   *87*

✔ **REVISION CHECKLIST: NARRATION**   *87*

EDITING A NARRATIVE ESSAY   *87*

GRAMMAR IN CONTEXT: AVOIDING RUN-ON SENTENCES   *88*

✔ **EDITING CHECKLIST: NARRATION**   *89*

➤ **A STUDENT WRITER: NARRATION**   *89*

➤ **SAMPLE STUDENT ESSAY: TIFFANY FORTE,** *MY FIELD OF DREAMS* 89
  Points for Special Attention *91*
  Focus on Revision *92*

  📄 **PEER EDITING WORKSHEET: NARRATION** *93*

VISUAL TEXT: MARVEL COMICS, From *Spider-Man* **(Comic Book)** *94*

SANDRA CISNEROS, *Only Daughter* *96*
  "Being only a daughter for my father meant my destiny would lead me to become someone's wife. That's what he believed."

MAYA ANGELOU, *Finishing School* *101*
  "It went without saying that all girls could iron and wash, but the finer touches around the home, like setting a table with real silver, baking roasts, and cooking vegetables without meat, had to be learned elsewhere. . . . During my tenth year, a white woman's kitchen became my finishing school."

BONNIE SMITH-YACKEL, *My Mother Never Worked* *108*
  "From her wheelchair she canned pickles, baked bread, ironed clothes, wrote dozens of letters weekly to her friends and her 'half dozen or more kids,' and made three patchwork housecoats and one quilt."

DANIEL GROSS, *Playing by the Rules* *114*
  "At the center of Parker Brothers' unlikely story, told by former executive Philip E. Orbanes in his recently published book, *The Game Makers,* lies an insight on the business of games, and on the game of business, that sprung from the mind of a teenager in Victorian New England."

MARTIN GANSBERG, *Thirty-Eight Who Saw Murder Didn't Call the Police* *120*
  "For more than half an hour 38 respectable, law-abiding citizens in Queens watched a killer stalk and stab a woman in three separate attacks. . . . Not one person telephoned the police during the assault; one witness called after the woman was dead."

GEORGE ORWELL, *Shooting an Elephant* *125*
  "But I did not want to shoot the elephant. I watched him beating his bunch of grass against his knees, with the preoccupied grandmotherly air that elephants have. It seemed to me that it would be murder to shoot him."

SHERMAN ALEXIE, *Indian Education* **(Fiction)** *134*
  "The farm town high school I play for is nicknamed the 'Indians,' and I'm probably the only actual Indian ever to play for a team with such a mascot."

  Writing Assignments for Narration *140*
  Collaborative Activity for Narration *141*
  Internet Assignment for Narration *141*

7 DESCRIPTION   *143*

WHAT IS DESCRIPTION?   *143*

USING DESCRIPTION   *144*
　　Understanding Objective and Subjective Description   *144*
　　Using Objective and Subjective Language   *147*
　　Selecting Details   *148*

PLANNING A DESCRIPTIVE ESSAY   *149*
　　Organizing Details   *149*
　　Using Transitions   *149*

STRUCTURING A DESCRIPTIVE ESSAY   *150*

REVISING A DESCRIPTIVE ESSAY   *150*
　　✔ **REVISON CHECKLIST: DESCRIPTION**   *151*

EDITING A DESCRIPTIVE ESSAY   *151*
　　GRAMMAR IN CONTEXT: AVOIDING MISPLACED AND DANGLING
　　　　MODIFIERS   *151*
　　✔ **EDITING CHECKLIST: DESCRIPTION**   *153*
　　➤ **STUDENT WRITERS: DESCRIPTION**   *153*
　　➤ SAMPLE STUDENT ESSAY: **JAMES GREGGS,** *BUILDING AND LEARNING*   *153*
　　　　Points for Special Attention   *155*
　　　　Focus on Revision   *156*
　　➤ SAMPLE STUDENT ESSAY: **MARY LIM,** *THE VALLEY OF WINDMILLS*   *156*
　　　　Points for Special Attention   *157*
　　　　Focus on Revision   *158*
　　　📄 PEER EDITING WORKSHEET: DESCRIPTION   *159*

VISUAL TEXT: VINCENT LAFORET, *Girls in Front of 9/11 Mural*
(Photo)   *160*

SUZANNE BERNE, *Ground Zero*   *162*

"Like me, perhaps, the people around me had in mind images from television and newspaper pictures: the collapsing buildings, the running office workers, the black plume of smoke against a bright blue sky. Like me, they were probably trying to superimpose those terrible images onto the industrious emptiness right in front of them."

LEAH HAGER COHEN, *Words Left Unspoken*   *168*

"My earliest memories of Sam Cohen are of his chin, which I remember as fiercely hard and pointy."

ISABEL ALLENDE, *The Amazon Queen*   *173*

"How shall I describe the Amazon? . . . From the airplane, it is a vast green world. Below, on the ground it is the kingdom of water: vapor, rain, rivers broad as oceans, sweat."

N. Scott Momaday, *The Way to Rainy Mountain*   *180*

"A single knoll rises out of the plain in Oklahoma, north and west of the Wichita Range. For my people, the Kiowas, it is an old landmark, and they gave it the name Rainy Mountain."

E. B. White, *Once More to the Lake*   *186*

"Summertime, oh summertime, pattern of life indelible, the fade-proof lake, the woods unshatterable, the pasture with the sweetfern and the juniper forever and ever."

Kate Chopin, *The Storm* **(Fiction)**   *194*

"They did not heed the crashing torrents, and the roar of the elements made her laugh as she lay in his arms. She was a revelation in that dim, mysterious chamber; as white as the couch she lay upon."

Writing Assignments for Description   *200*
Collaborative Activity for Description   *200*
Internet Assignment for Description   *201*

8 EXEMPLIFICATION   *203*

WHAT IS EXEMPLIFICATION?   *203*

USING EXEMPLIFICATION   *204*
   Using Examples to Explain and Clarify   *204*
   Using Examples to Add Interest   *204*
   Using Examples to Persuade   *205*
   Using Examples to Test Your Thesis   *205*

PLANNING AN EXEMPLIFICATION ESSAY   *206*
   Providing Enough Examples   *206*
   Choosing a Fair Range of Examples   *206*
   Using Transitions   *207*

STRUCTURING AN EXEMPLIFICATION ESSAY   *207*

REVISING AN EXEMPLIFICATION ESSAY   *208*

  ✔ **REVISION CHECKLIST: EXEMPLIFICATION**   *209*

EDITING AN EXEMPLIFICATION ESSAY   *209*

  GRAMMAR IN CONTEXT: USING COMMAS IN A SERIES   *209*

  ✔ **EDITING CHECKLIST: EXEMPLIFICATION**   *210*

  ➤ **STUDENT WRITERS: EXEMPLIFICATION**   *210*

  ➤ **SAMPLE STUDENT ESSAY: KRISTY BREDIN,** *JOB APPLICATION LETTER*   *211*
   Points for Special Attention   *212*
   Focus on Revision   *213*

  ➤ **SAMPLE STUDENT ESSAY: GRACE KU,** *MIDNIGHT*   *213*
   Points for Special Attention   *215*

Focus on Revision   *216*

📄 PEER EDITING WORKSHEET: EXEMPLIFICATION   *216*

VISUAL TEXTS: FOUR TATTOOS (Photos): ALEX WILLIAMS, *"Lisa Karen"*; JOEL GORDON, *"Rose"*; CHARLES GATEWOOD, *"Body Art"*; AND BOB DAEMMRICH, *"Jiminy Cricket"*   *218*

LAURENCE J. PETER AND RAYMOND HULL, *The Peter Principle*   *220*

"My Principle is the key to an understanding of all hierarchical systems, and therefore to an understanding of the whole structure of civilization."

DAVID J. BIRNBAUM, *The Catbird Seat*   *227*

"Cutting the lines at the Department of Motor Vehicles to renew my driver's license, getting out of speeding tickets and arriving late to work without a reprimand are my 'even uppers' for my physical limitations and for the difficulties caused by establishments not complying with the Americans with Disabilities Act."

PHIL PATTON, *Innovation*   *231*

"The impact of some innovations, such as jet planes, has been striking in its predictability. But small innovations have wrought surprisingly large and unexpected changes in daily life too. Here are enough innovations, large and small, to count on all 10 of what used to be called digits—your fingers."

BRENT STAPLES, *Just Walk On By: A Black Man Ponders His Power to Alter Public Space*   *240*

"It was in the echo of that terrified woman's footfalls that I first began to know the unwieldy inheritance I'd come into—the ability to alter public space in ugly ways."

DICK TERESI, *Star-Spangled Stupidity*   *246*

"This July 4 holiday will no doubt cause a lot of people 'to put out more flags,' to borrow a phrase from Evelyn Waugh's 1941 novel about wartime patriotism. All well and good. But can't it be done the right way? Since September 11, 2001, the American flag has come in for a strange kind of abuse from 'overnight patriots.'"

JONATHAN KOZOL, *The Human Cost of an Illiterate Society*   *252*

"Do we possess the character and courage to address a problem which so many nations, poorer than our own, have found it natural to correct?"

GRACE PALEY, *Samuel* (Fiction)   *262*

"Some boys are very tough. They're afraid of nothing. They are the ones who climb a wall and take a bow at the top. . . . They also jiggle and hop on the platform between the locked doors of the subway cars."

Writing Assignments for Exemplification   *265*
Collaborative Activity for Exemplification   *265*
Internet Assignment for Exemplification   *266*

9 PROCESS *267*

WHAT IS PROCESS? *267*
    Understanding Instructions *268*
    Understanding Process Explanations *268*

USING PROCESS *269*

PLANNING A PROCESS ESSAY *269*
    Accommodating Your Audience *269*
    Using Transitions *270*

STRUCTURING A PROCESS ESSAY *270*

REVISING A PROCESS ESSAY *271*

  ✔ **REVISION CHECKLIST: PROCESS** *271*

EDITING A PROCESS ESSAY *271*

  GRAMMAR IN CONTEXT: **AVOIDING UNNECESSARY SHIFTS** *272*

  ✔ **EDITING CHECKLIST: PROCESS** *274*

  ➤ **STUDENT WRITERS: PROCESS** *274*

  ➤ **SAMPLE STUDENT ESSAY: ERIC McGLADE,** *THE SEARCH* *274*
    Points for Special Attention *277*
    Focus on Revision *278*

  ➤ **SAMPLE STUDENT ESSAY: MELANY HUNT,** *MEDIUM ASH BROWN* *279*
    Points for Special Attention *280*
    Focus on Revision *281*

  📄 **PEER EDITING WORKSHEET: PROCESS** *282*

VISUAL TEXT: NIGEL HOLMES, *How to Cover Scratches on Furniture* **(Illustration)** *283*

MALCOLM X, *My First Conk* *285*

"My first view in the mirror blotted out the hurting. I'd seen some pretty conks, but when it's the first time, on your *own* head, the transformation, after the lifetime of kinks, is staggering."

MARCIA MULLER, *Creating a Female Sleuth* *290*

"The process of creating my sleuth, Sharon McCone, and plotting her first case—*Edwin of the Iron Shoes*—presented a number of technical problems. Because female sleuths are in themselves a rarity, my imaginary friend could not be too unusual or too much of a superwoman if modern readers—both male and female—were to identify with her."

JOSHUA PIVEN, DAVID BORGENICHT, AND JENNIFER WORICK, *How to Escape from a Bad Date* *297*

"If you do not think you will be able to change your appearance enough to slip past your date, you may have to find another way to depart. Back doors are the simplest; they are often located near the restrooms or are marked as fire exits. Do not open an emergency exit door if it is alarmed unless absolutely necessary; an alarm will only draw attention."

ARTHUR MILLER, *Get It Right: Privatize Executions* *305*

"People can be executed in places like Shea Stadium before immense paying audiences. . . . As with all sports events, a certain ritual would seem inevitable and would quickly become an expected part of the occasion."

JESSICA MITFORD, *The Embalming of Mr. Jones* *310*

"For those who have the stomach for it, let us part the formaldehyde curtain."

SHIRLEY JACKSON, *The Lottery* (Fiction) *317*

"There was a great deal of fussing to be done before Mr. Summers declared the lottery open. There were the lists to make up — of heads of families, heads of households in each family, members of each household in each family."

Writing Assignments for Process *325*
Collaborative Activity for Process *325*
Internet Assignment for Process *326*

10 CAUSE AND EFFECT *327*

WHAT IS CAUSE AND EFFECT? *327*

USING CAUSE AND EFFECT *328*
Understanding Main and Contributory Causes *329*
Understanding Immediate and Remote Causes *330*
Understanding Causal Chains *331*
Avoiding *Post Hoc* Reasoning *332*

PLANNING A CAUSE-AND-EFFECT ESSAY *333*
Purpose and Thesis *334*
Order and Sequence *334*
Using Transitions *334*

STRUCTURING A CAUSE-AND-EFFECT ESSAY *335*
Finding Causes *335*
Describing or Predicting Effects *336*

REVISING A CAUSE-AND-EFFECT ESSAY *336*
✔ **REVISION CHECKLIST: CAUSE AND EFFECT** *336*

EDITING A CAUSE-AND-EFFECT ESSAY *337*
GRAMMAR IN CONTEXT: AVOIDING "THE REASON IS BECAUSE"; USING *AFFECT* AND *EFFECT* CORRECTLY *337*
✔ **EDITING CHECKLIST: CAUSE AND EFFECT** *338*
➤ **A STUDENT WRITER: CAUSE AND EFFECT** *338*
➤ **SAMPLE STUDENT ESSAY: EVELYN PELLICANE, *THE IRISH FAMINE, 1845–1849*** *338*
Points for Special Attention *341*

Focus on Revision *342*

📄 PEER EDITING WORKSHEET: CAUSE AND EFFECT *342*

VISUAL TEXT: LOUIS REQUENA, *Major League Baseball Brawl*
(Photo) *344*

NORMAN COUSINS, *Who Killed Benny Paret?* *346*

" 'They don't come out to see a tea party,' he said evenly. 'They come out to
see the knockout. They come out to see a man hurt. If they think anything
else, they're kidding themselves.' "

MARIE WINN, *Television: The Plug-In Drug* *351*

"Television's contribution to family life has been an equivocal one. For while
it has, indeed, kept the members of the family from dispersing, it has not
served to bring them together."

KATHA POLLITT, *Why Boys Don't Play with Dolls* *361*

"Instead of looking at kids to 'prove' that differences in behavior by sex are
innate, we can look at the ways we raise kids as an index to how unfinished
the feminist revolution really is, and how tentatively it is embraced even by
adults who fully expect their daughters to enter previously male-dominated
professions and their sons to change diapers."

LAWRENCE OTIS GRAHAM, *The "Black Table" Is Still There* *366*

"What did the table say about the integration that was supposedly going on
in home rooms and gym classes? What did it say about the black kids? The
white kids? What did it say about me when I refused to sit there, day after
day, for three years?"

LINDA M. HASSELSTROM, *A Peaceful Woman Explains Why She Carries
a Gun* *371*

"People who have not grown up with the idea that they are capable of protecting themselves — in other words, most women — might have to work hard
to convince themselves of their ability, and of the necessity. Handgun ownership need not turn us into gunslingers, but it can be part of believing in,
and relying on, *ourselves* for protection."

ROBIN TOLMACH LAKOFF, *The Power of Words in Wartime* *377*

"In wartime, language must be created to enable combatants and noncombatants alike to see the other side as killable, to overcome the innate queasiness over the taking of human life. Soldiers, and those who remain at home,
learn to call their enemies by names that make them seem not quite human — inferior, contemptible and not like 'us.' "

JANICE MIRIKITANI, *Suicide Note* (Poetry) *382*

"I apologize.
Tasks do not come easily.
Each failure, a glacier.
Each disapproval, a bootprint.
Each disappointment,
ice above my river."

Writing Assignments for Cause and Effect   *385*
Collaborative Activity for Cause and Effect   *386*
Internet Assignment for Cause and Effect   *386*

11 COMPARISON AND CONTRAST   *387*

WHAT IS COMPARISON AND CONTRAST?   *387*

USING COMPARISON AND CONTRAST   *388*

PLANNING A COMPARISON-AND-CONTRAST ESSAY   *388*
Recognizing Comparison-and-Contrast Assignments   *389*
Establishing a Basis for Comparison   *389*
Selecting Points for Discussion   *390*
Formulating a Thesis Statement   *390*

STRUCTURING A COMPARISON-AND-CONTRAST ESSAY   *391*
Using Subject-by-Subject Comparison   *391*
Using Point-by-Point Comparison   *392*
Using Transitions   *393*

REVISING A COMPARISON-AND-CONTRAST ESSAY   *393*

✔ **REVISION CHECKLIST: COMPARISON AND CONTRAST**   *394*

EDITING A COMPARISON-AND-CONTRAST ESSAY   *394*

GRAMMAR IN CONTEXT: **USING PARALLELISM**   *394*

✔ **EDITING CHECKLIST: COMPARISON AND CONTRAST**   *395*

➤ **STUDENT WRITERS: COMPARISON AND CONTRAST**   *395*

➤ **SAMPLE STUDENT ESSAY: MARK COTHARN, *BRAINS VERSUS BRAWN***   *396*
Points for Special Attention   *399*
Focus on Revision   *400*

➤ **SAMPLE STUDENT ESSAY: MARIA TECSON, *A COMPARISON OF TWO WEB SITES ON ATTENTION DEFICIT DISORDER***   *401*
Points for Special Attention   *404*
Focus on Revision   *405*

📄**PEER EDITING WORKSHEET: COMPARISON AND CONTRAST**   **406**

Visual Texts: Auguste Rodin, *The Kiss,* and Robert Indiana, *LOVE* (Sculpture)   *407*

Bruce Catton, *Grant and Lee: A Study in Contrasts*   *409*

"When Ulysses S. Grant and Robert E. Lee met in the parlor of a modest house at Appomattox Court House, Virginia, on April 9, 1865, to work out the terms for the surrender of Lee's Army of Northern Virginia, a great chapter in American life came to a close, and a great new chapter began."

Bharati Mukherjee, *Two Ways to Belong in America*   *415*

"This is a tale of two sisters from Calcutta, Mira and Bharati, who have lived in the United States for some 35 years, but who find themselves on different sides in the current debate over the status of immigrants."

YI-FU TUAN, *Chinese Space, American Space* 421

"[T]he Chinese desire for stability and rootedness in place is prompted by the constant threat of war, exile, and the natural disasters of flood and drought. Forcible removal makes the Chinese keenly aware of their loss. By contrast, Americans move, for the most part, voluntarily."

JOHN DE GRAAF, DAVID WANN, AND THOMAS H. NAYLOR, *Swollen Expectations* 425

"Liberal economists argue that since about 1973 the real wages earned by middle-class Americans haven't really risen much . . . But one thing is incontestable: *We have a lot more stuff and much higher material expectations than previous generations did.*"

IAN FRAZIER, *Dearly Disconnected* 434

"I'm interested in pay phones in general these days, especially when I get the feeling that they are about to go away. Technology, in the form of sleek little phones in our pockets, has swept on by them and made them begin to seem antique."

DEBORAH TANNEN, *Sex, Lies, and Conversation* 440

"How can women and men have such different impressions of communication in marriage? Why the widespread imbalance in their interests and expectations?"

GWENDOLYN BROOKS, *Sadie and Maud* (Poetry) 447

"Maud went to college.
Sadie stayed at home.
Sadie scraped life
With a fine-tooth comb."

Writing Assignments for Comparison and Contrast *449*
Collaborative Activity for Comparison and Contrast *449*
Internet Assignment for Comparison and Contrast *450*

12   CLASSIFICATION AND DIVISION   451

WHAT IS CLASSIFICATION AND DIVISION? *451*
   Understanding Classification *452*
   Understanding Division *452*

USING CLASSIFICATION AND DIVISION *452*

PLANNING A CLASSIFICATION-AND-DIVISION ESSAY *453*
   Selecting and Arranging Categories *453*
   ✔ CHECKLIST: ESTABLISHING CATEGORIES *454*
   Formulating a Thesis Statement *454*
   Using Transitions *454*

STRUCTURING A CLASSIFICATION-AND-DIVISION ESSAY *455*

REVISING A CLASSIFICATION-AND-DIVISION ESSAY   *456*

✔ **REVISION CHECKLIST: CLASSIFICATION AND DIVISION**   *456*

EDITING A CLASSIFICATION-AND-DIVISION ESSAY   *457*

GRAMMAR IN CONTEXT: **USING A COLON TO INTRODUCE YOUR CATEGORIES**   *457*

✔ **EDITING CHECKLIST: CLASSIFICATION AND DIVISION**   *458*

➤ **A STUDENT WRITER: CLASSIFICATION AND DIVISION**   *458*

➤ **SAMPLE STUDENT ESSAY: JOSIE MARTINEZ, *WHAT I LEARNED (AND DIDN'T LEARN) IN COLLEGE***   *458*

Points for Special Attention   *461*

Focus on Revision   *462*

📄 **PEER EDITING WORKSHEET: CLASSIFICATION AND DIVISION**   *462*

Visual Texts: Ellis Island Immigration Museum/NPS, *Key to Chalk Marks Designating Medical Conditions of Immigrants, Ellis Island* (Chart)   *464*

Office of the Public Health Service Historian, *Eye Exam Administered to Immigrants, Ellis Island, 1910* (Photo)   *465*

William Zinsser, *College Pressures*   *466*

"What I wish for all students is some release from the clammy grip of the future. I wish them a chance to savor each segment of their education as an experience in itself and not as a grim preparation for the next step. I wish them the right to experiment, to trip and fall, to learn that defeat is as instructive as victory and is not the end of the world."

Carolyn Foster Segal, *The Dog Ate My Disk, and Other Tales of Woe*   *475*

"With a show of energy and creativity that would be admirable if applied to the (missing) assignments in question, my students persist, week after week, semester after semester, year after year, in offering excuses about why their work is not ready. Those reasons fall into several broad categories: the family, the best friend, the evils of dorm life, the evils of technology, and the totally bizarre."

Scott Russell Sanders, *The Men We Carry in Our Minds*   *481*

"So I was baffled when the women at college accused me and my sex of having cornered the world's pleasures. I think something like my bafflement has been felt by other boys (and by girls as well) who grew up in dirt-poor farm country, in mining country, in black ghettos, in Hispanic barrios, in the shadows of factories, in Third World nations—any place where the fate of men is as grim and bleak as the fate of women."

Amy Tan, *Mother Tongue*   *487*

"I spend a great deal of my time thinking about the power of language—the way it can evoke an emotion, a visual image, a complex idea, or a simple truth.

Language is the tool of my trade. And I use them all — all the Englishes I grew up with."

STEPHANIE ERICSSON, *The Ways We Lie*   *495*

"We lie. We all do. We exaggerate, we minimize, we avoid confrontation, we spare people's feelings, we conveniently forget, we keep secrets, we justify lying to the big-guy institutions."

EDWIN BROCK, *Five Ways to Kill a Man* (Poetry)   *505*

"These are, as I began, cumbersome ways
to kill a man. Simpler, direct, and much more neat
is to see that he is living somewhere in the middle
of the twentieth century, and leave him there."

Writing Assignments for Classification and Division   *507*
Collaborative Activity for Classification and Division   *507*
Internet Assignment for Classification and Division   *508*

13 DEFINITION *509*

WHAT IS DEFINITION?   *509*
    Understanding Formal Definitions   *509*
    Understanding Extended Definitions   *510*

USING DEFINITION   *510*

PLANNING A DEFINITION ESSAY   *511*
    Using Patterns of Development   *511*
    Using Other Strategies   *512*
    Phrasing Your Definition   *513*

STRUCTURING A DEFINITION ESSAY   *513*

REVISING A DEFINITION ESSAY   *514*

  ✔ **REVISION CHECKLIST: DEFINITION**   *514*

EDITING A DEFINITION ESSAY   *515*

  GRAMMAR IN CONTEXT: AVOIDING *IS WHEN* AND *IS WHERE*   *515*

  ✔ **EDITING CHECKLIST: DEFINITION**   *516*

  ➤ **A STUDENT WRITER: DEFINITION**   *516*

  ➤ **SAMPLE STUDENT ESSAY: AJOY MAHTAB,** *THE UNTOUCHABLE*   *516*
    Points for Special Attention   *519*
    Focus on Revision   *520*

  📄 **PEER EDITING WORKSHEET: DEFINITION**   *520*

VISUAL TEXT: U.S. CENSUS BUREAU, *U.S. Census 2000 Form* (Questionnaire)   *522*

JUDY BRADY, *I Want a Wife*   524

"My God, who *wouldn't* want a wife?"

JOSÉ ANTONIO BURCIAGA, *Tortillas*   528

"My earliest memory of *tortillas* is my *Mamá* telling me not to play with them. I had bitten eyeholes in one and was wearing it as a mask at the dinner table."

GAYLE ROSENWALD SMITH, *The Wife-Beater*   532

"The *Oxford Dictionary* defines the term *wife-beater* as:

'1. A man who physically abuses his wife and

2. Tank-style underwear shirts. Origin: based on the stereotype that physically abusive husbands wear that particular type of shirt.' "

REBECCA BLOOD, *What Is a Weblog?*   536

"Today there are hundreds of thousands of weblogs, and dozens of software products designed specifically to make updating them easier. They have evolved to encompass any subject matter and they reflect worldviews that range from the private world of the writer to the public world of culture and current events, and everything in between."

PAUL FUSSELL, *Stigmatic Uniforms*   544

"Sewn onto the common uniform were cloth badges, each identifying the crime that had landed the wearer in the camp: green triangle with numbers, a civil criminal; red triangle, a political criminal; pink triangle, a homosexual; red triangle with yellow star, a Jew."

PHILIP LEVINE, *What Work Is* **(Poetry)**   550

". . . You love your brother,
now suddenly you can hardly stand
the love flooding you for your brother,
who's not beside you or behind or
ahead because he's home trying to
sleep off a miserable night shift
at Cadillac so he can get up
before noon to study his German.
Works eight hours a night so he can sing
Wagner, the opera you hate most,
the worst music ever invented."

Writing Assignments for Definition   553
Collaborative Activity for Definition   554
Internet Assignment for Definition   554

14   ARGUMENTATION   555

WHAT IS ARGUMENTATION?   555

UNDERSTANDING ARGUMENTATION AND PERSUASION   556

PLANNING AN ARGUMENTATIVE ESSAY   557
    Choosing a Topic   557
    Taking a Stand   557
    Analyzing Your Audience   558
    Gathering and Documenting Evidence   558
    Dealing with the Opposition   561
    Understanding Rogerian Argument   562

✔ **CHECKLIST: GUIDELINES FOR USING ROGERIAN ARGUMENT**   563

USING DEDUCTIVE AND INDUCTIVE ARGUMENTS   563
    Using Deductive Arguments   563
    Using Inductive Arguments   565
    Using Toulmin Logic   566
    Recognizing Fallacies   567
    Using Transitions   570

STRUCTURING AN ARGUMENTATIVE ESSAY   571

REVISING AN ARGUMENTATIVE ESSAY   573

✔ **REVISION CHECKLIST: ARGUMENTATION**   573

EDITING AN ARGUMENTATIVE ESSAY   573

**GRAMMAR IN CONTEXT: USING COORDINATING AND SUBORDINATING
    CONJUNCTIONS**   574

✔ **EDITING CHECKLIST: ARGUMENTATION**   576

➤ **A STUDENT WRITER: ARGUMENTATION**   576

➤ **SAMPLE STUDENT ESSAY: MATT DANIELS, *AN ARGUMENT AGAINST THE
    ANNA TODD JENNINGS SCHOLARSHIP***   576
    Points for Special Attention   578
    Focus on Revision   580

▤ **PEER EDITING WORKSHEET: ARGUMENTATION**   580

VISUAL TEXT: AMERICAN CIVIL LIBERTIES UNION, *Thanks to Modern
Science . . .* **(Ad)**   582

THOMAS JEFFERSON, *The Declaration of Independence*   584

    "We hold these truths to be self-evident, that all men are created equal, that
    they are endowed by their Creator with certain unalienable rights, that
    among these are life, liberty and the pursuit of happiness."

ELIZABETH CADY STANTON, *Declaration of Sentiments and Resolutions,
Seneca Falls Convention, 1848*   590

    "The history of mankind is a history of repeated injuries and usurpations
    on the part of man toward woman, having in direct object the establishment
    of an absolute tyranny over her. To prove this, let the facts be submitted to a
    candid world."

MARTIN LUTHER KING JR., *Letter from Birmingham Jail*   597

    "For years now I have heard the word 'Wait!' It rings in the ear of every
    Negro with piercing familiarity. This 'Wait' has almost always meant 'Never.'

We must come to see, with one of our distinguished jurists, that 'justice too long delayed is justice denied.'"

DEBATE: **SHOULD U.S. CITIZENS BE REQUIRED TO CARRY NATIONAL IDENTITY CARDS?** *613*

WILLIAM SAFIRE, *The Threat of National ID*   *614*

"The universal use and likely abuse of the national ID — a discredit card — will trigger questions like: When did you begin subscribing to these publications, and why were you visiting that spicy or seditious Web site? Why are you afraid to show us your papers on demand?"

ALAN M. DERSHOWITZ, *Why Fear National ID Cards?*   *618*

"A national ID card would be much more effective in preventing terrorism than profiling millions of men simply because of their appearance."

DEBATE: **SHOULD GAY AND LESBIAN COUPLES BE ALLOWED TO ADOPT?**   *623*

TOM ADKINS, *Traditional Mother and Father: Still the Best Choice for Children*   *625*

"Without real data on alternatives, society is forced to favor the sure thing: a loving, responsible mother and father. That is still the best certain choice — not grandpa, not same-sex parents, and not single mothers, the single most highly correlated poverty factor for children."

BECKY BIRTHA, *Laws Should Support Loving Households, Straight or Not*   *630*

"The pediatricians say parents' sexual orientation alone cannot predict their ability to provide a supportive home environment for children. I wholeheartedly agree. Like race, gender, or being able-bodied, sexual orientation isn't linked to good or bad parenting."

DEBATE: **SHOULD THE DRAFT BE REINSTATED IN THE UNITED STATES?**   *635*

WILLIAM BROYLES JR., *A War for Us, Fought by Them*   *637*

"If this war is truly worth fighting, then the burdens of doing so should fall on all Americans. . . . If it's not worth your family fighting it, then it's not worth it, period. The draft is the truest test of public support for the administration's handling of the war, which is perhaps why the administration is so dead set against bringing it back."

RICK JAHNKOW, *For Those Who Believe We Need a Draft*   *643*

"The Pentagon was forced to give up the draft at the end of Vietnam, but it has been increasingly insinuating itself in institutions of socialization to

continue the process of militarization. If we brought back the draft,
it wouldn't remove the military from our schools or culture, it would
just make it easier to put more people through the militarization
process."

DEBATE: IS WAL-MART GOOD FOR AMERICA? *650*

KAREN DE COSTER AND BRAD EDMONDS, *The Case for Wal-Mart* *652*

"If the truth be told, Wal-Mart improves the lives of people in rural areas. . . .
When it comes to prices and service, try finding 70 percent off clearances at
your local mom-and-pop store or try going to that same store and returning
shoes you've worn for three months for a full-price refund with no questions asked."

LIZA FEATHERSTONE, *Down and Out in Discount America* *659*

"Wal-Mart routinely violates laws protecting workers' organizing rights
(workers have even been fired for union activity). It is a repeat offender on
overtime laws; in more than thirty states, workers have brought wage-and-
hour class-action suits against the retailer. In some cases, workers say, managers encouraged them to clock out and keep working; in others, managers
locked the doors and would not let employees go home at the end of their
shifts."

CASEBOOK: DOES MEDIA VIOLENCE CAUSE SOCIETAL VIOLENCE? *669*

SISSELA BOK, *Sizing Up the Effects* *671*

"As research evidence accumulates about the effects linked to media violence, it reinforces the commonsense view that violent programming influences viewers at least as much as the advertising directed at them for the
express purpose of arousing their desire for candy and toys. Both types of
exposure affect children most strongly to the degree that they are more suggestible and less critical of what is placed before them."

GERARD JONES, *Violent Media Is Good for Kids* *678*

"At its most fundamental level, what we call 'creative violence' — head-
bonking cartoons, bloody videogames, playground karate, toy guns — gives
children a tool to master their rage. . . . The world is uncontrollable and incomprehensible; mastering it is a terrifying, enraging task. Rage can be an
energizing emotion, a shot of courage to push us to resist greater threats,
take more control, than we ever thought we could."

OLIVER STONE, *Memo to John Grisham: What's Next — "A Movie Made Me Do It"?* *686*

"It gives me a shiver of fear when an influential lawyer and writer argues, as
Grisham does, that a particular work of art *should never have been allowed to be
made.*"

MICHAEL ZIMECKI, *Violent Films Cry "Fire" in Crowded Theaters*   691

"Film-inspired violence may not be 'imminent' in the constitutional sense, but the constitutional difference between 'I will kill you now' and 'I will kill you later' is cold comfort to the victims of movie-modeled murder."

Writing Assignments for Argumentation   697
Collaborative Activity for Argumentation   698
Internet Assignments for Argumentation   698

15   COMBINING THE PATTERNS   *703*

STRUCTURING AN ESSAY BY COMBINING THE PATTERNS   704
COMBINING THE PATTERNS: REVISING AND EDITING   704

GRAMMAR IN CONTEXT: AGREEMENT WITH INDEFINITE PRONOUNS   705

➤ A STUDENT WRITER: COMBINING THE PATTERNS   707

➤ SAMPLE STUDENT ESSAY: MICHAEL HUU TRUONG, *THE PARK*   707
Points for Special Attention   709
Focus on Revision   710

PEER EDITING WORKSHEET: COMBINING THE PATTERNS   711

LARS EIGHNER, *On Dumpster Diving*   712

"I have learned much as a scavenger. I mean to put some of what I have learned down here, beginning with the practical art of Dumpster diving and proceeding to the abstract."

VIRGINIA WOOLF, *The Death of the Moth*   728

"The struggle was over. The insignificant little creature now knew death. As I looked at the dead moth, this minute wayside triumph of so great a force over so mean an antagonist filled me with wonder. Just as life had been strange a few minutes before, so death was now as strange."

JONATHAN SWIFT, *A Modest Proposal*   733

"I have been assured by a very knowing American of my acquaintance in London, that a young healthy child well nursed is at a year old a most delicious, nourishing, and wholesome food, whether stewed, roasted, baked, or boiled; and I make no doubt that it will equally serve in fricasee or a ragout."

RICHARD RODRIGUEZ, *Strange Tools*   743

"What *did* I see in my books? I had the idea that they were crucial for my academic success, though I couldn't have said exactly how or why. In the sixth grade I simply concluded that what gave a book its value was some major idea or theme it contained. If that core essence could be mined and memorized, I would become learned like my teachers."

Writing Assignments for Combining the Patterns   750
Collaborative Activity for Combining the Patterns   750
Internet Assignment for Combining the Patterns   750

APPENDIX: USING RESEARCH IN YOUR WRITING *753*

STEP 1: CHOOSING A TOPIC *753*

STEP 2: TESTING YOUR TOPIC *754*

STEP 3: DOING RESEARCH *754*
　　Finding Information in the Library *754*
　　Finding Information on the Internet *756*

STEP 4: TAKING NOTES *757*
　　Paraphrasing *757*
　　Summarizing *758*
　　Quoting *759*

STEP 5: WATCHING OUT FOR PLAGIARISM *760*
　　Avoiding Common Errors That Lead to Plagiarism *761*
　　Avoiding Plagiarism with Online Sources *763*

STEP 6: DRAFTING A THESIS STATEMENT *763*

STEP 7: MAKING AN OUTLINE *764*

STEP 8: WRITING YOUR ESSAY *765*

STEP 9: DOCUMENTING YOUR SOURCES *767*
　　Parenthetical References in the Text *767*
　　The Works-Cited List *769*

➤ SAMPLE STUDENT RESEARCH ESSAY IN MLA STYLE: **CAITLIN BYRNE,**
　　AIRPORT INSECURITY *778*

Glossary *785*

Index *799*

Thematic Guide
to the Contents

Family Relationships

SANDRA CISNEROS, *Only Daughter* 96

LEAH HAGER COHEN, *Words Left Unspoken* 168

N. SCOTT MOMADAY, *The Way to Rainy Mountain* 180

E. B. WHITE, *Once More to the Lake* 186

KATE CHOPIN, *The Storm* 194

GRACE KU, *Midnight* 213

MARIE WINN, *Television: The Plug-In Drug* 351

JANICE MIRIKITANI, *Suicide Note* 382

BHARATI MUKHERJEE, *Two Ways to Belong in America* 415

GWENDOLYN BROOKS, *Sadie and Maud* 447

AMY TAN, *Mother Tongue* 487

PHILIP LEVINE, *What Work Is* 550

Language

HENRY LOUIS GATES JR., *"What's in a Name?"* 5

LEAH HAGER COHEN, *Words Left Unspoken* 168

JONATHAN KOZOL, *The Human Cost of an Illiterate Society* 252

ROBIN TOLMACH LAKOFF, *The Power of Words in Wartime* 377

DEBORAH TANNEN, *Sex, Lies, and Conversation* 440

AMY TAN, *Mother Tongue* 487

STEPHANIE ERICSSON, *The Ways We Lie* 495

GAYLE ROSENWALD SMITH, *The Wife-Beater* 532

VIRGINIA WOOLF, *The Death of the Moth* 728

Reading and Writing

SANDRA CISNEROS, *Only Daughter*   96
JONATHAN KOZOL, *The Human Cost of an Illiterate Society*   252
MARCIA MULLER, *Creating a Female Sleuth*   290
AMY TAN, *Mother Tongue*   487
REBECCA BLOOD, *What Is a Weblog?*   536
RICHARD RODRIGUEZ, *Strange Tools*   743

Education

LAURA BOBNAK, *The Price of Silence*   62
MAYA ANGELOU, *Finishing School*   101
SHERMAN ALEXIE, *Indian Education*   134
JONATHAN KOZOL, *The Human Cost of an Illiterate Society*   252
ERIC McGLADE, *The Search*   274
JANICE MIRIKITANI, *Suicide Note*   382
MARK COTHARN, *Brains versus Brawn*   396
JOSIE MARTINEZ, *What I Learned (and Didn't Learn) in College*   458
WILLIAM ZINSSER, *College Pressures*   466
CAROLYN FOSTER SEGAL, *The Dog Ate My Disk, and Other Tales
    of Woe*   475
AMY TAN, *Mother Tongue*   487
MATT DANIELS, *An Argument against the Anna Todd Jennings
    Scholarship*   576
RICHARD RODRIGUEZ, *Strange Tools*   743

Business and Work

BONNIE SMITH-YACKEL, *My Mother Never Worked*   108
DANIEL GROSS, *Playing by the Rules*   114
GEORGE ORWELL, *Shooting an Elephant*   125
JAMES GREGGS, *Building and Learning*   153
KRISTY BREDIN, *Job Application Letter*   211
GRACE KU, *Midnight*   213
LAURENCE J. PETER AND RAYMOND HULL, *The Peter Principle*   220
PHIL PATTON, *Innovation*   231
SCOTT RUSSELL SANDERS, *The Men We Carry in Our Minds*   481
PHILIP LEVINE, *What Work Is*   550
KAREN DE COSTER AND BRAD EDMONDS, *The Case for Wal-Mart*   652
LIZA FEATHERSTONE, *Down and Out in Discount America*   659

Sports

TIFFANY FORTE, *My Field of Dreams* 89

LOUIS REQUENA, *Major League Baseball Brawl* (Photo) 344

NORMAN COUSINS, *Who Killed Benny Paret?* 346

MARK COTHARN, *Brains versus Brawn* 396

Race and Culture

HENRY LOUIS GATES JR., *"What's in a Name?"* 5

MAYA ANGELOU, *Finishing School* 101

GEORGE ORWELL, *Shooting an Elephant* 125

SHERMAN ALEXIE, *Indian Education* 134

JAMES GREGGS, *Building and Learning* 153

MARY LIM, *The Valley of Windmills* 156

ISABEL ALLENDE, *The Amazon Queen* 173

N. SCOTT MOMADAY, *The Way to Rainy Mountain* 180

FOUR TATTOOS (Photos): ALEX WILLIAMS, *"Lisa Karen"*; JOEL GORDON, *"Rose"*; CHARLES GATEWOOD, *"Body Art"*; AND BOB DAEMMRICH, *"Jiminy Cricket"* 218

BRENT STAPLES, *Just Walk On By: A Black Man Ponders His Power to Alter Public Space* 240

JONATHAN KOZOL, *The Human Cost of an Illiterate Society* 252

MALCOLM X, *My First Conk* 285

LAWRENCE OTIS GRAHAM, *The "Black Table" Is Still There* 366

BHARATI MUKHERJEE, *Two Ways to Belong in America* 415

YI-FU TUAN, *Chinese Space, American Space* 421

GWENDOLYN BROOKS, *Sadie and Maud* 447

SCOTT RUSSELL SANDERS, *The Men We Carry in Our Minds* 481

AMY TAN, *Mother Tongue* 487

AJOY MAHTAB, *The Untouchable* 516

JOSÉ ANTONIO BURCIAGA, *Tortillas* 528

MATT DANIELS, *An Argument against the Anna Todd Jennings Scholarship* 576

MARTIN LUTHER KING JR., *Letter from Birmingham Jail* 597

TOM ADKINS, *Traditional Mother and Father: Still the Best Choice for Children* 625

BECKY BIRTHA, *Laws Should Support Loving Households, Straight or Not* 630

LARS EIGHNER, *On Dumpster Diving* 712

RICHARD RODRIGUEZ, *Strange Tools* 743

Gender

TIFFANY FORTE, *My Field of Dreams* 89
SANDRA CISNEROS, *Only Daughter* 96
KATE CHOPIN, *The Storm* 194
FOUR TATTOOS (Photos): ALEX WILLIAMS, *"Lisa Karen"*; JOEL GORDON,
    "Rose"; CHARLES GATEWOOD, *"Body Art"*; AND BOB DAEMMRICH, *"Jiminy
    Cricket"*; 218
GRACE PALEY, *Samuel* 262
MARCIA MULLER, *Creating a Female Sleuth* 290
JOSHUA PIVEN, DAVID BORGENICHT, AND JENNIFER WORICK, *How to Escape
    from a Bad Date* 297
KATHA POLLITT, *Why Boys Don't Play with Dolls* 361
LINDA M. HASSELSTROM, *A Peaceful Woman Explains Why She Carries
    a Gun* 371
DEBORAH TANNEN, *Sex, Lies, and Conversation* 440
SCOTT RUSSELL SANDERS, *The Men We Carry in Our Minds* 481
JUDY BRADY, *I Want a Wife* 524
GAYLE ROSENWALD SMITH, *The Wife-Beater* 532
ELIZABETH CADY STANTON, *Declaration of Sentiments
    and Resolutions* 590

Nature and the Environment

MARY LIM, *The Valley of Windmills* 156
ISABEL ALLENDE, *The Amazon Queen* 173
N. SCOTT MOMADAY, *The Way to Rainy Mountain* 180
E. B. WHITE, *Once More to the Lake* 186
KATE CHOPIN, *The Storm* 194
VIRGINIA WOOLF, *The Death of the Moth* 728

Media and Society

MARTIN GANSBERG, *Thirty-Eight Who Saw Murder Didn't Call
    the Police* 120
MARCIA MULLER, *Creating a Female Sleuth* 290
MARIE WINN, *Television: The Plug-In Drug* 351
MARIA TECSON, *A Comparison of Two Web Sites on Attention Deficit
    Disorder* 401
IAN FRAZIER, *Dearly Disconnected* 434
REBECCA BLOOD, *What Is a Weblog?* 536
SISSELA BOK, *Sizing Up the Effects* 671
GERARD JONES, *Violent Media Is Good for Kids* 678

OLIVER STONE, *Memo to John Grisham: What's Next — "A Movie Made Me Do It"?* 686
MICHAEL ZIMECKI, *Violent Films Cry "Fire" in Crowded Theaters* 691

History and Politics

GEORGE ORWELL, *Shooting an Elephant* 125
VINCENT LAFORET, *Girls in Front of 9/11 Mural* (Photo) 160
SUZANNE BERNE, *Ground Zero* 162
DICK TERESI, *Star-Spangled Stupidity* 246
ARTHUR MILLER, *Get It Right: Privatize Executions* 305
EVELYN PELLICANE, *The Irish Famine, 1845–1849* 338
ROBIN TOLMACH LAKOFF, *The Power of Words in Wartime* 377
BRUCE CATTON, *Grant and Lee: A Study in Contrasts* 409
BHARATI MUKHERJEE, *Two Ways to Belong in America* 415
JOHN DE GRAAF, DAVID WANN, AND THOMAS H. NAYLOR, *Swollen Expectations* 425
ELLIS ISLAND IMMIGRATION MUSEUM/NPS, *Key to Chalk Marks Designating Medical Conditions of Immigrants* (Chart) 464
OFFICE OF THE PUBLIC HEALTH SERVICE HISTORIAN, *Eye Exam Administered to Immigrants* (Photo) 465
EDWIN BROCK, *Five Ways to Kill a Man* 505
PAUL FUSSELL, *Stigmatic Uniforms* 544
AMERICAN CIVIL LIBERTIES UNION, *Thanks to Modern Science . . .* (Ad) 582
THOMAS JEFFERSON, *The Declaration of Independence* 584
ELIZABETH CADY STANTON, *Declaration of Sentiments and Resolutions* 590
MARTIN LUTHER KING JR., *Letter from Birmingham Jail* 597
WILLIAM SAFIRE, *The Threat of National ID* 614
ALAN M. DERSHOWITZ, *Why Fear National ID Cards?* 618
TOM ADKINS, *Traditional Mother and Father: Still the Best Choice for Children* 625
BECKY BIRTHA, *Laws Should Support Loving Households, Straight or Not* 630
WILLIAM BROYLES JR., *A War for Us, Fought by Them* 637
RICK JAHNKOW, *For Those Who Believe We Need a Draft* 643
JONATHAN SWIFT, *A Modest Proposal* 733
CAITLIN BYRNE, *Airport Insecurity* 778

Ethics

LAURA BOBNAK, *The Price of Silence* 62
MARTIN GANSBERG, *Thirty-Eight Who Saw Murder Didn't Call the Police* 120
GEORGE ORWELL, *Shooting an Elephant* 125
DAVID J. BIRNBAUM, *The Catbird Seat* 227

BRENT STAPLES, *Just Walk On By: A Black Man Ponders His Power to Alter Public Space*   240

JONATHAN KOZOL, *The Human Cost of an Illiterate Society*   252

ARTHUR MILLER, *Get It Right: Privatize Executions*   305

JESSICA MITFORD, *The Embalming of Mr. Jones*   310

SHIRLEY JACKSON, *The Lottery*   317

MARIE WINN, *Television: The Plug-In Drug*   351

ROBIN TOLMACH LAKOFF, *The Power of Words in Wartime*   377

CAROLYN FOSTER SEGAL, *The Dog Ate My Disk, and Other Tales of Woe*   475

STEPHANIE ERICSSON, *The Ways We Lie*   495

EDWIN BROCK, *Five Ways to Kill a Man*   505

PAUL FUSSELL, *Stigmatic Uniforms*   544

PHILIP LEVINE, *What Work Is*   550

AMERICAN CIVIL LIBERTIES UNION, *Thanks to Modern Science . . .* (Ad)   582

TOM ADKINS, *Traditional Mother and Father: Still the Best Choice for Children*   625

BECKY BIRTHA, *Laws Should Support Loving Households, Straight or Not*   630

WILLIAM BROYLES JR., *A War for Us, Fought by Them*   637

RICK JAHNKOW, *For Those Who Believe We Need a Draft*   643

SISSELA BOK, *Sizing Up the Effects*   671

Citizenship

VINCENT LAFORET, *Girls in Front of 9/11 Mural* (Photo)   160

SUZANNE BERNE, *Ground Zero*   162

DICK TERESI, *Star-Spangled Stupidity*   246

ARTHUR MILLER, *Get It Right: Privatize Executions*   305

ROBIN TOLMACH LAKOFF, *The Power of Words in Wartime*   377

BHARATI MUKHERJEE, *Two Ways to Belong in America*   415

JOHN DE GRAAF, DAVID WANN, AND THOMAS H. NAYLOR, *Swollen Expectations*   425

ELLIS ISLAND IMMIGRATION MUSEUM/NPS, *Key to Chalk Marks Designating Medical Conditions of Immigrants* (Chart)   464

OFFICE OF THE PUBLIC HEALTH SERVICE HISTORIAN, *Eye Exam Administered to Immigrants* (Photo)   465

AMERICAN CIVIL LIBERTIES UNION, *Thanks to Modern Science . . .* (Ad)   582

THOMAS JEFFERSON, *The Declaration of Independence*   584

ELIZABETH CADY STANTON, *Declaration of Sentiments and Resolutions*   590

MARTIN LUTHER KING JR., *Letter from Birmingham Jail*   597

WILLIAM SAFIRE, *The Threat of National ID*   614

ALAN M. DERSHOWITZ, *Why Fear National ID Cards?*   618

WILLIAM BROYLES JR., *A War for Us, Fought by Them*   637

RICK JAHNKOW, *For Those Who Believe We Need a Draft*   643

CAITLIN BYRNE, *Airport Insecurity*   778

Patterns for College Writing

A Rhetorical Reader
and Guide

make sure not distorting

1
Reading to Write: How to Use This Book

On a purely practical level, you will read the selections in this text to answer study questions and prepare for class discussions. More significantly, however, you will also read to evaluate the ideas of others, to form judgments, and to develop original viewpoints. By introducing you to new ideas and new ways of thinking about familiar concepts, reading prepares you to respond critically to the ideas of others and to develop ideas of your own. When you read critically, you can form opinions, exchange insights with others in conversation, ask and answer questions, and develop ideas that can be further explored in writing. For all of these reasons, reading is a vital part of your education.

Reading Critically

Reading is a two-way street. Readers are presented with a writer's ideas, but they also bring their own set of assumptions to what they read. After all, readers have different national, ethnic, cultural, and geographic backgrounds and different kinds of knowledge and experiences, so they may react differently to a particular essay or story. For example, readers from an economically and ethnically homogeneous suburban neighborhood may have difficulty understanding a story about class conflict, but these readers may also be more objective than readers who are struggling with such conflict in their own lives.

These differences in readers' responses do not mean that every interpretation is acceptable, that an essay or story or poem may mean whatever a reader wants it to mean. Readers must make sure they are not distorting a writer's words, overlooking (or ignoring) significant details, or seeing things in an essay or story that do not exist. It is not important for all readers to agree on a particular interpretation of a work. It *is* important, however, for each reader to develop an interpretation that the work itself supports.

The study questions that accompany the essays in this text encourage you to think critically about writers' ideas. Although some of the questions (particularly those listed under **Comprehension** assignments) call for fairly straightforward, factual responses, other questions (particularly the **Journal Entry** assignments) invite more complex responses that reflect your individual reaction to the selections.

Reading Actively

When you read an essay in this text, or any work that you expect to discuss in class (and perhaps to write about), you should read it carefully — and you should read it more than once.

Before You Read

Before you read, look over the essay to get an overview of its content. If the selection has a **headnote** — a paragraph or two about the author and the work — begin by reading it. (Note that each headnote in this text includes a **background** section, a discussion of the reading selection's cultural context.) Next, skim the work to get a general sense of the writer's ideas. As you read, note the title and any internal headings, as well as the use of boldface type, italics, and other design elements. Also pay special attention to the introductory and concluding paragraphs, where a writer is likely to make (or reiterate) key points.

As You Read

As you read, try to answer the questions in the following checklist.

> ✓ **CHECKLIST: Reading Actively**
>
> - What is the writer's general subject?
> - What is the writer's main point?
> - Does the writer seem to have a particular purpose in mind?
> - What kind of audience is the writer addressing?
> - What are the writer's assumptions about audience? About subject?
> - Are the writer's ideas consistent with your own?
> - Does the writer reveal any biases?
> - Do you have any knowledge that could challenge the writer's ideas?
> - Is any information missing?
> - Are any sequential or logical links missing?
> - Can you identify themes or ideas that also appear in other works you have read?
> - Can you identify parallels with your own experience?

Highlighting and Annotating

As you read and reread, be sure to record your reactions in writing. These notations will help you understand the writer's ideas and your own thoughts about these ideas. Every reader develops a different system of recording such responses, but many readers use a combination of *highlighting* and *annotating*.

When you **highlight**, you mark the text. You might, for example, underline important ideas, box key terms, number a series of related points, circle an unfamiliar word (or place a question mark beside it), draw vertical lines in the margin beside a particularly interesting passage, draw arrows to connect related points, or star discussions of the work's central issues or themes. T_{r+} /

When you **annotate**, you carry on a conversation with the text in marginal notes. You might, among other things, ask questions, suggest possible parallels with other reading selections or with your own experiences, argue with the writer's points, comment on the writer's style, or define unfamiliar terms and concepts.

The following paragraph, excerpted from Maya Angelou's "Finishing School" (page 101), illustrates a student's highlighting and annotating of a text.

Date written?

Why does she mention this?

(Recently) a white woman from Texas, who would quickly describe herself as a (liberal,) asked me about my hometown. When I told her that in Stamps my grandmother had owned the only Negro general merchandise store since the turn of the century, she exclaimed, "Why,

Serious or sarcastic?

you were a (debutante)." Ridiculous and even ludicrous. But Negro girls in small Southern towns, whether

Also true of boys? In North as well as South? True today?

poverty-stricken or just munching along on a few of life's necessities, were given as extensive and irrelevant

✳ preparations for adulthood as rich white girls shown in magazines. Admittedly the training was not the same. While white girls learned to waltz and sit gracefully with a tea cup balanced on their knees, we were lagging behind,

What are these values?

learning the (mid-Victorian values) with very little money to indulge them.

Remember that this process of highlighting and annotating is not an end in itself but a step toward understanding what you have read. Annotations suggest questions; in your search for answers, you may ask your instructor for clarification, or you may raise particularly puzzling or provocative points during class discussion or in small study groups. After your questions have been answered, you will be able to discuss and write about what you have read with greater confidence, accuracy, and authority.

The process you use when you react to a **visual text** — a photograph; an advertisement; a diagram, graph, or chart; or a work of fine art, for example — is much the same as the one you use when you respond to a written text. Here too, your goal is to understand the text, and highlighting and annotating a visual text can help you interpret it.

With visual texts, however, instead of identifying elements like particular words and ideas, you identify visual elements. These might include the use of color; the arrangement of shapes; the contrast between large and small or light and dark; and, of course, the particular images the visual includes.

The following photograph, one of four included in "Four Tattoos" (page 218), illustrates a student's highlighting and annotating of a visual text.

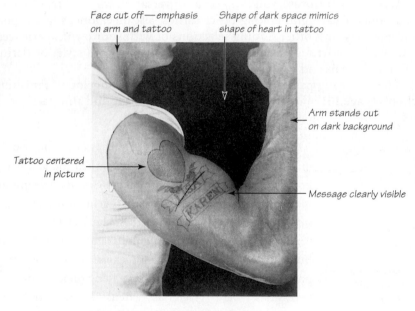

Alex Williams, "~~Lisa~~, Karen."

Reading the Essays in This Book

The selection that follows, "'What's in a Name?'" by Henry Louis Gates Jr., is typical of the essays in this text. It is preceded by a **headnote** that gives readers information about the author's life and career. This headnote includes a **background** section that provides a social, historical, and cultural context for the essay. As you read the headnote and the essay, highlight and annotate them carefully.

HENRY LOUIS GATES JR.

"What's in a Name?"

Henry Louis Gates Jr. was born in 1950 in Keyser, West Virginia, and grew up in the small town of Piedmont. Currently W. E. B. Du Bois Professor of Humanities and chair of the Afro-American Studies Department at Harvard, he has edited many collections of works by African-American writers and published several volumes of literary criticism. However, he is probably best known as a social critic whose books and articles for a general audience explore a wide variety of issues and themes, often focusing on issues of race and culture. In the following essay, which originally appeared in the journal *Dissent,* Gates recalls a childhood experience that occurred during the mid-1950s.

Background on the civil rights movement: In the mid-1950s, the first stirrings of the civil rights movement were under way, and in 1954 and 1955 the U.S. Supreme Court handed down decisions declaring racial segregation unconstitutional in public schools. Still, much of the country—particularly the South—remained largely segregated until Congress passed the Civil Rights Act of 1964, which prohibited discrimination based on race, color, religion, or national origin in businesses (such as restaurants and theaters) covered by interstate commerce laws, as well as in employment. This was followed by the Voting Rights Act of 1965, which guaranteed equal access to the polls, and the Civil Rights Act of 1968, which prohibited discrimination in housing and real estate. At the time of the experience Gates recalls here—before these laws were enacted—prejudice and discrimination against African Americans were the norm in many communities, including those outside the South.

The question of color takes up much space in these pages, but the question of color, especially in this country, operates to hide the graver questions of the self.

        – JAMES BALDWIN, 1961

. . . blood, darky, Tar Baby, Kaffir, shine . . . moor, blackamoor, Jim Crow, spook . . . quadroon, meriney, red bone, high yellow . . . Mammy, porch monkey, home, homeboy, George . . . spearchucker, schwarze, Leroy, Smokey . . . mouli, buck. Ethiopian, brother, sistah.

        – TREY ELLIS, 1989

I had forgotten the incident completely, until I read Trey Ellis's essay   1
"Remember My Name" in a recent issue of the *Village Voice* (June 13, 1989). But there, in the middle of an extended italicized list of the bynames of "the race" ("the race" or "our people" being the terms my parents used in polite or reverential discourse, "jigaboo" or "nigger" more commonly used in anger, jest, or pure disgust), it was: "George." Now the events of that very brief exchange return to mind so vividly that I wonder why I had forgotten it.

My father and I were walking home at dusk from his second job. He   2
"moonlighted" as a janitor in the evenings for the telephone company.
Every day but Saturday, he would come home at 3:30 from his regular job
at the paper mill, wash up, eat supper, then at 4:30 head downtown to his
second job. He used to make jokes frequently about a union official who
moonlighted. I never got the joke, but he and his friends thought it was
hilarious. All I knew was that my family always ate well, that my brother
and I had new clothes to wear, and that all of the white people in Piedmont, West Virginia, treated my parents with an odd mixture of resentment and respect that even we understood at the time had something
directly to do with a small but certain measure of financial security.

He had left a little early that evening because I was with him and I had   3
to be in bed early. I could not have been more than five or six, and we had
stopped off at the Cut-Rate Drug Store (where no black person in town
but my father could sit down to eat, and eat off real plates with real silverware) so that I could buy some caramel ice cream, two scoops in a wafer
cone, please, which I was busy licking when Mr. Wilson walked by.

Mr. Wilson was a very quiet man, whose stony, brooding, silent man-   4
ner seemed designed to scare off any overtures of friendship, even from
white people. He was Irish, as was one-third of our village (another third
being Italian), the more affluent among whom sent their children to
"Catholic School" across the bridge in Maryland. He had white straight
hair, like my Uncle Joe, whom he uncannily resembled, and he carried a
black worn metal lunch pail, the kind that Riley* carried on the television
show. My father always spoke to him, and for reasons that we never did
understand, he always spoke to my father.

"Hello, Mr. Wilson," I heard my father say.   5

"Hello, George."   6

I stopped licking my ice cream cone, and asked my Dad in a loud voice   7
why Mr. Wilson had called him "George."

"Doesn't he know your name, Daddy? Why don't you tell him your   8
name? Your name isn't George."

For a moment I tried to think of who Mr. Wilson was mixing Pop up   9
with. But we didn't have any Georges among the colored people in Piedmont; nor were there colored Georges living in the neighboring towns and
working at the mill.

"Tell him your name, Daddy."   10

"He knows my name, boy," my father said after a long pause. "He calls   11
all colored people George."

A long silence ensued. It was "one of those things," as my Mom would   12
put it. Even then, that early, I knew when I was in the presence of "one of
those things," one of those things that provided a glimpse, through a rent
curtain, at another world that we could not affect but that affected us.

---

* EDS. NOTE — The lead character in a 1950s television program titled *The Life of Riley*.

There would be a painful moment of silence, and you would wait for it to give way to a discussion of a black superstar such as Sugar Ray or Jackie Robinson.

"Nobody hits better in a clutch than Jackie Robinson."   13

"That's right. Nobody."   14

I never again looked Mr. Wilson in the eye.   15

• • •

Responding to an Essay

Once you have read an essay carefully and recorded your initial reactions to it, you should be able to respond to specific questions about it.

The study questions that follow each essay in this text will guide you through the rest of the reading process and help you to **think critically** about what you are reading. Five types of questions follow each essay:

- *Comprehension* questions help you to measure your understanding of what the writer is saying.

- *Purpose and Audience* questions ask you to consider why, and for whom, each selection was written and to examine the implications of the writer's choices in view of a particular purpose or intended audience.

- *Style and Structure* questions encourage you to examine the decisions the writer has made about elements such as arrangement of ideas, paragraphing, sentence structure, word choice, and imagery.

- *Vocabulary Projects* ask you to define certain words, to consider the connotations of others, and to examine the writer's reasons for selecting particular words or patterns of language.

- *Journal Entry* assignments ask you to respond informally to what you read and to speculate freely about related ideas — perhaps exploring ethical issues raised by the selection or offering your opinions about the writer's statements. Briefer, less polished, and less structured than full-length essays, journal entries not only allow you to respond critically to a reading selection but may also suggest ideas for more formal kinds of writing.

Following these sets of questions are three additional features:

- *Writing Workshop* assignments ask you to write essays structured according to the pattern of development explained and illustrated in the chapter.

- *Combining the Patterns* questions focus on the various patterns of development — other than the essay's dominant pattern — that the writer uses. These questions ask why a writer uses particular patterns (narration, description, exemplification, process, cause and effect, comparison and contrast, classification and division, definition), what each pattern contributes to the essay, and what other choices the writer might have had.

- *Thematic Connections* identify other readings in this book that deal with similar themes. Reading these related works will enhance your understanding and appreciation of the original work and perhaps give you material to write about.

Following are some examples of study questions and possible responses, as well as a **Writing Workshop** assignment and **Thematic Connections** for "'What's in a Name?'" (pages 5–7). The numbers in parentheses after quotations refer to the paragraphs in which the quotations appear.

Comprehension

1. *In paragraph 1, Gates wonders why he forgot about the exchange between his father and Mr. Wilson. Why do you think he forgot about it?* Gates may have forgotten about the incident simply because it was something that happened a long time ago or because such incidents were commonplace when he was a child. Alternatively, he may *not* have forgotten the exchange between his father and Mr. Wilson but pushed it out of his mind because he found it so painful. (After all, he says he never again looked Mr. Wilson in the eye.)

2. *How is the social status of Gates's family different from that of other African-American families in Piedmont, West Virginia? How does Gates account for this difference?* Gates's family is different from other African-American families in town in that they are treated with "an odd mixture of resentment and respect" (2) by whites. Although other blacks are not permitted to eat at the drugstore, Mr. Gates is. Gates attributes this social status to his family's "small but certain measure of financial security" (2). Even so, when Mr. Wilson insults Mr. Gates, the privileged status of the Gates family is revealed as false.

3. *What does Gates mean when he says, "It was 'one of those things,' as my Mom would put it" (12)?* Gates's comment indicates that the family learned to see such mistreatment as routine. In context, the word *things* in paragraph 12 refers to the kind of incident that gives Gates and his family a glimpse of the way the white world operates.

4. *Why does Gates's family turn to a discussion of a "black superstar" after a "painful moment of silence" (12) such as the one he describes?* Although Gates does not explain the family's behavior, we can infer that they speak of African-American heroes like prizefighter Sugar Ray Robinson and baseball player Jackie Robinson to make themselves feel better. Such discussions are a way of balancing the negative images of African Americans created by incidents such as the one Gates describes and of bolstering the low self-esteem the family felt as a result. These heroes seem to have won the respect denied to the Gates family; to mention them is to participate vicariously in their glory.

5. *Why do you think Gates "never again looked Mr. Wilson in the eye" (15)?* Gates may have felt that Mr. Wilson was somehow the enemy, not to be trusted, because he had insulted Gates's father. Or, he may have been ashamed to look him in the eye because he believed his father should have insisted on being addressed properly.

Purpose and Audience

1. *Why do you think Gates introduces his narrative with the two quotations he selects? How do you suppose he expects his audience to react to them? How do you react?* Gates begins with two quotations, both by African-American writers, written nearly thirty years apart. Baldwin's words seem to suggest that, in the United States, "the question of color" is a barrier to understanding "the graver questions of the self." That is, the labels *black* and *white* may mask more fundamental characteristics or issues. Ellis's list of names (many pejorative) for African Americans illustrates the fact that epithets can dehumanize people — they can, in effect, rob a person of his or her "self." This issue of the discrepancy between a name and what lies behind it is central to Gates's essay. In one sense, then, Gates begins with these two quotations because they are relevant to the issues he will discuss. More specifically, he is using the two quotations — particularly Ellis's string of unpleasant names — to arouse interest in his topic and provide an intellectual and emotional context for his story. He may also be intending to make his white readers uncomfortable and his black readers angry. How you react depends on your attitudes about race (and perhaps about language).

2. *What is the point of Gates's narrative? That is, why does he recount the incident?* Certainly Gates wishes to make readers aware of the awkward, and potentially dangerous, position of his father (and, by extension, of other African Americans) in a small southern town in the 1950s. He also shows us how names help to shape people's perceptions and actions: as long as Mr. Wilson can call all black men "George," he can continue to see them as insignificant and treat them as inferiors. The title of the piece suggests that the way names shape perceptions is the writer's main point.

3. *The title of this selection, which Gates places in quotation marks, is an allusion to act 2, scene 2, of Shakespeare's* Romeo and Juliet, *in which Juliet says, "What's in a name? That which we call a rose / By any other name would smell as sweet." Why do you think Gates chose this title? Does he expect his audience to recognize the quotation?* Because his work was originally published in a journal read by a well-educated audience, Gates probably expected readers to recognize the **allusion** (and also to know about 1950s race relations). Although Gates could not have been certain that all members of this audience would recognize the reference to *Romeo and Juliet,* he could have been reasonably sure that if they did, it would enhance their understanding of the selection. In Shakespeare's play, the two lovers are kept apart essentially because of their names: she is a Capulet and he is a Montague, and the two families are involved in a bitter feud. In the speech from which Gates takes the

title quotation, Juliet questions the logic of such a situation. In her view, what a person is called should not determine how he or she is regarded — and this, of course, is Gates's point as well. Even if readers do not recognize the allusion, however, the title still foreshadows the selection's focus on names.

Style and Structure

1. *Does paragraph 1 add something vital to the narrative, or would Gates's story make sense without the introduction? Could another kind of introduction work as well?* Gates's first paragraph supplies the context in which the incident is to be read — that is, it makes clear that Mr. Wilson's calling Mr. Gates "George" was not an isolated incident but part of a pattern of behavior that allowed those in positions of power to mistreat those they considered inferior. For this reason, it is an effective introduction. Although the narrative would make sense without paragraph 1, the story's full impact would probably not be as great. Still, Gates could have begun differently. For example, he could have started with the incident itself (paragraph 2) and interjected his comments about the significance of names later in the piece. He also could have begun with the exchange of dialogue in paragraphs 5 through 11 and then introduced the current paragraph 1 to supply the incident's context.

2. *What does the use of dialogue contribute to the narrative? Would the selection have a different impact without dialogue? Explain.* Gates was five or six years old when the incident occurred, and the dialogue helps to establish the child's innocence as well as his father's quiet acceptance of the situation. In short, the dialogue is a valuable addition to the piece because it creates two characters, one innocent and one resigned to injustice, both of whom contrast with the voice of the adult narrator: wise, worldly, but also angry and perhaps ashamed, the voice of a man who has benefited from the sacrifices of men like Gates's father.

3. *Why do you think Gates supplies the specific details he chooses in paragraphs 2 and 3? In paragraph 4? Is all this information necessary?* The details Gates provides in paragraphs 2 and 3 help to establish the status of his family in Piedmont; because readers have this information, the fact the family was ultimately disregarded and discounted by some whites emerges as deeply ironic. The information in paragraph 4 also contributes to this **irony**. Here we learn that Mr. Wilson was not liked by many whites, that he looked like Gates's Uncle Joe, and that he carried a lunch box — in other words, that he had no special status in the town apart from that conferred by race.

Vocabulary Projects

1. *Define each of the following words as it is used in this selection:*
   bynames (1) — nicknames
   measure (2) — extent or degree
   uncannily (4) — strangely
   ensued (12) — followed
   rent (12) — torn

2. *Consider the connotations of the words* colored *and* black, *both used by Gates to refer to African Americans. What different associations does each word have? Why does Gates use both—for example,* colored *in paragraph 9 and* black *in paragraph 12? What is your response to the father's use of the term* boy *in paragraph 11?* In the 1950s, when the incident Gates describes took place, the term *colored* was still widely used, along with *Negro,* to designate Americans of African descent. In the 1960s, the terms *Afro-American* and *black* replaced the earlier names, with *black* emerging as the preferred term and remaining dominant through the 1980s. Today, although *black* is preferred by some, *African American* is used more and more often. Because the term *colored* is the oldest designation, it may seem old-fashioned and even racist today; *black,* which connoted a certain degree of militancy in the 1960s, is probably now considered a neutral term by most people. Gates uses both words because he is speaking from two time periods. In paragraph 9, recreating the thoughts and words of a child in a 1950s southern town, he uses the term *colored;* in paragraph 12, the adult Gates, commenting in 1989 on the incident, uses *black.* The substitution of *African American* for the older terms might give the narrative a more contemporary flavor, but it might also seem awkward or forced—and, in paragraph 9, inappropriately formal. As far as the term *boy* is concerned, different readers are apt to have different responses. Although the father's use of the term can be seen as affectionate, it can also be seen as derisive in this context since it echoes the bigot's use of *boy* for all black males, regardless of age or accomplishments.   *derisive*

Journal Entry

Do you think Gates's parents should have used experiences like the one in " 'What's in a Name?' " to educate him about the family's social status in the community? Why do you think they chose instead to dismiss such incidents as "one of those things" (12)? Your responses to these questions should reflect your own opinions and judgments, based on your background and experiences as well as on your interpretation of the reading selection.

Writing Workshop

Write about a time when you, like Gates's father, could have spoken out in protest but chose not to. Would you make the same decision today? By the time you approach the Writing Workshop assignments, you will have read an essay, highlighted and annotated it, responded to study questions about it, discussed it in class, and perhaps considered its relationship to other essays in the text. Often, your next step will be to write an essay in response to one of the Writing Workshop questions. (Chapters 2–4 follow Laura Bobnak, a first-year composition student, through the process of writing an essay in response to this Writing Workshop assignment.)

Combining the Patterns   *exemplification—*

Although **narration** *is the pattern of development that dominates " 'What's in a Name?' " and gives it its structure, Gates also uses* **exemplification**, *presenting an extended example to support his thesis. What is this example? What does it illustrate?*

Would several brief examples have been more convincing? The extended example is the story of the encounter between Gates's father and Mr. Wilson, which compellingly illustrates the kind of behavior African Americans were often forced to adopt in the 1950s. Because Gates's introduction focuses on "the incident" (1), one extended example is enough (although he alludes to other incidents in paragraph 12).

Thematic Connections

- "Finishing School" (page 101)
- "The 'Black Table' Is Still There" (page 366)

As you read and think about the selections in this text, you should begin to see thematic links among them. Such parallels can add to your interest and understanding, as well as give you ideas for class discussion and writing. For example, Maya Angelou's "Finishing School," another autobiographical essay by an African-American writer, has many similarities with Gates's. Both essays describe the uneasy position of a pre-Civil-Rights-era black child expected to conform to the white world's unfair code of behavior, and both deal squarely with the importance of being called by one's name. In fact, paragraph 26 of "Finishing School" offers some helpful insights into the problem Gates examines. Another related work is Lawrence Otis Graham's "The 'Black Table' is Still There." The writer, an African-American man, returns in 1991 to his junior high school, where he sees the lunch tables as segregated as they were when he was a student there. Unlike Gates's essay, which discusses a specific incident that took place in the South in the 1950s, Graham's examines an ongoing situation that may apply to schools all over the United States. Thus, it provides a more current — and, perhaps, wider — context for discussing issues of race and class.

   In the process of thinking about Gates's narrative, discussing it in class, or preparing to write an essay on a related topic (such as the one listed under Writing Workshop), you might find it useful to consider (or reconsider) Angelou's and Graham's essays.

Responding to Other Texts

The first selection in Chapters 6 through 15 of this book is a visual text. It is followed by **Reading Images** questions, a **Journal Entry**, and **Thematic Connections** that will help you understand the image and shape your response to it.

   The final selection in each chapter, a story or poem, is followed by **Reading Literature** questions, a **Journal Entry**, and **Thematic Connections**.

   Note: At the end of each chapter, **Writing Assignments** offer additional practice in writing essays structured according to a particular pattern of development, a **Collaborative Activity** suggests an idea for a group project, and an **Internet Assignment** suggests an additional possibility for writing about the pattern.

PART ONE

The Writing Process

Every reading selection in this book is the result of a struggle between a writer and his or her material. If a writer's struggle is successful, the finished work is welded together without a visible seam, and readers have no sense of the frustration the writer experienced while rearranging ideas or hunting for the right word. Writing is no easy business, even for a professional writer. Still, although no simple formula for good writing exists, some approaches are easier and more productive than others.

At this point you may be asking yourself, "So what? What has this got to do with me? I'm not a professional writer." True enough, but during the next few years you will be doing a good deal of writing. Throughout your college career, you will write midterms, final exams, lab reports, essays, and research papers. In your professional life, you may write progress reports, proposals, business correspondence, and memos. As diverse as these tasks are, they have something in common: they can be made easier if you are familiar with the **writing process** — the process experienced writers follow to produce a piece of writing.

THE STAGES OF THE WRITING PROCESS

- **Invention** (also called **prewriting**)   During invention, you decide what to write about and gather information to support or explain what you want to say.
- **Arrangement**   During arrangement, you decide how you are going to organize your ideas.
- **Drafting and Revising**   During drafting and revising, you write several drafts as you reconsider your ideas and refine your style and structure.
- **Editing**   During editing, you correct grammar, punctuation, spelling, and mechanics.

Although the writing process is usually presented as a series of neatly defined steps, this model does not reflect the way people actually write. Ideas do not always flow easily, and the central point you set out to develop does not always wind up in the essay you ultimately write. In addition, writing often progresses in fits and starts, with ideas occurring sporadically or not at all. Surprisingly, much good writing occurs when a writer gets stuck or confused but continues to work until ideas take shape on the page or on the computer screen.

Because the writing process is so erratic, its stages overlap. Most writers engage in invention, arrangement, drafting and revision, and editing simultaneously — finding ideas, considering possible methods of organization, looking for the right words, and correcting grammar and punctuation all at the same time. In fact, writing is such an idiosyncratic process that no two writers approach the writing process in exactly the same way. Some people outline; others do not. Some take elaborate notes during the invention stage; others keep track of everything in their heads.

The writing process discussed throughout this book reflects the many choices writers make at various stages of composition. But regardless of writers' different approaches, one thing is certain: the more you write, the better acquainted you will become with your personal writing process and the better you will learn how to modify it to suit various writing tasks. The four chapters that follow will help you define your needs as a writer and understand your options as you approach writing assignments both in college and beyond.

2

Invention

Invention, or **prewriting**, is an important part of the writing process. At this stage, you discover what interests you about your subject and explore ideas to develop in your essay.

When you are given a writing assignment, you may be tempted to plunge into a first draft immediately. Before writing, however, you should be sure you understand your assignment and its limits, and you should think about what you want to say. Time spent on these concerns now will pay off later when you draft your essay.

Understanding Your Assignment

Almost everything you write in college will begin as an *assignment*. Some assignments will be direct and easy to understand:

Write about an experience that changed your life.

Discuss the procedure you used to synthesize ammonia.

Others will be more difficult and complex:

According to Wayne Booth, point of view is central to understanding modern fiction. In a short essay, discuss how Toni Morrison uses point of view in *Beloved*.

Before beginning to write, you need to understand what your assignment is asking you to do. If the assignment is written as a question, read it carefully several times, and underline its key words. If the assignment is read aloud by your instructor, be sure to copy it accurately. (A mistaken word—*analyze* for *compare,* for example—can make quite a difference.) If you are confused about anything, ask your instructor for clarification. Remember that no matter how well written an essay is, it will fall short if it does not address the assignment.

Setting Limits

Once you understand the assignment, you should consider its *length, purpose, audience,* and *occasion* and your own *knowledge* of the subject. Each of these factors helps you determine what you will say about your subject.

Length

Often, your instructor will specify the **length** of a paper, and this word or page limit has a direct bearing on your paper's focus. For example, you would need a narrower topic for a two-page essay than for a ten-page one. Similarly, you could not discuss a question as thoroughly during an hour-long exam as you might in a paper prepared over several days.

If your instructor sets no page limit, consider how the nature of the assignment suggests its length. A *summary* of a chapter or an article, for instance, should be much shorter than the original, whereas an *analysis* of a poem will most likely be longer than the poem itself. If you are uncertain about the appropriate length for your paper, consult your instructor.

Purpose

Your **purpose** also limits what you say and how you say it. For example, if you were writing a job application letter, you would not emphasize the same aspects of college life as you would in a letter to a friend. In the first case, you would want to persuade the reader to hire you, so you might include your grade-point average and a list of the relevant courses you took. In the second case, you would want to inform and perhaps entertain. To accomplish these aims, you might share anecdotes about dorm life or describe one of your favorite instructors. In each case, your purpose would help you determine what information to include to evoke a particular response in a specific audience.

In general, you can classify your purposes for writing according to your relationship to the audience. Thus, one purpose might be to express personal feelings or impressions to your readers. **Expressive writing** includes diaries, personal letters, journals, and often narrative and descriptive essays as well. Another purpose might be to inform readers about something. **Informative writing** includes essay exams, lab reports, book reports, expository essays, and some research papers. Your purpose might also be to persuade readers to think or act in a certain way. **Persuasive writing** includes editorials, argumentative essays, and many other essays and research papers.

In addition to these general purposes, you might have a more specific purpose—to analyze, entertain, hypothesize, assess, summarize, question, report, recommend, suggest, evaluate, describe, recount, request, instruct, and so on. For example, suppose you wrote a report on homelessness in your community. Your general purpose might be to *inform* readers of the situation, but you might also want to *assess* the problem and *instruct* readers how to help those in need.

Audience

To be effective, your essay should be written with a particular **audience** in mind. An audience can be an *individual* (your instructor, for example), or it can be a *group* (like your classmates or coworkers). Your essay can address a *specialized* audience (such as a group of medical doctors or economists) or a *general* or *universal* audience whose members have little in common (such as the readers of a newspaper or newsmagazine).

In college, your audience is usually your instructor, and your purpose in most cases is to demonstrate your mastery of the subject matter, your reasoning ability, and your competence as a writer. Other audiences may include classmates, professional colleagues, or members of your community. Considering the age and gender of your audience, its political and religious values, its social and educational level, and its interest in your subject may help you define it. Certainly, the approach you take in a report about homelessness in your community would depend on your intended audience. For example, a report written for students at a local middle school would be very different from one addressing a civic group or the city council—or the parents of those students.

Often, you will find that your audience is just too diverse to be categorized. In such cases, many writers imagine a general (or universal) audience and make points that they think will appeal to a variety of readers. Sometimes writers try to imagine one typical individual in the audience—perhaps a person they know—so that they can write to someone specific. At other times, writers identify a common denominator, a role that characterizes the entire audience. For instance, when a report on the dangers of smoking asserts, "Now is the time for health-conscious individuals to demand that cigarettes be removed from the market," it automatically casts its audience in the role of health-conscious individuals.

After you define your audience, you have to determine how much or how little its members know about your subject. This consideration helps you decide how much information your readers will need to understand the discussion. Are they highly informed? If so, you can make your points directly. Are they relatively uninformed? If this is the case, you will have to include definitions of key terms, background information, and summaries of basic research. Keep in mind that experts in one field will need background information in other fields. If, for example, you were writing an essay analyzing the characters in Joseph Conrad's *Heart of Darkness*, you could assume that the literature instructor who assigned the novel would not need a plot summary. However, if you wrote an essay for your history instructor that used *Heart of Darkness* to illustrate the evils of European colonialism in nineteenth-century Africa, you would probably include a short plot summary. (Even though your history instructor would know a lot about colonialism in Africa, she might not be familiar with Conrad's novel.)

Occasion

In general, the **occasion** for academic writing will be either an in-class writing exercise or an at-home assignment. In addition, different subject areas create different occasions for writing. A response suitable for a psychology or history class might not be acceptable for an English class.

Although college writing situations may seem artificial, they provide valuable practice for writing you do outside of college. Like college assignments, each writing task you do outside of school requires a special approach that suits the occasion. A memo to coworkers, for instance, will be less formal and more limited in scope than a report to a company's president. An email to members of an online discussion group might be strictly informational, whereas a letter to a state senator about preserving a local historic landmark would most likely be persuasive as well as informational.

Knowledge

What you know (and do not know) about a subject determines what you can say about it. Before writing about any subject, ask yourself the following questions:

- What do I know about the subject?
- What do I need to find out?
- What do I think about the subject?

Different writing situations require different kinds of knowledge. A personal essay will draw on your own experiences and observations; a term paper will require you to gain new knowledge through research. Sometimes you will be able to increase your knowledge about a topic easily because you already know a lot about the general subject. At other times, you may need to select a topic carefully so that you do not get out of your depth. In many cases, your page limit and the amount of time you are given to do the assignment will help you decide how much information you need to gather before you can begin.

✓ CHECKLIST: Setting Limits

LENGTH

- Has your instructor specified a length?
- Does the nature of your assignment suggest a length?

PURPOSE

- Is your general purpose to express personal feelings? To inform? To persuade?
- In addition to your general purpose, do you have any more specific purposes?
- Does your assignment provide any guidelines about purpose?

AUDIENCE

- Is your audience a group or an individual?
- Are you going to address a specialized or a general audience?
- Should you take into consideration the audience's age, gender, education, biases, or political or social values?
- Should you cast your audience in a particular role?
- How much can you assume your audience knows about your subject?
- How much interest does your audience have in your subject?

OCCASION

- Are you writing in class or at home?
- Are you addressing a situation outside the academic setting?
- What special approaches does your occasion for writing require?

KNOWLEDGE

- What do you know about your subject?
- What do you need to find out?
- What are your opinions about your subject?

Exercise 1

Decide whether or not each of the following topics is appropriate for the stated limits, and then write a few sentences to explain why each topic is or is not acceptable.

1. *A two-to-three-page paper*   A history of animal testing in medical research labs
2. *A two-hour final exam*   The effectiveness of bilingual education programs

3. *A one-hour in-class essay* An interpretation of one of Andy Warhol's paintings of Campbell's soup cans

4. *A letter to your college newspaper* A discussion of your school's policy on alcoholic beverages

Exercise 2

Make a list of the different audiences to whom you speak or write in your daily life. (Consider all the different people you see regularly, such as family members, your roommate, instructors, your boss, your friends, and so on.) Then, record your answers to the following questions:

1. Do you speak or write to each person in the same way and about the same things? If not, how do your approaches to these people differ?

2. List some subjects that would interest some of these people but not others. How do you account for these differences?

3. Choose one of the following subjects, and describe how you would speak or write to each audience about it.
   - A local political issue
   - Your favorite television show or Web site
   - Mandatory drug testing for all student athletes
   - Plagiarism

General to Specific

Moving from Subject to Topic

Although many essays begin as specific assignments or topics, some begin as broad areas of interest or concern. These **general subjects** always need to be narrowed to **specific topics** that can be discussed within the limits of the assignment. For example, a subject like stem-cell research could be interesting, but it is too complicated to write about for any college assignment except in a general way. You need to limit such a subject to a topic that can be covered within the time and space available.

GENERAL SUBJECT	SPECIFIC TOPIC
Stem-cell research	Using stem-cell research to cure multiple sclerosis
Herman Melville's *Billy Budd*	Billy Budd as a Christ figure
Constitutional law	One result of the *Miranda* ruling
The Internet	The uses of the Internet in elementary school classrooms

Two strategies can help you narrow a general subject to a specific topic: *questions for probing* and *freewriting*.

Questions for Probing

One way to move from a general subject to a specific topic is to examine your subject by asking a series of probing questions about it. These **questions for probing** are useful because they reflect how your mind operates — for instance, finding similarities and differences, or dividing a whole into its parts. By going through the questions on the following checklist, you can explore your subject systematically. Not all questions will work for every subject, but any single question may elicit many different answers, and each answer is a possible topic for your essay.

[handwritten note: that to narrow subject]

✓ CHECKLIST: **Questions for Probing**

What happened?
When did it happen?
Where did it happen?
Who did it?
What does it look like?
What are its characteristics?
What impressions does it make?
What are some typical cases or examples of it?
How did it happen?
What makes it work?
How is it made?
Why did it happen?
What caused it?
What does it cause?
What are its effects?
How is it like other things?
How is it different from other things?
What are its parts or types?
How can its parts or types be separated or grouped?
Do its parts or types fit into a logical order?
Into what categories can its parts or types be arranged?
On what basis can it be categorized?
How can it be defined?
How does it resemble other members of its class?
How does it differ from other members of its class?

When applied to a subject, some of these questions can yield many workable topics, including some you might never have considered had you not asked the questions. For example, by applying this approach to the general subject "the Brooklyn Bridge," you can generate more ideas and topics than you need:

> *What happened?* A short history of the Brooklyn Bridge
>
> *What does it look like?* A description of the Brooklyn Bridge
>
> *How is it made?* The construction of the Brooklyn Bridge
>
> *What are its effects?* The impact of the Brooklyn Bridge on American writers
>
> *How does it differ from other members of its class?* Innovations in the design of the Brooklyn Bridge

At this point in the writing process, you want to discover possible topics, and the more ideas you have, the wider your choice. Begin by writing down all the topics you think of. (You can repeat the process of probing several times to limit topics further.) Once you have a list of topics, eliminate those that do not interest you or are too complex or too simple to fit your assignment. When you have discarded these less promising topics, you should still have several left. You can then select the topic that best suits your paper's length, purpose, audience, and occasion, as well as your interests and your knowledge of the subject.

🖳 COMPUTER STRATEGY

You can store the questions for probing listed on page 21 in a file that you can open whenever you have a new subject. Make sure you keep a record of your answers. If the topic you have chosen is too difficult or too narrow, you can return to the questions-for-probing file and probe your subject again.

Exercise 3

Indicate whether each of the following is a general subject or a specific topic that is narrow enough for a short essay.

1. An argument against fast-food ads aimed at young children
2. A comparison of the salaries of professional basketball and football players
3. Cell phones and driving
4. Changes in U.S. immigration laws
5. Requiring college students to study a foreign language
6. The advantages of affirmative action
7. The advantages and disadvantages of pass/fail grading
8. Downloading music from the Internet

9. An analysis of a political cartoon in your local newspaper
10. The role of religion in people's lives

Exercise 4

In preparation for writing a 750-word essay, choose two of the following general subjects, and generate three or four specific topics from each by using as many of the questions for probing as you can.

1. Credit-card fraud
2. Censorship and the Internet
3. Identity theft
4. Gasoline prices
5. Substance abuse
6. Smoking
7. The minimum wage
8. Age discrimination
9. Women in combat
10. National ID cards
11. Reinstating the draft
12. Rising college tuition
13. Grading
14. Television reality shows
15. The death penalty

Freewriting

Another strategy for moving from subject to topic is **freewriting**. You can use freewriting at any stage of the writing process — for example, to generate supporting information or to find a thesis. However, freewriting is a particularly useful way to narrow a general subject or assignment. When you freewrite, you write for a fixed period, perhaps five or ten minutes, without stopping and without paying attention to spelling, grammar, or punctuation. Your goal is to get your ideas down on paper so that you can react to them and shape them. If you find you have nothing to say, write down anything until ideas begin to emerge — and in time they will. The secret is to *keep writing*. Try to focus on your subject, but don't worry if your ideas wander off in other directions. The object of freewriting is to let your ideas flow. Often your best ideas will come from the unexpected connections you make as you write.

After completing your freewriting, read what you have written and look for ideas you can write about. Some writers underline ideas they think they might explore in their essays. Any of these ideas could become essay topics, or they could become subjects for other freewriting exercises. You might want to freewrite again, using a new idea as your focus. This process of writing more and more narrowly focused freewriting exercises — called **looping** — can often yield a great deal of useful information and help you decide on a workable topic.

🖥 COMPUTER STRATEGY

If you do your freewriting on a computer, you may find that staring at your own words causes you to go blank or lose your spontaneity. One possible solution is to turn down the brightness until the screen becomes dark and then to freewrite. This technique allows you to block out distracting elements and concentrate on just your ideas. Once you finish freewriting, turn up the brightness, and see what you have. If you have an interesting idea, you can move it onto a new page and use it as the subject of a new freewriting exercise.

A STUDENT WRITER: Freewriting

After reading Henry Louis Gates Jr.'s "'What's in a Name?'" (page 5), Laura Bobnak, a student in a composition class, chose to write an essay in response to this Writing Workshop question:

> Write about a time when you, like Gates's father, could have spoken out in protest but chose not to. Would you make the same decision today?

In an attempt to narrow this assignment to a workable topic, Laura completed the following freewriting exercise:

> Write for ten minutes . . . ten minutes . . . at 9 o'clock in the morning — Just what I want to do in the morning — If you can't think of something to say, just write about anything. Right! Time to get this over with — An experience — should have talked — I can think of plenty of times I should have kept quiet! I should have brought coffee to class. I wonder what the people next to me are writing about. That reminds me. Next to me. Jeff Servin in chemistry. The time I saw him cheating. I was mad but I didn't do anything. I studied so hard and all he did was cheat. I was so mad. Nobody else seemed to care either. What's the difference between now and then? It's only a year and a half. . . . Honor code? Maturity? A lot of people cheated in high school. I bet I could write about this — Before and after, etc. My attitude then and now.

After some initial floundering, Laura discovered an idea that could be the basis for her essay. Although her discussion of the incident still had to be developed, Laura's freewriting had helped her discover a possible topic for her essay: a time she saw someone cheating and did not speak out.

Exercise 5

Do a five-minute freewriting exercise on one of the topics you generated in Exercise 4 (page 23).

Exercise 6

Read what you have just written, underline the most interesting ideas, and choose one idea as a topic you could write about in a short essay. Freewrite about this topic for another five minutes to narrow it further and to generate ideas for your essay. Underline the ideas that seem most useful.

Finding Something to Say

Once you have narrowed your subject to a workable topic, you need to find something to say about it. *Brainstorming* and *journal writing* are useful tools for generating ideas, and both can be helpful at this stage of the writing process (and whenever you need to find additional material).

Brainstorming

Brainstorming is a productive way of discovering ideas about your topic. You can brainstorm in a group, exchanging ideas with several students in your composition class and writing down the most useful ideas. You can also brainstorm on your own, quickly writing down every fact, idea, or detail you can think of that relates to your topic. Your notes might include words, phrases, statements, questions, or even drawings or diagrams. Jot them down in the order in which you think of them. Some of the items may be inspired by your class notes; others may be ideas you got from reading or from talking with friends; and still other items may be ideas you have begun to wonder about, points you thought of while moving from subject to topic, or thoughts that occurred to you as you brainstormed.

A STUDENT WRITER: **Brainstorming**

To narrow her topic further and find something to say about it, Laura Bobnak made the brainstorming notes shown on page 26. After reading these notes several times, Laura decided to concentrate on the differences between her current and earlier attitudes toward cheating. She knew that she could write a lot about this idea and relate it to the assignment, and she felt confident that her topic would be interesting both to her instructor and to the other students in the class.

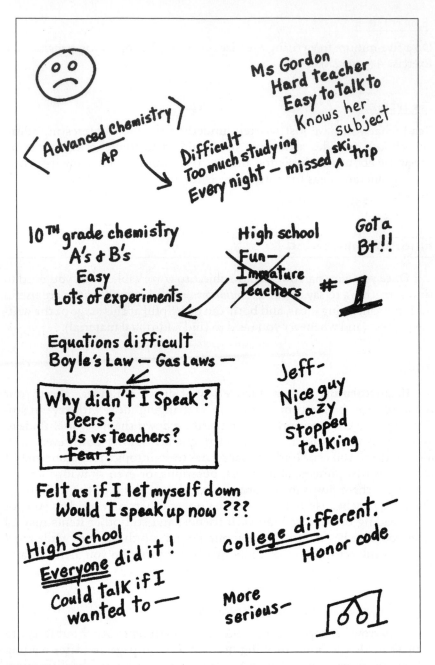

Brainstorming notes.

🖳 COMPUTER STRATEGY

If you are a good typist, brainstorming on your computer can save you time and effort. Your word-processing program makes it easy to create bulleted or numbered lists and gives you the flexibility to experiment with different ways of arranging and grouping items from your brainstorming notes.

Journal Writing

Journal writing can be a useful source of ideas at any stage of the writing process. Many writers routinely keep a journal, jotting down experiences or exploring ideas they may want to use when they write. They write journal entries even when they have no particular writing project in mind. Often these journal entries are the kernels from which longer pieces of writing develop. Your instructor may ask you to keep a writing journal, or you may decide to do so on your own. In either case, you will find your journal entries are likely to be more narrowly focused than freewriting or brainstorming, perhaps examining a small part of a reading selection or even one particular statement. Sometimes you will write in your journal in response to specific questions, such as the Journal Entry assignments that appear throughout this book. Assignments like these can help you start thinking about a reading selection that you may later discuss in class or write about.

A STUDENT WRITER: Journal Writing

In the following journal entry, Laura Bobnak explores one idea from her brainstorming notes — her thoughts about her college's honor code:

> At orientation the dean of students talked about the college's honor code. She talked about how we were a community of scholars who were here for a common purpose — to take part in an intellectual conversation. According to her, the purpose of the honor code is to make sure this conversation continues uninterrupted. This idea sounded dumb at first, but now it makes sense. If I saw someone cheating, I'd tell the instructor. First, though, I'd ask the student to go to the instructor. I don't see this as "telling" or "squealing." We're all here to get an education, and we should be able to assume everyone is being honest and fair. Besides, why should I go to all the trouble of studying while someone else does nothing and gets the same grade?

Even though Laura eventually included only a small part of this entry in her paper, writing in her journal helped her clarify her ideas about her topic.

🖳 COMPUTER STRATEGY

Keeping your journal in a computer file has some obvious advantages. Not only can you maintain a neat record of your ideas, but you can also easily move entries from your journal into an essay without retyping them.

Grouping Ideas

Once you have generated material for your essay, you will want to group ideas that belong together. *Clustering* and *outlining* can help you do this.

Clustering

Clustering is a way of visually arranging your ideas so that you can tell at a glance where ideas belong and whether or not you need to generate more information. Although you can use clustering at an earlier stage of the writing process, it is especially useful now for seeing how your ideas fit together. (Clustering can also help you narrow your paper's topic even further. If you find that your cluster diagram is too detailed, you can write about just one branch of the cluster.)

Begin clustering by writing your topic in the center of a sheet of paper. After circling the topic, surround it with the words and phrases that identify the major points you intend to discuss. (You can get ideas from your brainstorming notes, from your journal, and from your freewriting.) Circle these words and phrases, and connect them to the topic in the center. Next, construct other clusters of ideas relating to each major point, and draw lines connecting them to the appropriate point. By dividing and subdividing your points, you get more specific as you move outward from the center. In the process, you identify the facts, details, examples, and opinions that illustrate and expand your main points.

A STUDENT WRITER: Clustering

Because Laura Bobnak was not very visually oriented, she chose not to use this method of grouping her ideas. If she had, however, her cluster diagram might have looked like this:

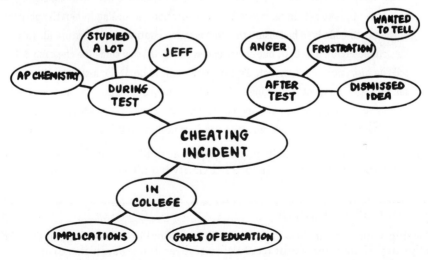

Making an Informal Outline

As an alternative or follow-up to clustering, you can organize your notes from brainstorming or other invention techniques into an **informal outline**. Informal outlines do not include all the major divisions and subdivisions of your paper nor indicate the relative importance of your ideas the way formal outlines do; they simply suggest the shape of your emerging essay. Quite often an informal outline is just a list of your major points presented in a tentative order. Sometimes, however, an informal outline will include supporting details or suggest a pattern of development.

🖳 COMPUTER STRATEGY

If you use a computer, you can easily arrange the notes you generated in your invention activities into an informal outline. You can make an informal outline by typing words or phrases from your notes and rearranging them until the order makes sense. Later, you can use the categories from this informal outline to construct a formal outline (see page 47).

A STUDENT WRITER: **Making an Informal Outline**

The following informal outline shows how Laura Bobnak grouped her ideas:

    During test
        Found test hard
        Saw Jeff cheating
    After test
        Got angry
        Wanted to tell
        Dismissed idea
    In college
        Implications of cheating
        Goals of education

Exercise 7

Continue your work on the topic you selected in Exercise 6 (page 25). Brainstorm about your topic; then, select the ideas you plan to write about in your essay, and use either clustering or an informal outline to help you group these ideas.

Understanding Thesis and Support

Once you have grouped your ideas, you need to consider your essay's thesis.

A **thesis** is the main idea of your essay, its central point. The concept of *thesis and support*—stating your thesis and developing ideas that explain and expand it—is central to college writing. The essays you write will consist of several paragraphs: an *introduction* that presents your thesis statement, several *body paragraphs* that develop and support your thesis, and a *conclusion* that reinforces your thesis and provides closure. Your thesis holds this structure together; it is the center the rest of your essay develops around.

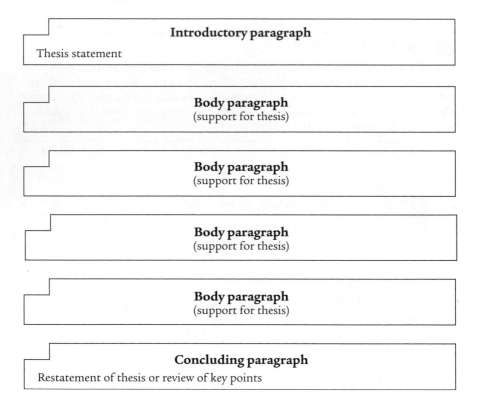

Introductory paragraph

Thesis statement

Body paragraph
(support for thesis)

Body paragraph
(support for thesis)

Body paragraph
(support for thesis)

Body paragraph
(support for thesis)

Concluding paragraph
Restatement of thesis or review of key points

Formulating a Thesis

Defining the Thesis Statement

A **thesis statement** is more than a *title*, an *announcement of your intent*, or a *statement of fact*. Although a descriptive title orients your readers, it is seldom detailed enough to reveal your essay's purpose or direction. An announcement of your intent can reveal more, but it is stylistically distracting. Finally, a statement of fact—such as a historical fact or a statistic—is typically a dead end and therefore cannot be developed into an essay. A statement like "Alaska became a state in 1959" or "Tuberculosis is highly contagious" or "The population of Greece is about ten million" provides your essay with no direction. However, a judgment or opinion *can* be an effective thesis—for instance, "The continuing threat of tuberculosis, particularly in the inner cities, suggests it is necessary to frequently test high-risk populations."

Title	Hybrid Cars: Pro and Con
Announcement	I will examine the pros and cons of hybrid cars that use both gasoline and electricity.
Statement of fact	Hybrid cars are more energy efficient than cars with standard gasoline engines.
Thesis statement	Hybrid cars that use both gasoline and electricity would decrease our country's dependence on foreign oil.
Title	Orwell's "A Hanging"
Announcement	This paper will discuss George Orwell's attitude toward the death penalty in his essay "A Hanging."
Statement of fact	In his essay, Orwell describes a hanging that he witnessed in Burma.
Thesis statement	In "A Hanging," George Orwell shows that capital punishment is not only brutal but also immoral.
Title	Speaking Out
Announcement	This essay will discuss a time when I could have spoken out but did not.
Statement of fact	Once I saw someone cheating and did not speak out.
Thesis statement	As I look back at the cheating I witnessed, I wonder why I kept silent and what would have happened if I had acted.

Deciding on a Thesis

No rules determine when you formulate your thesis; the decision depends on the scope and difficulty of your assignment, your knowledge of the subject, and your method of writing. When you know a lot about a subject, you may come up with a thesis before doing any invention activities (freewriting or brainstorming, for example). At other times, you may have to review all your material and then think of a single statement that communicates your position on the topic. Occasionally, your assignment may specify a thesis by telling you to take a particular position on a topic. Whatever the case, you should have a thesis statement in mind before you begin to write your first draft.

As you write, you will continue to discover new ideas, and you will probably move in directions that you did not anticipate. For this reason, the thesis statement you develop at this stage of the writing process is only *tentative*. Still, because a tentative thesis gives you guidance and purpose, it is essential at the initial stages of writing. As you draft your essay, review your thesis statement in light of the points you make, and revise it accordingly.

Stating Your Thesis

It is almost always a good idea to include a one-sentence statement of your thesis early in your essay. An effective thesis statement has three characteristics:

1. *An effective thesis statement clearly expresses your essay's main idea.* It does more than state your topic; it indicates what you will say about your topic, and it signals how you will approach your material. The following thesis statement, from the essay "Grant and Lee: A Study in Contrasts" by Bruce Catton (page 409), clearly communicates the writer's main idea:

> They [Grant and Lee] were two strong men, these oddly different generals, and they represented the strengths of two conflicting currents that, through them, had come into final collision.

This statement indicates that the essay will compare and contrast Grant and Lee. Specifically, it reveals that Catton will present the two Civil War generals as symbols of two historical currents that were also in opposition. If the statement had been less fully developed — for example, had Catton written, "Grant and Lee were quite different from each other" — it would have just echoed the essay's title.

2. *An effective thesis statement communicates your essay's purpose.* Whether your purpose is to evaluate or analyze or simply to describe or recount, your thesis statement should communicate that purpose to your readers. In general terms, your purpose may be to express personal feelings, to present information in a straightforward manner, or to persuade. Accordingly, your thesis can be *expressive,* conveying a mood or impression; it can be *informative,* perhaps listing the major points you will discuss or presenting an objective overview of the essay; or it can be *persuasive,* taking a strong stand or outlining the position you will argue.

Each of the following thesis statements communicates a different purpose:

To express feelings	The city's homeless families live in heartbreaking surroundings.
To inform	The plight of the homeless has become so serious that it is a major priority for many city governments.

To persuade   The best way to address the problems of the homeless is to renovate abandoned city buildings to cre-
ate suitable housing for homeless families.

3. *An effective thesis statement is clearly worded.*   To communicate your
essay's main idea, an effective thesis statement should be clearly and specifically worded. (It should also speak for itself. It is not necessary to write,
"My thesis is that . . ." or "The thesis of this paper is. . . .") The thesis statement should give an accurate indication of what follows and not mislead
readers about the essay's direction, emphasis, scope, content, or viewpoint.
Vague language, confusing abstractions, irrelevant details, and complex
terminology have no place in a thesis statement. Keep in mind, too, that
your thesis statement should not make promises that your essay is not
going to keep. For example, if you are going to discuss just the *effects* of new
immigration laws, your thesis statement should not emphasize the events
that led to their passage.

Your thesis statement cannot, of course, include every point you will
discuss in your essay. Still, it should be specific enough to indicate your
direction and scope. The statement "New immigration laws have failed to
stem the tide of illegal immigrants" does not give your essay much focus.
Which immigration laws will you be examining? Which illegal immigrants? The following sentence, however, *is* an effective thesis statement. It
clearly indicates what the writer is going to discuss, and it establishes a specific direction for the essay:

Because they do not take into account the economic causes of immigration, the 2002 immigration laws do little to decrease the number of illegal
immigrants coming from Mexico into the United States.

Implying a Thesis   *Implied thesis*

Like an explicitly stated thesis, an **implied thesis** conveys an essay's purpose, but it does not do so explicitly. Instead, the selection and arrangement
of the essay's ideas suggest the purpose. Professional writers sometimes prefer this option because an implied thesis is subtler than a stated thesis. (An
implied thesis is especially useful in narratives, descriptions, and some arguments, where an explicit thesis would seem heavy-handed or arbitrary.) In
most college writing, however, you should state your thesis to avoid any risk
of being misunderstood or of wandering away from your topic.

A STUDENT WRITER: Formulating a Thesis

After experimenting with different ways of arranging her ideas for her
essay, Laura Bobnak eventually summed them up in a tentative thesis
statement:

As I look back at the cheating I witnessed, I wonder why I kept silent and what
would have happened if I had acted.

Exercise 8

Assess the strengths and weaknesses of the following as thesis statements.

1. Myths are more than fairy tales.
2. Myths serve an important function in society.
3. Contrary to popular assumptions, myths are more than fairy tales; they express the underlying attitudes a society has toward important issues.
4. Today, almost two marriages in four will end in divorce.
5. Skiing, a popular sport for millions, is a major cause of winter injuries.
6. If certain reforms are not instituted immediately, the company will be bankrupt within two years.
7. Early childhood is an important period.
8. By using the proper techniques, parents can significantly improve the learning capabilities of their preschool children.
9. Fiction can be used to criticize society.
10. Fiction, in the hands of an able writer, can be a powerful tool for social change.

Exercise 9

Rewrite the following factual statements to make them effective thesis statements. Make sure each thesis statement is a clearly and specifically worded sentence.

1. A number of hospitals have refused to admit patients without health insurance because they fear that such patients do not have the resources to pay their bills.
2. Several Supreme Court decisions have said that art containing explicit sexual images is not necessarily pornographic.
3. Many women earn less money than men do, in part because they drop out of the workforce during their child-rearing years.
4. People who watch more than five hours of television a day tend to think the world is more violent than do people who watch less than two hours of television daily.
5. In recent years, the suicide rate among teenagers — especially middle- and upper-middle-class teenagers — has risen dramatically.

Exercise 10

Read the following sentences from *Broca's Brain* by Carl Sagan. Then, formulate a one-sentence thesis statement that summarizes the points Sagan makes about robots.

- "Robots, especially robots in space, have received derogatory notices in the press."

- "Each human being is a superbly constructed, astonishingly compact, self-ambulatory computer — capable on occasion of independent decision making and real control of his or her environment."
- "If we do send human beings to exotic environments, we must also send along food, air, water, waste recycling, amenities for entertainment, and companions."
- "By comparison, machines require no elaborate life-support systems, no entertainment, and no companionship, and we do not feel any strong ethical prohibitions against sending machines on one-way, or suicide, missions."
- "Even exceptionally simple computers — those that can be wired by a bright ten-year-old — can be wired to play perfect tic-tac-toe."
- "With this . . . set of examples of the state of development of machine intelligence, I think it is clear that a major effort over the next decade could produce much more sophisticated examples."
- "We appear to be on the verge of developing a wide variety of intelligent machines capable of performing tasks too dangerous, too expensive, too onerous, or too boring for human beings."
- "The main obstacle seems to be a very human problem, the quiet feeling that there is something threatening or 'inhuman' about machines."
- "But in many respects our survival as a species depends on our transcending such primitive chauvinisms."
- "There is nothing inhuman about an intelligent machine; it is indeed an expression of all those superb intellectual capabilities that only human beings . . . now possess."

Exercise 11

Go through as many steps as you need to formulate an effective thesis statement for the essay you have been working on.

3
Arrangement

Each of the tasks discussed in Chapter 2 represents choices you have to make about your topic and your material. Now, before you actually begin to write, you have another choice to make — how to arrange your material into an essay.

Recognizing a Pattern

Sometimes arranging your ideas will be easy because your assignment specifies a particular pattern of development. This may be the case in a composition class, where the instructor may assign a descriptive or a narrative essay. Also, certain assignments or exam questions suggest how your material should be structured. Probably no one will say to you, "Write a narrative," but you will have assignments that begin, "Give an account" or "Tell about." Likewise, teachers may not explicitly assign a process essay, but they may ask you to explain how something works. Similarly, an exam question might ask you to trace the circumstances leading up to an event. If you are perceptive, you will realize that this question calls for either a narrative or a cause-and-effect answer. The important thing is to recognize the clues such assignments give (or those you find in your topic or thesis statement) and to structure your essay accordingly.

One clue to structuring your essay may be found in the questions that proved most helpful when you probed your subject (see page 21). For example, if questions like "What happened?" and "When did it happen?" yielded the most useful information about your topic, you should consider structuring your paper as a narrative. The chart on page 38 links various questions to the patterns of development they suggest. Notice that the terms in the right-hand column — narration, description, and so on — identify patterns of development that can help order your ideas. Chapters 6 through 13 explain and illustrate each of these patterns.

✓ CHECKLIST: **Recognizing a Pattern**

Questions	Pattern
What happened? When did it happen? Where did it happen? Who did it?	Narration
What does it look like? What are its characteristics? What impression does it make?	Description
What are some typical cases or examples of it?	Exemplification
How did it happen? What makes it work? How is it made?	Process
Why did it happen? What caused it? What does it cause? What are its effects?	Cause and effect
How is it like other things? How is it different from other things?	Comparison and contrast
What are its parts or types? How can its parts or types be separated or grouped? Do its parts or types fit into a logical order? Into what categories can its parts or types be arranged? On what basis can it be categorized?	Classification and division
What is it? How does it resemble other members of its class? How does it differ from other members of its class?	Definition

Understanding the Parts of the Essay

No matter what pattern of development you use, your essay should have a beginning, a middle, and an end—that is, an *introduction,* a *body,* and a *conclusion.*

The Introduction

The **introduction** of your essay, usually one paragraph and rarely more than two, introduces your subject, creates interest, and often states your thesis.

You can introduce an essay and engage your readers' interest in a number of ways. Here are several options for beginning an essay (in each paragraph, the thesis statement is underlined):

1. You can give *background information* and then move directly to your thesis statement. This approach works well when you know the audience is already interested in your topic and you can come directly to the point. This strategy is especially useful for exams, where there is no need (or time) for subtlety.

> With inflation low, many companies have understandably lowered prices, and the oil industry should be no exception. Consequently, homeowners have begun wondering whether the high price of home heating oil is justified given the economic climate. It makes sense, therefore, for us to start examining the pricing policies of the major American oil companies.
>
> (economics essay)

2. You can introduce an essay with a *definition* of a relevant term or concept. (Keep in mind, however, that the "According to *Webster's Dictionary* . . ." formula is overused and trite.) This technique is especially useful for research papers or exams, where the meaning of a specific term is crucial.

> Democracy is a form of government in which power is given to and exercised by the people. This may be so in theory, but some recent elections have raised concerns about the future of democracy. Extensive voting-machine irregularities and "ghost voting" have jeopardized people's faith in the democratic process.
>
> (political science exam)

3. You can begin your essay with an *anecdote* or *story* that leads readers to your thesis.

> Upon meeting the famous author James Joyce, a young student stammered, "May I kiss the hand that wrote *Ulysses*?" "No!" said Joyce. "It did a lot of other things, too." As this exchange shows, Joyce was a person who valued humor. His sense of humor is present in his final work, *Finnegans Wake*, in which he uses humor to comment on the human condition.
>
> (English literature paper)

4. You can begin with a *question*.

> What was it like to live through the Holocaust? Elie Wiesel, in *One Generation After,* answers this question by presenting a series of accounts about ordinary people who found themselves imprisoned in Nazi death camps. As he does so, he challenges some of the assumptions we have about those who survived the Holocaust.   (sociology book report)

5. You can begin with a *quotation*. If it arouses interest, it can encourage your audience to read further.

> "The rich are different," F. Scott Fitzgerald said more than seventy years ago. Apparently, they still are. As an examination of the tax code shows, the wealthy receive many more benefits than the middle class or the poor do. (accounting paper)

6. You can begin with a *surprising statement*. An unexpected statement catches readers' attention and makes them want to read more.

> Believe it or not, most people who live in the suburbs are not white and rich. My family, for example, fits into neither of these categories. Ten years ago, my family and I came to the United States from Pakistan. My parents were poor then, and by some standards, they are still poor even though they both work two jobs. Still, they eventually saved enough to buy a small house in the suburbs of Chicago. Throughout the country, there are many suburban families like mine who are working hard to make ends meet so that their children can get a good education and go to college. (composition essay)

7. You can begin with a *contradiction*. You can open your essay with an idea that most people believe is true and then get readers' attention by showing that it is inaccurate or ill advised.

> Many people think that after the Declaration of Independence was signed in 1776, the colonists defeated the British army in battle after battle. This commonly held belief is incorrect. The truth is that the colonial army lost most of its battles. The British were defeated not because the colonial army was stronger, but because George Washington refused to be lured into a costly winner-take-all battle and because the British government lost interest in pursuing an expensive war three thousand miles from home. (history take-home exam)

8. You can begin with a *fact* or *statistic*.

> According to a recent government study, recipients of Medicare will spend billions of dollars on drugs over the next ten years. This is a very large amount of money, and it illustrates why lawmakers must do more to help older Americans with the cost of medications. Although the current legislation is an important first step, more must be done to help the elderly afford the drugs they need. (public policy essay)

No matter which strategy you select, your introduction should be consistent in tone with the rest of your essay. If it is not, it can misrepresent your intentions and even damage your credibility. (For this reason, it is a good idea not to write your introduction until after you have finished the rest of your rough draft.) A technical report, for instance, should have an introduction that reflects the formality and objectivity the occasion requires. The introduction to an autobiographical essay, however, should have a more informal, subjective tone.

Exercise 1

Look through magazine articles or the essays in this book, and find one example of each kind of introduction. Why do you think each introductory strategy was chosen? What other strategies might have worked?

The Body Paragraphs

The middle section, or **body**, of your essay develops your thesis. The body paragraphs present the support that convinces your audience your thesis is reasonable. To do so, each body paragraph should be *unified, coherent,* and *well developed.* It should also follow a particular pattern of development and should clearly support your thesis.

• *Each body paragraph should be unified.*   A paragraph has **unity** when every sentence relates directly to the main idea of the paragraph. Sometimes the main idea of a paragraph is explicitly stated in a **topic sentence**. Like a thesis statement, a topic sentence acts as a guidepost, making it easy for readers to follow the paragraph's discussion. Although the placement of a topic sentence depends on a writer's purpose and subject, beginning writers often make it the first sentence of a paragraph.

Sometimes the main idea of a paragraph is not stated but *implied* by the sentences in the paragraph. Professional writers frequently use this technique because they believe that in some situations — especially narratives and descriptions — a topic sentence can seem forced or awkward. As a beginning writer, however, you will find it helpful to use topic sentences to keep your paragraphs focused.

Whether or not you include a topic sentence, remember that each sentence in a paragraph should develop the paragraph's main idea. If the sentences in a paragraph do not support the main idea, the paragraph will lack unity.

In the following excerpt from a student essay, notice how the topic sentence (underlined) unifies the paragraph by summarizing its main idea:

> Built on the Acropolis overlooking the city of Athens in the fifth century B.C., the Parthenon illustrates the limitations of Greek architecture. As a temple of the gods, it was supposed to represent heavenly or divine perfection. However, although at first glance its structure seems perfectly symmetrical, on closer examination it becomes clear that this is not the case. As long as you stand in the center of any of its four sides to look at it, its form appears symmetrical. The strong Doric columns seem to be equally spaced, one next to another, along all four of its sides. But if you take a step to the right or left, the Parthenon's symmetry is destroyed.

The topic sentence, placed at the beginning of the paragraph, enables readers to grasp the writer's point immediately. The examples that follow all relate to that point, making the paragraph unified.

• *Each body paragraph should be coherent.* A paragraph is **coherent** if its sentences are smoothly and logically connected to one another. Coherence can be achieved through three techniques. First, you can repeat **key words** to carry concepts from one sentence to another and to echo important terms. Second, you can use **pronouns** to refer to key nouns in previous sentences. Finally, you can use **transitions**, words or expressions that show chronological sequence, cause and effect, and so on (see the list of transitions on page 43). These three strategies for connecting sentences—which you can also use to connect paragraphs within an essay—indicate for your readers the exact relationships among your ideas.

The following paragraph, from George Orwell's "Shooting an Elephant" (page 125), uses repeated key words, pronouns, and transitions to achieve coherence:

> I got up. The Burmans were already racing past me across the mud. It was obvious that the elephant would never rise again, but he was not dead. He was breathing very rhythmically with long rattling gasps, his great mound of a side painfully rising and falling. His mouth was wide open—I could see far down into the caverns of pale pink throat. I waited a long time for him to die, but his breathing did not weaken. Finally, I fired my two remaining shots into the spot where I thought his heart must be. The thick blood welled out of him like red velvet, but still he did not die. His body did not even jerk when the shots hit him, the tortured breathing continued without a pause. He was dying, very slowly and in great agony, but in some world remote from me where not even a bullet could damage him further. I felt that I had got to put an end to that dreadful noise. It seemed dreadful to see the great beast lying there, powerless to move and yet powerless to die, and not even to be able to finish him. I sent back for my small rifle and poured shot after shot into his heart and down his throat. They seemed to make no impression. The tortured gasps continued as steadily as the ticking of a clock.

Orwell keeps his narrative coherent by using transitional expressions (*already, finally, when the shots hit him*) to signal the passing of time. He uses pronouns (*he, his*) in nearly every sentence to refer back to the elephant, the topic of his paragraph. Finally, he repeats key words like *shots* and *die* (and its variants *dead* and *dying*) to link the whole paragraph's sentences together. The result is a coherent, cohesive whole.

• *Each body paragraph should be well developed.* A paragraph is **well developed** if it contains the **support**—examples, reasons, and so on— readers need to understand its main idea. If a paragraph is not adequately developed, readers will feel they have been given only a partial picture of the subject.

If you decide you need more information in a paragraph, you can look back at your brainstorming notes. If this doesn't help, you can freewrite or brainstorm again, talk with friends and instructors, read more about your

TRANSITIONS

SEQUENCE OR ADDITION

again	first, . . . second, . . . third	next
also	furthermore	one . . . another
and	in addition	still
besides	last	too
finally	moreover	

TIME

afterward	finally	simultaneously
as soon as	immediately	since
at first	in the meantime	soon
at the same time	later	subsequently
before	meanwhile	then
earlier	next	until
eventually	now	

COMPARISON

also	in the same way
likewise	similarly
in comparison	

CONTRAST

although	in contrast	on the one hand . . .
but	instead	on the other hand . . .
conversely	nevertheless	still
despite	nonetheless	whereas
even though	on the contrary	yet
however		

EXAMPLES

for example	specifically
for instance	that is
in fact	thus
namely	

CONCLUSIONS OR SUMMARIES

as a result	in summary
in conclusion	therefore
in short	thus

CAUSES OR EFFECTS

as a result	so
because	then
consequently	therefore
since	

topic, or (with your instructor's permission) do some research. Your assignment and your topic will determine the kind and amount of information you need.

TYPES OF SUPPORT

- **Examples**   Specific illustrations of a general idea or concept
- **Reasons**   Underlying causes or explanations
- **Facts**   Pieces of information that can be verified or proved
- **Statistics**   Numerical data (for example, results of studies by reputable authorities or organizations)
- **Details**   Parts or portions of a whole (for example, steps in a process)
- **Expert Opinions**   Statements by recognized authorities in a particular field
- **Personal Experiences**   Events that you lived through

✓ CHECKLIST: **Effective Support**

- **Support should be relevant.**   Body paragraphs should clearly relate to your essay's thesis. Irrelevant material—material that does not pertain to the thesis—should be deleted.
- **Support should be specific.**   Body paragraphs should contain support that is specific, not general or vague. Specific examples, clear reasons, and precise explanations engage readers and communicate your ideas to them.
- **Support should be adequate.**   Body paragraphs should contain enough facts, reasons, and examples to support your thesis. How much support you need depends on your audience, your purpose, and the scope of your thesis.
- **Support should be representative.**   Body paragraphs should present support that is typical, not atypical. For example, suppose you write a paper claiming that flu shots do not work. Your support for this claim is that your grandmother got the flu even though she was vaccinated. This example is not representative because studies show that most people who get vaccinated do not get the flu.
- **Support should be documented.**   Support that comes from research (print sources and the Internet, for example) should be documented. (For more information on proper documentation, see the Appendix.) **Plagiarism**—failure to document the ideas and words of others—is not only unfair but also dishonest. For this reason, be sure to use proper documentation to acknowledge your debt to your sources. (Keep in mind that words and ideas you borrow from the essays in this book must also be documented.)

The following student paragraph uses two examples to support its topic sentence:

> Just look at how males have been taught that extravagance is a positive characteristic. Scrooge, the main character of Dickens's *A Christmas Carol,* is portrayed as an evil man until he gives up his miserly ways and freely distributes gifts and money on Christmas day. This behavior, of course, is rewarded when people change their opinions about him and decide that he isn't such a bad person after all. Diamond Jim Brady is another interesting example. This individual was a nineteenth-century financier who was known for his extravagant taste in women and food. On any given night, he would eat enough food to feed at least ten of the numerous poor who roamed the streets of New York at that time. Yet, despite his selfishness and infantile self-gratification, Diamond Jim Brady's name has become associated with the good life.

• *Each body paragraph should follow a particular pattern of development.* In addition to making sure your body paragraphs are unified, coherent, and well developed, you need to organize each paragraph according to a specific pattern of development. (Chapters 6 through 13 each begin with a paragraph-length example of the pattern discussed in the chapter.)

• *Each body paragraph should clearly support the thesis statement.* No matter how many body paragraphs your essay has—three, four, five, or even more—each paragraph should introduce and develop an idea that supports the essay's thesis. Each paragraph's topic sentence should express one of these supporting points. The following diagram illustrates this thesis-and-support structure.

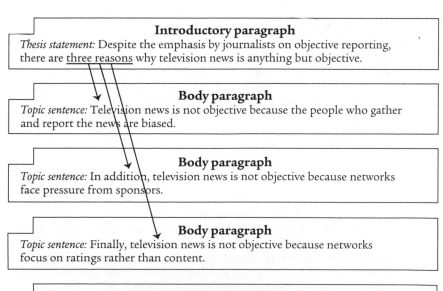

Introductory paragraph
Thesis statement: Despite the emphasis by journalists on objective reporting, there are <u>three reasons</u> why television news is anything but objective.

Body paragraph
Topic sentence: Television news is not objective because the people who gather and report the news are biased.

Body paragraph
Topic sentence: In addition, television news is not objective because networks face pressure from sponsors.

Body paragraph
Topic sentence: Finally, television news is not objective because networks focus on ratings rather than content.

Concluding paragraph
Restatement of thesis: Even though television journalists claim to strive for objectivity, the truth is that this ideal has been impossible to achieve.

Exercise 2

Choose a body paragraph from one of the essays in this book. Using the criteria discussed on pages 41–45, decide whether the paragraph is unified, coherent, and well developed.

Exercise 3

Choose one essay in this book, and underline its thesis statement. Then, determine how its body paragraphs support that thesis statement. (Note that in a long essay, several body paragraphs may develop a single supporting point, and some paragraphs may serve as transitions from one point to another.)

The Conclusion

Since readers remember best what they read last, your **conclusion** is extremely important. Always end your essay in a way that reinforces your thesis and your purpose.

Like your introduction, your conclusion is rarely longer than a paragraph. Regardless of its length, however, your conclusion should be consistent with the rest of your essay. It should not introduce points you have not discussed earlier. Frequently, a conclusion will restate the thesis, summarizing your essay's main idea in different words, or will review your key points. Like thesis statements, effective conclusions need no announcement, so you should avoid beginning them with the artificial phrase *In conclusion.*

Here are several ways to conclude an essay:

1. You can conclude your essay by *reviewing your key points* or *restating your thesis.*

> Rotation of crops provided several benefits. It enriched soil by giving it a rest; it enabled farmers to vary their production; and it ended the cycle of "boom or bust" that had characterized the prewar South's economy when cotton was the primary crop. Of course, this innovation did not solve all the economic problems of the postwar South, but it did lay the groundwork for the healthy economy this region enjoys today.   (history exam)

2. You can end a discussion of a problem with a *recommendation of a course of action.*

> While there is still time, American engineering has to reassess its priorities. We no longer have the luxury of exotic and wasteful experiments. Instead, we need technology grounded in common sense and economic feasibility. That the international space station presently orbiting the earth seems to have few practical applications illustrates how far we have strayed from old-fashioned common sense and ingenuity.
>
> (engineering ethics report)

3. You can conclude with a *prediction*. Be sure, however, that your prediction follows logically from the points you have made in the essay. Your conclusion is no place to make new points or change direction.

> It is too late to save parts of the great swamps in northern Florida, but it is not too late to preserve the Everglades in the southern part of the state. With intelligent planning and an end to the dam building program by the Army Corps of Engineers, we could halt the destruction of what Native Americans called the "Timeless Swamp."   (environmental science essay)

4. You can end with a relevant *quotation*.

> In *Walden,* Henry David Thoreau says, "The mass of men lead lives of quiet desperation." This sentiment is reinforced by a drive through the Hill District of our city. Perhaps the work of the men and women who run the clinic on Jefferson Street cannot totally change this situation, but it can give us hope to know that some people, at least, are working for the betterment of us all.   (public health essay)

Exercise 4

Look through magazine articles or the essays in this book, and find one example of each kind of conclusion. Why do you think each concluding strategy was chosen? What other strategies might have worked?

Constructing a Formal Outline

At this point, you may decide to construct a **formal outline** to guide you as you write your essay. Whereas informal outlines are preliminary lists that simply remind you which points to make, formal outlines are detailed, multilevel constructions that indicate the exact order in which you will present your points. The complexity of your assignment determines which type of outline you need. For a short paper, an informal outline like the one on page 29 is usually sufficient. For a longer, more complex essay, however, you may need a formal outline.

Begin constructing a formal outline by reviewing your thesis statement and all the ideas you compiled during invention. As you examine this material, you will see that some ideas seem more important than others. One way to construct a formal outline is to copy down the main headings from your informal outline. Then, arrange ideas from your brainstorming notes or cluster diagram as subheadings under the appropriate headings. As you work on your outline, make sure each idea you include supports your thesis. Ideas that don't fit should be reworded or discarded. As you revise your essay, continue to refer to your outline to make sure your thesis and support are logically related. The guidelines that follow will help you prepare a formal outline.

✓ CHECKLIST: **Constructing a Formal Outline**

- Write your thesis statement at the top of the page.
- Group main headings under roman numerals (*I, II, III, IV,* and so on), and place them flush with the left-hand margin.
- Indent each subheading under the first word of the heading above it. Use capital letters before major points and numbers before supporting details.
- Capitalize the first letter of the first word of each heading.
- Make your outline as simple as possible, avoiding overly complex divisions of ideas. (Try not to go beyond third-level headings—*1, 2, 3,* and so on.)
- Construct either a **topic outline**, with headings expressed as short phrases or single words ("Advantages and disadvantages"), or a **sentence outline**, with headings expressed as complete sentences ("The advantages of advanced placement chemistry outweigh the disadvantages"). *Never use both phrases and complete sentences in the same outline.*
- Express all headings at the same level in parallel terms. (If roman numeral *I* is a noun, *II, III,* and *IV* should also be nouns.)
- Make sure each heading contains at least two subdivisions. You cannot have a *1* without a *2* or an *A* without a *B*.
- Make sure your headings do not overlap.

A STUDENT WRITER: **Constructing a Formal Outline**

The topic outline Laura Bobnak constructed follows the guidelines discussed above. Notice that her outline focuses on the body of her paper and does not include the introduction or conclusion: these are usually developed after the body has been drafted. (Compare this formal outline with the informal outline on page 29 where Laura simply grouped her brainstorming notes under three general headings.)

Thesis statement: As I look back at the cheating I witnessed, I wonder why I kept silent and what would have happened if I had acted.

   I. The incident
      A. Test situation
      B. My observation
      C. My reactions
         1. Anger
         2. Silence
  II. Reasons for keeping silent
      A. Other students' attitudes
      B. My fears

   III. Current attitude toward cheating
       A. Effects of cheating on education
       B. Effects of cheating on students

This outline enabled Laura to arrange her points so that they supported her thesis. As she went on to draft her essay, the outline reminded her to emphasize the contrast between her present and former attitudes toward cheating.

🖳 COMPUTER STRATEGY

If you use a computer to construct a formal outline, you can easily arrange and rearrange your headings until your outline is logical and complete. (Your word-processing program will have an outline function that automatically indents and numbers items.) If you saved your prewriting notes in computer files, you can refer to them while working on your outline and perhaps add or modify headings to reflect what you find.

Exercise 5

Read the thesis statement you developed in Chapter 2, Exercise 11 (on page 35), as well as all the notes you made for the essay you are planning. Then, make a topic outline that lists the points you will discuss in your essay. When you are finished, check to make sure your outline conforms to the guidelines in the checklist on page 48.

4
Drafting and Revising

After you decide on a thesis and an arrangement for your ideas, you can begin to draft and revise your essay. Keep in mind that even as you carry out these activities, you may have to generate more material or revise your thesis statement.

Writing Your First Draft

The purpose of your **first draft** is to get your ideas down on paper so that you can react to them. Experienced writers know that the first draft is nothing more than a work in progress; it exists to be revised. With this in mind, you should be prepared to cross out and extensively rearrange material. In addition, don't be surprised if you think of new ideas as you write. If a new idea comes to you, take it to its conclusion. Some of the best writing comes from unexpected turns or accidents. The following guidelines will help you prepare your first draft.

✓ CHECKLIST: **Drafting**

- *Begin with the body paragraphs.* Because your essay will probably be revised extensively, don't take the time at this stage to write an introduction or conclusion. Let your thesis statement guide you as you draft the body paragraphs of your essay. When you have finished, you can write an appropriate introduction and conclusion.
- *Get your ideas down quickly.* Don't worry about grammar or word choice, and try not to interrupt the flow of your writing with concerns about style.
- *Take regular breaks as you write.* Don't write until you are so exhausted you can't think straight. Many writers divide their writing into stages, perhaps completing one or two body paragraphs and

(continued on next page)

(continued from previous page)
then taking a short break. This strategy is more efficient than trying to write a complete first draft without stopping.

- *Write with revision in mind.* Leave enough space between lines so that you will have room to make changes by hand on hard copy.
- *Leave yourself time to revise.* Remember, your first draft is a *rough draft*. All writing benefits from revision, so allow enough time to write two or more drafts.

A STUDENT WRITER: **Writing a First Draft**

Here is the first draft of Laura Bobnak's essay on the topic "Write about a time when you, like Henry Louis Gates's father, could have spoken out but chose not to. Would you make the same decision today?"

When I was in high school, I had an experience like the one Henry Louis Gates talks about in his essay. It was then that I saw a close friend cheat in chemistry class. As I look back at the cheating I witnessed, I wonder why I kept silent and what would have happened if I had acted.

1

The incident I am going to describe took place during the final exam for my advanced placement chemistry class. I had studied hard for it, but even so, I found the test difficult. As I struggled to balance a particularly difficult equation, I noticed that my friend Jeff Servin, who was sitting across from me, was acting strangely. I noticed that he was copying material from a paper. After watching him for a while, I dismissed the incident and got back to my test.

2

After the test was over, I began to think about what I had seen. The more I thought about it the angrier I got. It seemed unfair that I had studied for weeks to memorize formulas and equations while all Jeff had done was to copy them onto a cheat sheet. For a moment I considered going to the teacher, but I quickly rejected this idea. After all, cheating was something everybody did. Besides, I was afraid if I told on Jeff, my friends would stop talking to me.

3

Now that I am in college I see the situation differently. I find it hard to believe that I could ever have been so calm about cheating. Cheating is certainly something that students should not take for granted. It undercuts the education process and is unfair to teachers and to the majority of students who spend their time studying.

4

If I could go back to high school and relive the experience, I now know that I would have gone to the teacher. Naturally Jeff would have been angry at me, but at least I would have known I had the courage to do the right thing.

5

Exercise 1

Write a draft of the essay you have been working on in Chapters 2 and 3. Be sure to look back at all your notes as well as your outline.

Revising Your Essay

Revision is not something you do after your paper is finished. It is a continuing process during which you consider the logic and clarity of your ideas, as well as how effectively they are presented. Revision is not simply a matter of proofreading or editing, of crossing out one word and substituting another or correcting errors in spelling and punctuation; revision involves reexamining and rethinking what you have written. When you revise, you may find yourself adding and deleting extensively, reordering whole sentences or paragraphs as you reconsider what you want to communicate to your audience. Revision can take a lot of time, so don't be discouraged if you have to go through three or four drafts before you think your essay is ready to hand in. The following advice can help you when you revise your essay:

• *Give yourself a cooling-off period.* After you have written your first draft, put it aside for several hours or even a day or two if you can. This cooling-off period lets you distance yourself from your essay so that you can read it more objectively when you return to it. When you read it again, you will see things you missed the first time.

• *Revise on hard copy.* Because a printed-out draft shows you your entire paper and enables you to see your handwritten edits, you should always revise on hard copy instead of directly on the computer screen.

• *Read your draft aloud.* Before you revise, read your draft aloud to help you spot choppy sentences, missing words, or phrases that do not sound right.

• *Take advantage of opportunities to get feedback.* Your instructor may organize peer critique sessions, distribute a revision checklist, refer students to a writing center, or schedule one-on-one conferences. Make use of as many of these opportunities for feedback as you can; each offers you a different way of gaining information about what you have written.

• *Try not to get overwhelmed.* It is easy to become overwhelmed by all the feedback you get about your draft. To avoid this, approach revision as a systematic process. Don't just automatically make all the changes people suggest; consider the impact and the validity of each change. Also ask yourself whether comments suggest larger issues. For example, does a comment about choppy sentences in a paragraph simply suggest a need for you to add transitions, or does it require you to rethink your ideas?

• *Don't let your ego get in the way.* Everyone likes praise, and receiving negative criticism is never pleasant. Experienced writers know, however, that they must get feedback if they are going to improve their work. Learn to see criticism — whether from an instructor or from your peers — as a necessary (if painful) part of the revision process.

• *Revise in stages.* Deal with the large elements (essay and paragraph structure) before moving on to the smaller elements (sentence structure and word choice).

How you revise — what specific strategies you decide to use — depends on your own preference, your instructor's instructions, and the time available. Like the rest of the writing process, revision varies from student to student and from assignment to assignment. Four of the most useful revision strategies are *revising with a checklist, revising with an outline, revising with a peer critique,* and *revising with your instructor's comments.*

Revising with a Checklist

If you have time, you can use the following revision checklist, adapting it to your own writing process.

✓ REVISION CHECKLIST

- **Thesis statement**   Is your thesis statement clear and specific? Does it indicate the direction your essay is taking? Is it consistent with the body of your essay? If you departed from your essay's original direction while you were writing, you may need to revise your thesis statement so that it accurately sums up the ideas and information now contained in the body. Or, you may need to delete from the body any material that is unrelated to the thesis statement—or revise it so that it *is* relevant.

- **Body**   Are the body paragraphs unified? Coherent? Well developed? If not, you might have to add more facts or examples or smoother transitions. Does each body paragraph follow a particular pattern of development? Do the points you make in these paragraphs support your thesis?

- **Introduction and conclusion**   Are your introduction and your conclusion appropriate for your material, your audience, and your purpose? Are they interesting? Do they reinforce your thesis?

- **Sentences**   Are your sentences effective? Interesting? Varied in length and structure? Should any sentences be deleted, combined, or moved?

- **Words**   Should you make any substitutions?

- **Title**   Because it is the first thing in your essay that readers see, your title should create interest. Usually, single-word titles ("Love") and

---

cute ones ("The Cheery Cheerleader") do little to draw readers into your essay. To be effective, a title should reflect your purpose and your tone.

The titles of some of the essays in this book illustrate the various kinds of titles you can use:

Statement of essay's focus: "Grant and Lee: A Study in Contrasts"
Question: "Why Fear National ID Cards?"
Unusual angle: "Thirty-Eight Who Saw Murder Didn't Call the Police"
Controversy: "A Peaceful Woman Explains Why She Carries a Gun"
Provocative wording: "Sex, Lies, and Conversation"
Quotation: "The 'Black Table' Is Still There"
Humor: "The Dog Ate My Disk and Other Tales of Woe"

Revising with an Outline

If you do not have time to consult a detailed checklist, you can check your essay's structure by making a review **outline**. Either an informal outline or a formal one can show you whether you have omitted any important points. An outline can also show you whether your essay follows a particular pattern of development. Finally, an outline can clarify the relationship between your thesis statement and your body paragraphs.

Revising with a Peer Critique

Another revision strategy is seeking a **peer critique** — asking a friend to read your essay and comment on it. Sometimes a peer critique can be formal. An instructor may require students to exchange papers and evaluate their classmates' work according to certain standards, perhaps by completing a **peer editing worksheet**. (See pages 57–58 for an example.) Often, however, a peer critique is informal. Even if a friend is unfamiliar with your topic, he or she can still tell you honestly whether you are getting your point across — and maybe even advise you about how to communicate more effectively. (Remember, though, that your critic should be only your reader, not your ghostwriter.)

🖥 COMPUTER STRATEGY

When you revise, make sure you do not delete text you may need later. Move such information to the end of the draft or to a separate file. That way, if you change your mind about a deletion or if you find you need information you took out of a draft, you can recover it easily.

The use of peer critiques mirrors how people in the real world actually write. Businesspeople circulate reports to get feedback from coworkers; scientists and academics routinely collaborate when they write. (And, as you may have realized, even this book is the result of a collaboration.)

Your classmates can be quite helpful as you write the early drafts of your essay, providing suggestions that can guide you through the revision process. In addition, they can respond to questions you may have about your essay — for example, whether your introduction works or whether one of your supporting points needs more explanation. When friends ask *you* to critique their work, the following guidelines should help you.

✓ CHECKLIST: **Guidelines for Peer Critiques**

- *Be positive.* Remember that your purpose is to help other students improve their essays.
- *Be tactful.* Be sure to emphasize the good points about the essay. Mention one or two things the writer has done particularly well before you offer your suggestions.
- *Be specific.* Offer concrete suggestions about what the writer could do better. Vague words like *good* or *bad* provide little help.
- *Be involved.* If you are doing a critique orally, make sure you interact with the writer. Ask questions, listen to responses, and explain your comments.
- *Look at the big picture.* Don't focus on issues such as spelling and punctuation. You shouldn't expect these elements to be perfect in a first draft. At this stage, the clarity of the thesis statement, the effectiveness of the support, and the organization of the writer's ideas are much more important.
- *Be thorough.* When possible, write down and explain your comments, either on a form your instructor provides or in the margins of the draft you are reviewing.

Revising with Your Instructor's Comments

Your instructor's marginal comments on a draft of your essay can also help you revise by suggesting changes in content, arrangement, or style. For example, these comments may question your logic, suggest a clearer thesis statement, ask for more explicit transitions, recommend that a paragraph be relocated, or even propose a new direction for your essay. They may also recommend stylistic changes or ask you to provide more support in one or more of your body paragraphs. You may decide to incorporate these suggestions into the next draft of your essay, or you may decide not to. Whatever the case, you should take your instructor's comments seriously and make reading and responding to them a part of your revision process.

🖥 COMPUTER STRATEGY

A computer enables you to add, delete, and move information quickly and easily. Still, it is usually not a good idea to begin revising directly on the computer screen. Since most screens show only a portion of a page, the connections between ideas are hard to see and to keep track of. Even with the split-screen option that some word-processing programs offer, you usually cannot view one or more full pages of a draft at once or compare one draft to another. For these reasons, it is a good idea to revise on a hard copy of your essay. Once you have made your handwritten corrections, you can type them into your paper.

If your instructor encourages (or requires) you to schedule a one-on-one conference, come to the conference prepared. Read all your drafts carefully and bring a copy of your most recent draft as well as a list of any questions you may have. During the conference, you can ask your instructor to clarify marginal comments or to help you revise a particular section of your essay that is giving you trouble. Make sure you take notes during the conference so that you will have a record of what you and your instructor discussed. Remember that the more prepared for the conference you are, the more you will get out of it. (Some instructors use email to answer questions and to give students feedback.)

A STUDENT WRITER: Revising a First Draft

When she revised the first draft of her essay (page 52), Laura Bobnak followed the revision process discussed above. After writing her rough draft, she put it aside for a few hours and then reread it. Later, her instructor divided the class into pairs and had them read each other's essays and fill out **peer editing worksheets**. After reading and discussing the following worksheet (filled out by one of her classmates), Laura was able to focus on a number of areas that needed revision.

📄 **PEER EDITING WORKSHEET**

What is the essay's thesis? Is it clearly worded? Does it provide a focus for the rest of the essay? Is it appropriate for the assignment?

Thesis statement: "As I look back at the cheating I witnessed, I wonder why I kept silent and what would have happened if I had acted." I don't really think the thesis talks about the second part of the assignment — would you have done the same thing today?

How clearly are the body paragraphs related to the essay's thesis? Which topic sentences could be more focused?

(continued on next page)

(continued from previous page)

The topic sentences seem fine — each one seems to tell what the paragraph is about.

How do the body paragraphs develop the essay's main idea? Where could the writer have used more detail?

Each of the body paragraphs tells a part of the narrative, but, as I said before, the paragraph that deals with the second part of the assignment is missing. You could add more detail — I really can't picture everything you're talking about.

Can you follow the writer's ideas? Does the essay need transitions?

I have no problem following your ideas. Maybe you could have added some more transitions, but I think the essay moves OK.

Which points are especially clear? What questions do you have that are not answered in the essay?

I think you clearly explained what you didn't like about Jeff's cheating. I'm not sure what AP chemistry is like, though. Do people cheat because it's so hard?

If this were your essay, what would you change before you handed it in?

I'd change the thesis to make it reflect the assignment. I'd add more detail and explain more about AP chemistry. Also, what were the other students doing while the cheating was going on?

Overall, do you think the paper is effective? Explain.

Good paper; cheating is a big issue, and I think your story really gets this across.

A peer editing worksheet for each pattern of development appears at the end of the introductions for Chapters 6 through 15.

Points for Special Attention: First Draft

The Introduction

When she wrote her first draft, Laura knew she would eventually have to present more detail in her introduction. At this stage, though, she was more concerned with her thesis statement, and the students in her peer editing group agreed that it didn't address the second half of the assignment — to explain whether or not she would act differently today.

Keeping their comments in mind, Laura rewrote her introduction. First, she created a context for her discussion by specifically linking her story to

Gates's essay. Next, she decided to postpone mentioning her subject—cheating—until later in the paper, hoping this strategy would stimulate the curiosity of her readers and make them want to read further. Finally, she revised her thesis statement to reflect the specific wording of the assignment.

The Body Paragraphs

The students in her peer editing group also said Laura needed to expand her body paragraphs. Although she had expected that most of her readers would be familiar with courses like advanced placement chemistry, she discovered this was not the case. In addition, some students in her group thought she should expand the paragraph in which she described her reaction to the cheating. They wondered what the other students had thought about the incident. Did they know? Did they care? Laura's classmates were curious, and they thought other readers would be, too.

Before revising the body paragraphs, Laura did some brainstorming for additional ideas. She decided to describe the difficulty of advanced placement chemistry and the pressure the students in the class had felt. She also decided to summarize discussions she had had with several of her classmates after the test. In addition, she wanted to explain in more detail her present views on cheating; she felt that the paragraph presenting these ideas did not contrast enough with the paragraphs dealing with her high school experiences.

To make sure her sentences led smoothly into one another, Laura added transitions and rewrote entire sentences when necessary, signaling the progression of her thoughts by adding words and phrases such as *therefore, for this reason, for example,* and *as a result.* In addition, she tried to repeat key words so that important concepts would be reinforced.

The Conclusion

Laura's biggest concern as she revised was to make sure her readers would see the connection between her essay and the assignment. To make this connection clear, she decided to mention in her conclusion a specific effect the incident had on her: its impact on her friendship with Jeff. She also decided to link her reactions to those of Henry Louis Gates Jr. Like him, she had been upset by the actions of someone she knew. By employing this strategy, she was able to bring her essay full circle and develop an idea she had alluded to in her introduction. Thus, rewriting her conclusion helped Laura to reinforce her thesis statement and provide closure to her essay.

A STUDENT WRITER: Revising a Second Draft

The following draft incorporates Laura's revisions, as well as some preliminary editing of grammar and punctuation.

Speaking Out

In his essay "'What's in a Name?'" Henry Louis Gates Jr. recalls an incident   1
from his past in which his father did not speak up. Perhaps he kept silent because
he was afraid or because he knew that nothing he said or did would change the
situation in Piedmont, West Virginia. Although I have never encountered the kind
of prejudice Gates describes, I did have an experience in high school where, like
Gates's father, I could have spoken up but did not. As I now look back at the
cheating I witnessed, I know I would not make the same decision today.

The incident I am going to describe took place during the final examination   2
in my advanced placement chemistry class. The course was very demanding and
required hours of studying every night. Every day after school, I would meet with
other students to outline chapters and answer homework questions. Sometimes
we would even work on weekends. We would often ask ourselves whether we had
gotten in over our heads. As the semester dragged on, it became clear to me,
as well as to the other students in the class, that passing the course was not
something we could take for granted. Test after test came back with grades that
were well below the "As" and "Bs" I was used to getting in the regular chemistry
course I took in tenth grade. By the time we were ready to take the final exam,
most of us were worried that we would fail the course — despite the teacher's
assurances that she would mark on a curve.

The final examination for advanced placement chemistry was given on   3
a Friday morning from nine to twelve o'clock. As I struggled to balance a
particularly complex equation, I noticed that the person sitting across from me
was acting strangely. I thought I was imagining things, but as I stared I saw Jeff
Servin, my friend and study partner, fumbling with his test booklet. I realized
that he was copying material from a paper he had taped inside the cuff of his
shirt. After watching him for a while, I dismissed the incident and finished
my test.

Surprisingly, when I mentioned the incident to others in the class, they   4
all knew what Jeff had done. The more I thought about Jeff's actions, the
angrier I got. It seemed unfair that I had studied for weeks to memorize
formulas and equations while all Jeff had done was to copy them onto a cheat
sheet. For a moment I considered going to the teacher, but I quickly rejected
this idea. Cheating was nothing new to me or to others in my school. Many of
my classmates cheated at one time or another. Most of us saw school as a war
between us and the teachers, and cheating was just another weapon in our
arsenal. The worst crime I could commit would be to turn Jeff in. As far as I
was concerned, I had no choice. I fell in line with the values of my high school
classmates and dismissed the incident as "no big deal."

I find it hard to believe that I could ever have been so complacent about   5
cheating. The issues that were simple in high school now seem complex. I now
ask questions that never would have occurred to me in high school. Interestingly,
Jeff and I are no longer very close. Whenever I see him, I have the same reaction
Henry Louis Gates Jr. had when he met Mr. Wilson after he had insulted his
father — I have a hard time looking him in the eye.

Points for Special Attention: Second Draft

Laura could see that her second draft was stronger than her first, but
she decided to arrange a conference with her instructor to help her
improve her draft further.

The Introduction

Although Laura was satisfied with her introduction, her instructor
identified a problem. Laura had assumed that everyone reading her essay
would be familiar with Gates's essay. However, her instructor pointed out
that this might not be the case. So, he suggested that she add a brief explanation of the problems Gates's father had faced in order to accommodate
readers who didn't know about or remember Gates's comments.

The Body Paragraphs

After rereading her first body paragraph, Laura thought she could
sharpen its focus. Her instructor agreed, suggesting she delete the first sentence of the paragraph, which seemed too conversational. She also decided
she could delete the sentences that explained how difficult advanced placement chemistry was — even though she had added this material at the suggestion of a classmate. After all, cheating, not advanced placement
chemistry, was the subject of her paper. She realized that if she included
this kind of detail, she ran the risk of distracting readers with an irrelevant
discussion.

Her instructor also pointed out that in the second body paragraph,
the first and second sentences did not seem to be connected, so Laura
decided to connect these ideas by adding a short discussion of her own
reaction to the test. Her instructor also suggested that Laura add more
transitional words and phrases to this paragraph to clarify the sequence of
events she was describing. Phrases such as *at first* and *about a minute passed*
would help readers follow her discussion.

Laura thought the third body paragraph was her best, but, even so, she
felt she needed to add more material. She and her instructor decided she
should expand her discussion of the students' reactions to cheating. More

information—perhaps some dialogue—would help Laura make the point that cheating was condoned by the students in her class.

The Conclusion

Laura's conclusion began by mentioning her present attitude toward cheating and then suddenly shifted to the effect cheating had on her relationship with Jeff. Her instructor suggested that she revise by taking her discussion about her current view of cheating out of her conclusion and putting it in a separate paragraph. By doing this, she could focus her conclusion on the effect cheating had on both Jeff and her. This strategy enabled Laura to present her views about cheating in more detail and also helped her end her essay forcefully.

The Title

Laura's original title was only a working title, and now she wanted one that would create interest and draw readers into her essay. She knew, however, that a humorous, cute, or catchy title would undermine the seriousness of her essay. After she and her instructor rejected a number of possibilities, they decided on "The Price of Silence." This title was thought provoking and also descriptive, and it prepared readers for what was to follow in the essay.

A STUDENT WRITER: Preparing a Final Draft

Based on the decisions she made during and after her conference, Laura revised and edited her draft and handed in this final version of her essay.

The Price of Silence

Introduction (provides background)   In his essay "'What's in a Name?'" Henry Louis Gates Jr. recalls an incident from his past in which his father encountered prejudice and did not speak up. Perhaps he kept silent because he was afraid or because he knew that nothing he said or did would change the racial situation in Piedmont, West Virginia. Although I have never encountered the kind of prejudice Gates describes, I did have an experience in high school where, like Gates's father, I could have spoken out   *Thesis statement*   but did not. As I look back at the cheating incident that I witnessed, I realize that I have outgrown the immaturity and lack of confidence that made me keep silent.   1

Narrative begins   In my senior year in high school I, along with fifteen other students, took advanced placement chemistry. The course was very demanding and required hours of studying every   2 night. As the semester dragged on, it became clear to me, as well as to the other students in the class, that passing the course was not something we could take for granted. Test after test came back with grades that were well below the As and Bs I was used to getting in the regular chemistry course I had taken in tenth grade. By the time we were ready to take the final exam, most of us were worried that we would fail the course — despite the teacher's assurances that she would mark on a curve.

Key incident occurs

The final examination for advanced placement chemistry was given on a Friday morning between nine o'clock and noon. I had studied all that week, but, even so, I found the test difficult. I knew the material, but I had a hard time answering the long questions that were asked. As I struggled to balance a particularly complex equation, I noticed that the person sitting across from me was acting strangely. At first I thought I was imagining things, but as I stared I saw Jeff Servin, my friend and study partner, fumbling with his test booklet. About a minute passed before I realized that he was copying material from a paper he had taped to the inside of his shirt cuff. After a short time, I stopped watching him and finished my test.

3

Narrative continues: reactions to the incident

It was not until after the test that I began thinking about what I had seen. Surprisingly, when I mentioned the incident to others in the class, they all knew what Jeff had done. Some even thought that Jeff's actions were justified. "After all," one student said, "the test was hard." But the more I thought about Jeff's actions, the angrier I got. It seemed unfair that I had studied for weeks to memorize formulas and equations while all Jeff had done was copy them onto a cheat sheet. For a moment I considered going to the teacher, but I quickly rejected this idea. Cheating was nothing new to me or to others in my school. Many of my classmates cheated at one time or another. Most of us saw school as a war between us and the teachers, and cheating was just another weapon in our arsenal. The worst crime I could commit would be to turn Jeff

4

Narrative ends

in. As far as I was concerned, I had no choice. I fell in line with the values of my high school classmates and dismissed the incident as "no big deal."

Analysis of key incident

Now that I am in college, however, I see the situation differently. I find it hard to believe that I could ever have been

5

so complacent about cheating. The issues that were simple in high school now seem complex — especially in light of the honor code that I follow in college. I now ask questions that never would have occurred to me in high school. What, for example, are the implications of cheating? What would happen to the educational system if cheating became the norm? What are my obligations to all those who are involved in education? Aren't teachers and students interested in achieving a common goal? The answers to these questions give me a sense of the far-reaching effects of my failure to act. If confronted with the same situation today, I know I would speak out regardless of the consequences.

Reinforcement of thesis

Jeff Servin is now a first-year student at the state university and, like me, was given credit for chemistry. I feel certain that by not turning him in, I failed not only myself but also Jeff. I gave in to peer pressure instead of doing what I knew to be right. The worst that would have happened to Jeff had I spoken up is that he would have had to repeat chemistry in summer school. By doing so, he would have proven to himself that he could, like the rest of us in the class, pass on his own. In the long run, this knowledge would have served him better than the knowledge that he could cheat whenever he faced a difficult situation.

6

Conclusion (aftermath of incident)

Interestingly, Jeff and I are no longer very close. Whenever I see him, I have the same reaction Henry Louis Gates Jr. had when he met Mr. Wilson after he had insulted his father: I have a hard time looking him in the eye.

7

With each draft of her essay, Laura sharpened the focus of her discussion. In the process, she clarified her thoughts about her subject and reached some new and interesting conclusions. Although much of Laura's paper is a narrative, it also includes a contrast between her current ideas about cheating and the ideas she had in high school. Perhaps Laura could have explained the reasons behind her current ideas about cheating more fully. Even so, her paper gives a straightforward account of the incident and analyzes its significance without lapsing into clichés or simplistic moralizing. Especially effective is Laura's conclusion, in which she discusses the long-term effects of her experience. By placing this discussion at the end of her essay, she makes sure her readers will not lose sight of the implications of her experience.

Exercise 2

Use the checklist on page 54 to help you revise your draft. If you prefer, outline your draft and use that outline to help you revise.

Exercise 3

Have another student read your second draft. Then, using the student's peer critique as your guide, revise your draft.

Exercise 4

Using the essay on pages 62–64 as your guide, label the final draft of your own essay. In addition to identifying your introduction, conclusion, and thesis statement, you should also label the main points of your essay.

5
Editing and Proofreading

When you finish revising your essay, it is tempting to print it out, hand it in, and breathe a sigh of relief. This is one temptation you should resist. You still have to *edit* and *proofread* your paper to correct any small problems that may remain after you revise.

When you **edit**, you search for grammatical errors, check punctuation, look over your sentence style and word choice one last time, and correct misspellings. When you **proofread**, you look for surface errors, such as typos, incorrect spacing, or problems with your essay's format. The idea is to look carefully for any error, no matter how small, that might weaken your essay's message or undermine your credibility. Remember, this is your last chance to make sure your essay says exactly what you want it to say.

Editing for Grammar

As you edit, keep in mind that certain grammatical errors occur more frequently than others—and even more frequently in particular kinds of writing. By concentrating on these errors, as well as those errors you yourself are most likely to make, you will learn to edit your essays quickly and efficiently.

Learning the few rules that follow will help you identify the most common errors. Later on, when you practice writing essays in various patterns of development, you can use the **Grammar in Context** section in each chapter to help you correct any errors you find.

Be Sure Subjects and Verbs Agree

Subjects and verbs must agree in person and number. A singular subject takes a singular verb.

Stephanie Ericsson discusses ten kinds of liars.

A plural subject takes a plural verb.

Chronic liars are different from occasional liars.

Liars and plagiarists have a lot in common.

For more information on editing subject-verb agreement, see the Grammar in Context section of **Chapter 15 (page 705).**

Be Sure Verb Tenses Are Accurate and Consistent

Unintentional shifts in verb tense can be confusing to readers. Verb tenses in the same passage should be consistent unless you are referring to two different time periods.

Single time period:	*past tense* Lee surrendered to Grant on April 9, 1865, *past tense* and then he addressed his men.
Two different time periods:	In "Two Ways to Belong in America," Bharati *present tense* Mukherjee compares herself and her sister, *past tense* both of whom emigrated from India.

For more information on editing shifts in verb tenses, as well as unwarranted shifts in voice, person, and mood, see the Grammar in Context section of **Chapter 9 (page 272).**

Be Sure Pronoun References Are Clear

A pronoun is a word that takes the place of a noun in a sentence. Every pronoun should clearly refer to a specific **antecedent**, the word (a noun or pronoun) it replaces. Pronouns and antecedents must agree in person and number.

Singular pronouns refer to singular antecedents.

When she was attacked, Kitty Genovese was on her way home.

Plural pronouns refer to plural antecedents.

The people who watched the attack gave different reasons for their failure to help.

For more information on editing for pronoun-antecedent agreement with indefinite pronouns, see the Grammar in Context section of **Chapter 15 (page 705).**

Be Sure Sentences Are Complete

A **sentence** is a group of words that includes a subject and a verb and expresses a complete thought. A **fragment** is an incomplete sentence, one that is missing a subject, a verb, or both a subject and a verb — or that has a subject and a verb but does not express a complete thought.

Sentence:	Although it was written in 1963, Martin Luther King's "Letter from Birmingham Jail" remains powerful today.
Fragment (no subject):	Remains powerful today.
Fragment (no verb):	Martin Luther King's "Letter from Birmingham Jail."
Fragment (no subject or verb):	Written in 1963.
Fragment (includes subject and verb but does not express a complete thought):	Although it was written in 1963.

To correct a sentence fragment, you need to supply the missing part of the sentence (a subject, a verb, or both — or an entire independent clause). Often, you will find that the missing words appear in an adjacent sentence in your essay.

Be Careful Not to Run Sentences Together without Proper Punctuation

There are two kinds of **run-on sentences**: *comma splices* and *fused sentences*.

A **comma splice** is an error that occurs when two independent clauses are connected by just a comma.

Comma splice:	Women who live alone need to learn to protect themselves; sometimes this means carrying a gun.

A **fused sentence** is an error that occurs when two independent clauses are connected without any punctuation.

Fused sentence:	Residents of isolated rural areas may carry guns for protection, *but* sometimes these guns may be used against them.

For more information on editing run-on sentences, including additional ways to correct them, see the Grammar in Context section of **Chapter 6 (page 88).**

Be Careful to Avoid Misplaced and Dangling Modifiers

Modifiers are words and phrases that describe other words in a sentence. To avoid confusion, place modifiers as close as possible to the words they modify.

Limited by their illiteracy, millions of Americans are ashamed to seek help.

Hoping to draw attention to their plight, Jonathan Kozol wrote *Illiterate America.*

A **misplaced modifier** appears to modify the wrong word because it is placed incorrectly in the sentence. This placement can create an unintentionally humorous result.

Misplaced modifier:	Katha Pollitt questions whether a Tropical Splash Barbie is an appropriate gift for a girl with a plastic beach house. (*Does the girl have a plastic beach house?*)
Correct:	Katha Pollitt questions whether a Tropical Splash Barbie with a plastic beach house is an appropriate gift for a girl.

A dangling modifier "dangles" because it cannot logically describe any word in the sentence.

Dangling modifier:	Going back to his old junior high school, the "black table" was still there. (*Who went back to his old school?*)
Correct:	Going back to his old junior high school, Graham discovered that the "black table" was still there.

For more information on editing to correct misplaced and dangling modifiers, see the Grammar in Context section of **Chapter 7 (page 151).**

Be Sure Sentence Elements Are Parallel

Parallelism is the use of matching grammatical elements (words, phrases, clauses) to express the same or similar ideas. Used effectively — for example, with paired items or items in a series — parallelism makes the links between related ideas clear and emphasizes connections. **Faulty parallelism** — using items that are not parallel in a context in which parallelism is expected — makes ideas difficult to follow and will likely confuse your readers.

Paired items:	As Katha Pollitt points out, "boys still like trucks and girls still like dolls" (361). (*not* "boys still like trucks and dolls are preferred by girls")

Items in a series: Boys in the research study chose to play with blocks, trucks, and puzzles. (*not* "Boys in the research study chose to play with blocks or trucks and some also played with puzzles.")

For more information on using parallelism to strengthen your writing, see the Grammar in Context section of **Chapter 11 (page 394).**

✓ **CHECKLIST: Editing for Grammar**

- **Subject-verb agreement**   Do all your verbs agree with their subjects? Remember that singular subjects take singular verbs, and plural subjects take plural verbs.
- **Verb tenses**   Are all your verb tenses accurate and consistent? Have you avoided unnecessary shifts in tense?
- **Pronoun reference**   Do pronouns clearly refer to their antecedents?
- **Sentence fragments**   Does each group of words punctuated as a sentence have both a subject and a verb and express a complete thought? If not, can you correct the fragment by adding the missing words or by attaching it to an adjacent sentence?
- **Run-on sentences**   Have you been careful not to connect two independent clauses without the necessary punctuation? Have you avoided comma splices and fused sentences?
- **Modification**   Does every modifier point clearly to the word it modifies? Have you avoided misplaced and dangling modifiers?
- **Parallelism**   Have you used matching words, phrases, or clauses to express equivalent ideas? Have you avoided faulty parallelism?

For practice in editing for grammar, visit Exercise Central online at <bedfordstmartins.com/patterns>.

Editing for Punctuation

Like grammatical errors, certain punctuation errors are more common than others, particularly in certain contexts. By understanding a few punctuation rules, you can learn to identify and correct these errors in your writing.

Learn When to Use Commas — and When Not to Use Them

Commas separate certain elements of a sentence. They are used most often in the following situations:

- To separate an introductory phrase or clause from the rest of the sentence

  In "Only Daughter," Sandra Cisneros writes about her father.

According to Cisneros, he is very critical of her.

Although her father has six sons, she is the only daughter.

Note: Do not use a comma if a dependent clause follows an independent clause: She is the only daughter although her father has six sons. *(no comma)*

- To separate two independent clauses that are joined by a coordinating conjunction

  Cisneros tries to please her father, but he is not impressed.

- To separate elements in a series

  Cisneros has written stories, essays, poems, and a novel.

For more information on using commas in a series, see the Grammar in Context section of **Chapter 8 (page 209)**.

- To separate a **nonrestrictive clause** (a clause that does not supply information that is essential to the sentence's meaning) from the rest of the sentence

  Cisneros, who is the only daughter, feels her father would prefer her to be a son.

Note: Do not use commas to set off a **restrictive clause** (a clause that supplies information that is vital to the sentence's meaning).

The child who is overlooked is often the daughter. *(no commas)*

Learn When to Use Semicolons

Semicolons, like commas, separate certain elements of a sentence. However, semicolons separate only grammatically equivalent elements—for example, two closely related independent clauses.

In Burma, George Orwell learned something about the nature of imperialism; it was not an easy lesson.

Shirley Jackson's "The Lottery" is fiction; however, many early readers thought it was a true story.

In most cases, you use commas to separate items in a series. However, when one or more of the items in a series already include commas, separate the items with semicolons. This will make the sentence easier to follow.

Orwell set his works in Paris, France; London, England; and Moulmein, Burma.

Learn When to Use Quotation Marks

Quotation marks are used to set off quoted speech or writing.

At the end of his essay, E. B. White feels "the chill of death" (191).

Special rules govern the use of other punctuation marks with quotation marks:

- Commas and periods always go *inside* quotation marks.
- Colons and semicolons always go *outside* quotation marks.
- Question marks and exclamation points can go *either* inside or outside quotation marks, depending on whether or not they are part of the quoted material.

Quotation marks are also used to set off the titles of essays ("Once More to the Lake"), stories ("The Lottery"), and poems ("Five Ways to Kill a Man").

For information on formatting quotations in research papers, see the Appendix, **page 768.**

Learn When to Use Dashes and Colons

Dashes are occasionally used to set off and emphasize information within a sentence.

Jessica Mitford wrote a scathing critique of the funeral industry—and touched off an uproar. Her book *The American Way of Death* was widely read around the world.

However, because this usage is somewhat informal, dashes should be used in moderation in your college writing.

Colons are used to introduce lists, examples, and clarifications. A colon should always be preceded by a complete sentence.

Television has been criticized for three things: exposing children to sex, promoting gratuitous violence, and contributing to the decline of family life.

For more information on using colons, see the Grammar in Context section of **Chapter 12 (page 457).**

✓ CHECKLIST: **Editing for Punctuation**

- **Commas** Have you used commas when necessary—and only when necessary?
- **Semicolons** Have you used semicolons only between grammatically equivalent items?
- **Quotation marks** Have you used quotation marks to set off quoted speech or writing and to set off titles of essays, stories, and poems? Have you placed other punctuation correctly with quotation marks?
- **Dashes and colons** Have you used dashes in moderation? Is every colon that introduces a list, an example, or a clarification preceded by a complete sentence?

For practice in editing for punctuation, visit Exercise Central online at <bedfordstmartins.com/patterns>.

Exercise 1

Edit your essay for grammar and punctuation.

💻 COMPUTER STRATEGY

Just as you do when you revise, you should edit on a hard copy of your essay. Seeing your work on the printed page makes it easy for you to spot surface-level errors in grammar and punctuation. You can also run a grammar check to help you find grammar and punctuation errors, but you should keep in mind that grammar checkers are far from perfect. They often miss errors (such as faulty modification), and they frequently highlight areas of text (such as a long sentence) that may not contain an error.

Exercise 2

Run a grammar check, and then make any additional corrections you think are necessary.

Editing for Sentence Style and Word Choice

As you edit your essay for grammar and punctuation, you should also be looking one last time at how you construct sentences and choose words. To make your essay as clear, readable, and convincing as possible, your sentences should be not only correct but also concise and varied. In addition, every word should mean exactly what you want it to mean, and your language should be free of clichés.

Eliminate Awkward Phrasing

As you review your essay's sentences, check carefully for awkward phrasing, and do your best to smooth it out.

Awkward:	The reason Jefferson drafted the Declaration of Independence was because he felt the king was a tyrant.
Correct:	The reason Jefferson drafted the Declaration of Independence was that he felt the king was a tyrant.

For more information about this error, see the Grammar in Context section of Chapter 10 (page 337).

Awkward:	*Work* is where you earn money.
Correct:	*Work* is the activity you do to earn money.

For more information about this error, see the Grammar in Context section of Chapter 13 (page 515).

Be Sure Your Sentences Are Concise

A **concise** sentence is efficient; it is not overloaded with extra words and complicated constructions. To make sentences concise, you need to eliminate repetition and redundancy, delete empty words and expressions, and cut everything that is not absolutely necessary.

Wordy:	Brent Staples's essay "Just Walk On By" explores his feelings, thoughts, and ideas about various events and experiences that were painful to him as a black man living in a large metropolitan city.
Concise:	Brent Staples's essay "Just Walk On By" explores his ideas about his painful experiences as a black man living in a large city.

Be Sure Your Sentences Are Varied

To add interest to your paper, vary the length and structure of your sentences, and vary the way you open them.

- Mix long and short sentences.

  As time went on, and as he saw people's hostile reactions to him, Staples grew more and more uneasy. Then, he had an idea.

- Mix simple, compound, and complex sentences.

  Simple sentence (*one independent clause*): Staples grew more and more uneasy.

  Compound sentence (*two independent clauses*): Staples grew more and more uneasy, but he stood his ground.

  Complex sentence (*dependent clause, independent clause*): Although Staples grew more and more uneasy, he continued to walk in the neighborhood.

For more information on how to form compound and complex sentences, see the Grammar in Context section of Chapter 14 (page 574).

- Vary your sentence openings. Instead of beginning every sentence with the subject (particularly with a pronoun like *he* or *this*), begin some sentences with an introductory word, phrase, or clause that ties it to the preceding sentence.

  Dershowitz and Safire agree that a government-sponsored ID card is a controversial idea. For example, some people think that an ID card will mean the government is always watching them. Moreover, some people want to hide from creditors. Although these concerns are certainly valid, ID cards do have advantages.

Choose Your Words Carefully

- Choose **specific** words that identify particular examples and details.

  Vague: Violence in sports is a bad thing.

  Specific: Violence in boxing is a serious problem that threatens not just the lives of the boxers but also the sport itself.

- Avoid **clichés**, overused expressions that rely on tired figures of speech.

  Clichés: When he was hit, the boxer stood for a moment like a deer caught in the headlights, and then he fell to the ground like a ton of bricks.

  Revised: When he was hit, the boxer stood frozen for a moment, and then he fell to the ground.

✓ CHECKLIST: **Editing for Sentence Style and Word Choice**

- **Awkward phrasing**   Have you eliminated awkward constructions?
- **Concise sentences**   Have you eliminated repetition, empty phrases, and excess words? Is every sentence as concise as it can be?
- **Varied sentences**   Have you varied the length and structure of your sentences? Have you varied your sentence openings?
- **Word Choice**   Have you selected specific words? Have you eliminated clichés?

For practice in editing for sentence style and word choice, visit Exercise Central online at <bedfordstmartins.com/patterns>.

Exercise 3

Check your essay's sentence style and word choice.

Proofreading Your Essay

When you **proofread**, you check your essay for surface errors, such as commonly confused words, misspellings, faulty capitalization, and incorrect italic use; then, you check for typographical errors.

Check for Commonly Confused Words

Even if you have carefully considered your choice of words during the editing stage, you may have missed some errors. As you proofread, look carefully to see if you can spot any **commonly confused words:** *its* for *it's*, *there* for *their*, or *affect* for *effect*, for example.

For more information on how to distinguish between *affect* and *effect*, see the Grammar in Context section of **Chapter 10 (page 337).**

Check for Misspellings and Faulty Capitalization

It makes no sense to work hard on an essay and then undermine your credibility with spelling and mechanical errors. If you have any doubt about how a word is spelled or whether or not to capitalize it, check a dictionary (in book form or online).

Check for Correct Use of Underlining and Italics

Italics are required for titles of books and plays and for names of magazines and journals: *Life on the Mississippi, Hamlet, The Onion,* and *Publications of the Modern Language Association,* for example. However, your instructor may prefer that you underline these titles to indicate italics. When you proofread, make sure you have followed the required style.

Check for Typos

The last step in the proofreading process is to read carefully and hunt for typos. Make sure you have spaced correctly between words and have not accidentally typed an extra letter, omitted a letter, or transposed two letters.

✓ CHECKLIST: **Proofreading**

- **Commonly confused words**   Have you proofread for errors with words that are often confused with each other?
- **Misspelled words and faulty capitalization**   Have you proofread for errors in spelling and capitalization? Have you run a spell check?
- **Italics and underlining**   Have you underlined (or typed in italics) the titles of books and plays and the names of magazines and journals?
- **Typos**   Have you checked carefully to eliminate typing errors?

For more practice with proofreading, visit Exercise Central online at <bedfordstmartins.com/patterns>.

💻 **COMPUTER STRATEGY**

You should certainly run a spell check to help you locate misspelled words and incorrect strings of letters caused by typos, but keep in mind that a spell checker will not find every error. For example, it will not identify many misspelled proper nouns or foreign words, nor will it highlight words that are spelled correctly but used incorrectly—*work* for *word* or *form* for *from,* for example. For this reason, you must still proofread carefully—even if you run a spell check.

Exercise 4

Proofread your essay.

Checking Manuscript Format

The final thing to consider is manuscript format—how the paragraphs, sentences, and words look on the page. Your instructor will give you some general guidelines about format—telling you, for example, to type your last name and the page number at the top right of each page—and, of course, you should follow these guidelines. Students writing in the humanities usually follow the format illustrated below.

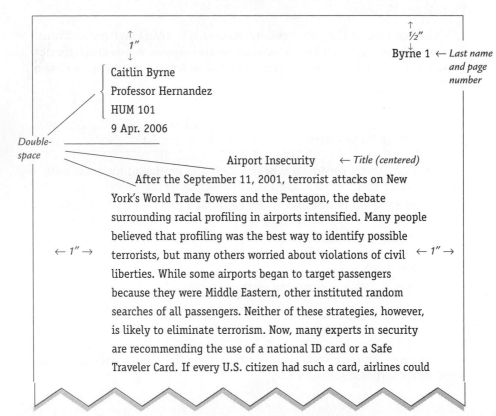

↑
1"
↓

↑
½"
↓

Byrne 1 ← *Last name and page number*

Caitlin Byrne
Professor Hernandez
HUM 101
9 Apr. 2006

Double-space

Airport Insecurity   ← *Title (centered)*

← 1" →

After the September 11, 2001, terrorist attacks on New York's World Trade Towers and the Pentagon, the debate surrounding racial profiling in airports intensified. Many people believed that profiling was the best way to identify possible terrorists, but many others worried about violations of civil liberties. While some airports began to target passengers because they were Middle Eastern, other instituted random searches of all passengers. Neither of these strategies, however, is likely to eliminate terrorism. Now, many experts in security are recommending the use of a national ID card or a Safe Traveler Card. If every U.S. citizen had such a card, airlines could

← 1" →

Use Visuals Responsibly.   If your instructor permits you to use visuals in your essay, choose them carefully. A visual should add something vital to your paper (for example, you might use a diagram to explain a complicated process, a chart or graph to clarify statistics, or a photograph to show an unusual structure). It should be located as close as possible to the section of the essay where it is discussed; this placement will provide context for the visual and make its purpose clear. Finally, you must document any visual that is not your original work. (For more on documentation, see the Appendix.)

✓ CHECKLIST: **Checking Manuscript Format**

- **Guidelines**   Have you followed your instructor's manuscript guidelines?
- **Spacing**   Have you double-spaced throughout?
- **Type size**   Have you used ten- or twelve-point type?
- **Paragraphing**   Have you indented the first line of every paragraph?
- **Visuals**   Have you inserted each visual in a logical place? Have you documented each borrowed visual?

Exercise 5

Make any necessary corrections to your essay's format, and then print out your final draft.

PART TWO

Readings for Writers

The relationship between reading and writing is a complex one. Sometimes you will write an essay based on your own experience; more often than not, however, you will respond in writing to something you have read. The essays in this book give you a chance to do both.

As you are probably aware, the fact that information appears in print or on the Internet does not mean you should take it at face value. Of course, many of the books and articles you read will be reliable, but some — especially material found on Web sites and in online discussion groups — will include contradictions, biased ideas, or even inaccurate or misleading information. For this reason, your goal should not be simply to understand what you read but to assess the credibility of the writers and, eventually, to judge the soundness of their ideas.

When you read the essays in this book, you should approach them critically. In other words, you should question (and sometimes challenge) the writer's ideas — and, in the process, try to create new interpretations that you can explore in your writing. Approaching a text in this way is not easy, for it requires you to develop your own analytical and critical skills and your own set of standards to help you judge and interpret what you read. Only after you have read and critically evaluated a text can you begin to draw your ideas together and write about them.

Every reading selection in Chapters 6 through 15 is accompanied by a series of questions intended to guide you through the reading process. In many ways, these questions are a warm-up for the intellectual workout of writing an essay. The more time you devote to them, the more you will develop your analytical skills. In a real sense, then, these questions will help you develop the critical thinking skills you will need when you write. In becoming a proficient reader, you will also gain confidence in yourself as a writer.

Each of the reading selections in Chapters 6 through 15 is organized around one dominant pattern of development. In your outside reading, however, you will often find more than one pattern used in a single piece of writing (as in Chapter 15, Combining the Patterns, page 703). When you write, then, do not feel you must follow these patterns blindly; instead, think of them as tools for making your writing more effective, and adapt them to your subject, your audience, and your writing purpose.

In addition to the reading selections, each chapter also includes a visual text — for example, a piece of fine art, an advertisement, or a photograph. By visually reinforcing the chapter's basic rhetorical concept, each visual text serves as a bridge to the chapter's essays. Following each visual is a set of questions designed to help you understand not just the image but also the pattern that is the chapter's focus.

6
Narration

What Is Narration?

Narration tells a story by presenting events in an orderly, logical sequence. In the following paragraph from "The Stone Horse," essayist Barry Lopez recounts the history of the exploration of the California desert:

Topic sentence

Narrative traces developments through the nineteenth century

Western man did not enter the California desert until the end of the eighteenth century, 250 years after Coronado brought his soldiers into the Zuni pueblos in a bewildered search for the cities of Cibola. The earliest appraisals of the land were cursory, hurried. People traveled *through* it, en route to Santa Fe or the California coastal settlements. Only miners tarried. In 1823 what had been Spain's became Mexico's, and in 1848 what had been Mexico's became America's; but the bare, jagged mountains and dry lake beds, the vast and uniform plains of creosote bush and yucca plants, remained as obscure as the northern Sudan until the end of the nineteenth century.

Narration can be the dominant pattern in many kinds of writing (as well as in speech). Histories, biographies, and autobiographies follow a narrative form, as do personal letters, diaries, and journals. Narration is the dominant pattern in many works of fiction and poetry, and it is an essential part of casual conversation. Narration also underlies folk and fairy tales and radio and television news reports. In short, anytime you tell what happened, you are using narration.

Using Narration

Although the purpose of a narrative may be simply to recount events or to create a particular mood or impression, in college writing a narrative essay is more likely to present a sequence of events for the purpose of supporting a thesis. For instance, in a narrative about a bad date, your purpose may be to show your readers that dating is a bizarre and often unpleasant ritual. Accordingly, you do not simply tell the story of your date. Rather, you select and arrange details to show your readers *why* dating is bizarre and unpleasant. As in any other kind of essay, you may state your thesis explicitly ("My experiences with dating have convinced me that this ritual should be abandoned entirely"), or you may imply your thesis through your selection and arrangement of events.

Narration can provide the structure for an entire essay, but narrative passages may also appear in essays that are not primarily narrative. In an argumentative essay supporting stricter gun-safety legislation, for example, you might devote one or two paragraphs to the story of a child accidentally killed by a handgun. In this chapter, however, we focus on narration as the dominant pattern of a piece of writing.

During your college career, many of your assignments will call for narration. In an English composition class, for instance, you may be asked to write about an experience that was important to your development as an adult; on a European history exam, you may need to relate the events that led to Napoleon's defeat at the Battle of Waterloo; and in a technical writing class, you may be asked to write a letter of complaint tracing a company's negligent actions. In each of these situations (as well as in many additional assignments), your writing has a primarily narrative structure, and the narrative supports a particular thesis.

The skills you develop in narrative writing will also help you in other kinds of writing. A *process essay,* such as an explanation of a laboratory experiment, is like a narrative because it outlines a series of steps in chronological order; a *cause-and-effect essay,* such as your answer to an exam question that asks you to analyze the events that caused the Great Depression, also resembles a narrative in that it traces a sequence of events. Although a process essay explains how to do something and a cause-and-effect essay explains why events occur, writing both these kinds of essays will be easier after you master narration. (Process essays and cause-and-effect essays are dealt with in Chapters 9 and 10, respectively.)

Planning a Narrative Essay

Including Enough Detail

Narratives, like other types of writing, need rich, specific details if they are to be convincing. Each detail should help to create a picture for the reader; even exact times, dates, and geographic locations can be helpful. Look, for example, at the following paragraph from the essay "My Mother Never Worked" by Bonnie Smith-Yackel, which appears later in this chapter:

> In the winter she sewed night after night, endlessly, begging cast-off clothing from relatives, ripping apart coats, dresses, blouses, and trousers

to remake them to fit her four daughters and son. Every morning and every evening she milked cows, fed pigs and calves, cared for chickens, picked eggs, cooked meals, washed dishes, scrubbed floors, and tended and loved her children. In the spring she planted a garden once more, dragging pails of water to nourish and sustain the vegetables for the family. In 1936 she lost a baby in her sixth month.

This list of details adds interest and authenticity to the narrative. The central figure in the narrative is a busy, productive woman, and readers know this because they are given an exhaustive catalog of her activities.

Varying Sentence Structure

When narratives present a long series of events, all the sentences can begin to sound alike: "She sewed dresses. She milked cows. She fed pigs. She fed calves. She cared for chickens." Such a predictable string of sentences may become monotonous for your readers. You can eliminate this monotony by varying your sentence structure—for instance, by using a variety of sentence openings or by combining simple sentences as Smith-Yackel does: "In the winter she sewed night after night, endlessly. . . . Every morning and every evening she milked cows, fed pigs and calves, cared for chickens."

Maintaining Clear Narrative Order

Many narratives present events in their exact order, moving from first event to last. Whether or not you follow a strict **chronological order** depends on the purpose of your narrative. If you are writing a straightforward account of a historical event or summarizing a record of poor management practices, you will probably want to move from beginning to end. In a personal-experience essay or a fictional narrative, however, you may want to engage your readers' interest by beginning with an event from the middle of your story, or even from the end, and then presenting the events that led up to it. You may also decide to begin in the present and then use one or more **flashbacks** (shifts into the past) to tell your story. To help readers follow the order of events in your narrative, it is very important to use correct verb tenses and clear transitions.

Using Accurate Verb Tenses. **Verb tense** is extremely important in writing that recounts events in a fixed order because tenses indicate temporal (time) relationships. When you write a narrative, you must be careful to keep verb tenses consistent and accurate so that your readers can follow the sequence of events. Naturally, you must shift tenses to reflect an actual time shift in your narrative. For instance, convention requires that you use present tense when discussing works of literature ("When Hamlet's mother *marries* his uncle . . . "), but a flashback to an earlier point in the story calls for a shift from present to past tense ("Before their marriage, Hamlet *was* . . . "). Nevertheless, you should avoid unwarranted shifts in verb tense; they will make your narrative confusing.

Using Transitions. Transitions — connecting words or phrases — help link events in time, enabling narratives to flow smoothly. Without them, narratives would lack coherence, and readers would be unsure of the correct sequence of events. Transitions indicate the order of events, and they also signal shifts in time. In narrative writing, the transitions commonly used for these purposes include *first, second, next, then, later, at the same time, meanwhile, immediately, soon, before, earlier, after, afterward, now,* and *finally*. In addition to these transitional words and phrases, specific time markers — such as *three years later, in 1927, after two hours,* and *on January 3* — indicate how much time has passed between events. (A more complete list of transitions appears on page 43.)

Structuring a Narrative Essay

Like other essays, a **narrative** essay has an introduction, a body, and a conclusion. If your essay's thesis is explicitly stated, it will, in most cases, appear in the **introduction**. The **body paragraphs** of your essay will recount the events that make up your narrative, following a clear and orderly plan. Finally, the **conclusion** will give your readers the sense that your narrative is complete, perhaps by restating your thesis or by summarizing key points or events.

Suppose you are assigned a short history paper about the Battle of Waterloo. You plan to support the thesis that if Napoleon had kept more troops in reserve, he might have defeated the British troops serving under Wellington. Based on this thesis, you decide that the best way to organize your paper is to present the five major phases of the battle in chronological order. An informal outline of your essay might look like this:

Introduction:	Thesis statement — If Napoleon had kept more troops in reserve, he might have broken Wellington's line with another infantry attack and thus won the Battle of Waterloo.
Phase 1 of the battle:	Napoleon attacked the Château of Hougoumont.
Phase 2 of the battle:	The French infantry attacked the British lines.
Phase 3 of the battle:	The French cavalry staged a series of charges against the British lines that had not been attacked before; Napoleon committed his reserves.

Phase 4 of the battle:	The French captured La Haye Sainte, their first success of the day but an advantage that Napoleon, having committed troops elsewhere, could not maintain without reserves.
Phase 5 of the battle:	The French infantry was decisively defeated by the combined thrust of the British infantry and the remaining British cavalry.
Conclusion:	Restatement of thesis or review of key points or events.

By discussing the five phases of the battle in chronological order, you clearly support your thesis. As you expand your informal outline into a historical narrative, exact details, dates, times, and geographic locations are extremely important. Without them, your statements are open to question. In addition, to keep your readers aware of the order of events, you must select appropriate transitional words and phrases and pay careful attention to verb tenses.

Revising a Narrative Essay

When you revise a narrative essay, consider the items on the revision checklist on page 54. In addition, pay special attention to the items on the following checklist, which apply specifically to revising narrative essays.

> ✓ REVISION CHECKLIST: **Narration**
>
> - Does your assignment call for narration?
> - Does your essay's thesis communicate the significance of the events you discuss?
> - Have you included enough specific detail?
> - Have you varied your sentence structure?
> - Is the order of events clear to readers?
> - Have you varied sentence openings to avoid monotony?
> - Do your transitions link events in time?

Editing a Narrative Essay

When you edit your narrative essay, follow the guidelines on the editing checklists on pages 71, 73, and 76. In addition, focus on the grammar, mechanics, and punctuation issues that are particularly relevant to narrative essays. One of these issues — avoiding run-on sentences — is discussed below.

GRAMMAR IN CONTEXT: Avoiding Run-On Sentences

....

When writing narrative essays, particularly personal narratives and essays that include dialogue, writers can easily lose sight of sentence boundaries and create **run-on sentences**. There are two kinds of run-on sentences: *fused sentences* and *comma splices*.

A **fused sentence** occurs when two sentences are incorrectly joined without punctuation.

TWO CORRECT SENTENCES:	"The sun came out hot and bright, endlessly, day after day. The crops shriveled and died" (Smith-Yackel 110).
FUSED SENTENCE:	The sun came out hot and bright, endlessly, day after day the crops shriveled and died.

A **comma splice** occurs when two sentences are incorrectly joined with just a comma.

COMMA SPLICE:	The sun came out hot and bright, endlessly, day after day, the crops shriveled and died.

Five Ways to Correct These Errors:

1. **Use a period to create two separate sentences.**

   The sun came out hot and bright, endlessly, day after day. The crops shriveled and died.

2. **Join the sentences with a comma and a coordinating conjunction** (*and, or, nor, for, so, but, yet*).

   The sun came out hot and bright, endlessly, day after day, and the crops shriveled and died.

3. **Join the sentences with a semicolon.**

   The sun came out hot and bright, endlessly, day after day; the crops shriveled and died.

4. **Join the sentences with a semicolon and a transitional word or phrase** (followed by a comma), such as *however, therefore,* or *for example.* (See page 43 for a list of transitional words and phrases.)

   The sun came out hot and bright, endlessly, day after day; eventually, the crops shriveled and died.

5. Create a complex sentence by adding a subordinating conjunction (*although, because, if,* and so on) or a relative pronoun (*who, which, that,* and so on) to one of the sentences.

As the sun came out hot and bright, endlessly, day after day, the crops shriveled and died.

For more practice in avoiding run-ons, visit Exercise Central at <bedfordstmartins.com/patterns/runons>.

✓ EDITING CHECKLIST: **Narration**

- Have you avoided run-on sentences?
- Do your verb tenses enable readers to follow the sequence of events?
- Have you avoided unnecessary tense shifts?
- If you use dialogue, have you punctuated it correctly and capitalized where necessary?

A STUDENT WRITER: **Narration**

The following essay is typical of the informal narrative writing many students are asked to do in English composition classes. It was written by Tiffany Forte in response to the assignment "Write an essay about a goal or dream you had when you were a child."

My Field of Dreams

Introduction   When I was young, I was told that when I grew up I 1
could be anything I wanted to be, and I always took for granted
that this was true. I knew exactly what I was going to be, and
I would spend hours dreaming about how wonderful my life
would be when I grew up. One day, though, when I did grow

Thesis statement   up, I realized that things had not turned out the way I had
always expected they would.

Narrative begins   When I was little, I never played with baby dolls or 2
Barbies. I wasn't like other little girls; I was a tomboy. I was the
only girl in the neighborhood where I lived, so I always played
with boys. We would play army or football or (my favorite)
baseball.

     Almost every summer afternoon, all the boys in my 3
neighborhood and I would meet by the big oak tree to get a
baseball game going. Surprisingly, I was always one of the first

to be picked for a team. I was very fast, and (for my size) I could hit the ball far. I loved baseball more than anything, and I wouldn't miss a game for the world.

My dad played baseball too, and every Friday night I would go to the field with my mother to watch him play. It was just like the big leagues, with lots of people, a snack bar, and lights that shone so high and bright you could see them a mile away. I loved to go to my dad's games. When all the other kids would wander off and play, I would sit and cheer on my dad and his team. My attention was focused on the field, and my heart would jump with every pitch.

Even more exciting than my dad's games were the major league games. The Phillies were my favorite team, and I always looked forward to watching them on television. My dad would make popcorn, and we would sit and watch in anticipation of a Phillies victory. We would go wild, yelling and screaming at all the big plays. When the Phillies would win, I would be so excited I couldn't sleep; when they would lose, I would go to bed angry just like my dad.

Key experience introduced (par. 6–7)

It was when my dad took me to my first major league baseball game that I decided I wanted to be a major league baseball player. The excitement began when we pulled into the parking lot of the old Veterans Stadium. There were thousands of cars. As we walked from the car to the stadium, my dad told me to hold on to his hand and not to let go no matter what. When we gave the man our tickets and entered the stadium, I understood why. There were mobs of people everywhere. They were walking around the stadium and standing in long lines for hot dogs, beer, and souvenirs. It was the most wonderful thing I had ever seen. When we got to our seats, I looked down at the tiny baseball diamond below and felt as if I were on top of the world.

The cheering of the crowd, the singing, and the chants were almost more than I could stand. I was bursting with enthusiasm. Then, in the bottom of the eighth inning, with the score tied and two outs, Mike Schmidt came up to bat and hit the game-winning home run. The crowd went crazy. Everyone in the whole stadium was standing, and I found myself yelling and screaming along with everyone else. When Mike Schmidt came out of the dugout to receive his standing ovation, I felt a lump

4

5

6

7

in my throat and butterflies in my stomach. He was everyone's hero that night, and I could only imagine the pride he must have felt. I slept the whole way home and dreamed of what it would be like to be the hero of the game.

Narrative continues

The next day, when I met with the boys at the oak tree, I   8 told them that when I grew up, I was going to be a major league baseball player. They all laughed at me and said I could never be a baseball player because I was a girl. I told them that they were all wrong and that I would show them.

Analysis of childhood experiences

In the years to follow I played girls' softball in a   9 competitive fast-pitch league, and I was very good. I always wanted to play baseball with the boys, but there were no mixed leagues. After a few years, I realized that the boys from the oak tree were right: I was never going to be a major league baseball player. I realized that what I had been told when I was younger wasn't the whole truth. What no one had bothered to tell me was that I could be anything I wanted to be — as long as it was something that was appropriate for a girl to do.

Conclusion

In time, I would get over the loss of my dream. I found new   10 dreams, acceptable for a young woman, and I moved on to other things. Still, every time I watch a baseball game and someone hits a home run, I get those same butterflies in my stomach and think, for just a minute, about what might have been.

Points for Special Attention

Introduction.   Tiffany's introduction is straightforward, yet it arouses reader interest by setting up a contrast between what she expected and what actually happened. Her optimistic expectation — that she could be anything she wanted to be — is contradicted by her thesis statement, encouraging readers to read on to discover how things turned out and why.

Thesis Statement.   Tiffany's assignment was to write about a goal or dream she had when she was a child, but her instructor made it clear that the essay should have an explicitly stated thesis that made a point about the goal or dream. Tiffany knew she wanted to write about her passion for baseball, but she also knew that just listing a series of events would not fulfill the assignment. Her thesis statement — "One day, though, when I did grow up, I realized that things had not turned out the way I had always expected they would" — puts her memories in context, suggesting that she will use them to support a general conclusion about the gap between dreams and reality.

Structure. The body of Tiffany's essay traces the chronology of her involvement with baseball — playing with the neighborhood boys, watching her father's games, watching baseball on television, and, finally, seeing her first major league game. Each body paragraph introduces a different aspect of her experience with baseball, culminating in the vividly described Phillies game. The balance of the essay (paragraphs 8–10) summarizes the aftermath of that game, gives a brief overview of Tiffany's later years in baseball, and presents her conclusion.

Detail. Personal narratives like Tiffany's need a lot of detail because the writers want readers to see and hear and feel what they did. To present an accurate picture, Tiffany includes all the significant sights and sounds she can remember: the big oak tree, the lights on the field, the popcorn, the excited cheers, the food and souvenir stands, the crowds, and so on. She also names Mike Schmidt ("everyone's hero"), his team, and the stadium where she saw him play. Despite all these details, though, she omits some important information — for example, how old she was at each stage of her essay.

Verb Tense. Maintaining clear chronological order is very important in narrative writing, where unwarranted shifts in verb tenses can confuse readers. Knowing this, Tiffany avoids unnecessary tense shifts. In her conclusion, she shifts from past to present tense, but this shift is both necessary and clear. Elsewhere she uses *would* to identify events that recurred regularly. For example, in paragraph 5 she says, "My dad *would* make popcorn" rather than "My dad *made* popcorn," which would suggest that he did so only once.

Transitions. Tiffany's skillful use of transitional words and expressions links her sentences and moves her readers smoothly through her essay. In addition to transitional words such as *when* and *then,* she uses specific time markers — "When I was little," "Almost every summer afternoon," "every Friday night," "As we walked," "The next day," "In the years to follow," and "After a few years" — to advance the narrative and carry her readers along.

Focus on Revision

In their responses to an earlier draft of Tiffany's essay, several students in her peer editing group recommended that she revise one particularly monotonous paragraph. (As one student pointed out, all its sentences began with the subject, making the paragraph seem choppy and its ideas disconnected.) Here is the paragraph from her draft:

> My dad played baseball too. I went to the field with my mother every Friday night to watch him play. It was just like the big leagues. There were lots of people and a snack bar. The lights shone so high and bright you could see them a mile away. I loved to go to my dad's games. All the other kids would wander off and play. I would sit and cheer on my dad and his team. My attention was focused on the field. My heart would jump with every pitch.

In the revised version of the paragraph (now paragraph 4 of her essay), Tiffany varies sentence length and opening strategies:

> My dad played baseball too, and every Friday night I would go to the field with my mother to watch him play. It was just like the big leagues, with lots of people, a snack bar, and lights that shone so high and bright you could see them a mile away. I loved to go to my dad's games. When all the other kids would wander off and play, I would sit and cheer on my dad and his team. My attention was focused on the field, and my heart would jump with every pitch.

After reading Tiffany's revised draft, another student suggested that she might still polish her essay a bit. For instance, she could add some dialogue, quoting the boys' taunts and her own reply in paragraph 8. She could also revise to eliminate **clichés** (overused expressions), substituting fresher, more original language for phrases such as "I felt a lump in my throat and butterflies in my stomach" and "felt as if I were on top of the world." In the next draft of her essay, Tiffany followed up on these suggestions. (A sample peer editing worksheet for narration appears below).

📄 **PEER EDITING WORKSHEET: Narration**

1. What point is the writer making about the essay's subject? Is this point explicitly stated in a thesis statement? If so, where? If not, is the essay's thesis clearly implied? Would a stated thesis be more effective?
2. Does the writer include enough detail? Where could more detail be added? What kind of detail? Be specific.
3. Does the writer vary sentence structure and avoid monotonous strings of similar sentences? Should some sentences be combined? If so, which ones? Can you suggest different openings for any sentences?
4. Is the order in which events occur clear? Should any events be relocated? Should any transitions be added to clarify relationships between events?
5. Are verb tenses consistent? Identify any verb tenses that you believe are incorrect.
6. Does the writer avoid run-on sentences?
7. What could the writer *add* to this essay?
8. What could the writer *take out* of this essay?
9. What is the essay's greatest strength? Why?
10. What is the essay's greatest weakness? What steps should the writer take to correct this problem?

The selections that follow illustrate some of the many possibilities open to writers of narratives. The first selection, a visual text, is followed by questions designed to illustrate how narration can operate in visual form.

From *Spider-Man* (Comic Book)

TM & © 2003, Marvel Characters Inc. Used with permission.

* * *

Reading Images

1. The five panels above tell part of a story of a conflict between Spider-Man and his enemy The Vulture. List the events depicted in the panels in the order shown.

2. What visual elements link each panel to the one that follows? Can you identify any verbal transitions? What additional transitional words and phrases might help to move readers from one panel to the next?

3. What do you think happened before the events depicted here? What do you suppose will happen next?

Journal Entry

Write a narrative paragraph summarizing the story told in these panels. Begin with a sentence that identifies the characters and the setting. Next, write a sentence that summarizes the events that might have preceded the first panel. Then, tell the story the pictures tell. In your last sentence, bring the sequence of events to a logical close. Be sure to use present tense and to include all necessary transitions.

Thematic Connections

- "Creating a Female Sleuth" (page 290)
- "Why Boys Don't Play with Dolls" (page 361)
- "Stigmatic Uniforms" (page 544)
- "Violent Media Is Good for Kids" (page 678)
- "The Park" (page 707)

Only Daughter

Born into a working-class family in 1954, Sandra Cisneros, the daughter of a Mexican-American mother and a Mexican father, spent much of her childhood shuttling between Chicago and Mexico City. A lonely, bookish child, Cisneros began writing privately at a young age but only began to find her voice when she was a creative-writing student at Loyola University and later at the University of Iowa Writers' Workshop. Her best-known works are the novel *The House on Mango Street* (1983) and the short-story collection *Woman Hollering Creek* (1991); she has also published several collections of poetry. Cisneros's latest novel, *Caramelo,* appeared in 2002.

Background on gender preference: In the following essay, which originally appeared in *Glamour* in 1990, Cisneros describes the difficulties of growing up as the only daughter in a Mexican-American family of six sons. Historically, sons have been valued over daughters in most cultures, as reflected in the following proverbs: "A house full of daughters is like a cellar full of sour beer" (Dutch); "Daughters pay nae [no] debts" (Scottish); "A stupid son is better than a crafty daughter" (Chinese); and "A virtuous son is the sun of his family" (Sanskrit). This was largely the case because limited employment opportunities for women meant that sons were more likely to be able to provide financial support for aging parents. Contemporary research suggests that while the preference for sons has diminished considerably in industrialized nations, a distinct preference for sons continues among many cultures in Asia and the Middle East, raising concerns among medical ethicists worldwide. And, even within the more traditional cultures of the industrialized world, old habits of mind regarding the role of women in society can die hard, as the attitudes of Cisneros's father suggest.

Once, several years ago, when I was just starting out my writing career, I was asked to write my own contributor's note for an anthology I was part of. I wrote: "I am the only daughter in a family of six sons. *That* explains everything." 1

Well, I've thought about that ever since, and yes, it explains a lot to me, but for the reader's sake I should have written: "I am the only daughter in a *Mexican* family of six sons." Or even: "I am the only daughter of a Mexican father and a Mexican-American mother." Or: "I am the only daughter of a working-class family of nine." All of these had everything to do with who I am today. 2

I was/am the only daughter and *only* a daughter. Being an only daughter in a family of six sons forced me by circumstance to spend a lot of time by myself because my brothers felt it beneath them to play with a *girl* in public. But that aloneness, that loneliness, was good for a would-be 3 writer — it allowed me time to think and think, to imagine, to read and prepare myself.

Being only a daughter for my father meant my destiny would lead me   4
to become someone's wife. That's what he believed. But when I was in the fifth grade and shared my plans for college with him, I was sure he understood. I remember my father saying, "*Que bueno, ni'ja,* that's good." That meant a lot to me, especially since my brothers thought the idea hilarious. What I didn't realize was that my father thought college was good for girls — good for finding a husband. After four years in college and two more in graduate school, and still no husband, my father shakes his head even now and says I wasted all that education.

In retrospect, I'm lucky my father believed daughters were meant for   5
husbands. It meant it didn't matter if I majored in something silly like English. After all, I'd find a nice professional eventually, right? This allowed me the liberty to putter about embroidering my little poems and stories without my father interrupting with so much as a "What's that you're writing?"

But the truth is, I wanted him to interrupt. I wanted my father to   6
understand what it was I was scribbling, to introduce me as "My only daughter, the writer." Not as "This is only my daughter. She teaches." *Es maestra* — teacher. Not even *profesora.*

In a sense, everything I have ever written has been for him, to win his   7
approval even though I know my father can't read English words, even though my father's only reading includes the brown-ink *Esto* sports magazines from Mexico City and the bloody *¡Alarma!* magazines that feature yet another sighting of *La Virgen de Guadalupe* on a tortilla or a wife's revenge on her philandering husband by bashing his skull in with a *molcajete* (a kitchen mortar made of volcanic rock). Or the *fotonovelas,* the little picture paperbacks with tragedy and trauma erupting from the characters' mouths in bubbles.

My father represents, then, the public majority. A public who is unin-   8
terested in reading, and yet one whom I am writing about and for, and privately trying to woo.

When we were growing up in Chicago, we moved a lot because of my   9
father. He suffered bouts of nostalgia. Then we'd have to let go of our flat, store the furniture with mother's relatives, load the station wagon with baggage and bologna sandwiches, and head south. To Mexico City.

We came back, of course. To yet another Chicago flat, another Chicago   10
neighborhood, another Catholic school. Each time, my father would seek out the parish priest in order to get a tuition break, and complain or boast: "I have seven sons."

He meant *siete hijos,* seven children, but he translated it as "sons." "I   11
have seven sons." To anyone who would listen. The Sears Roebuck employee who sold us the washing machine. The short-order cook where my father ate his ham-and-eggs breakfasts. "I have seven sons." As if he deserved a medal from the state.

My papa. He didn't mean anything by that mistranslation, I'm sure. 12
But somehow I could feel myself being erased. I'd tug my father's sleeve
and whisper: "Not seven sons. Six! and *one daughter.*"

When my oldest brother graduated from medical school, he fulfilled 13
my father's dream that we study hard and use this — our heads, instead of
this — our hands. Even now my father's hands are thick and yellow,
stubbed by a history of hammer and nails and twine and coils and springs.
"Use this," my father said, tapping his head, "and not this," showing us
those hands. He always looked tired when he said it.

Wasn't college an investment? And hadn't I spent all those years in 14
college? And if I didn't marry, what was it all for? Why would anyone go to
college and then choose to be poor? Especially someone who had always
been poor.

Last year, after ten years of writing professionally, the financial rewards 15
started to trickle in. My second National Endowment for the Arts Fellowship. A guest professorship at the University of California, Berkeley. My
book, which sold to a major New York publishing house.

At Christmas, I flew home to Chicago. The house was throbbing, same 16
as always; hot *tamales* and sweet *tamales* hissing in my mother's pressure
cooker, and everybody — my mother, six brothers, wives, babies, aunts,
cousins — talking too loud and at the same time, like in a Fellini film,
because that's just how we are.

I went upstairs to my father's room. One of my stories had just been 17
translated into Spanish and published in an anthology of Chicano writing,
and I wanted to show it to him. Ever since he recovered from a stroke two
years ago, my father likes to spend his leisure hours horizontally. And
that's how I found him, watching a Pedro Infante* movie on Galavisión†
and eating rice pudding.

There was a glass filmed with milk on the bedside table. There were 18
several vials of pills and balled Kleenex. And on the floor, one black sock
and a plastic urinal that I didn't want to look at but looked at anyway.
Pedro Infante was about to burst into song, and my father was laughing.

I'm not sure if it was because my story was translated into Spanish, or 19
because it was published in Mexico, or perhaps because the story dealt
with Tepeyac, the *colonia* my father was raised in and the house he grew up
in, but at any rate, my father punched the mute button on his remote control and read my story.

I sat on the bed next to my father and waited. He read it very slowly. As 20
if he were reading each line over and over. He laughed at all the right places
and read lines he liked out loud. He pointed and asked questions: "Is this
So-and-so?" "Yes," I said. He kept reading.

When he was finally finished, after what seemed like hours, my father 21
looked up and asked: "Where can we get more copies of this for the relatives?"

---

* EDS. NOTE — Mexican actor.
† EDS. NOTE — A Spanish-language cable channel.

Of all the wonderful things that happened to me last year, that was the   22
most wonderful.

• • •

Comprehension

1. What does Cisneros mean when she writes that being an only daughter in a family of six sons "explains everything" (1)?
2. What distinction does Cisneros make in paragraphs 2 and 3 between being "the only daughter" and being "*only* a daughter"?
3. What advantages does Cisneros see in being "the only daughter"? In being "*only* a daughter"?
4. Why does her father think she has wasted her education? What is her reaction to his opinion?
5. Why is her father's reaction to her story the "most wonderful" (22) thing that happened to Cisneros that year?

Purpose and Audience

1. Although Cisneros uses many Spanish words in her essay, in most cases she defines or explains these words. What does this decision tell you about her purpose and her audience?
2. What is Cisneros's thesis? What incidents and details support this thesis?
3. Do you think Cisneros intends to convey a sympathetic or an unsympathetic impression of her father? Explain.

Style and Structure

1. Where does Cisneros interrupt a narrative passage to comment on or analyze events? What does this strategy accomplish?
2. Are the episodes in this essay presented in chronological order? Explain.
3. What transitional expressions does Cisneros use to introduce new episodes?
4. Cisneros quotes her father several times. What do we learn about him from his words?
5. Why does Cisneros devote so much space to describing her father in paragraphs 17–21? How does this portrait compare to the one she presents in paragraphs 9–11?

Vocabulary Projects

1. Define each of the following words as it is used in this selection.

embroidering (5)   stubbed (13)

2. What is the difference in connotation between *sons* and *children*? Between *teacher* and *professor*? Do you think these distinctions are as significant as Cisneros seems to think they are? Explain.

Journal Entry

In what sense do the number and gender(s) of your siblings "explain everything" about who you are today?

Writing Workshop

1. Write a narrative essay consisting of a series of related episodes that show how you gradually gained the approval and respect of one of your parents, of another relative, or of a friend.
2. In "Only Daughter," Cisneros traces the development of her identity as an adult, as a female, and as a writer. Write a narrative essay tracing the development of your own personal or professional identity.
3. Are male and female children treated differently in your family? Have your parents had different expectations for their sons and daughters? Write a narrative essay recounting one or more incidents that illustrate these differences (or the lack of differences). If you and your siblings are all the same gender, or if you are an only child, write about another family you know well.

Combining the Patterns

Cisneros structures her essay as a narrative in which she is the main character and her brothers barely appear. To give her readers a clearer understanding of how her father's attitude toward her differs from his attitude toward her brothers, Cisneros could have added one or more paragraphs of **comparison and contrast**, focusing on the different ways she and her brothers are treated. What specific points of contrast do you think readers would find most useful? Where might such paragraphs be added?

Thematic Connections

- "My Field of Dreams" (page 89)
- "Words Left Unspoken" (page 168)
- "The Men We Carry in Our Minds" (page 481)
- "Strange Tools" (page 743)

Finishing School

Maya Angelou was born Marguerita Johnson in 1928 in St. Louis and spent much of her childhood in Stamps, Arkansas, living with her grandmother. She began her varied career as an actress and singer, appearing in several television dramas and films; in 1998, she made her debut as a director with the film *Down in the Delta*. In the 1960s, she served as northern coordinator for the Southern Christian Leadership Conference, the civil rights group organized by Martin Luther King Jr. A well-known poet, Angelou composed and read "On the Pulse of Morning" for Bill Clinton's 1993 presidential inauguration. The published version of the poem was a best-seller, and her recording of it won a Grammy award. She is currently on the faculty at Wake Forest University. It is likely, however, that Angelou will be best remembered for her series of autobiographical works, beginning with the critically acclaimed *I Know Why the Caged Bird Sings* (1969), which appeared when African-American literature was just beginning to flower.

Background on "finishing schools": In the following excerpt from *I Know Why the Caged Bird Sings*, Angelou recalls a difficult incident that occurred when she was growing up in racially segregated Stamps in the late 1930s. At this time, wealthy young white women, rather than complete a rigorous education, often attended "finishing schools," where they refined the social skills and artistic accomplishments deemed necessary for their future roles in polite society. Versions of such schools also existed (on a limited basis) for the daughters of black professionals in urban areas. However, children of the poor and the working class — both black and white — were expected to learn practical skills that would enable them to get jobs. Such employment opportunities for rural black people were limited by and large to farm work; black women were often limited to domestic service in white households, the role for which Angelou describes her training in this essay.

Recently a white woman from Texas, who would quickly describe herself as a liberal, asked me about my hometown. When I told her that in Stamps my grandmother had owned the only Negro general merchandise store since the turn of the century, she exclaimed, "Why, you were a debutante." Ridiculous and even ludicrous. But Negro girls in small Southern towns, whether poverty-stricken or just munching along on a few of life's necessities, were given as extensive and irrelevant preparations for adulthood as rich white girls shown in magazines. Admittedly the training was not the same. While white girls learned to waltz and sit gracefully with a tea cup balanced on their knees, we were lagging behind, learning the mid-Victorian values with very little money to indulge them. . . .

We were required to embroider and I had trunkfuls of colorful dish-   2
towels, pillowcases, runners, and handkerchiefs to my credit. I mastered
the art of crocheting and tatting, and there was a lifetime's supply of
dainty doilies that would never be used in sacheted dresser drawers. It went
without saying that all girls could iron and wash, but the finer touches
around the home, like setting a table with real silver, baking roasts, and
cooking vegetables without meat, had to be learned elsewhere. Usually at
the source of those habits. During my tenth year, a white woman's kitchen
became my finishing school.

Mrs. Viola Cullinan was a plump woman who lived in a three-bedroom   3
house somewhere behind the post office. She was singularly unattractive
until she smiled, and then the lines around her eyes and mouth which
made her look perpetually dirty disappeared, and her face looked like the
mask of an impish elf. She usually rested her smile until late afternoon
when her woman friends dropped in and Miss Glory, the cook, served
them cold drinks on the closed-in porch.

The exactness of her house was inhuman. This glass went here and   4
only here. That cup had its place and it was an act of impudent rebellion to
place it anywhere else. At twelve o'clock the table was set. At 12:15 Mrs.
Cullinan sat down to dinner (whether her husband had arrived or not). At
12:16 Miss Glory brought out the food.

It took me a week to learn the difference between a salad plate, a bread   5
plate, and a dessert plate.

Mrs. Cullinan kept up the tradition of her wealthy parents. She was   6
from Virginia. Miss Glory, who was a descendant of slaves that had worked
for the Cullinans, told me her history. She had married beneath her
(according to Miss Glory). Her husband's family hadn't had their money
very long and what they had "didn't 'mount to much."

As ugly as she was, I thought privately, she was lucky to get a husband   7
above or beneath her station. But Miss Glory wouldn't let me say a thing
against her mistress. She was very patient with me, however, over the
housework. She explained the dishware, silverware, and servants' bells. The
large round bowl in which soup was served wasn't a soup bowl, it was a
tureen. There were goblets, sherbet glasses, ice-cream glasses, wine glasses,
green glass coffee cups with matching saucers, and water glasses. I had a
glass to drink from, and it sat with Miss Glory's on a separate shelf from
the others. Soup spoons, gravy boat, butter knives, salad forks, and carving
platter were additions to my vocabulary and in fact almost represented a
new language. I was fascinated with the novelty, with the fluttering Mrs.
Cullinan and her Alice-in-Wonderland house.

Her husband remains, in my memory, undefined. I lumped him with   8
all the other white men that I had ever seen and tried not to see.

On our way home one evening, Miss Glory told me that Mrs. Cullinan   9
couldn't have children. She said that she was too delicate-boned. It was
hard to imagine bones at all under those layers of fat. Miss Glory went on
to say that the doctor had taken out all her lady organs. I reasoned that a

pig's organs included the lungs, heart, and liver, so if Mrs. Cullinan was walking around without those essentials, it explained why she drank alcohol out of unmarked bottles. She was keeping herself embalmed.

When I spoke to Bailey* about it, he agreed that I was right, but he also informed me that Mr. Cullinan had two daughters by a colored lady and that I knew them very well. He added that the girls were the spitting image of their father. I was unable to remember what he looked like, although I had just left him a few hours before, but I thought of the Coleman girls. They were very light-skinned and certainly didn't look very much like their mother (no one ever mentioned Mr. Coleman).   10

My pity for Mrs. Cullinan preceded me the next morning like the Cheshire cat's smile. Those girls, who could have been her daughters, were beautiful. They didn't have to straighten their hair. Even when they were caught in the rain, their braids still hung down straight like tamed snakes. Their mouths were pouty little cupid's bows. Mrs. Cullinan didn't know what she missed. Or maybe she did. Poor Mrs. Cullinan.   11

For weeks after, I arrived early, left late and tried very hard to make up for her barrenness. If she had her own children, she wouldn't have had to ask me to run a thousand errands from her back door to the back doors of her friends. Poor old Mrs. Cullinan.   12

Then one evening Miss Glory told me to serve the ladies on the porch. After I set the tray down and turned toward the kitchen, one of the women asked, "What's your name, girl?" It was the speckled-faced one. Mrs. Cullinan said, "She doesn't talk much. Her name's Margaret."   13

"Is she dumb?"   14

"No. As I understand it, she can talk when she wants to but she's usually quiet as a little mouse. Aren't you, Margaret?"   15

I smile at her. Poor thing. No organs and couldn't even pronounce my name correctly.   16

"She's a sweet little thing, though."   17

"Well, that may be, but the name's too long. I'd never bother myself. I'd call her Mary if I was you."   18

I fumed into the kitchen. That horrible woman would never have the chance to call me Mary because if I was starving I'd never work for her. . . .   19

That evening I decided to write a poem on being white, fat, old, and without children. It was going to be a tragic ballad. I would have to watch her carefully to capture the essence of her loneliness and pain.   20

The very next day, she called me by the wrong name. Miss Glory and I were washing up the lunch dishes when Mrs. Cullinan came to the doorway. "Mary?"   21

Miss Glory asked, "Who?"   22

---

* EDS. NOTE—Angelou's brother.

Mrs. Cullinan, sagging a little, knew and I knew. "I want Mary to go down to Mrs. Randall's and take her some soup. She's not been feeling well for a few days." 23

Miss Glory's face was a wonder to see. "You mean Margaret, ma'am. Her name's Margaret." 24

"That's too long. She's Mary from now on. Heat that soup from last night and put it in the china tureen and, Mary, I want you to carry it carefully." 25

Every person I knew had a hellish horror of being "called out of his name." It was a dangerous practice to call a Negro anything that could be loosely construed as insulting because of the centuries of their having been called niggers, jigs, dinges, blackbirds, crows, boots, and spooks. 26

Miss Glory had a fleeting second of feeling sorry for me. Then as she handed me the hot tureen she said, "Don't mind, don't pay that no mind. Sticks and stones may break your bones, but words . . . You know, I been working for her for twenty years." 27

She held the back door open for me. "Twenty years. I wasn't much older than you. My name used to be Hallelujah. That's what Ma named me, but my mistress give me 'Glory,' and it stuck. I likes it better too." 28

I was in the little path that ran behind the houses when Miss Glory shouted, "It's shorter too." 29

For a few seconds it was a tossup over whether I would laugh (imagine being named Hallelujah) or cry (imagine letting some white woman rename you for her convenience). My anger saved me from either outburst. I had to quit the job, but the problem was going to be how to do it. Momma wouldn't allow me to quit for just any reason. 30

"She's a peach. That woman is a real peach." Mrs. Randall's maid was talking as she took the soup from me, and I wondered what her name used to be and what she answered to now. 31

For a week I looked into Mrs. Cullinan's face as she called me Mary. She ignored my coming late and leaving early. Miss Glory was a little annoyed because I had begun to leave egg yolk on the dishes and wasn't putting much heart in polishing the silver. I hoped that she would complain to our boss, but she didn't. 32

Then Bailey solved my dilemma. He had me describe the contents of the cupboard and the particular plates she liked best. Her favorite piece was a casserole shaped like a fish and the green glass coffee cups. I kept his instructions in mind, so on the next day when Miss Glory was hanging out clothes and I had again been told to serve the old biddies on the porch, I dropped the empty serving tray. When I heard Mrs. Cullinan scream "Mary!" I picked up the casserole and two of the green glass cups in readiness. As she rounded the kitchen door I let them fall on the tiled floor. 33

I could never absolutely describe to Bailey what happened next, because each time I got to the part where she fell on the floor and screwed 34 up her ugly face to cry, we burst out laughing. She actually wobbled around on the floor and picked up shards of the cups and cried, "Oh, Momma. Oh, dear Gawd. It's Momma's china from Virginia. Oh Momma, I'm sorry."

Miss Glory came running in from the yard and the women from the porch crowded around. Miss Glory was almost as broken up as her mistress. "You mean to say she broke our Virginia dishes? What we gone do?"   35

Mrs. Cullinan cried louder. "That clumsy nigger. Clumsy little black nigger."   36

Old speckled-face leaned down and asked, "Who did it, Viola? Was it Mary? Who did it?"   37

Everything was happening so fast I can't remember whether her action preceded her words, but I know that Mrs. Cullinan said, "Her name's Margaret, goddamn it, her name's Margaret." And she threw a wedge of broken plate at me. It could have been the hysteria which put her aim off, but the flying crockery caught Miss Glory right over her ear and she started screaming.   38

I left the front door wide open so all the neighbors could hear.   39

Mrs. Cullinan was right about one thing. My name wasn't Mary.   40

●   ●   ●

Comprehension

1. What is Angelou required to do in the white woman's kitchen? Why are these tasks so important to Mrs. Cullinan?

2. Why does Angelou feel sorry for Mrs. Cullinan at first? When does her attitude change? Why?

3. Why does Mrs. Cullinan's friend recommend that Angelou be called "Mary" (18)? Why does this upset Angelou so deeply?

4. When Angelou decides she wants to quit, she realizes she cannot quit "for just any reason" (30). How does her brother Bailey help her resolve her dilemma?

5. What does Angelou actually learn through her experience?

Purpose and Audience

1. Do you think Angelou wrote this essay for southerners, for blacks, for whites, or for a general audience? Identify specific details that support your answer.

2. Angelou begins her narrative by summarizing a discussion between herself and a white woman. What purpose does she have for doing this?

3. What is Angelou's thesis?

Style and Structure

1. What image does the phrase *finishing school* usually call to mind? How is the use of this phrase **ironic** in view of its meaning in this selection?
2. How does Angelou signal the passage of time in this narrative? Identify some transitional phrases that move readers from one period to another.
3. How does the use of dialogue highlight the contrast between the black and the white characters? How does this contrast strengthen the narrative?
4. What details does Angelou use to describe Mrs. Cullinan and her home to the reader? How does this detailed description help to advance the narrative?

Vocabulary Projects

1. Define each of the following words as it is used in this selection.

   tatting (2)   pouty (11)   dilemma (33)
   sacheted (2)   barrenness (12)   shards (34)
   impudent (4)   ballad (20)
   embalmed (9)   construed (26)

2. According to your dictionary, what is the difference between *ridiculous* and *ludicrous* (1)? Between *soup bowl* and *tureen* (7)? Why do you think Angelou draws a distinction between the two words in each pair?
3. Try substituting an equivalent word for each of the following, paying careful attention to the context of each in the narrative.

   perpetually (3)   station (7)   biddies (33)
   exactness (4)   peach (31)

   Does Angelou's original choice seem more effective than your substitutions in all cases? Explain.

Journal Entry

Have you ever received any training or education that at the time you considered "extensive and irrelevant preparations for adulthood" (1)? Do you now see any value in the experience?

Writing Workshop

1. Think about a time in your life when someone in a position of authority treated you unjustly. How did you react? Write a narrative essay in which you recount the situation and your responses to it.

2. Have you ever been the victim of name calling—or found yourself doing the name calling? Summarize your experience, including dialogue and description that will help your readers understand your motivations and reactions. Include a thesis statement that conveys your present attitude toward the situation.

3. Write a narrative essay that includes a brief summary of an incident from a work of fiction—specifically, an incident that serves as a character's initiation into adulthood. In your essay, focus on how the experience helps the character grow up.

Combining the Patterns

Angelou's essay is a narrative, but it is rich with descriptive detail. Identify specific passages of the essay that are structured as **descriptions** of people and places. Is the description primarily visual, or does it incorporate other senses (sound, smell, taste, and touch) as well? Do you think any person, setting, or object should be described in greater detail? Explain.

Thematic Connections

- "Midnight" (page 213)
- "The 'Black Table' Is Still There" (page 366)
- "Letter from Birmingham Jail" (page 597)

My Mother Never Worked

Bonnie Smith-Yackel was born into a farm family in Willmar, Minnesota, in 1937. She began writing as a young homemaker in the early 1960s and for the next fourteen years published short stories, essays, and book reviews in such publications as *Catholic Digest, Minnesota Monthly,* and *Ms.* magazine, as well as in several local newspapers. As Smith-Yackel explains it, "The catalyst for writing the [following] essay shortly after my mother's death was recounting my telephone conversation with Social Security to the lawyer who was helping me settle my mother's estate. When I told him what the SS woman had said, he responded: 'Well, that's right. Your mother didn't work, you know.' At which point I stood and said, 'She worked harder throughout her life than you or a hundred men like you!' and stomped out of his office, drove home, sat down and wrote the essay in one sitting." Although this narrative essay, first published in *Women: A Journal of Liberation* in 1975, is based on personal experience, it also makes a broader statement about how society values "women's work."

> Background on Social Security benefits: Social Security is a federal insurance program that requires workers to contribute a percentage of their wages to a fund that they may draw benefits from if they become unemployed due to disability. After retirement, workers can receive a monthly income from this fund, which also provides a modest death benefit to survivors. The contribution is generally deducted directly from a worker's paycheck, and employers must contribute a matching amount. According to federal law, a woman who is a homemaker, who has never been a wage earner, is eligible for Social Security benefits only through the earnings of her deceased husband. (The same would be true for a man if the roles were reversed.) Therefore, a homemaker's survivors would not be eligible for the death benefit. Although the law has been challenged in the courts, the survivors of a homemaker who has never been a wage earner are still not entitled to a Social Security death benefit.

"Social Security Office." (The voice answering the telephone sounds very self-assured.)   1

"I'm calling about . . . my mother just died . . . I was told to call you and see about a . . . death-benefit check, I think they call it. . . ."   2

"I see. Was your mother on Social Security? How old was she?"   3

"Yes . . . she was seventy-eight. . . ."   4

"Do you know her number?"   5

"No . . . I, ah . . . don't you have a record?"   6

"Certainly. I'll look it up. Her name?"   7

"Smith. Martha Smith. Or maybe she used Martha Ruth Smith? . . . Sometimes she used her maiden name . . . Martha Jerabek Smith?"   8

"If you'd care to hold on, I'll check our records — it'll be a few minutes."   9
"Yes. . . ."   10

Her love letters — to and from Daddy — were in an old box, tied with   11
ribbons and stiff, rigid-with-age leather thongs: 1918 through 1920; hers
written on stationery from the general store she had worked in full-time
and managed, single-handed, after her graduation from high school in
1913; and his, at first, on YMCA or Soldiers and Sailors Club stationery
dispensed to the fighting men of World War I. He wooed her thoroughly
and persistently by mail, and though she reciprocated all his feelings for
her, she dreaded marriage. . . .

"It's so hard for me to decide when to have my wedding day — that's all.   12
I've thought about these last two days. I have told you dozens of times that I
won't be afraid of married life, but when it comes down to setting the date
and then picturing myself a married woman with half a dozen or more kids
to look after, it just makes me sick. . . . I am weeping right now — I hope that
some day I can look back and say how foolish I was to dread it all."

They married in February, 1921, and began farming. Their first baby, a   13
daughter, was born in January, 1922, when my mother was 26 years old.
The second baby, a son, was born in March, 1923. They were renting farms;
my father, besides working his own fields, also was a hired man for two
other farmers. They had no capital initially, and had to gain it slowly, working from dawn until midnight every day. My town-bred mother learned to
set hens and raise chickens, feed pigs, milk cows, plant and harvest a garden, and can every fruit and vegetable she could scrounge. She carried
water nearly a quarter of a mile from the well to fill her wash boilers in
order to do her laundry on a scrub board. She learned to shuck grain, feed
threshers, shock and husk corn, feed corn pickers. In September, 1925, the
third baby came, and in June, 1927, the fourth child — both daughters. In
1930, my parents had enough money to buy their own farm, and that
March they moved all their livestock and belongings themselves, 55 miles
over rutted, muddy roads.

In the summer of 1930 my mother and her two eldest children   14
reclaimed a 40-acre field from Canadian thistles, by chopping them all out
with a hoe. In the other fields, when the oats and flax began to head out,
the green and blue of the crops were hidden by the bright yellow of wild
mustard. My mother walked the fields day after day, pulling each mustard
plant. She raised a new flock of baby chicks — 500 — and she spaded up,
planted, hoed, and harvested a half-acre garden.

During the next spring their hogs caught cholera and died. No cash   15
that fall.

And in the next year the drought hit. My mother and father trudged   16
from the well to the chickens, the well to the calf pasture, the well to the
barn, and from the well to the garden. The sun came out hot and bright,
endlessly, day after day. The crops shriveled and died. They harvested half
the corn, and ground the other half, stalks and all, and fed it to the cattle
as fodder. With the price at four cents a bushel for the harvested crop, they

couldn't afford to haul it into town. They burned it in the furnace for fuel that winter.

In 1934, in February, when the dust was still so thick in the Minnesota air that my parents couldn't always see from the house to the barn, their fifth child — a fourth daughter — was born. My father hunted rabbits daily, and my mother stewed them, fried them, canned them, and wished out loud that she could taste hamburger once more. In the fall the shotgun brought prairie chickens, ducks, pheasant, and grouse. My mother plucked each bird, carefully reserving the breast feathers for pillows.   17

In the winter she sewed night after night, endlessly, begging cast-off clothing from relatives, ripping apart coats, dresses, blouses, and trousers to remake them to fit her four daughters and son. Every morning and every evening she milked cows, fed pigs and calves, cared for chickens, picked eggs, cooked meals, washed dishes, scrubbed floors, and tended and loved her children. In the spring she planted a garden once more, dragging pails of water to nourish and sustain the vegetables for the family. In 1936 she lost a baby in her sixth month.   18

In 1937 her fifth daughter was born. She was 42 years old. In 1939 a second son, and in 1941 her eighth child — and third son.   19

But the war had come, and prosperity of a sort. The herd of cattle had grown to 30 head; she still milked morning and evening. Her garden was more than a half acre — the rains had come, and by now the Rural Electricity Administration and indoor plumbing. Still she sewed — dresses and jackets for the children, housedresses and aprons for herself, weekly patching of jeans, overalls, and denim shirts. She still made pillows, using feathers she had plucked, and quilts every year — intricate patterns as well as patchwork, stitched as well as tied — all necessary bedding for her family. Every scrap of cloth too small to be used in quilts was carefully saved and painstakingly sewed together in strips to make rugs. She still went out in the fields to help with the haying whenever there was a threat of rain.   20

In 1959 my mother's last child graduated from high school. A year later the cows were sold. She still raised chickens and ducks, plucked feathers, made pillows, baked her own bread, and every year made a new quilt — now for a married child or for a grandchild. And her garden, that huge, undying symbol of sustenance, was as large and cared for as in all the years before. The canning, and now freezing, continued.   21

In 1969, on a June afternoon, mother and father started out for town so that she could buy sugar to make rhubarb jam for a daughter who lived in Texas. The car crashed into a ditch. She was paralyzed from the waist down.   22

In 1970 her husband, my father, died. My mother struggled to regain some competence and dignity and order in her life. At the rehabilitation institute, where they gave her physical therapy and trained her to live usefully in a wheelchair, the therapist told me: "She did fifteen pushups   23 today—fifteen! She's almost seventy-five years old! I've never known a woman so strong!"

From her wheelchair she canned pickles, baked bread, ironed clothes,   24
wrote dozens of letters weekly to her friends and her "half dozen or more kids," and made three patchwork housecoats and one quilt. She made balls and balls of carpet rags—enough for five rugs. And kept all her love letters.

"I think I've found your mother's records—Martha Ruth Smith; mar-   25
ried to Ben F. Smith?"

"Yes, that's right."   26

"Well, I see that she was getting a widow's pension. . . ."   27

"Yes, that's right."   28

"Well, your mother isn't entitled to our $255 death benefit."   29

"Not entitled! But why?"   30

The voice on the telephone explains patiently: 31

"Well, you see—your mother never worked."   32

• • •

Comprehension

1. What kind of work did Martha Smith do while her children were growing up? List some of the chores she performed.
2. Why aren't Martha Smith's survivors entitled to a death benefit when their mother dies?
3. How does the government define *work*?

Purpose and Audience

1. What point is the writer trying to make? Why do you suppose her thesis is never explicitly stated?
2. This essay appeared in *Ms.* magazine and other publications whose audiences are sympathetic to feminist goals. Could it just as easily have appeared in a magazine whose audience was not? Explain.
3. Smith-Yackel mentions relatively little about her father in this essay. How can you account for this?
4. This essay was first published in 1975. Do you think it is dated, or do you think the issues it raises are still relevant today?

Style and Structure

1. Is the essay's title effective? If so, why? If not, what alternate title can you suggest?
2. Smith-Yackel could have outlined her mother's life without framing it with the telephone conversation. Why do you think she includes this frame?

3. What strategies does Smith-Yackel use to indicate the passing of time in her narrative?

4. This narrative piles details one on top of another almost like a list. Why does the writer include so many details?

5. In paragraphs 20 and 21, what is accomplished by the repetition of the word *still*?

Vocabulary Projects

1. Define each of the following words as it is used in this selection.

scrounge (13)   rutted (13)   intricate (20)
shuck (13)   reclaimed (14)   sustenance (21)
shock (13)   flax (14)
husk (13)   fodder (16)

2. Try substituting equivalent words for those italicized in this sentence:

He *wooed* her *thoroughly* and *persistently* by mail, and though she *reciprocated* all his feelings for her, she *dreaded* marriage. . . (11).

How do your substitutions change the sentence's meaning?

3. Throughout her narrative, Smith-Yackel uses concrete, specific verbs. Review her choice of verbs, particularly in paragraphs 13–24, and comment on how such verbs serve the essay's purpose.

Journal Entry

Do you believe that a homemaker who has never been a wage earner should be entitled to a Social Security death benefit for her survivors? Explain your reasoning.

Writing Workshop

1. If you can, interview one of your parents or grandparents (or another person you know who reminds you of Smith-Yackel's mother) about his or her work, and write a chronological narrative based on what you learn. Include a thesis statement that your narrative can support.

2. Write Martha Smith's obituary as it might have appeared in her hometown newspaper. (If you are not familiar with the form of an obituary, read a few in your local paper.)

3. Write a narrative account of a typical day at the worst job you ever had. Include a thesis statement that expresses your negative feelings.

Combining the Patterns

Because of the repetitive nature of the farm chores Smith-Yackel describes in her narrative, some passages come very close to explaining a **process**, a series of repeated steps that always occur in a predictable order. Identify several such passages. If Smith-Yackel's essay were written entirely as a process explanation, what material would have to be left out? How would these omissions change the essay?

Thematic Connections

- "Midnight" (page 213)
- "I Want a Wife" (page 524)
- "What Work Is" (page 550)
- "Down and Out in Discount America" (page 659)

DANIEL GROSS

Playing by the Rules

Schooled at Cornell and Harvard universities, journalist Daniel Gross writes extensively about business, politics, and the economy as a contributor to the online magazine *Slate*, the *New York Times*, the *New Republic*, and various other publications. He also edits *STERNbusiness*, a journal published by New York University's Stern School of Business that focuses on management issues. A frequent guest on television and radio news programs, Gross has published three books: *Forbes' Greatest Business Stories of All Time* (1996); *Bull Run: Wall Street, the Democrats, and the New Politics of Personal Finance* (2000); and *Generations of Corning: 150 Years in the Life of a Global Corporation* (2001). The following essay about the career of George Parker and his company's popular board game Monopoly originally appeared in the November 2004 issue of the US Airways in-flight magazine, *Attaché*.

Background on the board game Monopoly: Monopoly was based on a game originally invented in 1903 and patented in 1904 by Elizabeth J. Magie. Called the Landlord's Game, it was, like most commercial games of its era, intended as instructional. Magie was a strong believer in a more equitable distribution of wealth among Americans, and she meant the Landlord's Game to show players how landowners grew wealthy to the detriment of their poorer tenants.

A variation of Magie's game allowed taxing property owners on their holdings and using those monies to buy utilities and railroads, which were then free to those who landed on them. Another option was to increase the "wages" awarded to players for rounding the board. Players around the country created their own versions of the game, calling it Auction Monopoly or simply Monopoly and substituting local street and place names for those in the original. When Charles Darrow encountered a version with Atlantic City, New Jersey, place names, he created a colorful playing board using them and marketed the game as his own. Later, when the Parker Brothers company brought out Darrow's version during the Great Depression, its intent was exactly the opposite of its originator's: the Parker Brothers version of Monopoly glorifies the acquisition of property and personal wealth.

There was a time when American children were able to amuse themselves by playing all sorts of games, with everything from rocks and sticks to dried nuts and shells. So the idea of getting kids — and more specifically their parents — to pay for entertainment that kids had otherwise found available for free is impressive. And to do so over time is even more impressive. But for 120 years, one board-game company has managed to make it look easy.

At the center of Parker Brothers' unlikely story, told by former executive Philip E. Orbanes in his recently published book, *The Game Makers,* lies an insight on the business of games, and on the game of business, that sprung from the mind of a teenager in Victorian New England.*   2

In 1883, George Parker, who lived near Boston, modified a simple card game to make "Banking." Encouraged by family and friends, he endeavored to have a publisher take it on. But the big-city businesses didn't see much in the teen's idea. So Parker raised $50, printed up 500 versions, and started selling Banking in the Boston area out of a suitcase. After high school, he went to work at the *Commercial Bulletin,* where older brother Edward was an editor.   3

But George was obsessed with creating and selling games. As a teenager covering the world of business, he straddled the worlds of childhood and adulthood, games and commerce. Today, academics study the theory of games. And video games are multi-billion-dollar businesses, enjoyed by adults as well as kids. But in Boston in the late 1880s, no such connections between the two seemingly exclusive realms were thought to exist. Nonetheless, as Orbanes notes, in the 1880s, Parker "came to see a relationship between the *strategies* that guided success in parlor games and the *principles* that enhanced success in the 'game' of business." The precocious lad codified them in 12 rules, many of which would be familiar to readers of today's management best-sellers. They included: "Know your goal and reach for it"; "Play by the rules but capitalize on them"; and "When faced with a choice, make the move with the most potential benefit versus risk."   4

Parker combined a rare ability to think strategically with an equally rare ability to grasp that real-world events and popular-culture phenomena could be quickly turned into profitable games. He created games based on the novels of Horatio Alger, and on Mark Twain's non-fiction bestseller *The Innocents Abroad.* When the Spanish-American War broke out in 1898, he published the game Siege of Havana.   5

A couple of years later, in 1901, Parker Brothers was incorporated, with George as president, former journalist Edward as treasurer, and middle brother Charles as vice president. Around the turn of the century, Parker Brothers brought over a British indoor-table-tennis game whose name derived from the sounds the ball made when struck by wooden paddles. Thanks to the company's marketing efforts, Ping-Pong became not just a popular game, but a competitive sport. And after the company brought mahjongg over from China, writes Orbanes, "The game became so popular that it sparked sales in all manner of Chinese accessories."   6

Parker Brothers' largest and most lasting breakthrough came during the Depression. The early 1930s were a difficult time for all American   7

---

* EDS. NOTE— Era corresponding to the reign of Britain's Queen Victoria (1837–1901) characterized by a high regard for proper behavior.

companies, but especially for those whose products were discretionary purchases. By 1934, the sales had fallen by two-thirds from the 1929 level. That spring, Robert Barton, George Parker's son-in-law, who had come to work for the company in 1931, did what the founder didn't have the heart to do. In the company's first significant workforce reduction, Barton fired every employee. (But he later hired them back.)

Being in such a retrenching condition, the firm wasn't in a mode to take on new products. So in 1934, George Parker rejected a game proffered by Charles Brace Darrow, a failed plumbing salesman from Philadelphia. Undaunted, Darrow did precisely what George Parker had done decades before: He published the game himself and sold it locally. The game, in which players could accumulate riches by moving around a board, while trading properties and railroads and building hotels and houses, caught on. While competing, lucky players might land on the Community Chest and receive a windfall; unlucky ones might pick a card ordering them to "go to jail." The game was, of course, Monopoly. 8

Darrow didn't have the capacity to turn his game into a blockbuster. And so Parker Brothers, presented with an opportune second chance, acquired Monopoly. Launched nationwide during the 1935 Christmas shopping season, it became an instant hit, selling 250,000 units. George Parker, then in his late 60s, turned to one of his youthful rules: "Bet heavily when the odds are long in your favor." Instead of resting after the Christmas season, Parker Brothers kicked Monopoly into a higher gear, ramping up production to 35,000 games per week. In a classic—and early—example of segmenting the market, Parker in 1936 developed six different editions of the game, ranging in price from $2 to $25. (The expensive one featured metal coins and a wooden board.) In 1936, 1.81 million copies were sold, and Parker Brothers was flush again. 9

George Parker died in 1952 at the age of 86. But in the post-war years, Parker Brothers continued to play by his rules. 10

In the 1950s, the company designed Risk, a game of geopolitical strategy that could in part be seen as mimicking Cold War* struggles. In the experimental '60s, the Ouija Board clicked with the psychedelic generation. Meanwhile, old stand-bys showed staying power. In 1967, the company sold 2.3 million Ouijas and 2 million of the 30-year-old Monopoly. 11

The past few decades haven't been all fun and games for Parker Brothers. After the company was sold to General Mills in 1968, many of George Parker's principles were cast aside. Worse, the 1970s saw the advent of electronic games like Atari and Pong, and the beginnings of a move away from cardboard and onto circuit boards. While Parker Brothers gamely attempted to keep up—Trivial Pursuit was a smash hit in the late 1980s—the new video-game environment didn't play to its strengths. 12

---

* EDS. NOTE—Referring to the intense competition and conflict between the communist Soviet Union and the United States and Western Europe beginning in the 1950s.

Parker Brothers was ultimately sold to toy giant Hasbro in 1991, where   13
it resides as a cherished brand. And some of George Parker's creations are
still with us in a very big way. Hasbro's most recent earnings release cited
Monopoly as one of the strongest performers. And in August, dozens of
athletes from around the globe competed in Athens for gold in table tennis,
another game that Parker originally popularized as Ping-Pong. But perhaps
the greatest legacy lies in his enduring rules, which offer something for athletes, game-playing kids, and business-running adults. The most universal,
perhaps, is Rule No. 4: "Learn from failure; build upon success."

• • •

Comprehension

1. What games did George Parker develop? What do these games have in
   common?
2. What is the difference between "the business of games" and "the game
   of business" (2)?
3. In what sense is the story of Parker Brothers' rise an "unlikely story" (2)?
4. What does Gross see as so unusual about George Parker? About
   Parker Brothers? What do you think accounts for the company's long
   success?
5. How would you characterize Gross's attitude toward George Parker
   and his company? Do you share his opinion?
6. Is this essay primarily about George Parker, about the company he
   founded, or about business strategy? Explain.
7. In what sense would you say that George Parker's life was an example
   of "playing by the rules"? In what sense, if any, did he break the rules?

Purpose and Audience

1. This essay was written for *Attaché,* the US Airways magazine, whose
   mission, as described on its Web site, is "to bring the best of the world
   to the business traveler." Why would this essay appeal to such an
   audience?
2. What central idea does Gross want to convey to his readers? State this
   idea in the form of a thesis.
3. Is Gross writing primarily to inform his readers about Parker's life, or
   does he have another purpose as well? Explain.

Style and Structure

1. The story Gross tells begins in paragraph 3. What functions do his
   essay's first two paragraphs serve?

2. Gross uses transitional words, such as *after* and *then,* to move his narrative along, and he also uses specific time markers, such as *around the turn of the century* and *by 1934,* to help his readers keep track of events. Give additional examples of transitional words and phrases used in the essay.

3. Gross quotes Philip E. Orbanes, author of a book about Parker Brothers. Would quotations by other experts have strengthened the essay? If so, what kind of experts? What other kinds of individuals might Gross have quoted? (For example, should he have quoted game theory experts? Parker's brothers? Parker himself?)

4. Does Gross's portrait of George Parker make him come alive as an individual? What else would you like to know about Parker? Why do you suppose Gross does not include this information?

Vocabulary Projects

1. Define each of the following words as it is used in this selection.

endeavored (3)	retrenching (8)	ramping (9)
straddled (4)	proffered (8)	flush (9)
codified (4)	undaunted (8)	advent (12)
discretionary (7)	opportune (9)	

2. George Parker was a businessman, and this essay uses the vocabulary of business management to describe Parker's progress. Give some examples of such vocabulary. Do you think this language is suitable for a general audience?

Journal Entry

In paragraphs 4, 9, and 13, Gross quotes some of Parker's 12 rules. Write a response to one of these rules. What do you think it means? How does it apply to your life?

Writing Workshop

1. Choose one of Parker's rules (quoted in the essay), and write an essay of your own in which the rule serves as the thesis statement. You can write about an experience from your personal or working life, or you can profile someone you know.

2. Write your "game autobiography." Begin by choosing five toys or games that you believe define various stages of your life. Then, tell the story of your life, using the toys and games you chose to help you show readers who you are and what you have done so far.

3. Imagine you are a successful executive writing a letter of advice to someone who wants to market a new game or toy. Using the future tense in the body of your letter, tell the prospective entrepreneur what

struggles he or she will face and what can be done to overcome them. (If you like, you may quote George Parker's rules in your letter.)

Combining the Patterns

At various points in his essay—for example, in paragraph 4—Gross compares Parker's games to the games of today. Do you think a **comparison-and-contrast** paragraph that explicitly discusses the differences between the two types of games would improve the essay? If so, where would such a paragraph go?

Thematic Connections

- "The Peter Principle" (page 220)
- "Innovation" (page 231)
- "Why Boys Don't Play with Dolls" (page 361)
- "Violent Media Is Good for Kids" (page 678)

MARTIN GANSBERG

Thirty-Eight Who Saw Murder Didn't Call the Police

Martin Gansberg (1920–1995), a native of Brooklyn, New York, was a reporter and editor for the *New York Times* for forty-three years. The following article, written for the *Times* two weeks after the 1964 murder it recounts, earned Gansberg an award for excellence from the Newspaper Reporters Association of New York. Gansberg's thesis, though not explicitly stated, still retains its power.

Background on the Kitty Genovese murder case: The events reported here took place on March 14, 1964, as contemporary American culture was undergoing a complex transition. The relatively placid years of the 1950s were giving way to more troubling times: the Civil Rights movement was leading to social unrest in the South and in northern inner cities; the escalating war in Vietnam was creating angry political divisions; President John F. Kennedy had been assassinated just four months earlier; violent imagery was increasing in television and film; crime rates were rising; and a growing drug culture was becoming apparent. The brutal, senseless murder of Kitty Genovese — and, more important, her neighbors' failure to respond immediately to her cries for help — became a nationwide, and even worldwide, symbol for what was perceived as an evolving culture of violence and indifference.

Recently, some of the details Gansberg mentions have been challenged. For example, as the *New York Times* now acknowledges, there were only two attacks on Ms. Genovese, not three; the first attack may have been shorter than first reported; the second attack may have occurred in the apartment house foyer, where neighbors would not have been able to see Genovese; and some witnesses may, in fact, actually *have* called the police. At the time, however, the world was shocked by the incident, and even today social scientists around the world debate the causes of "the Genovese syndrome."

For more than half an hour 38 respectable, law-abiding citizens in   1
Queens watched a killer stalk and stab a woman in three separate attacks
in Kew Gardens.

Twice their chatter and the sudden glow of their bedroom lights inter-   2
rupted him and frightened him off. Each time he returned, sought her out,
and stabbed her again. Not one person telephoned the police during the
assault; one witness called after the woman was dead.

That was two weeks ago today.   3

Still shocked is Assistant Chief Inspector Frederick M. Lussen, in   4
charge of the borough's detectives and a veteran of 25 years of homicide
investigations. He can give a matter-of-fact recitation on many murders.

But the Kew Gardens slaying baffles him — not because it is a murder, but because the "good people" failed to call the police.

"As we have reconstructed the crime," he said, "the assailant had three chances to kill this woman during a 35-minute period. He returned twice to complete the job. If we had been called when he first attacked, the woman might not be dead now."

This is what the police say happened beginning at 3:20 A.M. in the staid, middle-class, tree-lined Austin Street area:

Twenty-eight-year-old Catherine Genovese, who was called Kitty by almost everyone in the neighborhood, was returning home from her job as manager of a bar in Hollis. She parked her red Fiat in a lot adjacent to the Kew Gardens Long Island Rail Road Station, facing Mowbray Place. Like many residents of the neighborhood, she had parked there day after day since her arrival from Connecticut a year ago, although the railroad frowns on the practice.

She turned off the lights of her car, locked the door, and started to walk the 100 feet to the entrance of her apartment at 82-70 Austin Street, which is in a Tudor building, with stores in the first floor and apartments on the second.

The entrance to the apartment is in the rear of the building because the front is rented to retail stores. At night the quiet neighborhood is shrouded in the slumbering darkness that marks most residential areas.

Miss Genovese noticed a man at the far end of the lot, near a seven-story apartment house at 82-40 Austin Street. She halted. Then, nervously, she headed up Austin Street toward Lefferts Boulevard, where there is a call box to the 102nd Police Precinct in nearby Richmond Hill.

She got as far as a street light in front of a bookstore before the man grabbed her. She screamed. Lights went on in the 10-story apartment house at 82-67 Austin Street, which faces the bookstore. Windows slid open and voices punctuated the early-morning stillness.

Miss Genovese screamed: "Oh, my God, he stabbed me! Please help me! Please help me!"

From one of the upper windows in the apartment house, a man called down: "Let that girl alone!"

The assailant looked up at him, shrugged, and walked down Austin Street toward a white sedan parked a short distance away. Miss Genovese struggled to her feet.

Lights went out. The killer returned to Miss Genovese, now trying to make her way around the side of the building by the parking lot to get to her apartment. The assailant stabbed her again.

"I'm dying!" she shrieked. "I'm dying!"

Windows were opened again, and lights went on in many apartments. The assailant got into his car and drove away. Miss Genovese staggered to her feet. A city bus, 0–10, the Lefferts Boulevard line to Kennedy International Airport, passed. It was 3:35 A.M.

The assailant returned. By then, Miss Genovese had crawled to the back of the building, where the freshly painted brown doors to the apartment house held out hope for safety. The killer tried the first door; she wasn't there. At the second door, 82-62 Austin Street, he saw her slumped on the floor at the foot of the stairs. He stabbed her a third time — fatally. 18

It was 3:50 by the time the police received their first call, from a man who was a neighbor of Miss Genovese. In two minutes they were at the scene. The neighbor, a 70-year-old woman, and another woman were the only persons on the street. Nobody else came forward. 19

The man explained that he had called the police after much deliberation. He had phoned a friend in Nassau County for advice, and then he had crossed the roof of the building to the apartment of the elderly woman to get her to make the call. 20

"I didn't want to get involved," he sheepishly told police. 21

Six days later, the police arrested Winston Moseley, a 29-year-old business machine operator, and charged him with homicide. Moseley had no previous record. He is married, has two children and owns a home at 133-19 Sutter Avenue, South Ozone Park, Queens. On Wednesday, a court committed him to Kings County Hospital for psychiatric observation. 22

When questioned by the police, Moseley also said that he had slain Mrs. Annie May Johnson, 24, of 146-12 133d Avenue, Jamaica, on Feb. 29 and Barbara Kralik, 15, of 174-17 140th Avenue, Springfield Gardens, last July. In the Kralik case, the police are holding Alvin L. Mitchell, who is said to have confessed to that slaying. 23

The police stressed how simple it would have been to have gotten in touch with them. "A phone call," said one of the detectives, "would have done it." The police may be reached by dialing "0" for operator or SPring 7-3100. 24

Today witnesses from the neighborhood, which is made up of one-family homes in the $35,000 to $60,000 range with the exception of the two apartment houses near the railroad station, find it difficult to explain why they didn't call the police. 25

A housewife, knowingly if quite casually, said, "We thought it was a lovers' quarrel." A husband and wife both said, "Frankly, we were afraid." They seemed aware of the fact that events might have been different. A distraught woman, wiping her hands in her apron, said, "I didn't want my husband to get involved." 26

One couple, now willing to talk about that night, said they heard the first screams. The husband looked thoughtfully at the bookstore where the killer first grabbed Miss Genovese. 27

"We went to the window to see what was happening," he said, "but the light from our bedroom made it difficult to see the street." The wife, still apprehensive, added: "I put out the light and we were able to see better." 28

Asked why they hadn't called the police, she shrugged and replied: "I don't know." 29

A man peeked out from a slight opening in the doorway to his apart-   30
ment and rattled off an account of the killer's second attack. Why hadn't
he called the police at the time? "I was tired," he said without emotion. "I
went back to bed."

It was 4:25 A.M. when the ambulance arrived to take the body of Miss   31
Genovese. It drove off. "Then," a solemn police detective said, "the people
came out."

• • •

Comprehension

1. How much time elapsed between the first stabbing of Kitty Genovese
   and the time when the people finally came out?
2. What excuses do the neighbors make for not coming to Kitty
   Genovese's aid?

Purpose and Audience

1. This article appeared in 1964. What effect was it intended to have on
   its audience? Do you think it has the same impact today, or has its
   impact changed or diminished?
2. What is the article's main point? Why does Gansberg imply his thesis
   rather than state it explicitly?
3. What is Gansberg's purpose in describing the Austin Street area as
   "staid, middle-class, tree-lined" (6)?
4. Why do you suppose Gansberg provides the police department's
   phone number in his article? (Note that New York City did not have
   911 emergency service in 1964.)

Style and Structure

1. Gansberg is very precise in this article, especially in his references to
   time, addresses, and ages. Why?
2. The objective newspaper style is dominant in this article, but the
   writer's anger shows through. Point to words and phrases that reveal
   his attitude toward his material.
3. Because this article was originally set in the narrow columns of a
   newspaper, it has many short paragraphs. Would the narrative be
   more effective if some of these brief paragraphs were combined? If
   so, why? If not, why not? Give examples to support your answer.
4. Review the dialogue. Does it strengthen Gansberg's narrative? Would
   the article be more compelling without dialogue? Explain.
5. This article does not have a formal conclusion; nevertheless, the last
   paragraph sums up the writer's attitude. How?

Vocabulary Projects

1. Define each of the following words as it is used in this selection.

   stalk (1)   adjacent (7)   distraught (26)
   baffles (4)   punctuated (11)   apprehensive (28)
   staid (6)   sheepishly (21)

2. The word *assailant* appears frequently in this article. Why is it used so often? What impact is this repetition likely to have on readers? What other words could have been used?

Journal Entry

In a similar situation, would you have called the police? Would you have gone outside to help? What factors do you think might have influenced your decision?

Writing Workshop

1. In your own words, write a ten-sentence **summary** (see page 758) of the article. Try to reflect Gansberg's order and emphasis, as well as his ideas, and be sure to include all necessary transitions.

2. Rewrite the article as if it were a diary entry of one of the thirty-eight people who watched the murder. Summarize what you saw, and explain why you decided not to call for help. (You may invent details that Gansberg does not include.)

3. If you have ever been involved in or witnessed a situation in which someone was in trouble, write a narrative essay about the incident. If people failed to help the person in trouble, explain why you think no one acted. If people did act, tell how. Be sure to account for your own actions.

Combining the Patterns

Because the purpose of this newspaper article is to give basic factual information, it has no extended descriptions of the victim, the witnesses, or the crime scene. It also does not explain *why* those who watched did not act. Where might passages of **description** or **cause and effect** be added? How might such additions change the article's impact on readers? Do you think they would strengthen the article?

Thematic Connections

- "Samuel" (page 262)
- "The Lottery" (page 317)
- "Who Killed Benny Paret?" (page 346)
- "A Peaceful Woman Explains Why She Carries a Gun" (page 371)

GEORGE ORWELL

Shooting an Elephant

George Orwell (1903–1950) was born Eric Blair in Bengal, India, where his father was a British civil servant. Rather than attend university, Orwell joined the Imperial Police in neighboring Burma (now renamed Myanmar), where he served from 1922 to 1927. Finding himself increasingly opposed to British colonial rule, Orwell left Burma to live and write in Paris and London. A political liberal and a fierce moralist, Orwell is best known today for his novels *Animal Farm* (1945) and *1984* (1949), which portray the dangers of totalitarianism. In "Shooting an Elephant," written in 1936, he recalls an incident from his days in Burma that clarified his thinking about British colonial rule.

Background on British imperialism: The British had gradually taken over Burma through a succession of wars beginning in 1824; by 1885, the domination was complete. Like a number of other European countries, Britain had forcibly established colonial rule in countries throughout the world during the eighteenth and nineteenth centuries, primarily to exploit their natural resources. This empire building, known as *imperialism,* was justified by the belief that European culture was superior to the cultures of the indigenous peoples, particularly in Asia and Africa. Therefore, imperialist nations claimed, it was "the white man's burden" to bring civilization to these "heathen" lands. In most cases, such control could be achieved only through force. Anti-imperialist sentiment began to grow in the early twentieth century, but colonial rule continued until midcentury in much of the less-developed world. Not until the late 1940s did many European colonies begin to gain independence. The British ceded home rule to Burma in 1947.

In Moulmein, in Lower Burma, I was hated by large numbers of people — the only time in my life that I have been important enough for this to happen to me. I was sub-divisional police officer of the town, and in an aimless, petty kind of way anti-European feeling was very bitter. No one had the guts to raise a riot, but if a European woman went through the bazaars alone somebody would probably spit betel juice over her dress. As a police officer I was an obvious target and was baited whenever it seemed safe to do so. When a nimble Burman tripped me up on the football field and the referee (another Burman) looked the other way, the crowd yelled with hideous laughter. This happened more than once. In the end the sneering yellow faces of young men that met me everywhere, the insults hooted after me when I was at a safe distance, got badly on my nerves. The young Buddhist priests were the worst of all. There were several thousands of them in the town and none of them seemed to have anything to do except stand on street corners and jeer at Europeans.

All this was perplexing and upsetting. For at that time I had already   2
made up my mind that imperialism was an evil thing and the sooner I
chucked up my job and got out of it the better. Theoretically — and secretly,
of course — I was all for the Burmese and all against their oppressors, the
British. As for the job I was doing, I hated it more bitterly than I can perhaps make clear. In a job like that you see the dirty work of Empire at close
quarters. The wretched prisoners huddling in the stinking cages of the
lockups, the grey, cowed faces of the long-term convicts, the scarred but-
tocks of the men who had been flogged with bamboos — all these
oppressed me with an intolerable sense of guilt. But I could get nothing
into perspective. I was young and ill-educated and I had had to think out
my problems in the utter silence that is imposed on every Englishman in
the East. I did not even know that the British Empire is dying, still less did
I know that it is a great deal better than the younger empires that are going
to supplant it.* All I knew was that I was stuck between my hatred of the
empire I served and my rage against the evil-spirited little beasts who tried
to make my job impossible. With one part of my mind I thought of the
British Raj† as an unbreakable tyranny, as something clamped down, in
saecula saeculorum,‡ upon the will of prostrate peoples; with another part I
thought that the greatest joy in the world would be to drive a bayonet into a
Buddhist priest's guts. Feelings like these are the normal by-products of
imperialism; ask any Anglo-Indian official, if you can catch him off duty.

One day something happened which in a roundabout way was enlight-   3
ening. It was a tiny incident in itself, but it gave me a better glimpse than I
had had before of the real nature of imperialism — the real motives for
which despotic governments act. Early one morning the sub-inspector at a
police station the other end of the town rang me up on the phone and said
that an elephant was ravaging the bazaar. Would I please come and do
something about it? I did not know what I could do, but I wanted to see
what was happening and I got on to a pony and started out. I took my rifle,
an old .44 Winchester and much too small to kill an elephant, but I
thought the noise might be useful *in terrorem.*§ Various Burmans stopped
me on the way and told me about the elephant's doings. It was not, of
course, a wild elephant, but a tame one which had gone "must."** It had
been chained up, as tame elephants always are when their attack of "must"
is due, but on the previous night it had broken its chain and escaped. Its
mahout,†† the only person who could manage it when it was in that state,
had set out in pursuit, but had taken the wrong direction and was now
twelve hours' journey away, and in the morning the elephant had suddenly

---

   * EDS. NOTE — Orwell was writing in 1936, when Hitler and Stalin were in power and
World War II was only three years away.
   † EDS. NOTE — The former British rule of the Indian subcontinent.
   ‡ EDS. NOTE — From time immemorial.
   § EDS. NOTE — For the purpose of frightening.
  ** EDS. NOTE — Was in heat, a condition likely to wear off.
  †† EDS. NOTE — A keeper and driver of an elephant.

reappeared in the town. The Burmese population had no weapons and were quite helpless against it. It had already destroyed somebody's bamboo hut, killed a cow, and raided some fruit-stalls and devoured the stock; also it had met the municipal rubbish van and, when the driver jumped out and took to his heels, had turned the van over and inflicted violences upon it.

The Burmese sub-inspector and some Indian constables were waiting for me in the quarter where the elephant had been seen. It was a very poor quarter, a labyrinth of squalid bamboo huts, thatched with palm-leaf, winding all over a steep hillside. I remember that it was a cloudy, stuffy morning at the beginning of the rains. We began questioning people as to where the elephant had gone, and, as usual, failed to get any definite information. That is invariably the case in the East; a story always sounds clear enough at a distance, but the nearer you get to the scene of events the vaguer it becomes. Some of the people said that the elephant had gone in one direction, some said that he had gone in another, some professed not even to have heard of an elephant. I had almost made up my mind that the whole story was a pack of lies, when we heard yells a little distance away. There was a loud, scandalized cry of "Go away, child! Go away this instant!" and an old woman with a switch in her hand came round the corner of a hut, violently shooing away a crowd of naked children. Some more women followed, clicking their tongues and exclaiming; evidently there was something that the children ought not to have seen. I rounded the hut and saw a man's dead body sprawling in the mud. He was an Indian, a black Dravidian coolie,* almost naked, and he could not have been dead many minutes. The people said that the elephant had come suddenly upon him round the corner of the hut, caught him with its trunk, put its foot on his back, and ground him into the earth. This was the rainy season and the ground was soft, and his face had scored a trench a foot deep and a couple of yards long. He was lying on his belly with arms crucified and head sharply twisted to one side. His face was coated with mud, the eyes wide open, the teeth bared and grinning with an expression of unendurable agony. (Never tell me, by the way, that the dead look peaceful. Most of the corpses I have seen looked devilish.) The friction of the great beast's foot had stripped the skin from his back as neatly as one skins a rabbit. As soon as I saw the dead man I sent an orderly to a friend's house nearby to borrow an elephant rifle. I had already sent back the pony, not wanting it to go mad with fright and throw me if it smelled the elephant.

The orderly came back in a few minutes with a rifle and five cartridges, and meanwhile some Burmans had arrived and told us that the elephant was in the paddy[†] fields below, only a few hundred yards away. As I started forward practically the whole population of the quarter flocked out of the houses and followed me. They had seen the rifle and were all shouting excitedly that I was going to shoot the elephant. They had not shown much

4

5

---

* EDS. NOTE — An unskilled laborer.
† EDS. NOTE — Wet land for growing rice.

interest in the elephant when he was merely ravaging their homes, but it was different now that he was going to be shot. It was a bit of fun to them, as it would be to an English crowd; besides they wanted the meat. It made me vaguely uneasy. I had no intention of shooting the elephant—I had merely sent for the rifle to defend myself if necessary—and it is always unnerving to have a crowd following you. I marched down the hill, looking and feeling a fool, with the rifle over my shoulder and an ever-growing army of people jostling at my heels. At the bottom, when you got away from the huts, there was a metalled road and beyond that a miry waste of paddy fields a thousand yards across, not yet ploughed but soggy from the first rains and dotted with coarse grass. The elephant was standing eight yards from the road, his left side towards us. He took not the slightest notice of the crowd's approach. He was tearing up bunches of grass, beating them against his knees to clean them and stuffing them into his mouth.

I had halted on the road. As soon as I saw the elephant I knew with perfect certainty that I ought not to shoot him. It is a serious matter to shoot a working elephant—it is comparable to destroying a huge and costly piece of machinery—and obviously one ought not to do it if it can possibly be avoided. And at that distance, peacefully eating, the elephant looked no more dangerous than a cow. I thought then and I think now that his attack of "must" was already passing off; in which case he would merely wander harmlessly about until the mahout came back and caught him. Moreover, I did not in the least want to shoot him. I decided that I would watch him for a little while to make sure that he did not turn savage again, and then go home. 6

But at that moment I glanced round at the crowd that had followed me. It was an immense crowd, two thousand at the least and growing every minute. It blocked the road for a long distance on either side. I looked at the sea of yellow faces above the garish clothes—faces all happy and excited over this bit of fun, all certain that the elephant was going to be shot. They were watching me as they would watch a conjurer about to perform a trick. They did not like me, but with the magical rifle in my hands I was momentarily worth watching. And suddenly I realized that I should have to shoot the elephant after all. The people expected it of me and I had got to do it; I could feel their two thousand wills pressing me forward, irresistibly. And it was at this moment, as I stood there with the rifle in my hands, that I first grasped the hollowness, the futility of the white man's dominion in the East. Here was I, the white man with his gun, standing in front of the unarmed native crowd—seemingly the leading actor of the piece; but in reality I was only an absurd puppet pushed to and fro by the will of those yellow faces behind. I perceived in this moment that when the white man turns tyrant it is his own freedom that he destroys. He becomes a sort of hollow, posing dummy, the conventionalized figure of a sahib.* For it is 7

---

* EDS. NOTE—An official. The term was used among Hindus and Muslims in colonial India.

the condition of his rule that he shall spend his life in trying to impress the "natives," and so in every crisis he has got to do what the "natives" expect of him. He wears a mask, and his face grows to fit it. I had got to shoot the elephant. I had committed myself to doing it when I sent for the rifle. A sahib has got to act like a sahib; he has got to appear resolute, to know his own mind and do definite things. To come all that way, rifle in hand, with two thousand people marching at my heels, and then to trail feebly away, having done nothing — no, that was impossible. The crowd would laugh at me. And my whole life, every white man's life in the East, was one long struggle not to be laughed at.

But I did not want to shoot the elephant. I watched him beating his   8
bunch of grass against his knees, with the preoccupied grandmotherly air that elephants have. It seemed to me that it would be murder to shoot him. At that age I was not squeamish about killing animals, but I had never shot an elephant and never wanted to. (Somehow it always seems worse to kill a *large* animal.) Besides, there was the beast's owner to be considered. Alive, the elephant was worth at least a hundred pounds; dead, he would only be worth the value of his tusks, five pounds, possibly. But I had got to act quickly. I turned to some experienced-looking Burmans who had been there when we arrived, and asked them how the elephant had been behaving. They all said the same thing: he took no notice of you if you left him alone, but he might charge if you went too close to him.

It was perfectly clear to me what I ought to do. I ought to walk up to   9
within, say, twenty-five yards of the elephant and test his behavior. If he charged I could shoot, if he took no notice of me it would be safe to leave him until the mahout came back. But also I knew that I was going to do no such thing. I was a poor shot with a rifle and the ground was soft mud into which one would sink at every step. If the elephant charged and I missed him, I should have about as much chance as a toad under a steamroller. But even then I was not thinking particularly of my own skin, only of the watchful yellow faces behind. For at that moment, with the crowd watching me, I was not afraid in the ordinary sense, as I would have been if I had been alone. A white man mustn't be frightened in front of "natives"; and so, in general, he isn't frightened. The sole thought in my mind was that if anything went wrong those two thousand Burmans would see me pursued, caught, trampled on, and reduced to a grinning corpse like that Indian up the hill. And if that happened it was quite probable that some of them would laugh. That would never do. There was only one alternative. I shoved the cartridges into the magazine and lay down on the road to get a better aim.

The crowd grew very still, and a deep, low, happy sigh, as of people who   10
see the theatre curtain go up at last, breathed from innumerable throats. They were going to have their bit of fun after all. The rifle was a beautiful German thing with cross-hair sights. I did not then know that in shooting an elephant one would shoot to cut an imaginary bar running from ear-hole to ear-hole. I ought, therefore, as the elephant was sideways on, to

have aimed straight at his ear-hole; actually I aimed several inches in front of this, thinking the brain would be further forward.

When I pulled the trigger I did not hear the bang or feel the kick—one never does when a shot goes home—but I heard the devilish roar of glee that went up from the crowd. In that instant, in too short a time, one would have thought, even for the bullet to get there, a mysterious, terrible change had come over the elephant. He neither stirred nor fell, but every line on his body had altered. He looked suddenly stricken, shrunken, immensely old, as though the frightful impact of the bullet had paralyzed him without knocking him down. At last, after what seemed a long time—it might have been five seconds, I dare say—he sagged flabbily to his knees. His mouth slobbered. An enormous senility seemed to have settled upon him. One could have imagined him thousands of years old. I fired again into the same spot. At the second shot he did not collapse but climbed with desperate slowness to his feet and stood weakly upright, with legs sagging and head drooping. I fired a third time. That was the shot that did for him. You could see the agony of it jolt his whole body and knock the last remnant of strength from his legs. But in falling he seemed for a moment to rise, for as his hind legs collapsed beneath him he seemed to tower upwards like a huge rock toppling, his trunk reaching skywards like a tree. He trumpeted, for the first and only time. And then down he came, his belly towards me, with a crash that seemed to shake the ground even where I lay.

I got up. The Burmans were already racing past me across the mud. It was obvious that the elephant would never rise again, but he was not dead. He was breathing very rhythmically with long rattling gasps, his great mound of a side painfully rising and falling. His mouth was wide open—I could see far down into the caverns of pale pink throat. I waited a long time for him to die, but his breathing did not weaken. Finally I fired my two remaining shots into the spot where I thought his heart must be. The thick blood welled out of him like red velvet, but still he did not die. His body did not even jerk when the shots hit him, the tortured breathing continued without a pause. He was dying, very slowly and in great agony, but in some world remote from me where not even a bullet could damage him further. I felt that I had got to put an end to that dreadful noise. It seemed dreadful to see the great beast lying there, powerless to move and yet powerless to die, and not even to be able to finish him. I sent back for my small rifle and poured shot after shot into his heart and down his throat. They seemed to make no impression. The tortured gasps continued as steadily as the ticking of a clock.

In the end I could not stand it any longer and went away. I heard later that it took him half an hour to die. Burmans were bringing dahs* and baskets even before I left, and I was told they had stripped his body almost to the bones by the afternoon.

---

* Eds. note — Heavy knives.

Afterwards, of course, there were endless discussions about the shoot-   14
ing of the elephant. The owner was furious, but he was only an Indian and
could do nothing. Besides, legally I had done the right thing, for a mad elephant has to be killed, like a mad dog, if its owner fails to control it.
Among the Europeans opinion was divided. The older men said I was
right, the younger men said it was a damn shame to shoot an elephant for
killing a coolie, because an elephant was worth more than any damn Cor-
inghee coolie. And afterwards I was very glad that the coolie had been
killed; it put me legally in the right and it gave me a sufficient pretext for
shooting the elephant. I often wondered whether any of the others grasped
that I had done it solely to avoid looking a fool.

• • •

Comprehension

1. Why is Orwell "hated by large numbers of people" (1) in Burma? Why
   does he have mixed feelings toward the Burmese people?
2. Why do the local officials want something done about the elephant?
   Why does the crowd want Orwell to shoot the elephant?
3. Why does Orwell finally decide to kill the elephant? What makes him
   hesitate at first?
4. Why does Orwell say at the end that he was glad the coolie had been
   killed?

Purpose and Audience

1. One of Orwell's purposes in telling his story is to show how it gave
   him a glimpse of "the real nature of imperialism" (3). What does he
   mean? How does his essay illustrate this purpose?
2. Do you think Orwell wrote this essay to inform or to persuade his
   audience? How did Orwell expect his audience to react to his ideas?
   How can you tell?
3. What is the essay's thesis?

Style and Structure

1. What does Orwell's first paragraph accomplish? Where does the
   introduction end and the narrative itself begin?
2. The essay includes almost no dialogue. Why do you think Orwell's
   voice as narrator is the only one readers hear? Is the absence of dialogue a strength or a weakness? Explain.
3. Why do you think Orwell devotes so much attention to the elephant's
   misery (11–12)?

4. Orwell's essay includes a number of editorial comments, which appear within parentheses or dashes. How would you characterize these comments? Why are they set off from the text?

5. Consider the following statements: "Some of the people said that the elephant had gone in one direction, some said that he had gone in another" (4); "Among the Europeans opinion was divided. The older men said I was right, the younger men said it was a damn shame to shoot an elephant" (14). How do these comments reinforce the theme expressed in paragraph 2 ("All I knew was that I was stuck between my hatred of the empire I served and my rage against the evil-spirited little beasts")? What other comments reinforce this theme?

Vocabulary Projects

1. Define each of the following words as it is used in this selection.

baited (1)	despotic (3)	conjurer (7)
perplexing (2)	labyrinth (4)	dominion (7)
oppressors (2)	squalid (4)	magazine (9)
lockups (2)	professed (4)	cross-hair (10)
flogged (2)	ravaging (5)	remnant (11)
supplant (2)	miry (5)	trumpeted (11)
prostrate (2)	garish (7)	pretext (14)

2. Because Orwell is British, he frequently uses words or expressions that an American writer would not likely use. Substitute a contemporary American word or phrase for each of the following, making sure it is appropriate in Orwell's context.

raise a riot (1)	rubbish van (3)	a bit of fun (5)
rang me up (3)	inflicted violences (3)	I dare say (11)

What other expressions in Orwell's essay might need to be "translated" for a contemporary American audience?

Journal Entry

Do you think Orwell is a coward? Do you think he is a racist? Explain your feelings.

Writing Workshop

1. Orwell says that even though he hated British imperialism and sympathized with the Burmese people, he found himself a puppet of the system. Write a narrative essay about a time when you had to do something that went against your beliefs or convictions.

2. Orwell's experience taught him something not only about himself but also about something beyond himself—the way British imperialism

worked. Write a narrative essay that reveals how an incident in your life taught you something about some larger social or political force as well as about yourself.

3. Write an objective, factual newspaper article recounting the events Orwell describes.

Combining the Patterns

Implicit in this narrative essay is an extended **comparison and contrast** that highlights the differences between Orwell and the Burmese people. Review the essay, and list the most obvious differences Orwell perceives between himself and them. Do you think his perceptions are accurate? If all of the differences were set forth in a single paragraph, how might such a paragraph change your perception of Orwell's dilemma? Of his character?

Thematic Connections

- "Thirty-Eight Who Saw Murder Didn't Call the Police" (page 120)
- "Just Walk On By" (page 240)
- "The Power of Words in Wartime" (page 377)
- "The Untouchable" (page 516)
- "Stigmatic Uniforms" (page 544)

Indian Education (Fiction)

Sherman Alexie, the son of a Coeur d'Alene Indian father and a Spokane Indian mother, was born in 1966 and grew up on the Spokane Reservation in Wellpinit, Washington, home to some eleven hundred Spokane tribal members. A precocious child who endured much teasing from his fellow classmates on the reservation and who realized as a teenager that his educational opportunities there were extremely limited, Alexie made the unusual decision to attend high school off the reservation in nearby Reardon. Later a scholarship student at Gonzaga University, he received a bachelor's degree in American studies from Washington State University at Pullman. While in college, he began publishing poetry; within a year of graduation, his first collection, *The Business of Fancydancing* (1992), appeared. This was followed by *The Lone Ranger and Tonto Fistfight in Heaven* (1993), a short-story collection, and the novels *Reservation Blues* (1995) and *Indian Killer* (1996), all of which garnered numerous awards and honors. Alexie also wrote the screenplay for the film *Smoke Signals* (1998) and wrote and directed *The Business of Fancydancing* (2002). His most recent short-story collection is *Ten Little Indians* (2003).

Background on the U.S. government's "Indian schools": By the mid-1800s, most Native American tribes had been overwhelmed by the superior weapons of the U.S. military and confined to reservations. Beginning in the late 1800s and continuing into the 1950s, government policymakers established boarding schools for Native American youth to help them assimilate into the dominant culture and thus become "civilized." To this end, children were forcibly removed from their homes for long periods to separate them from native traditions. At the boarding schools, they were given a cursory academic education and spent most of their time studying Christian teachings and working to offset the cost of their schooling. Students were punished for speaking their own language or practicing their own religion. Responding to protests from the American Indian Movement in the 1970s, the government began to send fewer Native Americans to boarding schools and retreated from its goal of assimilation at boarding schools and at newly established reservation schools. Currently, government funding for Native American schools remains considerably lower than for other public schools, and students often make do with inadequate and antiquated facilities, equipment, and textbooks. In part because of such educational failures, few Native American students go on to college, and the incidence of alcohol and drug abuse among Native Americans is higher than in any other U.S. population.

First Grade

My hair was too short and my U.S. Government glasses were horn-rimmed, ugly, and all that first winter in school, the other Indian boys chased me from one corner of the playground to the other. They pushed me down, buried me in the snow until I couldn't breathe, thought I'd never breathe again.

They stole my glasses and threw them over my head, around my out-   2
stretched hands, just beyond my reach, until someone tripped me and sent me falling again, facedown in the snow.

I was always falling down; my Indian name was Junior Falls Down.   3
Sometimes it was Bloody Nose or Steal-His-Lunch. Once, it was Cries-Like-a-White-Boy, even though none of us had seen a white boy cry.

Then it was a Friday morning recess and Frenchy SiJohn threw snow-   4
balls at me while the rest of the Indian boys tortured some other *top-yogh-yaught* kid, another weakling. But Frenchy was confident enough to torment me all by himself, and most days I would have let him.

But the little warrior in me roared to life that day and knocked Frenchy   5
to the ground, held his head against the snow, and punched him so hard that my knuckles and the snow made symmetrical bruises on his face. He almost looked like he was wearing war paint.

But he wasn't the warrior. I was. And I chanted *It's a good day to die, it's a*   6
good day to die, all the way down to the principal's office.

Second Grade

Betty Towle, missionary teacher, redheaded and so ugly that no one   7
ever had a puppy crush on her, made me stay in for recess fourteen days straight.

"Tell me you're sorry," she said.   8

"Sorry for what?" I asked.   9

"Everything," she said and made me stand straight for fifteen minutes,   10
eagle-armed with books in each hand. One was a math book; the other was English. But all I learned was that gravity can be painful.

For Halloween I drew a picture of her riding a broom with a scrawny   11
cat on the back. She said that her God would never forgive me for that.

Once, she gave the class a spelling test but set me aside and gave me a   12
test designed for junior high students. When I spelled all the words right, she crumpled up the paper and made me eat it.

"You'll learn respect," she said.   13

She sent a letter home with me that told my parents to either cut my   14
braids or keep me home from class. My parents came in the next day and dragged their braids across Betty Towle's desk.

"Indians, indians, indians." She said it without capitalization. She   15
called me "indian, indian, indian."

And I said, *Yes, I am. I am Indian. Indian, I am.*   16

Third Grade

My traditional Native American art career began and ended with my   17
very first portrait: *Stick Indian Taking a Piss in My Backyard.*

As I circulated the original print around the classroom, Mrs. Schluter 18
intercepted and confiscated my art.

Censorship, I might cry now. *Freedom of expression,* I would write in edito- 19
rials to the tribal newspaper.

In third grade, though, I stood alone in the corner, faced the wall, and 20
waited for the punishment to end.

I'm still waiting. 21

Fourth Grade

"You should be a doctor when you grow up," Mr. Schluter told me, 22
even though his wife, the third grade teacher, thought I was crazy beyond
my years. My eyes always looked like I had just hit-and-run someone.

"Guilty," she said. "You always look guilty." 23

"Why should I be a doctor?" I asked Mr. Schluter. 24

"So you can come back and help the tribe. So you can heal people." 25

That was the year my father drank a gallon of vodka a day and the 26
same year that my mother started two hundred different quilts but never
finished any. They sat in separate, dark places in our HUD house and wept
savagely.

I ran home after school, heard their Indian tears, and looked in the 27
mirror. *Doctor Victor,* I called myself, invented an education, talked to my
reflection. *Doctor Victor to the emergency room.*

Fifth Grade

I picked up a basketball for the first time and made my first shot. No. I 28
missed my first shot, missed the basket completely, and the ball landed in
the dirt and sawdust, sat there just like I had sat there only minutes before.

But it felt good, that ball in my hands, all those possibilities and 29
angles. It was mathematics, geometry. It was beautiful.

At that same moment, my cousin Steven Ford sniffed rubber cement 30
from a paper bag and leaned back on the merry-go-round. His ears rang,
his mouth was dry, and everyone seemed so far away.

But it felt good, that buzz in his head, all those colors and noises. It 31
was chemistry, biology. It was beautiful.

Oh, do you remember those sweet, almost innocent choices that the Indian 32
boys were forced to make?

Sixth Grade

Randy, the new Indian kid from the white town of Springdale, got into 33
a fight an hour after he first walked into the reservation school.

Stevie Flett called him out, called him a squawman, called him a pussy,   34
and called him a punk.

Randy and Stevie, and the rest of the Indian boys, walked out into the   35
playground.

"Throw the first punch," Stevie said as they squared off.   36

"No," Randy said.   37

"Throw the first punch," Stevie said again.   38

"No," Randy said again.   39

"Throw the first punch!" Stevie said for the third time, and Randy   40
reared back and pitched a knuckle fastball that broke Stevie's nose.

We all stood there in silence, in awe.   41

That was Randy, my soon-to-be first and best friend, who taught me   42
the most valuable lesson about living in the white world: *Always throw the
first punch*.

Seventh Grade

I leaned through the basement window of the HUD house and kissed   43
the white girl who would later be raped by her foster-parent father, who was
also white. They both lived on the reservation, though, and when the headlines and stories filled the papers later, not one word was made of their color.

Just Indians being Indians, someone must have said somewhere and they   44
were wrong.

But on the day I leaned through the basement window of the HUD   45
house and kissed the white girl, I felt the good-byes I was saying to my
entire tribe. I held my lips tight against her lips, a dry, clumsy, and ultimately stupid kiss.

But I was saying good-bye to my tribe, to all the Indian girls and   46
women I might have loved, to all the Indian men who might have called me
cousin, even brother.

I kissed that white girl and when I opened my eyes, she was gone from   47
the reservation, and when I opened my eyes, I was gone from the reservation, living in a farm town where a beautiful white girl asked my name.

"Junior Polatkin," I said, and she laughed.   48

After that, no one spoke to me for another five hundred years.   49

Eighth Grade

At the farm town junior high, in the boys' bathroom, I could hear   50
voices from the girls' bathroom, nervous whispers of anorexia and bulimia.
I could hear the white girls' forced vomiting, a sound so familiar and natural to me after years of listening to my father's hangovers.

"Give me your lunch if you're just going to throw it up," I said to one of   51
those girls once.

I sat back and watched them grow skinny from self-pity.   52

*   *   *

Back on the reservation, my mother stood in line to get us commodities.   53
We carried them home, happy to have food, and opened the canned beef
that even the dogs wouldn't eat.

But we ate it day after day and grew skinny from self-pity.   54

There is more than one way to starve.   55

Ninth Grade

At the farm town high school dance, after a basketball game in an over-   56
heated gym where I had scored twenty-seven points and pulled down thirteen rebounds, I passed out during a slow song.

As my white friends revived me and prepared to take me to the emer-   57
gency room where doctors would later diagnose my diabetes, the Chicano
teacher ran up to us.

"Hey," he said. "What's that boy been drinking? I know all about these   58
Indian kids. They start drinking real young."

Sharing dark skin doesn't necessarily make two men brothers.   59

Tenth Grade

I passed the written test easily and nearly flunked the driving, but still   60
received my Washington State driver's license on the same day that Wally
Jim killed himself by driving his car into a pine tree.

No traces of alcohol in his blood, good job, wife and two kids.   61

"Why'd he do it?" asked a white Washington State trooper.   62

All the Indians shrugged their shoulders, looked down at the ground.   63

"Don't know," we all said, but when we look in the mirror, see the his-   64
tory of our tribe in our eyes, taste failure in the tap water, and shake with
old tears, we understand completely.

Believe me, everything looks like a noose if you stare at it long enough.   65

Eleventh Grade

Last night I missed two free throws which would have won the game   66
against the best team in the state. The farm town high school I play for is
nicknamed the "Indians," and I'm probably the only actual Indian ever to
play for a team with such a mascot.

This morning I pick up the sports page and read the headline: INDIANS   67
LOSE AGAIN.

Go ahead and tell me none of this is supposed to hurt me very much.   68

Twelfth Grade

I walk down the aisle, valedictorian of this farm town high school, and   69
my cap doesn't fit because I've grown my hair longer than it's ever been.

Later, I stand as the school-board chairman recites my awards, accomplishments, and scholarships.

I try to remain stoic for the photographers as I look toward the future.   70

Back home on the reservation, my former classmates graduate: a few can't   71
read, one or two are just given attendance diplomas, most look forward to
the parties. The bright students are shaken, frightened, because they don't
know what comes next.

They smile for the photographer as they look back toward tradition.   72

The tribal newspaper runs my photograph and the photograph of my for-   73
mer classmates side by side.

Postscript: Class Reunion

Victor said, "Why should we organize a reservation high school reunion?   74
My graduating class has a reunion every weekend at the Powwow Tavern."

• • •

Reading Literature

1. Instead of linking events with transitional phrases that establish
   chronology, Alexie uses internal headings to move readers through his
   story. How do these headings indicate the passage of time? Are these
   headings enough, or do you think Alexie should have opened each
   section of the story with a transitional phrase? (Try to suggest some
   possibilities.)
2. The narrator's experiences in each grade in school are illustrated by
   specific incidents. What do these incidents have in common? What do
   they reveal about the narrator? About his schools?
3. Explain the meaning of each of these statements in the context of the
   story:
   • "There is more than one way to starve" (55).
   • "Sharing dark skin doesn't necessarily make two men brothers" (59).
   • "Believe me, everything looks like a noose if you stare at it long
     enough" (65).

Journal Entry

What does the "Postscript: Class Reunion" section (74) tell readers about
Indian education? Is this information consistent with what we have
learned in the rest of the story, or does it come as a surprise? Explain.

Thematic Connections

• "College Pressures" (page 466)
• The Declaration of Independence (page 584)
• "Strange Tools" (page 743)

WRITING ASSIGNMENTS FOR NARRATION

1. Trace the path you expect to follow to establish yourself in your chosen profession, considering possible obstacles you may face and how you expect to deal with them. Include a thesis statement that conveys the importance of your goals. If you like, you may refer to some readings elsewhere in this book that focus on work — for example, "The Peter Principle" (page 220), "The Men We Carry in Our Minds" (page 481), or "What Work Is" (page 550).

2. Write a personal narrative looking back from some point in the far future on your own life as you hope others will see it. Use third person if you like, and write your own obituary; or use first person, assessing your life in a letter to your great-grandchildren.

3. Write a news article recounting in objective terms the events described in an essay elsewhere in this text — for example, "Who Killed Benny Paret?" (page 346) or "Grant and Lee: A Study in Contrasts" (page 409). Include a descriptive headline.

4. Write a historical narrative tracing the roots of your family or your hometown or community. Be sure to include specific detail, dialogue, and descriptions of people and places.

5. Write an account of one of these "firsts": your first date; your first serious argument with your parents; your first experience with physical violence or danger; your first extended stay away from home; your first encounter with someone whose culture was very different from your own; or your first experience with the serious illness or death of a close friend or relative. Make sure your essay includes a thesis statement your narrative can support.

6. Both George Orwell and Martin Gansberg deal with the consequences of failing to act. Write an essay or story recounting what would have happened if Orwell had *not* shot the elephant or if one of the eyewitnesses *had* called the police right away.

7. Maya Angelou's "finishing school" was Mrs. Cullinan's kitchen. Write about a similar person or place that helped you develop into the person you are today. What did you learn from this person or place, and how did this knowledge serve you later?

8. Write a short narrative essay summarizing what happened in one of the following: a short story, a television show, a conversation, a fable or fairy tale, or a narrative poem. Include as many details as you can.

9. Write a narrative about a time when you were an outsider, isolated because of social, intellectual, or ethnic differences between you and others. Did you resolve the problems your isolation created? Explain. If you like, you may refer to the Angelou or Orwell essays in this chapter or to "Just Walk On By" (page 240).

10. Imagine a meeting between any two people who appear in this chapter's reading selections. Using dialogue and narrative, write an account of this meeting.

11. Trace the history of an object of great value to you. If you do not know the object's history, you can research its history or create one based on

what you do know. Throughout the essay, use the object's history to reveal something about yourself. For example, a ring you inherited from your grandmother might illustrate your closeness to her; similarly, getting an autographed baseball might be the impetus for your interest in coaching a professional baseball team.

12. Using Alexie's story as a model, write the story of your own education.

13. List the ten books you have read that most influenced you at important stages of your life. Then, write your "literary autobiography," tracing your personal development through these books.

COLLABORATIVE ACTIVITY FOR NARRATION

Working with a group of students of about your own age, write a history of your television-viewing habits. Start by working individually to list all your most-watched television shows in chronological order, beginning as far back as you can remember. Then, compile a single list that reflects a consensus of the group's preferences, perhaps choosing one or two representative programs for each stage of your life (preschool, elementary school, and so on). Have a different student write a paragraph on each stage, describing the chosen programs in as much detail as possible. Finally, combine the individual paragraphs to create a narrative essay that traces the group's changing tastes in television shows. The essay's thesis statement should express what your group's television preferences reveal about your generation's development.

INTERNET ASSIGNMENT FOR NARRATION

Choose an important local or national event you remember hearing about, and use the following Web sites to help you locate newspaper or magazine articles about the event to find out more. Then, imagining you have witnessed the event firsthand, write a narrative of what you experienced. Refer to Martin Gansberg's "Thirty-Eight Who Saw Murder Didn't Call the Police" to see how to use dialogue in your narrative.

Poynter Institute
<poynter.org/links/>
A list of links to journalistic sources, including journalism organizations and libraries, research, newspapers, and radio and television channels.

The Len-Net Entertainment Web
<lni.net/cowabunga/>
This site offers links to media-related sites, including links to local newspapers across the United States.

Media Link
<kidon.com/media-link/index.php/>
This site offers links and in-depth information about news sources in virtually every nation in the world.

7
Description

What is Description?

You use **description** to tell readers about the physical characteristics of a person, place, or thing. Description relies on the five senses—sight, hearing, taste, touch, and smell. In the following paragraph from "Knoxville: Summer 1915," James Agee uses sight, sound, and touch to re-create a summer's evening for his audience:

Topic sentence

Description using sight

Description using touch

Description using sound

It is not of games children play in the evening that I want to speak now, it is of a contemporaneous atmosphere that has little to do with them; that of fathers and families, each in his space of lawn, his shirt fishlike pale in the unnatural light and his face nearly anonymous, hosing their lawns. The hoses were attached to spigots that stood out of the brick foundations of the houses. The nozzles were variously set but usually so there was a long sweet stream of spray, the nozzle wet in the hand, the water trickling the right forearm and the peeled-back cuff, and the water whishing out a long loose and low-curved cone, and so gentle a sound. First an insane noise of violence in the nozzle, then the still irregular sound of adjustment, then the smoothing into steadiness and a pitch as accurately tuned to the size and style of stream as any violin. So many qualities of sound out of one hose: so many choral differences out of those several hoses that were in earshot. Out of any one hose, the almost dead silence of the release, and the short still arch of the separate big drops, silent as a held breath, and the only noise the flattering noise on leaves and the slapped grass at the fall of each big drop. That, and the intense hiss with the intense stream; that, and

> the same intensity not growing less but growing
> more quiet and delicate with the turn of the nozzle,
> up to that extreme tender whisper when the water
> was just a wide bell of film.

A descriptive essay tells what something looks like or what it feels like, sounds like, smells like, or tastes like. However, description often goes beyond personal sense impressions: novelists can create imaginary landscapes, historians can paint word pictures of historical figures, and scientists can describe physical phenomena they have never actually seen. When you write description, you use language to create a vivid impression for your readers.

Writers of descriptive essays often use an **implied thesis** when they describe a person, place, or thing. This technique allows them to convey an essay's point subtly, through the selection and arrangement of details. When they use description to support a particular point, however, many writers prefer to use an **explicitly stated thesis**. This strategy lets readers see immediately what point the writer is making—for example, "The sculptures that adorn Philadelphia's City Hall are a catalog of nineteenth-century artistic styles." Whether you state or imply your thesis, the details of your descriptive essay must work together to create a single **dominant impression**—the mood or quality emphasized in the piece of writing. In many cases, your thesis may be just a statement of the dominant impression; sometimes, however, your thesis may go further and make a point about that dominant impression.

Using Description

Before we make judgments about the world, before we compare or contrast or classify our experiences, we describe. In your college writing, you use description in many different kinds of assignments. In a comparison-and-contrast essay, for example, you may describe the designs of two proposed buildings to show that one is more desirable than the other. In an argumentative essay, you may describe a fish kill in a local river to show that industrial waste dumping is a problem. Through description, you communicate your view of the world to your readers. If your readers come to understand or share your view, they are more likely to accept your observations, your judgments, and, eventually, your conclusions. Therefore, in almost every essay you write, knowing how to write effective description is important.

Understanding Objective and Subjective Description

Description can be objective or subjective. In an **objective description**, you focus on the object itself rather than on your personal reactions to it. Your purpose is to present a precise, literal picture of your subject. Many writing situations require exact descriptions of apparatus or conditions, and in these cases your goal is to construct an accurate picture for your audience. A biologist describing what he sees through a microscope and a historian describing a Civil War battlefield would both write objectively. The biologist would not, for instance, say how exciting his observations were, nor would the historian say how disappointed she was at the outcome of the battle. Many newspaper reporters also try to achieve this objectivity, as do writers of technical reports, scientific papers, and certain types of business correspondence. Still, objectivity is an ideal that writers strive for but never fully achieve. In fact, in selecting some details and leaving out others, writers are making subjective decisions.

In the following descriptive passage, Shakespearian scholar Thomas Marc Parrott aims for objectivity by giving his readers only the factual information they need to visualize Shakespeare's theater:

> The main or outer stage [of Shakespeare's theatre] was a large platform, which projected out into the audience. Sections of the floor could be removed to make such things as the grave in the grave digger's scene in *Hamlet,* or they could be transformed into trapdoors through which characters could disappear, as in *The Tempest.* The players referred to the space beneath the platform as the Hell. At the rear of the platform and at the same level was the smaller, inner stage, or alcove. . . . Above the alcove at the level of the second story, there was another curtained stage, the chamber. . . . The action of the play would move from one scene to another, using one, two, or all of them. Above the chamber was the music gallery; . . . and above this were the windows, "The Huts," where characters and lookouts could appear.

Note that Parrott is not interested in responding to or evaluating the theater he describes. Instead, he chooses words that convey sizes and directions, such as *large* and *above.*

Objective descriptions are sometimes accompanied by **visuals**, such as diagrams, drawings, or photographs. A well-chosen visual can enhance a description by enabling writers to avoid tedious passages of description that might confuse readers. To be effective, a visual should clearly illustrate what is being discussed and not introduce new or irrelevant material.

Look at the diagram that accompanies Parrott's description of Shakespeare's theater (page 146). Notice how this diagram makes the passage much easier to understand, helping readers to visualize the multiple stages where Shakespeare performed his plays.

🖳 COMPUTER STRATEGY

You can find visuals on the Internet, on DVDs, or on clip-art compilations. You can also scan pictures you find in print sources or download pictures you take with a digital camera. Once the visual is downloaded onto your computer as a file, you can cut and paste it into your essay. Remember, however, that all visual material you get from a source — whether print or Internet — must be documented.

Artist's rendering of the Globe Theatre, London.

In contrast to objective description, **subjective description** conveys your personal response to your subject. Your perspective is not necessarily expressed explicitly, in a direct statement. Often it is revealed indirectly, through your choice of words and phrasing. If an English composition assignment asks you to describe a place that has special meaning to you, you could give a subjective reaction to your topic by selecting and emphasizing details that show your feelings about the place. For example, you could write a subjective description of your room by focusing on particular objects — your desk, your window, and your bookshelves — and explaining the meanings these things have for you. Thus, your desk could be a "warm brown rectangle of wood whose surface reveals the scratched impressions of a thousand school assignments."

A subjective description should convey not just a literal record of sights and sounds but also their significance. For example, if you objectively described a fire, you might include its temperature, duration, and scope. In addition, you might describe, as accurately as possible, the fire's movement and intensity. If you subjectively described the fire, however, you would try to re-create for your audience a sense of how the fire made you feel — your reactions to the noise, to the dense smoke, to the sudden destruction.

In the following passage, notice how Mark Twain subjectively describes a sunset on the Mississippi River:

> I still kept in mind a certain wonderful sunset which I witnessed when steamboating was new to me. A broad expanse of the river was turned to

blood; in the middle distance the red hue brightened into gold, through which a solitary log came floating, black and conspicuous; in one place a long, slanting mark lay sparkling upon the water; in another the surface was broken by boiling, tumbling rings, that were as many-tinted as an opal.

In this passage, Twain conveys his strong emotional reaction to the sunset by using vivid, powerful images, such as the river "turned to blood," the "solitary log . . . black and conspicuous," and the "boiling, tumbling rings." He also chooses words that suggest great value, such as *gold* and *opal.*

Neither objective nor subjective description exists independently. Objective descriptions usually include some subjective elements, and subjective descriptions need some objective elements to convey a sense of reality. The skillful writer adjusts the balance between objectivity and subjectivity to suit the topic, thesis, audience, and purpose as well as occasion for writing.

Using Objective and Subjective Language

As the passages by Parrott and Twain illustrate, both objective and subjective descriptions depend on language to appeal to readers' senses. But these two types of description use language differently. Objective descriptions rely on precise, factual language that presents a writer's observations without conveying his or her attitude toward the subject. Subjective descriptions, however, often use richer and more suggestive language. They are more likely to rely on the **connotations** of words, their emotional associations, than on their **denotations**, or more direct meanings (such as those found in a dictionary). In addition, they may deliberately provoke the reader's imagination with striking phrases or vivid language, including **figures of speech** such as *simile, metaphor,* and *personification.*

A **simile** uses *like* or *as* to compare two dissimilar things. These comparisons occur frequently in everyday speech — for example, when someone claims to be "happy as a clam," "free as a bird," or "hungry as a bear." As a rule, however, you should avoid overused expressions like these in your writing. Effective writers constantly strive to create original similes. In his essay "The Way to Rainy Mountain," for instance, N. Scott Momaday uses a striking simile to describe the ruggedness of the Black Hills when he says, "the land was *like iron.*" In the same essay, he describes shadows from clouds "that move upon the grain *like water.*"

A **metaphor** compares two dissimilar things without using *like* or *as.* Instead of saying that something is *like* something else, a metaphor says it *is* something else. Twain uses a metaphor when he says, "A broad expanse of the river was turned to blood."

Personification speaks of concepts or objects as if they had life or human characteristics. If you say that the wind whispered or that an engine died, you are using personification.

In addition to these figures of speech, writers of subjective descriptions also use allusions to enrich their writing. An **allusion** is a reference to a person, place, event, or quotation that the writer assumes readers will recognize. In "Letter from Birmingham Jail" (page 597), for example, Martin Luther King Jr. enriches his argument by alluding to biblical passages and proverbs that he expects his audience of clergy to be familiar with.

Your purpose and audience determine whether you should use objective or subjective description. An assignment that specifically asks for reactions calls for a subjective description. Legal, medical, technical, business, and scientific writing assignments, however, usually require objective descriptions because their primary purpose is to give the audience factual information. Even in these areas, of course, figures of speech may be used. Scientists often use such language to describe an unfamiliar object or concept to an audience. In their pioneering article on the structure of DNA, for example, James Watson and Francis Crick use a simile when they describe a molecule of DNA as looking like two spiral staircases winding around each other.

Selecting Details

Sometimes inexperienced writers pack their descriptions with general words such as *nice, great, terrific,* or *awful,* substituting their own reactions to an object for the qualities of the object itself. To produce an effective description, however, you must do more than just *say* something is wonderful — you must use details that evoke this response in your readers, as Twain does with the sunset. (Twain does use the word *wonderful* at the beginning of his description, but he then goes on to supply many specific details that make the scene he describes vivid and specific.)

All good descriptive writing, whether objective or subjective, relies on specific detail. Your aim is not simply to *tell* readers what something looks like but to *show* them. Every person, place, or thing has its special characteristics, and you should use your powers of observation to detect them. Then, you need to select the specific words that will enable your readers to imagine what you describe. Don't be satisfied with "He looked angry" when you can say, "His face flushed, and one corner of his mouth twitched as he tried to control his anger." What's the difference? In the first case, you simply identify the man's emotional state. In the second, you provide enough detail so that readers can tell not only that he was angry but also how he revealed the intensity of his anger.

Of course, you could have provided even more detail by describing the man's beard, his wrinkles, or any number of other features. Keep in mind, however, that not all details are equally useful or desirable. You should include only those that contribute to the dominant impression you wish to create. Thus, in describing a man's face to show how angry he was, you would probably not include the shape of his nose or the color of his hair.

(After all, a person's hair color does not change when he or she gets angry.) In fact, the number of particulars you use is less important than their quality and appropriateness. You should select and use only those details relevant to your purpose.

Factors such as the level, background, and knowledge of your audience also influence the kinds of details you include. For example, a description of a DNA molecule written for first-year college students would contain more basic details than a description written for junior biology majors. In addition, the more advanced description would contain details — the sequence of amino acid groups, for instance — that might be inappropriate for first-year students.

Planning a Descriptive Essay

Organizing Details

When you plan a descriptive essay, you usually begin by writing down descriptive details in no particular order. You then arrange these details in a way that supports your thesis and communicates your dominant impression. As you consider how to arrange your details, keep in mind that you have a number of options. For example, you can move from a specific description of an object to a general description of other things around it. Or you can reverse this order, beginning with the general and proceeding to the specific. You can also progress from the least important feature to the most important one, from the smallest to the largest item, from the least unusual to the most unusual detail, or from left to right, right to left, top to bottom, or bottom to top. Another option is to combine approaches, using different organizing schemes in different parts of the essay. The strategy you choose depends on the dominant impression you want to convey, your thesis, and your purpose and audience.

Using Transitions

Be sure to include all the transitional words and phrases readers will need to follow your description. Without them, readers will have difficulty understanding the relationship between one detail and another. Throughout your description, especially in the topic sentences of your body paragraphs, use words or phrases indicating the spatial arrangement of details. In descriptive essays, the transitions commonly used include *above, adjacent to, at the bottom, at the top, behind, below, beyond, in front of, in the middle, next to, over, under, through,* and *within*. (A more complete list of transitions appears on page 43.)

Structuring a Descriptive Essay

Descriptive essays begin with an **introduction** that presents the **thesis** or establishes the **dominant impression** that the rest of the essay will develop. Each **body paragraph** includes details that support the thesis or convey the dominant impression. The **conclusion** reinforces the thesis or dominant impression, perhaps echoing an idea stated in the introduction or using a particularly effective simile or metaphor.

Suppose your English composition instructor has asked you to write a short essay describing a person, place, or thing. After thinking about the assignment for a day or two, you decide to write an objective description of the National Air and Space Museum in Washington, D.C., because you have visited it recently and many details are fresh in your mind. The museum is large and has many different exhibits, so you know you cannot describe them all. Therefore, you decide to concentrate on one, the heavier-than-air flight exhibit, and you choose as your topic the display you remember most vividly—Charles Lindbergh's airplane, *The Spirit of St. Louis*. You begin by brainstorming to recall all the details you can. When you read over your notes, you realize that the organizing scheme of your essay could reflect your actual experience in the museum. You decide to present the details of the airplane in the order in which your eye took them in, from front to rear. The dominant impression you wish to create is how small and fragile *The Spirit of St. Louis* appears, and your thesis statement communicates this impression. An informal outline for your essay might look like this:

Introduction:	Thesis statement—It is startling that a plane as small as *The Spirit of St. Louis* could fly across the Atlantic.
Front of plane:	Single engine, tiny cockpit
Middle of plane:	Short wing span, extra gas tanks
Rear of plane:	Limited cargo space filled with more gas tanks
Conclusion:	Restatement of thesis or review of key points or details

Revising a Descriptive Essay

When you revise a descriptive essay, consider the items on the revision checklist on pages 54–55. In addition, pay special attention to the items on the following checklist, which apply specifically to descriptive essays.

> ✓ **REVISION CHECKLIST: Description**
>
> - Does your assignment call for description?
> - Does your descriptive essay clearly communicate its thesis or dominant impression?
> - Is your description primarily objective or subjective?
> - If your description is primarily objective, have you used precise, factual language? Would your essay benefit from a diagram?
> - If your description is primarily subjective, have you used figures of speech as well as words that convey your feelings and emotions?
> - Have you included enough specific details?
> - Have you arranged your details in a way that supports your thesis and communicates your dominant impression?
> - Have you used the transitional words and phrases that readers need to follow your description?

Editing a Descriptive Essay

When you edit your descriptive essay, follow the guidelines in the editing checklists on pages 71, 73, and 76. In addition, focus on the grammar, mechanics, and punctuation issues particularly relevant to descriptive essays. One of these issues — avoiding misplaced and dangling modifiers — is discussed below.

GRAMMAR IN CONTEXT: Avoiding Misplaced and Dangling Modifiers

When writing descriptive essays, you use modifying words and phrases to describe people, places, and objects. Because these modifiers are important in descriptive essays, you need to place them correctly to ensure they clearly refer to the words they describe.

Avoiding Misplaced Modifiers   A **misplaced modifier** appears to modify the wrong word because it is placed incorrectly in the sentence. Sentences that contain these errors are always illogical and frequently humorous.

MISPLACED: E. B. White's son swam in the lake wearing an old bathing suit. (*Was the lake wearing a bathing suit?*)

(continued on next page)

(continued from previous page)

MISPLACED: In alliance with the Comanches, the southern Plains were ruled by the Kiowa. (*Did the southern Plains have an alliance with the Comanches?*)

In these sentences, the phrases *wearing an old bathing suit* and *in alliance with the Comanches* appear to modify words that they cannot logically modify. You can correct these errors and avoid confusion by moving each modifier as close as possible to the word it is supposed to modify.

CORRECT: Wearing an old bathing suit, E. B. White's son swam in the lake.

CORRECT: In alliance with the Comanches, the Kiowa ruled the southern Plains.

Avoiding Dangling Modifiers   A modifier "dangles" when it cannot logically modify any word that appears in the sentence. Often these **dangling modifiers** come at the beginning of sentences (as present or past participle phrases), where they illogically seem to modify the words that come immediately after them.

DANGLING: Determined to get a better look, the viewing platform next to St. Paul's Chapel was crowded. (*Who was determined to get a better look?*)

DANGLING: Standing on the corner, the cranes, jackhammers, and bulldozers worked feverishly at ground zero. (*Who was standing on the corner?*)

In the preceding sentences, the phrases *determined to get a better look* and *standing on the corner* seem to modify *the viewing platform* and *cranes, jackhammers, and bulldozers,* respectively. However, these sentences make no sense. How can a viewing platform get a better look? How can cranes, jackhammers, and bulldozers stand on a corner? The two sentences do not contain the words that the modifying phrases are supposed to describe. In each case, you can correct the problem by supplying the missing word and rewriting the sentence accordingly.

CORRECT: Determined to get a better look, people crowded the viewing platform next to St. Paul's Chapel.

CORRECT: Standing on the corner, people watched the cranes, jackhammers, and bulldozers work feverishly at ground zero.

For more practice in avoiding misplaced and dangling modifiers, visit Exercise Central at <bedfordstmartins.com/patterns/modifiers>.

✓EDITING CHECKLIST: **Description**

- Have you avoided misplaced modifiers?
- Have you avoided dangling modifiers?
- Have you used figures of speech effectively?
- Have you avoided general words such as *nice, great,* and *terrific*?

STUDENT WRITERS: Description

Each of the following student essays illustrates the principles of effective description. The first one, an objective description of a trailer, was written by James Greggs for a sociology class. The assignment was to write a description of the service-learning project he participated in with some classmates. The second essay, a subjective description of an area in Burma (renamed Myanmar after a military coup in 1989), was written by Mary Lim for her composition class. Her assignment was to write an essay about a place that had a profound effect on her.

Building and Learning

Introduction

Throughout the United States, houses reflect not only the lives of the people who live in them but also the diversity of the American population. Some are large and ostentatious, others are modest but well maintained, and still others are in need of repair. Unfortunately, most college students know little about homes other than those in their own neighborhood. I too was fairly sheltered until I participated in a service-learning project for my sociology class. For this project, I, along with some classmates, added a deck to a trailer where three elderly people lived.

Thesis statement

We gained a great deal of satisfaction from this project, and we also got to see a way of life that some of us never knew existed.

Description of area around the trailer

The trailer we worked on was located at the end of a small dirt road about thirty minutes from campus. Patches of green and brown grass dotted the land around the trailer, and in the far right-hand corner of the property stood three tall poplar trees. Although the bushes in the front of the trailer were trimmed, the woods behind the trailer were threatening to overrun the property. (We were told that members of a local church came once a month to trim the hedges and cut back the woods.) Dominating the right front corner of the lawn was a

1

2

circular concrete basin that looked like a large birdbath and housed a white well pipe with a rusted blue cap. About thirty feet to the left of the concrete basin stood a telephone pole and a bright red metal mailbox.

General description of the trailer

Like the property where it stood, the trailer was well maintained. It was approximately thirty-five feet long and six and a half feet high; it rested on cinderblocks, which raised it about three feet off the ground. Under the trailer was an overturned white plastic chair. The trailer itself was covered with sheets of white vinyl siding that ran horizontally, except for the bottom panels on the right side, which ran vertically. The vinyl panels closest to the roof were slightly discolored with dirt and green moss.

3

Specific description of the trailer

At the left end of the trailer was a small window — about two feet wide and one foot high. Next to the window was an aluminum door that was painted a dark brick red and outlined in green trim. It had one window at eye level that was divided by metal strips into four small sections. The number "24" in white plastic letters was glued to the door below this window. To the right of the door was a one-hundred-watt lightbulb in a black ceramic socket. Next to the light was a large window that was actually two vertical rows of three windows — each the same size as the small window on the left. Farther to the right were two of the smaller windows arranged vertically. Each of the small windows tilted upward at almost a ninety-degree angle and was framed with silver metal strips. On either side of each of these windows was a pair of green metal shutters.

4

Description of steps and walkway

The deck we built replaced the three white plastic steps that had led up to the trailer. A white metal handrail stood to the right side of these steps. It had been newly painted and was connected to the body of the trailer by a heart-shaped piece of metal. In front of the steps, two worn gray wooden boards, each about two feet wide and ten feet long, served as a walkway to the road.

5

Description of new deck

The finished deck provided a much better entranceway than the steps did and also gave the trailer a new look. It was not very large — ten feet by eight feet — but it extended from the doorway to the area underneath the windows immediately to the right of the door. We built the deck out of pressure-treated lumber so that it wouldn't rot or need painting. We also

6

built four steps that led from the deck to the lawn and
surrounded the deck with a wooden railing that ran down the
right side of the steps. After we finished, we bought two white
plastic chairs at a local thrift store and put them, along with
the chair that was under the trailer, on the deck.

Conclusion   Both the residents of the trailer and our class benefited   7
from the service-learning project. The residents of the trailer
were happy with the deck because it gave them a place to sit
when the weather was good. They also liked their trailer's new
look. Those of us who worked on the project expanded our view
of the world and learned how with just a little bit of work we
could make a difference in other people's lives.

Points for Special Attention

Objective Description. James Greggs, a student in a sociology
course that had a service-learning component, wrote this paper describing
the project in which he participated. James knew that his instructor
wanted an objective description because she told the class not to include
any subjective comments in the body of the paper. She told them that they
could, if they wished, discuss their feelings about the project in their introductions and conclusions.

Objective Language. Because his essay is an objective description,
James keeps his description straightforward. His factual, concrete language concentrates on the size, shape, and construction of the trailer as
well as on its surroundings. He uses specific measurements to convey the
dimensions of the trailer and to show the relationship of each part of the
trailer to the other parts, and he uses figures of speech to help his readers
visualize what he is describing—the "circular concrete basin that looked
like a large birdbath" (2), for example.

Structure. James structures his description by moving from far to
near. He begins by describing the land where the trailer stands. He then
directs his readers' attention to specific areas—for example, the woods
behind the trailer and the telephone pole and red mailbox in front of it.
James gives a general description of the trailer and then, as he moves from
left to right, considers its specific features. Finally, he focuses on the deck,
following a general description of the deck with specific details about its
construction. In his introduction, James provides the context for this
description and states his thesis; in his conclusion, he restates his thesis
and then evaluates his service-learning experience.

Selection of Detail. James's instructor defined his audience as people who would know what service learning is but who would not know about the specific project. For this reason, James does not include a definition of service learning or explain how it fits into the sociology curriculum. He does, however, provide a detailed description of the trailer and the work he and his classmates did.

Focus on Revision

The peer critics of James's paper identified three areas they thought needed work. One student said James should have included descriptions of the people who lived in the trailer. This student thought that without these descriptions, readers could not appreciate the impact the deck had on the residents. Another student suggested that James add more detail about the deck itself. She thought the deck should be the main focus of the paper, and for this reason, she thought James should spend more time describing it.

As a result of these criticisms, James decided to write a short paragraph (and insert it between paragraphs 2 and 3) describing the residents of the trailer. He also decided to add more detail about the deck itself—for example, the wishbone pattern formed by the floorboards and the decorative elements on the railing. Finally, a third student thought the description of the trailer's windows in paragraph 4 went on too long, so in his final draft James condensed paragraph 4.

Unlike "Building and Learning," Mary Lim's essay uses subjective description so that readers can share, as well as understand, her experience.

The Valley of Windmills

Introduction

In my native country of Burma, strange happenings and exotic scenery are not unusual, for Burma is a mysterious land that in some areas seems to have been ignored by time. Mountains stand jutting their rocky peaks into the clouds as they have for thousands of years. Jungles are so dense with exotic vegetation that human beings or large animals cannot even enter. But one of the most fascinating areas in Burma is *Description (identifying the scene)* the Valley of Windmills, nestled between the tall mountains near the fertile and beautiful city of Taungaleik. In this valley there is beautiful and breathtaking scenery, but there are also old, massive, and gloomy structures that can disturb a person deeply.

Description (moving toward the valley)

The road to Taungaleik twists out of the coastal flatlands into those heaps of slag, shale, and limestone that are the

1

2

Tennesserim Mountains in the southern part of Burma. The air grows rarer and cooler, and stones become grayer, the highway a little more precarious at its edges, until, ahead, standing in ghostly sentinel across the lip of a pass, is a line of squat forms.

Description (immediate view)

They straddle the road and stand at intervals up hillsides on either side. Are they boulders? Are they fortifications? Are they broken wooden crosses on graves in an abandoned cemetery?

These dark figures are windmills standing in the misty atmosphere. They are immensely old and distinctly evil, some merely turrets, some with remnants of arms hanging derelict from their snouts, and most of them covered with dark green moss. Their decayed but still massive forms seem to turn and

Description (more distant view)

sneer at visitors. Down the pass on the other side is a circular green plateau that lies like an arena below, where there are still more windmills. Massed in the plain behind them, as far as the eye can see, in every field, above every hut, stand ten thousand iron windmills, silent and sailless. They seem to await only a call from a watchman to clank, whirr, flap, and groan into action. Visitors suddenly feel cold. Perhaps it is a sense of loneliness, the cool air, the desolation, or the weirdness of the arcane windmills — but something chills them.

Conclusion

As you stand at the lip of the valley, contrasts rush as if to overwhelm you. Beyond, glittering on the mountainside like

Description (windmills contrasted with city)

a solitary jewel, is Taungaleik in the territory once occupied by the Portuguese. Below, on rolling hillsides, are the dark windmills, still enveloped in morning mist. These ancient

Thesis statement

windmills can remind you of the impermanence of life and the mystery that still surrounds these hills. In a strange way, the scene in the valley can disturb you, but it also can give you an insight into the contrasts that seem to define our lives here in my country.

3

4

Points for Special Attention

Subjective Description.   One of the first things her classmates noticed when they read Mary's essay was her use of vivid details. The road to Taungaleik is described in specific terms: it twists "out of the coastal flatlands" into the mountains, which are "heaps of slag, shale, and lime-stone." The iron windmills are decayed and stand "silent and sailless" on a green plateau that "lies like an arena." Through her use of detail, Mary

creates her dominant impression of the Valley of Windmills as dark, mysterious, and disquieting. The point of her essay — the thesis — is stated in the
last paragraph: the Valley of Windmills embodies the contrasts that characterize life in Burma.

Subjective Language.   By describing the windmills, Mary conveys
the sense of foreboding she felt. When she first introduces them, she questions whether these "squat forms" are "boulders," "fortifications," or "broken wooden crosses," each of which has a menacing connotation. After
telling readers what they are, she uses **personification**, describing the
windmills as dark, evil, sneering figures with "arms hanging derelict." She
sees them as ghostly sentinels awaiting "a call from a watchman" to spring
into action. With this figure of speech, Mary skillfully re-creates the
unearthly quality of the scene.

Structure.   Mary's purpose in writing this paper was to give her
readers the experience of actually being in the Valley of Windmills. She
uses an organizing scheme that takes readers along the road to Taungaleik,
up into the Tennesserim Mountains, and finally to the pass where the
windmills wait. From her perspective on the lip of the valley, she describes
the details closest to her and then those farther away, as if following the
movement of her eyes. She ends by bringing her readers back to the lip of
the valley, contrasting Taungaleik "glittering on the mountainside" with
the windmills "enveloped in morning mist." With her description, Mary
builds up to her thesis about the nature of life in her country. She with-
holds the explicit statement of her main point until her last paragraph,
when readers are fully prepared for it.

Focus on Revision

One of Mary's peer critics thought that the essay's thesis about life in
Burma needed additional support. The student pointed out that although
Mary's description is quite powerful, it does not really convey the contrasts
she alludes to in her conclusion.

Mary decided that adding another paragraph discussing something
about her life (perhaps her reasons for visiting the windmills) could help
supply this missing information. She could, for example, tell her readers
that right after her return from the valley, she found out that a friend had
been accidentally shot by border guards and that this event caused her to
characterize the windmills as she did. Such information would help
explain the passage's somber mood and underscore the ideas presented in
the conclusion.

PEER EDITING WORKSHEET: Description

1. What is the essay's dominant impression or thesis?

2. What points does the writer emphasize in the introduction? Should any other points be included? If so, which ones?

3. Would you characterize the essay as primarily an objective or subjective description? What leads you to your conclusion?

4. Point out some examples of figures of speech. Could the writer use figures of speech in other places? If so, where?

5. What specific details does the writer use to help readers visualize what is being described? Could the writer use more details anywhere? Would a visual have helped readers understand what is being described?

6. Are all the details necessary? Do any seem excessive or redundant? Are enough details provided to support the thesis or convey the dominant impression?

7. How are the details in the essay arranged? Would another arrangement be clearer or more effective?

8. List some transitional words and phrases the writer uses to help readers follow the discussion. Do any sentences need transitional words or phrases to link them to other sentences?

9. Do any sentences contain misplaced or dangling modifiers? If so, which ones?

10. How effective is the essay's conclusion? Does the conclusion reinforce the dominant impression?

The following selections illustrate various ways description can shape an essay. As you read them, pay particular attention to the differences between objective and subjective description. The first selection, a visual text, is followed by questions designed to illustrate how description can operate in visual form.

Girls in Front of 9/11 Mural (Photo)

• • •

Reading Images

1. The mural in the photograph above commemorates the first anniversary of the destruction of the towers at the World Trade Center by terrorists. What details does the mural include? What determines how these details are arranged?

2. What dominant impression do you think the photographer wants to create? How do the details in the photograph communicate this dominant impression?

3. Is the photographer who took the picture of the mural presenting a subjective or objective view of the subject? On what do you base your conclusion?

Journal Entry

What is the difference between the impact of the mural and the impact of the photo? Which do you find more moving? Why?

Thematic Connections

- "Ground Zero" (page 162)
- "Who Killed Benny Paret?" (page 346)
- "Five Ways to Kill a Man" (page 505)

SUZANNE BERNE

Ground Zero

Suzanne Berne grew up in Warrenton, Virginia, and Washington, D.C., and holds degrees from Wesleyan University and the Iowa Writers' Workshop at the University of Iowa. She has worked as a journalist and has also published book reviews and personal essays as well as two well-received novels, *A Crime in the Neighborhood* (1997) and *A Perfect Arrangement* (2001). She has taught writing at Harvard University and currently lives near Boston. In the following essay, which appeared on the *New York Times* op-ed page in April 2002, Berne describes a personal pilgrimage to the site of the former World Trade Center in New York City.

Background on the terrorist attacks of 9/11: The September 11, 2001, terrorist attacks that destroyed the twin towers of New York's World Trade Center and severely damaged the Pentagon stunned the nation and the world. People watched in horror as camera crews recorded the collapse of the towers while victims jumped to their deaths. The three hijacked aircraft that crashed into these targets, and a fourth that crashed into a field in rural Pennsylvania, caused the deaths of some three thousand people. An outpouring of grief, outrage, fear, and patriotism consumed the nation in the ensuing months as the possibility of war loomed large. While many, like Berne, have felt drawn to visit "ground zero" (as it has come to be called), some family members of the victims—particularly of those whose unidentified remains are still at the site—have expressed concern that it not become a tourist attraction. A memorial planned for the site will include two thirty-foot recesses occupying the twin towers' footprints, their walls cascading with water. Underground walkways will allow visitors access to pools at the bottom of the recesses, which will be surrounded by the names of the victims. The site will be surrounded by park land.

On a cold, damp March morning, I visited Manhattan's financial district, a place I'd never been, to pay my respects at what used to be the World Trade Center. Many other people had chosen to do the same that day, despite the raw wind and spits of rain, and so the first thing I noticed when I arrived on the corner of Vesey and Church Streets was a crowd.

Standing on the sidewalk, pressed against aluminum police barricades, wearing scarves that flapped into their faces and woolen hats pulled over their ears, were people apparently from everywhere. Germans, Italians, Japanese. An elegant-looking Norwegian family in matching shearling coats. People from Ohio and California and Maine. Children, middle-aged couples, older people. Many of them were clutching cameras and video recorders, and they were all craning to see across the street, where there was nothing to see.

At least, nothing is what it first looked like, the space that is now   3
ground zero. But once your eyes adjust to what you are looking at, "nothing" becomes something much more potent, which is absence.

But to the out-of-towner, ground zero looks at first simply like a con-   4
struction site. All the familiar details are there: the wooden scaffolding; the
cranes, the bulldozers and forklifts; the trailers and construction workers
in hard hats; even the dust. There is the pound of jackhammers, the steady
beep-beep-beep of trucks backing up, the roar of heavy machinery.

So much busyness is reassuring, and it is possible to stand looking at   5
the cranes and trucks and feel that mild curiosity and hopefulness so often
inspired by construction sites.

Then gradually your eyes do adjust, exactly as if you have stepped from   6
a dark theater into a bright afternoon, because what becomes most striking about this scene is the light itself.

Ground zero is a great bowl of light, an emptiness that seems weirdly   7
spacious and grand, like a vast plaza amid the dense tangle of streets in
lower Manhattan. Light reflecting off the Hudson River vaults into the
site, soaking everything—especially on an overcast morning—with a
watery glow. This is the moment when absence begins to assume a material
form, when what is not there becomes visible.

Suddenly you notice the periphery, the skyscraper shrouded in black   8
plastic, the boarded windows, the steel skeleton of the shattered Winter
Garden. Suddenly there are the broken steps and cracked masonry in front
of Brooks Brothers. Suddenly there are the firefighters, the waiting ambulance on the other side of the pit, the police on every corner. Suddenly
there is the enormous cross made of two rusted girders.

And suddenly, very suddenly, there is the little cemetery attached to St.   9
Paul's Chapel, with tulips coming up, the chapel and grounds miraculously undamaged except for a few plastic-sheathed gravestones. The iron
fence is almost invisible beneath a welter of dried pine wreaths, banners,
ribbons, laminated poems and prayers and photographs, swags of paper
cranes, withered flowers, baseball hats, rosary beads, teddy bears. And
flags, flags everywhere, little American flags fluttering in the breeze, flags
on posters drawn by Brownie troops, flags on T-shirts, flags on hats, flags
streaming by, tied to the handles of baby strollers.

It takes quite a while to see all of this; it takes even longer to come up   10
with something to say about it.

An elderly man standing next to me had been staring fixedly across the   11
street for some time. Finally he touched his son's elbow and said: "I watched
those towers being built. I saw this place when they weren't there." Then he
stopped, clearly struggling with, what for him, was a double negative, recall-
ing an absence before there was an absence. His son, waiting patiently, took
a few photographs. "Let's get out of here," the man said at last.

Again and again I heard people say, "It's unbelievable." And then they   12
would turn to each other, dissatisfied. They wanted to say something more

expressive, more meaningful. But it *is* unbelievable, to stare at so much devastation, and know it for devastation, and yet recognize that it does not
look like the devastation one has imagined.

Like me, perhaps, the people around me had in mind images from tele-   13
vision and newspaper pictures: the collapsing buildings, the running
office workers, the black plume of smoke against a bright blue sky. Like
me, they were probably trying to superimpose those terrible images onto
the industrious emptiness right in front of them. The difficulty of this
kind of mental revision is measured, I believe, by the brisk trade in World
Trade Center photograph booklets at tables set up on street corners.

Determined to understand better what I was looking at, I decided to   14
get a ticket for the viewing platform beside St. Paul's. This proved no easy
task, as no one seemed to be able to direct me to South Street Seaport,
where the tickets are distributed. Various police officers whom I asked for
directions waved me vaguely toward the East River, differing degrees of
boredom and resignation on their faces. Or perhaps it was a kind of incredulousness. Somewhere around the American Stock Exchange, I asked a
security guard for help and he frowned at me, saying, "You want tickets to
the disaster?"

Finally I found myself in line at a cheerfully painted kiosk, watching a   15
young juggler try to entertain the crowd. He kept dropping the four red
balls he was attempting to juggle, and having to chase after them. It was
noon; the next available viewing was at 4 P.M.

Back I walked, up Fulton Street, the smell of fish in the air, to wander   16
again around St. Paul's. A deli on Vesey Street advertised a view of the
World Trade Center from its second-floor dining area. I went in and
ordered a pastrami sandwich, uncomfortably aware that many people
before me had come to that same deli for pastrami sandwiches who would
never come there again. But I was here to see what I could, so I carried my
sandwich upstairs and sat down beside one of the big plate-glass windows.

And there, at last, I got my ticket to the disaster.   17

I could see not just into the pit now, but also its access ramp, which   18
trucks had been traveling up and down since I had arrived that morning.
Gathered along the ramp were firefighters in their black helmets and black
coats. Slowly they lined up, and it became clear that this was an honor
guard, and that someone's remains were being carried up the ramp toward
the open door of an ambulance.

Everyone in the dining room stopped eating. Several people stood up,   19
whether out of respect or to see better, I don't know. For a moment, everything paused.

Then the day flowed back into itself. Soon I was outside once more,   20
joining the tide of people washing around the site. Later, as I huddled with
a little crowd on the viewing platform, watching people scrawl their names
or write "God Bless America" on the plywood walls, it occurred to me that
a form of repopulation was taking effect, with so many visitors to this

place, thousands of visitors, all of us coming to see the wide emptiness where so many were lost. And by the act of our visiting—whether we are motivated by curiosity or horror or reverence or grief, or by something confusing that combines them all—that space fills up again.

•   •   •

Comprehension

1. What does Berne mean when she says that as her eyes adjust to what she is seeing, "'nothing' becomes something much more potent, which is absence" (3)?
2. Why does it take "quite a while" (10) to see all the details at ground zero? Why does it take "even longer" (10) to think of something to say about it?
3. According to Berne, how were the television pictures of ground zero different from the actual experience of seeing it?
4. How does the area around ground zero contrast with the site itself? How does Berne react to this contrast?
5. What does Berne mean in her conclusion when she says that with so many visitors coming to see ground zero, a form of "repopulation" (20) is taking place? Do you think she is being **ironic**?

Purpose and Audience

1. Does Berne state or imply her thesis? Why do you think she makes the decision she does? State Berne's thesis in your own words.
2. What is Berne's purpose in writing this essay?
3. What assumptions does Berne make about her readers' ideas about ground zero? How can you tell?

Style and Structure

1. Why does Berne begin her essay by saying she had never before visited Manhattan's financial district?
2. What organizational scheme does Berne use? What are the advantages and disadvantages of this scheme?
3. In paragraph 3, Berne says that ground zero at first looks like "nothing"; in paragraph 4, she says that it looks like a construction site. Then, in paragraph 7, she describes ground zero as "a great bowl of light." And finally, in her conclusion, she refers to it as a pit (18). Why do you think Berne describes ground zero in so many different ways?
4. Berne leaves a space between paragraphs 17 and 18. In what way does the space (as well as paragraph 17) reinforce a shift in the focus of her essay?

5. Why does Berne end her essay with a description of the crowd standing on the viewing platform? Why do you suppose she feels the need to include these observations?

6. In paragraphs 8 and 9, Berne repeats the word *suddenly*. What is the effect of this repetition? Could she have achieved this effect some other way?

Vocabulary Projects

1. Define each of the following words as it is used in this selection.

   shearling (2)   devastation (12)
   potent (3)   incredulousness (14)
   periphery (8)   repopulation (20)
   laminated (9)

2. A **paradox** is a seemingly contradictory statement that may nonetheless be true. Find examples of paradoxes in "Ground Zero." Why do you think Berne uses these paradoxes?

3. List ten striking visual details Berne uses to describe people and objects. Can you think of other details she could have used?

4. What does the term *ground zero* mean? What connotations does this term have?

Journal Entry

What did you feel when you first saw newspaper or magazine images of ground zero? How were your reactions similar to or different from Berne's?

Writing Workshop

1. Write an essay describing what you saw on the morning of September 11, 2001, when terrorists destroyed the World Trade Center. Make sure that you include an explicitly stated thesis and that you use your description to convey your reactions to the event.

2. Write a description of a place from several different vantage points, as Berne does. Make sure each of your perspectives provides different information about the place you are describing.

3. Write a subjective description of a scene you remember from your childhood. In your thesis statement and in your conclusion, explain how your adult impressions of the scene differ from those of your childhood.

Combining the Patterns

In addition to containing a great deal of description, this essay also uses **comparison and contrasts**. In paragraphs 1 through 10, what two ways of seeing ground zero does Berne compare? What points about each view of ground zero does she contrast?

Thematic Connections

- "Shooting an Elephant" (page 125)
- "Once More to the Lake" (page 186)
- "Why Fear National ID Cards?" (page 618)

Words Left Unspoken

Although she is not deaf, Leah Hager Cohen (b. 1967) lived for much of her childhood at the Lexington School for the Deaf in Queens, New York, where her mother was a teacher and her father was an administrator. (Both her paternal grandparents were deaf.) A graduate of the Columbia University School of Journalism, Cohen has been a writing instructor at Emerson College in Boston and an interpreter for deaf students in mainstream classes. Her books include *Glass, Paper, Beans: Revelations on the Nature and Value of Ordinary Things* (1997); *The Stuff of Dreams: Behind the Scenes of an American Community Theater* (2002); and *Without Apology: Girls, Women, and the Desire to Fight* (2005) as well as two novels, *Heat Lightning* (1998) and *Heart, You Bully, You Punk* (2004).

Background on deaf culture: Some one million deaf people live in the United States, and more than twenty million are hearing impaired. Hearing loss is often a result of the aging process, but children may also be born deaf or lose their hearing at an early age, usually because of inner ear or other infections. While improvements in hearing aids and cochlear implants have helped to mitigate some types of hearing loss, they are of only marginal help to those who are profoundly deaf. A growing segment of the deaf population has begun to urge that deafness be viewed not as an infirmity but as a cultural marker. Much debate has surrounded the question of whether deaf children should be educated to participate in the mainstream oral culture or whether they should be taught to communicate through sign language and thus become part of a deaf culture. One of Cohen's goals in *Train Go Sorry* (1994), the source of the following essay, was to convince readers that deafness is "not a pathology but a cultural identity."

My earliest memories of Sam Cohen are of his chin, which I remember as fiercely hard and pointy. Not pointy, my mother says, jutting; Grandpa had a strong, jutting chin. But against my very young face it felt like a chunk of honed granite swathed in stiff white bristles. Whenever we visited, he would lift us grandchildren up, most frequently by the elbows, and nuzzle our cheeks vigorously. This abrasive ritual greeting was our primary means of communication. In all my life, I never heard him speak a word I could understand.

Sometimes he used his voice to get our attention. It made a shapeless, gusty sound, like a pair of bellows sending up sparks and soot in a blacksmith shop. And he made sounds when he was eating, sounds that, originating from other quarters, would have drawn chiding or expulsion from the table. He smacked his lips and sucked his teeth; his chewing was moist and percussive; he released deep, hushed moans from the back of his throat, like a dreaming dog. And he burped out loud. Sometimes it was all Reba, Andy, and I could do not to catch one another's eyes and fall into giggles.

Our grandfather played games with us, the more physical the better. He loved that hand game: he would extend his, palms up, and we would hover ours, palms down, above his, and lower them, lower, lower, until they were just nesting, and *slap!* he'd have sandwiched one of our hands, trapping it between his. When we reversed, I could never even graze his, so fast would he snatch them away, like a big white fish.

He played three-card monte* with us, arranging the cards neatly between his long fingers, showing us once the jack of diamonds smirking, red and gold, underneath. And then, with motions as swift and implausible as a Saturday morning cartoon chase, his hands darted and faked and blurred and the cards lay still, face down and impassive. When we guessed the jack's position correctly, it was only luck. When we guessed wrong, he would laugh—a fond, gravelly sound—and pick up the cards and begin again.

He mimicked the way I ate. He compressed his mouth into dainty proportions as he nibbled air and carefully licked his lips and chewed tiny, precise bites, his teeth clicking, his eyelashes batting as he gazed shyly from under them. He could walk exactly like Charlie Chaplin and make nickels disappear, just vanish, from both his fists and up his sleeves; we never found them, no matter how we crawled over him, searching. All of this without any words.

He and my grandmother lived in the Bronx, in the same apartment my father and Uncle Max had grown up in. It was on Knox Place, near Mosholu Parkway, a three-room apartment below street level. The kitchen was a tight squeeze of a place, especially with my grandmother bending over the oven, blocking the passage as she checked baked apples or stuffed cabbage, my grandfather sitting with splayed knees at the dinette. It was easy to get each other's attention in there; a stamped foot sent vibrations clearly over the short distance, and an outstretched arm had a good chance of connecting with the other party.

The living room was ampler and dimmer, with abundant floor and table lamps to accommodate signed conversation. Little windows set up high revealed the legs of passersby. And down below, burrowed in black leather chairs in front of the television, we children learned to love physical comedy. Long before the days of closed captioning, we listened to our grandfather laugh out loud at the snowy black-and-white antics of Abbott and Costello, Laurel and Hardy, the Three Stooges.

During the time that I knew him, I saw his hairline shrink back and his eyes grow remote behind pairs of progressively thicker glasses. His athlete's

---

* Eds. note—A sleight-of-hand card game often played on urban streets; the dealer gets onlookers to place bets that they can pick the jack of diamonds.

bones shed some of their grace and nimbleness; they began curving in on themselves as he stood, arms folded across his sunken chest. Even his long, thin smile seemed to recede deeper between his nose and his prominent chin. But his hands remained lithe, vital. As he teased and argued and chatted and joked, they were the instruments of his mind, the conduits of his thoughts.

As far as anyone knows, Samuel Kolominsky was born deaf (according   9
to Lexington* records, his parents "failed to take note until child was about one and a half years old"). His birthplace was Russia, somewhere near Kiev. Lexington records say he was born in 1908; my grandmother says it was 1907. He was a child when his family fled the czarist pogroms. Lexington records have him immigrating in 1913, at age five; my grandmother says he came to this country when he was three. Officials at Ellis Island altered the family name, writing down Cohen, but they did not detect his deafness, so Sam sailed on across the last ribbon of water to America.

His name-sign at home: *Daddy*. His name-sign with friends: the thumb   10
and index finger, perched just above the temple, rub against each other like grasshopper legs. One old friend attributes this to Sam's hair, which was blond and thick and wavy. Another says it derived from his habit of twisting a lock between his fingers.

Lexington records have him living variously at Clara, Moore, Siegel,   11
Tehema, and Thirty-eighth streets in Brooklyn and on Avenue C in Manhattan. I knew him on Knox Place, and much later on Thieriot Avenue, in the Bronx. Wherever he lived, he loved to walk, the neighborhoods revolving silently like pictures in a Kinetoscope,† unfurling themselves in full color around him.

Shortly before he died, when I was thirteen, we found ourselves walk-   12
ing home from a coffee shop together on a warm night. My family had spent the day visiting my grandparents at their apartment. My grandmother and the rest of the family were walking half a block ahead; I hung back and made myself take my grandfather's hand. We didn't look at each other. His hand was warm and dry. His gait was uneven then, a long slow beat on the right, catch-up on the left. I measured my steps to his. It was dark except for the hazy pink cones of light cast by streetlamps. I found his rhythm, and breathed in it. That was the longest conversation we ever had.

He died before I was really able to converse in sign. I have never seen his   13
handwriting. I once saw his teeth, in a glass, on the bathroom windowsill. Now everything seems like a clue.

• • •

---

* EDS. NOTE — The Lexington School for the Deaf, where Cohen's grandfather was once a student.

† EDS. NOTE — A device for viewing a sequence of moving pictures as it rotates over a light source, creating the illusion of motion.

Comprehension

1. Why was Cohen's grandfather unable to speak? How did Cohen communicate with him?
2. What kind of relationship did Cohen have with her grandfather? Warm? Distant?
3. What is the significance of the essay's title? What does Cohen mean when she says, "That was the longest conversation we ever had" (12)?
4. In paragraph 13, Cohen says that now, after her grandfather's death, "everything seems like a clue." What does she mean?
5. What do you think the "words left unspoken" are? Is the speaker of these words Cohen, her grandfather, or both? Explain.

Purpose and Audience

1. Does "Words Left Unspoken" have an explicitly stated thesis? Why, or why not?
2. What dominant impression is Cohen trying to create in this essay? How successful is she?
3. How much do you think Cohen expects her readers to know about deaf culture? How can you tell?

Style and Structure

1. Why do you think Cohen begins her essay with a description of her grandfather's chin?
2. What is the organizing principle of this essay? Would another organizing principle be more effective? Explain.
3. Are you able to picture Cohen's grandfather after reading her description? Do you think she expects you to?
4. Does Cohen develop her description fully enough? At what points could she have provided more detail?
5. What figures of speech does Cohen use in this essay? Where might additional figures of speech be helpful?

Vocabulary Projects

1. Define each of the following words as it is used in this selection.

honed (1)	abundant (7)
expulsion (2)	prominent (8)
percussive (2)	lithe (8)
smirking (4)	conduits (8)
splayed (6)	gait (12)

2. Supply a synonym for each of the words listed. How is each synonym different from the original word?

Journal Entry

How does Cohen's grandfather fit the traditional stereotype of a grandfather? How does he not fit this stereotype?

Writing Workshop

1. Write a description of a person. Concentrate on one specific feature or quality you associate with this person (as Cohen does in her essay).
2. Choose three or four members of your family, and write a one-paragraph description of each. Combine these descriptions into a "family album" essay that has an introduction, a thesis statement, and a conclusion.
3. Write an essay describing your earliest memories of a family member or close family friend. Before you write, decide on the dominant impression you want to convey.

Combining the Patterns

Cohen uses **narration** to develop paragraph 9. Why does she include this narrative paragraph? Does it add to or detract from the dominant impression she wants to convey? Explain.

Thematic Connections

- "Only Daughter" (page 96)
- "The Way to Rainy Mountain" (page 180)
- "Mother Tongue" (page 487)

The Amazon Queen

Chilean writer Isabel Allende was born in 1942 in Lima, Peru, where her father held a diplomatic post. As a child, she lived in Chile, Bolivia, and Lebanon and then returned to Chile in 1958 to complete her education. She worked for the United Nations Food and Agricultural Organization both in South America and in Europe until 1965, when she again returned to Chile and began a career as a print and television journalist. Two years after the 1973 overthrow of her uncle, Salvador Allende, as president of Chile, she moved to Venezuela, where she wrote her first novel, the internationally best-selling *The House of the Spirits* (1982). Subsequent books include the novels *Eva Luna* (1989) and *Daughter of Fortune* (1999), the memoirs *Paula* (1994) and *My Invented Country* (2003), and several works for young adults. A naturalized U.S. citizen, Allende currently lives in California.

Background on the Amazon rain forest: Worlwide, rain forests provide a habitat for many plant and animal species. The vast, dense Amazon rain forest, which occupies much of South America, is the largest such forest on Earth, stretching for hundreds of miles from the banks of the Amazon River and its major tributaries, the Rio Negro and the Salomões River. Over the past quarter century, deforestation of the Amazon rain forest — to provide land for farming and raising livestock, to generate profits from the sale of timber, and to allow access to valuable mineral deposits — has led to the ongoing destruction of many thousands of square miles of habitat each year. Despite the World Wildlife Fund's call for "urgent, sweeping measures to save this area of global importance" and attempts by conservationists to initiate many programs for doing so, local governments and international business interests have been slow to respond. Adding to the problem of saving the Amazon rain forest is the argument that development would improve the economic lives of its indigenous peoples.

A powerful dream lead me to the Amazon. For three years I had been blocked, unable to write, with the feeling that the torrent of stories waiting to be told, which once had seemed inexhaustible, had dried up. Then one night I dreamed of four naked Indians emerging from the heart of South America carrying a large box, a gift for a conquistador.* And as they crossed jungles, rivers, mountains and villages, the box absorbed every sound, leaving the world in silence. The song of the birds, the murmuring of the wind, human stories, all were swallowed up. I awakened with the conviction that I must go there to look for that voracious box, where

1

---

* EDS. NOTE — Early Spanish conqueror of Central and South America.

perhaps I could find voices to nourish my inspiration. It took a year to realize that wondrous journey.

How shall I describe the Amazon? The Amazon occupies 60 percent of   2
Brazil — an area larger than India — and extends into Venezuela, Colombia and Peru. From the airplane, it is a vast green world. Below, on the ground it is the kingdom of water: vapor, rain, rivers broad as oceans, sweat.

I approached the Amazon through Manaus. The city is far from the   3
Atlantic coast, and appears on the map as a solid jungle. I imagined a village on stilts, ruled over by an anachronistic baroque theater. I had been told that during the height of the rubber boom, the city was so prosperous that its ladies sent their clothing to Paris to be laundered, but probably such tales were only legend.

It was a surprise to land in an effervescent city of a million habitants, a   4
free port, a center of a broad spectrum of businesses and trafficking, both legal and suspect. A wall of heat struck me in the face. The taxi took me along a highway bordered with luxuriant vegetation, then turned onto twisting little streets where the homes of the poor and the middle class were democratically interspersed, both far from the neighborhoods of the wealthy who live in luxurious fortresses under heavy guard.

The famous opera theater, remodeled, is still the major tourist attrac-   5
tion. During the last century, Europe's most famous opera stars traveled to Manaus to delight the rubber barons. The surrounding streets are paved with a mixture of stone and rubber to mute the wheels and horses' hooves during performances.

After seeing the theater, I had *piracucú,* the best fresh-water fish in the   6
world — delicious, but horrifying in appearance — served on a terrace in the port facing the incredible river, which in times of flood stretched out like an ocean.

I stayed in Manaus only a couple of days, then set out on a boat with a   7
powerful outboard motor. For an hour we traveled upstream at a suicidal pace, following the Rio Negro to the Ariaú Hotel, an eco-hotel constructed in the treetops. The hotel consists of several towers connected by passageways open to monkeys, parrots, coatis and every insect known to man. Chicken wire everywhere prevents animals from coming into the rooms, especially monkeys, which can wreak as much destruction as an elephant.

I took a walk through the thick undergrowth, led by a young *caboclo**   8
guide. It seemed to me that we walked for an eternity, but afterward I realized that the walk had been ridiculously short. Finally I understood the meaning of the last line of a famous Latin American novel: "He was swallowed up by the jungle." Compasses are useless here, and one can wander in circles forever.

The jungle is never silent; you hear birds, the screeching of animals,   9
stealthy footfalls. It smells of moss, of moistness, and sometimes you catch the waft of a sweet odor like rotted fruit. The heat is exhausting, but

---

* EDS. NOTE — An Indian with European and/or African ancestors.

beneath the dark canopy of the trees you can at least breathe. Out on the river the sun beats down unmercifully, although as long as the boat is moving, there is a breeze.

To inexpert eyes everything is uniformly green, but for the native the jungle is a diverse and endlessly rich world. The guide pointed out vines that collect pure water to drink, bark that relieves fevers, leaves used to treat diabetes, resins that close wounds, the sap of a tree that cures a cough, rubber for affixing points on arrows. Hospitals and doctors are beyond the reach of the *caboclos,* but they have a pharmacy in the forest plants — barely 10 percent of which have been identified. Some with poetic names are sold in the hotel: *mulateiro,* for beautiful skin: *breuzinho,* to improve memory and facilitate concentration during meditation; *guaraná,* to combat fatigue and hardness of heart; *macaranduba,* for coughs, weakness and lugubrious chest. 10

Another day we went to a native village, which was in fact the habitat of a single extended family. These were Sateré Maué Indians, who had been evicted from their lands and forced to emigrate to the city, where they ended up in a *favela,* or slum, dying of hunger. The owner of the Ariaú Hotel had given them some land where they could return to living in harmony with their traditions. We arrived at their village late one afternoon by boat, at the hour of mosquitoes. 11

We climbed a muddy hill to the clearing of the forest where, beneath a single palm roof, a bonfire blazed and a few hammocks were strung. One of the Indians spoke a little Portuguese, and he explained that they had planted mandioc* and soon they would have the necessary tools to process it. From the root they make flour, tapioca, bread — even a liquor. 12

I walked over to the fire to see what was cooking, and found an alligator about a meter in length, quartered like a chicken, with claws, teeth, eyes and hide intact, sadly roasting. Two piranhas were strung on a hook, along with something that resembled a muskrat. Later, after a good look at the skin, I saw it was a porcupine. I tried everything: the alligator tasted like dried and reconstituted codfish, the piranhas like smoke and the porcupine like petrified pig. The Indians were selling the modest crafts they make from seeds, sticks and feathers — and a long, badly cured boa skin, brittle and pathetic. 13

The *caboclos* are Indians with European or African blood, a mixing of races that began during the sixteenth century. Some are so poor they don't use money; they live from fishing and a few crops, trading for fuel, coffee, sugar, flour, matches and indispensable supplies. There are a few villages on land, but as the water rises more than 45 feet during the annual floods, submerging thousands of acres, people prefer to build houses on stilts or live in floating huts. 14

The dwellings are not divided into rooms, as the *caboclos* do not share the white man's urge for privacy. They have few possessions, barely what is 15

---

* EDS. NOTE — A tropical plant that produces an edible root.

needed for survival. The incentive of acquisition is unknown; people fish or hunt for the day's needs, because anything more than that spoils. Sometimes, if they catch more than their daily quota, they keep the live fish in bamboo baskets in the water. They cannot understand the white man's greed or his drive to get everywhere quickly.

All communication and transportation is by river. News can take   16
weeks to travel by word of mouth to the nearest radio, where it awaits its turn to be transmitted in the form of a telegram. As a result, the death of a family member may be learned a year after the fact, and a birth when the child is already walking. For the *caboclos,* time is measured in days by boat; life, in rainy seasons. What sense is there in rushing? Life, like the river, goes nowhere. The whole point is to keep afloat, paddling through an unchanging landscape.

A few months ago on the Alto Yavarí river, on the border between Peru   17
and Brazil, explorers discovered a tribe that had never had any contact with white civilization. To record that first encounter airplanes and helicopters laden with television cameras filled the air, while on the ground the Indians, surprised in the midst of the Stone Age, readied their arrows.

I admit with a touch of embarrassment that I bought a blowgun,   18
arrows and a pouch of the powerful poison curare that came directly from that tribe. The blowgun is nearly 10 feet long and I was not allowed to take it on the plane, but I hope that someday it will arrive in the mail. The arrows and curare are on my desk as I write, but I need to find a safer place for them. It would be difficult to explain if someone pricked a finger on a curare-poisoned arrow.

In comic contrast, Avon Ladies have invaded the Amazon, women who   19
go from door to door selling beauty products. I learned that one had recently been eaten by piranhas—a direct contradiction to the soothing words of the guide when he invited us to swim in the Rio Negro.

The Negro is as smooth as a dark mirror when it is calm, frightening   20
when storms erupt. In a glass, the water is a kind of amber color, like strong tea. It has a delicate, almost sweet flavor. One morning we left before dawn to see the sun rising on a red horizon and to watch the frolicking of rosy dolphins. Dolphins are among the few Amazonian creatures that are not eaten; the flesh tastes terrible and the skin is unusable. The Indians, nonetheless, still harpoon them to rip out their eyes and genitals to make amulets for virility and fertility. In that same river where the water is as warm as a soup and the dolphins frolic, where the previous afternoon we had watched some German tourists catch dozens of piranhas with a pole, a string and a bare hook, I had swum naked.

That night we went out in a canoe with a huge, battery-powered spot-   21
light to look at the alligators. The light blinded the fish, and in their terror some leaped into the boat. We saw bats and huge butterflies flying in the darkness. The boatman, an adolescent *caboclo* who spoke a little English and laughed openly at our discomfort, would beam his light into the tree roots and when he spotted a pair of red eyes would jump into the water. We

would hear a great thrashing and soon he would reemerge holding an alligator by the neck in his bare hand if it was small, with a cord around its muzzle if it was larger. We saw photographs of one they had caught the week before: It was longer than the boat. There are also more than 30 species of manta rays in those same waters, all very dangerous. And to think I had swum there!

After 10 days, we had — reluctantly — to leave. I did not find the four   22
naked Indians with their magic box, but when I returned home, I carried some bit of that vast greenness within me, like a treasure. For the sake of discipline, and because of superstition, I begin all my books on Jan. 8. On Jan. 8, 1997, I finally ended the three-year block I had suffered and was able to write again. My dream of the jungle was not without its reward.

•   •   •

Comprehension

1. Why did Allende go to the Amazon? What did she hope to accomplish there?
2. How does the Amazon appear to the inexpert visitor? What does the Amazon native see?
3. How is the culture of the Amazon Indians different from the "white man's" culture of Brazil?
4. What effect is contact with Brazilian culture having on the Amazon Indians? What is gained and what is lost by this contact?
5. In paragraphs 19–21, Allende describes the Rio Negro, with its piranhas, dolphins, alligators and many other insects and animals. How do people react to the river's wildlife? Do they all respond in the same way?
6. How is Allende's dream of the Amazon like or unlike what she actually experiences?

Purpose and Audience

1. At what point in the essay does Allende state her thesis?
2. What dominant impression does Allende try to create in her description? Is she successful?
3. What is Allende's attitude toward the Indians and their culture? Does she assume her readers share her feelings?

Style and Structure

1. In paragraph 1, Allende recounts a dream she had. What are the elements of this dream? What do you think they mean? How does her dream lead her to the Amazon?

2. In paragraph 2, Allende asks, "How shall I describe the Amazon?" How does she describe it? For example, how does she arrange the details in her description? What are the advantages and disadvantages of her organizing scheme? What other organizing scheme could she have used?

3. Is this essay an objective or a subjective description of the Amazon? What words and phrases in the essay lead you to your conclusion?

4. In paragraphs 17 and 19, Allende includes stories of helicopters, television crews, and Avon Ladies in the jungle. Why did she refer to them? What effect do they have on her essay?

5. How does Allende link her paragraphs? Should she have included more transitional words and phrases within (or between) paragraphs? Explain.

Vocabulary Projects

1. Define each of the following words as it is used in this selection.

torrent (1)	luxuriant (4)	reconstituted (13)
inexhaustible (1)	interspersed (4)	acquisition (15)
emerging (1)	mute (5)	quota (15)
voracious (1)	stealthy (9)	laden (17)
vapor (2)	canopy (9)	curare (18)
anachronistic (3)	resins (10)	amulets (20)
baroque (3)	lugubrious (10)	virility (20)
effervescent (4)	evicted (11)	

2. Make a list of the foreign words that Allende includes in her essay. How do these words help Allende create her dominant impression?

Journal Entry

Why do you think the trip helped to end Allende's writer's block?

Writing Workshop

1. Write a subjective description of a place you visited that changed how you look at the world. In your thesis statement and your conclusion, explain how the experience affected you.

2. Allende says that the Amazon Indians see the Amazon jungle differently from those who simply visit it. Think of a situation in which you were once a "visitor" but became a "native." Write an essay describing how gaining knowledge changed your perceptions.

3. In paragraph 13, Allende describes the food she ate when she stayed in the jungle. Write a letter to one of the Amazon Indians, describing the food you eat on a particular holiday. Assume the person you write to has had little contact with the outside world and is not familiar

with the food you describe. Be sure your essay conveys a clear dominant impression.

Combining the Patterns

In addition to describing the Amazon jungle, this essay also includes a great deal of **exemplification**. What specific points do the examples illustrate? Are these points stated in topic sentences, or are they implied?

Thematic Connections

- "Shooting an Elephant" (page 125)
- "The Human Cost of an Illiterate Society" (page 252)
- "The Death of the Moth" (page 728)

The Way to Rainy Mountain

N. Scott Momaday was born in 1934 in Lawton, Oklahoma, of Kiowa ancestry. He holds degrees from the University of New Mexico and Stanford University and has taught English at a number of colleges; he is currently Regents Professor at the University of Arizona. In 1969, Momaday won a Pulitzer Prize for his first novel, *House Made of Dawn* (1968). He followed this book with *The Way to Rainy Mountain* (1968), retelling Kiowa legends and folktales. His novel *The Ancient Child* was published in 1989, and he has also published collections of poetry and stories as well as a memoir, *The Names* (1976).

Background on the Kiowa: The following essay, excerpted from the introduction to *The Way to Rainy Mountain,* focuses both on the landscape of Momaday's childhood and on his Kiowa grandmother. The Kiowa tribe, originally from western Canada, migrated in the early 1700s to what is now western Montana. From there, they traveled to the Black Hills of South Dakota and later to the central plains of Oklahoma. Through their contact with the Crow Indians, they came to worship the sun, and an annual Sun Dance brought various autonomous groups of Kiowa together for a week of ritual. By the 1800s, the Kiowa were considered fierce warriors both by neighboring tribes and by settlers arriving from the East. They were famous buffalo hunters, using the animal for food as well as for the raw materials used in their daily lives. They were also skilled artists known for their intricate beadwork and paintings on buffalo hides depicting their culture, religion, and history. After tribal leaders signed treaties with the United States government in the late 1800s, many Kiowa were quick to assimilate, often doing so in a single generation. Like Momaday, those growing up in the twentieth century and later have often sought to embrace the heritage and traditions of their ancestors.

A single knoll rises out of the plain in Oklahoma, north and west of the Wichita Range. For my people, the Kiowas, it is an old landmark, and they gave it the name Rainy Mountain. The hardest weather in the world is there. Winter brings blizzards, hot tornadic winds arise in the spring, and in summer the prairie is an anvil's edge. The grass turns brittle and brown, and it cracks beneath your feet. There are green belts along the rivers and creeks, linear groves of hickory and pecan, willow and witch hazel. At a distance in July or August the steaming foliage seems almost to writhe in fire. Great green-and-yellow grasshoppers are everywhere in the tall grass, popping up like corn to sting the flesh, and tortoises crawl about on the red earth, going nowhere in the plenty of time. Loneliness is an aspect of the land. All things in the plain are isolate; there is no confusion of objects in the eye, but *one* hill or *one* tree or *one* man. To look upon that landscape in

the early morning, with the sun at your back, is to lose the sense of propor-
tion. Your imagination comes to life, and this, you think, is where Creation
was begun.

I returned to Rainy Mountain in July. My grandmother had died in the
spring, and I wanted to be at her grave. She had lived to be very old and at
last infirm. Her only living daughter was with her when she died, and I was
told that in death her face was that of a child.

I like to think of her as a child. When she was born, the Kiowas were
living that last great moment of their history. For more than a hundred
years they had controlled the open range from the Smoky Hill River to the
Red, from the headwaters of the Canadian to the fork of the Arkansas and
Cimarron. In alliance with the Comanches, they had ruled the whole of the
southern Plains. War was their sacred business, and they were among the
finest horsemen the world has ever known. But warfare for the Kiowas was
preeminently a matter of disposition rather than of survival, and they
never understood the grim, unrelenting advance of the U.S. Cavalry. When
at last, divided and ill-provisioned, they were driven onto the Staked Plains
in the cold rains of autumn, they fell into panic. In Palo Duro Canyon they
abandoned their crucial stores to pillage and had nothing then but their
lives. In order to save themselves, they surrendered to the soldiers at Fort
Sill and were imprisoned in the old stone corral that now stands as a military museum. My grandmother was spared the humiliation of those high
gray walls by eight or ten years, but she must have known from birth the
affliction of defeat, the dark brooding of old warriors.

Her name was Aho, and she belonged to the last culture to evolve in
North America. Her forebears came down from the high country in western Montana nearly three centuries ago. They were a mountain people, a
mysterious tribe of hunters whose language has never been positively classified in any major group. In the late seventeenth century they began a
long migration to the south and east. It was a long journey toward the
dawn, and it led to a golden age. Along the way the Kiowas were befriended
by the Crows, who gave them the culture and religion of the Plains. They
acquired horses, and their ancient nomadic spirit was suddenly free of the
ground. They acquired Tai-me, the sacred Sun Dance doll, from that
moment the object and symbol of their worship, and so shared in the
divinity of the sun. Not least, they acquired the sense of destiny, therefore
courage and pride. When they entered upon the southern Plains, they had
been transformed. No longer were they slaves to the simple necessity of
survival; they were a lordly and dangerous society of fighters and thieves,
hunters and priests of the sun. According to their origin myth, they
entered the world through a hollow log. From one point of view, their
migration was the fruit of an old prophecy, for indeed they emerged from a
sunless world.

Although my grandmother lived out her long life in the shadow of
Rainy Mountain, the immense landscape of the continental interior lay
like memory in her blood. She could tell of the Crows, whom she had never

seen, and of the Black Hills, where she had never been. I wanted to see in reality what she had seen more perfectly in the mind's eye, and traveled fifteen hundred miles to begin my pilgrimage.

Yellowstone, it seemed to me, was the top of the world, a region of deep lakes and dark timber, canyons and waterfalls. But, beautiful as it is, one might have the sense of confinement there. The skyline in all directions is close at hand, the high wall of the woods and deep cleavages of shade. There is a perfect freedom in the mountains, but it belongs to the eagle and the elk, the badger and the bear. The Kiowas reckoned their stature by the distance they could see, and they were bent and blind in the wilderness. 6

Descending eastward, the highland meadows are a stairway to the plain. In July the inland slope of the Rockies is luxuriant with flax and buckwheat, stonecrop and larkspur. The earth unfolds and the limit of the land recedes. Clusters of trees and animals grazing far in the distance cause the vision to reach away and wonder to build upon the mind. The sun follows a longer course in the day, and the sky is immense beyond all comparison. The great billowing clouds that sail upon it are shadows that move upon the grain like water, dividing light. Farther down, in the land of the Crows and Blackfeet, the plain is yellow. Sweet clover takes hold of the hills and bends upon itself to cover and seal the soil. There the Kiowas paused on their way; they had come to the place where they must change their lives. The sun is at home in the plains. Precisely there does it have the certain character of a god. When the Kiowas came to the land of the Crows, they could see the dark lees of the hills at dawn across the Bighorn River, the profusion of light on the grain shelves, the oldest deity ranging after the solstices. Not yet would they veer southward to the caldron of the land that lay below; they must wean their blood from the northern winter and hold the mountains a while longer in their view. They bore Tai-me in procession to the east. 7

A dark mist lay over the Black Hills, and the land was like iron. At the top of a ridge I caught sight of Devil's Tower upthrust against the gray sky as if in the birth of time the core of the earth had broken through its crust and the motion of the world was begun. There are things in nature that engender an awful quiet in the heart of man; Devil's Tower is one of them. Two centuries ago, because they could not do otherwise, the Kiowas made a legend at the base of the rock. My grandmother said: 8

> "Eight children were there at play, seven sisters and their brother. Suddenly the boy was struck dumb; he trembled and began to run upon his hands and feet. His fingers became claws, and his body was covered with fur. Directly there was a bear where the boy had been. The sisters were terrified; they ran, and the bear after them. They came to the stump of a great tree, and the tree spoke to them. It bade them climb upon it, and as they did so, it began to rise into the air. The bear came to kill them, but they were just beyond its reach. It reared against the tree and scored the bark all around with its claws. The seven sisters were borne into the sky, and they became the stars of the Big Dipper."

From that moment, and so long as the legend lives, the Kiowas have kinsmen in the night sky. Whatever they were in the mountains, they could be no more. However tenuous their well-being, however much they had suffered and would suffer again, they had found a way out of the wilderness.

My grandmother had a reverence for the sun, a holy regard that now is   9
all but gone out of mankind. There was a wariness in her, and an ancient awe. She was a Christian in her later years, but she had come a long way about, and she never forgot her birthright. As a child she had been to the Sun Dances; she had taken part in those annual rites, and by them she had learned the restoration of her people in the presence of Tai-me. She was about seven when the last Kiowa Sun Dance was held in 1887 on the Washita River above Rainy Mountain Creek. The buffalo were gone. In order to consummate the ancient sacrifice—to impale the head of a buffalo bull upon the medicine tree—a delegation of old men journeyed into Texas, there to beg and barter for an animal from the Goodnight herd. She was ten when the Kiowas came together for the last time as a living Sun Dance culture. They could find no buffalo; they had to hang an old hide from the sacred tree. Before the dance could begin, a company of soldiers rode out from Fort Sill under orders to disperse the tribe. Forbidden without cause the essential act of their faith, having seen the wild herds slaughtered and left to rot upon the ground, the Kiowas backed away forever from the medicine tree. That was July 20, 1890, at the great bend of the Washita. My grandmother was there. Without bitterness, and for as long as she lived, she bore a vision of deicide.

Now that I can have her only in memory, I see my grandmother in the   10
several postures that were peculiar to her: standing at the wood stove on a winter morning and turning meat in a great iron skillet; sitting at the south window, bent above her beadwork, and afterwards, when her vision had failed, looking down for a long time into the fold of her hands; going out upon a cane, very slowly as she did when the weight of age came upon her; praying. I remember her most often at prayer. She made long, rambling prayers out of suffering and hope, having seen many things. I was never sure that I had the right to hear, so exclusive were they of all mere custom and company. The last time I saw her she prayed standing by the side of her bed at night, naked to the waist, the light of a kerosene lamp moving upon her dark skin. Her long, black hair, always drawn and braided in the day, lay upon her shoulders and against her breasts like a shawl. I do not speak Kiowa, and I never understood her prayers, but there was something inherently sad in the sound, some merest hesitation upon the syllables of sorrow. She began in a high and descending pitch, exhausting her breath to silence; then again and again—and always the same intensity of effort, of something that is, and is not, like urgency in the human voice. Transported so in the dancing light among the shadows of her room, she seemed beyond the reach of time. But that was illusion; I think I knew that I should not see her again.

· · ·

Comprehension

1. What is the significance of the essay's title?
2. What does Momaday mean when he says that his grandmother was born when the Kiowas were living the "last great moment of their history" (3)?
3. How did meeting the Crows change the Kiowa?
4. What effect did the soldiers have on the religion of the Kiowa?
5. What significance does Momaday's grandmother have for him? What does she represent?

Purpose and Audience

1. Is Momaday writing only to express emotions, or does he have other purposes as well? Explain.
2. What assumptions does Momaday make about his audience? How do you know?
3. Why do you think Momaday includes the legend of Devil's Tower in his essay?

Style and Structure

1. Why do you think Momaday begins his essay with a description of Rainy Mountain?
2. What determines the order of the details in Momaday's description of his grandmother?
3. Why do you think Momaday ends his essay with a description of his grandmother praying?
4. Momaday includes many passages that describe landscapes. What do these descriptions add to readers' understanding of Momaday's grandmother?

Vocabulary Projects

1. Define each of the following words as it is used in this selection.

infirm (2)	billowing (7)	consummate (9)
preeminently (3)	profusion (7)	impale (9)
nomadic (4)	engender (8)	deicide (9)
luxuriant (7)	tenuous (8)	inherently (10)

2. Find three examples of figurative language in the essay. How do these examples help Momaday convey his impressions to his readers?

Journal Entry

Which people in your family connect you to your ethnic or cultural heritage? How do they do so?

Writing Workshop

1. Write an essay describing a grandparent or any other older person who has had a great influence on you. Make sure you include background information as well as a detailed physical description.
2. Describe a place that has played an important part in your life. Include a narrative passage conveying to your readers the place's significance.
3. Describe a ritual — such as a wedding or a confirmation — you have witnessed or participated in.

Combining the Patterns

Momaday weaves passages of **narration** throughout this descriptive essay. Bracket the narrative passages Momaday uses in this essay, and explain how each one helps him describe his grandmother.

Thematic Connections

- "Only Daughter" (page 96)
- "My Mother Never Worked" (page 108)
- "Indian Education" (page 134)
- "Words Left Unspoken" (page 168)

E. B. WHITE

Once More to the Lake

Elwyn Brooks White was born in 1899 in Mount Vernon, New York, and graduated from Cornell University in 1921. He joined the newly founded *New Yorker* in 1925 and was associated with the magazine until his death in 1985. In 1937, White moved his family to a farm in Maine and began a monthly column for *Harper's* magazine titled "One Man's Meat." A collection of some of these essays appeared under the same title in 1942. In addition to this and other essay collections, White published two popular children's books, *Stuart Little* (1945) and *Charlotte's Web* (1952). He also wrote a classic writer's handbook, *The Elements of Style* (1959), a revision of a text by one of his Cornell professors, William Strunk.

Background on continuity and change: In this 1941 *Harper's* essay, White writes of returning to a Maine lake where he and his parents began summering when he was a child thirty-seven years earlier. He takes along his son. In a sense, his essay is a reflection on continuity and change. While much had remained the same at this rural retreat in the years since 1904, the world outside had undergone a significant transformation. Auto and air travel had become commonplace; the invention of innumerable electrical appliances and machines had revolutionized the home and the workplace; movies had gone from primitive, silent black-and-white shorts to sophisticated productions with sound and sometimes color; and the rise of national advertising had spurred a new and greatly expanded generation of consumer products. Moreover, the country had suffered through World War I, enjoyed a great economic expansion, experienced a period of social revolution, and been devastated by a great economic depression with high rates of unemployment. Within this context, White relives his childhood through his son's eyes.

One summer, along about 1904, my father rented a camp on a lake in   1
Maine and took us all there for the month of August. We all got ringworm from some kittens and had to rub Pond's Extract on our arms and legs night and morning, and my father rolled over in a canoe with all his clothes on; but outside of that the vacation was a success and from then on none of us ever thought there was any place in the world like that lake in Maine. We returned summer after summer—always on August 1st for one month. I have since become a salt-water man, but sometimes in summer there are days when the restlessness of the tides and the fearful cold of the sea water and the incessant wind which blows across the afternoon and into the evening make me wish for the placidity of a lake in the woods. A few weeks ago this feeling got so strong I bought myself a couple of bass hooks and a spinner and returned to the lake where we used to go, for a week's fishing and to revisit old haunts.

I took along my son, who had never had any fresh water up his nose   2
and who had seen lily pads only from train windows. On the journey over
to the lake I began to wonder what it would be like. I wondered how time
would have marred this unique, this holy spot — the coves and streams, the
hills that the sun set behind, the camps and the paths behind the camps. I
was sure that the tarred road would have found it out and I wondered in
what other ways it would be desolated. It is strange how much you can
remember about places like that once you allow your mind to return into
the grooves which lead back. You remember one thing, and that suddenly
reminds you of another thing. I guess I remembered clearest of all the early
mornings, when the lake was cool and motionless, remembered how the
bedroom smelled of the lumber it was made of and the wet woods whose
scent entered through the screen. The partitions in the camp were thin and
did not extend clear to the top of the rooms, and as I was always the first
up I would dress softly so as not to wake the others, and sneak out into the
sweet outdoors and start out in the canoe, keeping close along the shore in
the long shadows of the pines. I remembered being very careful never to
rub my paddle against the gunwale for fear of disturbing the stillness of
the cathedral.

The lake had never been what you would call a wild lake. There were   3
cottages sprinkled around the shores, and it was in farming country
although the shores of the lake were quite heavily wooded. Some of the
cottages were owned by nearby farmers, and you would live at the shore
and eat your meals at the farmhouse. That's what our family did. But
although it wasn't wild, it was a fairly large and undisturbed lake and there
were places in it which, to a child at least, seemed infinitely remote and
primeval.

I was right about the tar: it led to within half a mile of the shore. But   4
when I got back there, with my boy, and we settled into a camp near a farmhouse and into the kind of summertime I had known, I could tell that it
was going to be pretty much the same as it had been before — I knew it,
lying in bed the first morning, smelling the bedroom, and hearing the boy
sneak quietly out and go off along the shore in a boat. I began to sustain
the illusion that he was I, and therefore, by simple transposition, that I was
my father. This sensation persisted, kept cropping up all the time we were
there. It was not an entirely new feeling, but in this setting it grew much
stronger. I seemed to be living a dual existence. I would be in the middle of
some simple act, I would be picking up a bait box or laying down a table
fork, or I would be saying something, and suddenly it would be not I but
my father who was saying the words or making the gesture. It gave me a
creepy sensation.

We went fishing the first morning. I felt the same damp moss covering   5
the worms in the bait can, and saw the dragonfly alight on the tip of my
rod as it hovered a few inches from the surface of the water. It was the
arrival of this fly that convinced me beyond any doubt that everything was
as it always had been, that the years were a mirage and there had been no

years. The small waves were the same, chucking the rowboat under the chin as we fished at anchor, and the boat was the same boat, the same color green and the ribs broken in the same places, and under the floor-boards the same freshwater leavings and débris — the dead helgramite,* the wisps of moss, the rusty discarded fishhook, the dried blood from yesterday's catch. We stared silently at the tips of our rods, at the dragonflies that came and went. I lowered the tip of mine into the water, tentatively, pensively dislodging the fly, which darted two feet away, poised, darted two feet back, and came to rest again a little farther up the rod. There had been no years between the ducking of this dragonfly and the other one — the one that was part of memory. I looked at the boy, who was silently watching his fly, and it was my hands that held his rod, my eyes watching. I felt dizzy and didn't know which rod I was at the end of.

We caught two bass, hauling them in briskly as though they were   6
mackerel, pulling them over the side of the boat in a businesslike manner without any landing net, and stunning them with a blow on the back of the head. When we got back for a swim before lunch, the lake was exactly where we had left it, the same number of inches from the dock, and there was only the merest suggestion of a breeze. This seemed an utterly enchanted sea, this lake you could leave to its own devices for a few hours and come back to, and find that it had not stirred, this constant and trustworthy body of water. In the shallows, the dark, water-soaked sticks and twigs, smooth and old, were undulating in clusters on the bottom against the clean ribbed sand, and the track of the mussel was plain. A school of minnows swam by, each minnow with its small individual shadow, doubling the attendance, so clear and sharp in the sunlight. Some of the other campers were in swimming, along the shore, one of them with a cake of soap, and the water felt thin and clear and unsubstantial. Over the years there had been this person with the cake of soap, this cultist, and here he was. There had been no years.

Up to the farmhouse to dinner through the teeming, dusty field, the   7
road under our sneakers was only a two-track road. The middle track was missing, the one with the marks of the hooves and the splotches of dried, flaky manure. There had always been three tracks to choose from in choosing which track to walk in; now the choice was narrowed down to two. For a moment I missed terribly the middle alternative. But the way led past the tennis court, and something about the way it lay there in the sun reassured me; the tape had loosened along the backline, the alleys were green with plantains and other weeds, and the net (installed in June and removed in September) sagged in the dry noon, and the whole place steamed with midday heat and hunger and emptiness. There was a choice of pie for dessert, and one was blueberry and one was apple, and the waitresses were the same country girls, there having been no passage of time, only the illu-

---

* EDS. NOTE — An insect larva often used as bait.

sion of it as in a dropped curtain — the waitresses were still fifteen; their hair had been washed, that was the only difference — they had been to the movies and seen the pretty girls with the clean hair.

Summertime, oh summertime, pattern of life indelible, the fade-proof lake, the woods unshatterable, the pasture with the sweetfern and the juniper forever and ever, summer without end; this was the background, and the life along the shore was the design, the cottages with their inno- cent and tranquil design, their tiny docks with the flagpole and the Ameri- can flag floating against the white clouds in the blue sky, the little paths over the roots of the trees leading from camp to camp and the paths lead- ing back to the outhouses and the can of lime for sprinkling, and at the souvenir counters at the store the miniature birch-bark canoes and the post cards that showed things looking a little better than they looked. This was the American family at play, escaping the city heat, wondering whether the newcomers in the camp at the head of the cove were "common" or "nice," wondering whether it was true that the people who drove up for Sunday dinner at the farmhouse were turned away because there wasn't enough chicken.

It seemed to me, as I kept remembering all this, that those times and those summers had been infinitely precious and worth saving. There had been jollity and peace and goodness. The arriving (at the beginning of August) had been so big a business in itself, at the railway station the farm wagon drawn up, the first smell of the pine-laden air, the first glimpse of the smiling farmer, and the great importance of the trunks and your father's enormous authority in such matters, and the feel of the wagon under you for the long ten-mile haul, and at the top of the last long hill catching the first view of the lake after eleven months of not seeing this cherished body of water. The shouts and cries of the other campers when they saw you, and the trunks to be unpacked, to give up their rich burden. (Arriving was less exciting nowadays, when you sneaked up in your car and parked it under a tree near the camp and took out the bags and in five minutes it was all over, no fuss, no loud wonderful fuss about trunks.)

Peace and goodness and jollity. The only thing that was wrong now, really, was the sound of the place, an unfamiliar nervous sound of the out- board motors. This was the note that jarred, the one thing that would sometimes break the illusion and set the years moving. In those other sum- mertimes all motors were inboard; and when they were at a little distance, the noise they made was a sedative, an ingredient of summer sleep. They were one-cylinder and two-cylinder engines, and some were make-and- break and some were jump-spark, but they all made a sleepy sound across the lake. The one-lungers throbbed and fluttered, and the twin-cylinder ones purred and purred, and that was a quiet sound too. But now the campers all had outboards. In the daytime, in the hot mornings, these motors made a petulant, irritable sound; at night, in the still evening when the afterglow lit the water, they whined about one's ears like mosquitoes. My boy loved our rented outboard, and his great desire was to achieve singlehanded mastery over it, and authority, and he soon learned the trick of choking it a little (but not too much), and the adjustment of the needle valve. Watching him I would remember the things you could do with the old one-cylinder engine with the heavy flywheel, how you could have it eating out of your hand if you got really close to it spiritually. Motor boats in those days didn't have clutches, and you would make a landing by shutting off the motor at the proper time and coasting in with a dead rudder. But there was a way of reversing them, if you learned the trick, by cutting the switch and putting it on again exactly on the final dying revolution of the flywheel, so that it would kick back against compression and begin reversing. Approaching a dock in a strong following breeze, it was difficult to slow up sufficiently by the ordinary coasting method, and if a boy felt he had complete mastery over his motor, he was tempted to keep it running beyond its time and then reverse it a few feet from the dock. It took a cool nerve, because if you threw the switch a twentieth of a second too soon you could catch the flywheel when it still had speed enough to go up past center, and the boat would leap ahead, charging bull-fashion at the dock.

We had a good week at the camp. The bass were biting well and the sun shone endlessly, day after day. We would be tired at night and lie down in the accumulated heat of the little bedrooms after the long hot day and the breeze would stir almost imperceptibly outside and the smell of the swamp drift in through the rusty screens. Sleep would come easily and in the morning the red squirrel would be on the roof, tapping out his gay routine. I kept remembering everything, lying in bed in the mornings — the small steamboat that had a long rounded stern like the lip of a Ubangi,* how quietly she ran on the moonlight sails, when the older boys played their mandolins and the girls sang and we ate doughnuts dipped in sugar, and how sweet the music was on the water in the shining night, and what it had felt like to think about girls then. After breakfast we would go up to the store and the things were in the same place — the minnows in a bottle, the plugs and spinners disarranged and pawed over by the youngsters from the boys' camp, the fig newtons and the Beeman's gum. Outside, the road was tarred and cars stood in front of the store. Inside, all was just as it had always been, except there was more Coca-Cola and not so much Moxie[†] and root beer and birch beer and sarsaparilla.[‡] We would walk out with a bottle of pop apiece and sometimes the pop would backfire up our noses and hurt. We explored the streams, quietly, where the turtles slid off the sunny logs and dug their way into the soft bottom; and we lay on the town wharf and fed worms to the tame bass. Everywhere we went I had trouble

11

---

* EDS. NOTE — A member of an African tribe known for wearing mouth ornaments that stretch the lips into a saucerlike shape.

† EDS. NOTE — A soft drink that was popular in the early twentieth century.

‡ EDS. NOTE — A sweetened carbonated beverage flavored with birch oil and sassafras.

making out which was I, the one walking at my side, the one walking in my pants.

One afternoon while we were there at that lake a thunderstorm came up. It was like the revival of an old melodrama that I had seen long ago with childish awe. The second-act climax of the drama of the electrical disturbance over a lake in America had not changed in any important respect. This was the big scene, still the big scene. The whole thing was so familiar, the first feeling of oppression and heat and a general air around camp of not wanting to go very far away. In midafternoon (it was all the same) a curious darkening of the sky, and a lull in everything that had made life tick; and then the way the boats suddenly swung the other way at their moorings with the coming of a breeze out of the new quarter, and the premonitory rumble. Then the kettle drum, then the snare, then the bass drum and cymbals, then crackling light against the dark, and the gods grinning and licking their chops in the hills. Afterward the calm, the rain steadily rustling in the calm lake, the return of light and hope and spirits, and the campers running out in joy and relief to go swimming in the rain, their bright cries perpetuating the deathless joke about how they were getting simply drenched, and the children screaming with delight at the new sensation of bathing in the rain, and the joke about getting drenched linking the generations in a strong indestructible chain. And the comedian who waded in carrying an umbrella.

When the others went swimming my son said he was going in too. He pulled his dripping trunks from the line where they had hung all through the shower, and wrung them out. Languidly, and with no thought of going in, I watched him, his hard little body, skinny and bare, saw him wince slightly as he pulled up around his vitals the small, soggy, icy garment. As he buckled the swollen belt suddenly my groin felt the chill of death.

• • •

Comprehension

1. How are the writer and his son alike? How are they different? What does White mean when he says, "I seemed to be living a dual existence" (4)?

2. In paragraph 5, White says that "no years" seemed to have gone by between past and present; elsewhere, he senses that things are different. How do you account for these conflicting feelings?

3. Why does White feel disconcerted when he discovers that the road to the farmhouse has two tracks, not three? What do you make of his comment that "now the choice was narrowed down to two" (7)?

4. How does sound "break the illusion and set the years moving" (10)?

5. What is White referring to in the essay's last sentence?

Purpose and Audience

1. What is the thesis of this essay? Is it stated or implied?
2. Do you think White expects the ending of his essay to surprise his audience? Explain.
3. What age group do you think this essay would appeal to most? Why?

Style and Structure

1. List the specific changes that have taken place on the lake. Does White emphasize these changes or play them down? Explain.
2. What ideas and images does White repeat throughout his essay? What is the purpose of this repetition?
3. White goes to great lengths to describe how things look, feel, smell, taste, and sound. How does this help him achieve his purpose in this essay?
4. How does White's conclusion echo the first paragraph of the essay?

Vocabulary Projects

1. Define each of the following words as it is used in this selection.

placidity (1)	pensively (5)	melodrama (12)
gunwale (2)	jollity (9)	premonitory (12)
primeval (3)	petulant (10)	perpetuating (12)
transposition (4)	imperceptibly (11)	languidly (13)

2. Underline ten words in the essay that refer to one of the five senses, and make a list of synonyms you could use for these words. How close do your substitutions come to capturing White's meaning?

Journal Entry

Do you identify more with the father or with the son in this essay? Why?

Writing Workshop

1. Write a description of a scene you remember from your childhood. In your essay, discuss how your current view of the scene differs from the view you had when you were a child.
2. Assume you are a travel agent. Write a descriptive brochure designed to bring tourists to the lake. Be specific, and stress the benefits White mentions in his essay.
3. Write an essay describing yourself from the perspective of one of your parents. Make sure your description conveys both the qualities your parent likes and the qualities he or she would want to change.

Combining the Patterns

White opens his essay with a short narrative about his first trip to the lake in 1904. How does this use of **narration** provide a context for the entire essay?

Thematic Connections

- "Only Daughter" (page 96)
- "Swollen Expectations" (page 425)
- "The Men We Carry in Our Minds" (page 481)

The Storm (Fiction)

Kate Chopin (1851–1904) was born Catherine O'Flaherty, the daughter of a St. Louis businessman father of Irish descent and a French-American mother. In 1870, she married Oscar Chopin and moved with him to New Orleans, where he was a cotton merchant. After suffering business reversals, the Chopins relocated to Cloutierville, Louisiana, to be closer to Oscar's extended Creole family. Oscar Chopin died suddenly in 1882, and Kate Chopin, left with six children to raise, returned to St. Louis. There she began writing short stories, many set in the colorful Creole country of central Louisiana, that appeared in a variety of popular publications. Her first collection, *Bayou Folk,* was published in 1894, followed by *A Night in Arcadie* in 1897. Her literary success was cut short, however, with the publication of her first novel, *The Awakening* (1899), a story of adultery that outraged many of her critics and readers because it was told sympathetically from a woman's perspective. Her work languished until the middle of the twentieth century, when it was rediscovered, largely by feminist literary scholars.

Background on Creole culture: The following story was probably written about the same time as *The Awakening,* but Chopin never attempted to publish it. Its frank sexuality — franker than that depicted in her controversial novel — and its focus on a liaison between two lovers (Calixta and Alcée) married to others would have been deemed too scandalous for middle-class readers of the day. Even within the more liberal Creole culture in which the story is set, Calixta's actions would have been outrageous. While Creole men were expected and even encouraged to have mistresses (usually black or mixed-race women), Creole wives were expected to remain true to their wedding vows. The Creoles themselves were descendants of the early Spanish and French settlers in Louisiana, and they lived lives quite separate from — and, they believed, superior to — those whose ancestors were British. Their language became a mix of French and English, as did their mode of dress and cuisine. A strong Creole influence can still be found in New Orleans and the surrounding Louisiana countryside; Mardi Gras, for example, is a Creole tradition.

I

The leaves were so still that even Bibi thought it was going to rain. Bobinôt, who was accustomed to converse on terms of perfect equality with his little son, called the child's attention to certain sombre clouds that were rolling with sinister intention from the west, accompanied by a sullen, threatening roar. They were at Friedheimer's store and decided to remain there till the storm had passed. They sat within the door on two empty kegs. Bibi was four years old and looked very wise.

"Mama'll be 'fraid, yes," he suggested with blinking eyes.   2

"She'll shut the house. Maybe she got Sylvie helpin' her this evenin'," 3
Bobinôt responded reassuringly.

"No; she ent got Sylvie. Sylvie was helpin' her yistiday," piped Bibi.   4

Bobinôt arose and going across to the counter purchased a can of   5
shrimps, of which Calixta was very fond. Then he returned to his perch on
the keg and sat stolidly holding the can of shrimps while the storm burst. It
shook the wooden store and seemed to be ripping great furrows in the distant field. Bibi laid his little hand on his father's knee and was not afraid.

II

Calixta, at home, felt no uneasiness for their safety. She sat at a side   6
window sewing furiously on a sewing machine. She was greatly occupied
and did not notice the approaching storm. But she felt very warm and
often stopped to mop her face on which the perspiration gathered in
beads. She unfastened her white sacque at the throat. It began to grow
dark, and suddenly realizing the situation she got up hurriedly and went
about closing windows and doors.

Out on the small front gallery she had hung Bobinôt's Sunday clothes   7
to air and she hastened out to gather them before the rain fell. As she
stepped outside, Alcée Laballière rode in at the gate. She had not seen him
very often since her marriage, and never alone. She stood there with
Bobinôt's coat in her hands, and the big rain drops began to fall. Alcée rode
his horse under the shelter of a side projection where the chickens had
huddled and there were plows and a harrow piled up in the corner.

"May I come and wait on your gallery till the storm is over, Calixta?" he   8
asked.

"Come 'long in, M'sieur Alcée."   9

His voice and her own startled her as if from a trance, and she seized   10
Bobinôt's vest. Alcée, mounting to the porch, grabbed the trousers and
snatched Bibi's braided jacket that was about to be carried away by a sudden gust of wind. He expressed an intention to remain outside, but it was
soon apparent that he might as well have been out in the open: the water
beat in upon the boards in driving sheets, and he went inside, closing the
door after him. It was even necessary to put something beneath the door to
keep the water out.

"My! what a rain! It's good two years sence it rain' like that," exclaimed   11
Calixta as she rolled up a piece of bagging and Alcée helped her to thrust it
beneath the crack.

She was a little fuller of figure than five years before when she married;   12
but she had lost nothing of her vivacity. Her blue eyes still retained their
melting quality; and her yellow hair, dishevelled by the wind and rain,
kinked more stubbornly than ever about her ears and temples.

The rain beat upon the low, shingled roof with a force and clatter that   13
threatened to break an entrance and deluge them there. They were in the

dining room—the sitting room—the general utility room. Adjoining was her bed room, with Bibi's couch along side her own. The door stood open, and the room with its white, monumental bed, its closed shutters, looked dim and mysterious.

Alcée flung himself into a rocker and Calixta nervously began to gather up from the floor the lengths of a cotton sheet which she had been sewing. 14

"If this keeps up, *Dieu sait** if the levees goin' to stan' it!" she exclaimed. 15

"What have you got to do with the levees?" 16

"I got enough to do! An' there's Bobinôt with Bibi out in that storm— if he only didn't left Friedheimer's!" 17

"Let us hope, Calixta, that Bobinôt's got sense enough to come in out of a cyclone." 18

She went and stood at the window with a greatly disturbed look on her face. She wiped the frame that was clouded with moisture. It was stiflingly hot. Alcée got up and joined her at the window, looking over her shoulder. The rain was coming down in sheets obscuring the view of far-off cabins and enveloping the distant wood in a gray mist. The playing of the lightning was incessant. A bolt struck a tall chinaberry tree at the edge of the field. It filled all visible space with a blinding glare and the crash seemed to invade the very boards they stood upon. 19

Calixta put her hands to her eyes, and with a cry, staggered backward. Alcée's arm encircled her, and for an instant he drew her close and spasmodically to him. 20

"*Bonté!*"† she cried, releasing herself from his encircling arm and retreating from the window, "the house'll go next! If I only knew w'ere Bibi was!" She would not compose herself; she would not be seated. Alcée clasped her shoulders and looked into her face. The contact of her warm, palpitating body when he had unthinkingly drawn her into his arms, had aroused all the old-time infatuation and desire for her flesh. 21

"Calixta," he said, "don't be frightened. Nothing can happen. The house is too low to be struck, with so many tall trees standing about. There! aren't you going to be quiet? say, aren't you?" He pushed her hair back from her face that was warm and steaming. Her lips were as red and moist as pomegranate seed. Her white neck and a glimpse of her full, firm bosom disturbed him powerfully. As she glanced up at him the fear in her liquid blue eyes had given place to a drowsy gleam that unconsciously betrayed a sensuous desire. He looked down into her eyes and there was nothing for him to do but to gather her lips in a kiss. It reminded him of Assumption.‡ 22

"Do you remember—in Assumption, Calixta?" he asked in a low voice broken by passion. Oh! she remembered; for in Assumption he had kissed 23

---

* EDS. NOTE—God knows.
† EDS. NOTE—Goodness!
‡ EDS. NOTE—a parish near New Orleans.

her and kissed and kissed her; until his senses would well nigh fail, and to save her he would resort to a desperate flight. If she was not an immaculate dove in those days, she was still inviolate; a passionate creature whose very defenselessness had made her defense, against which his honor forbade him to prevail. Now—well, now—her lips seemed in a manner free to be tasted, as well as her round, white throat and her whiter breasts.

They did not heed the crashing torrents, and the roar of the elements   24
made her laugh as she lay in his arms. She was a revelation in that dim, mysterious chamber; as white as the couch she lay upon. Her firm, elastic flesh that was knowing for the first time its birthright, was like a creamy lily that the sun invites to contribute its breath and perfume to the undying life of the world.

The generous abundance of her passion, without guile or trickery, was   25
like a white flame which penetrated and found response in depths of his own sensuous nature that had never yet been reached.

When he touched her breasts they gave themselves up in quivering   26
ecstasy, inviting his lips. Her mouth was a fountain of delight. And when he possessed her, they seemed to swoon together at the very borderland of life's mystery.

He stayed cushioned upon her, breathless, dazed, enervated, with his   27
heart beating like a hammer upon her. With one hand she clasped his head, her lips lightly touching his forehead. The other hand stroked with a soothing rhythm his muscular shoulders.

The growl of the thunder was distant and passing away. The rain beat   28
softly upon the shingles, inviting them to drowsiness and sleep. But they dared not yield.

The rain was over; and the sun was turning the glistening green world   29
into a palace of gems. Calixta, on the gallery, watched Alcée ride away. He turned and smiled at her with a beaming face; and she lifted her pretty chin in the air and laughed aloud.

III

Bobinôt and Bibi, trudging home, stopped without at the cistern to   30
make themselves presentable.

"My! Bibi, w'at will yo' mama say! You ought to be asham'. You oughtn'   31
put on those good pants. Look at 'em! An' that mud on yo' collar! How you got that mud on yo' collar, Bibi? I never saw such a boy!" Bibi was the picture of pathetic resignation. Bobinôt was the embodiment of serious solicitude as he strove to remove from his own person and his son's the signs of their tramp over heavy roads and through wet fields. He scraped the mud off Bibi's bare legs and feet with a stick and carefully removed all traces from his heavy brogans. Then, prepared for the worst—the meeting with an over-scrupulous housewife, they entered cautiously at the back door.

Calixta was preparing supper. She had set the table and was dripping   32
coffee at the hearth. She sprang up as they came in.

"Oh, Bobinôt! You back! My! but I was uneasy. W'ere you been during the rain? An' Bibi? he ain't wet? he ain't hurt?" She had clasped Bibi and was kissing him effusively. Bobinôt's explanations and apologies which he had been composing all along the way, died on his lips as Calixta felt him to see if he were dry, and seemed to express nothing but satisfaction at their safe return. **33**

"I brought you some shrimps, Calixta," offered Bobinôt, hauling the can from his ample side pocket and laying it on the table. **34**

"Shrimps! Oh, Bobinôt! you too good fo' anything!" and she gave him a smacking kiss on the cheek that resounded. "*J'vous réponds,** we'll have a feas' tonight! umph-umph!" **35**

Bobinôt and Bibi began to relax and enjoy themselves, and when the three sated themselves at table they laughed much and so loud that anyone might have heard them as far away as Laballière's. **36**

IV

Alcée Laballière wrote to his wife, Clarisse, that night. It was a loving letter, full of tender solicitude. He told her not to hurry back, but if she and the babies liked it at Biloxi, to stay a month longer. He was getting on nicely; and though he missed them, he was willing to bear the separation a while longer — realizing that their health and pleasure were the first things to be considered. **37**

V

As for Clarisse, she was charmed upon receiving her husband's letter. She and the babies were doing well. The society was agreeable; many of her old friends and acquaintances were at the bay. And the first free breath since her marriage seemed to restore the pleasant liberty of her maiden days. Devoted as she was to her husband, their intimate conjugal life was something which she was more than willing to forego for a while. **38**

So the storm passed and everyone was happy. **39**

• • •

Reading Literature

1. How does the storm help set in motion the action of the story? List the events caused by the storm.
2. Is the last line of the story to be taken literally, or is it meant to be **ironic** (that is, does it actually suggest the opposite meaning)? Explain.
3. What do the story's specific details tell us about Calixta?

---

* EDS. NOTE — I tell you.

Journal Entry

On one level, the story's title refers to the storm that takes place through much of the story. To what else could the story's title refer?

Thematic Connections

- "The Men We Carry in Our Minds" (page 481)
- "Sex, Lies, and Conversation" (page 440)
- "The Ways We Lie" (page 495)

WRITING ASSIGNMENTS FOR DESCRIPTION

1. Choose a character from a work of fiction or a film who you think is interesting. Write a descriptive essay conveying what makes this character so special.

2. Several of the essays in this chapter deal with the way journeys change how the writers see themselves. For example, in "Once More to the Lake," a visit to a campground forces E. B. White to confront his own mortality, and in "The Way to Rainy Mountain," a visit to the Black Hills in Oklahoma enables N. Scott Momaday to embrace his Native-American heritage. Write an essay describing a place that you traveled to. Make sure that, in addition to describing the place, you explain how it has influenced your perspective or taught you something about yourself.

3. Locate some photographs of your relatives. Describe three of these pictures, including details that provide insight into the lives of the people you discuss. Use your descriptive passages to support a thesis about your family.

4. Visit an art museum, and select a painting that interests you. Study it carefully, and then write an essay-length description of it. Before you write, decide how you will organize your details and whether you will write a subjective or an objective description. If possible, include a photograph of the painting in your essay.

5. Select an object you are familiar with, and write an objective description of it. Include a diagram.

6. Assume you are writing a letter to someone in another country who knows little about life in the United States. Describe to this person something you consider typically American — for example, a baseball stadium or a food court in a shopping mall.

7. Visit your college library, and write an objective description of the reference area. Be specific, and select an organizing scheme before you begin your essay. Your purpose is to acquaint students with some of the reference materials they will use.

8. Describe your neighborhood to a visitor who knows nothing about it. Include as much specific detail as you can.

9. After reading "Ground Zero," write a description of a sight or scene that fascinated, surprised, or shocked you. Your description should explain why you were so deeply affected by what you saw.

10. Write an essay describing an especially frightening horror film. What specific sights and sounds make this film so horrifying? Include a thesis statement assessing the film's success as a horror film. (Be careful not to merely summarize the plot of the film.)

COLLABORATIVE ACTIVITY FOR DESCRIPTION

Working in groups of three or four students, select a famous person — one you can reasonably expect your classmates to recognize. Then, work as a group to write a description of that individual, including as much physical detail as possible. (Avoid any details that will be an instant giveaway.) Give your description a general title—*politician, television star,* or *person in the news,* for example. Finally, have one person read the description aloud to the class, and see whether your classmates can guess the person's identity.

INTERNET ASSIGNMENT FOR DESCRIPTION

Visiting the following Web sites, find a painting or photograph that captures your interest. Imagine you are inside the scene depicted in the work, and write a description of what you see and experience. If the work includes a person, evoke that person's experience. This exercise calls for imagination—going beyond what you see in the painting or photograph to think about the effects of what you see on your other senses. Think about the details of the image—the mood, lighting, texture, color, brush strokes, or shadows—to help you capture the overall impression of the artwork.

Whitney Museum of American Art
<whitney.org>

The Museum of Modern Art
<moma.org>

International Center for Photography
<icp.org>

8
Exemplification

What Is Exemplification?

Exemplification uses one or more particular cases, or **examples**, to illustrate or explain a general point or an abstract concept. In the following paragraph from *Sexism and Language,* Alleen Pace Nilsen uses a number of well-chosen examples to illustrate her statement that the armed forces use words that have positive masculine connotations to encourage recruitment:

Topic sentence

    The armed forces, particularly the Marines, use the positive masculine connotation as part of their recruitment psychology. They promote the idea that to join the Marines (or the Army, Navy, or Air Force) guarantees that you will become a man. But this brings up a problem, because much of the work that is necessary to keep a large organization running is what is traditionally thought of as *woman's work.* Now, how can the Marines ask someone who has signed up for a *man-sized job* to do *woman's work?* Since they can't, they euphemize and give the jobs titles that are more prestigious or, at least, don't make people think of females. Wait-

Series of related examples

resses are called *orderlies,* secretaries are called *clerk-typists,* nurses are called *medics,* assistants are called *adjutants,* and cleaning up an area is called *policing* the area. The same kind of word glorification is used in civilian life to bolster a man's ego when he is doing such tasks as cooking and sewing. For example, a *chef* has higher prestige than a *cook* and a *tailor* has higher prestige than a *seamstress.*

Using Exemplification

You have probably noticed, when watching television talk shows or listening to classroom discussions, that the most interesting and persuasive exchanges occur when participants support their points with specific examples. Sweeping generalizations and vague statements are not nearly as effective as specific observations, anecdotes, details, and opinions. It is one thing to say, "The mayor is corrupt and should not be reelected" and another to illustrate your point by saying, "The mayor should not be reelected because he has fired two city workers who refused to contribute to his campaign fund, has put his family and friends on the city payroll, and has used public employees to make improvements to his home." The same principle applies to writing: many of the most effective essays use examples extensively. Exemplification is used in every kind of writing situation to explain and clarify, to add interest, and to persuade.

Using Examples to Explain and Clarify

On a midterm exam in a film course, you might write, "Even though horror movies seem modern, they really aren't." You may think your statement is perfectly clear, but if this is all you say about horror movies, you should not be surprised if your exam comes back with a question mark in the margin next to this sentence. After all, you have only made a general statement or claim about your subject. It is not specific, nor does it anticipate readers' questions about how horror movies are not modern. To be certain your audience knows exactly what you mean, state your point precisely: "Despite the fact horror movies seem modern, two of the most memorable ones are adaptations of nineteenth-century Gothic novels." Then, use examples to ensure clarity and avoid ambiguity. For example, you could illustrate your point by discussing two films — *Frankenstein,* directed by James Whale, and *Dracula,* directed by Todd Browning — and linking them to the nineteenth-century novels they are based on. With the benefit of these specific examples, readers would know what you mean — that the literary roots of such movies are in the past, not that their cinematic techniques or production methods are dated. Moreover, readers would know which particular horror movies you are discussing.

Using Examples to Add Interest

Writers use well-chosen examples to add interest as well as to clarify their points. Laurence J. Peter and Raymond Hull do this in their essay "The Peter Principle," which appears later in this chapter. Their claim that employees in a system rise to a level of authority where they are incompetent is not particularly engaging. This statement becomes interesting, however, when supported by specific examples — the affable foreman who becomes the indecisive supervisor, the exacting mechanic who becomes the disorganized foreman, and the effective battlefield general who becomes the ineffective and self-destructive field marshal.

When you use exemplification, look for examples that are interesting as well as pertinent. Test the effectiveness of your examples by putting yourself in your readers' place. If you don't find your essay lively and absorbing, chances are your readers won't either. If this is the case, try to add more thought-provoking and spirited examples. After all, your goal is to communicate ideas to your readers, and imaginative examples can make the difference between an engrossing essay and one that is a chore to read.

Using Examples to Persuade

Although you may use examples to explain your ideas or to add interest to your essay, examples are also an effective way of persuading people that what you are saying is reasonable and worth considering. A few well-chosen examples can provide effective support for otherwise unconvincing general statements. For instance, a broad statement that school districts across the country cannot cope with the numerous students with limited English skills is one that needs support. If you make such a statement on an exam, you need to back it up with appropriate examples — such as that in one state, North Carolina, the number of students with limited English skills increased from 8,900 in 1993 to 52,500 in 2003. Similarly, a statement in a biology paper that DDT should continue to be banned is unconvincing without persuasive examples such as these to support it:

- Although DDT has been banned since December 31, 1972, scientists are still finding traces in the eggs of various fish and waterfowl.
- Certain lakes and streams still cannot be used for sport and recreation because DDT levels are dangerously high, presumably because of farmland runoff.
- Because of its stability as a compound, DDT does not degrade quickly; therefore, existing residues will threaten the environment well into the twenty-first century.

Using Examples to Test Your Thesis

Examples can help you test your own ideas as well as the ideas of others. For instance, suppose you plan to write a paper for a composition class about students' writing skills. Your tentative thesis is that writing well is an inborn talent and that teachers can do little to help people write better. But is this really true? Has it been true in your own life? To test your point, you brainstorm about the various teachers you have had who tried to help you improve your writing.

As you assemble your list, you remember Mrs. Colson, a teacher you had in high school. She was strict, required lots of writing, and seemed to accept nothing less than perfection. At the time, neither you nor your classmates liked her; in fact, her nickname was Warden Colson. But looking back, you recall her one-on-one conferences, her organized lessons, and her pointed comments. You also remember her careful review of essay tests, and you realize that after completing her class, you felt much more comfortable taking such tests. When examining some papers you saved, you are surprised to see how much your writing actually improved during that year. These examples lead you to reevaluate your ideas and to revise your thesis. You conclude that even though some people seem to have a natural flair for writing, a good teacher can make a difference.

Planning an Exemplification Essay

Providing Enough Examples

Unfortunately, no general rule exists to tell you when you have enough examples to support your ideas. The number you use depends on your thesis statement. If, for instance, your thesis is that an educational institution, like a business, needs careful financial management, a detailed examination of one college or university could work well. In this case, a single example might provide all the information you need to make your point.

If, however, your thesis is that conflict between sons and fathers is a major theme in Franz Kafka's writing, more than one example would be necessary. A single example would show only that the theme is present in *one* of Kafka's works. In this case, the more examples you include, the more effectively you support your point. Of course, for some thesis statements, even several examples would not be enough. Examples alone, for instance, could not demonstrate convincingly that children from small families have more successful careers than children from large families. This thesis would have to be supported with a **statistical study** — that is, by collecting and interpreting numerical data representing a great many examples.

Choosing a Fair Range of Examples

Selecting a sufficient **range of examples** is just as important as choosing an appropriate number. If you want to persuade readers that Colin Powell was an able general, you should choose examples from several stages of his military career. Likewise, if you want to convince readers that outdoor advertising ruins the scenic views from major highways, you should discuss an area larger than your immediate neighborhood. Your objective in each case is to choose a cross section of examples to represent the full range of your topic.

Similarly, if you want to argue for a ban on smoking in all public buildings, you should not limit your examples to restaurants. To be convincing, you should include examples involving many public places, such as office buildings, hotel lobbies, and sports stadiums. For the same reason, one person's experience is not enough to support a conclusion about many others unless you can establish that the experience is typical.

If you decide you cannot cite a fair range of examples that support your thesis, reexamine it. Rather than switching to a new topic, try to narrow your thesis. After all, the only way your paper will be convincing is if your readers believe that your thesis is supported by your examples and that your examples fairly represent the scope of your topic.

Of course, to be convincing you must not only choose examples effectively but also *use* them effectively. You should keep your thesis statement in mind as you write, taking care not to get so involved with one example that you digress from your main point. No matter how carefully developed, no matter how specific, lively, and appropriate, your examples accomplish nothing if they do not support your essay's main idea.

Using Transitions

Be sure to use transitional words and phrases to introduce your examples. Without them, readers will have difficulty seeing the connection between an example and the general statement it is illustrating. In some cases, transitions will help you connect examples to your thesis statement ("*Another* successful program for the homeless provides telephone answering services for job seekers"). In other cases, transitions will link examples to topic sentences ("*For instance,* I have written articles for my college newspaper"). In exemplification essays, the most frequently used transitions include *for example, for instance, in fact, namely, specifically, that is,* and *thus.* (A more complete list of transitions appears on page 43.)

Structuring an Exemplification Essay

Exemplification essays usually begin with an **introduction** that includes the **thesis statement**, which is supported by examples in the body of the essay. Each **body paragraph** may develop a separate example, present a point illustrated by several brief examples, or explore one aspect of a single extended example that is developed throughout the essay. The **conclusion** reinforces the essay's main idea, perhaps restating the thesis. At times, however, variations of this basic pattern are advisable and even necessary. For instance, beginning your paper with a striking example might stimulate your reader's interest and curiosity; ending with one might vividly reinforce your thesis.

Exemplification presents one special organizational problem. If you do not select your examples carefully and arrange them effectively, your paper can become a thesis statement followed by a list or by ten or fifteen brief, choppy paragraphs. One way to avoid this problem is to develop your best examples fully in separate paragraphs and to discard the others. Another effective strategy is to group related examples together in one paragraph.

Within each paragraph, you can arrange examples **chronologically**, beginning with those that occurred first and moving to those that occurred later. You can also arrange examples **in order of increasing complexity**, beginning with the simplest and moving to the most difficult or complex. Finally, you can arrange examples **in order of importance**, beginning with those that are less significant and moving to those that are most significant or persuasive.

The following informal outline for an essay evaluating the nursing care at a hospital illustrates one way to arrange examples. Notice how the writer presents his examples in order of increasing importance under three general headings — *patient rooms, emergency room,* and *clinics.*

Introduction:	Thesis statement — Because of its focus on the patient, the nursing care at Montgomery Hospital can serve as a model for other medical facilities.

In Patient Rooms

Example 1:	Being responsive
Example 2:	Establishing rapport
Example 3:	Delivering bedside care

In Emergency Room

Example 4:	Staffing treatment rooms
Example 5:	Circulating among patients in the waiting room
Example 6:	Maintaining good working relationships with physicians

In Clinics

Example 7:	Preparing patients
Example 8:	Assisting during treatment
Example 9:	Instructing patients after treatment
Conclusion:	Restatement of thesis or review of key points or examples

Revising an Exemplification Essay

When you revise an exemplification essay, consider the items on the revision checklist on page 54. In addition, pay special attention to the items on the following checklist, which apply specifically to exemplification essays.

Editing an Exemplification Essay

When you edit your exemplification essay, follow the guidelines on the editing checklists on pages 71, 73, and 76. In addition, focus on the grammar, mechanics, and punctuation issues that are most relevant to exemplification essays. One of these issues — using commas in a series — is discussed here.

GRAMMAR IN CONTEXT: Using Commas in a Series

When you write an exemplification essay, you often use a series of examples to support a statement or to illustrate a point. When you use a series of three or more examples in a sentence, you must remember to separate them with commas.

- Always use commas to separate three or more items — words, phrases, or clauses — in a series.

In "Just Walk On By," Brent Staples says, "I was surprised, embarrassed, and dismayed all at once" (241).

In "Just Walk On By," Staples observes that the woman thought she was being stalked by a mugger, by a rapist, or by something worse (241).

In "The Peter Principle," Laurence Peter says, "For example my principal's main concerns were that all window shades be at the same level, that classrooms should be quiet, and that no one step on or near the rose beds" (Peter and Hull 220).

(continued on next page)

(continued from previous page)

According to Jonathan Kozol in "The Human Cost of an Illiterate Society," illiterates cannot help with homework, they cannot write notes to teachers, and they cannot read school notices (254).

Note: Although newspaper and magazine writers routinely leave out the comma before the last item in a series of three or more items, you should always include this comma in your college writing.

• Do not use a comma after the final element in a series of three or more items.

Incorrect: Staples was shocked, horrified, and disillusioned, to be taken for a mugger.

Correct: Staples was shocked, horrified, and disillusioned to be taken for a mugger.

• Do not use commas if all the elements in a series of three or more items are separated by coordinating conjunctions (*and, or, but,* and so on).

Peter and Hull believe that the Peter Principle controls everyone in business and in government and in education. (*no commas*)

For more practice in using commas in a series, visit Exercise Central at <bedfordstmartins.com/patterns/commas>.

EDITING CHECKLIST: Exemplification

• Have you used commas to separate three or more items in a series?
• Have you made sure not to use a comma after the last element in a series?
• Have you made sure not to use a comma in a series with items separated by coordinating conjunctions?
• Are all the elements in a series stated in **parallel** terms (see page 394)?

STUDENT WRITERS: Exemplification

Exemplification is frequently used in nonacademic writing situations, such as business reports, memos, and proposals. One of the most important situations for using exemplification* is in a letter you write to apply for a job. Kristy Bredin's letter of application to a prospective employer follows. (Grace Ku's essay on page 213 illustrates a more conventional academic use of exemplification.)

---

*EDS NOTE: In business letters, paragraphs are not indented and extra space is added between them.

1028 Geissinger Street
Bethlehem, PA 18018
September 7, 2005

Kim Goldstein
Rolling Stone
1290 Avenue of the Americas
New York, NY 10104

Dear Ms. Goldstein:

Introduction

Thesis statement

I am writing to apply for the editorial internship with Rolling   1
Stone magazine that you posted on Moravian College's
employment Web site. I believe that both my academic
experience and my experience in publishing qualify me for
the position you advertised.

Examples

I am currently a senior at Moravian College, where I am   2
majoring in English (with a concentration in creative writing)
and music. Throughout my college career, I have maintained a
3.4 average. After I graduate in May, I would like to find a full-
time job in publishing. For this reason, your internship is very
attractive. It would not only give me additional editorial and
administrative experience, but it would also give me insight into
a large-scale publishing operation. An internship at Rolling
Stone would also enable to me to read, edit, and possibly write
articles about popular music — a subject I like and have studied
extensively.

Examples

Throughout college, I have been involved in writing and editing.   3
I have served as both secretary and president of the Literary
Society and have written, edited, and published its annual
newsletter. I have also worked as a tutor in Moravian's Writing
Center; as a literature editor for the Manuscript, Moravian's
literary magazine; and as a features editor for the Comeneian,
the student newspaper. In these jobs I have gained a good deal
of practical experience in publishing as well as insight into
dealing with people. Finally, I acquired professional editing

experience this past semester when I worked as an intern for Taylor and Francis (Routledge) Publishing in New York.

Conclusion   I believe that my education and experience make me a   4
good candidate for your position. As your ad requested, I have enclosed my résumé, three letters of reference, information on Moravian's internship program, and several of my writing samples for your consideration. You can contact me by phone at (484) 625-6731 or by email at <stkab@moravian.edu>. I will be available for an interview anytime after September 23. I look forward to meeting with you to discuss my qualifications.

Sincerely,

Kristy Bredin

Kristy Bredin

Points for Special Attention

Organization.   Exemplification is ideally suited for letters of application. The only way Kristy Bredin can support her claims about her qualifications for the internship at *Rolling Stone* is to illustrate her educational and professional qualifications. For this reason, the body of her letter is divided into two categories—her educational record and her editorial experience. Each of the body paragraphs has a clear purpose and function. The second paragraph contains two examples pertaining to Kristy's educational record. The third paragraph contains examples of her editorial experience. These examples tell the prospective employer what qualifies Kristy for the internship. Within these two body paragraphs, she arranges her examples in order of increasing importance. Because her practical experience as an editor relates directly to the position she is applying for, Kristy considers this her strongest point and presents it last.

Kristy ends her letter on a strong note, expressing her willingness to be interviewed and giving the first date she will be available for an interview. Because people remember best what they read last, a strong conclusion is essential here, just as it is in other writing situations.

Persuasive Examples.   To support a thesis convincingly, examples should convey specific information, not generalizations. Saying "I am a good student who is not afraid of responsibility" means very little. It is far better to say, as Kristy does, "Throughout my college career, I have maintained a 3.4 average" and "I have served as both secretary and president of the Literary Society." A letter of application should specifically show a prospective employer how your strengths and background correspond to the employer's needs; well-chosen examples can help you accomplish this.

Focus on Revision

After reading her letter, the students in Kristy's peer editing group identified several areas that they thought needed work.

One student thought Kristy should have mentioned her computer experience: she had taken a desktop publishing course as an elective and worked with publishing and graphics software when she was the features editor of the student newspaper. Kristy agreed that this expertise would make her a more attractive candidate for the job and thought she could work these examples into her third paragraph.

Another student asked Kristy to explain how her experience as secretary and president of the Literary Society relates to the job she is applying for. If her purpose is to show that she can assume responsibility, she should say so; if it is to illustrate that she can supervise others, she should make this clear.

Finally, a student suggested that she expand the discussion of her internship with Taylor and Francis Publishing in New York. Examples of her duties there would be persuasive because they would give her prospective employer a clear idea of her editorial experience. (A peer editing worksheet for exemplification can be found on page 216.)

The following essay by Grace Ku was written for a composition class in response to the assignment "Write an essay about the worst job you (or someone you know) ever had."

Midnight

Introduction   It was eight o'clock, and I was staring at the television   1
set wondering what kind of lesson Dr. Huxtable would teach his children next on a rerun of The Cosby Show. I was glued to the set like an average eleven-year-old couch potato while leisurely eating cold Chef Boyardee spaghetti out of the can. As I watched the show, I gradually fell asleep on the floor fully clothed in a pair of jeans and a T-shirt, wondering when my parents would come home. Around midnight I woke up to a rustling noise: my parents had finally arrived from a long day at

Thesis statement

work. I could see in their tired faces the grief and hardship of working at a dry-cleaning plant.

Transitional paragraph provides background

Although my parents lived in the most technologically advanced country in the world, their working conditions were like those of nineteenth-century factory workers. Because they were immigrants with little formal education and spoke broken English, they could get jobs only as laborers. Therefore, they worked at a dry-cleaning plant that was as big as a factory, a place where hundreds of small neighborhood cleaners sent their clothes to be processed.

2

Series of brief examples: physical demands

At work, my parents had to meet certain quotas. Each day they had to clean and press several hundred garments — shirts, pants, and other clothing. By themselves, every day, they did the work of four laborers. The muscles of my mother's shoulders and arms grew hard as iron from working with the press, a difficult job even for a man. In addition to pressing, my father operated the washing machines. As a result, his work clothes always smelled of oil.

3

Example: long hours

Not only were my parents' jobs physically demanding, but they also required long hours. My parents went to work at five o'clock in the morning and came home between nine o'clock at night and midnight. Each day they worked over twelve hours at the dry-cleaning plant, where eight-hour workdays and labor unions did not exist. They were allowed to take only two ten- to twenty-minute breaks — one for lunch and one for dinner. They did not stop even when they were burned by a hot iron or by steam rising from a press. The scars on their arms made it obvious that they worked at a dry-cleaning plant. My parents' burned skin would blister and later peel off, exposing raw flesh. In time, these injuries would heal, but other burns would soon follow.

4

Example: frequent burns

Example: low pay

In addition to having to work long hours and suffering painful injuries, my parents were paid below minimum wage. Together their paychecks were equal to that of a single unionized worker (even though they did the work of four). They used this money to feed and care for a household of five people.

5

Conclusion

As my parents silently entered our home around midnight, they did not have to complain about their jobs. I could see their anguish in their faces and their fatigue in the

6

Restatement
of thesis

slow movements of their bodies. Even though they did not speak, their eyes said, "We hate our jobs, but we work so that our children will have better lives than we do."

Points for Special Attention

Organization.   Grace Ku begins her introduction by describing herself as an eleven-year-old sitting on the floor watching television. At first, her behavior seems typical of many American children, but two things suggest problems: first, she is eating her cold dinner out of a can, and, second, even though it is late in the evening, she is still waiting for her parents to return from work. This opening prepares readers for her thesis that her parents' jobs produce only grief and hardship.

In the body of her essay, Grace presents the examples that support her thesis statement. In paragraph 2, she sets the stage for the discussion to follow, explaining that her parents' working conditions were similar to those of nineteenth-century factory workers, and in paragraph 3, she presents a series of examples that illustrate how physically demanding her parents' jobs were. In the remaining body paragraphs, she gives three other examples to show how unpleasant the jobs were — how long her parents worked, how often they were injured, and how little they were paid. Grace concludes her essay by returning to the scene in her introduction, using a quotation that she wants to stay with her readers after they have finished the essay.

Enough Examples.   Certainly no single example, no matter how graphic, could adequately support the thesis of this essay. To establish the pain and difficulty of her parents' jobs, Grace uses several examples. Although additional examples would have added even more depth to the essay, the ones she uses are vivid and compelling enough to reinforce her thesis that her parents had to endure great hardship to make a living.

Range of Examples.   Grace selects examples that illustrate the full range of her subject. She draws from the daily experience of her parents and does not include atypical examples. She also includes enough detail so that her readers, who she assumes do not know much about working in a dry-cleaning plant, will understand her points. She does not, however, provide so much detail that her readers get bogged down and lose interest.

Effective Examples.   All of Grace's examples support her thesis statement. While developing these examples, she never loses sight of her main idea; consequently, she does not get sidetracked in irrelevant discussions. She also avoids the temptation to preach to her readers about the injustice of her parents' situation. By allowing her examples to speak for themselves, Grace presents a powerful portrait of her parents and their hardships.

Focus on Revision

After reading this draft, a peer critic thought Grace could go into more detail about her parents' situation and could explain her examples in more depth — perhaps writing about the quotas her parents had to meet or the other physical dangers of their jobs.

Grace herself thought she should expand the discussion in paragraph 5 about her parents' low wages, perhaps anticipating questions some of her readers might have about working conditions. For example, was it legal for her parents' employer to require them to work overtime without compensation or to pay them less than the minimum wage? If not, how was the employer able to get away with such practices?

Grace also thought she should move the information about her parents' work-related injuries from paragraph 4 to paragraph 3, where she discusses the physical demands of their jobs.

Finally, she decided to follow the advice of another student and include comments by her parents to make their experiences more immediate to readers.

📄 **PEER EDITING WORKSHEET: Exemplification**

1. What strategy does the writer use in the essay's introduction? Would another strategy be more effective?

2. What is the essay's thesis? Is it specific enough? Does it prepare readers for the essay that follows?

3. What specific points do the body paragraphs make? Are these points expressed in the topic sentences?

4. Does the writer use one example or several to illustrate each point? Should the writer use more examples? Fewer? Explain.

5. Does the writer use a sufficient range of examples? Are they explained in enough depth?

6. Do the examples add interest? How persuasive are they? List a few other examples that might be more persuasive.

7. What transitional words and phrases does the writer use to reinforce the connections between examples? Should any transitional words and phrases be added?

8. In what order are the examples presented? Would another order be more effective? Explain.

9. Has the writer used a series of three or more examples in a single sentence? If so, are these examples separated by commas?

10. What strategy does the writer use in the conclusion? What other strategy could be used?

The selections in this chapter all depend on exemplification to explain and clarify, to add interest, or to persuade. The first selection, a visual text, is followed by questions designed to illustrate how exemplification can operate in visual form.

ALEX WILLIAMS, JOEL GORDON,
CHARLES GATEWOOD, AND BOB DAEMMRICH*

Four Tattoos (Photos)

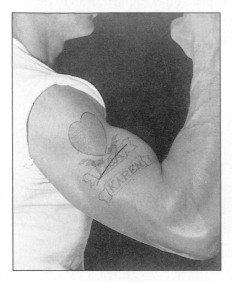

Alex Williams, "~~Lisa~~, Karen"

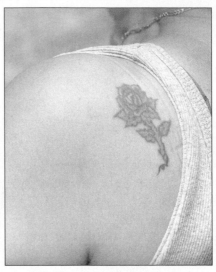

Joel Gordon, "Rose"

Bob Daemmrich, "Jiminy Cricket"

Charles Gatewood, "Body Art"

---

* Photos shown clockwise from top left.

• • •

Reading Images

1. How would you describe each of the four tattoos pictured on the previous page? List the prominent features of each, and then write two or three sentences that describe each of them.

2. After studying the four pictures (and reviewing your answer to question 1), write a one-sentence general statement that sums up your ideas about tattoos. For example, why do you think people get tattoos? Do you see them as a way for people to express themselves? As a way of demonstrating individuality? As a form of rebellion? As an impulsive act?

3. Do you think you have enough examples to support the general statement you made in question 2? Explain.

Journal Entry

Would you ever get a tattoo? Write a paragraph answering this question. Use your answers to the questions above to support the main idea in your topic sentence. (If you have a tattoo, explain why you decided to get it.)

Thematic Connections

- "Medium Ash Brown" (page 279)
- "My First Conk" (page 285)
- "The Embalming of Mr. Jones" (page 310)
- "The Wife-Beater" (page 532)

LAURENCE J. PETER AND RAYMOND HULL

The Peter Principle

Laurence J. Peter (1919–1990), an academic and education specialist, and Raymond Hull (1919–1985), a humorist and playwright, collaborated on the 1969 best-seller *The Peter Principle: Why Things Always Go Wrong*. In the preface to the book, Hull explained that he had become increasingly appalled at the number of problems people experienced with businesses and organizations, from those of trifling significance (bills going to an old address despite numerous attempts to give the business a new one) to ones of catastrophic importance (bridges collapsing only a few years after construction). Dr. Peter, Hull discovered during an impromptu conversation, had the explanation for such widespread ineptitude: within any hierarchy, employees tend to be promoted to a level where they are incompetent to perform the duties of the position. Within a short time of the publication of their book, the term *Peter Principle* had entered the language.

Background on corporations: During the 1950s, large corporations — touted as examples of an evolutionary leap forward in business organization structure — were widely perceived as models of efficiency. By the late 1960s, however, large bureaucracies seemed to be increasingly unresponsive, riddled with red tape, and demoralizing for workers. Peter and Hull's idea that most corporations were run by executives and managers who were simply out of their depth flew in the face of conventional 1950s wisdom and provided an explanation for 1960s corporate failings. The meteoric rise and subsequent crash of many Web-based business ventures in the late 1990s and the stunning demise in the years that followed of supposedly model corporations (such as Enron and WorldCom) suggest that Peter and Hull's analysis may still apply.

When I was a boy I was taught that the men upstairs knew what they were doing. I was told, "Peter, the more you know, the further you go." So I stayed in school until I graduated from college and then went forth into the world clutching firmly these ideas and my new teaching certificate. During the first year of teaching I was upset to find that a number of teachers, school principals, supervisors, and superintendents appeared to be unaware of their professional responsibilities and incompetent in executing their duties. For example my principal's main concerns were that all window shades be at the same level, that classrooms should be quiet, and that no one step on or near the rose beds. The superintendent's main concerns were that no minority group, no matter how fanatical, should ever be offended and that all official forms be submitted on time. The children's education appeared farthest from the administrator's mind.

At first I thought this was a special weakness of the school system in which I taught so I applied for certification in another province.* I filled out the special forms, enclosed the required documents, and complied willingly with all the red tape. Several weeks later, back came my application and all the documents!

No, there was nothing wrong with my credentials; the forms were correctly filled out; an official departmental stamp showed that they had been received in good order. But an accompanying letter said, "The new regulations require that such forms cannot be accepted by the Department of Education unless they have been registered at the Post Office to ensure safe delivery. Will you please remail the forms to the Department, making sure to register them this time?"

I began to suspect that the local school system did not have a monopoly on incompetence.

As I looked further afield, I saw that every organization contained a number of persons who could not do their jobs.

A Universal Phenomenon

Occupational incompetence is everywhere. Have you noticed it? Probably we have all noticed it.

We see indecisive politicians posing as resolute statesmen and the "authoritative source" who blames his misinformation on "situational imponderables." Limitless are the public servants who are indolent and insolent, military commanders whose behavioral timidity belies their dreadnought rhetoric, and governors whose innate servility prevents their actually governing. In our sophistication, we virtually shrug aside the immoral cleric, corrupt judge, incoherent attorney, author who cannot write, and English teacher who cannot spell. At universities we see proclamations authored by administrators whose own office communications are hopelessly muddled, and droning lectures from inaudible or incomprehensible instructors.

Seeing incompetence at all levels of every hierarchy — political, legal, educational, and industrial — I hypothesized that the cause was some inherent feature of the rules governing the placement of employees. Thus began my serious study of the ways in which employees move upward through a hierarchy, and of what happens to them after promotion.

For my scientific data hundreds of case histories were collected. Here are three typical examples.

---

* EDS. NOTE — An administrative district of a country, similar to a state; in this case, in Canada.

Municipal Government File, Case No. 17

J. S. Minion* was a maintenance foreman in the public works depart- 10
ment of Excelsior City. He was a favorite of the senior officials at City Hall.
They all praised his unfailing affability.

"I like Minion," said the superintendent of works. "He has good judg- 11
ment and is always pleasant and agreeable."

This behavior was appropriate for Minion's position: he was not sup- 12
posed to make policy, so he had no need to disagree with his superiors.

The superintendent of works retired and Minion succeeded him. Min- 13
ion continued to agree with everyone. He passed to his foreman every suggestion that came from above. The resulting conflicts in policy, and the
continual changing of plans, soon demoralized the department. Complaints poured in from the Mayor and other officials, from taxpayers and
from the maintenance-workers' union.

Minion still says "Yes" to everyone, and carries messages briskly back 14
and forth between his superiors and his subordinates. Nominally a superintendent, he actually does the work of a messenger. The maintenance
department regularly exceeds its budget, yet fails to fulfill its program of
work. In short, Minion, a competent foreman, became an incompetent
superintendent.

Service Industries File, Case No. 3

E. Tinker was exceptionally zealous and intelligent as an apprentice at 15
G. Reece Auto Repair Inc., and soon rose to journeyman mechanic. In this
job he showed outstanding ability in diagnosing obscure faults, and endless patience in correcting them. He was promoted to foreman of the repair
shop.

But here his love of things mechanical and his perfectionism became 16
liabilities. He will undertake any job that he thinks looks interesting, no
matter how busy the shop may be. "We'll work it in somehow," he says.

He will not let a job go until he is fully satisfied with it. 17

He meddles constantly. He is seldom to be found at his desk. He is 18
usually up to his elbows in a dismantled motor and while the man who
should be doing the work stands watching, other workmen sit around
waiting to be assigned new tasks. As a result the shop is always overcrowded with work, always in a muddle, and delivery times are often
missed.

Tinker cannot understand that the average customer cares little about 19
perfection—he wants his car back on time! He cannot understand that
most of his men are less interested in motors than in their pay checks. So
Tinker cannot get on with his customers or with his subordinates. He was
a competent mechanic, but is now an incompetent foreman.

---

* Some names have been changed, in order to protect the guilty.

Military File, Case No. 8

Consider the case of the late renowned General A. Goodwin. His   20
hearty, informal manner, his racy style of speech, his scorn for petty regulations, and his undoubted personal bravery made him the idol of his men.
He led them to many well-deserved victories.

When Goodwin was promoted to field marshal he had to deal, not   21
with ordinary soldiers, but with politicians and allied generalissimos.

He would not conform to the necessary protocol. He could not turn   22
his tongue to the conventional courtesies and flatteries. He quarreled with
all the dignitaries and took to lying for days at a time, drunk and sulking,
in his trailer. The conduct of the war slipped out of his hands into those of
his subordinates. He had been promoted to a position that he was incompetent to fill.

An Important Clue

In time I saw that all such cases had a common feature. The employee   23
had been promoted from a position of competence to a position of incompetence. I saw that, sooner or later, this could happen to every employee in
every hierarchy.

Hypothetical Case File, Case No. 1

Suppose you own a pill-rolling factory, Perfect Pill Incorporated. Your   24
foreman pill roller dies of a perforated ulcer. You need a replacement. You
naturally look among your rank-and-file pill rollers.

Miss Oval, Mrs. Cylinder, Mr. Ellipse, and Mr. Cube all show various   25
degrees of incompetence. They will naturally be ineligible for promotion.
You will choose—other things being equal—your most competent pill
roller, Mr. Sphere, and promote him to foreman.

Now suppose Mr. Sphere proves competent as foreman. Later, when   26
your general foreman, Legree, moves up to Works Manager, Sphere will be
eligible to take his place.

If, on the other hand, Sphere is an incompetent foreman, he will get no   27
more promotion. He has reached what I call his "level of incompetence."
He will stay there till the end of his career.

Some employees, like Ellipse and Cube, reach a level of incompetence   28
in the lowest grade and are never promoted. Some, like Sphere (assuming
he is not a satisfactory foreman), reach it after one promotion.

E. Tinker, the automobile repair-shop foreman, reached his level of   29
incompetence on the third stage of the hierarchy. General Goodwin
reached his level of incompetence at the very top of the hierarchy.

So my analysis of hundreds of cases of occupational incompetence led   30
me on to formulate *The Peter Principle:*

In a Hierarchy Every Employee Tends to Rise to His Level of Incompetence.

A New Science!

Having formulated the Principle, I discovered that I had inadvertently   31
founded a new science, hierarchiology, the study of hierarchies.

The term "hierarchy" was originally used to describe the system of   32
church government by priests graded into ranks. The contemporary meaning includes any organization whose members or employees are arranged
in order of rank, grade, or class.

Hierarchiology, although a relatively recent discipline, appears to have   33
great applicability to the fields of public and private administration.

This Means You!

My Principle is the key to an understanding of all hierarchical systems,   34
and therefore to an understanding of the whole structure of civilization. A
few eccentrics try to avoid getting involved with hierarchies, but everyone
in business, industry, trade-unionism, politics, government, the armed
forces, religion, and education is so involved. All of them are controlled by
the Peter Principle.

Many of them, to be sure, may win a promotion or two, moving from   35
one level of competence to a higher level of competence. But competence in
that new position qualifies them for still another promotion. For each
individual, for *you*, for *me*, the final promotion is from a level of competence to a level of incompetence.*

So, given enough time — and assuming the existence of enough ranks   36
in the hierarchy — each employee rises to, and remains at, his level of
incompetence. Peter's Corollary states:

> *In time, every post tends to be occupied by an employee who is incompetent to carry*
> *out its duties.*

Who Turns the Wheels?

You will rarely find, of course, a system in which *every* employee has   37
reached his level of incompetence. In most instances, something is being
done to further the ostensible purposes for which the hierarchy exists.

> *Work is accomplished by those employees who have not yet reached their level of*
> *incompetence.*

•   •   •

---

* The phenomena of "percussive sublimation" (commonly referred to as "being
kicked upstairs") and of "the lateral arabesque" are not, as the casual observer might
think, exceptions to the Principle. They are only pseudo-promotions. . . .

Comprehension

1. What things disillusioned Peter during his first year of teaching? What did he discover about organizations?
2. What is the Peter Principle? According to Peter and Hull, what happens when employees reach their "level of incompetence" (30)?
3. What do Peter and Hull mean by *hierarchiology* (31)? How did hierarchiology lead Peter to the Peter Principle?
4. If the Peter Principle operates in hierarchies such as corporations, who does the work?

Purpose and Audience

1. Is this essay aimed at a general audience or an expert audience? What led you to your conclusion?
2. What is the essay's thesis? At what point in the essay does the thesis statement appear? Why do you think Peter and Hull wait so long to state it?
3. How serious are Peter and Hull? What words or phrases indicate whether their purpose is to instruct or to entertain — or both?

Style and Structure

1. Why do you think Peter and Hull begin the essay with an example? Why do they present a series of brief examples before introducing the typical case histories?
2. Why do Peter and Hull say they collected hundreds of case histories for data? How are the three case histories analyzed here typical?
3. Does the use of hypothetical examples strengthen or weaken the writers' case? Explain.
4. Do Peter and Hull use a sufficiently wide range of examples? Explain.

Vocabulary Projects

1. Define each of the following words as it is used in this selection.

imponderables (7)	incomprehensible (7)	protocol (22)
indolent (7)	hypothesized (8)	subordinates (22)
insolent (7)	hierarchy (8)	eccentrics (34)
dreadnought (7)	minion (10)	ostensible (37)
inaudible (7)	dismantled (18)	

2. Do Peter and Hull use **figures of speech** in their discussion? Why do you think they do or do not?

Journal Entry

What examples of the Peter Principle have you encountered in your life?

Writing Workshop

1. Do Peter and Hull overstate their case? Write a letter to them in the form of an exemplification essay pointing out the weaknesses of their position.
2. Study a school, business, or organization that you know well. Write an exemplification essay showing how the Peter Principle applies (or does not apply).
3. Do you know someone who has progressed to the highest level of his or her incompetence? Supporting your thesis with a single example, write an exemplification essay showing how the Peter Principle applies.

Combining the Patterns

Peter and Hull use a series of narrative examples. What are the advantages and disadvantages of using **narration** here? Would other kinds of examples — such as statistics — have been more effective? Explain.

Thematic Connections

- "Playing by the Rules" (page 114)
- "Shooting an Elephant" (page 125)
- "Stigmatic Uniforms" (page 544)
- "What Work Is" (page 550)

DAVID J. BIRNBAUM

The Catbird Seat

David J. Birnbaum was born in 1963 in Brooklyn, New York, and is a graduate of New York University. A manager with AT&T, he also contributes essays to a number of publications. As he explains in the following essay, he lost the use of his legs in an auto accident and now uses a wheelchair to move about.

Background on the 1990 Americans with Disabilities Act: Approximately 19 percent of Americans, representing about 49 million people, have some form of disability, and almost half of these are considered severely disabled. An estimated 15 percent (about 38 million people) have disabilities that limit their physical activity.

The 1990 Americans with Disabilities Act, which Birnbaum refers to in paragraph 11, requires that reasonable accommodation be made in areas of educational opportunity, employment, government services, and access to businesses open to the general public, and it further prohibits discrimination against people with disabilities. Noncompliance with the act can result in fines, and perceived noncompliance has resulted in a number of lawsuits, which have raised questions about who can legitimately be considered disabled and what, in fact, constitutes "reasonable" accommodation. As Birnbaum suggests, due to various ambiguities in the wording of the act and to some of the loopholes contained in it, many establishments are still not in full compliance; this remains a sore point for advocates for the disabled.

1   I wasn't in a hurry to get back to my hospital room, but I had a lot on my mind. I was adjusting to my new fate, quadriplegia. Besides, I had been waiting at least three minutes for the elevator, which in teen-age time is three years. When I heard the ding, I dashed into the car, unintentionally cutting off the handful of other riders.

2   "What's the big hurry?" a pregnant woman asked. An elderly Asian man chimed in: "Leave the young man alone. He's in a wheelchair!"

3   That was the first time I felt my new place in society. A few months later, my friend Roy and I were in the back of a ticketholders' line that was clogging 34th Street waiting to see *The Empire Strikes Back* at the Murray Hill cinema. Suddenly an usher appeared and asked us to follow him into the theater. Despite the drizzle, the other patrons didn't seem to mind that we were cutting ahead. I was the only one in line that had a chair to sit in. Yet I didn't have to wait. Thereafter, I began to cut ahead often. Cashing a check at Chase, I'd ignore the velvet ropes and go straight to a teller. Registering for classes at N.Y.U., I cut three lines in one day: department approval, course selection, and, finally, registrar payment. Older people who only a few months earlier would have ignored a teen-ager with long

hair began acting very friendly. Senior citizens still smile at me 17 years after I crashed my car in Park Slope, breaking my neck, just days before my 18th birthday. Are they trying to cheer me up? Maybe they just see me as nonthreatening. They're probably thinking, "This guy is less than half my age, but I can still beat him up."

Soon after leaving the hospital, I realized I could now break rules. I   4
would sneak cans of beer into concerts at Madison Square Garden. At the queue where teen-agers are routinely patted down, the guards held up the process for me: "Please step back, we gotta wheelchair coming through!"

When I leave Staples, I tell the security guard that I need the plastic   5
shopping basket to carry my goods to my van. He nods his head trustingly, on the assumption that I'll unload and return it. I have five of these red baskets in my hallway closet. I don't know what I'm going to do with them. I just get a kick driving them home.

Before I left Jamaica last January, I hid a box of Cuban cigars in my can-   6
vas case. As I passed through customs at Newark International Airport, a woman in a brown uniform looked at my two large bags suspiciously. Perusing the card I filled out on the plane, she asked, "Nothing to declare?"

"Nothing."   7

"What's the canvas bag for?"   8

"It's a portable handicap shower seat," I replied truthfully.   9

"Oh . . . I'm so sorry. Go ahead."   10

Cutting the lines at the Department of Motor Vehicles to renew my   11
driver's license, getting out of speeding tickets and arriving late to work without a reprimand are my "even uppers" for my physical limitations and for the difficulties caused by establishments not complying with the Americans with Disabilities Act. I had to sit behind the last row in a theater, separated from my college friends, only once before I stopped being too proud to accept the senior citizens' discount offered by sympathetic employees. When the purser offered to bump me up into first class on that flight from Jamaica, I didn't say: "No, thank you. I've accepted my disability, I have a successful career and live independently. Please treat me like everyone else." I didn't care whether she was condescending, sympathizing or patronizing. I was just glad to be in "2B" sipping Chardonnay while I eyed the coach passengers frantically seeking space for their carry-on luggage and duty-free rum.

After sneaking my cigars through customs, I headed upstairs to get a   12
taxi. Three carloads of tired travelers, dragging luggage with and without wheels, were waiting for a single elevator to arrive. I waited like an Olympic sprinter anticipating the starting gun. I began inching my wheelchair forward, but accidentally wheeled over some guy's foot.

"Oww!" he turned around, saw my wheelchair and then followed ner-   13
vously with, "Oh, I'm ss . . . sss . . . sorry." He stepped to the side, leaving me perfectly positioned in front of the sliding aluminum doors. The "L" on the display lighted, the ding went off, the doors opened, and I swiftly pushed my chair forward into the car.

"What's wrong with you?" A well-tanned girl asked me angrily. I   14
looked her in the eye with cockiness, expecting my usual support from others. But it didn't come.

"Have some respect, for God's sake!" she continued, holding the door   15
open for a middle-aged man with dark glasses and a white cane.

There in the elevator, as everyone looked at me in disgust, I learned the   16
pecking order: blind trumps wheelchair; wheelchair trumps pregnant;
pregnant trumps old; old trumps whatever is left.

• • •

Comprehension

1. What "new place in society" does Birnbaum occupy after his accident
   (3)?
2. How does Birnbaum take advantage of his new status?
3. According to Birnbaum, how are cutting in line, avoiding speeding
   tickets, and getting to work late his "even uppers" (11)?
4. What incident causes Birnbaum to realize that the advantages he gets
   from his disability have limitations?

Purpose and Audience

1. What preconceptions about the disabled does Birnbaum assume his
   readers have? How can you tell?
2. Why does Birnbaum wait until paragraph 16 to state his thesis?
   Should he have stated it sooner? Explain.
3. Birnbaum is aiming his essay at a general audience. How would his
   essay be different if he were addressing health-care professionals?
   Other people with disabilities?
4. What is Birnbaum's purpose in writing this essay? For example, does
   he want to educate his readers? To persuade them? Or does he have
   some other purpose?

Style and Structure

1. Birnbaum's essay begins with an example. Is this an effective introductory strategy? Should he have used a more formal introduction?
2. All of Birnbaum's examples are drawn from his own experience. Does
   this reliance on personal experience make his essay less convincing
   than it would otherwise be? Explain.
3. How does Birnbaum arrange his examples? Is this arrangement effective? Explain.
4. How are the ideas in Birnbaum's first example (1–2) echoed in his
   conclusion?

Vocabulary Projects

1. Define each of the following words as it is used in this selection.

   quadriplegia (1)   patronizing (11)
   reprimand (11)   Chardonnay (11)
   purser (11)   trumps (16)
   condescending (11)

2. What terms does Birnbaum use to refer to his physical condition? What other terms could he have used? What different connotations do these terms have?

3. To "be in the catbird seat" means to have a position of power or prominence. Why does Birnbaum use this expression as his title? Is he being serious or **ironic**?

Journal Entry

Do you think people with disabilities have advantages that others do not have? Do you think Birnbaum should have special privileges because of his disability?

Writing Workshop

1. Write a letter to Birnbaum agreeing or disagreeing with his actions. Do you, for example, think he should reject the benefits conferred on him because he has a disability? Or, do you think that these benefits are justified given his physical limitations?

2. A **stereotype** is an oversimplified concept or image. Write an essay discussing three stereotypes of people with disabilities that many people share. How accurate are these stereotypes? What could (or should) be done to eliminate them?

3. Write an editorial for your school newspaper discussing how your school could do more to help students with physical disabilities. To support your thesis, include specific examples of changes that could be made.

Combining the Patterns

Choose four or five examples that Birnbaum uses in his essay. What other patterns of development does he use in presenting these examples? Does any single pattern predominate? If so, why?

Thematic Connections

- "Words Left Unspoken" (page 168)
- "The Men We Carry in Our Minds" (page 481)
- "On Dumpster Diving" (page 712)

PHIL PATTON

Innovation

New York Times columnist Phil Patton is also a contributing editor with *Esquire* and *Wired* magazines and has served as a commentator for CBS News and the History Channel. He has written extensively about automobile and other product design and was a consulting curator for the 1999 exhibition "Different Roads: Automobiles for the New Century" at the Museum of Modern Art in New York City. His books include *Made in USA: The Secret History of the Things That Made America* (1992); *Dreamland: Travels Inside the Secret World of Roswell and Area 51* (1998); and *Bug: The Strange Mutations of the World's Most Famous Automobile* (2004), about the history of the Volkswagen Beetle. Patton has also taught at the Columbia Graduate School of Journalism. In the following essay, which appeared in *American Heritage* in October 2004, Patton describes what he sees as the ten most important technological innovations of the past fifty years.

Background on patents: Patents as we know them originated with legislation passed by the British Parliament in 1642. These early patents were intended to encourage the development of innovative products and production techniques by granting to inventors exclusive rights to manufacture and market (and thus to benefit financially from) their inventions for fourteen years. While the U.S. Constitution includes a clause regarding intellectual property rights, the clause's wording is rather vague. Because George Washington, Thomas Jefferson, and other early government leaders recognized the importance of protecting inventors' rights as a spur to scientific innovation, patent legislation modeled on that of Great Britain was introduced in the first U.S. Congress in 1790. In 1793, a second Patent Act was passed. It was intended to streamline the process of granting of patents, to address the issue of patent disputes, and to establish a formal patent board. For the next forty years, the number of patent applications grew dramatically, and in 1836 a third Patent Act was passed to address the complaints of applicants. It authorized establishing an independent Patent Office, attempted to create conditions that would allow patents to be issued more quickly, and established procedures for distributing patent information to libraries for educational purposes. It also allowed for extending patent rights for seven years beyond the original fourteen. For the next seventy years, these improvements in patent legislation contributed significantly to the growth of American commerce and to the creation of the modern corporation. With minor changes, the 1836 legislation remains largely intact today.

"I can't imagine how we lived without it." So we often say about an innovation that has changed our lives. But about the changes that have been most deeply absorbed into the pores of daily routine, we could also often say, "I can't *remember* how we lived without it."

1

My finger no longer retains the muscle memory of a rotary dial phone. 2
I can no longer remember walking over to a television set to change the
channel. When I think of slipping into the back seat of my father's
Oldsmobile, I falsely remember fastening a seat belt. Old television shows
are magically remembered in color, and when I recall typing college term
papers in the early 1970s, I do so on a click-clacking plastic computer keyboard rather than a massive metal Royal.*

Such distortions may be the very definition of what has changed the 3
world most. The year 1954 saw the arrival of the first solar cells, developed
at Bell Labs. Boeing was testing a prototype of the 707, the intercontinental
jet airliner that would so change patterns of travel and consumption. Elvis
was cutting his first records. And computers were just starting to be connected by telephone lines in the creation of the Cold War[†] SAGE air
defense system. The broader implications of that development were hardly
imagined.

The impact of some innovations, such as jet planes, has been striking 4
in its predictability. But small innovations have wrought surprisingly large
and unexpected changes in daily life too. Here are enough innovations,
large and small, to count on all 10 of what used to be called digits — your
fingers.

1. Getting the Dish: The Power of the Satellite

It was all there in Arthur C. Clarke's famous article "Extra-Terrestrial 5
Relays" in *Wireless World* magazine in October 1945. Inspired by the discovery of German V2 rockets, which he believed could serve as boosters,
Clarke proposed launching earth satellites into geosynchronous orbit to
handle radio, telephone, and television communications. By 1962 Telstar
was beaming TV images between Europe and the United States.

Clarke understood that building ground networks no longer made 6
economic sense, a truth realized as countries all over the Third World
leapfrogged straight to wireless phones and satellite TV. The echoes of that
article are still resonating in such events as Rupert Murdoch's[‡] installation
as the TV baron of China. Satellite phones remain challenged by cost and
power demands, but their potential impact was illustrated a few years ago
by the poignant final moments of a trapped Mount Everest climber phon-
ing his wife with his last words and more recently by the pixelated pictures
from the Iraqi war front generated by satellite phones.

In the western North Carolina valley where my ancestors lived for a 7
century and a half, television reception was long limited by the mountains,

---

* EDS. NOTE — A brand of manual — that is, nonelectric — typewriter.
  [†] EDS. NOTE — The period beginning in the 1950s marked by political conflict
between the Soviet Union and the United States.
  [‡] EDS. NOTE — British publishing and telecommunications tycoon.

and the population was too poor and too sparse to justify investment by cable companies. My cousins and neighbors could see only two fuzzy channels before the arrival of the TV satellite dish. But then this area of Appalachia quickly came to have a remarkably high number of the dishes. Now the mountaineers can keep up with gossip about Hollywood stars as easily as with that about their cousins in the valley.

2. The Silicon Frontier: Technology as Manifest Destiny*

We've all heard by now of Moore's Law, the dictum laid down by the   8
Intel cofounder Gordon Moore in 1965 that holds that the number of transistors and therefore the capacity of a silicon chip must rise exponentially. The Intel 8088 processor in the first IBM PC had 29,000 transistors. Today's Pentium 4 has up to 178 million.

The importance of Moore's Law, however, lies not just in what chips   9
have done better and better — like running automobile engines more efficiently, regulating the browning of toast, and printing professional-looking flyers for the high school dance — but also in the pace at which their power has advanced, as relentlessly as did the frontier in the nineteenth century. Because of this, marketing and sales staffs have been able to set up a steady pattern of declining prices and new fashions in technology. "Adoption curves" have shot upward on the chart of time. Today's cutting-edge device for the "early adopter" is tomorrow's, or even today's, strip-mall commodity.

Technical advances just over the horizon are like the empty lands of   10
the nineteenth century. Exploitation of the manifest destiny of silicon has reinforced all the patterns of the Old West: speculation, competition, shootouts, and boomtowns and ghost towns.

3. Laser "Life"

For those of us who grew up on the promise of the laser as a powerful   11
ray gun, slicing up steel plate and boring holes through stone, the unexpected turn has been instead the spread of the low-power, low-cost laser.

It comes as no surprise that Boeing wants to mount antimissile lasers   12
on jets, but it's astonishing that the soldier in the field can pick out targets with his red laser pointer — and the regional sales manager can target data on his PowerPoint presentation with a pocket-size version of the same thing. We might have guessed that lasers would reshape the corneas of the myopic, but who would have anticipated the laser in a $30 device at the local Wal-Mart playing music or movies from discs?

---

* EDS. NOTE — The nineteenth century doctrine that the United States had a God-given right to expand West to the Pacific. Here, the term suggests a future development believed to be inevitable.

4. Pumping Calories: The Heat Pump

At Seaside, the planned town in the Florida Panhandle built in the 1970s to elaborate the ideas of the New Urbanism, the architecture melds old Charleston galleries with bungalows and farmhouses in an American village so archetypical it was used as the backdrop for the film *The Truman Show*. Picket fences are required by town ordinance. But look behind the fence of the majority of houses in Seaside, and you'll encounter the jarring sight of a mechanical minitower — a heat pump. 13

The heat pump changed Everytown, U.S.A., and helped create what we began in the early 1970s to call the Sunbelt. The device was developed just after World War II by Professor Carl Nielsen of Ohio State University and an engineer named J. Donald Kroeker, whose engineering firm installed the first commercial unit in the Equitable Building in Portland, Oregon, in 1948. Heat pumps were soon to be found in motels across America. 14

Basically air conditioners that can be reversed to provide low-demand heating systems, they made life tolerable in the Sunbelt, and at low cost. The heat pump removed the need for radiators or vented-air heat in much of the southern half of the country while supplanting the window-installed air-conditioning unit. It has flourished everywhere cooling is more important than heating and has supported our national dependence on low energy prices to make life sustainable in our fastest-growing areas. 15

5. The End of the Blues? The Mechanical Cotton Picker

The mechanical cotton picker killed Broadway, believes Jimmy Breslin. By driving poor blacks off the fields of the South to "Trailways and Greyhound bus depots for the long ride to New York City," he argues, it sent blacks moving "into the tenements that were vacated by whites," who themselves moved to the suburbs and abandoned Times Square. "Broadway would no longer be the place of guys and dolls." 16

The migration of African-Americans north and west out of the South is the greatest in American history, larger than that from the Dust Bowl* to California. Cotton-picking machinery, pioneered in the 1930s by the brothers John and Mack Rust, was mature by the late 1940s, but not until 1960 was a majority of the cotton crop harvested by machine. 17

The cotton picker soon became a key focus for historians studying the interaction of social and technological forces. The debate is charted in *The Second Great Emancipation: The Mechanical Cotton Picker, Black Migration, and How They Shaped the Modern South,* by Donald Holley. Did the migration of workers out of the South trigger the adoption of the picker and push the maturation of its technology? Or did the machine displace the workers? Did the appeal of greater freedom and prosperity in the rest of the country 18

---

* EDS. NOTE — An extensive drought in the Midwest in the early 1930s that caused many farm families to relocate to the West.

pull people off the land and into cities? Or did the disappearance of an agricultural society create a classic displaced proletariat?

What is not in doubt are the consequences: The growth of frequently   19
depressed inner-city neighborhoods and expanding suburban ones, and the transformation of the blues, in its new homes in Chicago and elsewhere, into rock 'n' roll and hip-hop.

6. Bar Codes and the Universal Product Code

Scanning your own groceries and avoiding the gum-chewing gossiping   20
checkout girl may be worth it for you, but it's even more worth it for the supermarket, with its just-in-time inventory. Much of America's recent productivity growth has been built on new sets of standards and means of marking products. The bar code is the most visible example of this.

The Universal Product Code was the first bar-code symbology widely   21
adopted, endorsed by the grocery industry in 1973. Product coding allows for quick price changes and has abetted the growth of the big-box discount store. Items can be tracked from port to rail to loading dock to shelf, thanks to containerized shipping that uses the codes. The consequence is lowered living costs.

Bar codes are just one of many industry standardizations that have   22
lowered costs and changed life. The American home has doubled in average square footage thanks in large part to standardized building materials (4-by-8-foot gypsum board and plywood, 2-by-4 studs 16 inches apart). Electronics is built on standards such as Windows compatibility, VHS, DVD, and so on. Coded product standards even rule the food in our kitchens. A banana that was once just a Chiquita is now a #4011.

7. Buckle Up: The Automobile Seat Belt

Can you recall a car without a seat belt? The movement to put seat   23
belts in the car began in 1954, when the American Medical Association first recommended them. Ford and Chrysler began to offer them as options a year later. By 1965 they were standard.

The push by safety advocates to require seat belts helped establish the   24
adversarial relationship between government and the automobile industry, which was accelerated by the Clean Air Act of 1970. Detroit grumbled, but the engineering achievement involved in developing the catalytic converter and the air bag, both of which Detroit argued were impractical, suggested that under pressure industry could do far more than it thought. For historians, the story indicated how effective "force fed" technology, demanded by government, could be. For philosophers, it challenged John Stuart Mill's classic liberal precept that government should not protect the individual from himself. Harley-riding libertarians, agreeing with Mill, have forced a rollback of mandatory helmet laws in some states. Will belt laws be unbuckled next?

8. Seeking Heat: The TV Remote Control

Today's children watch television in a wholly different way from those   25
of the 1950s. The remote control makes television an environment to be
moved through, not a schedule of successive programs. The result is grab-
'em-quick programming and short attention spans. Once families clus-
tered together to watch Ed Sullivan. Now a program waited for and seen
straight through is the exception rather than the rule.

While scientists at the remote Naval Ordnance Test Center at China   26
Lake were developing infrared heat-seeking guidance for the Sidewinder
air-to-air missile in the early 1950s, TV designers were struggling to find a
way to change channels from a distance. The first remote control, still
wired to the set, bore the apt name Lazy Bone. In 1955 a Zenith engineer
named Eugene Polley did away with the wire; his Flash-matic used light,
but it didn't work very well, so it was replaced by the Space Command,
which relied on ultrasound—frequencies beyond the range of the human
ear. The sounds were generated mechanically in a system that was part
chime, part tuning fork, because batteries were inadequate to power a wireless electric ultrasound system.

Not until the 1980s did cheap and dependable infrared technology   27
take over. Today 99 percent of all TV sets come with remote controls, and
restless fingers seek hot news and hot new stars unceasingly.

9. . . . And Going and Going: Better Batteries

We forget how much bigger and slower our portable devices used to be.   28
Remote controls and mobile phones and Game Boys have become possible
only with improvements in batteries. Hefty boom boxes are loaded with
companies of chunky C cells, but hearing aids, watches, and automobile
key fobs contain tiny button batteries that often outlast the devices they
power. The change began with the introduction of alkaline and nickel-
cadmium cells in the 1960s. Later decades saw nickel metal hydrides and
then lithium produce order-of-magnitude extensions in battery life. But
there have been tradeoffs. Most of the substances that make the best batteries are environmental hazards. Nickel, mercury, cadmium, and other
heavy metals tossed into landfills and incinerators are among the most
dangerous sources of pollutants. And while cell phones can remain on
standby for weeks, running a laptop for a whole airline flight across the
United States remains a challenge. The hope? That in the future miniature
fuel cells will replace batteries altogether.

10. Scoop! The French Fry Is King

In 1954 the first TV dinner arrived. It was a turkey-and-dressing meal   29
packaged in a segmented foil tray in a box printed up to look like a television screen. Frozen industrialized dinners heated in the home kitchen
looked like the culinary future. But in 1955 Ray Kroc began the national

franchising of McDonald's and signaled a different pattern, the industrialization of the restaurant kitchen, with machinery and methods allowing
the use of untrained labor. More and more meals would be eaten outside
the home as standardized chains spread.

Kroc's kitchen engineer, James Schindler, first broke down the burger   30
production system, the way Henry Ford had broken down auto manufacturing. Then he refined it, the way Toyota had with its just-in-time
automaking. Nothing better exemplified the system than the engineer
Ralph Weimer's fry scoop, a metal device that, when slipped onto a waxed
bag, measured out an order of fries with a single unskilled swipe.

McDonald's success has turned less on burgers than on fries, and the   31
fries in turn have depended on a whole supporting infrastructure. As critical to McDonald's as Ray Kroc himself was the spud king J. R. Simplot,
who produced Idaho russets with just the right water and sugar content
for proper caramelizing in cooking fat with just a touch of beef lard added.
And the potatoes created by a vast growing, freezing, and transportation
network end up in the hands of the worker wielding the scoop.

The scoop is an apt symbol of the power of the franchise itself, the   32
business-in-a-box approach that has sprinkled monad-like restaurants and
clothing stores across America and the world in the last half-century. What
McDonald's pioneered has been carried out by Starbucks and the Gap and
other chains. The colored signal lights that regulate restaurant machinery,
the step-by-step photos on training charts in fast-food kitchens, and the
just-in-time shelf arrangements at Gap stores — all are exact counterparts
of elements in modern automobile factories.

In the franchise nothing is left to chance — or to sheer stupidity. Not   33
long ago, after happily munching our Roy Rogers burgers, we smoothed
out the wrapper to discover a small circle printed on its interior. Inside the
circle were printed the words PLACE SANDWICH HERE.

•   •   •

Comprehension

1. According to Patton, what is the difference between saying, "I can't
   imagine how we lived without it" and "I can't *remember* how we lived
   without it" (1)? What examples does he give to explain this distinction?

2. How are technological advances and unexplored territories of the
   nineteenth century alike?

3. How did widespread use of the mechanical cotton picker displace
   African-American workers in the South? According to Patton, what
   were the consequences of this displacement?

4. How were American automobile companies forced to make safer cars?
   According to Patton, what did the automobile companies learn from
   this experience?

5. How is a McDonald's fast-food restaurant like an automobile factory? How has the standardization that McDonald's pioneered affected other businesses?

Purpose and Audience

1. This essay originally appeared in *American Heritage*, a magazine for readers who are interested in history. Based on this essay, do you think readers of *American Heritage* are likely to be experts who know a lot about history, or general readers?
2. What is the thesis of this essay? Where in the essay is it stated? Why do you think Patton states it where he does?
3. Do you think Patton has a serious point to make about technological innovation, or do you think his purpose is simply to entertain his readers and inform them about various inventions? Explain.

Style and Structure

1. In paragraph 3, Patton discusses innovations that occurred in 1954. Why do you think he chooses this year? How do these innovations lead him to his thesis?
2. In the body of his essay, Patton lists ten innovations. What do these innovations have in common? How do they support his thesis?
3. Patton uses numbers and boldfaced headings to introduce his ten innovations. Are these sufficient, or does he need to add specific topic sentences?
4. Do you think Patton uses too many examples? Would fewer examples have made the essay easier to understand?
5. Patton's essay does not have a formal conclusion. Do you think he needs one? Explain.

Vocabulary Projects

1. Define each of the following words as it is used in this selection.

innovation (1)	speculation (10)	successive (25)
retains (2)	myopic (12)	ordnance (26)
distortions (3)	archetypical (13)	fobs (28)
prototype (3)	displaced (18)	magnitude (28)
geosynchronous (5)	proletariat (18)	culinary (29)
poignant (6)	compatibility (22)	infrastructure (31)
sparse (7)	catalytic converter (24)	caramelizing (31)
dictum (8)	impractical (24)	franchise (32)
commodity (9)	libertarians (24)	counterparts (32)
exploitation (10)		

2. Underline the technical terms in this essay — for example, *prototype* and *geosynchronous*. After reviewing these words, decide how much (or how little) technical knowledge Patton assumed his readers would have. What would be gained or lost by substituting less technical terms for some (or all) of the terms Patton uses?

Journal Entry

Write a one-paragraph conclusion for this essay. Then, write a few sentences analyzing what your conclusion adds to the essay.

Writing Workshop

1. Make your own list of four or five technical innovations that affect your life — for example, cell phones and MP3 players. Then, write an essay in which you, like Patton, discuss why you couldn't live without these items.

2. Review Patton's list of ten innovations, and choose the two or three you think are the most important or influential. Then, write an essay considering the ways in which society would be different if these innovations had never come about. Use examples to illustrate your points.

3. Patton's essay discusses the ten biggest technological innovations. Make a list of five innovations that have occurred in other areas of American life — for example, home, education, entertainment, or the workplace. Then, write an essay discussing the innovations you listed. Make sure you include examples to illustrate your points.

Combining the Patterns

Patton uses a number of **cause-and-effect** paragraphs to illustrate the impact of his ten innovations on American society. What are the advantages of this strategy? Could he have used other patterns — for example, **comparison and contrast** — to illustrate how these innovations changed American life? Would these have added to the essay's impact? Explain.

Thematic Connections

- "The Human Cost of an Illiterate Society" (page 252)
- "The Plug-In Drug" (page 351)
- "Swollen Expectations" (page 425)
- "The Dog Ate My Disk — and Other Tales of Woe" (page 475)

BRENT STAPLES

Just Walk On By: A Black Man Ponders His Power to Alter Public Space

Born in Chester, Pennsylvania, in 1951, Brent Staples received his bachelor's degree from Widener University in 1973 and his doctorate in psychology from the University of Chicago in 1982. Staples joined the staff of the *New York Times* in 1985, writing on culture and politics, and he became a member of its editorial board in 1990. His columns appear regularly on the paper's op-ed pages. Staples has also written a memoir, *Parallel Time: Growing Up in Black and White* (1994), about his escape from the poverty and violence of his childhood.

Background on racial profiling: In "Just Walk On By," Staples reflects on the many times people have reacted to him as a potential threat solely because he was an African-American male. His essay can be read in light of current controversies surrounding racial profiling of criminal suspects, which occurs, according to the American Civil Liberties Union, "when the police target someone for investigation on the basis of that person's race, national origin, or ethnicity. Examples of profiling are the use of race to determine which drivers to stop for minor traffic violations ('driving while black') and the use of race to determine which motorists or pedestrians to search for contraband." Although law enforcement officials have often denied that they profile criminals solely on the basis of race, a number of studies have shown a high prevalence of police profiling directed primarily at African and Hispanic Americans. A number of states have enacted laws barring racial profiling, and some people have won court settlements when they objected to being interrogated by police solely because of their race. Since the terrorist attacks of September 11, 2001, people of Arab descent have been targets of heightened interest at airports and elsewhere, which has added to the continuing controversy surrounding the association of criminal behavior with particular ethnic groups.

My first victim was a woman — white, well dressed, probably in her early twenties. I came upon her late one evening on a deserted street in Hyde Park, a relatively affluent neighborhood in an otherwise mean, impoverished section of Chicago. As I swung onto the avenue behind her, there seemed to be a discreet, uninflammatory distance between us. Not so. She cast back a worried glance. To her, the youngish black man — a broad six feet two inches with a beard and billowing hair, both hands shoved into the pockets of a bulky military jacket — seemed menacingly close. After a few more quick glimpses, she picked up her pace and was

1

soon running in earnest. Within seconds she disappeared into a cross street.

That was more than a decade ago. I was 22 years old, a graduate student newly arrived at the University of Chicago. It was in the echo of that terrified woman's footfalls that I first began to know the unwieldy inheritance I'd come into—the ability to alter public space in ugly ways. It was clear that she thought herself the quarry of a mugger, rapist, or worse. Suffering a bout of insomnia, however, I was stalking sleep, not defenseless wayfarers. As a softy who is scarcely able to take a knife to a raw chicken—let alone hold it to a person's throat—I was surprised, embarrassed, and dismayed all at once. Her flight made me feel like an accomplice in tyranny. It also made it clear that I was indistinguishable from the muggers who occasionally seeped into the area from the surrounding ghetto. That first encounter, and those that followed, signified that a vast, unnerving gulf lay between nighttime pedestrians—particularly women—and me. And I soon gathered that being perceived as dangerous is a hazard in itself. I only needed to turn a corner into a dicey situation, or crowd some frightened, armed person in a foyer somewhere, or make an errant move after being pulled over by a policeman. Where fear and weapons meet—and they often do in urban America—there is always the possibility of death.

In that first year, my first away from my hometown, I was to become thoroughly familiar with the language of fear. At dark, shadowy intersections in Chicago, I could cross in front of a car stopped at a traffic light and elicit the *thunk, thunk, thunk, thunk* of the driver—black, white, male, or female—hammering down the door locks. On less traveled streets after dark, I grew accustomed to but never comfortable with people who crossed to the other side of the street rather than pass me. Then there were the standard unpleasantries with police, doormen, bouncers, cab drivers, and others whose business it is to screen out troublesome individuals *before* there is any nastiness.

I moved to New York nearly two years ago and I have remained an avid night walker. In central Manhattan, the near-constant crowd cover minimizes tense one-on-one street encounters. Elsewhere—visiting friends in SoHo, where sidewalks are narrow and tightly spaced buildings shut out the sky—things can get very taut indeed.

Black men have a firm place in New York mugging literature. Norman Podhoretz in his famed (or infamous) 1963 essay, "My Negro Problem—and Ours," recalls growing up in terror of black males; they "were tougher than we were, more ruthless," he writes—and as an adult on the Upper West Side of Manhattan, he continues, he cannot constrain his nervousness when he meets black men on certain streets. Similarly, a decade later, the essayist and novelist Edward Hoagland extols a New York where once "Negro bitterness bore down mainly on other Negroes." Where some see mere panhandlers, Hoagland sees "a mugger who is clearly screwing up his nerve to do more than just *ask* for money." But Hoagland has "the New

Yorker's quick-hunch posture for broken-field maneuvering," and the bad guy swerves away.

I often witness that "hunch posture," from women after dark on the warrenlike streets of Brooklyn where I live. They seem to set their faces on neutral and, with their purse straps strung across their chests bandolier style, they forge ahead as though bracing themselves against being tackled. I understand, of course, that the danger they perceive is not a hallucination. Women are particularly vulnerable to street violence, and young black males are drastically overrepresented among the perpetrators of that violence. Yet these truths are no solace against the kind of alienation that comes of being ever the suspect, against being set apart, a fearsome entity with whom pedestrians avoid making eye contact.

It is not altogether clear to me how I reached the ripe old age of 22 without being conscious of the lethality nighttime pedestrians attributed to me. Perhaps it was because in Chester, Pennsylvania, the small, angry industrial town where I came of age in the 1960s, I was scarcely noticeable against a backdrop of gang warfare, street knifings, and murders. I grew up one of the good boys, had perhaps a half-dozen fist fights. In retrospect, my shyness of combat has clear sources.

Many things go into the making of a young thug. One of those things is the consummation of the male romance with the power to intimidate. An infant discovers that random flailings send the baby bottle flying out of the crib and crashing to the floor. Delighted, the joyful babe repeats those motions again and again, seeking to duplicate the feat. Just so, I recall the points at which some of my boyhood friends were finally seduced by the perception of themselves as tough guys. When a mark cowered and surrendered his money without resistance, myth and reality merged— and paid off. It is, after all, only manly to embrace the power to frighten and intimidate. We, as men, are not supposed to give an inch of our lane on the highway; we are to seize the fighter's edge in work and in play and even in love; we are to be valiant in the face of hostile forces.

Unfortunately, poor and powerless young men seem to take all this nonsense literally. As a boy, I saw countless tough guys locked away; I have since buried several, too. They were babies, really—a teenage cousin, a brother of 22, a childhood friend in his mid-twenties—all gone down in episodes of bravado played out in the streets. I came to doubt the virtues of intimidation early on. I chose, perhaps even unconsciously, to remain a shadow—timid, but a survivor.

The fearsomeness mistakenly attributed to me in public places often has a perilous flavor. The most frightening of these confusions occurred in the late 1970s and early 1980s when I worked as a journalist in Chicago. One day, rushing into the office of a magazine I was writing for with a deadline story in hand, I was mistaken for a burglar. The office manager called security and, with an ad hoc posse, pursued me through the labyrinthine halls, nearly to my editor's door. I had no way of proving who I was. I could only move briskly toward the company of someone who knew me.

Another time I was on assignment for a local paper and killing time
before an interview. I entered a jewelry store on the city's affluent Near
North Side. The proprietor excused herself and returned with an enormous red Doberman pinscher straining at the end of a leash. She stood,
the dog extended toward me, silent to my questions, her eyes bulging
nearly out of her head. I took a cursory look around, nodded, and bade her
good night. Relatively speaking, however, I never fared as badly as another
black male journalist. He went to nearby Waukegan, Illinois, a couple of
summers ago to work on a story about a murderer who was born there.
Mistaking the reporter for the killer, police hauled him from his car at
gunpoint and but for his press credentials would probably have tried to
book him. Such episodes are not uncommon. Black men trade tales like
this all the time.

In "My Negro Problem—and Ours," Podhoretz writes that the hatred
he feels for blacks makes itself known to him through a variety of avenues—
one being his discomfort with that "special brand of paranoid touchiness"
to which he says blacks are prone. No doubt he is speaking here of black
men. In time, I learned to smother the rage I felt at so often being taken for
a criminal. Not to do so would surely have led to madness—via that special
"paranoid touchiness" that so annoyed Podhoretz at the time he wrote the
essay.

I began to take precautions to make myself less threatening. I move
about with care, particularly late in the evening. I give a wide berth to nervous people on subway platforms during the wee hours, particularly when
I have exchanged business clothes for jeans. If I happen to be entering a
building behind some people who appear skittish, I may walk by, letting
them clear the lobby before I return, so as not to seem to be following
them. I have been calm and extremely congenial on those rare occasions
when I've been pulled over by the police.

And on late-evening constitutionals along streets less traveled by, I
employ what has proved to be an excellent tension-reducing measure: I
whistle melodies from Beethoven and Vivaldi and the more popular classical composers. Even steely New Yorkers hunching toward nighttime destinations seem to relax, and occasionally they even join in the tune. Virtually
everybody seems to sense that a mugger wouldn't be warbling bright,
sunny selections from Vivaldi's *Four Seasons.* It is my equivalent of the cow-
bell that hikers wear when they know they are in bear country.

•   •   •

Comprehension

1. Why does Staples characterize the woman he encounters in paragraph 1
   as a "victim"?
2. What does Staples mean when he says he has the power to "alter public space" (2)?

3. Why does Staples walk the streets at night?

4. What things does Staples say contribute to "the making of a young thug" (8)? According to Staples, why are young, poor, and powerless men especially likely to become thugs?

5. How does Staples attempt to make himself less threatening?

Purpose and Audience

1. What is Staples's thesis? Does he state it or imply it?

2. Does Staples use logic, emotion, or a combination of the two to appeal to his readers? How appropriate is his strategy?

3. What preconceptions does Staples assume his audience has? How does he challenge these preconceptions?

4. What is Staples trying to accomplish with his first sentence? Do you think he succeeds? Why or why not?

Style and Structure

1. Why does Staples mention Norman Podhoretz? Could he make the same points without referring to Podhoretz's essay?

2. Staples begins his essay with an anecdote. How effective is this strategy? Do you think another opening strategy would be more effective? Explain.

3. Does Staples present enough examples to support his thesis? Are they representative? Would other types of examples be more convincing? Explain.

4. In what order does Staples present his examples? Would another order be more effective? Explain.

Vocabulary Projects

1. Define each of the following words as it is used in this selection.

discreet (1)	quarry (2)	constrain (5)
uninflammatory (1)	insomnia (2)	bravado (9)
billowing (1)	wayfarers (2)	constitutionals (14)

2. In his essay, Staples uses the word *thug*. List as many synonyms as you can for this word. Do all these words convey the same idea, or do they differ in their connotations? Explain.

Journal Entry

Have you ever been in a situation such as the ones Staples describes, where you perceived someone (or someone perceived you) as threatening? How did you react? After reading Staples's essay, do you think you would react the same way now?

Writing Workshop

1. Use your journal entry to help you write an essay using a single long example to support this statement: "When walking alone at night, you can (or cannot) be too careful."

2. Relying on examples from your own experience, write an essay discussing what part you think race plays in people's reactions to Staples. Do you think his perceptions are accurate?

3. How accurate is Staples's observation concerning the "male romance with the power to intimidate" (8)? What does he mean by this statement? What examples from your own experience support (or do not support) the idea that this "romance" is an element of male upbringing in our society?

Combining the Patterns

In paragraph 8, Staples uses **cause and effect** to demonstrate what goes "into the making of a young thug." Would several **examples** have better explained how a youth becomes a thug?

Thematic Connections

- "Finishing School" (page 101)
- "The 'Black Table' Is Still There" (page 366)
- "The Ways We Lie" (page 495)
- "The Wife Beater" (page 532)

Star-Spangled Stupidity

Dick Teresi is primarily a science writer who in 1978 was one of the cofounders of *Omni,* the first glossy magazine devoted to matters of science and science fiction. He has also contributed essays and reviews to *Discover,* the *New York Times Magazine, The Atlantic Monthly,* and the *New York Times Book Review.* The 1994 American Institute of Physics Award winner for Science Writing, Teresi is the coauthor, with physicist Leon Lederman, of *The God Particle: If the Universe Is the Answer, What Is the Question?* (1993) and author most recently of *Lost Discoveries: The Ancient Roots of Modern Science from the Babylonians to the Maya* (2002). In this 2004 op-ed piece for the *Wall Street Journal,* Teresi tackles a very different subject: the mistreatment of the American flag by self-styled patriots.

Background on the American flag: The early revolutionaries developed flags of various designs, the most common consisting of a representation of the British Union Jack (overlapping red and white crosses on a blue background) against a field of thirteen alternating red and white stripes. The origin of the substitution of thirteen stars on a blue background for the Union Jack is unclear. One story has it that George Washington, concerned that the use of the Union Jack smacked of British patriotism, roughed out a design that included 13 stars and stripes and brought it to Philadelphia upholsterer and seamstress Betsy Ross, who suggested arranging the stars in a circle. Supposedly, Ross sewed the first Stars and Stripes in the early summer of 1776, prior to the signing of the Declaration of Independence. (This story comes from her grandson, writing in the 1880s.) Officially, the stars and stripes of the American flag resulted from a resolution adopted by the Second Continental Congress at Philadelphia in 1777. After the admission of Kentucky and Vermont to the United States, the flag was expanded in 1794 to include fifteen stars and stripes, but it soon became apparent that the admission of subsequent states would require an unwieldy number of stripes, so it was determined that the stripes would return to thirteen to represent the thirteen original colonies and that the stars would represent the number of states. (The most recent redesign of the flag came in 1959 with the admission of Hawaii.) No protocol for the treatment of the flag, as described by Teresi, was developed until the Flag Code of 1923, passed into law in 1942 and amended in 1974.

This July 4 holiday will no doubt cause a lot of people "to put out more flags," to borrow a phrase from Evelyn Waugh's 1941 novel about wartime patriotism. All well and good. But can't it be done the right way? Since Sept. 11, 2001, the American flag has come in for a strange kind of abuse from "overnight patriots," as one long-suffering, third-generation former Marine, Robert Hudson Westover, puts it.

Shortly after the terrorist attacks, for example, I was taking my usual   2
bike ride on Route 47 in western Massachusetts when I heard an enormous
pickup truck bearing down on me. No problem. I veered toward the shoulder. Then, whap! I was belted about the face and shoulders by a plastic
American flag. Then, a fraction of a second later, whap! again. The rear
flag got me, too.

This guy had flags on all four fenders and a larger one horizontally   3
draped on the pickup bed. Later, as I passed the local XXX-rated video
store, I saw his truck, and others festooned with flags, parked in front. (I
guess if we don't exercise our right to view porn, then the terrorists have
won.) Each vehicle had flag poles inserted into every orifice in its chassis.

As the weeks wore on, I saw more and more vehicles with four or more   4
flags. A gas station on Route 9 erected six flags atop its pumps. The gas
station across the road responded with 14 flags. It was hard to decide
which station selling Arab oil was the more patriotic. On TV, I believe it
was CNN that was the first to display a cute little computer-generated wav-
ing flag next to its logo 24 hours a day. The National Football League kept
pace, sewing little flags on every team's uniform — to assure over-charged
fans, no doubt, that they weren't watching cut-rate Canadian football.

At the U.S. Post Office, I watched the local postmaster raise the flag   5
halfway, then leave it there. I asked if he'd like some help with that, and he
just glowered and walked briskly inside. My town of Amherst, Mass., got
into big trouble. From the common, says town manager Barry Del
Castilho, you can see seven proper flags (on poles with ropes for raising
and lowering — real flags), and on holidays we break out 29 "decorative"
flags (flags-on-a-stick). Certain citizens insisted that the town fly the decorative flags five months a year in the aftermath of 9/11. The town refused,
and this news hit the wire services and CNN, with all of us here branded as
un-American.

Flag abuse hasn't let up. Bakeries are designing "cake flags." Florists   6
offer red-white-and-blue "flag bouquets." This week my local doughnut
shop is selling a giant "flag doughnut." Do I eat it or salute it?

I have bristled under this star-spangled degradation for almost three   7
years. I like the American flag: the design, the colors and the way it has
evolved through the centuries to represent our ever-changing nation, rearranging its stars but never its stripes. I suspect many other Americans,
those who know what half-mast means, are bristling also but unwilling to
speak out, fearing to fault the errant flag wavers lest they themselves be
labeled unpatriotic. Independence Day seems like a good time to rebel
against this conspiracy of silence.

People are breaking rules they should have learned in sixth grade, in   8
the military or at Boy Scout camp. Here are just a few:

• The flag must be *lowered* to half-mast. This means it must be raised   9
first to the top of the pole, then brought down. Raising it only halfway
shows no respect for the person being honored. It says instead, "Thanks for
dying. You saved me the trouble of raising the flag to the top." By the way,

half-mast doesn't actually mean 50 percent. You fly the flag at three-quarters height.

• More is not better. On a vehicle, you are allowed one (1) decorative flag, 10 positioned at the right rear fender. And take it off at night or in bad weather.

• Get the flag off your pickup bed. Don't let it touch the ground or go 11 horizontal on any surface. There are some exceptions. Of course we want to see the flag on military caskets. If you captain an aircraft carrier, a large flag painted on the deck is handy so your pilots can identify you from the air. But the roof of your Ford Explorer is another matter.

• Those bins of little American flags you see at discount stores? Please. 12 Same deal as above. The basic rule is that the flag is a living thing and should be treated with respect.

• Flags on cakes, soda cans or beer mugs? No. The flag, or any part of 13 it, cannot be printed or impressed on anything designed for temporary use or consumption. Nor can it be printed on a receptacle. The same rule applies to clothing or the flags on NFL uniforms. A flag patch may, however, be worn on the uniforms of military personnel, firefighters and police. A fluttery flag embracing the CNN logo? Nuh uh. You can't use the flag in an advertisement or associate it with a product. CNN is a product. It was mind-numbing to watch my town portrayed as unpatriotic on a TV screen that displayed one of the most flagrant abuses of flag etiquette.

• Neither rain of day nor gloom of night may keep the Post Office 14 from its appointed rounds, but you can't leave your flag up in precipitation or after sundown unless it's illuminated. If your neighbor leaves a flag stuck to his SUV all night, affix a flashlight next to it to avoid the insult.

• Decorative flags: Those stationary flags that towns fly during holi- 15 days are meant only for special occasions. For one thing, they are fixed to poles and thus cannot be lowered to half-mast during days of national mourning. Our local patriots simply moved the flags on their sticks. This is half-assed, not half-mast. Part of the tribute is in the actual raising and lowering of the flag in public.

That's some of it. The rules are easily learned and spelled out in the 16 U.S. Code, Title 36, Chapter 10, available on the Internet at several sites. There are some fine points, but Lt. Col. Jack O'Brien, a professor of military science at Drexel University, says nitpicking isn't necessary.

For example, this July 4 weekend presents a quandary. The death of 17 President Reagan, according to the code, requires flags to be flown at half-mast for 30 days, through July 5. But on the holiday towns like to fly decorative flags that cannot be properly lowered to half-mast. This is not an infraction that upsets Lt. Col. O'Brien. He says to go ahead, fly the improper flags. Nor does it bother him that most people do not realize that on Memorial Day the flag should be flown half-mast until noon, then raised. It is fading or tattered flags, and especially commercial flag paraphernalia, that upset him.

The point isn't to intimidate or shame pick-up drivers or other well-   18
meaning flag-wavers. It is merely to suggest that, if you're going to be
patriotic, do it right. This isn't pedantry. It's simple respect.

Former Marine Westover often talks about the flag with his grandfa-   19
ther, George Westover, who survived the Pearl Harbor attack and later witnessed the raising of the flag on Iwo Jima. They're both weary of "flags up
all night, of flag patches on people's butts" and of being called unpatriotic
because they don't follow suit.

Oh, and about burning the flag. It's the only proper way to destroy it.   20

•   •   •

Comprehension

1. According to Teresi, what problems has increased patriotism caused
   for those, like him, who love the flag? What is the "strange kind of
   abuse" the flag has been subject to (1)?
2. What "conspiracy of silence" does Teresi think it is time to rebel
   against (7)? Why do you think he has kept quiet for almost three years
   since September 11?
3. According to Teresi, where do people generally learn the rules about
   how to treat the flag? Do you think he is correct?
4. What is the proper way to lower a flag to half-mast? Why does Teresi
   think this protocol is so important?
5. Teresi says he is not primarily concerned about the individual rules.
   What is his primary concern?

Purpose and Audience

1. What is Teresi's attitude toward his readers? How do you know? How
   much does he assume his readers know about flag etiquette?
2. Where in the essay does Teresi state his thesis? Why does he wait so
   long to state it?
3. In paragraph 16, Teresi refers readers to the U.S. Code for more rules
   about treating the flag. What purpose does he have? Do you think he
   actually expects readers to refer to the U.S. Code?
4. Do you think Teresi has a serious message to convey, or do you think
   he is just trying to entertain his readers? What do you think his message is?

Style and Structure

1. Why does Teresi begin his essay with several paragraphs of short
   examples? Would a single long example have been more effective?
   Explain.

2. How does Teresi introduce his list of rules? Should he have introduced them more formally? More fully?

3. Teresi presents his rules as a bulleted list. What would he have gained or lost by presenting these rules simply as paragraphs?

4. Teresi includes quotations both in his introduction and in his conclusion. What do these quotations add to his essay?

5. Teresi ends his essay with a one-sentence paragraph. Would his essay have been stronger without this sentence? Explain.

6. At times — for example, "Same deal as above" in paragraph 12 — Teresi uses a highly informal style. Does this style weaken his credibility? Explain.

Vocabulary Projects

1. Define each of the following words as it is used in this selection.

veered (2)	bristled (7)	quandary (17)
festooned (3)	degradation (7)	infraction (17)
orifice (3)	conspiracy (7)	paraphernalia (17)
logo (4)	flagrant (13)	intimidate (18)
briskly (5)	affix (14)	pedantry (18)
aftermath (5)	nitpicking (16)	

2. Teresi uses a number of colloquial words and phrases in his essay — for example, *guy* in paragraph 3. Underline as many of these informal words and phrases as you can. Then, substitute other words and phrases better suited for college writing. What effect do your changes have? Why do you think Teresi chose to use so many colloquial words and phrases? Do they help or hurt his essay?

Journal Entry

How do you react to the American flag? Do you think Teresi's essay makes a good point?

Writing Workshop

1. Review Teresi's list of rules for how to treat the flag. Decide which of these rules you think make sense and which do not. Then, write an essay presenting your conclusions. Remember, each of the rules you discuss will be an example that supports your thesis.

2. Write an essay making the case that it is not the flag itself but what it stands for that is important. Use examples from your own experience to support your thesis.

3. Recently, several members of Congress have talked about proposing legislation — or even an amendment to the United States Constitution — to prevent people from intentionally damaging the flag. Do

you think such a step is necessary? Write an essay presenting your opinion. Support your points with examples from your own experience as well as with references to Teresi's essay.

Combining the Patterns

This essay's main pattern of development is **exemplification**. Does Teresi use any other patterns? How would a paragraph of **comparison and contrast** — comparing how he treats the flag with the way others treat it — help support his thesis? Do you think Teresi should have included such a paragraph? Why, or why not?

Thematic Connections

- "Ground Zero" (page 162)
- "The Power of Words in Wartime" (page 377)
- "Two Ways to Belong in America" (page 415)
- The Declaration of Independence (page 584)

JONATHAN KOZOL

The Human Cost
of an Illiterate Society

Jonathan Kozol was born in Boston in 1936 and graduated from Harvard University in 1958. After studying in England, he began teaching in public schools in Boston's inner city. His experiences there provided the source material for his first book, *Death at an Early Age* (1967), a startling indictment of the system's failure to provide an adequate education to poor, mostly minority children. In the years since, Kozol—himself a child of privilege—has continued to use firsthand experience to write about the poorest in our society, sometimes angrily, sometimes movingly, but always with respect and sympathy. His books have focused on homelessness, on the inequities between schools in poor neighborhoods and those in affluent ones, and, most recently, on what he calls "apartheid schooling" in America.

Background on illiteracy in the United States: Kozol's *Illiterate America* (1985) examines the human and financial costs of illiteracy in the United States. The book estimates that more than 35 million Americans read below the level needed to function in society. A comprehensive survey published in 1993 seemed to support Kozol's estimates, reporting that more than 40 million adults—as much as 23 percent of the population—scored at the lowest of five levels on a series of standardized reading tests. Some critics have claimed that these results are misleading because the lowest level included some people who could not read at all and others who were functional readers who could perform some reading tasks. Still, literacy in the United States remains a matter of concern. In a recent report by the Educational Testing Service, analysis of the results of the 1993 U.S. study and a later international literacy study found that the United States ranked only twelfth in terms of literacy among twenty comparably wealthy nations and ranked first or second in terms of inequality in the distribution of literacy skills.

PRECAUTIONS. READ BEFORE USING.
Poison: Contains sodium hydroxide (caustic soda-lye).
Corrosive: Causes severe eye and skin damage, may cause blindness.
Harmful or fatal if swallowed.
If swallowed, give large quantities of milk or water.
Do not induce vomiting.
Important: Keep water out of can at all times to prevent contents
from violently erupting. . . .
—Warning on a can of Drano

Questions of literacy, in Socrates' belief, must at length be judged as   1
matters of morality. Socrates could not have had in mind the moral com-

promise peculiar to a nation like our own. Some of our Founding Fathers did, however, have this question in their minds. One of the wisest of those Founding Fathers (one who may not have been most compassionate but surely was more prescient than some of his peers) recognized the special dangers that illiteracy would pose to basic equity in the political construction that he helped to shape.

"A people who mean to be their own governors," James Madison wrote, "must arm themselves with the power knowledge gives. A popular government without popular information or the means of acquiring it, is but a prologue to a farce or a tragedy, or perhaps both." 2

Tragedy looms larger than farce in the United States today. Illiterate citizens seldom vote. Those who do are forced to cast a vote of questionable worth. They cannot make informed decisions based on serious print information. Sometimes they can be alerted to their interests by aggressive voter education. More frequently, they vote for a face, a smile, or a style, not for a mind or character or body of beliefs. 3

The number of illiterate adults exceeds by 16 million the entire vote cast for the winner in the 1980 presidential contest. If even one third of all illiterates could vote, and read enough and do sufficient math to vote in their self-interest, Ronald Reagan would not likely have been chosen president. There is, of course, no way to know for sure. We do know this: Democracy is a mendacious term when used by those who are prepared to countenance the forced exclusion of one third of our electorate. So long as 60 million people are denied significant participation, the government is neither of, nor for, nor by, the people. It is a government, at best, of those two-thirds whose wealth, skin color, or parental privilege allows them opportunity to profit from the provocation and instruction of the written word. 4

The undermining of democracy in the United States is one "expense" that sensitive Americans can easily deplore because it represents a contradiction that endangers citizens of all political positions. The human price is not so obvious at first. 5

Since I first immersed myself within this work I have often had the following dream: I find that I am in a railroad station or a large department store within a city that is utterly unknown to me and where I cannot understand the printed words. None of the signs or symbols is familiar. Everything looks strange: like mirror writing of some kind. Gradually I understand that I am in the Soviet Union. All the letters on the walls around me are Cyrillic. I look for my pocket dictionary but I find that it has been mislaid. Where have I left it? Then I recall that I forgot to bring it with me when I packed my bags in Boston. I struggle to remember the name of my hotel. I try to ask somebody for directions. One person stops and looks at me in a peculiar way. I lose the nerve to ask. At last I reach into my wallet for an ID card. The card is missing. Have I lost it? Then I remember that my card was confiscated for some reason, many years before. Around this point, I wake up in a panic. 6

This panic is not so different from the misery that millions of adult 7
illiterates experience each day within the course of their routine existence
in the U.S.A.

Illiterates cannot read the menu in a restaurant. 8

They cannot read the cost of items on the menu in the *window* of the 9
restaurant before they enter.

Illiterates cannot read the letters that their children bring home from 10
their teachers. They cannot study school department circulars that tell
them of the courses that their children must be taking if they hope to pass
the SAT exams. They cannot help with homework. They cannot write a letter to the teacher. They are afraid to visit in the classroom. They do not
want to humiliate their child or themselves.

Illiterates cannot read instructions on a bottle of prescription medi- 11
cine. They cannot find out when a medicine is past the year of safe consumption; nor can they read of allergenic risks, warnings to diabetics, or
the potential sedative effect of certain kinds of nonprescription pills. They
cannot observe preventive health care admonitions. They cannot read
about "the seven warning signs of cancer" or the indications of blood-
sugar fluctuations or the risks of eating certain foods that aggravate the
likelihood of cardiac arrest.

Illiterates live, in more than literal ways, an uninsured existence. They 12
cannot understand the written details on a health insurance form. They
cannot read the waivers that they sign preceding surgical procedures. Several women I have known in Boston have entered a slum hospital with the
intention of obtaining a tubal ligation and have emerged a few days later
after having been subjected to a hysterectomy. Unaware of their rights, in-
cognizant of jargon, intimidated by the unfamiliar air of fear and atmosphere of ether that so many of us find oppressive in the confines even of
the most attractive and expensive medical facilities, they have signed their
names to documents they could not read and which nobody, in the hectic
situation that prevails so often in those overcrowded hospitals that serve
the urban poor, had even bothered to explain.

Childbirth might seem to be the last inalienable right of any female 13
citizen within a civilized society. Illiterate mothers, as we shall see, already
have been cheated of the power to protect their progeny against the likelihood of demolition in deficient public schools and, as a result, against the
verbal servitude within which they themselves exist. Surgical denial of the
right to bear that child in the first place represents an ultimate denial, an
unspeakable metaphor, a final darkness that denies even the twilight
gleamings of our own humanity. What greater violation of our biological,
our biblical, our spiritual humanity could possibly exist than that which
takes place nightly, perhaps hourly these days, within such overburdened
and benighted institutions as the Boston City Hospital? Illiteracy has
many costs; few are so irreversible as this.

Even the roof above one's head, the gas or other fuel for heating that 14
protects the residents of northern city slums against the threat of illness in

the winter months become uncertain guarantees. Illiterates cannot read the lease that they must sign to live in an apartment which, too often, they cannot afford. They cannot manage check accounts and therefore seldom pay for anything by mail. Hours and entire days of difficult travel (and the cost of bus or other public transit) must be added to the real cost of whatever they consume. Loss of interest on the check accounts they do not have, and could not manage if they did, must be regarded as another of the excess costs paid by the citizen who is excluded from the common instruments of commerce in a numerate society.

"I couldn't understand the bills," a woman in Washington, D.C.,   15
reports, "and then I couldn't write the checks to pay them. We signed things we didn't know what they were."

Illiterates cannot read the notices that they receive from welfare offices   16
or from the IRS. They must depend on word-of-mouth instruction from the welfare worker—or from other persons whom they have good reason to mistrust. They do not know what rights they have, what deadlines and requirements they face, what options they might choose to exercise. They are half-citizens. Their rights exist in print but not in fact.

Illiterates cannot look up numbers in a telephone directory. Even if   17
they can find the names of friends, few possess the sorting skills to make use of the yellow pages; categories are bewildering and trade names are beyond decoding capabilities for millions of nonreaders. Even the emergency numbers listed on the first page of the phone book—"Ambulance," "Police," and "Fire"—are too frequently beyond the recognition of non-readers.

Many illiterates cannot read the admonition on a pack of cigarettes.   18
Neither the Surgeon General's warning nor its reproduction on the package can alert them to the risks. Although most people learn by word of mouth that smoking is related to a number of grave physical disorders, they do not get the chance to read the detailed stories which can document this danger with the vividness that turns concern into determination to resist. They can see the handsome cowboy or the slim Virginia lady lighting up a filter cigarette; they cannot heed the words that tell them that this product is (not "may be") dangerous to their health. Sixty million men and women are condemned to be the unalerted, high-risk candidates for cancer.

Illiterates do not buy "no-name" products in the supermarkets. They   19
must depend on photographs or the familiar logos that are printed on the packages of brand-name groceries. The poorest people, therefore, are denied the benefits of the least costly products.

Illiterates depend almost entirely upon label recognition. Many labels,   20
however, are not easy to distinguish. Dozens of different kinds of Campbell's soup appear identical to the nonreader. The purchaser who cannot read and does not dare to ask for help, out of the fear of being stigmatized (a fear which is unfortunately realistic), frequently comes home with something which she never wanted and her family never tasted.

Illiterates cannot read instructions on a pack of frozen food. Packages 21 sometimes provide an illustration to explain the cooking preparations; but illustrations are of little help to someone who must "boil water, drop the food — *within* its plastic wrapper — in the boiling water, wait for it to simmer, instantly remove."

Even when labels are seemingly clear, they may be easily mistaken. A 22 woman in Detroit brought home a gallon of Crisco for her children's dinner. She thought that she had bought the chicken that was pictured on the label. She had enough Crisco now to last a year — but no more money to go back and buy the food for dinner.

Recipes provided on the packages of certain staples sometimes tempt a 23 semiliterate person to prepare a meal her children have not tasted. The longing to vary the uniform and often starchy content of low-budget meals provided to the family that relies on food stamps commonly leads to ruinous results. Scarce funds have been wasted and the food must be thrown out. The same applies to distribution of food-surplus produce in emergency conditions. Government inducements to poor people to "explore the ways" by which to make a tasty meal from tasteless noodles, surplus cheese, and powdered milk are useless to nonreaders. Intended as benevolent advice, such recommendations mock reality and foster deeper feelings of resentment and of inability to cope. (Those, on the other hand, who cautiously refrain from "innovative" recipes in preparation of their children's meals must suffer the opprobrium of "laziness," "lack of imagination. . . .")

Illiterates cannot travel freely. When they attempt to do so, they 24 encounter risks that few of us can dream of. They cannot read traffic signs and, while they often learn to recognize and to decipher symbols, they cannot manage street names which they haven't seen before. The same is true for bus and subway stops. While ingenuity can sometimes help a man or woman to discern directions from familiar landmarks, buildings, cemeteries, churches, and the like, most illiterates are virtually immobilized. They seldom wander past the streets and neighborhoods they know. Geographical paralysis becomes a bitter metaphor for their entire existence. They are immobilized in almost every sense we can imagine. They can't move up. They can't move out. They cannot see beyond. Illiterates may take an oral test for drivers' permits in most sections of America. It is a questionable concession. Where will they go? How will they get there? How will they get home? Could it be that some of us might like it better if they stayed where they belong?

Travel is only one of many instances of circumscribed existence. 25 Choice, in almost all of its facets, is diminished in the life of an illiterate adult. Even the printed TV schedule, which provides most people with the luxury of preselection, does not belong within the arsenal of options in illiterate existence. One consequence is that the viewer watches only what appears at moments when he happens to have time to turn the switch. Another consequence, a lot more common, is that the TV set remains in operation night and day. Whatever the program offered at the hour when he walks into the room will be the nutriment that he accepts and swallows. Thus, to passivity, is added frequency—indeed, almost uninterrupted continuity. Freedom to select is no more possible here than in the choice of home or surgery or food.

"You don't choose," said one illiterate woman. "You take your wishes   26
from somebody else." Whether in perusal of a menu, selection of highways, purchase of groceries, or determination of affordable enjoyment, illiterate Americans must trust somebody else: a friend, a relative, a stranger on the street, a grocery clerk, a TV copywriter.

"All of our mail we get, it's hard for her to read. Settin' down and writ-   27
ing a letter, she can't do it. Like if we get a bill . . . we take it over to my sister-in-law. . . . My sister-in-law reads it."

Billing agencies harass poor people for the payment of the bills for   28
purchases that might have taken place six months before. Utility companies offer an agreement for a staggered payment schedule on a bill past due. "You have to trust them," one man said. Precisely for this reason, you end up by trusting no one and suspecting everyone of possible deceit. A submerged sense of distrust becomes the corollary to a constant need to trust. "They are cheating me. . . . I have been tricked. . . . I do not know. . . ."

Not knowing: This is a familiar theme. Not knowing the right word for   29
the right thing at the right time is one form of subjugation. Not knowing the world that lies concealed behind those words is a more terrifying feeling. The longitude and latitude of one's existence are beyond all easy apprehension. Even the hard, cold stars within the firmament above one's head begin to mock the possibilities for self-location. Where am I? Where did I come from? Where will I go?

"I've lost a lot of jobs," one man explains. "Today, even if you're a jani-   30
tor, there's still reading and writing. . . . They leave a note saying 'Go to room so-and-so. . . .' You can't do it. You can't read it. You don't know."

"The hardest thing about it is that I've been places where I didn't know   31
where I was. You don't know where you are. . . . You're lost."

"Like I said: I have two kids. What do I do if one of my kids starts chok-   32
ing? I go running to the phone. . . . I can't look up the hospital phone number. That's if we're at home. Out on the street, I can't read the sign. I get to a pay phone. 'Okay, tell us where you are. We'll send an ambulance.' I look at the street sign. Right there, I can't tell you what it says. I'd have to spell it out, letter for letter. By that time, one of my kids would be dead. . . . These are the kinds of fears you go with, every single day. . . ."

"Reading directions, I suffer with. I work with chemicals. . . . That's   33
scary to begin with. . . ."

"You sit down. They throw the menu in front of you. Where do you go   34
from there? Nine times out of ten you say, 'Go ahead. Pick out something for the both of us.' I've eaten some weird things, let me tell you!"

Menus. Chemicals. A child choking while his mother searches for a   35
word she does not know to find assistance that will come too late. Another

mother speaks about the inability to help her kids to read: "I can't read to them. Of course that's leaving them out of something they should have. Oh, it matters. You *believe* it matters! I ordered all these books. The kids belong to a book club. Donny wanted me to read a book to him. I told Donny: 'I can't read.' He said: 'Mommy, you sit down. I'll read it to you.' I tried it one day, reading from the pictures. Donny looked at me. He said, 'Mommy, that's not right.' He's only five. He knew I couldn't read. . . ."

A landlord tells a woman that her lease allows him to evict her if her   36
baby cries and causes inconvenience to her neighbors. The consequence of challenging his words conveys a danger which appears, unlikely as it seems, even more alarming than the danger of eviction. Once she admits that she can't read, in the desire to maneuver for the time in which to call a friend, she will have defined herself in terms of an explicit impotence that she cannot endure. Capitulation in this case is preferable to self-humiliation. Resisting the definition of oneself in terms of what one cannot do, what others take for granted, represents a need so great that other imperatives (even one so urgent as the need to keep one's home in winter's cold) evaporate and fall away in face of fear. Even the loss of home and shelter, in this case, is not so terrifying as the loss of self.

"I come out of school. I was sixteen. They had their meetings. The   37
directors meet. They said that I was wasting their school paper. I was wasting pencils. . . ."

Another illiterate, looking back, believes she was not worthy of her   38
teacher's time. She believes that it was wrong of her to take up space within her school. She believes that it was right to leave in order that somebody more deserving could receive her place.

Children choke. Their mother chokes another way: on more than   39
chicken bones.

People eat what others order, know what others tell them, struggle not   40
to see themselves as they believe the world perceives them. A man in California speaks about his own loss of identity, of self-location, definition:

"I stood at the bottom of the ramp. My car had broke down on the   41
freeway. There was a phone. I asked for the police. They was nice. They said to tell them where I was. I looked up at the signs. There was one that I had seen before. I read it to them: ONE WAY STREET. They thought it was a joke. I told them I couldn't read. There was other signs above the ramp. They told me to try. I looked around for somebody to help. All the cars was going by real fast. I couldn't make them understand that I was lost. The cop was nice. He told me: 'Try once more.' I did my best. I couldn't read. I only knew the sign above my head. The cop was trying to be nice. He knew that I was trapped. 'I can't send out a car to you if you can't tell me where you are.' I felt afraid. I nearly cried. I'm forty-eight years old. I only said: 'I'm on a one-way street. . . .' "

The legal problems and the courtroom complications that confront   42
illiterate adults have been discussed above. The anguish that may underlie such matters was brought home to me this year while I was working on

this book. I have spoken [in an earlier part of the book] of a sudden phone call from one of my former students, now in prison for a criminal offense. Stephen is not a boy today. He is twenty-eight years old. He called to ask me to assist him in his trial, which comes up next fall. He will be on trial for murder. He has just knifed and killed a man who first enticed him to his home, then cheated him, and then insulted him — as "an illiterate subhuman."

Stephen now faces twenty years to life. Stephen's mother was illiterate. 43
His grandparents were illiterate as well. What parental curse did not destroy was killed off finally by the schools. Silent violence is repaid with interest. It will cost us $25,000 yearly to maintain this broken soul in prison. But what is the price that has been paid by Stephen's victim? What is the price that will be paid by Stephen?

Perhaps we might slow down a moment here and look at the realities 44
described above. This is the nation that we live in. This is a society that most of us did not create but which our President and other leaders have been willing to sustain by virtue of malign neglect. Do we possess the character and courage to address a problem which so many nations, poorer than our own, have found it natural to correct?

The answers to these questions represent a reasonable test of our belief 45
in the democracy to which we have been asked in public school to swear allegiance.

· · ·

Comprehension

1. In what sense is illiteracy a danger to a democratic society?

2. According to Kozol, why do our reactions to the problem of illiteracy in America test our belief in democracy?

3. What does Kozol mean when he says that an illiterate person leads a "circumscribed existence" (25)? How does being illiterate limit a person's choices?

4. What legal problems and courtroom complications confront illiterate adults?

5. According to Kozol, what are people doing to solve the problem of illiteracy in the United States?

Purpose and Audience

1. What is Kozol's thesis? Where does he state it?

2. Kozol aims his essay at a general audience. How does he address the needs of this audience? How would his discussion differ if it were intended for an audience of reading specialists? Of politicians?

3. Is Kozol's purpose to inform, to persuade, to express emotions, or some combination of these three? Does he have additional, more specific purposes as well? Explain.

Style and Structure

1. Why does Kozol introduce his essay with references to Socrates and James Madison? How does this strategy help him support his thesis?
2. In paragraph 6, Kozol recounts a dream he often has. Why does he include this anecdote? How does it help him make the transition from his introduction to the body of his essay?
3. Kozol uses many short examples to make his point. Do you think fewer examples developed in more depth would be more effective? Why or why not?
4. How effective is Kozol's use of statistics? Do the statistics support or undercut his examples of the personal cost of illiteracy?

Vocabulary Projects

1. Define each of the following words as it is used in this selection.

prescient (1)	sedative (11)	opprobrium (23)
farce (2)	admonitions (11)	concession (24)
mendacious (4)	incognizant (12)	firmament (29)
countenance (4)	jargon (12)	capitulation (36)
Cyrillic (6)	numerate (14)	

2. Reread paragraphs 24 and 25, and determine which words or phrases convey Kozol's feelings toward his subject. Rewrite these two paragraphs, eliminating as much subjective language as you can. Do you think your changes make the paragraphs more (or less) appealing to a general audience? To a group of sociologists? To a group of reading teachers?

Journal Entry

Keep a detailed record of your activities for a day. Then, discuss the difficulty you would have carrying out each activity in your daily routine if you were illiterate.

Writing Workshop

1. Using your journal entry as a starting point, write an essay describing the tasks you would have difficulty accomplishing if you could not read. Include an explicit thesis statement, and use examples to illustrate your points.

2. Six hundred years ago, most people could not read, but they could still function in society. Similarly, many people today are not computer literate. Do you believe such people can still function well as citizens, as employees, and as parents?

3. Using Kozol's essay as source material, write an essay using as your thesis James Madison's statement, "A people who mean to be their own governors must arm themselves with the power knowledge gives" (2). Be sure to document any information you borrow from Kozol.

Combining the Patterns

Why does Kozol choose to end his essay with a **narrative** about Stephen, one of his former students, who is in jail awaiting trial for murder? How does this anecdote help Kozol set up his concluding remarks in paragraphs 44 and 45?

Thematic Connections

- "Words Left Unspoken" (page 168)
- "Mother Tongue" (page 487)
- "The Untouchable" (page 516)
- "Strange Tools" (page 743)

Samuel (Fiction)

Grace Paley (b. 1922) grew up in New York City and attended Hunter College there. Initially interested in poetry, she began writing short fiction in the 1950s while raising a family and participating in a number of political causes. Her stories have been published in the collections *Little Disturbances of Man* (1959), *Enormous Changes at the Last Minute* (1974), and *Later the Same Day* (1985). Her *Collected Stories* appeared in 1994 and was nominated for a National Book Award. "Samuel," originally published in *The Atlantic Monthly,* was reprinted in Paley's 1974 collection of stories.

Background on the generation gap: During the 1960s, the term *generation gap* was coined to describe the differences in attitudes toward drug use, the Vietnam War, fashion, music, lifestyle, and politics between parents and their teenage children. While generational differences have always existed, the gap between the "baby-boomers" and their parents seemed to be magnified significantly — perhaps because of the vast size of the baby-boom generation. "Samuel" is set during the 1960s and reflects the social and political upheaval within American society at that time. Much of the younger generation was rebelling against government policies and cultural conformity, while many older people felt fearful of or antagonistic toward the young people and minorities who were challenging the status quo. "Samuel" touches on these complexities and raises difficult questions about responsibility and loss.

Some boys are very tough. They're afraid of nothing. They are the ones who climb a wall and take a bow at the top. Not only are they brave on the roof, but they make a lot of noise in the darkest part of the cellar where even the super hates to go. They also jiggle and hop on the platform between the locked doors of the subway cars. 1

Four boys are jiggling on the swaying platform. Their names are Alfred, Calvin, Samuel, and Tom. The men and women in the cars on either side watch them. They don't like them to jiggle or jump but don't want to interfere. Of course some of the men in the cars were once brave boys like these. One of them had ridden the tail of a speeding truck from New York to Rockaway Beach without getting off, without his sore fingers losing hold. Nothing happened to him then or later. He had made a compact with other boys who preferred to watch: starting at Eighth Avenue and Fifteenth Street, he would get to some specified place, maybe Twenty-third and the river, by hopping the tops of the moving trucks. This was hard to do when one truck turned a corner in the wrong direction and the nearest truck was a couple of feet too high. He made three or four starts before succeeding. He had gotten this idea from a film at school called *The Romance of* 2

Logging. He had finished high school, married a good friend, was in a responsible job, and going to night school.

These two men and others looked at the four boys jumping and jig- 3
gling on the platform and thought, It must be fun to ride that way, especially now the weather is nice and we're out of the tunnel and way high over
the Bronx. Then they thought, These kids do seem to be acting sort of stupid. They *are* little. Then they thought of some of the brave things they had
done when they were boys and jiggling didn't seem so risky.

The ladies in the car became very angry when they looked at the four 4
boys. Most of them brought their brows together and hoped the boys
could see their extreme disapproval. One of the ladies wanted to get up and
say, be careful you dumb kids, get off that platform or I'll call a cop. But
three of the boys were Negroes and the fourth was something else she
couldn't tell for sure. She was afraid they'd be fresh and laugh at her and
embarrass her. She wasn't afraid they'd hit her, but she was afraid of
embarrassment. Another lady thought, Their mothers never know where
they are. It wasn't true in this particular case. Their mothers all knew that
they had gone to see the missile exhibit on Fourteenth Street.

Out on the platform, whenever the train accelerated, the boys would 5
raise their hands and point them up to the sky to act like rockets going off,
then they rat-tat-tatted the shatterproof glass pane like machine guns,
although no machine guns had been exhibited.

For some reason known only to the motorman, the train began a sud- 6
den slowdown. The lady who was afraid of embarrassment saw the boys
jerk forward and backward and grab the swinging guard chains. She had
her own boy at home. She stood up with determination and went to the
door. She slid it open and said, "You boys will be hurt. You'll be killed. I'm
going to call the conductor if you don't just go into the next car and sit
down and be quiet."

Two of the boys said, "Yes'm," and acted as though they were about to 7
go. Two of them blinked their eyes a couple of times and pressed their lips
together. The train resumed its speed. The door slid shut, parting the lady
and the boys. She leaned against the side door because she had to get off at
the next stop.

The boys opened their eyes wide at each other and laughed. The lady 8
blushed. The boys looked at her and laughed harder. They began to pound
each other's back. Samuel laughed the hardest and pounded Alfred's back
until Alfred coughed and the tears came. Alfred held tight to the chain
hook. Samuel pounded him even harder when he saw the tears. He said,
"Why you bawling? You a baby, huh?" and laughed. One of the men whose
boyhood had been more watchful than brave became angry. He stood up
straight and looked at the boys for a couple of seconds. Then he walked in
a citizenly way to the end of the car, where he pulled the emergency cord.
Almost at once, with a terrible hiss, the pressure of air abandoned the
brakes and the wheels were caught and held.

People standing in the most secure places fell forward, then backward. 9
Samuel had let go of his hold on the chain so he could pound Tom as well as
Alfred. All the passengers in the cars whipped back and forth, but he pitched
only forward and fell head first to be crushed and killed between the cars.

The train had stopped hard, halfway into the station, and the conductor 10
called at once for the trainmen who knew about this kind of death and how
to take the body from the wheels and brakes. There was silence except for passengers from the other cars who asked, What happened! What happened!
The ladies waited around wondering if he might be an only child. The men
recalled other afternoons with very bad endings. The little boys stayed close to
each other, leaning and touching shoulders and arms and legs.

When the policeman knocked at the door and told her about it, 11
Samuel's mother began to scream. She screamed all day and moaned all
night, though the doctors tried to quiet her with pills.

Oh, oh, she hopelessly cried. She did not know how she could ever find 12
another boy like that one. However, she was a young woman and she
became pregnant. Then for a few months she was hopeful. The child born
to her was a boy. They brought him to be seen and nursed. She smiled. But
immediately she saw that this baby wasn't Samuel. She and her husband
together have had other children, but never again will a boy exactly like
Samuel be known.

· · ·

Reading Literature

1. The story begins with the observation, "Some boys are very tough." Is
   Samuel really tough? What do you think Paley wants her readers to
   realize about Samuel?
2. What point do you think the story makes about bravery? Which of
   the characters do you consider brave? Why?
3. What effect does the incident have on the other characters? What do
   their reactions reveal about them?

Journal Entry

Do you consider Samuel a hero? Is it true, as the narrator asserts, that
"never again will a boy exactly like Samuel be known" (12)?

Thematic Connections

- "Thirty-Eight Who Saw Murder Didn't Call the Police" (page 120)
- "Who Killed Benny Paret?" (page 346)
- "Why Boys Don't Play with Dolls" (page 361)
- "The Men We Carry in Our Minds" (page 481)

WRITING ASSIGNMENTS FOR EXEMPLIFICATION

1. Interview several businesspeople in your community. Begin by explaining the Peter Principle to them if they are unfamiliar with it. Then, ask them to express their feelings about this concept, and take notes on their responses. Finally, write an essay about your findings that includes quotations from your notes.

2. Write a humorous essay about a ritual, ceremony, or celebration you experienced and the types of people who participated in it. Make a point about the event, and use the participants as examples to support your point.

3. Write an essay establishing that you are an optimistic (or pessimistic) person. Use examples to support your case.

4. If you could change three or four things at your school, what would they be? Use examples from your own experience to support your recommendations, and tie your recommendations together in your thesis statement.

5. Write an essay discussing two or three of the greatest challenges facing the United States today. If you like, you may refer to essays in this chapter, such as "Just Walk On By" (page 240) or "The Human Cost of an Illiterate Society" (page 252), or to essays elsewhere in this book, such as "Two Ways to Belong in America" (page 415) or "On Dumpster Diving" (page 712).

6. Using your family and friends as examples, write an essay suggesting some of the positive or negative characteristics of Americans.

7. Write an essay presenting your formula for achieving success in college. You may, if you wish, talk about things such as scheduling time, maintaining a high energy level, and learning how to relax. Use examples from your own experience to make your point. You may wish to refer to "College Pressures" (page 466).

8. Write an exemplification essay discussing how cooperation has helped you achieve some important goal. Support your thesis with a single well-developed example.

9. Choose an event that you believe illustrates a less-than-admirable moment in your life. Then, write an essay explaining your feelings.

10. The popularity of the TV show *American Idol* has revealed once again Americans' long-standing infatuation with music icons. Choose several pop groups or stars, old and new — such as Elvis Presley, the Beatles, Michael Jackson, Madonna, Jay-Z, Jennifer Lopez, Nirvana, Destiny's Child, and Eminem, to name only a few — and use them to illustrate the characteristics that you think make pop stars so appealing.

COLLABORATIVE ACTIVITY FOR EXEMPLIFICATION

The following passage appeared in a handbook given to parents of entering students at a midwestern university:

The freshman experience is like no other — at once challenging, exhilarating, and fun. Students face academic challenges as they are exposed to many new ideas. They also face personal challenges as they meet many new people from diverse backgrounds. It is a time to mature and grow. It is an opportunity to explore new subjects and familiar ones. There may be no more challenging and exciting time of personal growth than the first year of university study.

Working in groups of four, brainstorm to identify examples that support or refute the idea that there "may be no more challenging and exciting time of personal growth" than the first year of college. Then, choose one person from each group to tell the class the position the group took and explain the examples you collected. Finally, work together to write an essay that presents your group's position. Have one student write the first draft, two others revise this draft, and the last student edit and proofread the revised draft.

INTERNET ASSIGNMENT FOR EXEMPLIFICATION

Using examples from your own experience and from the Internet, write an exemplification essay explaining the importance of protecting the privacy rights of individuals. Use the following Web sites to gain an understanding of current privacy issues and policies.

Federal Trade Commission
<ftc.gov/privacy/index.html>
The FTC's site is designed to educate consumers and businesses about the importance of protecting the privacy of personal information.

Electronic Privacy Information Center
<epic.org>
This site has news articles and other information about privacy and civil liberties issues in the information age.

Privacy Times
<privacytimes.com>
Privacy Times is a newsletter that covers information law and policy.

9
Process

What Is Process?

A **process** essay explains how to do something or how something occurs. It presents a sequence of steps and shows how those steps lead to a particular result. In the following paragraph from *Language in Thought and Action,* the semanticist S. I. Hayakawa uses process to explain how a dictionary editor decides on a word's definition:

<table>
<tr>
<td>Process presents series of steps in chronological order</td>
<td>To define a word, then, the dictionary-editor places before him the stack of cards illustrating that word; each of the cards represents an actual use of the word by a writer of some literary or historical importance. He reads the cards carefully, discards some, rereads the rest, and divides up the stack according to what he thinks are the several senses of the word. Finally, he writes his definitions, following the hard-and-fast rule that each definition must be based on what the quotations in front of him reveal about the meaning of the word. The editor cannot be influenced by what he thinks</td>
</tr>
<tr>
<td>Topic sentence</td>
<td>a given word ought to mean. He must work according to the cards or not at all.</td>
</tr>
</table>

Process, like narration, presents events in chronological order. Unlike a narrative, however, a process essay explains a particular series of events that produces the same outcome whenever it is duplicated. Because these events form a sequence with a fixed order, clarity is extremely important. Whether your readers will actually perform the process or are simply trying to understand how it occurs, your essay must make clear the exact order of the individual steps, as well as their relationships to one another and to the process as a whole. This means you need to provide clear, logical transitions between the steps in a process, and you also need to present the steps in *strict* chronological order — that is, in the exact order in which they occur or are to be performed.

Depending on its purpose, a process essay can be either a set of *instructions* or a *process explanation.*

Understanding Instructions

The purpose of **instructions** is to enable readers to perform a process. A recipe, a handout about using your library's online databases, and the operating manual for your DVD player are all written in the form of instructions. So are directions for locating an office building in Washington, D.C., or for driving from Houston to Pensacola. Instructions use the present tense and, like commands, they use the imperative mood, speaking directly to readers: "*Disconnect* the system, and *check* the electrical source."

Understanding Process Explanations

The purpose of a **process explanation** is not to enable readers to perform a process but to help them understand how it is carried out. Such essays may examine anything from how silkworms spin their cocoons to how Michelangelo and Leonardo da Vinci painted their masterpieces on plaster walls and ceilings.

A process explanation may use the first person *(I, we)* or the third *(he, she, it, they)*, the past tense or the present. Because its readers need to understand the process, not perform it, a process explanation does not use the second person *(you)* or the imperative mood (commands). The style of a process explanation varies, depending on whether a writer is explaining a process that takes place regularly or one that occurred in the past and also depending on whether the writer or someone else carries out the steps. The following chart suggests the stylistic options available to writers of process explanations.

	First person	*Third person*
Present tense	"After I place the chemicals in the tray, I turn out the lights in the darkroom." *(habitual process performed by the writer)*	"After photographers place the chemicals in the tray, they turn out the lights in the darkroom." *(habitual process performed by someone other than the writer)*
Past tense	"After I placed the chemicals in the tray, I turned out the lights in the darkroom." *(process performed in the past by the writer)*	"After the photographer placed the chemicals in the tray, she turned out the lights in the darkroom." *(process performed in the past by someone other than the writer)*

Using Process

College writing frequently calls for instructions or process explanations. In a biology paper on genetic testing, you might devote a paragraph to an explanation of the process of amniocentesis; in an editorial about the negative side of fraternity life, you might include a brief outline of the process of pledging. You can also organize an entire paper around a process pattern: in a literature essay, you might trace a fictional character's steps in reaching some new insight; on a finance midterm, you might explain the procedure for approving a commercial loan.

You can use either kind of process writing to persuade or simply to present information. If its purpose is persuasive, a process essay may take a strong stand, such as "Applying for food stamps is a needlessly complex process that discourages many qualified recipients" or "The process of slaughtering baby seals is inhumane and sadistic." Many process essays, however, communicate nothing more debatable than the procedure for blood typing. Even in such a case, though, a process should have a clear thesis statement that identifies the process and perhaps tells why it is performed: "Typing their own blood can familiarize students with some fundamental laboratory procedures."

Planning a Process Essay

As you plan a process essay, remember that your primary goal is to depict the process accurately. This means you need to distinguish between what usually or always happens and what occasionally or rarely happens, between necessary steps and optional ones. You should also mentally test all the steps in sequence to be sure the process really works as you say it does, checking carefully for omitted steps or incorrect information. If you are writing about a process you witnessed, try to test the accuracy of your explanation by observing the process again.

Accommodating Your Audience

As you write, remember to keep your readers' needs in mind. When necessary, explain the reasons for performing the steps, describe unfamiliar materials or equipment, define terms, and warn readers about possible problems that may occur during the process. (Sometimes you may even need to include illustrations.) Besides complete information, your readers need a clear and consistent discussion without ambiguities or digressions. For this reason, you should avoid unnecessary shifts in tense, person, voice, and mood. You should also be careful not to omit articles (*a, an,* and *the*) so that your discussion moves smoothly, like an essay—not abruptly, like a cookbook.

Using Transitions

Throughout your essay, be sure to use transitional words and phrases to ensure that each step, each stage, and each paragraph leads logically to the next. Transitions such as *first, second, meanwhile, after this, next, then, at the same time, when you have finished,* and *finally* help to establish sequential and chronological relationships so that readers can follow the process. A more complete list of transitions appears on page 43.

Structuring a Process Essay

Like other essays, a process essay generally consists of three sections. The **introduction** identifies the process and indicates why and under what circumstances it is performed. This section may include information about materials or preliminary preparations, or it may present an overview of the process, perhaps even listing its major stages. The paper's thesis is also usually stated in the introduction.

Each paragraph in the **body** of the essay typically treats one major stage of the process. Each stage may group several steps, depending on the nature and complexity of the process. These steps are presented in chronological order, interrupted only for essential definitions, explanations, or cautions. Every step must be included and must appear in its proper place.

A short process essay may not need a formal **conclusion**. If an essay does have a conclusion, however, it will often briefly review the procedure's major stages. Such an ending is especially useful if the paper has outlined a technical procedure that may seem complicated to general readers. The conclusion may also reinforce the thesis by summarizing the results of the process or explaining its significance.

Suppose you are taking a midterm examination in a course in childhood and adolescent behavior. One essay question calls for a process explanation: "Trace the stages that children go through in acquiring language." After thinking about the question, you formulate the following thesis statement: "Although individual cases may differ, most children acquire language in a predictable series of stages." You then plan your essay and develop an informal outline, which might look like this:

Introduction:	Thesis statement—Although individual cases may differ, most children acquire language in a predictable series of stages.
First stage (two to twelve months):	Prelinguistic behavior, including "babbling" and appropriate responses to nonverbal cues.
Second stage (end of first year):	Single words as commands or requests; infant catalogs his or her environment.

Third stage (beginning of second year):	Expressive jargon (flow of sounds that imitates adult speech); real words along with jargon.
Fourth and final stage (middle of second year to beginning of third year):	Two-word phrases; longer strings; missing parts of speech.
Conclusion:	Restatement of thesis or review of major stages of process.

This essay, when completed, will show not only what the stages of the process are but also how they relate to one another. In addition, it will support the thesis that children learn language through a well-defined process.

Revising a Process Essay

When you revise a set of instructions or a process explanation, consider the items on the revision checklist on page 54. In addition, pay special attention to the items on the following checklist, which apply specifically to revising process essays.

> ✓ REVISION CHECKLIST: **Process**
>
> - Does your assignment call for a set of instructions or a process explanation?
> - Does your essay's style clearly and consistently indicate whether you are writing a set of instructions or a process explanation?
> - Does your essay have a clearly stated thesis that identifies the process and perhaps tells why it is (or was) performed?
> - Have you included all necessary reminders and cautions?
> - Have you included all necessary steps?
> - Are the steps presented in strict chronological order?
> - Do transitions clearly indicate where one step ends and the next begins?

Editing a Process Essay

When you edit your process essay, follow the guidelines on the editing checklists on pages 71, 73, and 76. In addition, focus on the grammar, mechanics, and punctuation issues that are particularly relevant to process essays. One of these issues—avoiding unnecessary shifts in tense, person, voice, and mood—is discussed below.

GRAMMAR IN CONTEXT: Avoiding Unnecessary Shifts

To explain a process to readers, you need to use consistent verb **tense** (past or present), **person** (second or third), **voice** (active or passive), and **mood** (statements or commands). Unnecessary shifts in tense, person, voice, or mood can confuse readers and make it difficult for them to follow your process.

Avoiding Shifts in Tense   Use present tense for a process that is performed regularly.

"The body is first laid out in the undertaker's morgue—or rather, Mr. Jones is reposing in the preparation room—to be readied to bid the world farewell" (Mitford 311).

Use past tense for a process that was performed in the past.

"He peeled the potatoes and thin-sliced them into a quart-sized Mason fruit jar" (Malcolm X 286).

Shift from present to past tense only when you need to indicate a change in time: Usually, I study several days before a test, but this time I studied the night before.

Avoiding Shifts in Person   In process explanations, use first or third person.

FIRST PERSON (*I*):	"Now that I had my sleuth, the next question was what kind of case she should solve" (Muller 292).
FIRST PERSON (*WE*):	"We decided to use my bathroom to dye our hair" (Hunt 279)
THIRD PERSON (*HE*):	"The embalmer, having allowed an appropriate interval to elapse, returns to the attack, but now he brings into play the skill and equipment of sculptor and cosmetician" (Mitford 313).

In instructions, use second person.

SECOND PERSON (*YOU*):	"If you sometimes forget to pay bills, or if you have large student loans, you may have a problem" (McGlade 274).

When you give instructions, be careful not to shift from third to second person.

INCORRECT:	If a person sometimes forgets to pay bills, or if someone has large student loans, you may have a problem.
CORRECT:	If you sometimes forget to pay bills, or if you have large student loans, you may have a problem. (second person)

Avoiding Shifts in Voice   Use active voice when you want to emphasize the person performing the action.

"During the final typing of the manuscript, I checked and rechecked my clues" (Muller 294).

Use passive voice to emphasize the action itself, not the person performing it.

"The patching and filling completed, Mr. Jones is now shaved, washed, and dressed" (Mitford 314).

Do not shift between the active and the passive voice, especially within a sentence, unless your intent is to change your emphasis.

INCORRECT:	The first draft of my essay was completed, and then I started the second draft.
CORRECT:	I completed the first draft of my essay, and then I started the second draft. (active voice)

Avoiding Shifts in Mood   Use the indicative mood (statements) for process explanations.

"He draped the towel around my shoulders, over my rubber apron, and began again vaselining my hair" (Malcolm X 286).

Use the imperative mood (commands) only in instructions.

"Call a friend or relative for help" (Piven et al. 297).

Be careful not to shift from the imperative mood to the indicative mood.

INCORRECT:	First, check your credit report for errors, and you should report any errors you find.
CORRECT:	First, check your credit report for errors, and report any errors you find. (imperative)
CORRECT	First, you should check your credit report for errors, and you should report any errors you find. (indicative)

For more practice in avoiding unnecessary shifts, visit Exercise Central at <bedfordstmartins.com/patterns/shifts>.

✓ EDITING CHECKLIST: Process

- Have you used commas correctly in a series of three or more steps, including a comma before the *and*?
- Have you used parallel structure for items in a series?
- Have you avoided unnecessary shifts in tense?
- Have you avoided unnecessary shifts in person?
- Have you avoided unnecessary shifts in voice?
- Have you avoided unnecessary shifts in mood?

STUDENT WRITERS: Process

The following two student essays, written for a composition class, are process essays. The first essay, "The Search," gives readers instructions on how to find an apartment. It was written by Eric McGlade in response to the assignment, "Write an essay giving practical advice about how to do something most people you know will need to do at one time or another." The second essay, Melany Hunt's "Medium Ash Brown" (page 279), is a process explanation.

The Search

Introduction

In the last four years, I have moved eight times, living in three dorm rooms, two summer sublets, and three apartments in three different cities. I would not recommend this experience to anyone. Finding an apartment is time consuming, stressful, and *Thesis statement* expensive, so the best advice is to stay where you are. However, if you must move, here are a few tips to help you survive the search. 1

First major stage of process: before the search

Before you begin your search, take some time to plan. First, figure out what you can afford. (Here's a hint — you can afford less than you think.) Most experts say you should spend *First step: review your finances* no more than one-third of your net income on rent. Find a budgeting worksheet and see for yourself how car insurance, electricity, and cable can add up. Remember, your new landlord may charge a security deposit and the first month's rent, and there may be pet, parking, cleaning, or moving-in fees. 2

Second step: check your credit history

Next, consider your credit history. If you sometimes forget to pay bills, or if you have large student loans, you may have a problem. Landlords usually run a credit check on potential renters. If you are particularly concerned about your credit rating, order a credit report from one of the three main 3 credit bureaus: TransUnion, Equifax, or Experian. If you find that your credit isn't perfect, don't panic. First, check your credit report for errors, and report any errors you find to the credit bureau. Second, adopt good financial habits immediately. Start paying bills on time, and try to consolidate any debts at a lower interest rate. If a landlord does question your credit, be prepared to explain any extenuating circumstances of the past and to point out your current good behavior.

Third step: consider where to live

After you know what you can afford, you need to figure   4
out where you want to (and can afford to) live. Keep in mind important factors such as how close the apartment is to your school or workplace and how convenient the neighborhood is. Is public transportation located nearby? Is on-street parking available? Can you easily get to a supermarket, coffee shop, convenience store, and Laundromat? If possible, visit each potential neighborhood both during the day and at night. A business district may be bustling during the day but deserted (and perhaps dangerous) at night. If you visit both early and late, you will get a more accurate impression of how safe the neighborhood feels.

Fourth step: consider a roommate

During this stage, consider if you are willing to live with   5
a roommate. You will sacrifice privacy, but you will be able to afford a better apartment. If you do decide to live with a roommate, the easiest way to proceed is to find a friend who also needs an apartment. If this isn't possible, try to find an apartment that comes with a roommate — one with one roommate moving out but the other roommate remaining in the apartment. The third option is to find another apartment seeker and go apartment hunting together. Some Web sites, such as www.roommates.com, cater to this type of search, but, unfortunately, most require a fee. However, your school housing office might have a list of apartment hunters.

Transitional paragraph

Now, you are ready to start looking. You can find the   6
perfect apartment through a real estate agent, by checking your local newspaper or school's housing listings, by asking your friends and family, or by visiting Web sites such as www.craigslist.org.

Second major stage of process: during the search

Each of these methods has pros and cons. A real estate   7
agent might help you find your dream apartment quickly, but you will usually have to pay for this speedy service. As for

First step: do research

newspaper listings, stick to your local paper; unless you are looking for a second vacation home in Maui, national newspapers are not your best bet. An even better idea is to check your school's housing listings, where you are likely to find fellow students in search of apartments in your price range.

Second step: spread the word

Meanwhile, spread the word. Tell everyone you know that you are apartment hunting. Your stepsister's uncle's mother-in-law may live in a building with a newly vacant apartment. This method isn't the most efficient, but the results can be amazing. As a bonus, you will receive practical advice about your neighborhood, such as what to watch out for and what problems other renters have had.   8

Third step: try craigslist

Finally, if you are hunting in a major city, I have but one word: Craigslist. Craigslist.org provides free apartment listings arranged by city and neighborhood. You can hunt for an apartment by price, by number of bedrooms, or by length of lease. If you are on a tight moving schedule and need a place immediately, this Web site is especially helpful because of the sheer volume of its listings. Craigslist also has the added benefit of providing a general price range for your ideal neighborhood.   9

Fourth step: visit apartments

Once you have identified some possibilities, it's time to visit the apartments. Get a good look at each one. Is it furnished or unfurnished? Look closely at the kitchen. Are all the appliances in good working order? How big is your bedroom? Will your bed fit? How much closet space will you have? Are there phone, cable, and Internet hook-ups? Is it a sunny apartment (south facing), or is it dark (north facing)? Ask about the landlord. Does he or she respond quickly to complaints? In the bathroom, turn on the faucets in the sink and shower; check for rust and poor water pressure. As you walk through the apartment, check the cell-phone reception (leaning out the window of your bathroom to talk on the phone is not fun). Most important, do not forget to take notes. After seeing fourteen apartments, you may confuse Apartment A, with the six pets and funny smell, with Apartment G, with the balcony and renovated kitchen.   10

Third major stage of process: after the search

And now, at last, the search is over: you have found your apartment. Congratulations! Unfortunately, your work is not yet over. Now, it is time to read your lease. It will be long and   11

First step: check your lease boring, but it is a very important document. Among other things, your lease should specify the length of the lease, a rent due date, late fees for rent, the amount of the security deposit, and the conditions required for the return of the security deposit. If you have decided to live with a roommate, you might ask the landlord to divide the rent on your lease. This way, if your roommate moves to Brazil, you will not have to pay his share of the rent. Be sure to read your lease thoroughly and bring up any concerns with your landlord.

Second step: get insurance and activate utilities Before you move in, you have a few more things to do: 12
get renter's insurance to protect you from theft or damage to your possessions; arrange to get your utilities hooked up; submit a change-of-address form at the post office; and inform your bank or credit-card company about your future move. Finally, start packing!

Conclusion If you plan ahead and shop smart, you can find your   13
perfect apartment. Remember to figure out what you can afford, check out the neighborhoods, consider a roommate, use multiple search methods, and take careful notes when you visit potential apartments. Yes, happy endings do occur. I am now in the third month of a two-year lease, and I have no plans for moving anytime soon.

Points for Special Attention

Introduction.   The first paragraph of Eric McGlade's essay begins by giving readers some background on his own experience as an apartment hunter. This strategy gives him some credibility, establishing him as an "expert" who can explain the process. Eric then narrows his focus to the difficulties of apartment hunting and ends his introduction with a thesis statement telling readers that the process can be made easier.

Structure.   Eric divides his essay into the three major stages of apartment hunting: what to do before, during, and after the search. After his introduction, Eric includes four paragraphs that explain what to do before the search gets under way. In paragraphs 6 through 10, he explains how to go about the actual hunt for an apartment. Then, in paragraphs 11 and 12, he tells readers what they should do after they locate an apartment (but before they move in). In his conclusion, he restates his thesis, summarizes the steps in the process, and returns to his own experience to reassure readers that a positive outcome is possible.

Purpose and Style.   Because Eric's assignment asked him to give practical advice for a process readers could expect to perform, he decided to write the essay as a set of instructions. Therefore, he uses the second person ("If *you* find that *your* credit isn't perfect, don't panic") and the present tense, with many of his verbs in the form of commands ("First, *figure* out what you can afford").

Transitions.   To make his essay clear and easy to follow, Eric includes transitions that indicate the order in which each step is to be performed ("First," "Next," "Now," "Meanwhile," "Finally," and so on), as well as expressions such as "During this stage." He also includes transitional sentences to move his essay from one stage of the process to the next:

- "Before you begin your search, take some time to plan" (2).
- "Now, you are ready to start looking" (6).
- "Once you have identified some possibilities, it's time to visit the apartments" (10).
- "And now, at last, the search is over: you have found your apartment" (11).

Finally, paragraph 6 serves as a transitional paragraph, moving readers from the preliminary steps to the start of the actual search for an apartment.

Focus on Revision

When he met with his peer editing group, Eric found that they had all gone through the apartment-hunting process and therefore had some practical suggestions to make. In the draft they reviewed, Eric included a good deal of information about his own experiences, but his readers felt those narratives, although amusing, were distracting and got in the way of the process. Eric agreed, and he deleted these anecdotes. His readers thought that mentioning his experiences briefly in his introduction would be sufficient, but Eric decided to return briefly to his own story in his conclusion, adding the two "happy ending" sentences that now conclude his essay. In addition, he followed his readers' suggestion to add a review of the steps of the process to his conclusion to help readers remember what they had read. These additions gave him a fully developed conclusion.

In terms of his essay's content, his reviewers were most concerned with paragraph 10, which they felt seemed to rush through a very important part of the process: visiting the apartments. They also observed that the information in this paragraph was not arranged in any logical order and that Eric had failed to mention other considerations (for example, whether the apartment needed repairs or painting, whether it was noisy, whether it included air conditioning). One reader suggested that Eric expand his discussion and divide the information into two separate paragraphs, one on the apartment's mechanical systems (plumbing, electricity, and so on) and another on its physical appearance (size of rooms, light, and so on). In the final draft of his essay, Eric did just that. (A sample peer editing worksheet for process appears on page 282.)

In contrast to "The Search," Melany Hunt's essay is a process explanation. It was written in response to the assignment, "Write an essay explaining a process that changed your appearance in some way."

Medium Ash Brown

Introduction

The beautiful chestnut-haired woman pictured on the box seemed to beckon to me. I reached for the box of Medium Ash Brown hair dye just as my friend Veronica grabbed the box labeled Sparkling Sherry. I can't remember our reasons for wanting to change our hair color, but they seemed to make sense at the time. Maybe we were just bored. I do remember that the idea of transforming our appearance came up unexpectedly. Impulsively, we decided to change our hair *Thesis statement* color — and, we hoped, ourselves — that very evening. Now I know that some impulses should definitely be resisted. 1

Materials assembled

We decided to use my bathroom to dye our hair. Inside each box of hair color, we found two little bottles and a small tube wrapped in a page of instructions. Attached to the instruction page itself were two very large, one-size-fits-all plastic gloves, which looked and felt like plastic sandwich bags. The directions recommended having some old towels around to soak up any spills or drips that might occur. Under the sink we found some old, frayed towels that I figured my mom had *First stage of* forgotten about, and we spread them around the bathtub. After *process: preparing* we put our gloves on, we began the actual dyeing process. First *the dye* we poured the first bottle into the second, which was half-full of some odd-smelling liquid. The smell was not much better after we combined the two bottles. The directions advised us to cut off a small section of hair to use as a sample. For some reason, we decided to skip this step. 2

Second stage of
process: applying
the dye

At this point, Veronica and I took turns leaning over the tub to wet our hair for the dye. The directions said to leave the dye on the hair for fifteen to twenty minutes, so we found a 3 little timer and set it for fifteen minutes. Next, we applied the dye to our hair. Again, we took turns, squeezing the bottle in order to cover all our hair. We then wrapped the old towels around our sour-smelling hair and went outside to get some fresh air.

Third stage of process: rinsing

After the fifteen minutes were up, we rinsed our hair. According to the directions, we were to add a little water and scrub as if we were shampooing our hair. The dye lathered up, and we rinsed our hair until the water ran clear. So far, so good.   4

Last stage of process: applying conditioner

The last part of the process involved applying the small tube of conditioner to our hair (because dyed hair becomes brittle and easily damaged). We used the conditioner as directed, and then we dried our hair so that we could see the actual color. Even before I looked in the mirror, I heard Veronica's gasp.   5

Outcome of process

"Nice try," I said, assuming she was just trying to make me nervous, "but you're not funny."   6

"Mel," she said, "look in the mirror." Slowly, I turned around. My stomach turned into a lead ball when I saw my reflection. My hair was the putrid greenish-brown color of a winter lawn, dying in patches yet still a nice green in the shade.   7

The next day in school, I wore my hair tied back under a baseball cap. I told only my close friends what I had done. After they were finished laughing, they offered their deepest, most heartfelt condolences. They also offered many suggestions — none very helpful — on what to do to get my old hair color back.   8

Conclusion

It is now three months later, and I still have no idea what prompted me to dye my hair. My only consolation is that I resisted my first impulse — to dye my hair a wild color, like blue or fuchsia. Still, as I wait for my hair to grow out, and as I assemble a larger and larger collection of baseball caps, it is small consolation indeed.   9

Points for Special Attention

Structure.   In her opening paragraph, Melany's thesis statement makes it very clear that the experience she describes is not one she would recommend to others. The temptation she describes in her introduction's first few sentences lures readers into her essay, just as the picture on the box lured her. Her second paragraph lists the contents of the box of hair dye and explains how she and her friend assembled the other necessary materials. Then, she explains the first stage in the process: preparing the dye. Paragraphs 3–5 describe the other stages in the process in chronological order, and paragraphs 6–8 record Melany's and Veronica's reactions to their experiment. In paragraph 9, Melany sums up the impact of her experience and once again expresses her annoyance with herself for her impulsive act.

Purpose and Style.   Melany's purpose is not to enable others to duplicate the process she explains; on the contrary, she wants to discourage readers from doing what she did. Consequently, she presents her process not as a set of instructions but as a process explanation, using first person and past tense to explain the actions of herself and her friend. She also largely eliminates cautions and reminders that her readers, who are not likely to undertake the process, will not need to know.

Detail.   Melany's essay includes vivid descriptive detail that gives readers a clear sense of the process and its outcome. Throughout, her emphasis is on the negative aspects of the process—the "odd-smelling liquid" and the "putrid greenish-brown color" of her hair, for instance—and this emphasis is consistent with her essay's purpose.

Transitions.   To move readers smoothly through the process, Melany includes clear transitions ("First," "At this point," "Next," "then") and clearly identifies the beginning of the process ("After we put our gloves on, we began the actual dyeing process") and the end ("The last part of the process").

Focus on Revision

Students who read Melany's essay thought it was clearly written and structured and that its ironic, self-mocking tone was well suited to her audience and purpose. They felt, however, that some minor revisions would make her essay even more effective. Specifically, they thought that paragraph 2 began too abruptly: paragraph 1 recorded the purchase of the hair dye, and paragraph 2 opened with the sentence "We decided to use my bathroom to dye our hair," leaving readers wondering how much time had passed between purchase and application. Because the thesis rests on the idea of the foolishness of an impulsive gesture, it is important for readers to understand that the girls presumably went immediately from the store to Melany's house.

After thinking about this criticism, Melany decided to write a clearer opening for paragraph 2: "As soon as we paid for the dye, we returned to my house, where, eager to begin our transformation, we locked ourselves in my bathroom. Inside each box. . . ." She also decided to divide paragraph 2 into two paragraphs, one describing the materials and another beginning with "After we put our gloves on," which introduces the first step in the process.

Another possible revision Melany considered was developing Veronica's character further. Although both girls purchase and apply hair color, readers never learn what happens to Veronica. Melany knew she could easily add a brief paragraph after paragraph 7, describing Veronica's "Sparkling Sherry" hair in humorous terms, and she planned to do so in her paper's final draft.

📄 **PEER EDITING WORKSHEET: Process**

1. What process does this essay describe? How familiar were you with this process before you read the essay?
2. Does the writer include all the information the audience needs? Is any vital step or piece of information missing? Is any step or piece of information irrelevant? Is any necessary definition, explanation, or caution missing or incomplete?
3. Is the essay a set of instructions or a process explanation? How can you tell? Why do you think the writer chose this strategy rather than the alternative? Do you think this was the right choice?
4. Does the writer consistently follow the stylistic conventions for the strategy—instructions or process explanation—he or she has chosen?
5. Are the steps presented in clear, logical order? Are they grouped logically into paragraphs? Should any steps be combined or relocated? If so, which ones?
6. Does the writer use enough transitions to move readers through the process? Should any transitions be added? If so, where? Do the transitions clearly indicate the logical and sequential relationships between steps?
7. Does the writer avoid confusing shifts in tense, person, voice, and mood?
8. Is the essay interesting? What descriptive details would add interest to the essay? Would a visual be helpful?
9. How would you characterize the writer's opening strategy? Is it appropriate for his or her purpose and audience? What alternative strategy might be more effective?
10. How would you characterize the writer's closing strategy? Would a different conclusion be more effective? Explain.

The reading selections that follow illustrate how varied the uses of process writing can be. The first selection, a visual text, is followed by questions designed to illustrate how process can operate in visual form.

NIGEL HOLMES

How to Cover Scratches on Furniture (Illustration)

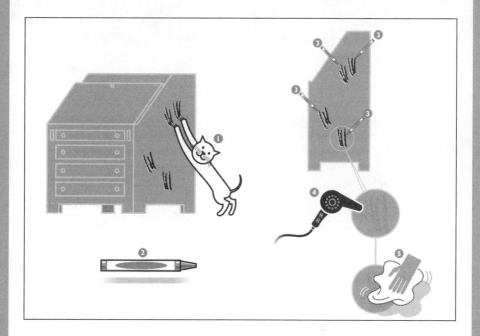

• • •

Reading Images

1. Look closely at the series of illustrations. Do the illustrations give you enough information to enable you to perform the process? What specific details, if any, are missing?

2. Consulting the illustrations, list the steps involved in the process of covering cat scratches on furniture. Is the step labeled number 1 actually part of the process? Explain.

3. What cautions or reminders might be helpful to someone who wanted to follow these instructions?

Journal Entry

Write a one-paragraph set of instructions (straightforward or humorous) for removing cat scratches from furniture. Using commands and present tense, explain each step in order. Then, add an introductory sentence to identify the process and a concluding sentence to sum it up.

Thematic Connections

- "Innovation" (page 231)
- "I Want a Wife" (page 524)

My First Conk

Malcolm X was born Malcolm Little in Omaha, Nebraska, in 1925. As a young man, he had a number of run-ins with the law, and he wound up in prison on burglary charges before he was twenty-one. There he pursued his education and was influenced by the writings of Elijah Muhammed, the founder of the Black Muslims (now known as the Nation of Islam), a black separatist organization. On his release from prison, Malcolm X became a highly visible member of this group and a disciple of its leader. He left the movement in 1963, later converting to orthodox Islam and founding a rival African-American political organization. He was assassinated in 1965.

Background on conks and other African-American hair styles: *The Autobiography of Malcolm X* (written with Alex Haley) was published in 1964. The following excerpt from that book describes the painful and painstaking process many African-American men once endured to achieve a style of straight hair called a "conk." (The term probably comes from Congolene, the brand name of one commercial hair straightener.) First popularized in the 1920s by black entertainers such as Cab Calloway, the style continued to be fashionable until the 1960s, when more natural styles, including the Afro, became a symbol of black pride, and conked hair came to be seen as a self-loathing attempt to imitate whites. Ironically, perhaps, some contemporary African Americans still distinguish between "good" (that is, naturally straight) and "bad" (that is, naturally curly) hair. Today, cosmetically straightened hair (a process that is no longer so arduous) is considered one fashion option among many, including shaved heads, closely cropped hair, braids, cornrows, and dreadlocks.

1 Shorty soon decided that my hair was finally long enough to be conked. He had promised to school me in how to beat the barber shops' three- and four-dollar price by making up congolene, and then conking ourselves.

2 I took the little list of ingredients he had printed out for me, and went to a grocery store, where I got a can of Red Devil lye, two eggs, and two medium-sized white potatoes. Then at a drugstore near the poolroom, I asked for a large jar of vaseline, a large bar of soap, a large-toothed comb and a fine-toothed comb, one of those rubber hoses with a metal spray-head, a rubber apron, and a pair of gloves.

3 "Going to lay on that first conk?" the drugstore man asked me. I proudly told him, grinning, "Right!"

4 Shorty paid six dollars a week for a room in his cousin's shabby apartment. His cousin wasn't at home. "It's like the pad's mine, he spends so much time with his woman," Shorty said. "Now, you watch me—"

He peeled the potatoes and thin-sliced them into a quart-sized Mason   5
fruit jar, then started stirring them with a wooden spoon as he gradually
poured in a little over half the can of lye. "Never use a metal spoon; the lye
will turn it black," he told me.

A jelly-like, starchy-looking glop resulted from the lye and potatoes,   6
and Shorty broke in the two eggs, stirring real fast — his own conk and dark
face bent down close. The congolene turned pale-yellowish. "Feel the jar,"
Shorty said. I cupped my hand against the outside, and snatched it away.
"Damn right, it's hot, that's the lye," he said. "So you know it's going to
burn when I comb it in — it burns bad. But the longer you can stand it, the
straighter the hair."

He made me sit down, and he tied the string of the new rubber apron   7
tightly around my neck, and combed up my bush of hair. Then, from the
big vaseline jar, he took a handful and massaged it hard all through my hair
and into the scalp. He also thickly vaselined my neck, ears and forehead.
"When I get to washing out your head, be sure to tell me anywhere you feel
any little stinging," Shorty warned me, washing his hands, then pulling on
the rubber gloves, and tying on his own rubber apron. "You always got to
remember that any congolene left in burns a sore into your head."

The congolene just felt warm when Shorty started combing it in. But   8
then my head caught fire.

I gritted my teeth and tried to pull the sides of the kitchen table   9
together. The comb felt as if it was raking my skin off.

My eyes watered, my nose was running. I couldn't stand it any longer; I   10
bolted to the washbasin. I was cursing Shorty with every name I could
think of when he got the spray going and started soap lathering my head.

He lathered and spray-rinsed, lathered and spray-rinsed, maybe ten or   11
twelve times, each time gradually closing the hot-water faucet, until the
rinse was cold, and that helped some.

"You feel any stinging spots?"   12

"No," I managed to say. My knees were trembling.   13

"Sit back down, then. I think we got it all out okay."   14

The flame came back as Shorty, with a thick towel, started drying my   15
head, rubbing hard. *"Easy, man, easy!"* I kept shouting.

"The first time's always worst. You get used to it better before long.   16
You took it real good, homeboy. You got a good conk."

When Shorty let me stand up and see in the mirror, my hair hung   17
down in limp, damp strings. My scalp still flamed, but not as badly; I could
bear it. He draped the towel around my shoulders, over my rubber apron,
and began again vaselining my hair.

I could feel him combing, straight back, first the big comb, then the   18
fine-tooth one.

Then, he was using a razor, very delicately, on the back of my neck.   19
Then, finally, shaping the sideburns.

My first view in the mirror blotted out the hurting. I'd seen some   20
pretty conks, but when it's the first time, on your *own* head, the transformation, after the lifetime of kinks, is staggering.

The mirror reflected Shorty behind me. We both were grinning and   21
sweating. And on top of my head was this thick, smooth sheen of shining
red hair — real red — as straight as any white man's.

How ridiculous I was! Stupid enough to stand there simply lost in   22
admiration of my hair now looking "white," reflected in the mirror in
Shorty's room. I vowed that I'd never again be without a conk, and I never
was for many years.

This was my first really big step toward self-degradation: when I   23
endured all of that pain, literally burning my flesh to have it look like a
white man's hair. I had joined that multitude of Negro men and women in
America who are brainwashed into believing that the black people are "inferior" — and white people "superior" — that they will even violate and muti-
late their God-created bodies to try to look "pretty" by white standards.

Look around today, in every small town and big city, from two-bit cat-   24
fish and soda-pop joints into the "integrated" lobby of the Waldorf-Astoria,
and you'll see conks on black men. And you'll see black women wearing
these green and pink and purple and red and platinum-blonde wigs.
They're all more ridiculous than a slapstick comedy. It makes you wonder if
the Negro has completely lost his sense of identity, lost touch with himself.

You'll see the conk worn by many, many so-called "upper class" Negroes,   25
and, as much as I hate to say it about them, on all too many Negro entertainers. One of the reasons that I've especially admired some of them, like Lionel
Hampton and Sidney Poitier, among others, is that they have kept their natural hair and fought to the top. I admire any Negro man who has never had
himself conked, or who has had the sense to get rid of it — as I finally did.

I don't know which kind of self-defacing conk is the greater shame —   26
the one you'll see on the heads of the black so-called "middle class" and
"upper class," who ought to know better, or the one you'll see on the heads
of the poorest, most downtrodden, ignorant black men. I mean the legal-
minimum-wage ghetto-dwelling kind of Negro, as I was when I got my first
one. It's generally among these poor fools that you'll see a black kerchief
over the man's head, like Aunt Jemima; he's trying to make his conk last
longer, between trips to the barbershop. Only for special occasions is this
kerchief-protected conk exposed — to show off how "sharp" and "hip" its
owner is. The ironic thing is that I have never heard any woman, white or
black, express any admiration for a conk. Of course, any white woman with
a black man isn't thinking about his hair. But I don't see how on earth a
black woman with any race pride could walk down the street with any
black man wearing a conk — the emblem of his shame that he is black.

To my own shame, when I say all of this, I'm talking first of all about   27
myself — because you can't show me any Negro who ever conked more
faithfully than I did. I'm speaking from personal experience when I say of
any black man who conks today, or any white-wigged black woman, that if
they gave the brains in their heads just half as much attention as they do
their hair, they would be a thousand times better off.

· · ·

Comprehension

1. What exactly is a conk? Why does Malcolm X want to get his hair conked? What does the conk symbolize to him at the time he gets it? What does it symbolize at the time he writes about it?

2. List the materials Shorty asks Malcolm X to buy. Is the purpose of each explained? If so, where?

3. Outline the major stages in the procedure Malcolm X describes. Are they presented in chronological order? Which, if any, of the major stages are out of place?

Purpose and Audience

1. Why was this selection written as a process explanation instead of as a set of instructions?

2. This selection has an explicitly stated thesis that makes its purpose clear. What is this thesis?

3. *The Autobiography of Malcolm X* was published in 1964, when many African Americans regularly straightened their hair. Is the thesis of this excerpt from the book still relevant today?

4. Why do you think Malcolm X includes so many references to the pain and discomfort he endured as part of the process?

5. What is the relationship between Malcolm X's personal experience and his universal statement about conking?

Style and Structure

1. Identify some of the transitional words Malcolm X uses to move from step to step.

2. Only about half of this selection is devoted to the process explanation. Where does the process begin? Where does it end?

3. In paragraphs 22–26, Malcolm X encloses several words in quotation marks, occasionally prefacing them with the phrase *so-called*. What is the effect of these quotation marks?

Vocabulary Projects

1. Define each of the following words as it is used in this selection.

vowed (22)	mutilate (23)	downtrodden (26)
self-degradation (23)	slapstick (24)	emblem (26)
multitude (23)	self-defacing (26)	

2. Because this is an informal piece of writing, Malcolm X uses many **colloquialisms** and **slang** terms. Substitute a more formal word for each of the following.

beat (1)	glop (6)	"sharp" (26)
pad (4)	real (6)	"hip" (26)

Evaluate the possible impact of your substitutions. Do they improve the essay or weaken it?

Journal Entry

Did you ever engage in behavior that you later came to view as unacceptable as your beliefs changed or as your social consciousness developed? What made you change your attitude toward this behavior?

Writing Workshop

1. Write a process explanation of an unpleasant experience you or someone you know has often gone through to conform to others' standards of physical beauty (for instance, dieting or undertaking strenuous exercise). Include a thesis statement that conveys your disapproval of the process.
2. Rewrite Malcolm X's process explanation as he might have written it when he still considered conking a desirable process, worth all the trouble. Include all his steps, but change his thesis and choose words that make conking sound painless and worthwhile.
3. Rewrite this essay as a set of instructions that Shorty might have written for a friend about to help someone conk his hair. Begin by telling the friend what materials to purchase.

Combining the Patterns

Although "My First Conk" is very detailed, it does not include an extended **definition** of a conk. Do you think a definition paragraph should be added? If so, where could it be inserted? What patterns could be used to develop such a definition?

Thematic Connections

- "Finishing School" (page 101)
- "Medium Ash Brown" (page 279)
- "Stigmatic Uniforms" (page 544)

MARCIA MULLER

Creating a Female Sleuth

Marcia Muller (b. 1944) grew up in Detroit and received her B.A. in English and her M.A. in journalism from the University of Michigan. She wrote for magazines and worked for an editorial service before publishing her first novel, *Edwin of the Iron Shoes* (1977), a detective story featuring private investigator Sharon McCone as its central character. Since then, Muller has written more than twenty books in the McCone series, most recently *The Dangerous Hour* (2004), as well as mysteries solved by other female sleuths. The winner of many awards, she has also edited a number of fiction collections, often with her husband, mystery writer Bill Pronzini. In this essay, first published in *The Writer* in 1978, Muller explains how she created Sharon McCone.

Background on the fictional detective: Most critics trace the fictional detective back to Edgar Allan Poe's 1841 short story "The Murders in the Rue Morgue" and later Poe tales centering on the brilliant and eccentric amateur C. Auguste Dupin. The English writer Wilkie Collins published what is considered the first detective novel, *The Moonstone,* in 1868. Some twenty years later, Arthur Conan Doyle introduced Sherlock Holmes, probably literature's most famous detective. The genre blossomed in the early twentieth century, when scores of new detective series appeared, with central characters such as G. K. Chesterton's cerebral priest, Father Brown; Dorothy L. Sayers's genteel Lord Peter Wimsey; S. S. Van Dine's wealthy connoisseur Philo Vance; and the hardboiled private investigators Sam Spade and Philip Marlowe (both precursors of a long line of fictional PIs), created by Dashiell Hammett and Raymond Chandler, respectively. While some series were devoted to amateur female sleuths—such as Agatha Christie's elderly Jane Marple and plucky teenager Nancy Drew (ghostwritten by various writers, all using the pseudonym Carolyn Keene)—and although P. D. James's police inspector Cordelia Gray appeared in 1972, Muller's Sharon McCone was the first fictional female private investigator. She was soon joined by Sue Grafton's Kinsey Millhone, Liza Cody's Anna Lee, and Sara Paretsky's V. I. Warshawski, among many others.

Several years ago, a friend handed me my first whodunit as I was about to embark on a long bus ride. I finished the book before I reached my destination and, upon arrival, went straight to the paperback racks for another. I was hooked. 1

In the years that followed, my puzzle-prone friends and I noticed that one figure was missing from the mystery scene. There were scores of male sleuths, both hard- and soft-boiled. There were old ladies with knitting needles and noses for secrets. There were even a few dedicated and hard- 2 working policewomen. But nowhere, at that time, could we find a female private eye.

Obviously, I decided, if I wanted to read about such a character, I would first have to write about her. 3

The process of creating my sleuth, Sharon McCone, and plotting her first case — *Edwin of the Iron Shoes* — presented a number of technical problems. Because female sleuths are in themselves a rarity, my imaginary friend could not be too unusual or too much of a superwoman if modern readers — both male and female — were to identify with her. She also needed to have a background that would make her choice of profession believable. 4

On the other hand, like all detectives, she had to be somewhat larger than life. She had to be the sort of person who would do things you and I might never dream of: stalk her quarry through the highways and byways of the city; stand her ground with hostile cops; grapple hand-to-hand with dangerous criminals. 5

In order to reconcile these seeming opposites, I chose to give Sharon a normal, perhaps pedestrian, family background and upbringing that produced a well-adjusted, uncomplicated adult. Sharon's problems are those we've all experienced at one time: an affectionate but nosy mother who, fortunately, lives 500 miles away; the frustration of not finding a decent job after graduating from college with a sociology major; the lack of an interesting man in one's life; too high a rent for too small a studio apartment. 6

Marital status, which affects a female investigator's freedom of movement far more than a male's, was easy to decide, particularly when the police lieutenant in charge of Sharon's first murder case turned out to be attractive, if a bit of a smart-aleck. Sharon is single. 7

For the background that would qualify her for a career as a private investigator, I chose department-store security, a relatively easy field to break into. Where else could a nice girl learn to fire a .38 Special or flip a grown man over with a judo hold? I decided that Sharon was bored with guarding dresses on the sales floor, had gone off to college, and then returned to investigative work when she realized the demand for sociologists was nil. Further training with a big security agency equipped her for a position as staff investigator at a San Francisco legal cooperative in time for her first big case. 8

With this plausible basis for my sleuth's choice of occupation and a number of down-to-earth character traits, I gave my imagination free rein. I wanted to make Sharon's physical attributes stand out in the reader's mind, and at the same time to avoid the old, overused mirror-on-the-wall device ("As I stood before the mirror and brushed my hair, I thought about the case and noticed gray strands among the black"). Therefore, I decided to make Sharon a person with Scotch-Irish ancestry, whose one-eighth Shoshone Indian blood dominates her appearance. Her unusual looks, coupled with her name, cause people to comment, "McCone? But you look like an Indian!" — and this enabled me to dispense with a great deal of description. 9

Larger Than Life

Now I was really getting into the larger-than-life qualities, or, more 10
accurately, the larger-than-author traits. Sharon is much taller than I, so
she can more easily wrestle with criminals. She never has to worry about
her weight, presumably because she does not sit at a typewriter all day. She
is more independent than the average soul, delights in asserting herself,
and, of course, is much braver.

These admirable qualities were all very well to list, but the next prob- 11
lem was how to express them in action. When I began writing up her first
case, I found my heroine in a given situation and asked myself: "All right,
what would *I* do?" The answer, inevitably, was something like "Run." Since
this was not working out, I conditioned myself to think of what I would do
if I were brave, tall, an expert at judo, and so on, each time taking it a step
farther. I discovered it was better to have Sharon act ridiculously brave,
even foolhardy, and moderate her actions later, than to start off timidly,
because a timid response to a situation was more difficult to correct in a
rewrite.

Touchier yet was the problem of emotional balance: how was Sharon 12
to deal with the rough situations that came up in the course of her work
without sacrificing her femininity? The qualities of empathy and intuition
would be great assets to her, because as a woman she might realize or even
be told things that ordinary investigative methods would not turn up.
Still, she couldn't cry at every bump and bruise, or lose her gun in her
purse at the crucial moment. Again, I constantly had to consider what I
would do if I were a trained professional, how I would condition and curb
my natural responses. I constantly made adjustments for this balance in
every draft of the novel, and am still making adjustments now, as I guide
my sleuth through her second case.

A mechanical aid in getting acquainted with my character was writing 13
the biographical sketch, a detailed run-down on Sharon's history, preferences and opinions from her own point of view. I wrote this in the first person, as if she were standing up to introduce herself to a group. Throughout
the writing process, this "biography" was there to help refresh my memory
as to details. It was no substitute, however, for getting to know my character through writing about her.

Two Rules for Plotting

Now that I had my sleuth, the next question was what kind of case she 14
should solve. In short, what was my plot to be?

I had a setting I wanted to explore: an enclave of antique and junk 15
shops, loosely based on several such areas in San Francisco, and I wanted to
center on one particular shop containing an assortment of strange objects,
including a department store mannequin named Edwin, who wore a pair
of ornate iron shoes. I also had a problem for Sharon to solve: the dead

body of the proprietor on the floor of the shop, with Edwin as the only witness to the murder.

With this in mind, I began to play the game of "what if." I started with   16
the very obvious questions: What if the proprietor had a fortune in antiques hidden in the shop? What if she had a jealous lover? What if several powerful real-estate syndicates were after the land the shop was on? What if, beneath her ordinary exterior, the victim hid some criminal secret? The answers to these and other often laughable questions gave the basis for my solution.

Knowing my solution was the real key to a plot that held together. I   17
needed to have some ending, however tentative, in mind at all times, or I couldn't plant clues or make my suspects act properly suspicious. Without a solution, I didn't know what the clues pointed to or why my characters needed to behave strangely. This has become my first unbreakable rule of plotting.

My second unbreakable rule, to keep the plot as flexible as possible, may   18
sound like a direct contradiction to the first. I found, however, that I had to be willing to modify my original solution or even throw it out and replace it with another when characters and events indicated this was necessary.

For example, I reached a point in my whodunit where all the loose ends   19
were tying up nicely. Everything pointed to my chosen killer, his motives were coming clear, and my sleuth had won over the nasty police lieutenant by her clever use of logic. Elated, I took a breath to count pages and realized that I was only halfway through the book!

This is the kind of situation in which you need all the flexibility you   20
can muster. I looked over what I had written and concluded that this would be not only a very short book, but also a very boring one. Everything pointed clearly to the killer. His motives were too pat and ordinary. I began once more to play "what if."

What if, at the height of his bedazzlement with Sharon's logic, the   21
police lieutenant receives a phone call, and then smugly announces to her that the supposed murderer himself was dead? That he was knifed in his own apartment, in fact, and that the apartment had been searched?

Of course, the answer was that I had to get myself a new killer. What if   22
the sleazy bail bondsman that the victim had been consorting with . . . ? The new solution was more interesting all around, and it gave me the extra pages I needed.

Plot Control

This experience taught me the difficulty of keeping the plot of a who-   23
dunit in hand even after you think you know what it is. I had to keep track of events that happened weeks, even years, before my opening action, all of which led up to the initial crime. There were also facts that had to be withheld from the reader as long as possible, and clues the reader had to be given. A number of characters were engaged in suspicious activities that

may or may not have had something to do with the murder. How was I to keep track of all this?

Several mechanical devices helped. The first, a sketch of what really happened, was like a well-detailed short story. I started at the beginning of my mystery, two years before the murder, when the antique shop proprietor needed a great deal more money than her shop could bring in. I followed the course of events from there to the day she ended up dead on the shop floor, and finally ended the sketch with the arrest of her killer. The sketch was available for reference as my plot unfolded and the past was explained. And, in accordance with the flexibility rule, it was discarded and rewritten when the solution changed.   24

A second device was the sketch of each main character. While not as detailed as the biography of the heroine, it contained much the same types of information: background, important life events, outstanding physical and personality traits. These sketches helped me keep the characters' motivations in mind and to keep details about their lives consistent.   25

The most useful device for plot control was my time chart. It took the form of a grid, with major characters plotted across the top and chapters or time frames plotted down the side; it covered the same period as the sketch of what really happened.   26

In the squares under each character on the chart, I noted what he or she was doing during every time period. In this way, I avoided such embarrassing situations as finding that the murderer was really with my detective when he was supposed to have been doing in his second victim. I usually plotted only three to five chapters ahead at a time, finding that the things characters said and did often suggested new complications or scenes. However, I imagine this type of chart could be adapted nicely to complete preplanning as well.   27

The rewrite was my final check of how well my plot hung together. This was when I went back and inserted clues I had forgotten, brought out necessary facets of a suspect's character, and smoothed over inconsistencies and cut and cleaned up style. My experience with rewrites has been rewarding: the wicked-looking bone-handled knife which, as the murder weapon, plays a large part in my whodunit, didn't even exist until the rewrite, when a critic friend pointed out that a small paring knife made a pretty silly instrument of violent death.   28

During the final typing of the manuscript, I checked and rechecked my clues. I believe in playing fair with the reader, and I wanted to make sure I'd given him every clue Sharon came across in solving the case. Rather than have Sharon say: "I realized something that told me who the killer was," I had her carry on a mental conversation with Edwin, the heavy-footed mannequin. At its end, she says: "Edwin, why didn't you tell me?" The conversation provides the reader with all the clues he needs to solve the murders along with Sharon. And I will be delighted to hear of readers who solve my whodunit ahead of my sleuth!   29

• • •

Comprehension

1. According to Muller, what motivated her to create her "female sleuth"?
2. Muller believed that her detective had to be someone readers could identify with and yet also someone "larger than life" (5). Why? List some of the characteristics that help Sharon McCone satisfy both these requirements.
3. What advantages does Muller's fictional detective have because she is female? What disadvantages does she have?
4. What are Muller's "unbreakable rule[s] of plotting" (17–18)? Why are they "unbreakable"?
5. What problems did Muller encounter in plotting her novel? How did she solve them? What "mechanical devices" (24) did she devise to help her control her plot?

Purpose and Audience

1. This essay was first published in 1978, a year after the first Sharon McCone detective novel appeared in print. Are today's readers more or less likely to be interested in the development of the female detective? Explain.
2. Do you think Muller expects her audience to be familiar with the conventions of a typical detective story? How can you tell?
3. Muller states her thesis in paragraph 3. Paraphrase this one-sentence paragraph. Should she have stated her thesis earlier? Explain.

Style and Structure

1. Where does the actual discussion of the process of creating a female sleuth begin? How does Muller signal the start of this process to her readers?
2. List the major stages in the process Muller followed to create Sharon McCone.
3. What transitional expressions does Muller use to guide readers through the process and to connect one stage to the next?
4. Are any of the elements that are typically included in a process explanation missing from this essay? For example, does Muller include warnings and reminders? If so, where? If not, why not?
5. Although Muller is a professional writer discussing her craft, her style is, for the most part, quite informal. Give examples of her informal language. What does Muller gain by using this kind of language instead of more formal language?

Vocabulary Projects

1. Define each of the following words as it is used in this selection.

   quarry (5)   foolhardy (11)
   pedestrian (6)   elated (19)
   nil (8)   pat (20)
   plausible (9)   facets (28)

2. Muller's essay includes a number of words traditionally associated with detective stories — for example, *sleuth* (title) and *whodunit* (1). What other such words can you identify? What do they add to the essay?

3. What adjectives does Muller use to describe Sharon McCone? Which of these adjectives, if any, could not be used to describe a male detective?

Journal Entry

Review the steps in Muller's writing process, and compare them with the steps in the writing process outlined in Chapters 2 through 5 of this text. How are the two processes alike? How are they different? How do you account for the differences?

Writing Workshop

1. Rewrite Muller's process explanation as a brief "how-to" essay aimed at writers who want to write a detective story.

2. Write a process explanation telling how you would write a story that features another kind of nontraditional detective — for example, a member of an ethnic or racial minority or a person with a disability. What "technical problems" would you have, and how would you solve them?

3. Write a process essay explaining how you would create a different kind of character altogether — for example, a villain in a romance novel or a movie superhero with unusual powers.

Combining the Patterns

Although this essay explains a process, Muller uses a good deal of **description** as well. Is this description primarily *subjective* or *objective*? Should Muller have included additional passages of description?

Thematic Connections

- "Why Boys Don't Play with Dolls" (page 361)
- "A Peaceful Woman Explains Why She Carries a Gun" (page 371)
- "Sex, Lies, and Conversation" (page 440)
- Declaration of Sentiments and Resolutions (page 590)

JOSHUA PIVEN, DAVID BORGENICHT,
AND JENNIFER WORICK

How to Escape from a Bad Date

Joshua Piven and David Borgenicht are the authors of the runaway best-seller *The Worst-Case Scenario Survival Handbook* (1999), having consulted numerous experts to enable them to provide advice for such dilemmas as "How to Break into a Parked Car" and "How to Escape from a Mountain Lion." The book's success sparked a series that now includes *The Worst-Case Scenario Survival Handbook: Travel* (2001), *The Worst-Case Scenario Survival Handbook: Holidays* (2002), *The Worst-Case Scenario Survival Handbook: College* (2004), and *The Worst-Case Scenario Survival Handbook: Weddings* (2005) as well as the reality-television show *Worst-Case Scenario*. In 2002, they collaborated on *The Worst-Case Scenario Survival Handbook: Dating and Sex* with Jennifer Worick, who is also the author of *My Fabulous Life: Musings on a Marvelous Me* (2001), *Nancy Drew's Guide to Life* (2001), and *The Action Heroine's Handbook* (2003).

Background on self-help and "how-to" books: The United States has a long history of "how-to," advice, and self-improvement books dating back to Benjamin Franklin's *Poor Richard's Almanack* (1732–1757), but, beginning in the 1930s, the genre proliferated when publications such as Dale Carnegie's *How to Win Friends and Influence People* topped the best-seller lists. The "Self-Help" and "How-To" sections are now among the largest in many bookstores, and the success of the "for Dummies" series suggests the wide range of topics covered by such advice books. The books in the *Worst-Case Scenario* series, however, are generally shelved in bookstores' "Humor" sections because they offer tongue-in-cheek advice not really intended to be followed. Such parodies have been popular at least since Shepherd Mead's 1952 *How to Succeed in Business without Really Trying;* other examples include *The Official Preppy Handbook* (1980) and *Life for Real Dummies* (1998). (The *Sex and Dating* volume of the *Worst-Case Scenario* series parodies such relationship-oriented how-to books as 1999's *The Rules: Time-Tested Secrets for Capturing the Heart of Mr. Right.*)

Fake an Emergency

1. Excuse Yourself from the Table.

Tell your date that you are going to the restroom to "wash up." Take your cell phone with you. If you do not have one, locate a restaurant phone that's out of your date's line of vision. Bring a restaurant matchbook or a business card that includes the restaurant's phone number. 1

2. Call a Friend or Relative for Help.

Tell them to call you (either on your cell phone or on the restaurant's phone) and pretend there has been an emergency. Believable emergencies are: 2

- Personal Crisis: "My friend just broke up with her husband — she's having a breakdown. I have to go."
- Business Crisis: "My boss just called — she's in Seattle for a major presentation, and has lost all her files. I have to e-mail them to her immediately."
- Health Crisis: "My sister just called — our grandmother is alone and ill."

3. Leave Quickly before Your Date Can Protest.

Apologize, but refuse any attempt your date makes to accompany you. If you leave swiftly and without hesitation, your date won't have time to understand what's happening or to object.

3

Slip Away Unnoticed

1. Identify Your Escape Route.

Observe your surroundings. Take note of the exits, especially the back doors. Look for the best way out and an alternative.

4

2. Plan to Alter Your Appearance.

Think about your most distinctive features and figure out how to hide or disguise them. The person you are trying to leave is going to see a figure moving past and away at a distance and will be focusing on the first impression. If you are not familiar to him and are uninteresting, you will not get a second look.

5

3. Excuse Yourself from the Table.

Move to the restroom or any private area with a mirror to begin your transformation. Your date will probably wait only two or three minutes before expecting you to return, so act quickly, before he begins looking for you.

6

4. Add or Remove Clothing.

Layering garments will change your body shape and even suggest a different gender. A long coat will obscure your body type. Hats are especially useful because they conceal your hair and facial features. Eyeglasses, whether added or removed, work wonders. A shopping bag is a handy prop and can be used to hold your belongings.

7

5. Change Your Walk and Posture.

If you usually walk quickly, move slowly. If you stand up straight, hunch over. To alter your gait, slip a pebble in one shoe or bind one of your knees with a piece of string or cloth.

8

6. Use or Remove Cosmetics.

Lipstick can change the shape of your mouth, heighten the color in your cheeks and nose, and even give you tired eyes if dabbed and blended

9

Add—or remove—eyeglasses. Roll or unroll your sleeves; tuck in or untuck your blouse. Modify your hairstyle.

on your eyelids. An eyebrow pencil can be used to add age lines, change the shape of your eyes and brows, or create facial hair.

7. Change Your Hairstyle or Color.

A rubberband, hairspray, water, or any gooey substance can be useful for changing a hairstyle, darkening your hair, or altering a hairline. Borrow flour from the kitchen to lighten or gray your hair color.

10

8. Adopt a Cover Role.

A waiter in the restaurant may have an apron and be carrying a tray. If   11
you can manage to procure these items, add or subtract a pair of eyeglasses,
and alter your hairline or hairstyle, you can become invisible as you are
moving out of the restaurant, into the kitchen, and out the rear door. Or
you can take on the role of a maintenance worker; carry a convenient pot-
ted plant out the front door and no one will think twice.

9. Make Your Move.

Do not look at your date.   12

Slip Out the Window

If you do not think you will be able to change your appearance enough   13
to slip past your date, you may have to find another way to depart. Back
doors are the simplest; they are often located near the restrooms or are
marked as fire exits. Do not open an emergency exit door if it is alarmed
unless absolutely necessary; an alarm will only draw attention. If there are
no accessible alternate doors, you will need to find a window.

1. Locate a Usable Window.

Avoid windows with chicken wire or large plate glass. Bathroom win-   14
dows often work best. If you are not on the ground floor, be sure there is a
fire escape.

2. Attempt to Open the Window.

Do not immediately break the window, no matter how dire your need   15
to get out.

3. Prepare to Break the Window if You Cannot Open It.

Make sure no one is around. If you can, lock the bathroom door.   16

4. Find an Implement to Break the Window.

Try to avoid using your elbow, fist, or foot. Suitable implements are: 17

- Wastebasket
- Toilet plunger
- Handbag or briefcase
- Paper towel dispenser

5. Strike the Center of the Glass with the Implement.

If the hand holding the implement will come within a foot of the win-   18
dow as you break it, wrap it with a jacket or sweater before attempting to
break the glass. If no implement is available, use your heavily wrapped
hand; be sure you wrap your arm as well, beyond the elbow.

Strike the center of the glass with the implement.

6. Punch Out Any Remaining Shards of Glass.

Cover your fist with a jacket or sweater before removing the glass.   19

7. Make Your Escape.

Do not worry about any minor nicks and cuts. Run.   20

Get Your Date to Leave

1. Say Something Offensive.

If you know your date is of a particular religion or ethnicity, make   21
inappropriate comments.

2. Behave Inappropriately.

Do things that you think he will find unattractive or distasteful: chew   22
with your mouth open, eat with your fingers, argue with the waiter, close
your eyes and pretend to sleep, light matches and drop them on your plate,
ignore everything he says, and/or call someone else on your cell phone.

3. Send Your Date on a "Fool's Errand."

• Tell him you want to go to a specific nightclub, but explain that it gets very crowded and that if you are not in line by a certain time (say, fifteen minutes from then), you won't get in. Tell your date that you have arranged to have your friend stop by the restaurant with guest passes, but that if your date does not go ahead to the nightclub to get in line, you'll never make it inside. If your date wants your cell phone number, give the number willingly but make sure you change one digit. Promise you will see your date within half an hour. Never show.

• Fake an allergy attack, and insist that he leave in search of the appropriate over-the-counter allergy medicine. Explain that you must have been allergic to something in the drink/appetizer/food/taxicab, and that if you do not obtain your medicine you will break out in hives. When your date dutifully leaves, slip away.

Be Aware

Blind dates are the riskiest form of dating—it is best to check out a potential suitor extensively before the date.

• Have a friend agree to check out your potential suitor and call you before you enter the bar/restaurant. Send your friend in with a cell phone. Situate yourself at a bar nearby, and await her call. Have her contact you when she has identified the mark.

• If you discover unsavory facts about someone you're supposed to meet, call immediately to cancel the date. Blame work and say that you have to stay late at the office, or say that you're experiencing car trouble. A more permanent solution is to say that an old flame has reentered your life; this will prevent your blind date from calling you again and asking for a rain check.

• • •

Comprehension

1. According to the authors, what four basic strategies can someone use who wants to escape from a bad date?
2. Which of the four strategies seems most plausible? Why?
3. What kind of date do the authors seem to be imagining? Where does the date take place? How can you tell? Can the "escape" strategies the authors describe be modified for other kinds of dates as well?

Purpose and Audience

1. Do the authors expect readers to take their advice seriously? How do you know?

2. What purpose do visuals usually serve in instructions? What purpose do the visuals serve in this selection?

3. What thesis is implied in this set of instructions? Write a sentence that could serve as the thesis statement. Should such a sentence be added? If so, where?

4. Is the intended audience of this selection men, women, or both? How can you tell?

5. The writers never define what they mean by a "bad date." Why not?

Style and Structure

1. This selection is neither structured nor formatted like the other essays in this text. What does it include that other essays do not? What elements are missing that other essays include?

2. What features tell you this is a set of instructions rather than a process explanation?

3. Instructions are directed at people who will actually perform the process described. Is that the case here? Explain.

4. Where do the authors include the cautions and reminders that characterize instructions? Are these warnings and reminders actually necessary here?

5. Look carefully at the steps listed under each of the essay's five strategy headings. How do the authors move readers from one step to the next? Would transitional words and expressions be helpful additions? If so, which ones? Explain.

Vocabulary Projects

1. Define each of the following words as it is used in this selection.

   obscure (7)   dire (15)
   gait (8)   implement (17)
   procure (11)   unsavory (24)

2. Despite its informal style and tone, "How to Escape from a Bad Date" uses some terms — for example, "escape route" (4) and "prop" (7) — designed to make it sound like an authentic set of instructions. Identify other examples of such language. Do these expressions make the selection seem more serious? More credible?

Journal Entry

Think about a date you wanted to "escape" from but couldn't. Which of the strategies presented here might have been useful to you?

Writing Workshop

1. Although this is a humorous essay, the writers nevertheless do give some useful advice. Write a new version of these instructions, including only steps that you see as realistic and sensible. In your introduction, give some reasons someone might need to escape from a date; in your conclusion, make recommendations for avoiding this problem in the future.

2. Rewrite one of the selection's four strategy sections, replacing the authors' specific advice with your own advice — for example, your own steps for faking an emergency or getting your date to leave. Add an introduction and a conclusion to make your instructions into a complete essay.

3. Write a set of instructions for how to escape from a bad party.

Combining the Patterns

"How to Escape from a Bad Date" presents the steps in a process but considers neither the causes nor the effects of the "escape." What might cause someone to need to escape from a date? What might the effects of such an escape be? Should the authors have included sections of **cause and effect** to answer these questions?

Thematic Connections

- "Sex, Lies, and Conversation" (page 440)
- "The Dog Ate My Disk, and Other Tales of Woe" (page 475)
- "The Ways We Lie" (page 495)

ARTHUR MILLER

Get It Right: Privatize Executions

One of the leading playwrights of the twentieth century, Arthur Miller
(1915–2005), was born in New York City. He began writing plays while a
student at the University of Michigan and had his first play produced on
Broadway in 1944. Though it was not a success, his next Broadway production, *All My Sons* (1947), received positive reviews and the New York
Drama Critics' Circle Award. However, it was his 1949 play *Death of a Salesman* that established Miller as a major voice in the American theater:
opening to ecstatic reviews, it went on to win the Pulitzer Prize. Another
important play, *The Crucible* (1953), was set during the Salem witch trials
of the late seventeenth century but written as an allegory for the persecu-
tion of suspected Communists in the 1950s. (Miller himself was called
before the House Un-American Activities Committee and convicted of
contempt of Congress because he refused to cooperate by naming one-
time Communist sympathizers.) While his plays from the 1960s on did
not achieve the success of his earlier works, Miller's artistic legacy is
assured; his moral vision, as evidenced in the following 1992 essay, continues to move readers and playgoers around the world.

Background on public executions: Public executions of convicted felons
can be traced back at least as far as the ancient civilizations of Greece and
Rome and were common in European countries until well into the nineteenth century (public executions were conducted in England, for example, until 1868). Over time, they have been carried out by crucifixion,
stoning, burning at the stake, and beheading, among other methods.
However, by the 1600s in England and in the American colonies, public
executions were most often accomplished by hanging, usually in a public
square. These hangings, which were meant to teach spectators a moral lesson, ironically took on a festive, carnival-like air and were considered a
form of free entertainment. By the early 1800s, authorities in a number of
states began to require that hangings be performed in the privacy of
prisons—in part because the crowds witnessing them had become so
rowdy and in part because it was felt that public executions could stir sentiments against capital punishment. Still, public executions persisted in
some areas of the United States until the twentieth century; the last was
performed in 1936 in Owensboro, Kentucky. Today, public executions
continue in countries operating under Muslim law and under repressive
regimes, such as that of North Korea. The debate over public executions
moved again to the forefront in the United States in 2001 when the execution of Timothy McVeigh, convicted of the 1995 bombing in Oklahoma
City that killed 168 people, was witnessed via closed-circuit television by
family members of some of the victims.

The time has come to consider the privatization of executions. 1

There can no longer be any doubt that government — society itself — is 2
incapable of doing anything right, and this certainly applies to the executions of convicted criminals.

At present, the thing is a total loss, to the convicted person, to his fam- 3
ily and to society. It need not be so.

People can be executed in places like Shea Stadium before immense 4
paying audiences. The income from the spectacle could be distributed to
the prison that fed and housed him or to a trust fund for prisoner rehabilitation and his own family and/or girlfriend, as he himself chose.

The condemned would of course get a percentage of the gate, to be 5
negotiated by his agent or a promoter, if he so desired.

The take would, without question, be sizable, considering the immense 6
number of Americans in favor of capital punishment. A $200 to $300 ring-
side seat would not be excessive, with bleachers going for, say, $25.

As with all sports events, a certain ritual would seem inevitable and 7
would quickly become an expected part of the occasion. The electric chair
would be set on a platform, like a boxing ring without the rope, around
second base.

Once the audience was seated, a soprano would come forward and sing 8
"The Star-Spangled Banner." When she stepped down, the governor, holding a microphone, would appear and describe the condemned man's
crimes in detail, plus his many failed appeals.

Then the governor would step aside and a phalanx of police officers or 9
possibly National Guard or Army troops would mount the platform and
surround the condemned. This climactic entrance might be accompanied
by a trumpet fanfare or other musical number by the police or Army band,
unless it was thought to offend good taste.

Next, a minister or priest would appear and offer a benediction, asking 10
God's blessing on the execution.

The condemned, should he desire, could make a short statement and 11
even a plea of innocence. This would only add to the pathos of the occasion and would of course not be legally binding. He would then be
strapped into the chair.

Finally, the executioner, hooded to protect himself from retaliation, 12
would proceed to the platform. He would walk to a console where, on a
solemn signal from the governor, he would pull the switch.

The condemned man would instantly surge upward against his bind- 13
ings, with smoke emitting from his flesh. This by itself would provide a
most powerful lesson for anyone contemplating murder. For those not
contemplating murder, it would be a reminder of how lucky they are to
have been straight and honest in America.

For the state, this would mean additional income; for the audience, an 14
intense and educational experience — people might, for example, wish to
bring their children.

And for the condemned, it would have its achievement aspect, because 15
he would know that he had not lived his life for nothing.

Some might object that such proceedings are so fundamentally attrac-   16
tive that it is not too much to imagine certain individuals contemplating
murder in order to star in the program. But no solution to any profound
social problem is perfect.

Finally, and perhaps most important, it is entirely possible that after   17
witnessing a few dozen privatized executions, the public might grow tired
of the spectacle — just as it seizes on all kinds of entertainment only to lose
interest once their repetitiousness becomes too tiresomely apparent.

Then perhaps we might be willing to consider the fact that in execut-   18
ing prisoners we merely add to the number of untimely dead without
diminishing the number of murders committed.

At that point, the point of boredom, we might begin asking why it is   19
that Americans commit murder more often than any other people. At the
moment, we are not bored enough with executions to ask this question;
instead, we are apparently going to demand more and more of them, most
probably because we never get to witness any in person.

My proposal would lead us more quickly to boredom and away from   20
our current gratifying excitement — and ultimately perhaps to a wiser use
of alternating current.

•   •   •

Comprehension

1. What process does Miller describe?
2. List the individual steps in the process.
3. Which of Miller's recommendations are most outrageous? Is any part
   of his scheme actually plausible?
4. In paragraph 6, Miller notes that many Americans support capital punishment. Do you think Miller is one of these people? Why, or why not?
5. Why, according to Miller, do executions need to be privatized rather
   than performed by the government?
6. What specific benefits does Miller say will result from his scheme?
7. In paragraph 20, Miller suggests that his proposal might ultimately
   lead to "a wiser use of alternating current." What does he mean?

Purpose and Audience

1. This essay begins with an abrupt statement of a very controversial thesis. Why does Miller choose this approach? How successful is it?
2. What kind of reaction do you think Miller would like to get from his
   audience? For instance, does he want them to be amused? Shocked?
   Guilty? Angry? Explain.
3. What is Miller's real purpose in writing this essay? What does he hope
   to accomplish?

Style and Structure

1. Because this essay was first published in a newspaper and set in columns, it has relatively short paragraphs. Which paragraphs, if any, could be combined? Which would you leave as they are? Are there any advantages to using one- or two-sentence paragraphs in this essay?

2. Where does the actual process begin? Where does it end?

3. What words and phrases does Miller use to link the steps in the process? Do you think he needs any additional transitions? If so, where?

4. Much of this essay's tone is ironic, and Miller clearly intends that many of his statements not be taken literally. How do you suppose he expects readers to react to each of the following?
   - "unless it was thought to offend good taste" (9)
   - "he would know that he had not lived his life for nothing" (15)
   - "no solution to any profound social problem is perfect" (16)

5. Miller seems to suggest that executions are not unlike sporting events. How, according to Miller, are they alike? Is this a valid **analogy**?

Vocabulary Projects

1. Define each of the following words as it is used in this selection.

   privatization (1)   fanfare (9)
   phalanx (9)   pathos (11)
   climactic (9)   emitting (13)

2. Miller repeats variations of the word *execution* many times. What alternatives does he have? What different connotations does each of your possible substitutions suggest?

Journal Entry

Many people who support capital punishment see it as a deterrent to crime. Do you believe that the death penalty discourages people from committing capital crimes? Do you think Miller's scheme, if enacted, would be a deterrent?

Writing Workshop

1. Using the past tense, rewrite the process section of Miller's essay from the point of view of someone who has just witnessed a public execution. Give the condemned person an identity, a history, and a family, and explain the crime for which he or she is being punished. In your thesis, take a stand on whether or not this person deserves to be executed.

2. Write a letter to the editor of a newspaper expressing your strong disapproval of the idea of public executions. Use the steps in the process to support your position. To convince readers this practice is inhumane, add descriptive details — for example, about the observers' reactions and the sensationalist TV news coverage.

Combining the Patterns

Although the body of this essay is structured as a process, the essay as a whole makes a powerful **argument**. Does Miller have a debatable thesis? Do you think he needs more evidence to support his thesis, or is the process itself enough? Does he consider the possible objections of his audience? Does he refute these objections?

Thematic Connections

- "Shooting an Elephant" (page 125)
- "The Lottery" (page 317)
- "Who Killed Benny Paret?" (page 346)
- "Five Ways to Kill a Man" (page 505)
- "The Death of the Moth" (p. 728)

JESSICA MITFORD

The Embalming of Mr. Jones

Jessica Mitford (1917–1996) was born in Batsford Mansion, England, to a wealthy, aristocratic family. She rebelled against her sheltered upbringing, became involved in left-wing politics, and eventually immigrated to the United States. Mitford wrote two volumes of autobiography—*Daughters and Rebels* (1960), about her eccentric family, and *A Fine Old Conflict* (1976). In the 1950s, she began a career in investigative journalism, which produced the books *The American Way of Death* (1963), about abuses in the funeral business; *Kind and Usual Punishment* (1973), about the U.S. prison system; and *The American Way of Birth* (1992), about the crisis in American obstetrical care.

Background on the funeral industry: "The Embalming of Mr. Jones" is excerpted from *The American Way of Death,* a scathing critique of the funeral industry in the United States. The book prompted angry responses from morticians but also led to increased governmental regulation, culminating in a 1984 Federal Trade Commission ruling requiring funeral homes to disclose in writing the prices for all goods and services, as well as certain consumer rights; barring funeral homes from forcing consumers to purchase more than they really want; and forbidding funeral directors from misleading consumers regarding state laws governing the disposal of bodies. Still, industry critics charge that many abuses continue. While funeral services can be purchased for less than a thousand dollars, the standard rate is between two and four thousand dollars — and it can go much higher. The difference in cost is based largely on the price of a casket, and grieving family members are often strongly pressured into buying the most expensive caskets, which may be marked up as much as 500 percent. Advocates for reform suggest that consumers choose cremation over burial (of the approximately 2.5 million people who died in the United States in 2003, only some 700,000 were cremated) and that they hold memorial services in churches or other settings, where costs are much lower than in funeral homes.

Embalming is indeed a most extraordinary procedure, and one must wonder at the docility of Americans who each year pay hundreds of millions of dollars for its perpetuation, blissfully ignorant of what it is all about, what is done, how it is done. Not one in ten thousand has any idea of what actually takes place. Books on the subject are extremely hard to come by. They are not to be found in most libraries or bookshops.

In an era when huge television audiences watch surgical operations in the comfort of their living rooms, when, thanks to the animated cartoon, the geography of the digestive system has become familiar territory even to the nursery school set, in a land where the satisfaction of curiosity about almost all matters is a national pastime, the secrecy surrounding embalming can, surely, hardly be attributed to the inherent gruesomeness of the subject. Custom in this regard has within this century suffered a complete reversal. In the early days of American embalming, when it was performed in the home of the deceased, it was almost mandatory for some relative to stay by the embalmer's side and witness the procedure. Today, family members who might wish to be in attendance would certainly be dissuaded by the funeral director. All others, except apprentices, are excluded by law from the preparation room.

A close look at what does actually take place may explain in large measure the undertaker's intractable reticence concerning a procedure that has become his major *raison d'être.** Is it possible he fears that public information about embalming might lead patrons to wonder if they really want this service? If the funeral men are loath to discuss the subject outside the trade, the reader may, understandably, be equally loath to go on reading at this point. For those who have the stomach for it, let us part the formaldehyde curtain. . . .

3

The body is first laid out in the undertaker's morgue — or rather, Mr. Jones is reposing in the preparation room — to be readied to bid the world farewell.

4

The preparation room in any of the better funeral establishments has the tiled and sterile look of a surgery, and indeed the embalmer-restorative artist who does his chores there is beginning to adopt the term "dermasurgeon" (appropriately corrupted by some mortician-writers as "demisurgeon") to describe his calling. His equipment, consisting of scalpels, scissors, augers, forceps, clamps, needles, pumps, tubes, bowls, and basin, is crudely imitative of the surgeon's as is his technique, acquired in a nine- or twelve-month post-high-school course in an embalming school. He is supplied by an advanced chemical industry with a bewildering array of fluids, sprays, pastes, oils, powders, creams, to fix or soften tissue, shrink or distend it as needed, dry it here, restore the moisture there. There are cosmetics, waxes, and paints to fill and cover features, even plaster of Paris to replace entire limbs. There are ingenious aids to prop and stabilize the cadaver: a Vari-Pose Head Rest, the Edwards Arm and Hand Positioner, the Repose Block (to support the shoulders during the embalming), and the Throop Foot Positioner, which resembles an old-fashioned stocks.

5

Mr. John H. Eckels, president of the Eckels College of Mortuary Science, thus describes the first part of the embalming procedure: "In the hands of a skilled practitioner, this work may be done in a comparatively short time and without mutilating the body other than by slight incision — so slight that it scarcely would cause serious inconvenience if made upon a living person. It is necessary to remove all the blood, and doing this not only helps in the disinfecting, but removes the principal cause of disfigurements due to discoloration."

6

---

* EDS. NOTE — Reason for being (French).

Another textbook discusses the all-important time element: "The earlier this is done, the better, for every hour that elapses between death and embalming will add to the problems and complications encountered. . . ." Just how soon should one get going on the embalming? The author tells us, "On the basis of such scanty information made available to this profession through its rudimentary and haphazard system of technical research, we must conclude that the best results are to be obtained if the subject is embalmed before life is completely extinct—that is, before cellular death has occurred. In the average case, this would mean within an hour after somatic death." For those who feel that there is something a little rudimentary, not to say haphazard, about this advice, a comforting thought is offered by another writer. Speaking of fears entertained in early days of premature burial, he points out, "One of the effects of embalming by chemical injection, however, has been to dispel fears of live burial." How true; once the blood is removed, chances of live burial are indeed remote.

To return to Mr. Jones, the blood is drained out through the veins and replaced by embalming fluid pumped in through the arteries. As noted in *The Principles and Practices of Embalming,* "every operator has a favorite injection and drainage point—a fact which becomes a handicap only if he fails or refuses to forsake his favorites when conditions demand it." Typical favorites are the carotid artery, femoral artery, jugular vein, subclavian vein. There are various choices of embalming fluid. If Flextone is used, it will produce a "mild, flexible rigidity. The skin retains a velvety softness, the tissues are rubbery and pliable. Ideal for women and children." It may be blended with B. and G. Products Company's Lyf-Lyk tint, which is guaranteed to reproduce "nature's own skin texture . . . the velvety appearance of living tissue." Suntone comes in three separate tints: Suntan; Special Cosmetic Tint, a pink shade "especially indicated for young female subjects"; and Regular Cosmetic Tint, moderately pink.

About three to six gallons of a dyed and perfumed solution of formaldehyde, glycerin, borax, phenol, alcohol, and water is soon circulating through Mr. Jones, whose mouth has been sewn together with a "needle directed upward between the upper lip and gum and brought out through the left nostril," with the corners raised slightly "for a more pleasant expression." If he should be buck-toothed, his teeth are cleaned with Bon Ami and coated with colorless nail polish. His eyes, meanwhile, are closed with flesh-tinted eye caps and eye cement.

The next step is to have at Mr. Jones with a thing called a trocar. This is a long, hollow needle attached to a tube. It is jabbed into the abdomen, poked around the entrails and chest cavity, the contents of which are pumped out and replaced with "cavity fluid." This done, and the hole in the abdomen sewed up, Mr. Jones's face is heavily creamed (to protect the skin from burns which may be caused by leakage of the chemicals), and he is covered with a sheet and left unmolested for a while. But not for long— there is more, much more, in store for him. He has been embalmed, but not yet restored, and the best time to start restorative work is eight to ten hours after embalming, when the tissues have become firm and dry.

The object of all this attention to the corpse, it must be remembered, is   11
to make it presentable for viewing in an attitude of healthy repose. "Our
customs require the presentation of our dead in the semblance of normal-
ity . . . unmarred by the ravages of illness, disease or mutilation," says Mr. J.
Sheridan Mayer in his *Restorative Art.* This is rather a large order since few
people die in the full bloom of health, unravaged by illness and unmarked
by some disfigurement. The funeral industry is equal to the challenge: "In
some cases the gruesome appearance of a mutilated or disease-ridden subject may be quite discouraging. The task of restoration may seem impossible and shake the confidence of the embalmer. This is the time for
intestinal fortitude and determination. Once the formative work is begun
and affected tissues are cleaned or removed, all doubts of success vanish. It
is surprising and gratifying to discover the results which may be obtained."

The embalmer, having allowed an appropriate interval to elapse,   12
returns to the attack, but now he brings into play the skill and equipment
of sculptor and cosmetician. Is a hand missing? Casting one in plaster of
Paris is a simple matter. "For replacement purposes, only a cast of the back
of the hand is necessary; this is within the ability of the average operator
and is quite adequate." If a lip or two, a nose or an ear should be missing,
the embalmer has at hand a variety of restorative waxes with which to
model replacements. Pores and skin texture are simulated by stippling
with a little brush, and over this cosmetics are laid on. Head off? Decapitation cases are rather routinely handled. Ragged edges are trimmed, and
head joined to torso with a series of splints, wires, and sutures. It is a good
idea to have a little something at the neck — a scarf or high collar — when
time for viewing comes. Swollen mouth? Cut out tissue as needed from
inside the lips. If too much is removed, the surface contour can easily be
restored by padding with cotton. Swollen necks and cheeks are reduced by
removing tissue through vertical incisions made down each side of the
neck. "When the deceased is casketed, the pillow will hide the suture incisions. . . . as an extra precaution against leakage, the suture may be painted
with liquid sealer."

The opposite condition is more likely to present itself — that of emaci-   13
ation. His hypodermic syringe now loaded with massage cream, the
embalmer seeks out and fills the hollowed and sunken areas by injection.
In this procedure the backs of the hands and fingers and the underchin
area should not be neglected.

Positioning the lips is a problem that recurrently challenges the inge-   14
nuity of the embalmer. Closed too tightly, they tend to give a stern, even
disapproving expression. Ideally, embalmers feel, the lips should give the
impression of being ever so slightly parted, the upper lip protruding
slightly for a more youthful appearance. This takes some engineering,
however, as the lips tend to drift apart. Lip drift can sometimes be reme-
died by pushing one or two straight pins through the inner margin of the
lower lip and then inserting them between the two front upper teeth. If Mr.
Jones happens to have no teeth, the pins can just as easily be anchored in
his Armstrong Face Former and Denture Replacer. Another method to

maintain lip closure is to dislocate the lower jaw, which is then held in its new position by a wire run through holes which have been drilled through the upper jaws at the midline. As the French are fond of saying, *il faut souffrir pour être belle.**

If Mr. Jones has died of jaundice, the embalming fluid will very likely turn him green. Does this deter the embalmer? Not if he has intestinal fortitude. Masking pastes and cosmetics are heavily laid on, burial garments and casket interiors are color-correlated with particular care, and Jones is displayed beneath rose-colored lights. Friends will say, "How *well* he looks." Death by carbon monoxide, on the other hand, can be rather a good thing from an embalmer's viewpoint: "One advantage is the fact that this type of discoloration is an exaggerated form of a natural pink coloration." This is nice because the healthy glow is already present and needs but little attention.

The patching and filling completed, Mr. Jones is now shaved, washed, and dressed. Cream-based cosmetic, available in pink, flesh, suntan, brunette, and blonde, is applied to his hands and face, his hair is shampooed and combed (and, in the case of Mrs. Jones, set), his hands manicured. For the horny-handed son of toil special care must be taken; cream should be applied to remove ingrained grime, and the nails cleaned. "If he were not in the habit of having them manicured in life, trimming and shaping is advised for better appearance — never questioned by kin."

Jones is now ready for casketing (this is the present participle of the verb "to casket"). In this operation his right shoulder should be depressed slightly "to turn the body a bit to the right and soften the appearance of lying flat on the back." Positioning the hands is a matter of importance, and special rubber positioning blocks may be used. The hands should be cupped slightly for a more lifelike, relaxed appearance. Proper placement of the body requires a delicate sense of balance. It should lie as high as possible in the casket, yet not so high that the lid, when lowered, will hit the nose. On the other hand, we are cautioned, placing the body too low "creates the impression that the body is in a box."

Jones is next wheeled into the appointed slumber room where a few last touches may be added — his favorite pipe placed in his hand or, if he was a great reader, a book propped into position. (In the case of little Master Jones a Teddy bear may be clutched.) Here he will hold open house for a few days, visiting hours 10 A.M. to 9 P.M.

·   ·   ·

Comprehension

1. How, according to Mitford, has the public's knowledge of embalming changed? How does she explain this change?

---

* EDS. NOTE — It is necessary to suffer in order to be beautiful.

2. To what other professionals does Mitford compare the embalmer? Are these analogies flattering or critical? Explain.

3. What are the major stages in the process of embalming and restoration?

Purpose and Audience

1. Mitford's purpose in this essay is to convince her audience of something. What is her thesis?

2. Do you think Mitford expects her audience to agree with her thesis? How can you tell?

3. In one of her books, Mitford refers to herself as a *muckraker,* one who informs the public of misconduct. Does she achieve this status here? Cite specific examples.

4. Mitford's tone in this essay is subjective, even judgmental. What effect does her tone have on you? Does it encourage you to trust her? Should she have presented her facts in a more objective way? Explain.

Style and Structure

1. Identify the stylistic features that distinguish this process explanation from a set of instructions.

2. In this selection, as in many process essays, a list of necessary materials comes before the procedure. What additional details does Mitford include in her list in paragraph 5? How do these additions affect you?

3. Locate Mitford's remarks about the language of embalming. How do her comments about euphemisms, newly coined words, and other aspects of language help to support her thesis?

4. Throughout the essay, Mitford quotes various experts. How does she use their remarks to support her thesis?

5. What phrases serve as transitions between the various stages of Mitford's process?

6. Mitford uses a good deal of sarcasm and biased language in this essay. Identify some examples. Does this kind of language strengthen or weaken her essay?

Vocabulary Projects

1. Define each of the following words as it is used in this selection.

perpetuation (1)	rudimentary (7)	stippling (12)
inherent (2)	haphazard (7)	emaciation (13)
mandatory (2)	entertained (7)	recurrently (14)
dissuaded (2)	pliable (8)	jaundice (15)
intractable (3)	repose (11)	toil (16)
reticence (3)	unravaged (11)	
loath (3)	fortitude (11)	

2. Substitute another word for each of the following.

territory (2)   ingenious (5)   presentable (11)
gruesomeness (2)   jabbed (10)

What effect does each of your changes have on Mitford's meaning?

3. Reread paragraphs 5–9 carefully. Then, list all the words in this section of the essay that suggest surgical technique and all the words that suggest cosmetic artistry. What do your lists tell you about Mitford's intent in these paragraphs?

Journal Entry

What are your thoughts about how your religion or culture deals with death and dying? What practices, if any, make you uncomfortable? Why?

Writing Workshop

1. Rewrite this process explanation as a set of instructions for undertakers, condensing it so that your essay is about five hundred words long. Unlike Mitford, keep your essay objective.

2. In the role of a funeral director, write a letter to Mitford taking issue with her essay. Explain the practice of embalming as necessary and practical. Unlike Mitford, design your process explanation to defend the practice.

3. Write an explanation of a process you personally find disgusting — or delightful. Make your attitude clear in your thesis statement and in your choice of words.

Combining the Patterns

Although Mitford structures this essay as a process, many passages rely heavily on subjective **description**. Where is her focus on descriptive details most obvious? What is her purpose in describing particular individuals and objects as she does? How do these descriptive passages help to support her essay's thesis?

Thematic Connections

- "My First Conk" (page 285)
- "The Ways We Lie" (page 495)
- "A Modest Proposal" (page 733)

SHIRLEY JACKSON

The Lottery (Fiction)

Shirley Jackson (1919–1965) was born in California and graduated from Syracuse University in 1940. She is best known for her subtly macabre stories of horror and suspense, most notably her best-selling novel *The Haunting of Hill House* (1959), which Stephen King has called "one of the greatest horror stories of all time." She also published wryly humorous reflections on her experiences as a wife and mother of four children. Many of her finest stories and novels were not anthologized until after her death.

Background on the initial reaction to "The Lottery": "The Lottery" first appeared in *The New Yorker* in 1948, three years after the end of World War II. Jackson was living somewhat uneasily in the New England college town of Bennington, Vermont, a village very similar to the setting of "The Lottery." She felt herself an outsider there, a sophisticated intellectual in an isolated, closely knit community suspicious of strangers. Here, Jackson (whose husband was Jewish) experienced frequent encounters with anti-Semitism. At the time, the full atrocity of Germany's wartime program to exterminate Jews, now called the Holocaust, had led many social critics to contemplate humanity's terrible capacity for evil. Most Americans, however, wished to put the horrors of the war behind them, and many readers reacted with outrage to Jackson's tale of an annual small-town ritual, calling it "nasty," "nauseating," and even "perverted." Others, however, immediately recognized its genius, its power, and its many layers of meaning. This classic tale is now one of the most widely anthologized of twentieth-century short stories.

The morning of June 27th was clear and sunny, with the fresh warmth of a full-summer day; the flowers were blossoming profusely and the grass was richly green. The people of the village began to gather in the square, between the post office and the bank, around ten o'clock; in some towns there were so many people that the lottery took two days and had to be started on June 26th, but in this village, where there were only about three hundred people, the whole lottery took less than two hours, so it could begin at ten o'clock in the morning and still be through in time to allow the villagers to get home for noon dinner. 1

The children assembled first, of course. School was recently over for the summer, and the feeling of liberty sat uneasily on most of them; they tended to gather together quietly for a while before they broke into boisterous play, and their talk was still of the classroom and the teacher, of books and reprimands. Bobby Martin had already stuffed his pockets full of stones, and the other boys soon followed his example, selecting the smoothest and roundest stones; Bobby and Harry Jones and Dickie 2

Delacroix—the villagers pronounced his name "Dellacroy"—eventually made a great pile of stones in one corner of the square and guarded it against the raids of the other boys. The girls stood aside, talking among themselves, looking over their shoulders at the boys, and the very small children rolled in the dust or clung to the hands of their older brothers or sisters.

Soon the men began to gather, surveying their own children, speaking of planting and rain, tractors and taxes. They stood together, away from the pile of stones in the corner, and their jokes were quiet and they smiled rather than laughed. The women, wearing faded house dresses and sweaters, came shortly after their menfolk. They greeted one another and exchanged bits of gossip as they went to join their husbands. Soon the women, standing by their husbands, began to call to their children, and the children came reluctantly, having to be called four or five times. Bobby Martin ducked under his mother's grasping hand and ran, laughing, back to the pile of stones. His father spoke up sharply, and Bobby came quickly and took his place between his father and his oldest brother.   3

The lottery was conducted—as were the square dances, the teenage club, the Halloween program—by Mr. Summers, who had time and energy to devote to civic activities. He was a round-faced, jovial man and he ran the coal business, and people were sorry for him, because he had no children and his wife was a scold. When he arrived in the square, carrying the black wooden box, there was a murmur of conversation among the villagers, and he waved and called "Little late today, folks." The postmaster, Mr. Graves, followed him, carrying a three-legged stool, and the stool was put in the center of the square and Mr. Summers set the black box down on it. The villagers kept their distance, leaving a space between themselves and the stool, and when Mr. Summers said, "Some of you fellows want to give me a hand?" there was a hesitation before two men, Mr. Martin and his oldest son, Baxter, came forward to hold the box steady on the stool while Mr. Summers stirred up the papers inside it.   4

The original paraphernalia for the lottery had been lost long ago, and the black box now resting on the stool had been put into use even before Old Man Warner, the oldest man in town, was born. Mr. Summers spoke frequently to the villagers about making a new box, but no one liked to upset even as much tradition as was represented by the black box. There was a story that the present box had been made with some pieces of the box that had preceded it, the one that had been constructed when the first people settled down to make a village here. Every year, after the lottery, Mr. Summers began talking about a new box, but every year the subject was allowed to fade off without anything's being done. The black box grew shabbier each year; by now it was no longer completely black but splintered badly along one side to show the original wood color, and in some places faded and stained.   5

Mr. Martin and his oldest son, Baxter, held the black box securely on the stool until Mr. Summers had stirred the papers thoroughly with his   6 hand. Because so much of the ritual had been forgotten or discarded, Mr. Summers had been successful in having slips of paper substituted for the chips of wood that had been used for generations. Chips of wood, Mr. Summers had argued, had been all very well when the village was tiny, but now that the population was more than three hundred and likely to keep on growing, it was necessary to use something that would fit more easily into the black box. The night before the lottery, Mr. Summers and Mr. Graves made up the slips of paper and put them in the box, and it was then taken to the safe of Mr. Summers' coal company and locked up until Mr. Summers was ready to take it to the square the next morning. The rest of the year, the box was put away, sometimes one place, sometimes another; it had spent one year in Mr. Graves' barn and another year underfoot in the post office, and sometimes it was set on a shelf in the Martin grocery and left there.

There was a great deal of fussing to be done before Mr. Summers   7
declared the lottery open. There were the lists to make up — of heads of families, heads of households in each family, members of each household in each family. There was the proper swearing-in of Mr. Summers by the postmaster, as the official of the lottery; at one time, some people remembered, there had been a recital of some sort, performed by the official of the lottery, a perfunctory, tuneless chant that had been rattled off duly each year; some people believed that the official of the lottery used to stand just so when he said or sang it, others believed that he was supposed to walk among the people, but years and years ago this part of the ritual had been allowed to lapse. There had been, also, a ritual salute, which the official of the lottery had had to use in addressing each person who came up to draw from the box, but this also had changed with time, until now it was felt necessary only for the official to speak to each person approaching. Mr. Summers was very good at all this; in his clean white shirt and blue jeans, with one hand resting carelessly on the black box, he seemed very proper and important as he talked interminably to Mr. Graves and the Martins.

Just as Mr. Summers finally left off talking and turned to the as-   8
sembled villagers, Mrs. Hutchinson came hurriedly along the path to the square, her sweater thrown over her shoulders, and slid into place in the back of the crowd. "Clean forgot what day it was," she said to Mrs. Delacroix, who stood next to her, and they both laughed softly. "Thought my old man was out back stacking wood," Mrs. Hutchinson went on, "and then I looked out the window and the kids were gone, and then I remembered it was the twenty-seventh and came a-running." She dried her hands on her apron, and Mrs. Delacroix said, "You're in time, though. They're still talking away up there."

Mrs. Hutchinson craned her neck to see through the crowd and found   9
her husband and children standing near the front. She tapped Mrs. Delacroix on the arm as a farewell and began to make her way through the crowd. The people separated good-humoredly to let her through; two or

three people said, in voices just loud enough to be heard across the crowd, "Here comes your Missus, Hutchinson," and "Bill, she made it after all." Mrs. Hutchinson reached her husband, and Mr. Summers, who had been waiting, said cheerfully, "Thought we were going to have to get on without you, Tessie." Mrs. Hutchinson said, grinning, "Wouldn't have me leave m'dishes in the sink, now, would you, Joe?" and soft laughter ran through the crowd as the people stirred back into position after Mrs. Hutchinson's arrival.

"Well, now," Mr. Summers said soberly, "guess we better get started, get   10
this over with, so's we can go back to work. Anybody ain't here?"

"Dunbar," several people said. "Dunbar, Dunbar."   11

Mr. Summers consulted his list. "Clyde Dunbar," he said. "That's   12
right. He's broke his leg, hasn't he? Who's drawing for him?"

"Me, I guess," a woman said, and Mr. Summers turned to look at her.   13
"Wife draws for her husband," Mr. Summers said. "Don't you have a grown boy to do it for you, Janey?" Although Mr. Summers and everyone else in the village knew the answer perfectly well, it was the business of the official of the lottery to ask such questions formally. Mr. Summers waited with an expression of polite interest while Mrs. Dunbar answered.

"Horace's not but sixteen yet," Mrs. Dunbar said regretfully. "Guess I   14
gotta fill in for the old man this year."

"Right," Mr. Summers said. He made a note on the list he was holding.   15
Then he asked, "Watson boy drawing this year?"

A tall boy in the crowd raised his hand. "Here," he said. "I'm drawing   16
for m'mother and me." He blinked his eyes nervously and ducked his head as several voices in the crowd said things like "Good fellow, Jack," and "Glad to see your mother's got a man to do it."

"Well," Mr. Summers said, "guess that's everyone. Old Man Warner   17
make it?"

"Here," a voice said, and Mr. Summers nodded.   18

A sudden hush fell on the crowd as Mr. Summers cleared his throat   19
and looked at the list. "All ready?" he called. "Now, I'll read the names — heads of families first — and the men come up and take a paper out of the box. Keep the paper folded in your hand without looking at it until everyone has had a turn. Everything clear?"

The people had done it so many times that they only half listened to   20
the directions; most of them were quiet, wetting their lips, not looking around. Then Mr. Summers raised one hand high and said, "Adams." A man disengaged himself from the crowd and came forward. "Hi, Steve," Mr. Summers said, and Mr. Adams said, "Hi, Joe." They grinned at one another humorlessly and nervously. Then Mr. Adams reached into the black box and took out a folded paper. He held it firmly by one corner as he turned and went hastily back to his place in the crowd, where he stood a little apart from his family, not looking down at his hand.

"Allen." Mr. Summers said. "Anderson. . . . Betham."   21

"Seems like there's no time at all between lotteries any more," Mrs.   22
Delacroix said to Mrs. Graves in the back row. "Seems like we got through
the last one only last week."

"Time sure goes fast," Mrs. Graves said.   23

"Clark.... Delacroix."   24

"There goes my old man," Mrs. Delacroix said. She held her breath   25
while her husband went forward.

"Dunbar," Mr. Summers said, and Mrs. Dunbar went steadily to the   26
box while one of the women said, "Go on, Janey," and another said, "There
she goes."

"We're next," Mrs. Graves said. She watched while Mr. Graves came   27
around from the side of the box, greeted Mr. Summers gravely, and
selected a slip of paper from the box. By now, all through the crowd there
were men holding the small folded papers in their large hands, turning
them over and over nervously. Mrs. Dunbar and her two sons stood
together, Mrs. Dunbar holding the slip of paper.

"Harburt.... Hutchinson."   28

"Get up there, Bill," Mrs. Hutchinson said, and the people near her   29
laughed.

"Jones."   30

"They do say," Mr. Adams said to Old Man Warner, who stood next to   31
him, "that over in the north village they're talking of giving up the lottery."

Old Man Warner snorted. "Pack of crazy fools," he said. "Listening to   32
the young folks, nothing's good enough for *them.* Next thing you know,
they'll be wanting to go back to living in caves, nobody work any more, live
that way for a while. Used to be a saying about 'Lottery in June, corn be
heavy soon.' First thing you know, we'd all be eating stewed chickweed and
acorns. There's *always* been a lottery," he added petulantly. "Bad enough to
see young Joe Summers up there joking with everybody."

"Some places have already quit lotteries," Mrs. Adams said.   33

"Nothing but trouble in *that,*" Old Man Warner said stoutly. "Pack of   34
young fools."

"Martin." And Bobby Martin watched his father go forward.   35
"Overdyke.... Percy."

"I wish they'd hurry," Mrs. Dunbar said to her older son. "I wish they'd   36
hurry."

"They're almost through," her son said.   37

"You get ready to run tell Dad," Mrs. Dunbar said.   38

Mr. Summers called his own name and then stepped forward precisely   39
and selected a slip from the box. Then he called, "Warner."

"Seventy-seventh year I been in the lottery," Old Man Warner said as he   40
went through the crowd. "Seventy-seventh time."

"Watson." The tall boy came awkwardly through the crowd. Someone   41
said, "Don't be nervous, Jack," and Mr. Summers said, "Take your time,
son."

"Zanini."   42

After that, there was a long pause, a breathless pause, until Mr. Summers, holding his slip of paper in the air, said, "All right fellows." For a minute, no one moved, and then all the slips of paper were opened. Suddenly, all the women began to speak at once, saying, "Who is it," "Who's got it?," "Is it the Dunbars?," "Is it the Watsons?" Then the voices began to say, "It's Hutchinson. It's Bill," "Bill Hutchinson's got it."   43

"Go tell your father," Mrs. Dunbar said to her older son.   44

People began to look around to see the Hutchinsons. Bill Hutchinson   45
was standing quiet, staring down at the paper in his hand. Suddenly, Tessie Hutchinson shouted to Mr. Summers, "You didn't give him time enough to take any paper he wanted. I saw you. It wasn't fair!"

"Be a good sport, Tessie," Mrs. Delacroix called, and Mrs. Graves said,   46
"All of us took the same chance."

"Shut up, Tessie," Bill Hutchinson said.   47

"Well, everyone," Mr. Summers said, "That was done pretty fast, and   48
now we've got to be hurrying a little more to get it done in time." He consulted his next list. "Bill," he said, "you draw for the Hutchinson family. You got any other households in the Hutchinsons?"

"There's Don and Eva," Mrs. Hutchinson yelled. "Make *them* take their   49
chance!"

"Daughters draw with their husbands' families, Tessie," Mr. Summers   50
said gently. "You know that as well as anyone else."

"It wasn't *fair*," Tessie said.   51

"I guess not, Joe," Bill Hutchinson said regretfully. "My daughter   52
draws with her husband's family, that's only fair. And I've got no other family except the kids."

"Then, as far as drawing for families is concerned, it's you," Mr. Summers said in explanation, "and as far as drawing for households is concerned, that's you, too. Right?"   53

"Right," Bill Hutchinson said.   54

"How many kids, Bill?" Mr. Summers asked formally.   55

"Three," Bill Hutchinson said. "There's Bill, Jr., and Nancy, and little   56
Dave. And Tessie and me."

"All right, then," Mr. Summers said. "Harry, you got their tickets back?"   57

Mr. Graves nodded and held up the slips of paper. "Put them in the   58
box, then," Mr. Summers directed. "Take Bill's and put it in."

"I think we ought to start over," Mrs. Hutchinson said, as quietly as she   59
could. "I tell you it wasn't *fair*. You didn't give him time enough to choose. *Every*body saw that."

Mr. Graves had selected the five slips and put them in the box, and he   60
dropped all the papers but those onto the ground, where the breeze caught them and lifted them off.

"Listen, everybody," Mrs. Hutchinson was saying to the people around   61
her.

"Ready, Bill?" Mr. Summers asked, and Bill Hutchinson, with one   62
quick glance around at his wife and children, nodded.

"Remember," Mr. Summers said, "take the slips and keep them folded   63
until each person has taken one. Harry, you help little Dave." Mr. Graves
took the hand of the little boy, who came willingly with him up to the box.
"Take a paper out of the box, Davy," Mr. Summers said. Davy put his hand
into the box and laughed. "Take just *one* paper," Mr. Summers said. "Harry,
you hold it for him." Mr. Graves took the child's hand and removed the
folded paper from the tight fist and held it while little Dave stood next to
him and looked up at him wonderingly.

"Nancy next," Mr. Summers said. Nancy was twelve, and her school   64
friends breathed heavily as she went forward, switching her skirt, and took
a slip daintily from the box. "Bill, Jr.," Mr. Summers said, and Billy, his face
red and his feet over-large, nearly knocked the box over as he got a paper
out. "Tessie," Mr. Summers said. She hesitated for a minute, looking
around defiantly, and then set her lips and went up to the box. She
snatched a paper out and held it behind her.

"Bill," Mr. Summers said, and Bill Hutchinson reached into the box   65
and felt around, bringing his hand out at last with the slip of paper in it.

The crowd was quiet. A girl whispered, "I hope it's not Nancy," and the   66
sound of the whisper reached the edges of the crowd.

"It's not the way it used to be," Old Man Warner said clearly. "People   67
ain't the way they used to be."

"All right," Mr. Summers said. "Open the papers. Harry, you open little   68
Dave's."

Mr. Graves opened the slip of paper and there was a general sigh   69
through the crowd as he held it up and everyone could see that it was
blank. Nancy and Bill, Jr., opened theirs at the same time, and both
beamed and laughed, turning around to the crowd and holding their slips
of paper above their heads.

"Tessie," Mr. Summers said. There was a pause, and then Mr. Summers   70
looked at Bill Hutchinson, and Bill unfolded his paper and showed it. It
was blank.

"It's Tessie," Mr. Summers said, and his voice was hushed. "Show us   71
her paper, Bill."

Bill Hutchinson went over to his wife and forced the slip of paper out   72
of her hand. It had a black spot on it, the black spot Mr. Summers had
made the night before with the heavy pencil in the coal-company office.
Bill Hutchinson held it up, and there was a stir in the crowd.

"All right, folks," Mr. Summers said. "Let's finish quickly."   73

Although the villagers had forgotten the ritual and lost the original   74
black box, they still remembered to use stones. The pile of stones the boys
had made earlier was ready; there were stones on the ground with the blow-
ing scraps of paper that had come out of the box. Mrs. Delacroix selected a
stone so large she had to pick it up with both hands and turned to Mrs.
Dunbar. "Come on," she said. "Hurry up."

Mrs. Dunbar had small stones in both hands, and she said, gasping for   75
breath, "I can't run at all. You'll have to go ahead and I'll catch up with you."

The children had stones already, and someone gave little Davy   76
Hutchinson a few pebbles.

Tessie Hutchinson was in the center of a cleared space by now, and she   77
held her hands out desperately as the villagers moved in on her. "It isn't
fair," she said. A stone hit her on the side of the head.

Old Man Warner was saying, "Come on, come on, everyone." Steve   78
Adams was in the front of the crowd of villagers, with Mrs. Graves beside
him.

"It isn't fair, it isn't right," Mrs. Hutchinson screamed, and then they   79
were upon her.

· · ·

Reading Literature

1. List the stages in the process of the lottery. Then, identify passages
   explaining the reasons behind each step. How logical are these explanations?
2. What is the significance that the process has continued essentially
   unchanged for so many years? What does this fact suggest about the
   people in the town?
3. Do you see this story as an explanation of a brutal process carried out
   in one town, or do you see it as a universal statement about dangerous
   tendencies in modern society — or in human nature? Explain your reasoning.

Journal Entry

What do you think it would take to stop a process like the lottery? What
could be done — and who would have to do it?

Thematic Connections

- "Thirty-Eight Who Saw Murder Didn't Call the Police" (page 120)
- "Shooting an Elephant" (page 125)
- "Samuel" (page 262)
- "Get It Right: Privatize Executions" (page 305)

WRITING ASSIGNMENTS FOR PROCESS

1. Jessica Mitford describes the process of doing a job. Write an essay summarizing the steps you took in applying for, performing, or quitting a job.

2. Write a set of instructions explaining in objective terms how the lottery Shirley Jackson describes should be conducted. Imagine you are setting these steps down in writing for generations of your fellow townspeople to follow.

3. Write a consumer-oriented article for your school newspaper explaining how to apply for financial aid, a work-study job, a student internship, or permanent employment in your field.

4. List the steps in the process you follow when you study for an important exam. Then, interview two friends about how they study, and take notes about their usual routine. Finally, combine the most helpful strategies into a set of instructions aimed at students entering your school.

5. Write a set of instructions explaining how to use a print reference work or an online database you are familiar with. Assume your audience is not familiar with the research tool you are using.

6. Think of a series of steps in a bureaucratic process, a process you had to go through to accomplish something—getting a driver's license or becoming a U.S. citizen, for instance. Write an essay explaining that process, and include a thesis statement that evaluates the efficiency of that process.

7. Imagine you have encountered a visitor from another country (or another planet) who is not familiar with a social ritual you take for granted. Try to outline the steps involved in the ritual you are familiar with—for instance, choosing sides for a game or pledging a fraternity or sorority.

8. Write a process essay explaining how you went about putting together a collection, a scrapbook, a portfolio, or an album of some kind. Be sure your essay makes clear why you collected or compiled your materials.

9. Explain how a certain ritual or ceremony is conducted in your religion. Make sure someone of another faith could understand the process, and include a thesis statement that explains why the ritual is important.

10. Think of a process you believe should be modified or discontinued. (Examples might include getting a passport or applying to college.) Formulate a persuasive thesis that presents your negative feelings, and then explain the process so that you make your objections clear to your readers.

11. Write an essay explaining a process you experienced but would not recommend to others—for example, getting a tattoo or a body piercing.

12. Give readers instructions for participating in a potentially dangerous but worthwhile physical process—for example, rock climbing or white-water rafting. Be sure to include all necessary cautions.

COLLABORATIVE ACTIVITY FOR PROCESS

Working with three other students, create an illustrated instructional pamphlet to help new students survive four of your college's first "ordeals"—for example, registering for classes, purchasing textbooks, eating in the cafeteria, and moving into a dorm. Before beginning, decide as a group which processes to write about, whether you want your pamphlet to be practical and serious or humorous and irreverent, and what kind of illustrations it should include. Then, decide who will write about which process—each student should do one—and who will provide the illustrations. When all of you are ready, assemble your individual efforts into a single unified piece of writing.

INTERNET ASSIGNMENT FOR PROCESS

Write a letter to a friend giving instructions for doing Internet research for a school project. Before you start to write, visit the following Web sites about the Internet so that you can better understand the process your friend will need to go through when conducting this research, and think carefully about what resources and steps will be most useful.

Conducting Research on the Internet
<library.albany.edu/internet/research.html>
This site, sponsored by the University at Albany libraries, offers a list of ways to search the Internet and includes links to other Internet tutorials.

Using the Internet
<sofweb.vic.edu.au/internet/research.htm>
This site offers information on planning how you will use the Internet for research projects, strategies for searching and evaluating resources, and a helpful worksheet of questions to think about when evaluating sources.

Bedford/St. Martin's Interactive Research Tutorials
<bedfordstmartins.com/english_research/demos.htm>
This site offers tutorials on such skills as conducting Web searches and using online library catalogs.

10
Cause and Effect

What Is Cause and Effect?

Process describes *how* something happens; **cause and effect** analyzes *why* something happens. Cause-and-effect essays examine causes, describe effects, or do both. In the following paragraph, journalist Tom Wicker considers the effects of a technological advance on a village in India:

Cause

Effects

Topic sentence

When a solar-powered water pump was provided for a well in India, the village headman took it over and sold the water, until stopped. The new liquid abundance attracted hordes of unwanted nomads. Village boys who had drawn water in buckets had nothing to do, and some became criminals. The gap between rich and poor widened, since the poor had no land to benefit from irrigation. Finally, village women broke the pump, so they could gather again around the well that had been the center of their social lives. Moral: technological advances have social, cultural, and economic consequences, often unanticipated.

Cause and effect, like narration, links situations and events together in time, with causes preceding effects. But causality involves more than sequence: cause-and-effect analysis explains why something happened — or is happening — and predicts what probably will happen.

Sometimes many different causes can be responsible for one effect. For example, as the following diagram illustrates, many elements may contribute to an individual's decision to leave his or her country of origin for the United States:

Causes *Effect*

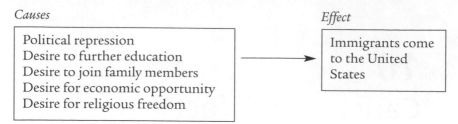

Similarly, a single cause can produce many different effects. Immigration, for instance, has had a variety of effects on the United States:

Cause *Effects*

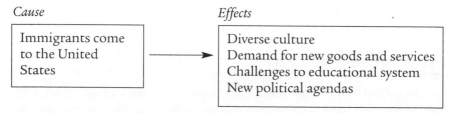

Using Cause and Effect

Of course, causal relationships are rarely as neat as the boxes above suggest; in fact, such relationships are often subtle and complex. As you examine situations that seem suited to cause-and-effect analysis, you will discover that most complex situations involve numerous causes and many different effects.

Consider this example. For more than twenty years, from the 1960s to the 1980s, the college-board scores of high school seniors steadily declined. The decline began soon after television became popular, and therefore many people concluded that the two events were connected. This idea is plausible because children did seem to be reading less to watch television more, and reading comprehension is one of the chief skills the tests evaluate.

But many other elements might have contributed to the decline of test scores. During the same period, for example, many schools reduced the number of required courses and deemphasized traditional subjects and skills, such as reading. Adults were reading less than they used to, and perhaps they were not encouraging their children to read. Furthermore, during the 1960s and 1970s, many colleges changed their policies and admitted students who previously would not have qualified. These new admission standards encouraged students who would not have taken college boards in earlier years to take the tests. Therefore, the scores may have been lower because they measured the top third of high school seniors rather than the top fifth. In any case, the reason for the lower scores is not clear. Perhaps television was the main cause after all, but nobody knows for sure. In such a case, it is easy—too easy—to claim a cause-and-effect relationship without the evidence to support it.

Just as the drop in scores may have had many causes, television watching may have had many effects. For instance, it may have made those same students better observers and listeners even if they did less well on standardized written tests. It may have encouraged them to have a national or even international outlook instead of a narrower local perspective. In other words, even if watching television did limit young people in some ways, it might also have expanded their horizons in other ways.

To give a balanced analysis, try to consider all causes and effects, not just the most obvious ones or the first ones you think of. For example, suppose a professional basketball team, recently stocked with the best players money can buy, has had a mediocre season. Because the individual players are talented and were successful under other coaches, fans blame the current coach for the team's losing streak and want him fired. But is the coach alone responsible? Maybe the inability of the players to function well as a team contributed to their poor performance. Perhaps some of the players are suffering from injuries, personal problems, or drug dependency. Or maybe the drop in attendance at games has affected the team's morale. Clearly, other elements besides the new coach could have caused the losing streak. (And, of course, the team's losing streak might have any number of consequences, from declining attendance at games to the city's refusal to build a new arena.) When you write about such a situation, you need to carefully identify these complex causes and effects.

Understanding Main and Contributory Causes

Even when you have identified several causes of an effect, one—the main cause—is always more important than the others, the contributory causes. Understanding the distinction between the **main** (most important) **cause** and the **contributory** (less important) **causes** is vital for planning a cause-and-effect paper because once you identify the main cause, you can emphasize it in your paper and downplay the other causes. How, then, can you tell which cause is most important? Sometimes the main cause is obvious, but often it is not, as the following example shows.

During one winter a number of years ago, an unusually large amount of snow accumulated on the roof of the Civic Center Auditorium in Hartford, Connecticut, and the roof fell in. Newspapers reported that the weight of the snow had caused the collapse, and they were partly right. Other buildings, however, had not been flattened by the snow, so the main cause seemed to lie elsewhere. Insurance investigators eventually decided that the roof design, not the weight of the snow (which was a contributory cause), was the main cause of the collapse.

These cause-and-effect relationships are shown in this diagram:

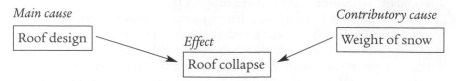

Because the main cause is not always the most obvious one, you should be sure to consider the significance of each cause very carefully as you plan your essay—and to continue to evaluate the importance of each cause as you write and revise.

Understanding Immediate and Remote Causes

Another important distinction is the difference between an immediate cause and a remote cause. An **immediate cause** closely precedes an effect and is therefore relatively easy to recognize. A **remote cause** is less obvious, perhaps because it involves something in the past or far away. Assuming that the most obvious cause is always the most important can be dangerous as well as shortsighted.

For example, consider again the Hartford roof collapse. Most people agreed that the snow was the immediate, or most obvious, cause of the roof collapse. But further study by insurance investigators suggested remote causes that were not so apparent. The design of the roof was the most important remote cause of the collapse, but other remote causes were also examined. Perhaps the materials used in the roof's construction were partly to blame. Maybe maintenance crews had not done their jobs properly, or necessary repairs had not been made. If you were the insurance investigator analyzing the causes of this event, you would want to assess all possible contributing factors rather than just the most obvious. If you did not consider the remote as well as the immediate causes, you would reach an oversimplified and perhaps incorrect conclusion.

This diagram shows the cause-and-effect relationships summarized above:

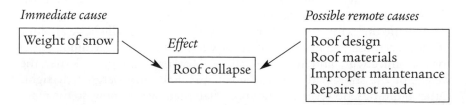

Remember, remote causes can be extremely important. In the roof-collapse situation, as we have seen, a remote cause—the roof design—was actually the main cause of the accident.

Understanding Causal Chains

Sometimes an effect can also be a cause. This is true in a **causal chain**, where A causes B, B causes C, C causes D, and so on, as shown here:

A
Cause ⎯⎯⎯⎯⟶ B
           Effect
       (Cause) ⎯⎯⎯⟶ C
                  Effect
               (Cause) ⎯⎯⎯⟶ D
                            Effect
                      (Cause) ⎯⎯⎯⟶ E
                                       Effect

In causal chains, the result of one action is the cause of another. Leaving out any link in the chain, or putting any link in improper order, destroys the logic and continuity of the chain.

A simple example of a causal chain starts with the conclusion of World War II in 1945. Beginning in 1946, as thousands of American soldiers returned home, the U.S. birth rate began to rise dramatically. As the numbers of births increased, the creation of goods and services to meet the needs of this growing population also increased. As advertisers competed to attract this group's attention to various products, the so-called baby-boom generation became more visible. Consequently, baby-boomers were perceived as more powerful—as both voters and consumers. As a result, this group's emergence became a major factor in shaping American political, social, cultural, and economic life.

Here is another example of a causal chain. In the past thirty years, the bicycle as a form of transportation for children has become increasingly rare, with fewer than one percent of children now riding bicycles to school. In addition, fewer children ride bicycles for recreation. Causes cited for this decline include the absence of sidewalks in many newer suburban communities, parents' rising fears about crime and traffic accidents, the rise in the number of students who schedule back-to-back after-school activities (perhaps due in part to the increased number of households with both parents working), the growing popularity of computer games, and the increased availability of after-school jobs for teenagers (who often need cars, not bikes, to get to work). The decreasing number of children who ride bikes has contributed to a corresponding steady decline, since the 1970s, in the sale of bicycles.

As a result of the decline in bicycle sales, bicycle thefts have decreased sharply, and bicycle deaths involving children under sixteen have also dropped dramatically (although this is due in part to increased use of helmets). However, the number of American children who are obese has doubled since the mid-1980s—in part because children get less and less exercise. So, factors such as fewer sidewalks and more working teenagers have led to a decline in bicycle sales, which in turn has had a far-reaching impact.

If your analysis of a situation reveals a causal chain, this discovery can be useful in your writing. The very operation of a causal chain suggests an organizational pattern for a paper, and following the chain helps you to discuss items in their logical order. Be careful, however, to keep your emphasis on the causal connections and not to lapse into narration.

Avoiding *Post Hoc* Reasoning

When developing a cause-and-effect paper, you should not assume that just because event A *precedes* event B, event A has *caused* event B. This illogical assumption, called ***post hoc* reasoning**, equates a chronological sequence with causality. When you fall into this trap—assuming, for instance, that you failed an exam because a black cat crossed your path the day before—you are mistaking coincidence for causality.

Consider a classic example of *post hoc* reasoning. Until the late nineteenth century, many scientists accepted the notion of spontaneous generation—that is, they believed living things could arise directly from nonliving matter. To support their beliefs, they pointed to specific situations. For instance, they observed that maggots, the larvae of the housefly, seemed to arise directly from the decaying flesh of dead animals.

These scientists were confusing sequence with causality, assuming that just because the presence of decaying meat preceded the appearance of maggots, the two were connected in a causal relationship. In fact, because the dead animals were exposed to the air, flies were free to lay eggs in the animals' bodies, and these eggs hatched into maggots. Therefore, the living maggots were not a direct result of the presence of nonliving matter. Although these scientists were applying the best technology and scientific theory of their time, hindsight reveals that their conclusions were not valid.

A more recent example of *post hoc* reasoning occurred after medical researchers published findings reporting that female centenarians—women who reached the age of one hundred—were four times as likely to have given birth when they were past forty as were women in a control group who died at the age of seventy-three. Researchers saw no causal connection between childbirth after forty and long life, suggesting only that the centenarians might have been predisposed to live longer because they reached menopause later than the other women. Local television newscasts and tabloid newspapers, however, misinterpreted the study's implications, presenting the relationship between late childbearing and long life as a causal one. In a vivid example of *post hoc* reasoning, one promotional spot for a local television newscast proclaimed, "Having kids late in life can help you live longer."

In your writing, as well as in your observations, it is neither logical nor fair to assume that a causal relationship exists unless clear, strong evidence supports the connection. When you revise a cause-and-effect paper, make sure you have not confused words such as *because, therefore,* and *consequently* (words that indicate a causal relationship) with words such as *subsequently, later,* and *afterward* (words that indicate a chronological relationship). When you use a word like *because,* you are signaling to readers that you are telling *why* something happened; when you use a word like *later,* you are only showing *when* it happened.

The ability to identify and analyze cause-and-effect relationships; to distinguish causes from effects and recognize causal chains; and to distinguish immediate from remote, main from contributory, and logical from illogical causes are all skills that will improve your writing. Understanding the nature of the cause-and-effect relationship will help you decide when and how to use this pattern in a paper.

Planning a Cause-and-Effect Essay

After you have sorted out the cause-and-effect relationships you will write about, you are ready to plan your paper. You have three basic options — to discuss causes, to discuss effects, or to discuss both causes and effects. Often your assignment will suggest which of these options to use. Here are a few likely topics for cause-and-effect treatment:

Focus on finding causes	Discuss the factors that contributed to the declining population of state mental hospitals in the 1960s. (social work paper)
	Identify some possible causes of collective obsessional behavior. (psychology exam)
Focus on describing or predicting effects	Evaluate the probable effects of moving elementary school children from a highly structured classroom to a relatively open classroom. (education paper)
	Discuss the impact of World War I on two of Ernest Hemingway's characters. (literature exam)
Focus on both causes and effects	The 1840s were volatile years in Europe. Choose one social, political, or economic event that occurred during those years, analyze its causes, and briefly note how the event influenced later developments in European history. (history exam)

Purpose and Thesis

Of course, a cause-and-effect essay usually does more than just enumerate causes or effects. For example, an economics paper treating the major effects of the Vietnam War on the U.S. economy could be a straightforward presentation of factual information — an attempt to inform readers of the war's economic impact. It is more likely, however, that the paper would indicate the significance of the war's effects, not just list them. In fact, cause-and-effect analysis often requires you to judge various factors so that you can assess their relative significance.

When you formulate a thesis statement, be sure it identifies the relationships among the specific causes or effects you will discuss. This thesis statement should tell your readers three things: the issues you plan to consider, the position you will take, and whether your emphasis is on causes, effects, or both. Your thesis statement may also indicate explicitly or implicitly the cause or effect you consider most important and the order in which you will present your points.

Order and Sequence

When deciding on the sequence in which you will present causes or effects, you have several options. One option, of course, is chronological order: you can present causes or effects in the order in which they occurred. Another option is to introduce the main cause first and then the contributory causes — or you can do just the opposite. If you want to stress positive consequences, begin by briefly discussing the negative ones; if you plan to emphasize negative results, summarize the less important positive effects first. Still another possibility is to begin by dismissing any events that were *not* causes and then explain what the real causes were. This method is especially effective if you think your readers are likely to jump to *post hoc* conclusions. Finally, you can begin with the most obvious causes or effects and move on to more subtle factors — and then to your analysis and conclusion.

Using Transitions

Cause-and-effect essays rely on clear transitions — *the first cause, the second cause; one result, another result* — to distinguish causes from effects and to help move readers through the discussion. In essays that analyze complex causal relationships, transitions are even more important because they can help readers distinguish main from contributory causes (*the most important cause, another cause*) and immediate from remote causes (*the most obvious cause, a less apparent cause*). Transitions are also essential in a causal chain, where they can help readers sort out the sequence (*then, next*), as well as the causal relationships (*because, as a result, for this reason*). A more complete list of transitions appears on page 43.

Structuring a Cause-and-Effect Essay

Finding Causes

Suppose you are planning the social work paper mentioned earlier: "Discuss the factors that contributed to the declining population of state mental hospitals in the 1960s." Your assignment specifies an effect—the declining population of state mental hospitals—and asks you to discuss possible causes, which might include the following:

- An increasing acceptance of mental illness in our society
- Prohibitive costs of in-patient care
- Increasing numbers of mental health professionals, facilitating treatment outside of hospitals

Many health professionals, however, believe that the most important cause was the development and use of psychotropic drugs, such as chlorpromazine (Thorazine), which can alter behavior. To emphasize this cause in your paper, you could formulate the following thesis statement:

Less important causes	Although society's increasing acceptance of the mentally ill, the high cost of in-patient care, and the rise in the number of mental health profession-
Effect	als were all influential in reducing the population of state mental hospitals, the most important
Most important cause	cause of this reduction was the development and use of psychotropic drugs.

This thesis statement fully prepares your readers for your essay. It identifies the points you will consider, and it reveals your position—your assessment of the relative significance of the causes you identify. It states the less important causes first and indicates their secondary importance with *although*. In the body of your essay, the less important causes would come first so that the essay could gradually build up to the most convincing material. An informal outline for your paper might look like this:

Introduction:	Thesis statement—Although society's increasing acceptance of the mentally ill, the high cost of in-patient care, and the rise in the number of mental health professionals were all influential in reducing the population of state mental hospitals, the most important cause of this reduction was the development and use of psychotropic drugs.
First cause:	Increasing acceptance of the mentally ill
Second cause:	High cost of in-patient care
Third cause:	Rise in the number of mental health professionals
Fourth (and most important) cause:	Development and use of psychotropic drugs
Conclusion:	Restatement of thesis or summary of key points

Describing or Predicting Effects

Suppose you were planning the education paper mentioned earlier: "Evaluate the probable effects of moving elementary school children from a highly structured classroom to a relatively open classroom." Here you would focus on effects rather than on causes. After brainstorming and deciding which specific points to discuss, you might formulate this thesis statement:

Cause	Moving children from a highly structured class-room to a relatively open one is desirable because it
Effects	is likely to encourage more independent play, more flexibility in forming friendship groups, and, ultimately, more creativity.

This thesis statement clearly tells readers the stand you will take and the main points you will consider in your essay. The thesis also clearly specifies that these points are *effects* of the open classroom. After introducing the cause, your essay would treat these three effects in the order they are presented in the thesis statement, building up to the most important point. An informal outline of your paper might look like this:

Introduction:	Thesis statement—Moving children from a highly structured classroom to a relatively open one is desirable because it is likely to encourage more independent play, more flexibility in forming friendship groups, and, ultimately, more creativity.
First effect:	More independent play
Second effect:	More flexible friendship groups
Third (and most important) effect:	More creativity
Conclusion:	Restatement of thesis or summary of key points

Revising a Cause-and-Effect Essay

When you revise a cause-and-effect essay, consider the items on the revision checklist on page 54. In addition, pay special attention to the items on the following checklist, which apply specifically to cause-and-effect essays.

✓ **REVISION CHECKLIST: Cause and Effect**

- Does your assignment call for a discussion of causes, of effects, or of both causes and effects?
- Does your essay have a clearly stated thesis that indicates your focus and the significance of the causes and effects you discuss?

- Have you considered all possible causes and all possible effects?
- Have you distinguished between the main (most important) cause and the contributory (less important) causes?
- Have you distinguished between immediate and remote causes?
- Have you identified a causal chain in your reasoning?
- Have you avoided *post hoc* reasoning?
- Have you used transitional words and phrases to show how the causes and effects you discuss are related?

Editing a Cause-and-Effect Essay

When you edit your cause-and-effect essay, follow the guidelines on the editing checklists on pages 71, 73, and 76. In addition, focus on the grammar, mechanics, and punctuation issues that are particularly relevant to cause-and-effect essays. Two of these issues — avoiding faulty "the reason is because" constructions and using *affect* and *effect* correctly — are discussed here.

GRAMMAR IN CONTEXT: Avoiding "The reason is because"; Using *Affect* and *Effect* Correctly

Avoiding "the reason is because"   When you discuss causes and effects, you may find yourself writing the phrase "the reason is." If you follow this phrase with *because* ("the reason is *because*"), you will create an error.

The word *because* means "for the reason that." Therefore, it is redundant to say "the reason is because" (which literally means "the reason is for the reason that"). You can correct this error by substituting *that* for *because* ("the reason is *that*").

INCORRECT: Robin Tolmach Lakoff believes that one reason soldiers are able to kill in wartime is because they use language to dehumanize their enemies (377).

CORRECT: Robin Tolmach Lakoff believes that one reason soldiers are able to kill in wartime is that they use language to dehumanize their enemies (377).

Using *Affect* and *Effect* Correctly   When you write a cause-and-effect essay, you will most likely use the words *affect* and *effect* quite often. For this reason, it is important that you know the difference between *affect* and *effect*.

(continued on next page)

(continued from previous page)

Affect, usually a verb, means "to influence."

Hasselstrom believes that carrying a gun has <u>affected</u> her life in a positive way (371).

Effect, usually a noun, means "a result."

Hasselstrom believes that carrying a gun has had a positive <u>effect</u> on her life (371).

Note: *Effect* can also be a verb meaning "to bring about" ("She worked hard to <u>effect</u> change in the community").

For more practice in avoiding faulty constructions and commonly confused words, visit Exercise Central at <bedfordstmartins.com/patterns/faultyconstructions> or <bedfordstmartins.com/patterns/confusedwords>.

✓ **EDITING CHECKLIST: Cause and Effect**

- Have you used verb tenses correctly to distinguish among events that happened earlier, at the same time, and later?
- Have you placed a comma **after** every dependent clause introduced by *because* ("Because the rally was so crowded, we left early") but *not* used a comma **before** a dependent clause introduced by *because* ("We left early because the rally was so crowded")?
- Have you used "the reason is that" (not "the reason is because")?
- Have you used *affect* and *effect* correctly?

A STUDENT WRITER: Cause and Effect

The following midterm exam, written for a history class, analyzes both the causes and the effects of the Irish potato famine that occurred during the 1840s. Notice how the writer, Evelyn Pellicane, concentrates on causes but also discusses briefly the effects of this tragedy, just as the exam question directs.

Question: The 1840s were volatile years in Europe. Choose one social, political, or economic event that occurred during those years, analyze its causes, and briefly note how the event influenced later developments in European history.

The Irish Famine, 1845-1849

Thesis statement   The Irish famine, which brought hardship and tragedy to 1

Ireland during the 1840s, was caused and prolonged by four

basic factors: the failure of the potato crop, the landlord-tenant system, errors in government policy, and the long-standing prejudice of the British toward Ireland.

First cause

The immediate cause of the famine was the failure of the potato crop. In 1845, potato disease struck the crop, and potatoes rotted in the ground. The 1846 crop also failed, and before long people were eating weeds. The 1847 crop was healthy, but there were not enough potatoes to go around, and in 1848 the blight struck again, leading to more and more evictions of tenants by landlords.

Second cause

The tenants' position on the land had never been very secure. Most had no leases and could be turned out by their landlords at any time. If a tenant owed rent, he was evicted — or, worse, put in prison, leaving his family to starve. The threat of prison caused many tenants to leave their land; those who could leave Ireland did so, sometimes with money provided by their landlords. Some landlords did try to take care of their tenants, but most did not. Many were absentee landlords who spent their rent money abroad.

Third cause

Government policy errors, although not an immediate cause of the famine, played an important role in creating an unstable economy and perpetuating starvation. In 1846, the government decided not to continue selling corn, as it had during the first year of the famine, claiming that low-cost purchases of corn by Ireland had paralyzed British trade by interfering with free enterprise. Therefore, 1846 saw a starving population, angry demonstrations, and panic; even those with money were unable to buy food. Still, the government insisted that if it sent food to Ireland, prices would rise in the rest of the United Kingdom and that this would be unfair to hardworking English and Scots. As a result, no food was sent. Throughout the years of the famine, the British government aggravated an already grave situation: they did nothing to improve agricultural operations, to help people adjust to another crop, to distribute seeds, or to reorder the landlord-tenant system that made the tenants' position so insecure.

Fourth cause

At the root of this poor government policy was the long-standing British prejudice against the Irish. Hostility between the two countries went back some six hundred years, and the British were simply not about to inconvenience themselves to save the

Irish. When the Irish so desperately needed grain to replace the damaged potatoes, it was clear that grain had to be imported from England. This meant, however, that the Corn Laws, which had been enacted to keep the price of British corn high by taxing imported grain, had to be repealed. The British were unwilling to repeal the Corn Laws. Even when they did supply cornmeal, they made no attempt to explain to the Irish how to cook this unfamiliar food. Moreover, the British government was determined to make Ireland pay for its own poor, so it forced the collection of taxes. Since many landlords could not collect the tax money, they were forced to evict their tenants. The British government's callous and indifferent treatment of the Irish has been called genocide.

Effects   As a result of this devastating famine, the population   6
of Ireland was reduced from about nine million to about six and one-half million. During the famine years, men roamed the streets looking for work, begging when they found none. Epidemics of "famine fever" and dysentery reduced the population drastically. The most important historical result of the famine, however, was the massive immigration to the United States, Canada, and Great Britain of poor, unskilled people who had to struggle to fit into a skilled economy and who brought with them a deep-seated hatred of the British. (This same hatred remained strong in Ireland itself — so strong that at the time of World War II, Ireland, then independent, remained neutral rather than coming to England's aid.) Irish immigrants faced slums, fever epidemics, joblessness, and hostility — even anti-Catholic and anti-Irish riots — in Boston, New York, London, Glasgow, and Quebec. In Ireland itself, poverty and discontent continued, and by 1848 those emigrating from Ireland included a more highly skilled class of farmers, the ones Ireland needed to recover and to survive.

Conclusion (includes   The Irish famine, one of the great tragedies of the   7
restatement of thesis)   nineteenth century, was a natural disaster compounded by the insensitivity of the British government and the archaic agricultural system of Ireland. Although the deaths that resulted depleted Ireland's resources even more, the men and women who immigrated to other countries permanently enriched those nations.

Points for Special Attention

Structure.   This is a relatively long essay; if it were not so clearly organized, it would be difficult to follow. Because the essay was to focus primarily on causes, Evelyn first introduces the effect — the famine itself — and then considers its causes. After she examines the causes, she moves on to the results of the famine, treating the most important result last. In this essay, then, the famine is first treated as an effect and then, toward the end, as a cause. In fact, it is the central link in a causal chain.

Evelyn devotes one paragraph to her introduction and one to each cause; she sums up the famine's results in a separate paragraph and devotes the final paragraph to her conclusion. (Depending on a particular paper's length and complexity, more — or less — than one paragraph may be devoted to each cause or effect.) An informal outline for her paper might look like this:

Introduction (including thesis statement)
First cause: Failure of the potato crop
Second cause: The landlord-tenant system
Third cause: Errors in government policy
Fourth cause: British prejudice
Results of the famine
Conclusion

Because Evelyn saw all the causes as important and interrelated, she did not present them in order of increasing importance. Instead, she begins with the immediate cause of the famine — the failure of the potato crop — and then digs more deeply until she arrives at the most remote cause, British prejudice. The immediate cause is also the main (most important) cause, for the other situations had existed before the famine began.

Transitions.   The cause-and-effect relationships in this essay are both subtle and complex because Evelyn considers a series of relationships as well as an intricate causal chain. Throughout the essay, many words suggest cause-and-effect connections: *brought, caused, leading to, therefore, as a result, so, since,* and the like. These words help readers sort out the causal connections.

Answering an Exam Question.   Before planning and writing her answer, Evelyn read the exam question carefully. She saw that it asked for both causes and effects but that its wording directed her to spend more time on causes ("analyze") than on effects ("briefly note"), so she organized her discussion to conform to these directions. In addition, she indicated *explicitly* which were the causes ("government policy . . . played an important role") and which were the effects ("The most important historical result").

Evelyn's purpose was to convey factual information and, in doing so, to demonstrate her understanding of the course material. Rather than waste her limited time choosing a clever opening strategy or making elaborate attempts to engage her audience, Evelyn began her essay with a direct statement of her thesis.

Evelyn was obviously influenced by outside sources; the ideas in the essay are not completely her own. Because this was an exam, however, and because the instructor expected that students would base their essays on class notes and assigned readings, Evelyn did not have to document her sources.

Focus on Revision

Because this essay was written as an exam answer, Evelyn had no time — and no need — to revise it further. If she had been preparing this assignment outside of class, however, she might have done more. For example, she could have added a more arresting opening, such as a brief eyewitness account of the famine's effects. Her conclusion — appropriately brief and straightforward for an exam answer — could also have been strengthened, perhaps with the addition of information about the nation's eventual recovery. Finally, adding statistics, quotations by historians, or a brief summary of Irish history before the famine could have further enriched the essay.

📄   **PEER EDITING WORKSHEET: Cause and Effect**

1. Paraphrase the essay's thesis. Is it explicitly stated? Should it be?
2. Does the essay focus on causes, effects, or both? Does the thesis statement clearly identify this focus? If not, how should the thesis statement be revised?
3. Does the writer consider *all* relevant causes or effects? Are any key causes or effects omitted? Are any irrelevant causes or effects included?
4. Make an informal outline of the essay. What determines the order of the causes or effects? Is this the most effective order? If not, what revisions do you suggest?
5. List the transitional words and phrases used to indicate causal connections. Are any additional transitions needed? If so, where?
6. Does the writer avoid *post hoc* reasoning? Are all causal connections logical?
7. Does the writer explain each cause or effect clearly and convincingly? Are more examples or details needed to help readers understand causal connections? If so, where?

8. Do you agree with the writer's interpretation of the cause-and-effect relationships examined in this essay? Do you agree with his or her conclusions? Why or why not?

9. Has the writer avoided illogical "the reason is because" constructions?

10. Are *affect* and *effect* used correctly?

All the selections that follow focus on cause-and-effect relationships. Some readings focus on causes, others on effects. The first selection, a visual text, is followed by questions designed to illustrate how cause and effect can operate in visual form.

LOUIS REQUENA

Major League Baseball Brawl (Photo)

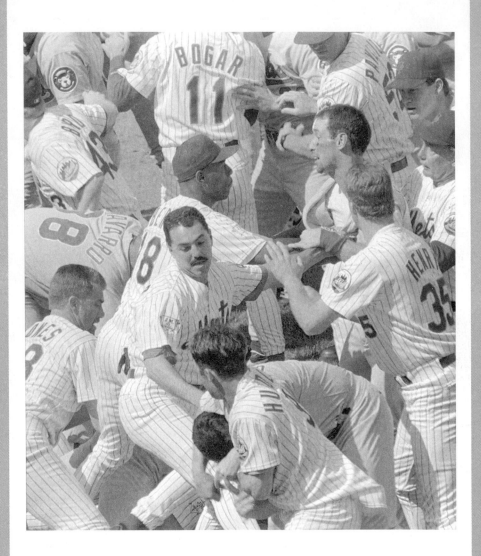

• • •

Reading Images

1. Study the photo above. What might have caused the situation on the field? Consider remote as well as immediate causes.

2. What outcomes might you expect from this fight? Consider the effects on the players on the field, on the players waiting in the dugout, and on the fans in the stands.

3. Consider the fight on the field as part of a causal chain. Diagram that chain of events, using arrows to point from one event to the next.

Journal Entry

Write a paragraph suggesting ways to prevent situations such as the one shown in the picture. For example, might high fines deter players from losing their tempers?

Thematic Connections

- "My Field of Dreams" (page 89)
- "Who Killed Benny Paret?" (page 346)
- "Sizing Up the Effects" (page 671)

NORMAN COUSINS

Who Killed Benny Paret?

Norman Cousins (1915–1990) was born in Union City, New Jersey, and graduated from Columbia University's Teachers College in 1933. He began his career in journalism writing for the *New York Evening Post* and *Current History* magazine. In 1940, Cousins joined the *Saturday Review,* where he served as editor from 1942 to 1978. A noted social critic, Cousins lectured widely on world affairs. An adjunct professor in the department of psychiatry at the UCLA School of Medicine from 1978 until his death, he is particularly remembered for his many books urging a positive outlook to combat illness, including *Anatomy of an Illness* (1979).

Background on the hazards of boxing: Cousins's 1962 essay "Who Killed Benny Paret?" focuses on a brutal boxing match at Madison Square Garden between Emile Griffith and Benny (Kid) Paret — a fight that led to Paret's death after nine days in a coma. The event, witnessed by millions of shocked television viewers, is the subject of a 2004 documentary, *Ring of Fire*. The fight went twelve rounds and ended with Griffith driving Paret onto the ropes and relentlessly beating him. Some newspapers reported that Griffith was angry because Paret had questioned his manhood, calling him, in Spanish (Paret was Cuban), a *maricón* (a derogatory name for a gay man). In the aftermath of the fight, many demanded that boxing be banned altogether. As a result, a number of rules for professional boxing were changed, but boxing remains an inherently dangerous sport. More than five hundred ring deaths have occurred in the past century; as recently as 2005, a professional boxer died following a knockout in the ring. In addition, many boxers suffer from chronic latent brain damage, known medically as *dementia pugilistica*. In answering the question posed by his essay's title, Cousins takes a strong stand against violence in boxing.

Sometime about 1935 or 1936 I had an interview with Mike Jacobs, the   1
prize-fight promoter. I was a fledgling reporter at that time; my beat was education but during the vacation season I found myself on varied assignments, all the way from ship news to sports reporting. In this way I found myself sitting opposite the most powerful figure in the boxing world.

There was nothing spectacular in Mr. Jacobs' manner or appearance;   2
but when he spoke about prize fights, he was no longer a bland little man but a colossus who sounded the way Napoleon must have sounded when he reviewed a battle. You knew you were listening to Number One. His saying something made it true.

We discussed what to him was the only important element in success-   3
ful promoting — how to please the crowd. So far as he was concerned, there was no mystery to it. You put killers in the ring and the people filled your

arena. You hire boxing artists—men who are adroit at feinting, parrying, weaving, jabbing, and dancing, but who don't pack dynamite in their fists—and you wind up counting your empty seats. So you searched for the killers and sluggers and maulers—fellows who could hit with the force of a baseball bat.

I asked Mr. Jacobs if he was speaking literally when he said people 4
came out to see the killer.

"They don't come out to see a tea party," he said evenly. "They come 5
out to see the knockout. They come out to see a man hurt. If they think
anything else, they're kidding themselves."

Recently, a young man by the name of Benny Paret was killed in the 6
ring. The killing was seen by millions; it was on television. In the twelfth
round, he was hit hard in the head several times, went down, was counted
out, and never came out of the coma.

The Paret fight produced a flurry of investigations. Governor Rocke- 7
feller was shocked by what happened and appointed a committee to assess
the responsibility. The New York State Boxing Commission decided to
find out what was wrong. The District Attorney's office expressed its concern. One question that was solemnly studied in all three probes concerned the action of the referee. Did he act in time to stop the fight?
Another question had to do with the role of the examining doctors who
certified the physical fitness of the fighters before the bout. Still another
question involved Mr. Paret's manager; did he rush his boy into the fight
without adequate time to recuperate from the previous one?

In short, the investigators looked into every possible cause except the 8
real one. Benny Paret was killed because the human fist delivers enough
impact, when directed against the head, to produce a massive hemorrhage
in the brain. The human brain is the most delicate and complex mechanism in all creation. It has a lacework of millions of highly fragile nerve
connections. Nature attempts to protect this exquisitely intricate machinery by encasing it in a hard shell. Fortunately, the shell is thick enough to
withstand a great deal of pounding. Nature, however, can protect a man
against everything except man himself. Not every blow to the head will kill
a man—but there is always the risk of concussion and damage to the brain.
A prize fighter may be able to survive even repeated brain concussions and
go on fighting, but the damage to his brain may be permanent.

In any event, it is futile to investigate the referee's role and seek to 9
determine whether he should have intervened to stop the fight earlier.
That is not where the primary responsibility lies. The primary responsibility lies with the people who pay to see a man hurt. The referee who stops a
fight too soon from the crowd's viewpoint can expect to be booed. The
crowd wants the knockout; it wants to see a man stretched out on the canvas. This is the supreme moment in boxing. It is nonsense to talk about
prize fighting as a test of boxing skills. No crowd was ever brought to its
feet screaming and cheering at the sight of two men beautifully dodging

and weaving out of each other's jabs. The time the crowd comes alive is when a man is hit hard over the heart or the head, when his mouthpiece flies out, when the blood squirts out of his nose or eyes, when he wobbles under the attack and his pursuer continues to smash at him with pole-axe impact.

Don't blame it on the referee. Don't even blame it on the fight man- 10 agers. Put the blame where it belongs — on the prevailing mores that regard prize fighting as a perfectly proper enterprise and vehicle of entertainment. No one doubts that many people enjoy prize fighting and will miss it if it should be thrown out. And that is precisely the point.

· · ·

Comprehension

1. Why, according to Mike Jacobs, do people come to see a prizefight? Does Cousins agree with him?

2. What was the immediate cause of Paret's death? What remote causes did the investigators consider? What, according to Cousins, was the main cause? That is, where does the "primary responsibility" (9) lie?

3. Why does Cousins believe "it is futile to investigate the referee's role" (9)?

4. Cousins ends his essay with "And that is precisely the point." What is the "point" he refers to?

Purpose and Audience

1. This persuasive essay has a strong thesis. What is it?

2. This essay appeared on May 5, 1962, a month after Paret died. What do you suppose its impact was on its audience? Do you think the impact on readers is the same today?

3. At whom is this essay aimed — boxing enthusiasts, sportswriters, or a general audience? On what do you base your conclusion?

4. Does Cousins expect his audience to agree with his thesis? How does he try to win sympathy for his position?

Style and Structure

1. Does Cousins include enough detail to convince readers? Explain. Where, if anywhere, might more detail be helpful?

2. Sort out the complex cause-and-effect relationships discussed in paragraph 9.

3. What strategy does Cousins use in his conclusion? Is it effective? Explain your reasoning.

Vocabulary Projects

1. Define each of the following words as it is used in this selection.

   promoter (1)   feinting (3)   lacework (8)
   fledgling (1)   parrying (3)   encasing (8)
   colossus (2)   maulers (3)   intervened (9)

2. The specialized vocabulary of boxing is prominent in this essay, but the facts Cousins presents would apply equally well to any sport in which violence is a potential problem.

   a. Imagine you are writing a similar essay about football, hockey, rugby, or another sport. Think about your audience, and substitute an appropriate equivalent word or phrase for each of the following:

      promoter (1)   feinting, parrying, weaving,   knockout (5)
      prize fights (2)   jabbing, and dancing (3)   referee (7)
      in the ring (3)   killers and sluggers   fighters/fight (7)
      boxing artists (3)   and maulers (3)

   b. Rewrite this sentence so that it suits the sport you have chosen: "The crowd wants the knockout; it wants to see a man stretched out on the canvas. . . . It is nonsense to talk about prize fighting as a test of boxing skills. No crowd was ever brought to its feet screaming and cheering at the sight of two men beautifully dodging and weaving out of each other's jabs" (9).

Journal Entry

Do Cousins's graphic descriptions convince you that boxing should be outlawed? Explain.

Writing Workshop

1. Write a cause-and-effect essay examining how the demands of the public affect a professional sport. (You might examine violence in hockey or football, for example, or how an individual player cultivates an image for the fans.)

2. Write a cause-and-effect essay about a time when, in response to peer pressure, you encouraged someone to do something you felt was dishonest or unwise. Be sure to identify the causes for your actions.

3. Why do you think a young person might turn to a career in boxing? Write a cause-and-effect essay examining the possible motives.

Combining the Patterns

This essay begins with five paragraphs of **narration** that summarize a meeting between Cousins and Mike Jacobs. What function does this narrative introduction serve in the essay? Once Paret's death is mentioned and the persuasive portion of the essay begins, Cousins never resumes the narrative. Do you think he should have returned to this narrative? If so, where might he have continued the story?

Thematic Connections

- "Thirty-Eight Who Saw Murder Didn't Call the Police" (page 120)
- "Shooting an Elephant" (page 125)
- "Get It Right: Privatize Executions" (page 305)
- "The Lottery" (page 317)

MARIE WINN

Television: The Plug-In Drug

Marie Winn was born in 1936 in Prague, in what is now the Czech Republic, and came to the United States in 1939. She was educated at Radcliffe College and Columbia University. As a freelance writer, Winn has contributed articles to the *New York Times Magazine, Parade,* and *Smithsonian* magazine. She has written books for children and also for parents and teachers, including *The Plug-In Drug: Television, Computers, and Family Life* (1977, revised 2002) and *Children without Childhood* (1983). Her recent work has focused on urban wildlife; in 1998, she published *Red-Tails in Love: A Wildlife Drama in Central Park,* and she is currently working on a book about animal life in New York City's Central Park after dark.

Background on television and its effects on children: Referred to as early as 1961 as a "vast wasteland" (by the then-chairman of the Federal Communications Commission), television has had its critics all along, particularly in relation to the effects of television watching on children. Some three thousand books and articles have been published on the subject, and current research suggests that the average young person in the United States watches twenty-one hours of television a week (which, with the proliferation of cable channels devoted to children and the spread of videos and DVDs, may be a low estimate). Studies show that children who spend three or more hours a day in front of the set do less schoolwork, have poorer reading and social skills, and are more likely to be overweight. In addition, much controversy surrounds the effects of television violence and advertising on young viewers. In this excerpt from *The Plug-In Drug,* Winn considers the effects of television not only on children but also on how family members relate to one another. Winn's observations are even more relevant now than when she originally wrote her essay: today a large majority of children live in a household with three or more television sets, and 56 percent have one in their own rooms.

Not much more than fifty years after the introduction of television into American society, the medium has become so deeply ingrained in daily life that in many states the TV set has attained the rank of a legal necessity, safe from repossession in case of debt along with clothes and cooking utensils. Only in the early years after television's introduction did writers and commentators have sufficient perspective to separate the activity of watching television from the actual content it offers the viewer. In those days writers frequently discussed the effects of television on family life. However, a curious myopia afflicted those first observers: almost without exception they regarded television as a favorable, beneficial, indeed, wondrous influence upon the family.

"Television is going to be a real asset in every home where there are children," predicted a writer in 1949.

"Television will take over your way of living and change your children's habits, but this change can be a wonderful improvement," claimed another commentator.

"No survey's needed, of course, to establish that television has brought the family together in one room," wrote the *New York Times*'s television critic in 1949.

The early articles about television were almost invariably accompanied by a photograph or illustration showing a family cozily sitting together before the television set, Sis on Mom's lap, Buddy perched on the arm of Dad's chair, Dad with his arm around Mom's shoulder. Who could have guessed that twenty or so years later Mom would be watching a drama in the kitchen, the kids would be looking at cartoons in their room, while Dad would be taking in the ball game in the living room?

Of course television sets were enormously expensive when they first came on the market. The idea that by the year 2000 more than three quarters of all American families would own two or more sets would have seemed preposterous. The splintering of the multiple-set family was something the early writers did not foresee. Nor did anyone imagine the number of hours children would eventually devote to television, the changes television would effect upon child-rearing methods, the increasing domination of family schedules by children's viewing requirements—in short, the power of television to dominate family life.

As children's consumption of the new medium increased together with parental concern about the possible effects of so much television viewing, a steady refrain helped soothe and reassure anxious parents. "Television always enters a pattern of influences that already exist: the home, the peer group, the school, the church and culture generally," wrote the authors of an early and influential study of television's effects on children. In other words, if the child's home life is all right, parents need not worry about the effects of too much television watching.

But television did not merely influence the child; it deeply influenced that "pattern of influences" everyone hoped would ameliorate the new medium's effects. Home and family life have changed in important ways since the advent of television. The peer group has become television-oriented, and much of the time children spend together is occupied by television viewing. Culture generally has been transformed by television. Participation in church and community activities has diminished, with television a primary cause of this change. Therefore it is improper to assign to television the subsidiary role its many apologists insist it plays. Television is not merely one of a number of important influences upon today's child. Through the changes it has made in family life, television emerges as *the* important influence in children's lives today.

The Quality of Life

Television's contribution to family life has been an equivocal one. For   9
while it has, indeed, kept the members of the family from dispersing, it has
not served to bring them together. By its domination of the time families
spend together, it destroys the special quality that distinguishes one family
from another, a quality that depends to a great extent on what a family
does, what special rituals, games, recurrent jokes, familiar songs, and
shared activities it accumulates.

Yet parents have accepted a television-dominated family life so com-   10
pletely that they cannot see how the medium is involved in whatever problems they might be having. A first-grade teacher reports:

> I have one child in the group who's an only child. I wanted to find out
> more about her family life because this little girl was quite isolated from
> the group, didn't make friends, so I talked to her mother. Well, they don't
> have time to do anything in the evening, the mother said. The parents
> come home after picking up the child at the baby-sitter's. Then the
> mother fixes dinner while the child watches TV. Then they have dinner
> and the child goes to bed. I said to this mother. "Well, couldn't she help
> you fix dinner? That would be a nice time for the two of you to talk," and
> the mother said, "Oh, but I'd hate to have her miss *Zoom*. It's such a good
> program!"

Several decades ago a writer and mother of two boys aged three and   11
seven described her family's television schedule in a newspaper article.
Though some of the programs her kids watched then have changed, the
situation she describes remains the same for great numbers of families
today:

> We were in the midst of a full-scale War. Every day was a new battle and
> every program was a major skirmish. We agreed it was a bad scene all
> around and were ready to enter diplomatic negotiations. . . . In principle
> we have agreed on 2½ hours of TV a day, *Sesame Street, Electric Company*
> (with dinner gobbled up in between) and two half-hour shows between 7
> and 8:30, which enables the grown-ups to eat in peace and prevents the
> two boys from destroying one another. Their pre-bedtime choice is dread-
> ful, because, as Josh recently admitted, "There's nothing much on I really
> like." So . . . it's *What's My Line* or *To Tell the Truth*. . . . Clearly there is a need
> for first-rate children's shows at this time. . . .

Consider the "family life" described here: Presumably the father comes   12
home from work during the *Sesame Street–Electric Company* stint. The children are either watching television, gobbling their dinner, or both. While
the parents eat their dinner in peaceful privacy, the children watch another
hour of television. Then there is only a half-hour left before bedtime, just
enough time for baths, getting pajamas on, brushing teeth, and so on. The
children's evening is regimented with an almost military precision. They
watch their favorite programs, and when there is "nothing much on I really

like," they watch whatever else is on—because *watching* is the important thing. Their mother does not see anything amiss with watching programs just for the sake of watching; she only wishes there were some first-rate children's shows on at those times.

Without conjuring up fantasies of bygone eras with family games and long, leisurely meals, the question arises: isn't there a better family life available than this dismal, mechanized arrangement of children watching television for however long is allowed them, evening after evening?   13

Of course, families today still do things together at times: go camping in the summer, go to the zoo on a nice Sunday, take various trips and expeditions. But their ordinary daily life together is diminished—those hours of sitting around at the dinner table, the spontaneous taking up of an activity, the little games invented by children on the spur of the moment when there is nothing else to do, the scribbling, the chatting, and even the quarreling, all the things that form the fabric of a family, that define a childhood. Instead, the children have their regular schedule of television programs and bedtime, and the parents have their peaceful dinner together.   14

The author of the quoted newspaper article notes that "keeping a family sane means mediating between the needs of both children and adults." But surely the needs of the adults in that family were being better met than the needs of the children. The kids were effectively shunted away and rendered untroublesome, while their parents enjoyed a life as undemanding as that of any childless couple. In reality, it is those very demands that young children make upon a family that lead to growth, and it is the way parents respond to those demands that builds the relationships upon which the future of the family depends. If the family does not accumulate its backlog of shared experiences, shared everyday experiences that occur and recur and change and develop, then it is not likely to survive as anything other than a caretaking institution.   15

Family Rituals

Ritual is defined by sociologists as "that part of family life that the family likes about itself, is proud of and wants formally to continue." Another text notes that "the development of a ritual by a family is an index of the common interest of its members in the family as a group."   16

What has happened to family rituals, those regular, dependable, recurrent happenings that gave members of a family a feeling of belonging to a home rather than living in it merely for the sake of convenience, those experiences that act as the adhesive of family unity far more than any material advantages?   17

Mealtime rituals, going-to-bed rituals, illness rituals, holiday rituals— how many of these have survived the inroads of the television set?   18

A young woman who grew up near Chicago reminisces about her childhood and gives an idea of the effects of television upon family rituals: 19

As a child I had millions of relatives around — my parents both come from relatively large families. My father had nine brothers and sisters. And so every holiday there was this great swoop-down of aunts, uncles, and millions of cousins. I just remember how wonderful it used to be. These thousands of cousins would come and everyone would play and ultimately, after dinner, all the women would be in the front of the house, drinking coffee and talking, all the men would be in the back of the house, drinking and smoking, and all the kids would be all over the place, playing hide and seek. Christmas time was particularly nice because everyone always brought all their toys and games. Our house had a couple of rooms with go-through closets, so there were always kids running in a great circle route. I remember it was just wonderful.

And then all of a sudden one year I remember becoming suddenly aware of how different everything had become. The kids were no longer playing Monopoly or Clue or the other games we used to play together. It was because we had a television set which had been turned on for a football game. All of that socializing that had gone on previously had ended. Now everyone was sitting in front of the television set, on a holiday, at a family party! I remember being stunned by how awful that was. Somehow the television had become more attractive.

As families have come to spend more and more of their time together   20
engaged in the single activity of television watching, those rituals and pastimes that once gave family life its special quality have become more and more uncommon. Not since prehistoric times, when cave families hunted, gathered, ate, and slept, with little time remaining to accumulate a culture of any significance, have families been reduced to such a sameness.

Real People

The relationships of family members to each other are affected by tele-   21
vision's powerful competition in both obvious and subtle ways. For surely the hours that children spend in a one-way relationship with television people, an involvement that allows for no communication or interaction, must have some effect on their relationships with real-life people.

Studies show the importance of eye-to-eye contact, for instance, in   22
real-life relationships, and indicate that the nature of one's eye-contact patterns, whether one looks another squarely in the eye or looks to the side or shifts one's gaze from side to side, may play a significant role in one's success or failure in human relationships. But no eye contact is possible in the child-television relationship, although in certain children's programs people purport to speak directly to the child and the camera fosters this illusion by focusing directly upon the person being filmed. How might such a distortion affect a child's development of trust, of openness, of an ability to relate well to *real* people?

Bruno Bettelheim suggested an answer: 23

Children who have been taught, or conditioned, to listen passively most of the day to the warm verbal communications coming from the TV screen, to the deep emotional appeal of the so-called TV personality, are often unable to respond to real persons because they arouse so much less feeling than the skilled actor. Worse, they lose the ability to learn from reality because life experiences are much more complicated than the ones they see on the screen. . . .

A teacher makes a similar observation about her personal viewing experiences: 24

> I have trouble mobilizing myself and dealing with real people after watching a few hours of television. It's just hard to make that transition from watching television to a real relationship. I suppose it's because there was no effort necessary while I was watching, and dealing with real people always requires a bit of effort. Imagine, then, how much harder it might be to do the same thing for a small child, particularly one who watches a lot of television every day.

But more obviously damaging to family relationships is the elimination of opportunities to talk and converse, or to argue, to air grievances between parents and children and brothers and sisters. Families frequently use television to avoid confronting their problems, problems that will not go away if they are ignored but will only fester and become less easily resolvable as time goes on.   25

A mother reports: 26

> I find myself, with three children, wanting to turn on the TV set when they're fighting. I really have to struggle not to do it because I feel that's telling them this is the solution to the quarrel — but it's so tempting that I often do it.

A family therapist discusses the use of television as an avoidance mechanism: 27

> In a family I know the father comes home from work and turns on the television set. The children come and watch with him and the wife serves them their meal in front of the set. He then goes and takes a shower, or works on the car or something. She then goes and has her own dinner in front of the television set. It's a symptom of a deeper-rooted problem, sure. But it would help them all to get rid of the set. It would be far easier to work on what the symptom really means without the television. The television simply encourages a double avoidance of each other. They'd find out more quickly what was going on if they weren't able to hide behind the TV. Things wouldn't necessarily be better, of course, but they wouldn't be anesthetized.

A number of research studies done when television was a relatively new medium demonstrated that television interfered with family activities and the formation of family relationships. One survey showed that 78 percent of the respondents indicated no conversation taking place during viewing except at specified times such as commercials. The study noted: "The tele-   28 vision atmosphere in most households is one of quiet absorption on the part of family members who are present. The nature of the family social life during a program could be described as 'parallel' rather than interactive, and the set does seem to dominate family life when it is on." Thirty-six percent of the respondents in another study indicated that television viewing was the only family activity participated in during the week.

The situation has only worsened during the intervening decades. When 29 the studies were made, the great majority of American families had only one television set. Though the family may have spent more time watching TV in those early days, at least they were all together while they watched. Today the vast majority of all families have two or more sets, and nearly a third of all children live in homes with four or more TVs. The most telling statistic: almost 60 percent of all families watch television during meals, and not necessarily at the same TV set. When do they talk about what they did that day? When do they make plans, exchange views, share jokes, tell about their triumphs or little disasters? When do they get to be a real family?

Undermining the Family

Of course television has not been the only factor in the decline of fam- 30 ily life in America. The steadily rising divorce rate, the increase in the number of working mothers, the trends towards people moving far away from home, the breakdown of neighborhoods and communities — all these have seriously affected the family.

Obviously the sources of family breakdown do not necessarily come 31 from the family itself, but from the circumstances in which the family finds itself and the way of life imposed upon it by those circumstances. As Urie Bronfenbrenner has suggested:

> When those circumstances and the way of life they generate undermine relationships of trust and emotional security between family members, when they make it difficult for parents to care for, educate, and enjoy their children, when there is no support or recognition from the outside world for one's role as a parent, and when time spent with one's family means frustration of career, personal fulfillment, and peace of mind, then the development of the child is adversely affected.

Certainly television is not the single destroyer of American family life. 32 But the medium's dominant role in the family serves to anesthetize parents into accepting their family's diminished state and prevents them from struggling to regain some of the richness the family once possessed.

One research study alone seems to contradict the idea that television 33 has a negative impact on family life. In their important book *Television and the Quality of Life,* sociologists Robert Kubey and Mihaly Csikszentmihalyi observe that the heaviest viewers of TV among their subjects were "no less likely to spend time with their families" than the lightest viewers. Moreover, those heavy viewers reported feeling happier, more relaxed, and satisfied when watching TV with their families than light viewers did. Based on

these reports, the researchers reached the conclusion that "television viewing harmonizes with family life."

Using the same data, however, the researchers made another observa- 34
tion about the heavy and light viewers: ". . . families that spend substantial
portions of their time together watching television are likely to experience
greater percentages of their family time feeling relatively passive and
unchallenged compared with families who spend small proportions of
their time watching TV."

At first glance the two observations seem at odds: the heavier viewers 35
feel happy and satisfied, yet their family time is more passive and unchal-
lenging — less satisfying in reality. But when one considers the nature of
the television experience, the contradiction vanishes. Surely it stands to
reason that the television experience is instrumental in preventing viewers
from recognizing its dulling effects, much as a mind-altering drug might
do.

In spite of everything, the American family muddles on, dimly aware 36
that something is amiss but distracted from an understanding of its plight
by an endless stream of television images. As family ties grow weaker and
vaguer, as children's lives become more separate from their parents', as parents' educational role in their children's lives is taken over by the media,
the school, and the peer group, family life becomes increasingly more
unsatisfying for both parents and children. All that seems to be left is love,
an abstraction that family members know is necessary but find great difficulty giving to each other since the traditional opportunities for expressing it within the family have been reduced or eliminated.

•   •   •

Comprehension

1. How did early observers view television? How, in general, does Winn's
   view differ from theirs?

2. How has the nature of family television viewing changed since its
   inception? How does Winn account for this change?

3. How does television keep families apart? In what sense does Winn see
   television as a threat to the very nature of the family?

4. What definition of *ritual* does Winn quote (16)? According to Winn,
   how has television affected such rituals?

5. What other factors besides television does Winn see as having a negative effect on the family?

Purpose and Audience

1. Winn states her thesis in paragraph 8. What is it?

2. In paragraphs 23 and 31, Winn quotes two noted psychologists. What effect do you think she expects their words to have on her audience?

3. What effect do you believe the young woman's testimony in paragraph 19 is calculated to have on Winn's readers?

4. Do you think Winn presents enough evidence to support her thesis? Explain your position.

5. In paragraph 20, Winn makes an **analogy** between modern families and cave families. What is her purpose in doing this? Is this a valid analogy?

Style and Structure

1. Winn does not state her thesis until paragraph 8. What does she do in the paragraphs preceding this?

2. The length of Winn's paragraphs varies considerably. What effect do you think short paragraphs such as paragraphs 2, 3, 4, and 18 are likely to have on readers?

3. From what sources does Winn draw the many quotations she uses in this essay? How does the varied nature of these quotations help support her thesis?

4. This essay includes four headings: "The Quality of Life," "Family Rituals," "Real People," and "Undermining the Family." What functions do these headings serve? Could they be omitted? Should they be?

5. At the end of the essay, Winn addresses the findings of a study that contradicts her thesis. Should she also have addressed other issues that might have challenged her thesis? If so, which ones? Do you think she adequately refutes the study's conclusions? Does placing the opposing study at the end of the essay strengthen or weaken her essay? Explain.

6. This is a fairly long essay. Is it *too* long? What, if anything, could Winn have cut?

Vocabulary Projects

1. Define each of the following words as it is used in this selection.

myopia (1)	recurrent (9)	inroads (18)
preposterous (6)	regimented (12)	purport (22)
splintering (6)	leisurely (13)	fosters (22)
ameliorate (8)	mechanized (13)	fester (25)
advent (8)	mediating (15)	diminished (32)
subsidiary (8)	shunted (15)	amiss (36)
apologists (8)	rendered (15)	abstraction (36)
equivocal (9)	adhesive (17)	

2. One effect of television has been on our vocabulary: television has spawned new words (for example, *sitcom*) and suggested new uses for old words (for instance, *tube*). List as many television-inspired words as you can, and define each.

Journal Entry

What effects—positive or negative—do you think television has had on your life? What would your life be like without it?

Writing Workshop

1. Write an essay in which you consider the effects (including any possible future effects) on the American family of one of these inventions: the cell phone, email, the microwave, the VCR and DVD player, the iPod, or Xbox.
2. Write a cause-and-effect essay discussing the *positive* effects of television on American society.
3. Winn's essay, although recently updated for this book, is more than thirty-five years old, and both television and viewers have changed considerably since she wrote "Television: The Plug-In Drug." Write a cause-and-effect essay about television considering developments that Winn does not take into account—for example, the popularity of reality-based programs and the availability of satellite dishes.

Combining the Patterns

Winn's essay relies on several patterns of development besides cause and effect. Where does she use **narration? Definition? Exemplification?** Why does she use each of these patterns?

Thematic Connections

- "Once More to the Lake" (page 186)
- "The Human Cost of an Illiterate Society" (page 252)
- "Sizing Up the Effects" (page 671)

KATHA POLLITT

Why Boys Don't Play with Dolls

Katha Pollitt (b. 1949) grew up in Brooklyn, New York, and now lives on Manhattan's Upper West Side. A graduate of Radcliffe College, she won the *Mademoiselle* undergraduate poetry contest in 1971. Pollitt has taught in the graduate writing program at New York University and the graduate program in liberal studies at the New School for Social Research, and she has published hundreds of book reviews and essays, as well as poetry, in a variety of periodicals, including *The Nation, The New Yorker, Harper's, Mother Jones,* and *Dissent.* A popular lecturer on feminist issues, she has also written the books *Reasonable Creatures: Essays on Women and Feminism* (1994) and *Subject to Debate: Sense and Dissents on Women, Politics, and Culture* (2001).

Background on gender-specific toys: In the following essay, which originally appeared in the *New York Times Magazine,* Pollitt considers the effects of gender stereotyping as it is reflected in the different toys given to little girls and to little boys. While the twentieth century saw the introduction of many toys that appealed to both girls and boys—wagons, pogo sticks, board games, hula hoops, and video games such as Pokémon—the majority of toys were marketed either for boys or for girls: at the turn of the century, train sets and cap guns for boys, baby dolls and crayons for girls; ten years later, Erector sets and toy cars for boys, Raggedy Ann dolls for girls. The introduction of the Easy Bake oven in the 1950s was matched by a proliferation of cowboy gear for boys. In the 1960s, the must-have toys were G.I. Joe and Hot Wheels versus the Barbie Doll; in the 1970s, action figures versus Holly Hobbie dolls; in the 1980s, He-Man and Masters of the Universe versus She-Ra and My Little Pony. Among the more recent popular toys introduced for boys was the Robosapien Remote Control Robot; girls got the Bratz dolls ("with a passion for fashion") and the Diva Starz fashion dolls.

It's 28 years since the founding of NOW,* and boys still like trucks and girls still like dolls. Increasingly, we are told that the source of these robust preferences must lie outside society—in prenatal hormonal influences, brain chemistry, genes—and that feminism has reached its natural limits. What else could possibly explain the love of preschool girls for party dresses or the desire of toddler boys to own more guns than Mark from Michigan.

True, recent studies claim to show small cognitive differences between the sexes: he gets around by orienting himself in space, she does it by remembering landmarks. Time will tell if any deserve the hoopla with

---

* EDS. NOTE—The National Organization for Women (NOW) was founded in 1966.

which each is invariably greeted, over the protests of the researchers themselves. But even if the results hold up (and the history of such research is not encouraging), we don't need studies of sex-differentiated brain activity in reading, say, to understand why boys and girls still seem so unalike.

The feminist movement has done much for some women, and something for every woman, but it has hardly turned America into a playground free of sex roles. It hasn't even got women to stop dieting or men to stop interrupting them.

Instead of looking at kids to "prove" that differences in behavior by sex are innate, we can look at the ways we raise kids as an index to how unfinished the feminist revolution really is, and how tentatively it is embraced even by adults who fully expect their daughters to enter previously male-dominated professions and their sons to change diapers.

I'm at a children's birthday party. "I'm sorry," one mom silently mouths to the mother of the birthday girl, who has just torn open her present — Tropical Splash Barbie. Now, you can love Barbie or you can hate Barbie, and there are feminists in both camps. But *apologize* for Barbie? Inflict Barbie, against your own convictions, on the child of a friend you know will be none too pleased?

Every mother in that room had spent years becoming a person who had to be taken seriously, not least by herself. Even the most attractive, I'm willing to bet, had suffered over her body's failure to fit the impossible American ideal. Given all that, it seems crazy to transmit Barbie to the next generation. Yet to reject her is to say that what Barbie represents — being sexy, thin, stylish — is unimportant, which is obviously not true, and children know it's not true.

Women's looks matter terribly in this society, and so Barbie, however ambivalently, must be passed along. After all, there are worse toys. The Cut and Style Barbie styling head, for example, a grotesque object intended to encourage "hair play." The grown-ups who give that probably apologize, too.

How happy would most parents be to have a child who flouted sex conventions? I know a lot of women, feminists, who complain in a comical, eyeball-rolling way about their sons' passion for sports: the ruined weekends, obnoxious coaches, macho values. But they would not think of discouraging their sons from participating in this activity they find so foolish. Or do they? Their husbands are sports fans, too, and they like their husbands a lot.

Could it be that even sports-resistant moms see athletics as part of manliness? That if their sons wanted to spend the weekend writing up their diaries, or reading, or baking, they'd find it disturbing? Too antisocial? Too lonely? Too gay?

Theories of innate differences in behavior are appealing. They let parents off the hook — no small recommendation in a culture that holds moms, and sometimes even dads, responsible for their children's every misstep on the road to bliss and success.

They allow grown-ups to take the path of least resistance to the domi-   11
nant culture, which always requires less psychic effort, even if it means
more actual work: just ask the working mother who comes home
exhausted and nonetheless finds it easier to pick up her son's socks than
make him do it himself. They let families buy for their children, without
too much guilt, the unbelievably sexist junk that the kids, who have been
watching commercials since birth, understandably crave.

But the thing the theories do most of all is tell adults that the *adult*   12
world — in which moms and dads still play by many of the old rules even as
they question and fidget and chafe against them — is the way it's supposed
to be. A girl with a doll and a boy with a truck "explain" why men are from
Mars and women are from Venus, why wives do housework and husbands
just don't understand.

The paradox is that the world of rigid and hierarchical sex roles evoked   13
by determinist theories is already passing away. Three-year-olds may indeed
insist that doctors are male and nurses female, even if their own mother is
a physician. Six-year-olds know better. These days, something like half of
all medical students are female, and male applications to nursing school
are inching upward. When tomorrow's three-year-olds play doctor, who's
to say how they'll assign the roles?

With sex roles, as in every area of life, people aspire to what is possible   14
and conform to what is necessary. But these are not fixed, especially today.
Biological determinism may reassure some adults about their present, but
it is feminism, the ideology of flexible and converging sex roles, that fits
our children's future. And the kids, somehow, know this.

That's why, if you look carefully, you'll find that for every kid who fits   15
a stereotype, there's another who's breaking one down. Sometimes it's the
same kid — the boy who skateboards *and* takes cooking in his after-school
program; the girl who collects stuffed animals *and* A-pluses in science.

Feminists are often accused of imposing their "agenda" on children.   16
Isn't that what adults always do, consciously or unconsciously? Kids aren't
born religious, or polite, or kind, or able to remember where they put their
sneakers. Inculcating these behaviors, and the values behind them, is a
tremendous amount of work, involving many adults. We don't have a
choice, really, about *whether* we should give our children messages about
what it means to be male and female — they're bombarded with them from
morning till night.

The question, as always, is what do we want those messages to be?   17

•   •   •

Comprehension

1. How does Pollitt assess the accomplishments of the feminist movement?

2. Who (or what) does Pollitt blame for the fact that the "feminist revolution" is "unfinished" (4)?

3. Why, according to Pollitt, do mothers continue to "transmit Barbie to the next generation" (6)? Does she think they are wrong to do so? Explain.

4. How does Pollitt account for the fact that women do not discourage their sons from playing sports? Does she think they should?

5. What is Pollitt's asessment of "theories of innate differences in behavior" (10) between girls and boys?

6. What dangers does Pollitt see in encouraging girls to play with dolls and boys to play with trucks? Do you see any dangers in this behavior?

7. What **paradox** does Pollitt identify beginning in paragraph 13? Why is this a paradox?

8. In paragraph 14, Pollitt says, "With sex roles, as in every area of life, people aspire to what is possible and conform to what is necessary." What does she mean?

Purpose and Audience

1. What is Pollitt's thesis? Does she state it explicitly? Do you agree with her?

2. In paragraphs 5–7, Pollitt relates an anecdote about a birthday party. What purpose does this anecdote serve in the essay?

3. How does Pollitt expect her audience to react to her essay? Do you think she wants them to change their behavior or simply to reexamine their priorities? Explain.

Style and Structure

1. According to Pollitt, what is the main cause of the gender differences in toy preferences? What other causes does she suggest? Can you think of others?

2. Use a causal chain to explain why a female child might choose to play with dolls instead of with trucks.

3. When Pollitt says, "A girl with a doll and a boy with a truck 'explain' why . . . wives do housework and husbands just don't understand" (12), is she guilty of *post hoc* reasoning? Explain.

4. Pollitt ends her essay with a one-sentence conclusion. Is this an effective strategy, or should she have developed the paragraph further — for example, by suggesting answers to the question she poses?

Vocabulary Projects

1. Define each of the following words as it is used in this selection.

robust (1)	flouted (8)	hierarchical (13)
cognitive (2)	innate (10)	determinist (13)
hoopla (2)	chafe (12)	inculcating (16)

2. Throughout this essay, Pollitt often uses the word *kids* rather than *children*. What different connotations do these two words have? Do you think her frequent use of *kids* is a good strategy?

Journal Entry

In the essay's first sentence, Pollitt says that "boys still like trucks and girls still like dolls." Do your experiences and observations support this conclusion?

Writing Workshop

1. Write a cause-and-effect essay titled "Why Girls Don't Play with Trucks." Support your thesis with information from your personal experience and observations.
2. How do you think playing with Barbie dolls might actually change the way a young girl thinks or behaves? Write a cause-and-effect essay explaining the specific effects of playing with this particular doll.
3. What kinds of toys or games do you see as having a negative effect on young children? Write a cause-and-effect essay that identifies and accounts for these negative consequences. In your conclusion, make some recommendations on how to solve the problems these toys or games create.

Combining the Patterns

Although this is a cause-and-effect essay, it also compares boys and girls (and, by extension, men and women). What specific differences does Pollitt see between the two genders? Do you think she should have spent more time on developing a **comparison and contrast** between males and females? What additional information would she have had to provide?

Thematic Connections

- "My Field of Dreams" (page 89)
- "Sex, Lies, and Conversation" (page 440)
- "I Want a Wife" (page 524)

LAWRENCE OTIS GRAHAM

The "Black Table" Is Still There

Lawrence Otis Graham was born in 1962 into one of the few African-American families then living in an upper-middle-class community in Westchester County, near New York City. A graduate of Princeton University and Harvard Law School, Graham works as a corporate attorney in Manhattan and teaches at Fordham University. He is the author of some dozen books, most recently *Our Kind of People: Inside the Black Middle Class* (1999) and *Proversity: Getting Past Face Value* (2001). The following essay, originally published in the *New York Times* in 1991, is included in Graham's 1995 essay collection, *Member of the Club: Reflections on Life in a Racially Polarized Society*.

Background on school segregation: In "The 'Black Table' Is Still There," Graham returns to his largely white junior high school and discovers to his dismay how little has changed since the 1970s. Since the 1950s, the United States government has strongly supported integration of public schools. For example, the Supreme Court in 1955 found segregation of public schools unconstitutional; the Civil Rights Act of 1964 required public school systems to implement integration programs; and in 1971, the Supreme Court upheld court-ordered busing as a means of achieving integration. The results of these policies were dramatic. From the mid-1960s to 1972, the number of African-American students attending desegregated schools jumped from 12 percent to 44 percent. By the 1990s, however, this had begun to change as the Supreme Court began to lift desegregation orders in response to local school boards' promises to desegregate voluntarily through magnet schools and the like. A study published in 2003 showed that two-thirds of African-American students attend schools that are predominantly minority and more than 5 percent attend schools that are 99 to 100 percent minority, a significant rise since 1989. Ironically, as Graham observes, when students are given the choice, self-segregation seems to be the norm.

During a recent visit to my old junior high school in Westchester 1
County, I came upon something that I never expected to see again, something that was a source of fear and dread for three hours each school morning of my early adolescence: the all-black lunch table in the cafeteria of my predominantly white suburban junior high school.

As I look back on 27 years of often being the first and only black per- 2
son integrating such activities and institutions as the college newspaper, the high school tennis team, summer music camps, our all-white suburban neighborhood, my eating club at Princeton, or my private social club at Harvard Law School, the one scenario that puzzled me the most then and now is the all-black lunch table.

Why was it there? Why did the black kids separate themselves? What 3
did the table say about the integration that was supposedly going on in
home rooms and gym classes? What did it say about the black kids? The
white kids? What did it say about me when I refused to sit there, day after
day, for three years?

Each afternoon, at 12:03 P.M., after the fourth period ended, I found 4
myself among 600 12-, 13-, and 14-year-olds who marched into the
brightly-lit cafeteria and dashed for a seat at one of the 27 blue formica
lunch tables.

No matter who I walked in with — usually a white friend — no matter 5
what mood I was in, there was one thing that was certain: I would not sit at
the black table.

I would never consider sitting at the black table. 6

What was wrong with me? What was I afraid of? 7

I would like to think that my decision was a heroic one, made in order 8
to express my solidarity with the theories of integration that my community was espousing. But I was just 12 at the time, and there was nothing
heroic in my actions.

I avoided the black table for a very simple reason: I was afraid that by 9
sitting at the black table I'd lose all my white friends. I thought that by sitting there I'd be making a racist, anti-white statement.

Is that what the all-black table means? Is it a rejection of white people? 10
I no longer think so.

At the time, I was angry that there was a black lunch table. I believed 11
that the black kids were the reason why other kids didn't mix more. I was
ready to believe that their self-segregation was the cause of white bigotry.

Ironically, I even believed this after my best friend (who was white) told 12
me I probably shouldn't come to his bar mitzvah because I'd be the only
black and people would feel uncomfortable. I even believed this after my
Saturday afternoon visit, at age 10, to a private country club pool prompted
incensed white parents to pull their kids from the pool in terror.

In the face of this blatantly racist (anti-black) behavior I still somehow 13
managed to blame only the black kids for being the barrier to integration
in my school and my little world. What was I thinking?

I realize now how wrong I was. During that same time, there were at 14
least two tables of athletes, an Italian table, a Jewish girls' table, a Jewish
boys' table (where I usually sat), a table of kids who were into heavy metal
music and smoking pot, a table of middle-class Irish kids. Weren't these
tables just as segregationist as the black table? At the time, no one thought
so. At the time, no one even acknowledged the segregated nature of these
other tables.

Maybe it's the color difference that makes all-black tables or all-black 15
groups attract the scrutiny and wrath of so many people. It scares and
angers people; it exasperates. It did those things to me, and I'm black.

As an integrating black person, I know that my decision *not* to join the 16
black lunch table attracted its own kinds of scrutiny and wrath from my

classmates. At the same time that I heard angry words like "Oreo" and "white boy" being hurled at me from the black table, I was also dodging impatient questions from white classmates: "Why do all those black kids sit together?" or "Why don't you ever sit with the other blacks?"

The black lunch table, like those other segregated tables, is a comment   17
on the superficial inroads that integration has made in society. Perhaps I should be happy that even this is a long way from where we started. Yet, I can't get over the fact that the 27th table in my junior high school cafeteria is still known as the "black table" — 14 years after my adolescence.

• • •

Comprehension

1. What exactly is the "black table"?

2. In paragraph 1, Graham says that on a recent visit to his old junior high school he "came upon something that [he] never expected to see again." Why do you think the sight of the all-black lunch table was such a surprise to him?

3. In Graham's junior high school, what factors determined where students sat?

4. Why didn't Graham sit at the "black table" when he was in junior high?

5. When he was a junior high school student, whom did Graham blame for the existence of the exclusively black lunch table? Whom or what does he now see as the cause of the table's existence?

Purpose and Audience

1. What is Graham's thesis?

2. Rather than introducing outside supporting information — such as statistics, interviews with educators, or sociological studies — Graham relies on his own opinions and on anecdotal evidence to support his thesis. Do you think this is enough? Explain.

3. Why does Graham give background information about himself in this essay — for example, in paragraphs 2 and 12? How does this information affect your reaction to him as a person? Your reaction to his essay? Do you think he needs to supply additional information about himself or his junior high school? If so, what kind of information would be helpful?

4. Do you think Graham's primary purpose here is to criticize a system he despises, to change his audience's views about segregated lunch tables, or to justify his own behavior? Explain your conclusion.

5. In paragraph 5, Graham tells readers that he usually entered the cafeteria with a white friend; in paragraph 12, he reveals that his best friend was white. Why do you suppose he wants his audience to know these facts?

Style and Structure

1. Throughout his essay Graham asks **rhetorical questions**. Identify as many of these questions as you can. Are they necessary? Provocative? Distracting? Explain.

2. In paragraph 16, Graham quotes his long-ago classmates. What do these quotations reveal? Should he have included more of them?

3. Is Graham's focus on finding causes, describing effects, or both? Explain.

4. This essay uses first-person pronouns and contractions. Do you think Graham would have more credibility if he used a less personal and more formal style?

Vocabulary Projects

1. Define each of the following words as it is used in this selection.

   scenario (2)   incensed (12)   scrutiny (15)
   espousing (8)   blatantly (13)   inroads (17)

2. Does the phrase *black table* have a negative connotation for you? Do you think Graham intends it to? What other names could he give to the table that might present it in a more neutral, even positive, light? What names could he give to the other tables he lists in paragraph 14?

Journal Entry

Graham sees the continued presence of the "black table" as a serious problem. Do you agree?

Writing Workshop

1. In paragraph 14, Graham mentions other lunch tables that were limited to certain groups and asks, "Weren't these tables just as segregationist as the black table?" Answer his question in a cause-and-effect essay explaining why you believe "black tables" still exist.

2. In addition to self-segregated lunch tables, many colleges also have single-race social clubs, dormitories, fraternities, and even graduation ceremonies. Do you see such self-segregation as something that divides our society (that is, as a cause) or as something that reflects divisions that already exist (that is, as an effect)? Write an essay discussing this issue, supporting your thesis with examples from your own experience.

3. Do the people at your school or workplace tend to segregate themselves according to race, gender, or some other principle? Do you see a problem in such behavior? Write a memo to your school's dean of students or to your employer explaining what you believe causes this pattern and what effects, positive or negative, you have observed.

Combining the Patterns

In paragraph 14, Graham uses **classification and division**. What is he categorizing? What categories does he identify? What other categories might he include? Why is this pattern of development particularly appropriate for this essay?

Thematic Connections

- "Indian Education" (page 134)
- "Just Walk On By" (page 240)
- "College Pressures" (page 466)

LINDA M. HASSELSTROM

A Peaceful Woman Explains
Why She Carries a Gun

Linda M. Hasselstrom (b. 1943) grew up in rural South Dakota in a cattle ranching family. After receiving a master's degree in journalism from the University of Missouri, she returned to South Dakota to run her own ranch and now divides her time between South Dakota and Cheyenne, Wyoming. A highly respected poet, essayist, and writing teacher, she often focuses on everyday life in the American West in her work. Her publications include the poetry collections *Caught by One Wing* (1984), *Roadkill* (1987), and *Dakota Bones* (1991); the essay collection *Land Circle* (1991); and several books about ranching, including *Feels Like Far: A Rancher's Life on the Great Plains* (1999) and *Between Grass and Sky: Where I Live and Work* (2002). In this essay from *Land Circle*, Hasselstrom explains her reluctant decision to become licensed to carry a concealed handgun.

   Background on incidences of sexual assault: Hasselstrom's gun ownership can certainly be considered in the context of the ongoing debate over how (and even whether) stricter gun safety measures should be enacted in the United States. Equally important, however, is the fact that her reason for carrying a gun is to protect herself from sexual assault. A study by the Bureau of Justice Statistics found that in 2002, more than 200,000 women reported being sexually assaulted in this country. It is estimated that only one in six instances of sexual assault is actually reported to the police, so the number of such attacks is, in reality, much higher.

I am a peace-loving woman. But several events in the past 10 years have convinced me I'm safer when I carry a pistol. This was a personal decision, but because handgun possession is a controversial subject, perhaps my reasoning will interest others.   1

I live in western South Dakota on a ranch 25 miles from the nearest town: for several years I spent winters alone here. As a free-lance writer, I travel alone a lot — more than 100,000 miles by car in the last four years. With women freer than ever before to travel alone, the odds of our encountering trouble seem to have risen. Distances are great, roads are deserted, and the terrain is often too exposed to offer hiding places.   2

A woman who travels alone is advised, usually by men, to protect herself by avoiding bars and other "dangerous situations," by approaching her car like an Indian scout, by locking doors and windows. But these precautions aren't always enough. I spent years following them and still found myself in dangerous situations. I began to resent the idea that just because I am female, I have to be extra careful.   3

A few years ago, with another woman, I camped for several weeks in the   4
West. We discussed self-defense, but neither of us had taken a course in it.
She was against firearms, and local police told us Mace was illegal. So we
armed ourselves with spray cans of deodorant tucked into our sleeping
bags. We never used our improvised Mace because we were lucky enough to
camp beside people who came to our aid when men harassed us. But on
one occasion we visited a national park where our assigned space was less
than 15 feet from other campers. When we returned from a walk, we found
our closest neighbors were two young men. As we gathered our cooking
gear, they drank beer and loudly discussed what they would do to us after
dark. Nearby campers, even families, ignored them: rangers strolled past,
unconcerned. When we asked the rangers point-blank if they would protect us, one of them patted my shoulder and said, "Don't worry, girls.
They're just kidding." At dusk we drove out of the park and hid our camp
in the woods a few miles away. The illegal spot was lovely, but our enjoyment of that park was ruined. I returned from the trip determined to
reconsider the options available for protecting myself.

At that time, I lived alone on the ranch and taught night classes in   5
town. Along a city street I often traveled, a woman had a flat tire, called for
help on her CB radio, and got a rapist who left her beaten. She was afraid
to call for help again and stayed in her car until morning. For that reason,
as well as because CBs work best along line-of-sight, which wouldn't help
much in the rolling hills where I live, I ruled out a CB.

As I drove home one night, a car followed me. It passed me on a narrow   6
bridge while a passenger flashed a blinding spotlight in my face. I braked
sharply. The car stopped, angled across the bridge, and four men jumped
out. I realized the locked doors were useless if they broke the windows of
my pickup. I started forward, hoping to knock their car aside so I could
pass. Just then another car appeared, and the men hastily got back in their
car. They continued to follow me, passing and repassing. I dared not go
home because no one else was there. I passed no lighted houses. Finally
they pulled over to the roadside, and I decided to use their tactic: fear.
Speeding, the pickup horn blaring, I swerved as close to them as I dared as
I roared past. It worked: they turned off the highway. But I was frightened
and angry. Even in my vehicle I was too vulnerable.

Other incidents occurred over the years. One day I glanced out at a   7
field below my house and saw a man with a shotgun walking toward a
pond full of ducks. I drove down and explained that the land was posted. I
politely asked him to leave. He stared at me, and the muzzle of the shotgun
began to rise. In a moment of utter clarity I realized that I was alone on the
ranch, and that he could shoot me and simply drive away. The moment
passed: the man left.

One night, I returned home from teaching a class to find deep tire ruts   8
in the wet ground of my yard, garbage in the driveway, and a large gas tank
empty. A light shone in the house: I couldn't remember leaving it on. I was
too embarrassed to drive to a neighboring ranch and wake someone up. An

hour of cautious exploration convinced me the house was safe, but once inside, with the doors locked, I was still afraid. I kept thinking of how vulnerable I felt, prowling around my own house in the dark.

My first positive step was to take a kung fu class, which teaches evasive   9
or protective action when someone enters your space without permission. I learned to move confidently, scanning for possible attackers. I learned how to assess danger and techniques for avoiding it without combat.

I also learned that one must practice several hours every day to be good   10
at kung fu. By that time I had married George: when I practiced with him, I learned how *close* you must be to your attacker to use martial arts, and decided a 120-pound woman dare not let a six-foot, 220-pound attacker get that close unless she is very, very good at self-defense. I have since read articles by several women who were extremely well trained in the martial arts, but were raped and beaten anyway.

I thought back over the times in my life when I had been attacked or   11
threatened and tried to be realistic about my own behavior, searching for anything that had allowed me to become a victim. Overall, I was convinced that I had not been at fault. I don't believe myself to be either paranoid or a risk-taker, but I wanted more protection.

With some reluctance I decided to try carrying a pistol. George had   12
always carried one, despite his size and his training in martial arts. I practiced shooting until I was sure I could hit an attacker who moved close enough to endanger me. Then I bought a license from the county sheriff, making it legal for me to carry the gun concealed.

But I was not yet ready to defend myself. George taught me that the   13
most important preparation was mental: convincing myself I could actually *shoot a person*. Few of us wish to hurt or kill another human being. But there is no point in having a gun; in fact, gun possession might increase your danger unless you know you can use it. I got in the habit of rehearsing, as I drove or walked, the precise conditions that would be required before I would shoot someone.

People who have not grown up with the idea that they are capable of   14
protecting themselves — in other words, most women — might have to work hard to convince themselves of their ability, and of the necessity. Handgun ownership need not turn us into gunslingers, but it can be part of believing in, and relying on, *ourselves* for protection.

To be useful, a pistol has to be available. In my car, it's within instant   15
reach. When I enter a deserted rest stop at night, it's in my purse, with my hand on the grip. When I walk from a dark parking lot into a motel, it's in my hand, under a coat. At home, it's on the headboard. In short, I take it with me almost everywhere I go alone.

Just carrying a pistol is not protection; avoidance is still the best   16
approach to trouble. Subconsciously watching for signs of danger, I believe I've become more alert. Handgun use, not unlike driving, becomes instinctive. Each time I've drawn my gun — I have never fired it at another human being — I've simply found it in my hand.

I was driving the half-mile to the highway mailbox one day when I saw   17
a vehicle parked about midway down the road. Several men were standing
in the ditch, relieving themselves. I have no objection to emergency urina-
tion, but I noticed they'd dumped several dozen beer cans in the road.
Besides being ugly, cans can slash a cow's feet or stomach.

The men noticed me before they finished and made quite a perfor-   18
mance out of zipping their trousers while walking toward me. All four of
them gathered around my small foreign car, and one of them demanded
what the hell I wanted.

"This is private land. I'd appreciate it if you'd pick up the beer cans."   19

"What beer cans?" said the belligerent one, putting both hands on the   20
car door and leaning in my window. His face was inches from mine, and the
beer fumes were strong. The others laughed. One tried the passenger door,
locked; another put his foot on the hood and rocked the car. They circled,
lightly thumping the roof, discussing my good fortune in meeting them
and the benefits they were likely to bestow upon me. I felt very small and
very trapped and they knew it.

"The ones you just threw out," I said politely.   21

"I don't see no beer cans. Why don't you get out here and show them to   22
me, honey?" said the belligerent one, reaching for the handle inside my door.

"Right over there," I said, still being polite. " — there, and over there." I   23
pointed with the pistol, which I'd slipped under my thigh. Within one
minute the cans and the men were back in the car and headed down the
road.

I believe this incident illustrates several important principles. The men   24
were trespassing and knew it: their judgment may have been impaired by
alcohol. Their response to the polite request of a woman alone was to use
their size, numbers, and sex to inspire fear. The pistol was a response in the
same language. Politeness didn't work: I couldn't match them in size or
number. Out of the car, I'd have been more vulnerable. The pistol just
changed the balance of power. It worked again recently when I was driving
in a desolate part of Wyoming. A man played cat-and-mouse with me for 30
miles, ultimately trying to run me off the road. When his car passed mine
with only two inches to spare, I showed him my pistol, and he disappeared.

When I got my pistol, I told my husband, revising the old Colt slogan,   25
"God made men *and women,* but Sam Colt made them equal." Recently I
have seen a gunmaker's ad with a similar sentiment. Perhaps this is an idea
whose time has come, though the pacifist inside me will be saddened if the
only way women can achieve equality is by carrying weapons.

We must treat a firearm's power with caution. "Power tends to corrupt,   26
and absolute power corrupts absolutely," as a man (Lord Acton) once said.
A pistol is not the only way to avoid being raped or murdered in today's
world, but, intelligently wielded, it can shift the balance of power and provide a measure of safety.

•   •   •

Comprehension

1. According to Hasselstrom, why does she carry a gun? In one sentence, summarize her rationale.
2. List the specific events that led Hasselstrom to her decision to carry a gun.
3. Other than carrying a gun, what means of protecting herself did Hasselstrom try? Why did she find them unsatisfactory? Can you think of other strategies she could have adopted instead of carrying a gun?
4. Where in the essay does Hasselstrom express her reluctance to carry a gun?
5. In paragraph 13, Hasselstrom says, "Gun possession might increase your danger unless you know you can use it." Where else does she touch on the possible pitfalls of carrying a gun?
6. What does Hasselstrom mean when she says, "The pistol just changed the balance of power" (paragraph 24)?

Purpose and Audience

1. How does paragraph 1 establish Hasselstrom's purpose for writing this essay? What other purpose might she have?
2. What purpose does paragraph 5 serve? Is it necessary?
3. Do you think this essay is aimed at men, at women, or at both? Why?
4. Do you think Hasselstrom expects her readers to agree with her position? Where does she indicate that she expects them to challenge her? How does she address this challenge?

Style and Structure

1. This essay is written in the first person, and it relies heavily on personal experience. Do you see this as a strength or a weakness? Explain.
2. What is the main cause in this cause-and-effect essay—that is, what is the most important reason Hasselstrom gives for carrying a gun? Can you identify any contributory causes?
3. Could you argue that simply being a woman is justification enough for carrying a gun? Do you think this is Hasselstrom's position? Explain.
4. Think of Hasselstrom's essay as the first step in a possible causal chain. What situations might result from her decision to carry a gun?
5. In paragraph 25, Hasselstrom says, "The pacifist inside me will be saddened if the only way women can achieve equality is by carrying weapons." In her title and elsewhere in the essay, Hasselstrom characterizes herself as a "peaceful woman." Do you think she is successful in using language like this to portray herself as a peace-loving woman who only reluctantly carries a gun?

Vocabulary Projects

1. Define each of the following words as it is used in this selection.

   posted (7)   belligerent (20)   wielded (26)
   muzzle (7)   bestow (20)

2. Some of the words and phrases Hasselstrom uses in this essay suggest that she sees her pistol as an equalizer, something that helps to compensate for her vulnerability. Identify the words and phrases she uses to characterize her gun in this way.

Journal Entry

Do you agree that carrying a gun is Hasselstrom's only choice, or do you think she could take other steps to ensure her safety? Explain.

Writing Workshop

1. Hasselstrom lives in a rural area, and the scenarios she describes apply to rural life. Rewrite this essay as "A Peaceful Urban (or Suburban) Woman Explains Why She Carries a Gun."

2. What reasons might a "peace-loving" man have for carrying a gun? Write a cause-and-effect essay outlining such a man's motives, using any of Hasselstrom's reasons that might apply to him as well.

3. Write a cause-and-effect essay presenting reasons to support a position that opposes Hasselstrom's: "A Peaceful Woman (or Man) Explains Why She (or He) Will Not Carry a Gun."

Combining the Patterns

Several times in her essay, Hasselstrom uses **narrative** to support her position. Identify these narrative passages. Are they absolutely essential to the essay? Could they be briefer? Could some be deleted? Explain.

Thematic Connections

- "Shooting an Elephant" (page 125)
- "Just Walk On By" (page 240)
- "The Wife-Beater" (page 532)

ROBIN TOLMACH LAKOFF

The Power of Words in Wartime

Linguist Robin Tolmach Lakoff was born in Brooklyn, New York, in 1942 and holds degrees from Radcliffe College, Indiana University, and Harvard University. She has been on the faculty of the University of California at Berkeley since 1971. Her first book, *Language and Woman's Place* (1975), was a groundbreaking study of the effect of language on gender roles. Other important works include *Talking Power: The Politics of Language in Our Lives* (1990) and *The Language War* (2000), an analysis of language, politics, and the media. The following essay appeared on the op-ed page of the *New York Times* in May 2004.

Background on what wartime enemies have called Americans: During World War II, the German Nazis denigrated Americans as "mongrels" (because the U.S. population was made up of so many nationalities), creating an image of Americans as ill-bred animals. To the Japanese, Americans were "monsters" and "devils" as well as "mongrels," and American soldiers were referred to in Japanese films of the time simply as "they" or "them." During the subsequent Korean War, Korean communist propaganda called Americans "apes" and "beasts," while during the Vietnam War, Vietnamese communists referred to Americans generally as "imperialists" and to American soldiers as "killers" and "American aggressors." More recently, extremists in the Muslim world have referred to America as "the Great Satan," echoing the words of Iran's Ayatollah Khomeini, and to Americans in general as "infidels."

An American soldier refers to an Iraqi prisoner as "it." A general speaks not of "Iraqi fighters" but of "the enemy." A weapons manufacturer doesn't talk about people but about "targets." 1

Bullets and bombs are not the only tools of war. Words, too, play their part. 2

Human beings are social animals, genetically hard-wired to feel compassion toward others. Under normal conditions, most people find it very difficult to kill. 3

But in war, military recruits must be persuaded that killing other people is not only acceptable but even honorable. 4

The language of war is intended to bring about that change, and not only for soldiers in the field. In wartime, language must be created to enable combatants and noncombatants alike to see the other side as killable, to overcome the innate queasiness over the taking of human life. Soldiers, and those who remain at home, learn to call their enemies by names that make them seem not quite human — inferior, contemptible and not like "us." 5

The specific words change from culture to culture and war to war. The   6
names need not be obviously demeaning. Just the fact that *we* can name
them gives us a sense of superiority and control. If, in addition, we give
them nicknames, we can see them as smaller, weaker and childlike — not
worth taking seriously as fully human.

The Greeks and Romans referred to everyone else as "barbarians" —   7
etymologically those who only babble, only go "barbar." During the American Revolution, the British called the colonists "Yankees," a term with a
history that is still in dispute. While the British intended it disparagingly,
the Americans, in perhaps the first historical instance of reclamation,
made the word their own and gave it a positive spin, turning the derisive
song "Yankee Doodle" into our first, if unofficial, national anthem.

In World War I, the British gave the Germans the nickname "Jerries,"   8
from the first syllable of German. In World War II, Americans referred to
the Japanese as "Japs."

The names may refer to real or imagined cultural and physical differ-   9
ences that emphasize the ridiculous or the repugnant. So in various wars,
the British called the French "Frogs." Germans have been called "Krauts," a
reference to weird and smelly food. The Vietnamese were called "slopes"
and "slants." The Koreans were referred to simply as "gooks."

The war in Iraq has added new examples. Some American soldiers refer   10
to the Iraqis as "hadjis," used in a derogatory way, apparently unaware that
the word, which comes from the Arabic term for a pilgrimage to Mecca, is
used as a term of respect for older Muslim men.

The Austrian ethologist Konrad Lorenz suggested that the more   11
clearly we see other members of our own species as individuals, the harder
we find it to kill them.

So some terms of war are collective nouns, encouraging us to see the   12
enemy as an undifferentiated mass, rather than as individuals capable of
suffering. Crusaders called their enemy "the Saracen," and in World War I,
the British called Germans "the Hun."

American soldiers are trained to call those they are fighting against   13
"the enemy." It is easier to kill an enemy than an Iraqi.

The word "enemy" itself provides the facelessness of a collective noun.   14
Its nonspecificity also has a fear-inducing connotation; enemy means simply "those we are fighting," without reference to their identity.

The terrors and uncertainties of war make learning this kind of lan-   15
guage especially compelling for soldiers on the front. But civilians back
home also need to believe that what their country is doing is just and necessary, and that the killing they are supporting is in some way different
from the killing in civilian life that is rightly punished by the criminal justice system. The use of the language developed for military purposes by
civilians reassures them that war is not murder.

The linguistic habits that soldiers must absorb in order to fight make   16
atrocities like those at Abu Ghraib virtually inevitable. The same language
that creates a psychological chasm between "us" and "them," and enables

American troops to kill in battle, makes enemy soldiers fit subjects for torture and humiliation. The reasoning is: They are not really human, so they will not feel the pain.

Once language draws that line, all kinds of mistreatment become   17
imaginable, and then justifiable. To make the abuses at Abu Ghraib unthinkable, we would have to abolish war itself.

• • •

Comprehension

1. According to Lakoff, exactly what power do words have in wartime?
2. Do you think Lakoff attributes too much power to language in the circumstances she describes, or do you think she is right?
3. Do you see this essay as primarily about language or about war? Explain.
4. In paragraph 16, Lakoff says, "The linguistic habits that soldiers must absorb in order to fight make atrocities like those at Abu Ghraib virtually inevitable." Do you agree, or do you think she is exaggerating?
5. When Lakoff discusses U.S. enemies — for example, the Germans and the Japanese in World War II and the Iraqi insurgents today — she does not mention that among these groups, too, language is used to dehumanize their enemies. Do you think this information is implicit, or does her failure to illustrate that, in times of war, Americans are also *victims* of the power of words weaken her essay?

Purpose and Audience

1. Paraphrase Lakoff's thesis. Do you think most readers would be likely to accept this thesis? Does Lakoff convince you?
2. In paragraph 11, Lakoff paraphrases Konrad Lorenz. What purpose does this paragraph serve?
3. Is Lakoff's primary purpose to analyze language, or is this essay really about something else? Explain.

Style and Structure

1. Lakoff opens her essay with a series of examples. Is this an effective opening strategy? What other options did she have?
2. In this cause-and-effect essay, is language a cause, an effect, or both? Explain.
3. What words does Lakoff use to signal to readers that she is focusing on cause-and-effect relationships?
4. What other factors, besides language, might cause soldiers (and civilians) to see their enemies as "inferior, contemptible and not like

'us'" (5)? Does Lakoff consider these other factors? If not, do you think she should have?

5. Lakoff considers language the main, or most important, cause of our ability to dehumanize our enemies. Do you agree, or do you see it as just a contributory cause? In what sense can it also be seen as a remote cause? Explain.

6. Lakoff focuses here on one effect of language on people's behavior. What other effects do you think such language might have on the people who use it?

7. In paragraphs 7–9, Lakoff lists historical examples to support her thesis. Do such examples constitute sufficient support? What other kinds of support might she have used?

8. Do you see Lakoff's central argument as logical, or do you think she is guilty of *post hoc* reasoning?

Vocabulary Projects

1. Define each of the following words as it is used in this selection.

   innate (5)   derogatory (10
   etymologically (7)   ethologist (11)
   disparagingly (7)   undifferentiated (12)
   reclamation (7)   chasm (16)

2. In this essay on a very serious topic, Lakoff uses colloquialisms such as "hard-wired" (3) and "spin" (7). Can you identify other examples? Do you think such language is appropriate?

Journal Entry

Lakoff asserts that language can make it easier for us to dismiss or discount our enemies. Do you think the kind of pejorative names Lakoff discusses can also have such power in situations outside of wartime?

Writing Workshop

1. Write a cause-and-effect essay explaining how derogatory terms applied to particular groups of people — for example, people from developing nations, day laborers or migrant workers, or individuals with disabilities — make it possible for others to ignore, dislike, or even mistreat them.

2. Young children often direct hurtful language at their peers without recognizing or understanding its impact. What effects does such language have on children? Write an essay discussing the power of words on the playground.

Combining the Patterns

Although Lakoff focuses primarily on causes and effects, this essay also relies heavily on **exemplification**. Are some of her examples more convincing than others? Should other kinds of examples be added?

Thematic Connections

- "'What's in a Name?'" (page 5)
- "Shooting an Elephant" (page 125)
- "The Embalming of Mr. Jones" (page 310)
- "The Ways We Lie" (page 495)
- "The Untouchable" (page 516)

Suicide Note (Poetry)

Janice Mirikitani, a third-generation Japanese American, was born in San Francisco in 1942 and graduated from the University of California at Los Angeles in 1962. In her poetry, Mirikitani often considers how racism in the United States affects Asian Americans, particularly the thousands of Japanese Americans held in internment camps during World War II. Her collections include *Awake in the River* (1978), *Shedding Silence* (1987), and *We, the Dangerous: New and Selected Poems* (1995). She has also edited anthologies of Japanese-American and developing-nation literature, as well as several volumes giving voice to children living in poverty. For many years, she has been president of the Glide Foundation, which sponsors outreach programs for the poor and homeless of San Francisco. Mirikitani is the current poet laureate of San Francisco.

Background on teenage suicide: The following poem, which appears in *Shedding Silence,* takes the form of a suicide note written by a young Asian-American college student to her family and reveals the extreme pressure to excel placed on her by her parents and her culture. The theme, however, has considerable relevance beyond the Asian-American community. Tragically, some five thousand teenagers and young adults commit suicide annually in the United States (there are thirty to fifty times as many attempts), and suicide is the third leading cause of death among fifteen- to twenty-four-year-olds. Among college students, suicide is the second leading cause of death; some one thousand college students take their lives every year. Indicating the extent of the problem, in 2004 Congress passed a bill, signed into law by President Bush, authorizing funding of $82 million for programs to help prevent youth suicides.

> How many notes written . . .
> ink smeared like birdprints in snow.

not good enough   not pretty enough   not smart enough

dear mother and father.
I apologize   5
for disappointing you.
I've worked very hard,

not good enough

harder, perhaps to please you.
If only I were a son, shoulders broad   10
as the sunset threading through pine,

I would see the light in my mother's
eyes, or the golden pride reflected
in my father's dream
of my wide, male hands worthy of work   15
and comfort.
I would swagger through life
muscled and bold and assured,
drawing praises to me
like currents in the bed of wind, virile   20
with confidence.

    not good enough   not strong enough   not good enough

I apologize.
Tasks do not come easily.
Each failure, a glacier.   25
Each disapproval, a bootprint.
Each disappointment,
ice above my river.
So I have worked hard.

            not good enough   30

My sacrifice I will drop
bone by bone, perched
on the ledge of my womanhood,
fragile as wings.

            not strong enough   35

It is snowing steadily
surely not good weather
for flying — this sparrow
sillied and dizzied by the wind
on the edge.   40

            not smart enough

I make this ledge my altar
to offer penance.
This air will not hold me,
the snow burdens my crippled wings,   45
my tears drop like bitter cloth
softly into the gutter below.

    not good enough   not strong enough   not smart enough

Choices thin as shaved
ice. Notes shredded   50
drift like snow

on my broken body,
cover me like whispers
of sorries
sorries.   55
Perhaps when they find me
they will bury
my bird bones beneath
a sturdy pine
and scatter my feathers like   60
unspoken song
over this white and cold and silent
breast of earth.

• • •

Reading Literature

1. An author's note that originally introduced this poem explained the
    main cause of the student's death:

    An Asian-American college student was reported to have jumped to her
    death from her dormitory window. Her body was found two days later
    under a deep cover of snow. Her suicide note contained an apology to her
    parents for having received less than a perfect four-point grade average.

    What other causes might have contributed to her suicide?

2. Why does the speaker believe her life would be happier if she were
    male? Do you think she is correct?

3. What words, phrases, and images are repeated in this poem? What
    effect do these repetitions have on you?

Journal Entry

Whom (or what) do you blame for teenage suicides such as the one the
poem describes? How might such deaths be eliminated?

Thematic Connections

- "Only Daughter" (page 96)
- "College Pressures" (page 466)
- "The Death of the Moth" (page 728)

WRITING ASSIGNMENTS FOR CAUSE AND EFFECT

1. "Thirty-Eight Who Saw Murder Didn't Call the Police" (page 120), "Who Killed Benny Paret?" (page 346), and "On Dumpster Diving" (page 712) all encourage readers, either directly or indirectly, to take action rather than remain uninvolved. Using information gleaned from these essays (or from others in the text) as support for your thesis, write an essay exploring either the possible consequences of apathy, the possible causes of apathy, or both.

2. Write an updated version of one of this chapter's essays. For example, you might explore the kinds of pressure Lawrence Otis Graham ("The 'Black Table' Is Still There") might face as a middle-school student today.

3. Various technological and social developments have contributed to the decline of formal letter writing. One of these is the telephone; others are text-messaging and email. Consider some other possible causes, and write an essay explaining why letter writing has all but disappeared. You may also consider the *effects* (both positive and negative) of this development.

4. How do you account for the popularity of one of the following: blogs, hip-hop, video games, home schooling, reality TV, fast food, or sensationalist tabloids such as the *Star*? Write an essay considering remote as well as immediate causes for the success of the phenomenon you choose.

5. Between 1946 and 1964, the U.S. birth rate increased considerably. Some of the effects attributed to this "baby boom" include the 1960s antiwar movement, an increase in the crime rate, and the development of the women's movement. Write an essay exploring some possible effects on the nation's economy and politics of the baby-boom generation's growing older. What trends would you expect to find now that the first baby boomers have turned sixty?

6. Write an essay tracing a series of events in your life that constitutes a causal chain. Indicate clearly both the sequence of events and the causal connections among them, and be careful not to confuse coincidence with causality.

7. Consider the effects, or possible effects, of one of these scientific developments on your life, on the lives of your contemporaries, or on both: genetic engineering, space exploration, the Internet, or human cloning. Consider negative as well as positive effects.

8. Almost half of American marriages now end in divorce. To what do you attribute this high divorce rate? Be as specific as possible, citing "case studies" of families you are familiar with.

9. What do you see as the major cause of any one of these problems: acquaintance rape, binge drinking among college students, voter apathy, school shootings, or academic cheating? Based on your identification of its causes, formulate some specific solutions for the problem you select.

10. Write an essay considering the likely effects of a severe, protracted shortage of one of the following commodities: food, rental housing, flu vaccine, computer hardware, or reading matter. You may consider a community-, city-, or statewide shortage or a nation- or worldwide crisis.

11. Write an essay exploring the causes, effects, or both of increased violence among children in the United States. If you choose to cite the media as a main cause, you may refer to the essays on media violence in Chapter 14, "Argumentation."

12. Write an essay exploring the causes and effects of the trend toward longer lifespans among adults in contemporary times. (An example of a cause might be advances in medicine; an effect could be a larger population of senior citizens.) In your thesis statement, be sure to focus on what this trend might mean for future generations — politically, socially, and economically.

COLLABORATIVE ACTIVITY FOR CAUSE AND EFFECT

Working in groups of four, discuss your thoughts about the increasing homeless population, and then list four effects the presence of homeless people is having on you, your community, and our nation. Assign each member of your group to write a paragraph explaining one of the effects the group identifies. Then, arrange the paragraphs by increasing importance, moving from the least to the most significant consequence. Finally, work together to turn your individual paragraphs into an essay: write an introduction, a conclusion, and transitions between paragraphs, and include a thesis statement in paragraph 1.

INTERNET ASSIGNMENT FOR CAUSE AND EFFECT

Write an essay describing the effects of food irradiation, genetically modified food, or the use of pesticides on consumers' health. Visit the following Web sites to learn about the possible advantages and disadvantages of these food industry practices.

American Council on Science and Health
<acsh.org/index.html>
This Web site gives information of the consumer education consortium, the American Council on Science and Health (ACSH). It contains information on issues related to food, nutrition, chemicals, the environment, and health.

Center for Food Safety & Applied Nutrition
<vm.cfsan.fda.gov>
The site contains an overview and history of the Food and Drug Administration, as well as articles and information on specific programs and special topics such as biotechnology, food labeling, and nutrition.

Organic Consumers Association (OCA)
<organicconsumers.org/organlink.htm>
The OCA is a grassroots nonprofit organization that deals with issues of food safety, industrial agriculture, genetic engineering, corporate accountability, and environmental sustainability. Its Web site offers an overview of the pro-organic, anti-irradiation, and anti–genetically engineered food positions but also includes general information and a vast archive of articles from newspapers, magazines, and other publications on these subjects.

11
Comparison and Contrast

What Is Comparison and Contrast?

In the narrowest sense, *comparison* shows how two or more things are similar, and *contrast* shows how they are different. In most writing situations, however, the two related processes of **comparison and contrast** are used together. In the following paragraph from *Disturbing the Universe*, scientist Freeman Dyson compares and contrasts two different styles of human endeavor, which he calls "the gray and the green":

Topic sentence (outlines elements of comparison)	<u>In everything we undertake, either on earth or in the sky, we have a choice of two styles, which I call the gray and the green.</u> The distinction between the gray and green is not sharp. Only at the extremes of the spectrum can we say without qualification, this is green and that is gray. The difference between green and gray is better explained by examples than by definitions. Factories are gray, gardens are green. Physics is gray, biology is green. Plutonium is gray, horse manure is green. Bureaucracy is gray, pioneer communities are green. Self-reproducing machines are gray, trees and children are green. Human technology is gray, God's technology is green. Clones are gray, clades* are green. Army field manuals are gray, poems are green.
Point-by-point comparison	

A special form of comparison, called **analogy**, explains one thing by comparing it to a second, more familiar thing. In the following paragraph from *The Shopping Mall High School*, Arthur G. Powell, Eleanor Farrar, and David K. Cohen use analogy to shed light on the nature of contemporary American high schools:

---

* EDS. NOTE—A group of organisms that evolved from a common ancestor.

If Americans want to understand their high schools at work, they should imagine them as shopping malls. Secondary education is another consumption experience in an abundant society. Shopping malls attract a broad range of customers with different tastes and purposes. Some shop at Sears, others at Woolworth's or Bloomingdale's. In high schools a broad range of students also shop. They too can select from an astonishing variety of products and services conveniently assembled in one place with ample parking. Furthermore, in malls and schools many different kinds of transactions are possible. Both institutions bring hopeful purveyors and potential purchasers together. The former hope to maximize sales but can take nothing for granted. Shoppers have a wide discretion not only about what to buy but also about whether to buy.

Using Comparison and Contrast

Throughout our lives, we are bombarded with information from newspapers, television, radio, the Internet, and personal experience: the police strike in Memphis; city workers walk out in Philadelphia; the Senate debates government spending; taxes are raised in New Jersey. Somehow we must make sense of the jumbled facts and figures that surround us. One way we have of understanding information like this is to put it side by side with other data and then to compare and contrast. Do the police in Memphis have the same complaints as the city workers in Philadelphia? What are the differences between the two situations? Is the national debate on spending analogous to the New Jersey debate on taxes? How do they differ? We make similar distinctions every day about matters that directly affect us. When we make personal decisions, we consider alternatives, asking ourselves whether one option seems better than another. Should I major in history or business? What job opportunities will each major offer me? Should I register as a Democrat or a Republican, or should I join a third party? What are the positions of each political party on government spending, health care, and taxes? To answer questions like these, we use comparison and contrast.

Planning a Comparison-and-Contrast Essay

Because comparison and contrast is central to our understanding of the world, this way of thinking is often called for in papers and on essay exams:

Compare and contrast the attitudes toward science and technology expressed in Fritz Lang's *Metropolis* and George Lucas's *Star Wars*. (film)

What are the similarities and differences between mitosis and meiosis? (biology)

Discuss the relative merits of establishing a partnership or setting up a corporation. (business law)

Discuss the advantages and disadvantages of bilingual education. (education)

Recognizing Comparison-and-Contrast Assignments

You are not likely to sit down and say to yourself, "I think I'll write a comparison-and-contrast essay today. Now what can I write about?" Instead, your assignment will suggest comparison and contrast, or you will decide comparison and contrast suits your purpose. In the preceding examples, for instance, the instructors have phrased their questions to tell students how to treat the material. When you read these questions, certain key words and phrases — *compare and contrast, similarities and differences, relative merits, advantages and disadvantages* — indicate you should use a comparison-and-contrast pattern to organize your essay. Sometimes you may not even need a key phrase. Consider the question, "Which of the two Adamses, John or Samuel, had the greater influence on the timing and course of the American Revolution?" Here the word *greater* is enough to suggest a contrast.

Even when your assignment is not worded to suggest comparison and contrast, your purpose may point to this pattern of development. For instance, when you evaluate, you frequently use comparison and contrast. If, as a student in a management course, you are asked to evaluate two health-care systems, you can begin by researching the standards experts use in their evaluations. You can then compare each system's performance with those standards and contrast the systems with each other, concluding perhaps that both systems meet minimum standards but that one is more cost efficient than the other. Or, if you are evaluating two of this year's new cars for a consumer newsletter, you might establish some criteria — fuel economy, safety features, handling, comfort, style — and compare and contrast the cars on each criterion. If each of the cars is better in different categories, your readers will have to decide which features matter most to them.

Establishing a Basis for Comparison

Before you can compare and contrast two things, you must be sure a **basis for comparison** exists — that the two things have enough in common to justify the comparison. For example, although cats and dogs are very different, they share several significant elements: they are mammals, they make good pets, and they are affectionate companions. Without these shared elements, there would be no basis for analysis and nothing of importance to discuss.

A comparison should lead you beyond the obvious. For instance, at first the idea of a comparison-and-contrast essay based on an analogy between bees and people might seem absurd: after all, these two creatures differ in species, physical structure, and intelligence. In fact, their differences are so obvious that an essay based on them might seem pointless. But after further analysis, you might decide that bees and people have quite a few similarities. Both are social animals that live in complex social structures, and both have tasks to perform and roles to fulfill in their respective societies. Therefore, you *could* write about them, but you would focus on the common elements that seem most provocative — social structures and roles — rather than on dissimilar elements. If you tried to draw an analogy between bees and SUVs or humans and golf tees, however, you would run into trouble. Although some points of comparison could be found, they would be trivial. Why bother to point out that both bees and SUVs can travel great distances or that both people and tees are needed to play golf? Neither statement establishes a significant basis for comparison.

When two subjects are very similar, the contrast may be worth writing about. And, when two subjects are not very much alike, you may find that the similarities are enlightening.

Selecting Points for Discussion

After you decide which subjects to compare and contrast, you need to select the points you want to discuss. You do this by determining your emphasis — on similarities, differences, or both — and the major focus of your paper. If your purpose in comparing two types of house plants is to explain that one is easier to grow than the other, you would select points having to do with plant care, not those having to do with plant biology.

When you compare and contrast, make sure you treat the same (or at least similar) elements for each subject you discuss. For instance, if you were going to compare and contrast two novels, you might consider the following elements in both works:

NOVEL A	NOVEL B
Minor characters	Minor characters
Major characters	Major characters
Themes	Themes

Try to avoid the common error of discussing entirely different elements for each subject. Such an approach obscures any basis for comparison that might exist. The two novels, for example, could not be meaningfully compared or contrasted if you discussed dissimilar elements:

NOVEL A	NOVEL B
Minor characters	Author's life
Major characters	Plot
Themes	Symbolism

Formulating a Thesis Statement

After selecting the points you want to discuss, you are ready to formulate your thesis statement. This **thesis statement** should tell readers what to expect in your essay, identifying not only the subjects to be compared and contrasted but also the point you will make about them. Your thesis statement should also indicate whether you will concentrate on similarities or differences or both. In addition, it may list the points of comparison and contrast in the order in which they will be discussed in the essay.

The structure of your thesis statement can indicate the emphasis of your essay. As the following sentences illustrate, a thesis statement should highlight the essay's central concern by presenting it in the independent, rather than the dependent, clause of the sentence. Notice that the structure of the first thesis statement emphasizes similarities, while the structure of the second highlights differences:

> Despite the fact television and radio are distinctly different media, they use similar strategies to appeal to their audiences.

> Although Melville's *Moby-Dick* and London's *The Sea Wolf* are both about the sea, the minor characters, major characters, and themes of *Moby-Dick* establish its greater complexity.

Structuring a Comparison-and-Contrast Essay

Like every other type of essay in this book, a comparison-and-contrast essay has an **introduction**, several **body paragraphs**, and a **conclusion**. Within the body of your paper, you can use either of two basic comparison-and-contrast strategies — **subject by subject** or **point by point**. As you might expect, each organizational strategy has advantages and disadvantages. In general, you should use subject-by-subject comparison when your purpose is to emphasize overall similarities or differences, and you should use point-by-point comparison when your purpose is to emphasize individual points of similarity or difference.

Using Subject-by-Subject Comparison

In a **subject-by-subject comparison**, you essentially write a separate essay about each subject, but you discuss the same points for both subjects. Use your basis for comparison to guide your selection of points, and arrange these points in some logical order, usually in order of their increasing significance. The following informal outline illustrates a subject-by-subject comparison:

Introduction:	Thesis statement — Despite the fact that television and radio are distinctly different media, they use similar strategies to appeal to their audiences.

Television audiences
    Point 1:   Men
    Point 2:   Women
    Point 3:   Children

Radio audiences
  Point 1:   Men
  Point 2:   Women
  Point 3:   Children
  Conclusion: Restatement of thesis or review of key points

Subject-by-subject comparisons are most appropriate for short, uncomplicated papers. In longer papers, where you might make many points about each subject, this organizational strategy demands too much of your readers, requiring them to keep track of all your points throughout your paper. In addition, because of the length of each section, your paper may seem like two completely separate essays. For longer or more complex papers, then, it is often best to use point-by-point comparison.

Using Point-by-Point Comparison

In a **point-by-point comparison**, you first make a point about one subject and then follow it with a comparable point about the other. This alternating pattern continues throughout the body of your essay until all your points have been made. The following informal outline illustrates a point-by-point comparison:

Introduction: Thesis statement — Although Melville's *Moby-Dick* and London's *The Sea Wolf* are both about the sea, the minor characters, major characters, and themes of *Moby-Dick* establish its greater complexity.
Minor characters
  Book 1:   *The Sea Wolf*
  Book 2:   *Moby-Dick*
Major characters
  Book 1:   *The Sea Wolf*
  Book 2:   *Moby-Dick*
Themes
  Book 1:   *The Sea Wolf*
  Book 2:   *Moby-Dick*
Conclusion: Restatement of thesis or review of key points

Point-by-point comparisons are especially useful for longer, more complicated essays in which you discuss many different points. (If you treat only one or two points of comparison, you should consider a subject-by-subject organization.) In a point-by-point essay, readers can follow comparisons or contrasts more easily and do not have to wait several paragraphs to find out, for example, the differences between minor characters in *Moby-Dick* and *The Sea Wolf* or to remember on page five what was said on page three. Nevertheless, it is easy to fall into a monotonous, back-and-forth movement between points when you write a point-by-point comparison. To avoid this problem, vary your sentence structure as you move from point to point.

Using Transitions

Transitions are especially important in comparison-and-contrast essays because you must supply readers with clear signals that identify individual similarities and differences. Without these cues, readers will have trouble following your discussion and may lose track of the significance of the points you are making. Some transitions indicating comparison and contrast are listed in the following box. (A more complete list of transitions appears on page 43.)

USEFUL TRANSITIONS FOR COMPARISON AND CONTRAST

COMPARISON

in comparison	like
in the same way	likewise
just as . . . so	similarly

CONTRAST

although	nevertheless
but	nonetheless
conversely	on the contrary
despite	on the one hand . . . on the other hand
even though	still
however	unlike
in contrast	whereas
instead	yet

Longer essays frequently include **transitional paragraphs** that connect one part of an essay to another. A transitional paragraph can be a single sentence that signals a shift in focus or a longer paragraph that provides a concise summary of what was said before. In either case, transitional paragraphs enable readers to pause and consider what has already been said before moving on to a new subject.

Revising a Comparison-and-Contrast Essay

When you revise your comparison-and-contrast essay, consider the items on the revision checklist on page 54. In addition, pay special attention to the items on the following checklist, which apply specifically to comparison-and-contrast essays.

> ✓ REVISION CHECKLIST: **Comparison and Contrast**
>
> - Does your assignment call for comparison and contrast?
> - What basis for comparison exists between the two subjects you are comparing?
> - Does your essay have a clear thesis statement that identifies both the subjects you are comparing and the points you are making about them?
> - Do you discuss the same or similar points for both subjects?
> - If you have written a subject-by-subject comparison, have you included a transition paragraph that connects the two sections of the essay?
> - If you have written a point-by-point comparison, have you included appropriate transitions and varied your sentence structure to indicate your shift from one point to another?
> - Is the organizational strategy of your essay suited to your purpose?
> - Have you included transitional words and phrases that indicate whether you are discussing similarities or differences?

Editing a Comparison-and-Contrast Essay

When you edit your comparison-and-contrast essay, follow the guidelines on the editing checklists on pages 71, 73, and 76. In addition, focus on the grammar, mechanics, and punctuation issues that are particularly relevant to comparison-and-contrast essays. One of these issues — using parallel structure — is discussed below.

GRAMMAR IN CONTEXT: Using Parallelism

Parallelism — the use of matching nouns, verbs, phrases, or clauses to express the same or similar ideas — is frequently used in comparison-and-contrast essays to emphasize the similarities or differences between one point or subject and another.

- Always use parallel structure with paired items or with items in a series.

"I am an American citizen and she is not" (Mukherjee 415).

"For women, as for girls, intimacy is the fabric of relationships, and talk is the thread from which it is woven" (Tannen 441).

"Lee was tidewater Virginia, and in his background were family, culture, and tradition . . . the age of chivalry transplanted to a New World which was making its own legends and its own myths" (Catton 410).

According to Bruce Catton, Lee was <u>strong</u>, <u>aristocratic</u>, and <u>dedicated to the Confederacy</u> (410).

• Be sure to use parallel structure with paired items linked by correlative conjunctions (*not only/but also, both/and, neither/nor, either/or,* and so on).

"In everything we undertake, **either** <u>on earth</u> **or** <u>in the sky</u>, we have a choice of two styles, which I call the gray and the green" (Dyson 387).

Not only does <u>Catton admire Grant</u>, **but** he **also** <u>respects him</u>.

• Finally, use parallel structure to emphasize the contrast between paired items linked by *as* or *than.*

According to Deborah Tannen, women's conversation is **as** <u>frustrating for men</u> **as** <u>men's is for women</u> (Tannen 443).

As Deborah Tannen observes, most men are socialized <u>to communicate through actions</u> **rather than** <u>to communicate through conversation</u> (441).

For more practice in using parallelism, visit Exercise Central at <bedford stmartins.com/patterns/parallelism>.

✓EDITING CHECKLIST: **Comparison and Contrast**

- Have you used parallel structure with parallel elements in a series?
- Have you used commas to separate three or more parallel elements in a series?
- Have you used parallel structure with paired items linked by correlative conjunctions?
- Have you used parallel structure with paired items linked by *as* or *than*?

STUDENT WRITERS: Comparison and Contrast

Both of the following essays illustrate comparison and contrast. The first, by Mark Cotharn, is a subject-by-subject comparison. It was written for a composition class whose instructor asked students to write an essay comparing two educational experiences. The second, by Maria Tecson, is a point-by-point comparison. It was written for a class in educational psychology whose instructor asked students to compare two Web sites about a health issue and to determine which is the more reliable information source.

Brains versus Brawn

Introduction

When people think about discrimination, they usually 1
associate it with race or gender. But discrimination can take
other forms. For example, a person can gain an unfair advantage
at a job interview by being attractive, by knowing someone who
works at the company, or by being able to talk about something
(like sports) that has nothing to do with the job. Certainly, the
people who do not get the job would claim that they were
discriminated against, and to some extent they would be
right. As a high school athlete, I experienced both sides of
discrimination. When I was a sophomore, I benefited from
discrimination. When I was a junior, however, I was penalized
by it, treated as if there were no place for me in a classroom. As

Thesis statement a result, I learned that discrimination, whether it helps you or
(emphasizing hurts you, is wrong.
differences)

First subject: At my high school, football was everything, and the 2
Mark helped by entire town supported the local team. In the summer,
discrimination merchants would run special football promotions. Adults would

Status of football wear shirts with the team's logo, students would collect money
to buy equipment, and everyone would go to the games and
cheer the team on. Coming out of junior high school, I was
considered an exceptional athlete who was eventually going
to start as varsity quarterback. Because of my status, I was
enthusiastically welcomed by the high school. Before I entered
the school, the varsity coach visited my home, and the principal
called my parents and told them how well I was going to do.

Treatment by teachers I knew that high school would be different from junior 3
high, but I wasn't prepared for the treatment I received from my
teachers. Many of them talked to me as if I were their friend,
not their student. My math teacher used to keep me after class
just to talk football; he would give me a note so I could be late
for my next class. My biology teacher told me I could skip the
afternoon labs so that I would have some time for myself before
practice. Several of my teachers told me that during football
season, I didn't have to hand in homework because it might
distract me during practice. My Spanish teacher even told me
that if I didn't do well on a test, I could take it over after the
season. Everything I did seemed to be perfect.

Mark's reaction to Despite this favorable treatment, I continued to study 4
treatment hard. I knew that if I wanted to go to a good college, I would

have to get good grades, and I resented the implication that the only way I could get good grades was by getting special treatment. I had always been a good student, and I had no intention of changing my study habits now that I was in high school. Each night after practice, I stayed up late outlining my notes and completing my class assignments. Any studying I couldn't do during the week, I would complete on the weekends. Of course my social life suffered, but I didn't care. I was proud that I never took advantage of the special treatment my teachers were offering me.

Transitional paragraph: signals shift from one subject to another

Then, one day, the unthinkable happened. The township 5 redrew the school-district lines, and I suddenly found myself assigned to a new high school — one that was academically more demanding than the one I attended and, worse, one that had a weak football team. When my parents appealed to the school board to let me stay at my current school, they were told that if the board made an exception for me, it would have to make exceptions for others, and that would lead to chaos. My principal and my coach also tried to get the board to change its decision, but they got the same response. So, in my junior year, at the height of my career, I changed schools.

Second subject: Mark hurt by discrimination

Unlike the people at my old school, no one at my new 6 school seemed to care much about high school football. Many of the students attended the games, but their primary focus was on getting into college. If they talked about football at all, they

Status of football

usually discussed the regional college teams. As a result, I didn't have the status I had when I attended my former school. When I met with the coach before school started, he told me the football team was weak. He also told me that his main goal was to make sure everyone on the team had a chance to play. So, even though I would start, I would have to share the quarterback position with two seniors. Later that day, I saw the principal, who told me that although sports were an important part of school, academic achievement was more important. He made it clear that I would play football only as long as my grades did not suffer.

Treatment by teachers

Unlike the teachers at my old school, the teachers at my 7 new school did not give any special treatment to athletes. When I entered my new school, I was ready for the challenge. What I was not ready for was the hostility of most of my new teachers.

From the first day, in just about every class, my teachers made it obvious that they had already made up their minds about what kind of student I was going to be. Some teachers told me I shouldn't expect any special consideration just because I was the team's quarterback. One even said in front of the class that I would have to study as hard as the other students if I expected to pass. I was hurt and embarrassed by these comments. I didn't expect anyone to give me anything, and I was ready to get the grades I deserved. After all, I had gotten good grades up to this point, and I had no reason to think that the situation would change. Even so, my teachers' preconceived ideas upset me.

Mark's reaction to treatment

Just as I had in my old school, I studied hard, but I didn't know how to deal with the prejudice I faced. At first, it really bothered me and even affected my performance on the football field. However, after awhile, I decided that the best way to show my teachers that I was not the stereotypical jock was to prove to them what kind of student I really was. In the long run, far from discouraging me, their treatment motivated me, and I decided to work as hard in the classroom as I did on the football field. By the end of high school, not only had the team won half of its games (a record season), but I had also proved to my teachers that I was a good student. (I still remember the surprised look on the face of my chemistry teacher when she handed my first exam back to me and told me that I had received the second highest grade in the class.)

8

Conclusion

Before I graduated, I talked to the teachers about how they had treated me during my junior year. Some admitted they had been harder on me than on the rest of the students, but others denied they had ever discriminated against me. Eventually, I realized that some of them would never understand what they had done. Even so, my experience did have some positive effects. I learned that you should judge people on their merits, not by your own set of assumptions. In addition, I learned that although some people are talented intellectually, others have special skills that should also be valued. And, as I found out, discriminatory treatment, whether it helps you or hurts you, is no substitute for fairness.

9

Restatement of thesis

Points for Special Attention

Basis for Comparison.   Mark knew he could easily compare his two experiences. Both involved high school, and both focused on the treatment he had received as an athlete. In one case, Mark was treated better than other students because he was the team's quarterback; in the other, he was stereotyped as a "dumb jock" because he was a football player. Mark also knew that his comparison would make an interesting (and perhaps unexpected) point — that discrimination is unfair even when it gives a person an advantage.

Selecting Points for Comparison.   Mark wanted to make certain that he would discuss the same (or at least similar) points for the two experiences he was going to compare. As he planned his essay, he consulted his brainstorming notes and made the following informal outline:

EXPERIENCE 1 (gained an advantage)	EXPERIENCE 2 (was put at a disadvantage)
Status of football	Status of football
Treatment by teachers	Treatment by teachers
My reaction	My reaction

Structure.   Mark's essay makes three points about each of the two experiences he compares. Because his purpose was to convey the overall differences between the two experiences, he decided to use a subject-by-subject strategy. In addition, Mark thought he could make his case more convincingly if he discussed the first experience fully before moving on to the next one, and he believed readers would have no trouble keeping his individual points in mind as they read. Of course, Mark could have decided to do a point-by-point comparison. He rejected this strategy, though, because he thought that shifting back and forth between subjects would distract readers from his main point.

Note: In Mark's case, a subject-by-subject comparison made more sense than a point-by-point comparison. Occasionally, however, the choice is a matter of preference — a writer might simply like one strategy better than the other.

Transitions.   Without adequate transitions, a subject-by-subject comparison can read like two separate essays. Notice that in Mark's essay, paragraph 5 is a **transitional paragraph** that connects the two sections of the essay. In it, Mark sets up the comparison by telling how he suddenly found himself assigned to another high school.

In addition to connecting the sections of an essay, transitional words and phrases can identify individual similarities or differences. Notice, for example, how the transitional word *however* emphasizes the contrast between the following sentences from paragraph 1:

WITHOUT TRANSITION

When I was a sophomore, I benefited from discrimination. When I was a junior, I was penalized by it.

WITH TRANSITION

When I was a sophomore, I benefited from discrimination. When I was a junior, *however,* I was penalized by it.

Topic Sentences.   Like transitional phrases, topic sentences help to guide readers through an essay. When reading a comparison-and-contrast essay, readers can easily forget the points being compared, especially if the paper is long or complex. Direct, clearly stated topic sentences act as guideposts, alerting readers to the comparisons and contrasts you are making. For example, Mark's straightforward topic sentence at the beginning of paragraph 5 dramatically signals the movement from one experience to the other ("Then, one day, the unthinkable happened"). In addition, as in any effective comparison-and-contrast essay, each point discussed in connection with one subject is also discussed in connection with the other. Mark's topic sentences reinforce this balance:

FIRST SUBJECT

At my high school, football was everything, and the entire town supported the local team.

SECOND SUBJECT

Unlike the people at my old school, no one at my new school seemed to care much about high school football.

Focus on Revision

Mark's peer critics thought he could have spent more time talking about what he did to counter the preconceptions about athletes that teachers in *both* his schools had.

One student pointed out that the teachers at both schools seemed to think athletes were weak students. The only difference was that the teachers at Mark's first school were willing to make allowances for athletes, while the teachers at his second school were not. The student thought that although Mark alluded to this fact, he should have made his point more explicitly. After rereading his essay, along with his classmates' comments, Mark decided to add information about how demanding football practice was. Without this information, readers would have a hard time understanding how difficult it was for him to keep up with his studies.

Another peer critic thought Mark should concede that some student athletes *do* fit the teachers' stereotypes (although many do not). This information would reinforce his thesis and help him demonstrate how unfair his treatment was. (A sample peer editing worksheet for comparison and contrast appears on page 406.)

Unlike the preceding essay, Maria Tecson's paper is a point-by-point comparison.

A Comparison of Two Web Sites on Attention Deficit Disorder

Introduction   At first glance, the National Institute of Mental Health   1
(NIMH) Web site on Attention Deficit Hyperactivity Disorder (www.nimh.nih.gov) and AdultADD.com — two Web sites on Attention Deficit Disorder (ADD) — look a lot alike. Both have good designs, informative headings, and links to other Web sites. Because anyone can publish on the Internet, however, Web sites cannot be judged simply on how they look. Colorful graphics and an appealing layout can often hide shortcomings

Thesis statement   that make sites unsuitable for use as research sources. As a
(emphasizing differences) comparison of the NIMH and AdultADD.com Web sites shows, one site is definitely a better source of information than the other.

First point: comparing   The first difference between the two Web sites is the   2
homepages   design of their homepages. The nimh.nih.gov homepage looks
NIMH homepage   clear and professional. For example, the logos, tabs, links, search boxes, and text columns are placed carefully on the page (see fig. 1). Words are spelled correctly; tabs help users to navigate; and content is arranged topically, with headers such as "What is Attention Deficit Hyperactivity Disorder?" and "Signs & Symptoms." The text, set in columns, looks like a newspaper page. Throughout the Web site, links connect to a reference page that lists sources for articles, and footnotes give source information. In addition, the nimh.nih.gov site contains links to other Web sites, both governmental and academic. Finally, the site accommodates sight-disabled people by giving them the option of viewing enlarged text.

Adult ADD homepage   The AdultADD.com homepage looks more open than the   3
NIMH homepage; it has less text and contains fewer design elements (see fig. 2). Even so, the arrangement of text on the page, the no-nonsense style, and the lack of misspellings indicate that it has been carefully designed. The homepage is

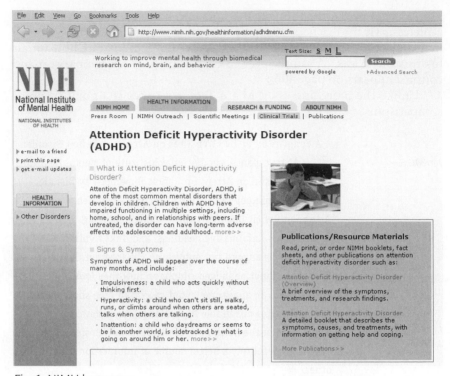

Fig. 1. NIMH homepage.

straightforward and businesslike and looks like a PowerPoint slide. It is easy to navigate and contains simple headings, such as "Find a Physician" and "Treatment for Adults." Despite the clean, direct design, however, the layout raises a question: why isn't this site linked to any other Web sites about ADD or ADHD? Unlike nimh.nih.gov, the AdultADD.com Web site has no footnotes and no reference page. In addition, it does not accommodate sight-disabled users.

Second point: comparing sponsors

Another difference between the two Web sites is who posted them. One look at the URL for the NIMH Web site indicates that it is a *.gov* — a Web site created by a branch of the United States government. The logo in the upper left-hand corner of the homepage identifies the National Institute of Mental Health (NIMH) as the sponsor of the site. In addition, every article on the Web site has a listed author, so users know who is responsible for the content. Clicking the "About NIMH" tab

NIMH site sponsor

4

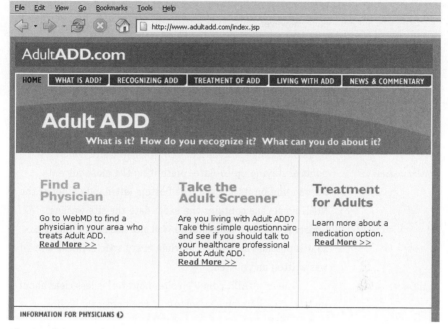

Fig. 2. Adult ADD homepage.

on the upper-right of the homepage takes users to a description of NIMH, as well as to contact information. Here visitors to the site find out that NIMH is part of the National Institutes of Health, which is, in turn, a part of the U.S. Department of Health and Human Services. Furthermore, NIMH is the "lead Federal agency for research on mental and behavioral disorders." This description also makes clear the NIMH Web site's purpose: to give the American public the latest information about ADHD. For this reason, the Web site lists all the medications used to treat ADHD and evaluates the various treatment options available to patients.

AdultADD site sponsor   The URL for the AdultADD.com Web site ends with *.com,*   5
indicating that it is a commercial site that promotes a product. It is not immediately clear, however, who (or what) sponsors the Web site. The home page has no corporate logo and no identifying information. Across the top of the homepage are a series of links — "What is ADD?" "Recognizing ADD," and so on. Each of these links leads to a page that contains a video clip of a television commercial that promotes Strattera, a new drug manufactured by the Eli Lilly pharmaceutical company for the

treatment of ADD. If you click on the links in the middle of the page, however, you never encounter this information. For this reason, there is a good possibility that much of the information these links lead to is biased. In other words, Lilly seems to be highlighting treatments that involve its own product and disregarding treatments that involve products made by other pharmaceutical companies.

Third point: comparing frequency of updates

NIMH updates

A final difference between the two Web sites is how frequently they are updated. The NIMH Web site makes a point of staying up-to-date, presenting the most current information on its subject. The bottom left-hand corner of the NIMH homepage contains the exact date the site was last updated, and each page on the Web site has a different date, so it is possible to determine when every article on the site was written and posted.

6

AdultADD updates

The AdultADD.com Web site, however, is less clear about updates. The date on the bottom of the homepage indicates only that the Web site was copyrighted in 2003; it does not indicate when the Web site itself was updated. This omission makes it very difficult for patients to determine how current the information on the site actually is.

7

Conclusion

A comparison of the NIMH Web site and adultADD.com Web site shows some clear differences between the two. The NIMH Web site makes it easy for users to find out who posted the site, who wrote material on it, and when the site was last updated. The AdultADD.com Web site, however, tries to hide its commercial purpose and makes it difficult for visitors to find out who wrote the material posted on the site and when it was last updated. For these reasons, the NIMH Web site is a more trustworthy source of information than the AdultADD.com Web site.

8

Restatement of thesis

Points for Special Attention

Structure.   Maria's purpose in writing this essay was to examine two Web sites that deal with Attention Deficit Hyperactivity Disorder and to determine which is the better, more reliable source of information. She structured her essay as the point-by-point comparison, carefully discussing the same points for each subject. With this method of organization, she can be sure her readers will understand the specific differences between the NIMH Web site and AdultADD.com Web site. Had Maria used a subject-by-subject comparison, her readers would have had to keep turning back to match the points she made about one Web site with those she made about the other.

Topic Sentences.   Without clear topic sentences, Maria's readers would have had difficulty determining where each discussion of the NIMH Web site ended and each one about the AdultADD.com Web site began. Maria uses topic sentences to distinguish the two subjects of her comparison and to make the contrast between them clear.

> The nimh.nih.gov homepage looks clear and professional.

> The AdultADD.com homepage looks more open than the NIMH homepage; it has less text and contains fewer design elements.

> One look at the Uniform Resource Locator (URL) for the NIMH Web site indicates that it is a *.gov*—a Web site created by a branch of the United States government.

> The URL for the AdultADD.com Web site ends with *.com,* indicating that it is a commercial site that promotes a product.

> The NIMH Web site makes a point of staying up-to-date, presenting the most current information on its subject.

> The AdultADD.com Web site, however, is less clear about updates.

Transitions.   In addition to clear and straightforward topic sentences, Maria included transitional sentences to help readers move through the essay. These sentences identify the three points of contrast in the essay and, by establishing a parallel structure, they form a pattern that reinforces the essay's thesis.

> The first difference between the two Web sites is the design of their homepages.

> Another difference between the two Web sites is who posted them.

> A final difference between the two Web sites is how frequently they are updated.

Focus on Revision

Maria's peer critics thought the greatest strength of her essay was its use of detail, which made the contrast between the two Web sites clear, but they thought that even more detail would improve her essay. For example, in paragraph 6, Maria could include a few titles of the articles the NIMH Web site lists, along with their dates of publication. In paragraph 7, she could also list some of the specific information on the AdultADD.com Web site and explain why it is necessary to know when the information was written and posted. Maria agreed with these suggestions. She also thought she could improve her conclusion: although it summed up the main points of her essay, it contained little that would stay with readers after they finished. A sentence or two to caution readers about the need to carefully evaluate the information they find on Web sites would be an improvement.

📄 **PEER EDITING WORKSHEET: Comparison and Contrast**

1. Does the essay have a clearly stated thesis? What is it?
2. What two things are being compared? What basis for comparison exists between the two?
3. Does the essay treat the same or similar points for each of its two subjects? List the points discussed.

   FIRST SUBJECT   SECOND SUBJECT
   a.   a.
   b.   b.
   c.   c.
   d.   d.

   Are these points discussed in the same order for both subjects? Are the points presented in parallel terms?
4. Does the essay use a point-by-point or subject-by-subject strategy? Is this the best choice? Why?
5. Are transitional words and phrases used appropriately to identify points of comparison and contrast? List some of the transitions used.
6. Are additional transitions needed? If so, where?
7. How could the introductory paragraph be improved?
8. How could the concluding paragraph be improved?
9. What could the writer add to this essay?
10. What could the writer take out of this essay?

The selections that follow illustrate both subject-by-subject and point-by-point comparisons. The first selection, a pair of visual texts, is followed by questions designed to illustrate how comparison and contrast can operate in visual form.

The Kiss (Sculpture)

LOVE (Sculpture)

. . .

Reading Images

1. What significant characteristics do the two sculptures pictured above and on the preceding page share? Do they share enough characteristics to establish a basis for comparison? Explain.

2. Make a list of points you could discuss if you were comparing the two sculptures.

3. What general statement could you make about these two sculptures? Do the points you listed in question 2 provide enough support for this general statement?

Journal Entry

How does each sculpture convey the idea of love? Which one do you believe conveys this idea more effectively? Why?

Thematic Connections

- "The Storm" (page 194)
- "How to Escape from a Bad Date" (page 297)
- "Sex, Lies, and Conversation" (page 440)

BRUCE CATTON

Grant and Lee: A Study in Contrasts

Bruce Catton (1899–1978) was born in Petoskey, Michigan, and attended Oberlin College. His studies were interrupted by his service during World War I, after which he worked as a journalist and then for various government agencies. Catton edited *American Heritage* magazine from 1954 until his death. He was a notable authority on the American Civil War; among his many books on the subject are *Mr. Lincoln's Army* (1951); *A Stillness at Appomattox* (1953), which won both a Pulitzer Prize and a National Book Award; and *Gettysburg: The Final Fury* (1974). Catton also wrote a memoir, *Waiting for the Morning Train* (1972), in which he recalls listening as a young boy to the reminiscences of Union Army veterans.

Background on Grant and Lee: "Grant and Lee: A Study in Contrasts," which first appeared in a collection of historical essays titled *The American Story,* focuses on the two generals who headed the opposing armies during the Civil War (1861–1865). Robert E. Lee led the Army of Northern Virginia, the backbone of the Confederate forces, throughout much of the war. Ulysses S. Grant was named commander in chief of the Union troops in March 1864. By the spring of 1865, although it seemed almost inevitable that the Southern forces would be defeated, Lee made an attempt to lead his troops to join another Confederate army in North Carolina. Finding himself virtually surrounded by Grant's forces near the small town of Appomattox Court House, Lee chose to surrender to Grant. The following essay considers these two great generals in terms of both their differences and their important similarities.

1   When Ulysses S. Grant and Robert E. Lee met in the parlor of a modest house at Appomattox Court House, Virginia, on April 9, 1865, to work out the terms for the surrender of Lee's Army of Northern Virginia, a great chapter in American life came to a close, and a great new chapter began.

2   These men were bringing the Civil War to its virtual finish. To be sure, other armies had yet to surrender, and for a few days the fugitive Confederate government would struggle desperately and vainly, trying to find some way to go on living now that its chief support was gone. But in effect it was all over when Grant and Lee signed the papers. And the little room where they wrote out the terms was the scene of one of the poignant, dramatic contrasts in American history.

3   They were two strong men, these oddly different generals, and they represented the strengths of two conflicting currents that, through them, had come into final collision.

4   Back of Robert E. Lee was the notion that the old aristocratic concept might somehow survive and be dominant in American life.

Lee was tidewater Virginia, and in his background were family, culture,   5
and tradition . . . the age of chivalry transplanted to a New World which
was making its own legends and its own myths. He embodied a way of life
that had come down through the age of knighthood and the English country squire. America was a land that was beginning all over again, dedicated
to nothing much more complicated than the rather hazy belief that all men
had equal rights and should have an equal chance in the world. In such a
land Lee stood for the feeling that it was somehow of advantage to human
society to have pronounced inequality in the social structure. There should
be a leisure class, backed by ownership of land; in turn, society itself should
be keyed to the land as the chief source of wealth and influence. It would
bring forth (according to this deal) a class of men with a strong sense of
obligation to the community; men who lived not to gain advantage for
themselves, but to meet the solemn obligations which had been laid on them
by the very fact that they were privileged. From them the country would get
its leadership; to them it could look for the higher values — of thought, of
conduct, of personal deportment — to give it strength and virtue.

Lee embodied the noblest elements of this aristocratic ideal. Through   6
him, the landed nobility justified itself. For four years, the Southern states
had fought a desperate war to uphold the ideals for which Lee stood. In the
end, it almost seemed as if the Confederacy fought for Lee; as if he himself
was the Confederacy . . . the best thing that the way of life for which the
Confederacy stood could ever have to offer. He had passed into legend
before Appomattox. Thousands of tired, underfed, poorly clothed Confederate soldiers, long since past the simple enthusiasm of the early days of
the struggle, somehow considered Lee the symbol of everything for which
they had been willing to die. But they could not quite put this feeling into
words. If the Lost Cause, sanctified by so much heroism and so many
deaths, had a living justification, its justification was General Lee.

Grant, the son of a tanner on the Western frontier, was everything Lee   7
was not. He had come up the hard way and embodied nothing in particular
except the eternal toughness and sinewy fiber of the men who grew up
beyond the mountains. He was one of a body of men who owed reverence
and obeisance to no one, who were self-reliant to a fault, who cared hardly
anything for the past but who had a sharp eye for the future.

These frontier men were the precise opposites of the tidewater aristo-   8
crats. Back of them, in the great surge that had taken people over the
Alleghenies and into the opening Western country, there was a deep,
implicit dissatisfaction with a past that had settled into grooves. They
stood for democracy, not from any reasoned conclusion about the proper
ordering of human society, but simply because they had grown up in the
middle of democracy and knew how it worked. Their society might have
privileges, but they would be privileges each man had won for himself.
Forms and patterns meant nothing. No man was born to anything, except
perhaps to a chance to show how far he could rise. Life was competition.

Yet along with this feeling had come a deep sense of belonging to a   9
national community. The Westerner who developed a farm, opened a shop,
or set up in business as a trader, could hope to prosper only as his own
community prospered — and his community ran from the Atlantic to the
Pacific and from Canada down to Mexico. If the land was settled, with
towns and highways and accessible markets, he could better himself. He
saw his fate in terms of the nation's own destiny. As its horizons expanded,
so did his. He had, in other words, an acute dollars-and-cents stake in the
continued growth and development of his country.

And that, perhaps, is where the contrast between Grant and Lee   10
becomes most striking. The Virginia aristocrat, inevitably, saw himself in
relation to his own region. He lived in a static society which could endure
almost anything except change. Instinctively, his first loyalty would go to
the locality in which that society existed. He would fight to the limit of
endurance to defend it, because in defending it he was defending everything that gave his own life its deepest meaning.

The Westerner, on the other hand, would fight with an equal tenacity   11
for the broader concept of society. He fought so because everything he
lived by was tied to growth, expansion, and a constantly widening horizon.
What he lived by would survive or fall with the nation itself. He could not
possibly stand by unmoved in the face of an attempt to destroy the Union.
He would combat it with everything he had, because he could only see it as
an effort to cut the ground out from under his feet.

So Grant and Lee were in complete contrast, representing two diamet-   12
rically opposed elements in American life. Grant was the modern man
emerging; beyond him, ready to come on the stage, was the great age of
steel and machinery, of crowded cities and a restless burgeoning vitality.
Lee might have ridden down from the old age of chivalry, lance in hand,
silken banner fluttering over his head. Each man was the perfect champion
of his cause, drawing both his strengths and his weaknesses from the
people he led.

Yet it was not all contrast, after all. Different as they were — in back-   13
ground, in personality, in underlying aspiration — these two great soldiers
had much in common. Under everything else, they were marvelous fighters. Furthermore, their fighting qualities were really very much alike.

Each man had, to begin with, the great virtue of utter tenacity and   14
fidelity. Grant fought his way down the Mississippi Valley in spite of acute
personal discouragement and profound military handicaps. Lee hung on
in the trenches at Petersburg after hope itself had died. In each man there
was an indomitable quality . . . the born fighter's refusal to give up as long
as he can still remain on his feet and lift his two fists.

Daring and resourcefulness they had, too; the ability to think faster   15
and move faster than the enemy. These were the qualities which gave Lee
the dazzling campaigns of Second Manassas and Chancellorsville and won
Vicksburg for Grant.

Lastly, and perhaps greatest of all, there was the ability, at the end, to 16
turn quickly from war to peace once the fighting was over. Out of the way
these two men behaved at Appomattox came the possibility of a peace of
reconciliation. It was a possibility not wholly realized, in the years to come,
but which did, in the end, help the two sections to become one nation
again . . . after a war whose bitterness might have seemed to make such a
reunion wholly impossible. No part of either man's life became him more
than the part he played in this brief meeting in the McLean house at Appomattox. Their behavior there put all succeeding generations of Americans
in their debt. Two great Americans, Grant and Lee—very different, yet
under everything very much alike. Their encounter at Appomattox was one
of the great moments of American history.

• • •

Comprehension

1. What took place at Appomattox Court House on April 9, 1865? Why
   did the meeting at Appomattox signal the closing of "a great chapter
   in American life" (1)?
2. How does Robert E. Lee represent aristocracy? How does Ulysses S.
   Grant represent Lee's opposite?
3. According to Catton, where is it that "the contrast between Grant and
   Lee becomes most striking" (10)?
4. What similarities does Catton see between the two men?
5. Why, according to Catton, are "succeeding generations of Americans"
   (16) in debt to Grant and Lee?

Purpose and Audience

1. Catton's purpose in contrasting Grant and Lee is to make a general
   statement about the differences between two currents in American
   history. Summarize these differences. Do you think the differences
   still exist today? Explain.
2. Is Catton's purpose in comparing Grant and Lee the same as his purpose in contrasting them? That is, do their similarities also make a
   statement about U.S. history? Explain.
3. State the essay's thesis in your own words.

Style and Structure

1. Does Catton use subject-by-subject or point-by-point comparison?
   Why do you think he chooses the strategy he does?
2. In this essay, topic sentences are extremely helpful to the reader.
   Explain the functions of the following sentences: "Grant . . . was everything Lee was not" (7); "So Grant and Lee were in complete contrast"

(12); "Yet it was not all contrast, after all" (13); and "Lastly, and perhaps greatest of all . . ." (16).

3. Catton uses transitions skillfully in his essay. Identify the transitional words or expressions that link each paragraph to the preceding one.

4. Why do you suppose Catton provides the background for the meeting at Appomattox but presents no information about the dramatic meeting itself?

Vocabulary Projects

1. Define each of the following words as it is used in this selection.

poignant (2)	obeisance (7)	tenacity (14)
chivalry (5)	implicit (8)	fidelity (14)
deportment (5)	inevitably (10)	indomitable (14)
sanctified (6)	diametrically (12)	reconciliation (16)
embodied (7)	burgeoning (12)	
sinewy (7)	aspiration (13)	

2. Look up **synonyms** for each of the following words, and determine whether each would be as effective as the word used in this essay. Explain your choices.

deportment (5)	obeisance (7)	indomitable (14)
sanctified (6)	diametrically (12)	

Journal Entry

Compare your attitudes about the United States to those held by Grant and by Lee. Which man do you agree with?

Writing Workshop

1. Write a "study in contrasts" about two people you know well — two teachers, your parents, two relatives, two friends — or about two fictional characters you are very familiar with. Be sure to include a thesis statement.

2. Write a dialogue between two people you know that reveals their contrasting attitudes toward school, work, or any other subject.

3. Write an essay about two individuals from a period of American history other than the Civil War to make the same points Catton makes. Do some research if necessary.

Combining the Patterns

In several places, Catton uses **exemplification** to structure a paragraph. For instance, in paragraph 7, he uses examples to support the topic sentence "Grant, the son of a tanner on the Western frontier, was everything

Lee was not." Identify three paragraphs that use examples to support the topic sentence, and bracket the examples. How do these examples in these paragraphs reinforce the similarities and differences between Grant and Lee?

Thematic Connections

- "Star-Spangled Stupidity" (page 246)
- The Declaration of Independence (page 584)
- "Letter from Birmingham Jail" (page 597)

Two Ways to Belong in America

Born in 1940 in Calcutta, India, novelist Bharati Mukherjee attended the University of Calcutta before immigrating to the United States in 1961. After receiving an M.F.A. from the University of Iowa, she moved with her husband to Canada, where she taught at McGill University. Now a naturalized U.S. citizen, she teaches at the University of California at Berkeley. Mukherjee's novels include *Tiger's Daughter* (1972), *Jasmine* (1989), *Leave It to Me* (1997), *Desirable Daughters* (2002), and *The Tree Bride* (2004); her story collections are *Darkness* (1975) and the prize-winning *The Middleman and Other Stories* (1988). Her fiction often explores the tensions between the traditional role of women in Indian society and their very different role in the United States.

Background on U.S. immigration policy: The following essay, originally published in 1996, was written in response to proposals in Congress (eventually defeated) to enact legislation denying government benefits, such as Social Security, to resident aliens. Not to be confused with illegal immigrants, resident aliens — also called *legal permanent residents* — are immigrants who live in the United States legally, sometimes for their whole lives, but do not apply for citizenship. Most work and pay taxes like any citizen. According to the 2000 census, the United States population includes more than 30 million foreign-born residents, accounting for about 11 percent of the population. Of these, 9.3 million are legal permanent residents, 9.2 million are naturalized citizens, and an estimated 8.5 million are in the country illegally; most of the rest are refugees seeking political asylum and students and temporary workers with visas. Although various issues related to immigration policy have been hotly debated for many years, particularly as large numbers of immigrants entered the country in the 1990s, the terrorist attacks of September 2001 have led to greater restrictions on and closer screenings of foreigners who want to enter the United States, especially those applying for student visas.

This is a tale of two sisters from Calcutta, Mira and Bharati, who have lived in the United States for some 35 years, but who find themselves on different sides in the current debate over the status of immigrants. I am an American citizen and she is not. I am moved that thousands of long-term residents are finally taking the oath of citizenship. She is not. 1

Mira arrived in Detroit in 1960 to study child psychology and pre-school education. I followed her a year later to study creative writing at the University of Iowa. When we left India, we were almost identical in appearance and attitude. We dressed alike, in saris; we expressed identical views on politics, social issues, love, and marriage in the same Calcutta convent- 2 school accent. We would endure our two years in America, secure our degrees, then return to India to marry the grooms of our father's choosing.

Instead, Mira married an Indian student in 1962 who was getting his business administration degree at Wayne State University. They soon acquired the labor certifications necessary for the green card of hassle-free residence and employment. 3

Mira still lives in Detroit, works in the Southfield, Mich., school system, and has become nationally recognized for her contributions in the fields of pre-school education and parent-teacher relationships. After 36 years as a legal immigrant in this country, she clings passionately to her Indian citizenship and hopes to go home to India when she retires. 4

In Iowa City in 1963, I married a fellow student, an American of Canadian parentage. Because of the accident of his North Dakota birth, I bypassed labor-certification requirements and the race-related "quota" system that favored the applicant's country of origin over his or her merit. I was prepared for (and even welcomed) the emotional strain that came with marrying outside my ethnic community. In 33 years of marriage, we have lived in every part of North America. By choosing a husband who was not my father's selection, I was opting for fluidity, self-invention, blue jeans and T-shirts, and renouncing 3,000 years (at least) of caste-observant, "pure culture" marriage in the Mukherjee family. My books have often been read as unapologetic (and in some quarters overenthusiastic) texts for cultural and psychological "mongrelization." It's a word I celebrate. 5

Mira and I have stayed sisterly close by phone. In our regular Sunday morning conversations, we are unguardedly affectionate. I am her only blood relative on this continent. We expect to see each other through the looming crises of aging and ill health without being asked. Long before Vice President Gore's "Citizenship U.S.A." drive, we'd had our polite arguments over the ethics of retaining an overseas citizenship while expecting the permanent protection and economic benefits that come with living and working in America. 6

Like well-raised sisters, we never said what was really on our minds, but we probably pitied one another. She, for the lack of structure in my life, the erasure of Indianness, the absence of an unvarying daily core. I, for the narrowness of her perspective, her uninvolvement with the mythic depths or the superficial pop culture of this society. But, now, with the scapegoatings of "aliens" (documented or illegal) on the increase, and the targeting of long-term legal immigrants like Mira for new scrutiny and new self-consciousness, she and I find ourselves unable to maintain the same polite discretion. We were always unacknowledged adversaries, and we are now, more than ever, sisters. 7

"I feel used," Mira raged on the phone the other night. "I feel manipulated and discarded. This is such an unfair way to treat a person who was invited to stay and work here because of her talent. My employer went to the I.N.S. and petitioned for the labor certification. For over 30 years, I've 8

MIRA'S POV

invested my creativity and professional skills into the improvement of *this* country's pre-school system. I've obeyed all the rules, I've paid my taxes, I love my work, I love my students, I love the friends I've made. How dare America now change its rules in midstream? If America wants to make new rules curtailing benefits of legal immigrants, they should apply only to immigrants who arrive after those rules are already in place."

To my ears, it sounded like the description of a long-enduring, comfortable yet loveless marriage, without risk or recklessness. Have we the right to demand, and to expect, that we be loved? (That, to me, is the subtext of the arguments by immigration advocates.) My sister is an expatriate, professionally generous and creative, socially courteous and gracious, and that's as far as her Americanization can go. She is here to maintain an identity, not to transform it.

I asked her if she would follow the example of others who have decided   10
to become citizens because of the anti-immigration bills in Congress. And here, she surprised me. "If America wants to play the manipulative game, I'll play it, too," she snapped. "I'll become a U.S. citizen for now, then change back to India when I'm ready to go home. I feel some kind of irrational attachment to India that I don't to America. Until all this hysteria against legal immigrants, I was totally happy. Having my green card meant I could visit any place in the world I wanted to and then come back to a job that's satisfying and that I do very well."

In one family, from two sisters alike as peas in a pod, there could not be   11
a wider divergence of immigrant experience. America spoke to me — I married it — I embraced the demotion from expatriate aristocrat to immigrant nobody, surrendering those thousands of years of "pure culture," the saris, the delightfully accented English. She retained them all. Which of us is the freak?

Mira's voice, I realize, is the voice not just of the immigrant South   12
Asian community but of an immigrant community of the millions who have stayed rooted in one job, one city, one house, one ancestral culture, one cuisine, for the entirety of their productive years. She speaks for greater numbers than I possibly can. Only the fluency of her English and the anger, rather than fear, born of confidence from her education, differentiate her from the seamstresses, the domestics, the technicians, the shop owners, the millions of hard-working but effectively silenced documented immigrants as well as their less fortunate "illegal" brothers and sisters.

Nearly 20 years ago, when I was living in my husband's ancestral   13
homeland of Canada, I was always well-employed but never allowed to feel part of the local Quebec or larger Canadian society. Then, through a Green Paper that invited a national referendum on the unwanted side effects of "nontraditional" immigration, the Government officially turned against its immigrant communities, particularly those from South Asia.

betrayal

I felt then the same sense of betrayal that Mira feels now. I will never   14
forget the pain of that sudden turning, and the casual racist outbursts the
Green Paper elicited. That sense of betrayal had its desired effect and drove
me, and thousands like me, from the country.

Mira and I differ, however, in the ways in which we hope to interact   15
with the country that we have chosen to live in. She is happier to live in
America as expatriate Indian than as an immigrant American. I need to feel
like a part of the community I have adopted (as I tried to feel in Canada as
well). I need to put roots down, to vote and make the difference that I can.
The price that the immigrant willingly pays, and that the exile avoids, is
the trauma of self-transformation.

. . .

Comprehension

1. At first, how long did Mukherjee and her sister intend to stay in
   America? Why did they change their plans?

2. What does Mukherjee mean when she says she welcomed the "emotional strain" of "marrying outside [her] ethnic community" (5)?

3. In what ways is Mukherjee different from her sister? What kind of
   relationship do they have?

4. Why does Mukherjee's sister feel used? Why does she say that America
   has "'change[d] its rules in midstream'" (8)?

5. According to Mukherjee, how is her sister like all immigrants who
   "have stayed rooted in one job, one city, one house, one ancestral culture, one cuisine, for the entirety of their productive years" (12)?

Purpose and Audience

1. What is Mukherjee's thesis? At what point does she state it?

2. At whom is Mukherjee aiming her remarks? Immigrants like herself?
   Immigrants like her sister? General readers? Explain.

3. What is Mukherjee's purpose? Is she trying to inform? To move readers to action? To accomplish something else? Explain.

Style and Structure

1. What basis for comparison exists between Mukherjee and her sister?
   Where in the essay does Mukherjee establish this basis?

2. Is this essay a point-by-point or a subject-by-subject comparison? Why
   do you think Mukherjee chose the option she did?

3. What points does Mukherjee discuss for each subject? Should she
   have discussed any other points?

4. What transitional words and phrases does Mukherjee use to signal shifts from one point to another?

5. How effective is Mukherjee's conclusion? Does it summarize the essay's major points? Would another strategy be more effective? Explain.

Vocabulary Projects

1. Define each of the following words as it is used in this selection.

certifications (3)   superficial (7)   divergence (11)
mongrelization (5)   scrutiny (7)   expatriate (11)
perspective (7)   discretion (7)   saris (11)
mythic (7)   curtailing (8)   trauma (15)

2. What, according to Mukherjee, is the difference between an *immigrant* and an *exile* (15)? What are the connotations of these two words? Do you think the distinction Mukherjee makes is valid?

Journal Entry

Do you think Mukherjee respects her sister's decision? From your perspective, which sister has made the right choice?

Writing Workshop

1. Assume the sister, Mira, has just read Mukherjee's essay and wants to respond to it. Write a letter from Mira comparing her position about assimilation to that of Mukherjee. Make sure you explain Mira's position and address Mukherjee's points about assimilation.

2. Have you ever moved from one town or city to another? Write an essay comparing the two places. Your thesis statement should indicate whether you are emphasizing similarities or differences and convey your opinion of the new area. (If you have never moved, write an essay comparing two places you are familiar with — your college and your high school, for example.)

3. Assume you had to move to another country. Where would you move? Would you, like Mukherjee, assimilate into your new culture, or would you, like her sister, retain your own cultural values? Write an essay comparing life in your new country to life in the United States. Make sure your thesis reflects your attitude toward assimilation. If you have already moved from another country, compare your life in the United States with your life in your country of origin.

Combining the Patterns

Do you think Mukherjee should have used **cause and effect** to structure a section explaining why she and her sister are so different? Explain what such a section would add to or take away from the essay.

Thematic Connections

- "Only Daughter" (page 96)
- "The Way to Rainy Mountain" (page 180)
- "The Untouchable" (page 516)
- "Strange Tools" (page 743)

YI-FU TUAN

Chinese Space, American Space

Born in 1930 in Tientsin, China, Yi-Fu Tuan received degrees from Oxford University in England and the University of California at Berkeley. An internationally recognized scholar, he has taught at the University of New Mexico and the University of Minnesota and is now professor emeritus of geography at the University of Wisconsin at Madison, where he was a popular teacher. He is the author of numerous articles, and his books include *Topophilia: A Study of Environmental Perception, Attitudes, and Values* (1974); *Space and Place: The Perspectives of Experience* (1977); *Dominance and Affection: The Making of Pets* (1984); *Cosmos and Hearth: A Cosmopolite's View* (1996); and *Dear Colleague: Common and Uncommon Observations* (2002).

Background on Chinese homes: Modest, very private homes surrounding a central courtyard, as described by Tuan in this essay, are still common in many parts of China. Often 150 or more years old, houses in China are typically occupied by the same family for many generations. Such homes (particularly those in rural areas), with small rooms and no indoor plumbing or central heating, would be considered quite basic by Western standards. Kitchens are especially small compared with American kitchens and generally feature few, if any, appliances. Because many such homes are occupied by extended families, personal living space is much smaller than in the average American home, which has grown considerably over the past few decades. Since the early 1990s, as the Communist government of China has encouraged private enterprise, larger, more Western-style houses have begun to spring up on the outskirts of cities, and many urban professionals now occupy highrise apartments, which have proliferated in Chinese metropolitan areas. The traditional Chinese connection to place that Tuan writes about is fading among a younger, more ambitious generation that increasingly emulates Western attitudes and lifestyles.

Americans have a sense of space, not of place. Go to an American home in exurbia, and almost the first thing you do is drift toward the picture window. How curious that the first compliment you pay your host inside his house is to say how lovely it is outside his house! He is pleased that you should admire his vistas. The distant horizon is not merely a line separating earth from sky, it is a symbol of the future. The American is not rooted in his place, however lovely: his eyes are drawn by the expanding space to a point on the horizon, which is his future.

By contrast, consider the traditional Chinese home. Blank walls enclose it. Step behind the spirit wall and you are in a courtyard with perhaps a miniature garden around a corner. Once inside his private compound you are wrapped in an ambiance of calm beauty, an ordered world of buildings, pavement, rock, and decorative vegetation. But you have no distant view: nowhere does space open out before you. Raw nature in such a home is experienced only as weather, and the only open space is the sky above. The Chinese is rooted in his place. When he has to leave, it is not for the promised land on the terrestrial horizon, but for another world altogether along the vertical, religious axis of his imagination.

The Chinese tie to place is deeply felt. Wanderlust is an alien sentiment. The Taoist classic *Tao Te Ching* captures the ideal of rootedness in place with these words: "Though there may be another country in the neighborhood so close that they are within sight of each other and the crowing of cocks and barking of dogs in one place can be heard in the other, yet there is no traffic between them; and throughout their lives the two peoples have nothing to do with each other." In theory if not in practice, farmers have ranked high in Chinese society. The reason is not only that they are engaged in a "root" industry of producing food but that, unlike pecuniary merchants, they are tied to the land and do not abandon their country when it is in danger.

Nostalgia is a recurrent theme in Chinese poetry. An American reader of translated Chinese poems may well be taken aback — even put off — by the frequency, as well as the sentimentality, of the lament for home. To understand the strength of this sentiment, we need to know that the Chinese desire for stability and rootedness in place is prompted by the constant threat of war, exile, and the natural disasters of flood and drought. Forcible removal makes the Chinese keenly aware of their loss. By contrast, Americans move, for the most part, voluntarily. Their nostalgia for home town is really longing for a childhood to which they cannot return; in the meantime the future beckons and the future is "out there," in open space. When we criticize American rootlessness, we tend to forget that it is a result of ideals we admire, namely, social mobility and optimism about the future. When we admire Chinese rootedness, we forget that the word "place" means both a location in space and position in society: to be tied to place is also to be bound to one's station in life, with little hope of betterment. Space symbolizes hope; place, achievement and stability.

· · ·

Comprehension

1. According to Tuan, what is the difference between *space* and *place*?
2. How are American and Chinese homes different? What do these differences reveal about Chinese and American cultures?
3. How does the classic work *Tao Te Ching* explain the Chinese idea of "rootedness" (3)? How does the farmer exemplify this idea?
4. What in Chinese history accounts for the people's tie to place?

5. How does Tuan explain American rootlessness? What does space symbolize to Americans?

Purpose and Audience

1. Does Tuan assume his readers are familiar with both Chinese and American cultures, or does he assume they are more familiar with one than the other? Explain.
2. At what point in his essay does Tuan state his thesis? Why does he state it where he does?
3. What do you think Tuan hoped to accomplish by writing his essay? Do you think he was successful?

Style and Structure

1. Is this essay a point-by-point or subject-by-subject comparison? Why do you think Tuan chose this way to organize his comparison-contrast essay?
2. Tuan begins his essay by discussing his first subject. Should he have begun instead with a paragraph introducing his two subjects?
3. This essay devotes only one paragraph to the American sense of space; the rest of the essay deals with the Chinese sense of place. Should Tuan have written a more evenly balanced discussion? Why do you think he devotes so little space to discussing America?
4. Does Tuan seem to favor one culture's values over the other's? Is he writing from the point of view of a Chinese person or an American?
5. In addition to having no formal introduction, Tuan's essay has no concluding paragraph. What, if anything, constitutes his conclusion? Would his essay have benefited from a separate concluding paragraph? Explain.

Vocabulary Projects

1. Define each of the following words as it is used in this selection.

exurbia (1)	Taoist (3)
vistas (1)	pecuniary (3)
rooted (1)	nostalgia (4)
terrestrial (2)	lament (4)
axis (2)	beckons (4)
wanderlust (3)	stability (4)

2. Make a list of the adjectives Tuan uses to describe American culture. Then, make another list of the words he uses to describe Chinese culture. What qualities do these words emphasize?

Journal Entry

Are you someone who values place over space, or do you value space more than place?

Writing Workshop

1. Write an essay discussing how your ties to your home or your community differ from those of a friend or a parent. Be specific, and limit your discussion to just a few areas.

2. If you have ever visited another country, list the difference between life in that country and life in the United States. Then, write an essay presenting your conclusions about the differences between the two countries in the form of a comparison-and-contrast essay.

3. Write an essay discussing whether you are a person who values space or place. In your essay, examine such factors as how often you have moved and how long you and your family have lived in the same area.

Combining the Patterns

At several points in his essay—in paragraph 4, for example—Tuan uses **cause and effect**. Identify some of these paragraphs. Why does Tuan include these sections? What do they contribute to the essay?

Thematic Connections

- "Ground Zero" (page 162)
- "Once More to the Lake" (page 186)
- "Mother Tongue" (page 487)
- "The Untouchable" (page 516)

JOHN DE GRAAF, DAVID WANN, AND THOMAS H. NAYLOR

Swollen Expectations

Over the past several decades, John De Graaf has written and produced some fifteen programs for public television, including *Running Out of Time, For Earth's Sake: The Life and Times of David Brower, Circle of Plenty, Green Plans,* and *Genetic Time Bomb.* He has received more than a hundred awards for his filmmaking. David Wann is a former official with the Environmental Protection Agency who now writes extensively about sustainable lifestyles. He is the author of the books *Biologic: Designing with Nature to Protect the Environment* (1990), *Deep Design: Pathways to a Livable Future* (1996), and *The Zen of Gardening in the High and Arid West* (2003). Thomas H. Naylor is professor emeritus of economics at Duke University, where he taught for thirty years. An international strategic management consultant to governments and corporations in more than thirty nations, Naylor has authored or coauthored a number of books, including *The Gorbachev Strategy: Opening a Closed Society* (1988), *The Search for Meaning* (1994), and *Downsizing the U.S.A.* (1997). The following chapter from the three authors' book *Affluenza: The All Consuming Epidemic* (2001) is based on a television program by De Graaf likening the American passion for consumption to a disease.

   Background on American consumerism in the 1950s: The 1950s were a time of relative prosperity in the United States. Following the economic hardships produced by the Depression of the 1930s and the war years of the 1940s (when goods were scarce), the 1950s saw an explosion in American consumerism. The postwar economy was booming, incomes doubled over the decade, and the government's G.I. Bill provided low-cost mortgages to veterans, so many more Americans could own their own homes, often in new suburban developments. Television sets were within the price range of the average consumer, and soon a majority of American families owned one, along with other basic appliances, such as a range, a refrigerator, and a washing machine (clothes dryers and dishwashers were much rarer). Still, as the following selection points out, material expectations were considerably lower in the 1950s than they are for many today. The average home was far smaller. People generally had many fewer possessions, as demonstrated by the fewer and smaller closets built into most 1950s homes. And, while car ownership became increasingly common over the decade, most households owned only one car. The average family traveled modestly as well, generally vacationing in spots that could easily be reached by car; airline travel was, by and large, limited to the wealthy.

Take a walk down memory lane. Way down. If you're as old as we are, 1
your memories carry you back to the 1950s, at least. The Second World
War and the Great Depression were over, and America was on the move.
Suburban houses going up everywhere. New cars rolling from the assembly

lines and out onto new pavement. Ground breaking for the National Defense Interstate Highway System, soon to stretch from sea to shining sea. A TV dinner (introduced in 1953) in every oven.

"It's a great life, eh Bob?" a man in a '50s commercial intones as a young couple and their tow-headed son sit on a couch watching the tube. "And tomorrow will be even better, for you and for all the people." Of course, the great life wasn't great for the millions who were poor or discriminated against. And even for middle-class America, it wasn't worry-free. On the same day in 1957 (October 4th) that *Leave It To Beaver* premiered on American television, those pesky Russians shot Sputnik* into space. Nikita Kruschev† promised to bury us "in the peaceful field of economic competition." We know how that came out.

But 1957 was important for another less-heralded reason. It was the year the percentage of Americans describing themselves as "very happy" reached a peak never to be exceeded for the rest of the Twentieth Century.[1] The following year, a year when Americans bought 200 million "hula hoops," economist John Kenneth Galbraith published an influential book calling the United States "the affluent society."

We *felt* richer then than we do now. Most Americans today don't really think of themselves as affluent, says psychologist Paul Wachtel, "even though in terms of Gross National Product we have more than twice as much as we did then. Everybody's house has twice as much stuff in it. But the feeling of affluence, the experience of well-being, is no higher and perhaps even lower."[2]

Liberal economists argue that since about 1973 the real wages earned by middle-class Americans haven't really risen much and, for many workers, have actually declined. Young couples talk of not being able to afford what their parents had. By contrast, conservative economists contend that the rate of inflation as calculated by the federal government has been overstated and, therefore, that real wages have actually risen considerably. But one thing is incontestable: *We have a lot more stuff and much higher material expectations than previous generations did.*

Starter Castles

Take housing, for example. The average size of new homes is now more than double what it was in the 1950s, while families are smaller. LaNita Wacker, who owns Dream House Realty in Seattle, has been selling homes for more than a quarter of a century. She takes us on a drive through the neighborhoods near her office to explain what's happened.

She shows us houses built during every decade since World War II and describes how they've gotten bigger and bigger. Right after World War II, Wacker points out, 750 square feet was the norm (in Levittown, for ex-

---

* EDS. NOTE — The first artificial satellite.
† EDS. NOTE — Premier of the Soviet Union during the 1950s and 1960s.

ample). "Then in the '50s," she says, "they added 200 square feet, so 950 was the norm." By the '60s, 1,100 square feet was typical, and by the '70s, 1,350. Now it's 2,300.

LaNita Wacker started selling homes in 1972, "right about the time we   8
moved from a single bath to the demand for a double bath."[3] Two-car garages came in then too, and by the late '80s many homes were being built with three-car garages. That's 600 to 900 square feet of garage space alone, "as much square footage as an entire family used in the early '50s," Wacker says. "It would house an entire family. But we have acquired a lot of stuff to store."

To drive the point home, Wacker takes us by a huge home with a four-   9
car garage. Expensive cars and a boat are parked outside. The owner comes out wondering why LaNita is so interested in his place. "I own Dream House Realty," she says. "And yours is a dream house." "It was built to the specifications of my charming wife," the man replies with a laugh. "So why four garages?" asks LaNita. "It's probably because of storage," the man replies, explaining that the garages are filled with family possessions. "You never have enough storage so you can never have enough garages," he adds cheerfully. LaNita asks if he has children. "They're gone now," he replies. "It's just me and the wife."

The four-car garage is an exception, no doubt. But everyone expects   10
larger homes now. "A master bedroom in the '50s would be about 130 square feet," explains Wacker. "Now, even in moderately priced homes, you're talking about maybe 300 square feet devoted to the master bed-room."

In recent years more than ever, homes have become a symbol of con-   11
spicuous consumption, as beneficiaries of the recent stock market boom and unparalleled economic expansion have begun, in many communities, to buy real estate, bulldoze existing (and perfectly functional) homes and replace them with megahouses of 10,000 square feet and more. "Starter castles," some have named them. Others call them "Monster Homes."

On America's Streets of Dreams, the competition is fierce. McMan-   12
sions ... Double McMansions ... Deluxe McMansions ... Deluxe McMan-sions with Cheese . . . Full Garage Deals . . . each one a little bigger and glitzier, popping up like mushrooms in a frenzy of home wars. In places like the spectacular mountain towns of the West, many such megahomes are actually *second homes,* mere vacation destinations for the newly rich.

Better than Tail Fins

A similar story presents itself with automobiles. In 1957, when Ford   13
had a better idea called the Edsel,* cars were big and chromey, but they were far from the sophisticated machines we drive today. A 1960 Ford com-mercial shows crowds of people admiring new Fairlanes, Thunderbirds,

---

* Eds. note — A famously unsuccessful Ford model.

and Falcons, surrounded by twinkling stars as if touched by Tinkerbell. It is, the ad proclaims, "the Wonderful New World of Ford." But in that wonderful new world, much of what we now take for granted as standard automobile features wasn't even available in luxury models.

In 1960, for example, fewer than five percent of new cars had air conditioning. Now ninety percent do. Mike Sillivan, a veteran Toyota salesman in Seattle, says that "today, people's expectations are much higher. They want amenities — power steering, power brakes as standard, premium sound systems."[4] The car of today is a different animal from that of a generation ago. Filled with computer technology. And, after a decade's hiatus following the "energy crisis" of the mid '70s, big is back.

Until the recent price hike, gasoline costs for Americans were at an all-time low in real dollar terms. Worries about fuel efficiency were forgotten as we bought gas-guzzling four-wheel drive wagons called sport utility vehicles (some call them Suburban Assault Vehicles). In the late '90s half of all new cars sold were SUVs and light trucks, exempted from federal fuel efficiency standards. Roomy, comfy, and costly, SUVs just keep getting bigger.

Car Wars

Until recently, the 18-foot-long Chevy Suburban set the standard for gigantism. Now, not to be outdone, Ford has introduced the Excursion, a 7,000-pound titan that is a foot longer than the Suburban. Ford Motors Chairman William Ford even apologized for making so many SUVs, calling his Excursion "the Ford Valdez"* for its propensity to consume fuel. He condemned SUVs as wasteful and polluting, but said Ford would continue to manufacture them anyway because they are extremely profitable.

"For a lot of people an SUV is a status symbol," says car salesman Sillivan. "So they're willing to pay the thirty- to forty-odd thousand dollars to drive one of these vehicles."

Never one to give up without a fight, General Motors has come charging back at Ford, acquiring ownership of the Hummer, a more luxurious version of the military transport vehicle used during the Gulf War. GM is "placing a big bet that the decade-long trend toward ever larger and more aggressive-looking sport utility vehicles would continue," according to *The New York Times*.[5] "It's like a tank with fashion," says one teenager quoted by the *Times*. The kid says he loves the Hummer because "I like something where I can look down into another car and give that knowing smile that says 'I'm bigger than you.' It makes me feel powerful." More than a foot wider than the Excursion, the Hummer retails for $93,000. GM predicts these behemoths will be especially popular in (we are not making this up) Manhattan, which is probably a good thing because you need to be on the

---

* EDS. NOTE — Alaskan site of a dangerous 1989 oil tanker spill.

viewing platform of the Empire State Building to see over them. But now what will Ford counter with, an even bigger SUV called The Extinction?

Weightless Tourism

Hummers on the streets of Manhattan. You might call them Saddam's revenge. Or Ho-Hummers, if you compare them with yet another way to drop nearly a hundred grand. Check out spacevoyages.com to find out what may be the ultimate in swollen expectations. Just plop down $98 K, including a $6 K deposit, and you, dear reader, can be an astronaut. Sometime between 2003 and 2005, you'll be able to take a two-hour trip on a rocket ship and spend about five weightless minutes in actual outer space. Besides that, you'll get an "original and exclusive Space Adventures suborbital flight certificate," a flight training suit, astronaut wings, a medallion, a travel bag, photos, and a lifetime membership in the Space Adventurers Club—all for less than a hundred thousand dollars. If that sounds like a deal, you might want to stick a thermometer in your mouth right away. Ten . . . nine . . . eight . . .*   19

Let's Do Lunch

Consider food. The '50s did give us TV dinners. Turkey, peas, and mashed potatoes in a throwaway tray for sixty-nine cents, thank you Swanson's. As kids, we considered them delectable. Our standard diets were pretty bland. Exotic meant soggy egg rolls, chow mein, and chop suey. Mexican was tacos and tamales (how did we cope without chimichangas and chalupas?). Thai wasn't even part of our vocabulary. Now, city streets and even suburban malls sport a United Nations of restaurants. We remember waiting for certain fruits and vegetables to be in season. Now, there is no season; everything is always available. When it's winter here, it's summer in New Zealand, after all. Yet we often feel deprived. Strawberries lose their flavor when you can have them all the time. More choices and more diversity certainly aren't a bad thing, but they come at a cost. The exotic quickly becomes commonplace and boring, requiring ever newer and more expensive menus.   20

Take coffee. Until recently, we took it as watery brown stuff made bearable by gobs of sugar. Now, specialty coffees are everywhere. NPR radio host Scott Simon was surprised a few years ago when he stopped at a service station in rural Washington State. In the station's mini-mart was an espresso stand with so many types of coffee drinks to offer that Simon longed for an Italian dictionary to identify them. No need. The kid behind the counter with his baseball cap on backwards knew them all.   21

---

* EDS. NOTE — As of this writing, private space vehicles are not expected to take paying passengers until at least 2007.

Eating out used to be a special occasion. Now we spend more money   22
on restaurant food than on the food we cook ourselves. Swelling expectations. Swelling stomachs too, but that's another symptom.

Invention Is the Mother of Necessity

Consider, also, the kinds of goods that were deemed luxuries as   23
recently as 1970, but are now found in well over half of U.S. homes, and
thought of by a majority of Americans as necessities: dishwashers, clothes
dryers, central heating and air conditioning, color and cable TV.[6] And back
in 1970, there were no microwave ovens, VCRs, CD players, cell phones, fax
machines, compact discs, leaf blowers, Pokemon, or personal computers.
Now, more than half of us take all of these goods for granted and would
feel deprived without them. Well, OK, so you wouldn't feel deprived without Pokemon.

There always seems to be a "better" model that we've just gotta have.   24
Writing about Compaq's new iPaq 3600 Pocket PC, *Seattle Times* technology reporter Paul Andrews warns that the iPaq, with its "sleek Porsche-like
case and striking color screen," costs $500 more than an ordinary Palm
Pilot. "But without the color display, music, and photos of the iPaq, life
seems pretty dull," he laments.[7]

And take travel. We drive twice as much per capita as we did a half cen-   25
tury ago, and fly an amazing twenty-five times as much.[8] Middle-income
Americans seldom ventured more than a few hundred miles from home
then, even during two-week summer vacations. Now, many of us (not just
the rich) expect to spend occasional long weekends in Puerto Vallarta, or
(in the case of New Yorkers) in Paris. Everywhere, humble motels have been
replaced by elegant "inns," humble resorts by Club Meds. Now, "I need a
vacation" means I need to change continents for a few days.

The Changing Joneses

"Greed has infected our society. It is the worst infection," says the real   26
Patch Adams, the doctor who was portrayed by Robin Williams in a popular Hollywood film.[9] He's right only to a degree. It may be fear rather than
greed that primarily drives our swelling expectations. Fear of not succeeding in the eyes of others. In one magazine ad from the '50s, readers are
encouraged to "keep up with the Joneses" by driving what they're driving: a
Chevy. A Chevy sedan at that, not even a Corvette. Just about the cheapest
car around, even then.

But the mythical Joneses don't drive Chevrolets any more. And they're   27
no longer your next door neighbors either, folks who make roughly what
you do. Economist Juliet Schor studied people's attitudes about consumption in a large corporation and found that most Americans now compare
themselves with coworkers or television characters when they think about
what they "need."

But corporations have become increasingly stratified economically in recent years. One frequently comes into contact with much-better-paid colleagues than oneself. Their cars, clothes, and travel plans reflect their higher incomes, yet set the standards for everyone in the firm. 28

Likewise, says Schor, "TV shows a very inflated standard of living relative to what the true standard of living of the American public is. People on television tend to be upper middle class or even rich, and people who watch a lot of TV have highly inflated views of what the average American has. For example, people who are heavy TV watchers vastly exaggerate the number of Americans with swimming pools, tennis courts, maids, and planes, and their own expectations of what they should have also become inflated, so they tend to spend more and save less."[10] 29

Schor says that as the gap between rich and poor grew during the 1980s, people with relatively high incomes began to feel deprived in comparison to those who were suddenly making even more. "They started to feel 'poor on $100,000 a year' as the well-known phrase puts it, because they were comparing themselves to the Donald Trumps and the other newly wealthy." It happened all the way down the income line, Schor says. "Everybody felt worse compared to the role models, those at the top." Polls now show that Americans believe they need $75,000 (for a family of four) just to lead a "minimum" middle-class life. 30

I've Got Mine, Jack

In the years just after World War II the super-rich sought to conceal their profligacy, but since Ronald Reagan's first inaugural ball many have begun to flaunt it again. As economist Robert Frank points out, there's been a rush on $15,000 purses, $10,000 watches, even $65 million private jets. Twenty million Americans now own big-screen TVs costing at least $2,000 each. Some buy their children $5,000 life-size reproductions of Darth Vader and $18,000 replicas of Range Rovers, $25,000 birthday parties and million-dollar Bar Mitzvahs.[11] 31

Thus from the hot zones of popular culture and stratified workplaces, our new Joneses—consciously or otherwise—spread the affluenza virus, swelling our expectations as never before. And stuffing us up. 32

• • •

Endnotes

1. David Meyer, *The American Paradox,* p. 136.
2. Personal interview, April 1996.
3. Personal interview, September 1996.
4. Personal interview, September 1996.
5. Keith Bradshear, "GM Has High Hopes for Road Warriors," *New York Times,* August 6, 2000.

6. See the wealth of information on changing expectations in Richard McKenzie's *The Paradox of Progress*.

7. Paul Andrews, "Compaq's new iPac may be the PC for your pocket," *Seattle Times*, November 5, 2000.

8. *All-Consuming Passion*, p. 4.

9. Personal interview, October 1987.

10. Personal interview, May 1997.

11. James Lardner, "The Urge to Splurge," *U.S. News and World Report*, May 24, 1998.

Comprehension

1. Why do De Graaf, Wann, and Naylor think that 1957 was an important year? What is odd about the fact that most Americans today do not consider themselves affluent?

2. What do liberal economists say about wages? How do their ideas differ from those of conservative economists?

3. How are houses built today different from those built in the 1950s, 1960s, 1970s, and 1980s? How are these differences significant?

4. According to the authors, why do Americans seem to be buying bigger and bigger automobiles? What do the authors see as the implications of this trend?

5. What do most Americans compare themselves to when they form their attitudes about consumption? How do these comparisons cause dissatisfaction?

Purpose and Audience

1. At what point do the authors state their thesis? Why do they state it where they do?

2. What preconceptions do the authors seem to have about their readers? How can you tell?

3. What is the authors' purpose? To instruct? To persuade? To entertain? Do they have any other purpose? Explain.

Style and Structure

1. Why do the authors begin with "a walk down memory lane" (1)? What does this look at the past contribute to the essay?

2. What two things are the authors comparing? Is this selection organized as a subject-by-subject or a point-by-point comparison? Why do you think the authors chose the strategy they did?

3. What purpose do the headings serve? Are these headings helpful, or do they just get in the way?

4. What transitions do the authors use to signal their movement from one point to another?

5. What strategy do the authors use in their conclusion? Is the strategy effective? Why or why not?

Vocabulary Projects

1. Define each of the following words as it is used in this selection.

intones (2)	consumption (11)	exotic (20)
affluent (3)	hiatus (14)	stratified (28)
inflation (5)	status (17)	conceal (31)
conspicuous (11)	behemoths (18)	flaunt (31)

2. In their conclusion, the authors coin (invent) a new word: *affluenza*. What two words did they use to form this new word? What do you think this word means? Did the authors have to coin a word, or could they have used a word already in the language? Explain.

Journal Entry

Do you think the authors characterize society accurately, or do they over-state their case? For example, do you know people who suffer from *affluenza*?

Writing Workshop

1. Write an essay comparing your home or car to the ones the authors discuss in their essay.
2. Interview your parents or grandparents, and ask them about the trends the authors discuss. Then, write an essay agreeing or disagreeing with their thesis. Support your thesis by comparing the authors' observations to those of the people you interviewed.
3. Do you expect to be more or less affluent than your parents? Write an essay comparing where your parents are now to where you expect to be when you are their age. Your essay can be either serious or humorous.

Combining the Patterns

This essay contains a number of **exemplification** paragraphs—for example, paragraphs 6 and 9. What do these paragraphs add to the essay? Would more such paragraphs be helpful?

Thematic Connections

- "Once More to the Lake" (page 186)
- "Innovation" (page 231)
- "The Human Cost of an Illiterate Society" (page 252)
- "The 'Black Table' Is Still There" (page 366)
- "On Dumpster Diving" (page 712)

IAN FRAZIER

Dearly Disconnected

Born in 1951 in Cleveland, Ohio, Ian Frazier graduated from Harvard University, where he was on the staff of the *Harvard Lampoon*. He went on to become a *New Yorker* staff writer for many years, and his first books were the humor collections *Dating Your Mom* (1986) and *Nobody Better, Better Than Nobody* (1987). His later works, beginning with *Great Plains* (1989) and including most recently *The Fish's Eye: Essays about Angling and the Out of Doors* (2002), have often focused on his love of rural Montana, where he spends part of each year. Frazier also writes about American culture and society in essays such as the following ode to the pay telephone.

Background on pay telephones: Telephone technology was perfected in 1876, and the first United States telephone company was organized in 1878. The popularity of this new invention spread quickly, and by 1880 close to 200,000 telephones were in use nationwide. The earliest pay telephones were often installed in hotels and other businesses open to the public and supervised by attendants who collected money directly from users. The first coin-operated telephone was installed in a Hartford, Connecticut, bank in 1889, and by 1902 the United States had 81,000 pay phones. The first outdoor pay telephone appeared on a Cincinnati corner in 1905, but such phones were not immediately popular, perhaps because people did not wish to have private conversations on a public street. Early telephone booths—especially those in hotel lobbies—were often elaborate, carpeted closets constructed of expensive woods, but later in the century metal and glass booths became more common. As of 1960, the Bell Company had installed one million pay telephones in the United States. These phones were, of course, a boon to people who could not afford home service. Moreover, in the days before cell phones, pay phones were virtually the only means that people away from their homes and offices had for calling others.

Before I got married I was living by myself in an A-frame cabin in northwestern Montana. The cabin's interior was a single high-ceilinged room, and at the center of the room, mounted on the rough-hewn log that held up the ceiling beam, was a telephone. I knew no one in the area or indeed the whole state, so my entire social life came to me through that phone. The woman I would marry was living in Sarasota, Florida, and the distance between us suggests how well we were getting along at the time. We had not been in touch for several months; she had no phone. One day she decided to call me from a pay phone. We talked for a while, and after her coins ran out I jotted the number on the wood beside my phone and called her back. A day or two later, thinking about the call, I wanted to talk to her again. The only number I had for her was the pay phone number I'd written down.

1

The pay phone was on the street some blocks from the apartment   2
where she stayed. As it happened, though, she had just stepped out to do
some errands a few minutes before I called, and she was passing by on the
sidewalk when the phone rang. She had no reason to think that a public
phone ringing on a busy street would be for her. She stopped, listened to it
ring again, and picked up the receiver. Love is pure luck; somehow I had
known she would answer, and she had known it would be me.

Long afterwards, on a trip to Disney World in Orlando with our two   3
kids, then aged six and two, we made a special detour to Sarasota to show
them the pay phone. It didn't impress them much. It's just a nondescript
Bell Atlantic pay phone on the cement wall of a building, by the vestibule.
But its ordinariness and even boringness only make me like it more; ordinary places where extraordinary events have occurred are my favorite kind.
On my mental map of Florida that pay phone is a landmark looming above
the city it occupies, and a notable, if private, historic site.

I'm interested in pay phones in general these days, especially when I get   4
the feeling that they are about to go away. Technology, in the form of sleek
little phones in our pockets, has swept on by them and made them begin to
seem antique. My lifelong entanglement with pay phones dates me; when I
was young they were just there, a given, often as stubborn and uncongenial
as the curbstone underfoot. They were instruments of torture sometimes.
You had to feed them fistfuls of change in those pre-phone-card days, and
the operator was a real person who stood maddeningly between you and
whomever you were trying to call. And when the call went wrong, as communication often does, the pay phone gave you a focus for your rage. Pay
phones were always getting smashed up, the receivers shattered to bits
against the booth, the coin slots jammed with chewing gum, the cords
yanked out and unraveled to the floor.

You used to hear people standing at pay phones and cursing them. I   5
remember the sound of my own frustrated shouting confined by the glass
walls of a phone booth—the kind you don't see much anymore, with a
little ventilating fan in the ceiling that turned on when you shut the
double-hinged glass door. The noise that fan made in the silence of a
phone booth was for a while the essence of romantic, lonely-guy melancholy for me. Certain specific pay phones I still resent for the unhappiness
they caused me, and others I will never forgive, though not for any fault of
their own. In the C concourse of the Salt Lake City airport there's a row of
pay phones set on the wall by the men's room just past the concourse
entry. While on a business trip a few years ago, I called home from a phone
in that row and learned that a friend had collapsed in her apartment and
was in the hospital with brain cancer. I had liked those pay phones before,
and had used them often; now I can't even look at them when I go by.

There was always a touch of seediness and sadness to pay phones, and   6
a sense of transience. Drug dealers made calls from them, and shady types
who did not want their whereabouts known, and otherwise respectable
people planning assignations, and people too poor to have phones of their

own. In the movies, any character who used a pay phone was either in trouble or contemplating a crime. Pay phones came with their own special atmospherics and even accessories sometimes — the predictable bad smells and graffiti, of course, as well as cigarette butts, soda cans, scattered pamphlets from the Jehovah's Witnesses, and single bottles of beer (empty) still in their individual, street-legal paper bags. Mostly, pay phones evoked the mundane: "Honey, I'm just leaving. I'll be there soon." But you could tell that a lot of undifferentiated humanity had flowed through these places, and that in the muteness of each pay phone's little space, wild emotion had howled.

Once, when I was living in Brooklyn, I read in the newspaper that a 7 South American man suspected of dozens of drug-related contract murders had been arrested at a pay phone in Queens. Police said that the man had been on the phone setting up a murder at the time of his arrest. The newspaper story gave the address of the pay phone, and out of curiosity one afternoon I took a long walk to Queens to take a look at it. It was on an undistinguished street in a middle-class neighborhood, by a florist's shop. By the time I saw it, however, the pay phone had been blown up and/or fire-bombed. I had never before seen a pay phone so damaged; explosives had blasted pieces of the phone itself wide open in metal shreds like frozen banana peels, and flames had blackened everything and melted the plastic parts and burned the insulation off the wires. Soon after, I read that police could not find enough evidence against the suspected murderer and so had let him go.

The cold phone outside a shopping center in Bigfork, Montana, from 8 which I called a friend in the West Indies one winter when her brother was sick; the phone on the wall of the concession stand at Redwood Pool, where I used to stand dripping and call my mom to come and pick me up; the sweaty phones used almost only by men in the hallway outside the maternity ward at Lenox Hill Hospital in New York; the phone by the driveway of the Red Cloud Indian School in South Dakota where I used to talk with my wife while priests in black slacks and white socks chatted on a bench nearby; the phone in the old wood-paneled phone booth with leaded glass windows in the drugstore in my Ohio hometown — each one is as specific as a birthmark, a point on earth unlike any other. Recently I went back to New York City after a long absence and tried to find a working pay phone. I picked up one receiver after the next without success. Meanwhile, as I scanned down the long block, I counted half a dozen or more pedestrians talking on their cell phones.

It's the cell phone, of course, that's putting the pay phone out of busi- 9 ness. The pay phone is to the cell phone as the troubled and difficult older sibling is to the cherished newborn. People even treat their cell phones like babies, cradling them in their palms and beaming down upon them lovingly as they dial. You sometimes hear people yelling on their cell phones, but almost never yelling at them. Cell phones are toylike, nearly magic, and we get a huge kick out of them, as often happens with technological advances until the new wears off. Somehow I don't believe people had a similar honeymoon period with pay phones back in their early days, and they certainly have no such enthusiasm for them now. When I see a cell-phone user gently push the little antenna and fit the phone back into its brushed-vinyl carrying case and tuck the case inside his jacket beside his heart, I feel sorry for the beat-up pay phone standing in the rain.

People almost always talk on cell phones while in motion — driving, 10 walking down the street, riding on a commuter train. The cell phone took the transience the pay phone implied and turned it into VIP-style mobility and speed. Even sitting in a restaurant, the person on a cell phone seems importantly busy and on the move. Cell-phone conversations seem to be unlimited by ordinary constraints of place and time, as if they represent an almost-perfect form of communication whose perfect state would be telepathy.

And yet no matter how we factor the world away, it remains. I think 11 this is what drives me so nuts when a person sitting next to me on a bus makes a call from her cell phone. Yes, this busy and important caller is at no fixed point in space, but nevertheless I happen to be beside her. The job of providing physical context falls on me; I become her call's surroundings, as if I'm the phone booth wall. For me to lean over and comment on her cell-phone conversation would be as unseemly and unexpected as if I were in fact a wall; and yet I have no choice, as a sentient person, but to hear what my chatty fellow traveler has to say.

Some middle-aged guys like me go around complaining about this 12 kind of thing. The more sensible approach is just to accept it and forget about it, because there's not much we can do. I don't think that pay phones will completely disappear. Probably they will survive for a long while as clumsy old technology still of some use to those lagging behind, and as a backup if ever the superior systems should temporarily fail. Before pay phones became endangered I never thought of them as public spaces, which of course they are. They suggested a human average; they belonged to anybody who had a couple of coins. Now I see that, like public schools and public transportation, pay phones belong to a former commonality our culture is no longer quite so sure it needs.

I have a weakness for places — for old battlefields, car-crash sites, 13 houses where famous authors lived. Bygone passions should always have an address, it seems to me. Ideally, the world would be covered with plaques and markers listing the notable events that occurred at each par-ticular spot. A sign on every pay phone would describe how a woman broke up with her fiancé here, how a young ballplayer learned that he had made the team. Unfortunately, the world itself is fluid, and changes out from under us; the rocky islands that the pilot Mark Twain was careful to avoid in the Mississippi are now stone outcroppings in a soybean field. Mean-while, our passions proliferate into illegibility, and the places they occur can't hold them. Eventually pay phones will become relics of an almost-vanished landscape, and of a time when there were fewer of us and our stories were on an earlier page. Romantics like me will have to reimagine our passions as they are — unmoored to earth, like an infinitude of cell-phone messages flying through the atmosphere.

• • •

Comprehension

1. Why does Frazier see the pay phone in Florida as a "landmark" and a "historic site" (3)?
2. Why are pay phones in danger of disappearing?
3. Why does Frazier feel nostalgic about pay phones?
4. How are cell phones different from pay phones?
5. What bothers Frazier most about cell phones?

Purpose and Audience

1. At what point in the essay does Frazier state his thesis? Why do you think he states it where he does?
2. What preconceptions about pay phones does Frazier seem to think his readers have? How can you tell?
3. What is Frazier's purpose in this essay? To instruct? To convince? To entertain? Does he have some other purpose? Explain.
4. Does the title of this essay accurately reflect its thesis? Suggest some other titles Frazier could have used.

Style and Structure

1. Why does Frazier open his essay with a story about how he phoned his wife? What does this story add to his essay?
2. Is this essay organized as a subject-by-subject or a point-by-point comparison? Why do you think Frazier chose this strategy?
3. What transition does Frazier use to signal his movement from one subject to another?
4. Does Frazier make the same (or similar) points about both pay phones and cell phones? Should he have made any other points?
5. What strategy does Frazier use in his conclusion? Is this strategy effective? Why, or why not?

Vocabulary Projects

1. Define each of the following words as it is used in this selection.

A-frame (1)	curbstone (4)	concourse (5)
nondescript (3)	unraveled (4)	assignations (6)

evoked (6)	muteness (6)	proliferate (13)
mundane (6)	concession stand (8)	infinitude (13)
undifferentiated (6)	commonality (12)	

2. This essay includes a number of rather difficult words. Choose a paragraph that contains several of these words (paragraph 6, for example), and rewrite it in more accessible language. Then, evaluate what has been gained and lost with your substitutions.

Journal Entry

Identify an object you feel as intensely about as Frazier feels about pay phones, and explain the role this object has played in your life.

Writing Workshop

1. Write an essay in which you, like Frazier, tell how a technological device—a cell phone or a digital camera, for example—changed your life. Make sure you compare your life before you began using the object with your life after you started to use it. Your essay can be either serious or humorous.

2. Write an essay comparing an example of new technology with an example of old technology—email and regular mail, for example. Make sure you discuss the positive and negative aspects of each.

3. Interview your parents or grandparents, and ask them about their attitudes toward cell phones. Then, write an essay comparing their attitudes to your own.

Combining the Patterns

This essay contains a number of **exemplification** paragraphs—for example, paragraphs 7 and 8. What do these paragraphs add to the essay?

Thematic Connections

- "Once More to the Lake" (page 186)
- "Innovation" (page 231)
- "Television: The Plug-In Drug" (page 351)
- "The Dog Ate My Disk, and Other Tales of Woe" (page 475)

DEBORAH TANNEN

Sex, Lies, and Conversation

Deborah Tannen was born in Brooklyn, New York, in 1945. She graduated from the State University of New York at Binghamton, was awarded a doctorate from the University of California at Berkeley, and currently teaches at Georgetown University. Tannen has written and edited several scholarly books on the problems of communicating across cultural, class, ethnic, and sexual divides. She has also presented her research to the general public in newspapers and magazines and in her best-selling books *That's Not What I Meant!* (1986), *You Just Don't Understand: Women and Men in Conversation* (1990), and *Talking from 9 to 5* (1994). Her latest book is *I Only Say This Because I Love You* (2001).

Background on men's and women's communication styles: "Sex, Lies, and Conversation" was written in conjunction with the publication of *You Just Don't Understand,* which Tannen wrote because the single chapter in *That's Not What I Meant!* on the difficulties men and women in the United States have communicating with one another had gotten such an overwhelming response. She realized the chapter might raise some controversy — that discussing their different communication styles might be used to malign men or to put women at a disadvantage — and indeed some critics have seen her work as reinforcing stereotypes. Still, her work on the subject, along with that of other writers (most notably John Gray in his *Men Are from Mars, Women Are from Venus* series), has proved enormously popular, and much research (and debate) occurs about male and female differences in terms of brain function, relational styles and expectations, and evolutionary roles.

I was addressing a small gathering in a suburban Virginia living room — a women's group that had invited men to join them. Throughout the evening, one man had been particularly talkative, frequently offering ideas and anecdotes, while his wife sat silently beside him on the couch. Toward the end of the evening, I commented that women frequently complain that their husbands don't talk to them. This man quickly concurred. He gestured toward his wife and said, "She's the talker in our family." The room burst into laughter; the man looked puzzled and hurt. "It's true," he explained. "When I come home from work I have nothing to say. If she didn't keep the conversation going, we'd spend the whole evening in silence."

This episode crystallizes the irony that although American men tend to talk more than women in public situations, they often talk less at home. And this pattern is wreaking havoc with marriage.

The pattern was observed by political scientist Andrew Hacker in the late '70s. Sociologist Catherine Kohler Riessman reports in her new book *Divorce Talk* that most of the women she interviewed — but only a few of the men — gave lack of communication as the reason for their divorces. Given the current divorce rate of nearly 50 percent, that amounts to millions of cases in the United States every year — a virtual epidemic of failed conversation.

In my own research, complaints from women about their husbands   4
most often focused not on tangible inequities such as having given up the chance for a career to accompany a husband to his, or doing far more than their share of daily life-support work like cleaning, cooking, social arrangements, and errands. Instead, they focused on communication: "He doesn't listen to me," "He doesn't talk to me." I found, as Hacker observed years before, that most wives want their husbands to be, first and foremost, conversational partners, but few husbands share this expectation of their wives.

In short, the image that best represents the current crisis is the stereo-   5
typical cartoon scene of a man sitting at the breakfast table with a newspaper held up in front of his face, while a woman glares at the back of it, wanting to talk.

Linguistic Battle of the Sexes

How can women and men have such different impressions of commu-   6
nication in marriage? Why the widespread imbalance in their interests and expectations?

In the April issue of *American Psychologist*, Stanford University's Eleanor   7
Maccoby reports the results of her own and others' research showing that children's development is most influenced by the social structure of peer interactions. Boys and girls tend to play with children of their own gender, and their sex-separate groups have different organizational structures and interactive norms.

I believe these systematic differences in childhood socialization make   8
talk between women and men like cross-cultural communication, heir to all the attraction and pitfalls of that enticing but difficult enterprise. My research on men's and women's conversations uncovered patterns similar to those described for children's groups.

For women, as for girls, intimacy is the fabric of relationships, and talk   9
is the thread from which it is woven. Little girls create and maintain friendships by exchanging secrets; similarly, women regard conversation as the cornerstone of friendship. So a woman expects her husband to be a new and improved version of a best friend. What is important is not the individual subjects that are discussed but the sense of closeness, of a life shared, that emerges when people tell their thoughts, feelings, and impressions.

Bonds between boys can be as intense as girls', but they are based less   10
on talking, more on doing things together. Since they don't assume talk is the cement that binds a relationship, men don't know what kind of talk women want, and they don't miss it when it isn't there.

Boys' groups are larger, more inclusive, and more hierarchical, so boys   11
must struggle to avoid the subordinate position in the group. This may
play a role in women's complaints that men don't listen to them. Some
men really don't like to listen, because being the listener makes them feel
one-down, like a child listening to adults or an employee to a boss.

But often when women tell men, "You aren't listening," and the men   12
protest, "I am," the men are right. The impression of not listening results
from misalignments in the mechanics of conversation. The misalignment
begins as soon as a man and a woman take physical positions. This became
clear when I studied videotapes made by psychologist Bruce Dorval of children and adults talking to their same-sex best friends. I found that at every
age, the girls and women faced each other directly, their eyes anchored on
each other's faces. At every age, the boys and men sat at angles to each
other and looked elsewhere in the room, periodically glancing at each
other. They were obviously attuned to each other, often mirroring
each other's movements. But the tendency of men to face away can give
women the impression they aren't listening even when they are. A young
woman in college was frustrated: Whenever she told her boyfriend she
wanted to talk to him, he would lie down on the floor, close his eyes, and
put his arm over his face. This signaled to her, "He's taking a nap." But he
insisted he was listening extra hard. Normally, he looks around the room,
so he is easily distracted. Lying down and covering his eyes helped him concentrate on what she was saying.

Analogous to the physical alignment that women and men take in   13
conversation is their topical alignment. The girls in my study tended to
talk at length about one topic, but the boys tended to jump from topic to
topic. The second-grade girls exchanged stories about people they knew.
The second-grade boys teased, told jokes, noticed things in the room, and
talked about finding games to play. The sixth-grade girls talked about
problems with a mutual friend. The sixth-grade boys talked about 55 different topics, none of which extended over more than a few turns.

Listening to Body Language

Switching topics is another habit that gives women the impression   14
men aren't listening, especially if they switch to a topic about themselves.
But the evidence of the 10th-grade boys in my study indicates otherwise.
The 10th-grade boys sprawled across their chairs with bodies parallel and
eyes straight ahead, rarely looking at each other. They looked as if they
were riding in a car, staring out the windshield. But they were talking
about their feelings. One boy was upset because a girl had told him he had
a drinking problem, and the other was feeling alienated from all his
friends.

Now, when a girl told a friend about a problem, the friend responded   15
by asking probing questions and expressing agreement and understanding. But the boys dismissed each other's problems. Todd assured Richard

that his drinking was "no big problem" because "sometimes you're funny when you're off your butt." And when Todd said he felt left out, Richard responded, "Why should you? You know more people than me."

Women perceive such responses as belittling and unsupportive. But   16
the boys seemed satisfied with them. Whereas women reassure each other by implying, "You shouldn't feel bad because I've had similar experiences," men do so by implying, "You shouldn't feel bad because your problems aren't so bad."

There are even simpler reasons for women's impression that men don't   17
listen. Linguist Lynette Hirschman found that women make more listener-noise, such as "mhm," "uhuh," and "yeah," to show "I'm with you." Men, she found, more often give silent attention. Women who expect a stream of listener-noise interpret silent attention as no attention at all.

Women's conversational habits are as frustrating to men as men's are   18
to women. Men who expect silent attention interpret a stream of listener-noise as overreaction or impatience. Also, when women talk to each other in a close, comfortable setting, they often overlap, finish each other's sentences, and anticipate what the other is about to say. This practice, which I call "participatory listenership," is often perceived by men as interruption, intrusion, and lack of attention.

A parallel difference caused a man to complain about his wife, "She   19
just wants to talk about her own point of view. If I show her another view, she gets mad at me." When most women talk to each other, they assume a conversationalist's job is to express agreement and support. But many men see their conversational duty as pointing out the other side of an argument. This is heard as disloyalty by women, and refusal to offer the requisite support. It is not that women don't want to see other points of view, but that they prefer them phrased as suggestions and inquiries rather than as direct challenges.

In his book *Fighting for Life*, Walter Ong points out that men use   20
"agonistic," or warlike, oppositional formats to do almost anything; thus discussion becomes debate, and conversation a competitive sport. In contrast, women see conversation as a ritual means of establishing rapport. If Jane tells a problem and June says she has a similar one, they walk away feeling closer to each other. But this attempt at establishing rapport can backfire when used with men. Men take too literally women's ritual "troubles talk," just as women mistake men's ritual challenges for real attack.

The Sounds of Silence

These differences begin to clarify why women and men have such dif-   21
ferent expectations about communication in marriage. For women, talk creates intimacy. Marriage is an orgy of closeness: you can tell your feelings and thoughts, and still be loved. Their greatest fear is being pushed away. But men live in a hierarchical world, where talk maintains independence

and status. They are on guard to protect themselves from being put down and pushed around.

This explains the paradox of the talkative man who said of his silent   22
wife, "She's the talker." In the public setting of a guest lecture, he felt challenged to show his intelligence and display his understanding of the lecture. But at home, where he has nothing to prove and no one to defend
against, he is free to remain silent. For his wife, being home means she is
free from the worry that something she says might offend someone, or
spark disagreement, or appear to be showing off; at home she is free to
talk.

The communication problems that endanger marriage can't be fixed   23
by mechanical engineering. They require a new conceptual framework
about the role of talk in human relationships. Many of the psychological
explanations that have become second nature may not be helpful, because
they tend to blame either women (for not being assertive enough) or men
(for not being in touch with their feelings). A sociolinguistic approach by
which male-female conversation is seen as cross-cultural communication
allows us to understand the problem and forge solutions without blaming
either party.

Once the problem is understood, improvement comes naturally, as it   24
did to the young woman and her boyfriend who seemed to go to sleep
when she wanted to talk. Previously, she had accused him of not listening,
and he had refused to change his behavior, since that would be admitting
fault. But then she learned about and explained to him the differences in
women's and men's habitual ways of aligning themselves in conversation.
The next time she told him she wanted to talk, he began, as usual, by lying
down and covering his eyes. When the familiar negative reaction bubbled
up, she reassured herself that he really was listening. But then he sat up
and looked at her. Thrilled, she asked why. He said, "You like me to look at
you when we talk, so I'll try to do it." Once he saw their differences as cross-
cultural rather than right and wrong, he independently altered his behavior.

Women who feel abandoned and deprived when their husbands won't   25
listen to or report daily news may be happy to discover their husbands trying to adapt once they understand the place of small talk in women's relationships. But if their husbands don't adapt, the women may still be
comforted that for men, this is not a failure of intimacy. Accepting the difference, the wives may look to their friends or family for that kind of talk.
And husbands who can't provide it shouldn't feel their wives have made
unreasonable demands. Some couples will still decide to divorce, but at
least their decisions will be based on realistic expectations.

In these times of resurgent ethnic conflicts, the world desperately   26
needs cross-cultural understanding. Like charity, successful cross-cultural
communication should begin at home.

• • •

Comprehension

1. What pattern of communication does Tannen identify at the beginning of her essay?
2. According to Tannen, what do women complain about most in their marriages?
3. What gives women the impression that men do not listen?
4. What characteristics of women's speech do men find frustrating?
5. According to Tannen, what can men and women do to remedy the communication problems that exist in most marriages?

Purpose and Audience

1. What is Tannen's thesis?
2. What is Tannen's purpose in writing this essay? Do you think she wants to inform or to persuade? On what do you base your conclusion?
3. Is Tannen writing for an expert audience or for an audience of general readers? To men, women, or both? How can you tell?

Style and Structure

1. What does Tannen gain by stating her thesis in paragraph 2 of the essay? Would there be any advantage in postponing the thesis statement until the end? Explain.
2. Is this essay a subject-by-subject or a point-by-point comparison? What does Tannen gain by organizing her essay the way she does?
3. Throughout her essay, Tannen cites scholarly studies and quotes statistics. How effectively does this information support her points? Could she have made a strong case without this material? Why, or why not?
4. Would you say Tannen's tone is hopeful, despairing, sarcastic, angry, or something else? Explain.
5. Tannen concludes her essay with a far-reaching statement. What do you think she hopes to accomplish with this conclusion? Is she successful? Explain your reasoning.

Vocabulary Projects

1. Define each of the following words as it is used in this selection.

concurred (1)	pitfalls (8)	rapport (20)
crystallizes (2)	subordinate (11)	ritual (20)
inequities (4)	misalignment (12)	orgy (21)
imbalance (6)	analogous (13)	sociolinguistic (23)
peer (7)	alienated (14)	forge (23)
organizational (7)	intrusion (18)	

2. Where does Tannen use professional **jargon** in this essay? Would the essay be more or less effective without these words? Explain.

Journal Entry

Based on your own observations of male-female communication, how accurate is Tannen's analysis? Can you relate an anecdote from your own life that illustrates (or contradicts) her thesis?

Writing Workshop

1. In another essay, Tannen contrasts the communication patterns of male and female students in classroom settings. After observing a few of your own classes, write an essay also drawing a comparison between the communication patterns of your male and female classmates.

2. Write an essay comparing the way male and female characters speak in films or on television. Use examples to support your points.

3. Write an essay comparing the vocabulary used in two different sports. Does one sport use more violent language than the other? For example, baseball uses the terms *bunt* and *sacrifice,* and football uses the terms *blitz* and *bomb*. Use as many examples as you can to support your points.

Combining the Patterns

Tannen begins her essay with an anecdote. Why does she begin with a paragraph of **narration**? How does this story set the tone for the rest of the essay?

Thematic Connections

- "Why Boys Don't Play with Dolls" (page 361)
- "The Men We Carry in Our Minds" (page 481)
- "I Want a Wife" (page 524)
- "The Wife-Beater" (page 532)

Sadie and Maud (Poetry)

Poet Gwendolyn Brooks (1917–2000) was born in Topeka, Kansas, and graduated from Wilson Junior College in Chicago, where she lived most of her life. She was on the faculty of Columbia College and Northeastern Illinois State College, and she was named the poet laureate of Illinois. Her first volume of poetry was *A Street in Bronzeville* (1945), named for the African-American neighborhood on the South Side of Chicago where she grew up. Among her many later collections are *Annie Allen* (1949), for which she was the first African American to win a Pulitzer Prize; *Riot* (1969), based on the violent unrest that gripped many inner-city neighborhoods following the assassination of Martin Luther King Jr.; and *Blacks* (1987). She also published books for children, a novel, and two volumes of her memoirs. The following poem is from *A Street in Bronzeville*.

Background on African Americans in the 1940s: Because restrictive laws in Chicago in the 1940s prevented blacks from buying property outside of Bronzeville, the area was home to African Americans from all income levels as well as to many thriving black-owned businesses. Still, the opportunities available to women like Sadie and Maud in the 1940s were limited. Only about 12 percent of African Americans completed four years of high school (although numbers were higher in the North than in the South), and many fewer went on to college. Six out of ten African-American women were employed in low-paying domestic service positions, while fewer than one percent held professional positions, primarily as teachers in segregated schools.

Maud went to college.
Sadie stayed at home.
Sadie scraped life
With a fine-tooth comb.

She didn't leave a tangle in.   5
Her comb found every strand.
Sadie was one of the livingest chits
In all the land.

Sadie bore two babies
Under her maiden name.   10
Maud and Ma and Papa
Nearly died of shame.

When Sadie said her last so-long
Her girls struck out from home.

(Sadie had left as heritage   15
Her fine-tooth comb.)

Maud, who went to college,
Is a thin brown mouse.
She is living all alone
In this old house.   20

•   •   •

Reading Literature

1. What two ideas is Brooks comparing in the poem? How does the
    speaker let readers know when she is shifting her focus from one sub-
    ject to another?
2. How accurate do you think the speaker's portrayals are? Is the speaker
    stereotyping the two women?
3. What comment do you think the poem is making about education?
    About society? About women? About African-American women?

Journal Entry

Brooks wrote "Sadie and Maud" in 1945. What changes do you think she
would have to make if she wrote her poem today?

Thematic Connections

- "Finishing School" (page 101)
- Declaration of Sentiments and Resolutions (page 590)
- "Strange Tools" (page 743)

WRITING ASSIGNMENTS FOR COMPARISON AND CONTRAST

1. Find a description of the same news event in two different magazines or newspapers. Write a comparison-and-contrast essay discussing the similarities and differences between the two stories.

2. In the library, locate two children's books on the same subject — one written in the 1950s and one written within the past ten years. Write an essay discussing which elements are the same and which are different. Include a thesis statement about the significance of the differences between the two books.

3. Write an essay about a relative or friend you have known since you were a child. Consider how your opinion of this person is different now from what it was then.

4. Write an essay comparing and contrasting the expectations that college professors and high school teachers have for their students. Cite your own experiences as examples.

5. Since you started college, how have you changed? Write an essay that answers this question.

6. Taking careful notes, watch a local television news program and then a national news broadcast. Write an essay comparing the two programs, paying particular attention to the news content and to the journalists' broadcasting styles.

7. Write an essay comparing your own early memories of school with those of a parent or an older relative.

8. How are the attitudes toward education different among students who work to finance their own education and students who do not? Your thesis statement should indicate what differences exist and why.

9. Compare and contrast the college experiences of commuters and students who live in dorms on campus. Interview people in your classes to use as examples.

10. Write an essay comparing any two groups that have divergent values — vegetarians and meat eaters or smokers and nonsmokers, for example.

11. How is being a participant — playing a sport or acting in a play, for instance — different from being a spectator? Write a comparison-and-contrast essay in which you answer this question.

COLLABORATIVE ACTIVITY FOR COMPARISON AND CONTRAST

Form groups of four students. Assume your college has hired these groups as consultants to suggest solutions for several problems students have been complaining about. Select the four areas — food, campus safety, parking, and class scheduling, for example — you think need improvement. Then, as a group, write a short report to your college describing the present conditions in these areas, and compare them to the improvements you envision. (Be sure to organize your report as a comparison-and-contrast essay.) Finally, have one person from each group read the group's report to the class. Decide as a class which group has the best suggestion.

INTERNET ASSIGNMENT FOR COMPARISON AND CONTRAST

Write an essay comparing and contrasting the media coverage of men's and women's professional athletics. Use the following Web sites to familiarize yourself with how the media covers men's and women's sports.

CNN Sports Illustrated
<sportsillustrated.cnn.com>
This site offers up-to-the-minute sports coverage.

ESPN.com
<espn.go.com>
This site covers both men's and women's sports teams on both collegiate and professional levels.

Feminist Majority Foundation
<feminist.org/sports/>
This site includes a spotlight on women's sports, links to sports magazines, information on grants and scholarships for athletes, and links to publications covering such topics as inequity and sex discrimination in sports.

12
Classification and Division

What Is Classification and Division?

Division is the process of breaking a whole into parts; **classification** is the process of sorting individual items into categories. In the following paragraph from "Pregnant with Possibility," Gregory J. E. Rawlins divides Americans into categories based on their access to computer technology:

Topic sentence identifies categories

Today's computer technology is rapidly turning us into three completely new races: the superpoor, the rich, and the superrich. The superpoor are perhaps eight thousand in every ten thousand of us. The rich—me and you—make up most of the remaining two thousand, while the superrich are perhaps the last two of every ten thousand. Roughly speaking, the decisions of two superrich people control what almost two thousand of us do, and our decisions, in turn, control what the remaining eight thousand do. These groups are really like races since the group you're born into often determines which group your children will be born into.

Through **classification and division**, we can make sense of seemingly random ideas by putting scattered bits of information into useful, coherent order. By breaking a large group into smaller categories and assigning individual items to larger categories, we can identify relationships between a whole and its parts and relationships among the parts themselves. Remember, though, that classification involves more than simply comparing two items or enumerating examples; when you classify, you sort examples into a variety of different categories.

In countless practical situations, classification and division brings order to chaos. Items in a Sunday newspaper are *classified* in clearly defined sections—international news, sports, travel, entertainment, and so on—

so that hockey scores, for example, are not mixed up with real estate listings. Similarly, department stores are *divided* into different departments so that managers can assign merchandise to particular areas and shoppers can know where to look for a particular item. Thus, order is brought to newspapers and department stores—and to supermarkets, biological hierarchies, and libraries—when a whole is divided into categories or sections and individual items are assigned to one or another of these subgroups.

Understanding Classification

Even though the interrelated processes of classification and division invariably occur together, they are two separate operations. When you **classify**, you begin with individual items and sort them into categories. Since a given item invariably has several different attributes, it can be classified in various ways. For example, the most obvious way to classify the students who attend your school might be according to their year in college. But you could also classify students according to their major, racial or ethnic background, home state, grade-point average, or any number of other principles. The **principle of classification** you choose—the quality your items have in common—would depend on how you wish to approach the members of this large and diverse group.

Understanding Division

Division is the opposite of classification. When you **divide**, you start with a whole (an entire class) and break it into its individual parts. For example, you might start with the large general class *television shows* and divide it into categories: *comedy, drama, action/adventure, reality shows,* and so forth. You could then divide each of these still further. *Action/adventure programs,* for example, might include *Westerns, crime dramas, spy dramas,* and so on—and each of these categories could be further divided as well. Eventually, you would need to identify a particular principle of classification to help you assign specific programs to one category or another—that is, to classify them.

Using Classification and Division

Whenever you write an essay, you use classification and division to bring order to the invention stage of the writing process. For example, when you brainstorm, as Chapter 2 explains, you begin with your paper's topic and list all the related points you can think of. Next, you *divide* your topic into logical categories and *classify* the items in your brainstorming notes into one category or another, perhaps narrowing, expanding, or eliminating some categories — or some points — as you go along. This sorting and grouping enables you to condense and shape your material until it eventually suggests a thesis and the main points your essay will develop.

More specifically, certain topics and questions, because of the way they are worded, immediately suggest a classification-and-division pattern. Suppose, for example, you are asked, "What kinds of policies can be implemented to reduce the nation's budget deficit?" Here, the word *kinds* suggests classification and division. Other words — such as *types, varieties, aspects,* and *categories* — can also indicate that this pattern is called for.

Planning a Classification-and-Division Essay

Once you decide to use a classification-and-division pattern, you need to identify a **principle of classification**. Every group of people, things, or ideas can be categorized in many ways. When you are at your college bookstore with limited funds, the cost of different books may be the only principle of classification you use when deciding which ones to buy. As you consider which books to carry across campus, however, weight may matter more. Finally, as you study and read, the usefulness of the books will determine which ones you concentrate on. Similarly, when you organize an essay, the principle of classification you choose is determined by your writing situation — your assignment, your purpose, your audience, and your special knowledge and interests.

Selecting and Arranging Categories

After you define your principle of classification and apply it to your topic, you should select your categories by dividing a whole class into parts and grouping a number of different items together within each part. Next, you should decide how you will treat the categories in your essay. Just as a comparison-and-contrast essay makes comparable points about its subjects, so your classification-and-division essay should treat all categories similarly. When you discuss comparable points for each category, your readers are able to understand your distinctions among categories as well as your definition of each category.

Finally, you should arrange your categories in some logical order so that readers can see how the categories are related and what their relative importance is. Whatever order you choose, it should be consistent with your purpose and with your essay's thesis.

✓ CHECKLIST: **Establishing Categories**

- **All the categories should derive from the same principle.** If you decide to divide *television shows* into *soap operas, crime shows,* and the like, it is not logical to include *children's programs,* for this category results from one principle (target audience) while the others result from another principle (genre). Similarly, if you were classifying undergraduates at your school according to their year, you would not include the category *students receiving financial aid.*

- **All the categories should be at the same level.** In the series *comedy, drama, action/adventure,* and *Westerns,* the last item, *Westerns,* does not belong because it is at a lower level—that is, it is a subcategory of *action/adventure.* Likewise, *sophomores* (a subcategory of *undergraduates*) does not belong in the series *undergraduates, graduate students, continuing education students.*

- **You should treat all categories that are significant and relevant to your discussion.** Include enough categories to make your point, with no important omissions and no overlapping categories. In a review of a network's fall television lineup, the series *sitcoms, soap operas, crime shows,* and *detective shows* is incomplete because it omits important categories such as *news programs, game shows, reality shows,* and *documentaries;* moreover, *detective shows* may overlap with *crime shows.* In the same way, the series *freshmen, sophomores, juniors,* and *transfers* is illogical: the important group *seniors* has been omitted, and *transfers* may include *freshmen, sophomores,* and *juniors.*

Formulating a Thesis Statement

Like other kinds of essays, a classification-and-division essay should have a thesis. Your **thesis statement** should identify your subject, introduce the categories you will discuss, and perhaps show readers the relationships of your categories to one another and to the subject as a whole. In addition, your thesis statement should tell your readers why your categories are significant or establish their relative value. For example, simply listing different kinds of investments would be pointless. Instead, your thesis statement might note their relative strengths and weaknesses and perhaps make recommendations based on your assessment. Similarly, a research paper about a writer's major works would accomplish little if it merely categorized his or her writings. Instead, your thesis statement should communicate your evaluation of these works, perhaps demonstrating that some deserve higher public regard than others.

Using Transitions

When you write a classification-and-division essay, you use transitional words and phrases both to introduce your categories (*the first category, one category,* and so on) and to move readers from one category to the next (*the second category, the next category, another category,* and so on). In addition, transitional words and expressions can show readers the relationships between categories — for example, whether one category is more important than another (*a more important category, the most important category,* and so on). A more complete list of transitions appears on page 43.

Structuring a Classification-and-Division Essay

Once you have formulated your essay's thesis and established your categories, you should plan your classification-and-division essay around the same three major sections that other essays have: *introduction, body,* and *conclusion.* Your **introduction** should orient your readers by mentioning your topic, the principle for classifying your material, and the individual categories you plan to discuss; your thesis is also usually stated in the introduction. In the subsequent **body paragraphs**, you should treat the categories one by one in the same order as in your introduction. Finally, your **conclusion** should restate your thesis, summing up the points you have made and perhaps considering their implications.

Suppose you are preparing a research paper on Mark Twain's nonfiction works for an American literature course. You have read selections from *Roughing It, Life on the Mississippi,* and *The Innocents Abroad.* Besides these travel narratives, you have read parts of Twain's autobiography and some of his correspondence and essays. When you realize that the works you have studied can easily be classified as four different types of Twain's nonfiction — travel narratives, essays, letters, and autobiography — you decide to use classification and division to structure your essay. Therefore, you first divide the large class *Twain's nonfiction prose* into major categories — his travel narratives, essays, autobiography, and letters. Then, you classify the individual works, assigning each work to one of these categories, which you will discuss one at a time. Your purpose is to persuade readers to reconsider the reputations of some of these works, and you word your thesis statement accordingly. You might then prepare a formal outline like the one that follows for the body of your paper:

> *Thesis statement:* Most readers know Mark Twain as a novelist, but his nonfiction works — his travel narratives, essays, letters, and especially his autobiography — deserve more attention.
> I. Travel narratives
>   A. *Roughing It*
>   B. *The Innocents Abroad*
>   C. *Life on the Mississippi*
> II. Essays
>   A. "Fenimore Cooper's Literary Offenses"
>   B. "How to Tell a Story"
>   C. "The Awful German Language"

III. Letters
    A. To W. D. Howells
    B. To his family
IV. Autobiography

Because this will be a long essay, each of the outline's divisions will have several subdivisions, and each subdivision might require several paragraphs.

This outline illustrates all the characteristics of an effective classification-and-division essay. To begin with, Twain's nonfiction works are classified according to a single principle of classification—literary genre. (Depending on your purpose, of course, another principle—such as theme or subject matter—could work just as well.) The outline also reveals that the paper's categories are on the same level (each is a different literary genre) and that all relevant categories are included. Had you left out *essays,* for example, you would have been unable to classify several significant works of nonfiction.

This outline also arranges the four categories so that they will support your thesis most effectively. Because you believe Twain's travel narratives are somewhat overrated, you plan to discuss them early in your paper. Similarly, because you think the autobiography would make your best case for the merit of the nonfiction works as a whole, you decide it should be placed last. (Of course, you could arrange your categories in several other orders, such as shorter to longer works or least to most popular, depending on the thesis your paper will support.)

Finally, this outline reminds you to treat all categories comparably in your paper. Your case would be weakened if, for example, you inadvertently skipped style in your discussion of Twain's letters while discussing style for every other category. This omission might lead your readers to suspect that you had not done enough research on the letters or that the style of Twain's letters did not measure up to the style of his other works.

Revising a Classification-and-Division Esssay

When you revise a classsification-and-division essay, consider the items on the revision checklist on page 54. In addition, pay special attention to the items on the following checklist, which apply specifically to revising classification-and-division essays.

✓ **REVISION CHECKLIST: Classification and Division**

- Does your assignment call for classification and division?
- Have you identified a principle of classification for your material?

- Have you identified the categories you plan to discuss and decided how you will treat them?
- Have you arranged your categories in a logical order?
- Have you treated all categories similarly?
- Does your essay have a clearly stated thesis that identifies your subject and the categories you will discuss and indicates the significance of your classification?
- Have you used transitional words and phrases to show the relationships among categories?

Editing a Classification-and-Division Essay

When you edit your classification-and-division essay, you should follow the guidelines on the editing checklists on pages 71, 73, and 76. In addition, you should focus on the grammar, mechanics, and punctuation issues that are particularly relevant to classification-and-division essays. One of these issues — using a colon to introduce your categories — is discussed below.

GRAMMAR IN CONTEXT: Using a Colon to Introduce Your Categories

When you state the thesis of a classification-and-division essay, you often give readers an overview by listing the categories you will discuss. You introduce this list of categories with a **colon**, a punctuation mark whose purpose is to direct readers to look ahead for a series, list, clarification, or explanation.

When you use a colon to introduce your categories, the colon must be preceded by a complete sentence.

CORRECT: "I see four kinds of pressure working on college students today: economic pressure, parental pressure, peer pressure, and self-induced pressure" (Zinsser 467).

INCORRECT: Four kinds of pressure working on college students today are: economic pressure, parental pressure, peer pressure, and self-induced pressure.

In any list or series of three or more categories, the categories should be separated by commas, with a comma preceding the *and* that separates the last two items. This last comma prevents confusion by ensuring that readers will be able to see at a glance exactly how many categories you are discussing.

(continued on next page)

(continued from previous page)

CORRECT: economic pressure, parental pressure, peer pressure, and self-induced pressure (four categories)

INCORRECT: economic pressure, parental pressure, peer pressure and self-induced pressure (without the final comma, it might appear you are only discussing three categories)

Note: Items in a list or series are always stated in **parallel** terms.

For more practice in using colons correctly, visit Exercise Central at <bedfordstmartins.com/patterns/colons>.

✓ **EDITING CHECKLIST: Classification and Division**

- Do you introduce your list of categories with a colon preceded by a complete sentence?
- Are the items on your list of categories separated by commas?
- Do you include a comma before the *and* that connects the last two items in your list?
- Do you state the items on your list in parallel terms?

A STUDENT WRITER: Classification and Division

The following classification-and-division essay was written by Josie Martinez for an education course. Her assignment was to look back at her own education and to consider what she had learned so far. The essay divides a whole — college classes — into four categories.

What I Learned (and Didn't Learn) in College

Introduction   College classes are as varied as the students who take   1
them. As a result, a class that is perfect for one student — in size, format, subject matter, and teaching style — may be the same class that another student hates and learns little or nothing from. Nevertheless, despite the variety of experiences that different students have with different courses, most

Categories listed   college classes can be classified into one of four categories: ideal classes, worthless classes, disappointing classes, and unexpectedly valuable classes.

Categories explained   First are courses that students love — ideal learning   2
environments in which they enjoy both the subject matter and

the professor-student interaction. Far from these ideal courses are those that students find completely worthless in terms of subject matter, atmosphere, and teaching style. Somewhere between these two extremes are two kinds of courses that can be classified into another pair of opposites: courses that students expect to enjoy and to learn much from but are disappointing and courses that students are initially not interested in but that exceed their expectations. Knowing that these four categories exist can help students accept the fact that one disappointing class is not a disaster.

Thesis statement

First category: ideal class   One of the best courses I have taken so far as a college   3
student was my Shakespeare class. The professor who taught it had a great sense of humor and was liberal in terms of what she allowed in her classroom — for example, controversial Shakespeare adaptations and virtually any discussion, relevant or irrelevant. The students in the class — English majors and non-English majors, those who were interested in the plays as theater and those who preferred to study them as literature — shared an enthusiasm for Shakespeare, and they were eager to engage in lively discussions of the material. This class gave us a thorough knowledge of Shakespeare's plays (tragedies, histories, comedies) as well as an understanding of his life. We also developed our analytical skills through our discussions of the plays and films, as well as through special projects, which included a character profile presentation and an abstract art presentation relating a work of art to one of the plays. This class was an ideal learning environment not only because of the wealth of material we were exposed to but also because of the respect with which our professor treated us: we were her colleagues, and she was as willing to learn from us as we were to learn from her.

Second category: worthless class   In contrast to this ideal class, one of the most worthless   4
courses I have taken in college was Movement Education. As an education major, I expected to like this class, and several other students who had taken it told me it was both easy and enjoyable. The class consisted of playing children's games and learning the theory behind what made certain activities appropriate and inappropriate for children of various ages. The only requirement for this class was that we had to write note

cards explaining how to play each game so that we could use them for reference in our future teaching experiences. Unfortunately, I never really enjoyed the games we played, and I have long since discarded my note cards and forgotten how to play the games — or even what they were.

Third category: disappointing class

Although I looked forward to taking Introduction to Astronomy, I was very disappointed in this class. I had hoped to satisfy my curiosity about the universe outside our solar system, but the instructor devoted most of the semester to a detailed study of the earth and the other bodies in our own solar system. In addition, a large part of our work included charting orbits and processing distance equations — work that I found both difficult and boring. Furthermore, we spent little class time learning how to use a telescope and locate objects in the sky. In short, I gained little information from the class, learning only how to solve equations I would never confront again and how to chart orbits that had already been charted.

Fourth category: unexpectedly valuable class

In direct contrast to my astronomy class, a religion class called Paul and the Early Church was much more rewarding than I had anticipated. Having attended Catholic school for thirteen years, I assumed this course would offer me little that was new to me. However, because the class took a historical approach to studying Paul's biblical texts, I found that I learned more about Christianity than I had in all my previous religion classes. We learned about the historical validity of Paul and other texts in the Bible and how they were derived from various sources and passed orally through several generations before being written down and translated into different languages. We approached the texts from a linguistic perspective, determining the significance of certain words and how various meanings can be derived from different translations of the same passage. This class was unlike any of my other religion classes in that it encouraged me to study the texts objectively, leaving me with a new and valuable understanding of material I had been exposed to for most of my life.

Conclusion

Although each student's learning experience in college will be different — because every student has a different learning style, is interested in different subjects, and takes courses at different schools taught by different professors — all

5

6

7

Summary of four categories

college students' experiences are similar in one respect. All students will encounter the same kinds of courses: those that are ideal, those that are worthless, those that they learn little from despite their interest in the subject, and those that they learn from and become engaged in despite their low

Restatement of thesis

expectations. Understanding that these categories exist is important because it can teach students that even if one course is a disappointment, another may be more interesting — or even exciting. For this reason, they should not be discouraged by a course they do not like; the best classes are almost certainly still in their future.

Points for Special Attention

Thesis and Support.   Josie's purpose in writing this essay was to communicate to her professor and the other students in her education class what she had learned from the classes she had taken so far in college. Knowing that few, if any, students in her class would have taken any of the same courses, Josie knew she had to provide a lot of detail. She was also careful to include a thesis that made her purpose clear to her readers.

Organization.   As she reviewed the various courses she had taken and took stock of their strengths and weaknesses, Josie saw a classification scheme emerging. As soon as she noticed this, she organized her material into four categories. Rather than discuss the four kinds of classes from best to worst or from worst to best, Josie decided to present them as two opposing pairs: ideal class and worthless class, surprisingly disappointing class and unexpectedly worthwhile class.

Overview of Categories.   In paragraph 1, Josie lists the four categories she plans to discuss in her essay. Then, in paragraph 2, she gives readers an overview of these categories to help prepare them for her thesis.

Transitions between Categories.   Josie uses clear topic sentences to move readers from one category to the next and indicate the relationship of each category to another.

"One of the best college courses I have taken so far as a college student was my Shakespeare class." (3)

"In contrast to this ideal class, one of the most worthless courses I have taken in college was Movement Education." (4)

"Although I looked forward to taking Introduction to Astronomy, I was very disappointed in this class." (5)

"In direct contrast to my astronomy class, a religion class called Paul and the Early Church was much more rewarding than I had anticipated." (6)

These four sentences distinguish the four categories from one another and also help to communicate Josie's direction and emphasis.

Focus on Revision

An earlier draft of Josie's essay, which she discussed with her classmates in a peer editing session, did not include very helpful topic sentences. Instead, the sentences were vague and unfocused:

"One class I took in college was a Shakespeare course."

"Another class I took was Movement Education."

"I looked forward to taking Introduction to Astronomy."

"My experience with a religion class was very different."

Although her first two paragraphs listed the categories and explained how they differed, Josie's classmates advised her to revise her topic sentences so that it would be clear which category she was discussing in each body paragraph. Josie took the advice of her peer editing group and revised these topic sentences. After reading her next draft, she felt confident that her categories — listed in paragraph 1 and repeated in paragraph 2, in her topic sentences, and again in her conclusion — were clear and distinct.

Even after making these revisions, however, Josie felt her paper needed some additional fine-tuning. For example, in her final draft, she planned to add some material to paragraphs 4 and 5. At first, because she had dismissed Movement Education as completely worthless and Introduction to Astronomy as disappointing, Josie felt she did not have to say much about them. When she reread her paper, however, she realized she needed to explain the shortcomings of the two classes more fully so that her readers would understand why these classes had little value for her.

📄 **PEER EDITING WORKSHEET: Classification and Division**

1. What thesis does the body of the essay support? Is this thesis explicitly stated?
2. What whole is being divided into parts in this essay? Into what general categories is the whole divided?
3. Is each category clearly identified and explained? If not, what revisions can you suggest? (For example, can you suggest a different title for a particular category?)
4. Does the writer list the categories to be discussed? Is the list introduced by a colon (preceded by a complete sentence)?

5. Are the categories arranged in a logical order, one that indicates their relationships to one another and their relative importance? If not, how could they be rearranged?

6. Does the writer treat all relevant categories and no irrelevant ones? Which categories, if any, should be added, deleted, or combined?

7. Does the writer include all necessary items, and no unnecessary ones, within each category? What additional items could be added? Should any items be located elsewhere?

8. Does the writer treat all categories similarly, discussing comparable points for each? Should any additional points be discussed? If so, where?

9. Do topic sentences clearly signal the movement from one category to the next? Should any topic sentences be strengthened to mark the boundaries between categories more clearly? If so, which ones?

10. Could the writer use another pattern of development to structure this essay? Is classification and division the best choice? Explain.

Each of the following selections is developed by means of classification and division. In some cases, the pattern is used to explain ideas; in others, it is used to persuade the reader. The first selection, a pair of visual texts, is followed by questions designed to illustrate how classification and division can operate in visual form.

Key to Chalk Marks Designating Medical Conditions of Immigrants, Ellis Island (Chart)

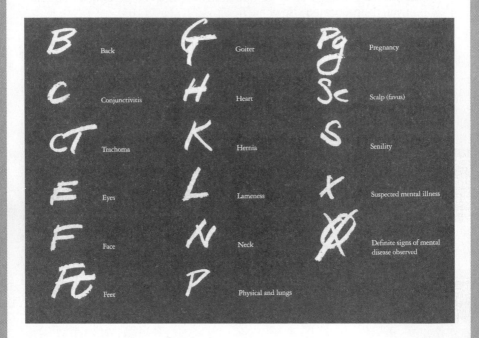

B — Back	G — Goiter	Pg — Pregnancy
C — Conjunctivitis	H — Heart	Sc — Scalp (favus)
CT — Trachoma	K — Hernia	S — Senility
E — Eyes	L — Lameness	X — Suspected mental illness
F — Face	N — Neck	Ø — Definite signs of mental disease observed
Ft — Feet	P — Physical and lungs	

• • •

Reading Images

1. The photo on this page shows symbols, written on chalk on immigrants' clothing, representing medical conditions that could disqualify them from entry into the United States. The photo on the next page depicts immigrants lined up for exams to check for the presence of one such condition — trachoma, a contagious eye disease. What different principles of classification might be used to assign the symbols into categories? Which principle of classification seems to make the most sense? Why?

2. Guided by the principle of classification you selected in question 1, arrange the various symbols into three or four logical categories. Are there any that do not fit into your classification scheme?

Eye Exam Administered to Immigrants, Ellis Island, 1910 (Photo)

• • •

3. What medical conditions do you think might disqualify an immigrant for entry into the United States today? List some possible criteria for exclusion, and arrange these criteria into categories.

Journal Entry

Do you think the United States should exclude any potential immigrants solely for medical reasons? Why or why not?

Thematic Connections

- "Words Left Unspoken" (page 168)
- "The Catbird Seat" (page 227)
- "Why Fear National ID Cards?" (page 618)

WILLIAM ZINSSER

College Pressures

Born in 1922 in New York City, William Zinsser graduated from Princeton University in 1944. He worked at the *New York Herald Tribune* as a feature and editorial writer, and he was a columnist for *Life* magazine and the *New York Times*. Zinsser has also taught English at Yale University and is the author of numerous books on writing, including *On Writing Well: The Classic Guide to Writing Nonfiction* (twenty-fifth anniversary edition, 2001) and *Writing about Your Life: A Journey into the Past* (2004). He has also written works on American culture, including *Spring Training* (1989), about the culture of baseball, and *Easy to Remember: Great American Songwriters and Their Songs* (2001).

Background on college pressures today: Although the following essay focuses on the kinds of pressures facing Yale students in 1979, many of these remain relevant for college students today: the need to develop time management and study skills appropriate for college work, the desire for good grades, the desire to meet familial expectations, and the need to find employment in a competitive job market after graduation. In addition, many college students today face pressures unknown to most students in the late 1970s. According to the U.S. Department of Education's National Center for Education Statistics, only about 25 percent of current undergraduates fit the "traditional" model of eighteen- to twenty-two-year-old full-time students still supported primarily by their parents. Increasingly, college undergraduates are adults, supporting themselves—and sometimes families—and funding their own education through full- or part-time employment. Moreover, the average student faces some $18,900 of college-related debt by the time he or she graduates.

Dear Carlos: I desperately need a dean's excuse for my chem midterm which will begin in about 1 hour. All I can say is that I totally blew it this week. I've fallen incredibly, inconceivably behind.   1

Carlos: Help! I'm anxious to hear from you. I'll be in my room and won't leave it until I hear from you. Tomorrow is the last day for. . . .   2

Carlos: I left town because I started bugging out again. I stayed up all night to finish a take home make-up exam and am typing it to hand in on the 10th. It was due on the 5th. P.S. I'm going to the dentist. Pain is pretty bad.   3

Carlos: Probably by Friday I'll be able to get back to my studies. Right now I'm going to take a long walk. This whole thing has taken a lot out of me.   4

Carlos: I'm really up the proverbial creek. The problem is I really *bombed* the history final. Since I need that course for my major. . . .   5

Carlos: Here follows a tale of woe. I went home this weekend, had to help   6
my Mom, & caught a fever so didn't have much time to study. My professor . . .

Carlos: Aargh! Nothing original but everything's piling up at once. To be   7
brief, my job interview . . .

Hey Carlos, good news! I've got mononucleosis.   8

Who are these wretched supplicants, scribbling notes so laden with   9
anxiety, seeking such miracles of postponement and balm? They are men
and women who belong to Bradford College, one of the twelve residential
colleges at Yale University, and the messages are just a few of the hundreds
that they left for their dean, Carlos Hortas — often slipped under his door
at 4 A.M. — last year.

But students like the ones who wrote those notes can also be found on   10
campuses from coast to coast — especially in New England and at many
other private colleges across the country that have high academic standards and highly motivated students. Nobody could doubt that the notes
are real. In their urgency and their gallows humor they are authentic voices
of a generation that is panicky to succeed.

My own connection with the message writers is that I am master of   11
Bradford College. I live in its Gothic quadrangle and know the students
well. (We have 485 of them.) I am privy to their hopes and fears — and also
to their stereo music and their piercing cries in the dead of night ("Does
anybody ca-a-are?"). If they went to Carlos to ask how to get through
tomorrow, they come to me to ask how to get through the rest of their
lives.

Mainly I try to remind them that the road ahead is a long one and that   12
it will have more unexpected turns than they think. There will be plenty
of time to change jobs, change careers, change whole attitudes and
approaches. They don't want to hear such liberating news. They want a
map — right now — that they can follow unswervingly to career security,
financial security, Social Security, and, presumably, a prepaid grave.

What I wish for all students is some release from the clammy grip of   13
the future. I wish them a chance to savor each segment of their education
as an experience in itself and not as a grim preparation for the next step. I
wish them the right to experiment, to trip and fall, to learn that defeat is as
instructive as victory and is not the end of the world.

My wish, of course, is naive. One of the few rights that America does   14
not proclaim is the right to fail. Achievement is the national god, venerated
in our media — the million-dollar athlete, the wealthy executive — and glo-
rified in our praise of possessions. In the presence of such a potent state
religion, the young are growing up old.

I see four kinds of pressure working on college students today: eco-   15
nomic pressure, parental pressure, peer pressure, and self-induced pressure. It is easy to look around for villains — to blame the colleges for

charging too much money, the professors for assigning too much work, the parents for pushing their children too far, the students for driving themselves too hard. But there are no villains, only victims.

"In the late 1960s," one dean told me, "the typical question that I got from students was 'Why is there so much suffering in the world?' or 'How can I make a contribution?' Today it's 'Do you think it would look better for getting into law school if I did a double major in history and political science, or just majored in one of them?'" Many other deans confirmed this pattern. One said: "They're trying to find an edge — the intangible something that will look better on paper if two students are about equal."   16

Note the emphasis on looking better. The transcript has become a sacred document, the passport to security. How one appears on paper is more important than how one appears in person. *A* is for Admirable and *B* is for Borderline, even though, in Yale's official system of grading, *A* means "excellent" and *B* means "very good." Today, looking very good is no longer good enough, especially for students who hope to go on to law school or medical school. They know that entrance into the better schools will be an entrance into the better law firms and better medical practices where they will make a lot of money. They also know that the odds are harsh. Yale Law School, for instance, matriculates 170 students from an applicant pool of 3,700; Harvard enrolls 550 from a pool of 7,000.   17

It's all very well for those of us who write letters of recommendation for our students to stress the qualities of humanity that will make them good lawyers or doctors. And it's nice to think that admission officers are really reading our letters and looking for the extra dimension of commitment or concern. Still, it would be hard for a student not to visualize these officers shuffling so many transcripts studded with *A*s that they regard a *B* as positively shameful.   18

The pressure is almost as heavy on students who just want to graduate and get a job. Long gone are the days of the "gentleman's *C*," when students journeyed through college with a certain relaxation, sampling a wide variety of courses — music, art, philosophy, classics, anthropology, poetry, religion — that would send them out as liberally educated men and women. If I were an employer I would rather employ graduates who have this range and curiosity than those who narrowly pursued safe subjects and high grades. I know countless students whose inquiring minds exhilarate me. I like to hear the play of their ideas. I don't know if they're getting *A*s or *C*s, and I don't care. I also like them as people. The country needs them, and they will find satisfying jobs. I tell them to relax. They can't.   19

Nor can I blame them. They live in a brutal economy. Tuition, room, and board at most private colleges now comes to at least $7,000, not counting books and fees.* This might seem to suggest that the colleges are get-   20

---

* Eds. note — Zinsser's essay was published in 1979; the figures quoted for tuition and other expenses would be much higher today.

ting rich. But they are equally battered by inflation. Tuition covers only 60 percent of what it costs to educate a student, and ordinarily the remainder comes from what colleges receive in endowments, grants, and gifts. Now the remainder keeps being swallowed by cruel costs — higher every year — of just opening the doors. Heating oil is up. Insurance is up. Postage is up. Health-premium costs are up. Everything is up. Deficits are up. We are witnessing in America the creation of a brotherhood of paupers — colleges, parents, and students, joined by the common bond of debt.

Today it is not unusual for a student, even if he works part time at col- 21 lege and full time during the summer, to accrue $5,000 in loans after four years — loans that he must start to repay within one year after graduation. Exhorted at commencement to go forth into the world, he is already behind as he goes forth. How could he not feel under pressure throughout college to prepare for this day of reckoning? I have used "he" incidentally, only for brevity. Women at Yale are under no less pressure to justify their expensive education to themselves, their parents, and society. In fact, they are probably under more pressure. For although they leave college superbly equipped to bring fresh leadership to traditionally male jobs, society hasn't yet caught up with this fact.

Along with economic pressure goes parental pressure. Inevitably, the 22 two are deeply intertwined.

I see many students taking pre-medical courses with joyless tenacity. 23 They go off to their labs as if they were going to the dentist. It saddens me because I know them in other corners of their life as cheerful people.

"Do you want to go to medical school?" I ask them. 24

"I guess so," they say, without conviction, or "Not really." 25

"Then why are you going?" 26

"Well, my parents want me to be a doctor. They're paying all this 27 money and . . ."

Poor students, poor parents. They are caught in one of the oldest webs 28 of love and duty and guilt. The parents mean well; they are trying to steer their sons and daughters toward a secure future. But the sons and daughters want to major in history or classics or philosophy — subjects with no "practical" value. Where's the payoff on the humanities? It's not easy to persuade such loving parents that the humanities do indeed pay off. The intellectual faculties developed by studying subjects like history and classics — an ability to synthesize and relate, to weigh cause and effect, to see events in perspective — are just the faculties that make creative leaders in business or almost any general field. Still, many fathers would rather put their money on courses that point toward a specific profession — courses that are pre-law, pre-medical, pre-business, or, as I sometimes heard it put, "pre-rich."

But the pressure on students is severe. They are truly torn. One part of 29 them feels obliged to fulfill their parents' expectations; after all, their parents are older and presumably wiser. Another part tells them that the expectations that are right for their parents are not right for them.

I know a student who wants to be an artist. She is very obviously an artist and will be a good one — she has already had several modest exhibits. Meanwhile she is growing as a well-rounded person and taking humanistic subjects that will enrich the inner resources out of which her art will grow. But her father is strongly opposed. He thinks that an artist is a "dumb" thing to be. The student vacillates and tries to please everybody. She keeps up with her art somewhat furtively and takes some of the "dumb" courses her father wants her to take — at least they are dumb courses for her. She is a free spirit on a campus of tense students — no small achievement in itself — and she deserves to follow her muse.

Peer pressure and self-induced pressure are also intertwined, and they begin almost at the beginning of freshman year.

"I had a freshman student I'll call Linda," one dean told me, "who came in and said she was under terrible pressure because her roommate, Barbara, was much brighter and studied all the time. I couldn't tell her that Barbara had come in two hours earlier to say the same thing about Linda."

The story is almost funny — except that it's not. It's symptomatic of all the pressures put together. When every student thinks every other student is working harder and doing better, the only solution is to study harder still. I see students going off to the library every night after dinner and coming back when it closes at midnight. I wish they could sometimes forget about their peers and go to a movie. I hear the clacking of typewriters in the hours before dawn. I see the tension in their eyes when exams are approaching and papers are due: *"Will I get everything done?"*

Probably they won't. They will get sick. They will get "blocked." They will sleep. They will oversleep. They will bug out. *Hey Carlos, help!*

Part of the problem is that they do more than they are expected to do. A professor will assign five-page papers. Several students will start writing ten-page papers to impress him. Then more students will write ten-page papers, and a few will raise the ante to fifteen. Pity the poor student who is still just doing the assignment.

"Once you have twenty or thirty percent of the student population deliberately overexerting," one dean points out, "it's bad for everybody. When a teacher gets more and more effort from his class, the student who is doing normal work can be perceived as not doing well. The tactic works, psychologically."

Why can't the professor just cut back and not accept longer papers? He can, and he probably will. But by then the term will be half over and the damage done. Grade fever is highly contagious and not easily reversed. Besides, the professor's main concern is with his course. He knows his students only in relation to the course and doesn't know that they are also overexerting in their other courses. Nor is it really his business. He didn't sign up for dealing with the student as a whole person and with all the emotional baggage the student brought along from home. That's what deans, masters, chaplains, and psychiatrists are for.

To some extent this is nothing new: a certain number of professors   38
have always been self-contained islands of scholarship and shyness, more
comfortable with books than with people. But the new pauperism has
widened the gap still further, for professors who actually like to spend time
with students don't have as much time to spend. They also are overexerting. If they are young, they are busy trying to publish in order not to per-
ish, hanging by their fingernails onto a shrinking profession. If they are
old and tenured, they are buried under the duties of administering departments — as departmental chairmen or members of committees — that have
been thinned out by the budgetary axe.

Ultimately it will be the students' own business to break the circles in   39
which they are trapped. They are too young to be prisoners of their parents' dreams and their classmates' fears. They must be jolted into believing
in themselves as unique men and women who have the power to shape
their own future.

"Violence is being done to the undergraduate experience," says Carlos   40
Hortas. "College should be open-ended: at the end it should open many,
many roads. Instead, students are choosing their goal in advance, and their
choices narrow as they go along. It's almost as if they think that the country has been codified in the type of jobs that exist — that they've got to fit
into certain slots. Therefore, fit into the best-paying slot.

"They ought to take chances. Not taking chances will lead to a life of   41
colorless mediocrity. They'll be comfortable. But something in the spirit
will be missing."

I have painted too drab a portrait of today's students, making them   42
seem a solemn lot. That is only half of their story; if they were so dreary I
wouldn't so thoroughly enjoy their company. The other half is that they
are easy to like. They are quick to laugh and to offer friendship. They are
not introverts. They are usually kind and are more considerate of one
another than any student generation I have known.

Nor are they so obsessed with their studies that they avoid sports and   43
extracurricular activities. On the contrary, they juggle their crowded hours
to play on a variety of teams, perform with musical and dramatic groups,
and write for campus publications. But this in turn is one more cause of
anxiety. There are too many choices. Academically, they have 1,300 courses
to select from; outside class they have to decide how much spare time they
can spare and how to spend it.

This means that they engage in fewer extracurricular pursuits than   44
their predecessors did. If they want to row on the crew and play in the sym-
phony they will eliminate one; in the '60s they would have done both. They
also tend to choose activities that are self-limiting. Drama, for instance, is
flourishing in all twelve of Yale's residential colleges as it never has before.
Students hurl themselves into these productions — as actors, directors, carpenters, and technicians — with a dedication to create the best possible
play, knowing that the day will come when the run will end and they can
get back to their studies.

They also can't afford to be the willing slave of organizations like the   45
Yale Daily News. Last spring at the one-hundredth anniversary banquet of
that paper — whose past chairmen include such once and future kings as
Potter Stewart, Kingman Brewster, and William F. Buckley, Jr.* — much was
made of the fact that the editorial staff used to be small and totally committed and that "newsies" routinely worked fifty hours a week. In effect
they belonged to a club; Newsies is how they defined themselves at Yale.
Today's student will write one or two articles a week, when he can, and he
defines himself as a student. I've never heard the word Newsie except at the
banquet.

If I have described the modern undergraduate primarily as a driven   46
creature who is largely ignoring the blithe spirit inside who keeps trying to
come out and play, it's because that's where the crunch is, not only at Yale
but throughout American education. It's why I think we should all be worried about the values that are nurturing a generation so fearful of risk and
so goal-obsessed at such an early age.

I tell students that there is no one "right" way to get ahead — that each   47
of them is a different person, starting from a different point and bound for
a different destination. I tell them that change is a tonic and that all the
slots are not codified nor the frontiers closed. One of my ways of telling
them is to invite men and women who have achieved success outside the
academic world to come and talk informally with my students during the
year. They are heads of companies or ad agencies, editors of magazines,
politicians, public officials, television magnates, labor leaders, business
executives, Broadway producers, artists, writers, economists, photographers, scientists, historians — a mixed bag of achievers.

I ask them to say a few words about how they got started. The students   48
assume that they started in their present profession and knew all along
that it was what they wanted to do. Luckily for me, most of them got into
their field by a circuitous route, to their surprise, after many detours. The
students are startled. They can hardly conceive of a career that was not pre-
planned. They can hardly imagine allowing the hand of God or chance to
nudge them down some unforeseen trail.

•   •   •

Comprehension

1. What advice does Zinsser give students when they bring their problems to him?
2. What does Zinsser wish for his students? Why does he believe his wish
   is naive?

---

* EDS. NOTE — Stewart is a former U.S. Supreme Court Justice, Brewster is a former
president of Yale, and Buckley is a conservative editor and columnist.

3. What four kinds of pressure does Zinsser identify?

4. Whom does Zinsser blame for the existence of these pressures? Explain.

5. How, according to Zinsser, is his evaluation of students different from their own and from their potential employers' assessments?

6. Why does Zinsser believe that women are probably under even more pressure than men? Do you agree with him?

7. How does what Zinsser calls the "new pauperism" (38) affect professors?

8. Who, according to Zinsser, is ultimately responsible for eliminating college pressures? Explain.

9. In what sense are sports and other extracurricular activities another source of anxiety for students? How do students adapt to this pressure?

Purpose and Audience

1. In your own words, state Zinsser's thesis. Is his intent in this essay simply to expose a difficult situation or to effect change? Explain.

2. On what kind of audience do you think this essay would have the most significant impact: students, teachers, parents, potential employers, graduate school admissions committees, or college administrators? Why?

3. What do you think Zinsser hopes to accomplish in paragraphs 42–46? How would the essay be different without this section?

4. What assumptions does Zinsser make about his audience? Do you think these assumptions are valid? Explain.

Style and Structure

1. Evaluate the essay's introductory strategy. What impact do you think the notes to Carlos are likely to have on readers?

2. Identify the boundaries of Zinsser's actual classification. How does he introduce the first category? How does he indicate that his treatment of the final category is complete?

3. What function do paragraphs 22 and 31 serve in the essay?

4. Zinsser is careful to explain that when he refers to students as *he*, he includes female students as well. However, he also refers to professors as *he* (for example, in paragraphs 35–37). Assuming that not all professors at Yale are male, what other stylistic options does Zinsser have in this situation?

5. At various points in the essay, Zinsser quotes deans and students at Yale. What is the effect of these quotations?

6. Zinsser notes that his categories are "intertwined" (22, 31). In what ways do the categories overlap? Does this overlap weaken the essay? Explain.

7. What, if anything, seems to determine the order of Zinsser's categories? Is this order effective? Why, or why not?

Vocabulary Projects

1. Define each of the following words as it is used in this selection.

proverbial (5)	intangible (16)	blithe (46)
supplicants (9)	accrue (21)	tonic (47)
balm (9)	exhorted (21)	codified (47)
privy (11)	tenacity (23)	
venerated (14)	faculties (28)	

2. At times Zinsser uses religious language—*national god, sacred document*—to describe the students' quest for success. Identify other examples of such language, and explain why it is used.

Journal Entry

Which of the pressures Zinsser identifies has the strongest impact on you? Why? Do you have any other pressures Zinsser does not mention?

Writing Workshop

1. Zinsser describes problems students faced at an elite private college in the late 1970s. Are the pressures you experience as a college student similar to or different from the ones Zinsser identifies? Classify your own college pressures, and write an essay with a thesis statement that takes a strong stand against the forces responsible for these pressures.
2. Write a classification essay supporting a thesis about college students' drive for success. Categorize students you know either by the degree of their need to succeed or by the different ways in which they wish to succeed.
3. Zinsser takes a negative view of the college pressures he identifies. Using his four categories, write an essay arguing that, in the long run, these pressures are not only necessary but also valuable.

Combining the Patterns

Exemplification is an important secondary pattern in this classification-and-division essay. Identify as many passages of exemplification as you can. What do these examples add to Zinsser's essay? What other kinds of examples might be helpful to readers?

Thematic Connections

- "The 'Black Table' Is Still There" (page 366)
- "Suicide Note" (page 382)
- "The Dog Ate My Disk, and Other Tales of Woe" (page 475)

CAROLYN FOSTER SEGAL

The Dog Ate My Disk, and Other Tales of Woe

Carolyn Foster Segal (b. 1950) grew up in Bay Shore, New York, and earned her master's and doctoral degrees in English from Lehigh University. She is a member of the English faculty at Cedar Crest College in Allentown, Pennsylvania. Segal has published poetry, fiction, and essays in a number of publications, including the *Chronicle of Higher Education,* where the following essay originally appeared. She sums up her ideas about writing as follows: "Writing — and it does not matter if it is writing about a feature of the landscape, an aspect of human nature, or a work of literature — begins with observation. The other parts are curiosity, imagination, and patience." She has received hundreds of responses from other instructors corroborating the experiences she describes here.

Background on academic integrity: While the concept of college honor codes in the United States goes back to one developed by students at the University of Virginia in 1840, reports of widespread cheating on college campuses in the early 1990s brought renewed interest in such codes. (Surveys show that more than three-quarters of college students have cheated at least once during their schooling, and an even greater number see cheating as the norm among successful students.) In 1992, the Center for Academic Integrity was established to help colleges and universities find ways to promote "honesty, trust, fairness, respect, and responsibility" among students and faculty members. Its original twenty-five-member group has grown to include more than two hundred institutions, and many other colleges have adopted its goals as well. The main focus of most honor codes revolves around discouraging plagiarism — copying the work of others and presenting the work of others as one's own — and various forms of cheating on tests. The Center for Academic Integrity sees promoting individual honesty as the fundamental issue underlying all of these concerns. While falsifying an excuse for being unprepared for class may seem like a minor infraction, it is still considered a breach of academic integrity.

Taped to the door of my office is a cartoon that features a cat explaining to his feline teacher, "The dog ate my homework." It is intended as a gently humorous reminder to my students that I will not accept excuses for late work, and it, like the lengthy warning on my syllabus, has had absolutely no effect. With a show of energy and creativity that would be admirable if applied to the (missing) assignments in question, my students persist, week after week, semester after semester, year after year, in offering excuses about why their work is not ready. Those reasons fall into several broad categories: the family, the best friend, the evils of dorm life, the evils of technology, and the totally bizarre.

The Family

The death of the grandfather/grandmother is, of course, the grand- 2
mother of all excuses. What heartless teacher would dare to question a student's grief or veracity? What heartless student would lie, wishing death on
a revered family member, just to avoid a deadline? Creative students may
win extra extensions (and days off) with a little careful planning and fuller
plot development, as in the sequence of "My grandfather/grandmother is
sick"; "Now my grandfather/grandmother is in the hospital"; and finally,
"We could all see it coming — my grandfather/grandmother is dead."

Another favorite excuse is "the family emergency," which (always) goes 3
like this: "There was an emergency at home, and I had to help my family."
It's a lovely sentiment, one that conjures up images of Louisa May
Alcott's* little women rushing off with baskets of food and copies of *Pil-
grim's Progress,*† but I do not understand why anyone would turn to my
most irresponsible students in times of trouble.

The Best Friend

This heartwarming concern for others extends beyond the family to 4
friends, as in, "My best friend was up all night and I had to (a) stay up with
her in the dorm, (b) drive her to the hospital, or (c) drive to her college
because (1) her boyfriend broke up with her, (2) she was throwing up blood
[no one catches a cold anymore; everyone throws up blood], or (3) her
grandfather/grandmother died."

At one private university where I worked as an adjunct, I heard an 5
interesting spin that incorporated the motifs of both best friend and dead
relative: "My best friend's mother killed herself." One has to admire the
cleverness here: A mysterious woman in the prime of her life has allegedly
committed suicide, and no professor can prove otherwise! And I admit I
was moved, until finally I had to point out to my students that it was
amazing how the simple act of my assigning a topic for a paper seemed to
drive large numbers of otherwise happy and healthy middle-aged women
to their deaths. I was careful to make that point during an off week, during
which no deaths were reported.

The Evils of Dorm Life

These stories are usually fairly predictable; almost always feature the 6
evil roommate or hallmate, with my student in the role of the innocent victim; and can be summed up as follows: My roommate, who is a horrible
person, likes to party, and I, who am a good person, cannot concentrate on

---

* EDS. NOTE — Nineteenth-century sentimental novelist, author of *Little Women.*

† EDS. NOTE — Eighteenth-century allegory by John Bunyan describing a Christian's
journey from the City of Destruction to the Celestial City.

my work when he or she is partying. Variations include stories about the two people next door who were running around and crying loudly last night because (a) one of them had boyfriend/girlfriend problems; (b) one of them was throwing up blood; or (c) someone, somewhere, died. A friend of mine in graduate school had a student who claimed that his roommate attacked him with a hammer. That, in fact, was a true story; it came out in court when the bad roommate was tried for killing his grandfather.

The Evils of Technology

The computer age has revolutionized the student story, inspiring almost as many new excuses as it has Internet businesses. Here are just a few electronically enhanced explanations: 7

- The computer wouldn't let me save my work.
- The printer wouldn't print.
- The printer wouldn't print this disk.
- The printer wouldn't give me time to proofread.
- The printer made a black line run through all my words, and I know you can't read this, but do you still want it, or wait, here, take my disk. File name? I don't know what you mean.
- I swear I attached it.
- It's my roommate's computer, and she usually helps me, but she had to go to the hospital because she was throwing up blood.
- I did write to the newsgroup, but all my messages came back to me.
- I just found out that all my other newsgroup messages came up under a diferent name. I just want you to know that its really me who wrote all those messages, you can tel which ones our mine because I didnt use the spelcheck! But it was yours truely :) Anyway, just in case you missed those messages or dont belief its my writting. I'll repeat what I sad: I thought the last movie we watched in clas was borring.

The Totally Bizarre

I call the first story "The Pennsylvania Chain Saw Episode." A commuter student called to explain why she had missed my morning class. She had gotten up early so that she would be wide awake for class. Having a bit of extra time, she walked outside to see her neighbor, who was cutting some wood. She called out to him, and he waved back to her with the saw. Wouldn't you know it, the safety catch wasn't on or was broken, and the blade flew right out of the saw and across his lawn and over her fence and across her yard and severed a tendon in her right hand. So she was calling me from the hospital, where she was waiting for surgery. Luckily, she reassured me, she had remembered to bring her paper and a stamped envelope   8 (in a plastic bag, to avoid bloodstains) along with her in the ambulance, and a nurse was mailing everything to me even as we spoke.

That wasn't her first absence. In fact, this student had missed most of the class meetings, and I had already recommended that she withdraw from the course. Now I suggested again that it might be best if she dropped the class. I didn't harp on the absences (what if even some of this story were true?). I did mention that she would need time to recuperate and that making up so much missed work might be difficult. "Oh, no," she said, "I can't drop this course. I had been planning to go on to medical school and become a surgeon, but since I won't be able to operate because of my accident, I'll have to major in English, and this course is more important than ever to me." She did come to the next class, wearing — as evidence of her recent trauma — a bedraggled Ace bandage on her left hand.

You may be thinking that nothing could top that excuse, but in fact I have one more story, provided by the same student, who sent me a letter to explain why her final assignment would be late. While recuperating from her surgery, she had begun corresponding on the Internet with a man who lived in Germany. After a one-week, whirlwind Web romance, they had agreed to meet in Rome, to rendezvous (her phrase) at the papal Easter Mass. Regrettably, the time of her flight made it impossible for her to attend class, but she trusted that I — just this once — would accept late work if the pope wrote a note.

• • •

Comprehension

1. What is Segal's thesis? Does she state it in her essay? What exactly is she classifying here?

2. In paragraph 3, Segal says, "I do not understand why anyone would turn to my most irresponsible students in times of trouble." Do you see this comment as fair?

3. Which of the excuses Segal discusses do you see as valid? Which do you see as just excuses? Why?

4. Do you see Segal as rigid and unsympathetic, or do you think her frustration is justified? Do you think her students are irresponsible procrastinators or simply overworked?

5. What lessons do you think Segal would like her students to learn from her? Would reading this essay teach them what she wants them to learn?

Purpose and Audience

1. This essay was originally published in the *Chronicle of Higher Education*, a periodical for college teachers. How do you think these readers responded to the essay? How might college students respond?

2. Do you see Segal's purpose here as to entertain, to let off steam, to criticize, or to change students' habits? Explain.

3. In paragraph 7, Segal lists some specific excuses in one category, paraphrasing students' remarks and even imitating their grammar and style. Why does she do this? Is it an effective strategy?

Style and Structure

1. In paragraph 1, Segal lists the five categories she plans to discuss. Is this list necessary?

2. Are Segal's categories mutually exclusive, or do they overlap? Could she combine any categories? Can you think of any categories she does not include?

3. What determines the order in which Segal introduces her categories? Is this order logical, or should she present her categories in a different order?

4. Does Segal discuss comparable points for each category? What points, if any, need to be added?

5. Segal frequently uses **sarcasm** in this essay. Give some examples. Given her original audience, do you think this tone is appropriate? How do you react to her sarcasm?

6. Throughout her essay, Segal returns again and again to two excuses: "my grandfather/grandmother died" and "throwing up blood." Locate different versions of these excuses in the essay. Why do you think she singles out these two excuses?

7. Although Segal deals with a serious academic problem, she includes many expressions — such as "Wouldn't you know it" (8) — that give her essay an informal tone. Identify some other examples. What is your reaction to the essay's casual, offhand tone?

8. Review the category Segal calls "The Evils of Technology." Can you add to her list? Can you create subcategories?

Vocabulary Projects

1. Define each of the following words as it is used in this selection.

feline (1)	adjunct (5)
veracity (2)	harp (9)
revered (2)	bedraggled (9)
conjures (3)	rendezvous (10)

2. Every profession has its own unique terms. What terms in this essay characterize the writer as a college professor?

Journal Entry

Do you think this essay is funny? Explain your reaction.

Writing Workshop

1. Write a letter to Segal explaining why your English paper will be late, presenting several different kinds of excuses for your paper's lateness. Be sure to acknowledge the inadequacies of the excuses Segal lists before you present your own superior excuses.

2. Write an essay identifying four or five categories of legitimate excuses for handing in work late. If you like, you can use narrative examples from your own life as a student to explain each category.

3. Using a light (or even sarcastic) tone, write an essay identifying several different categories of teachers in terms of their shortcomings — for instance, teachers who do not cover the assigned work or teachers who do not grade papers in a timely fashion. Be sure to give specific examples of teachers in each category.

Combining the Patterns

In paragraphs 8–10, Segal uses **narration** to tell two stories. What do these stories add to her essay? Do you think she should have added more stories like these to her essay? If so, where?

Thematic Connections

- "Thirty-Eight Who Saw Murder Didn't Call the Police" (page 120)
- "College Pressures" (page 466)
- "The Ways We Lie" (page 495)

The Men We Carry in Our Minds

Scott Russell Sanders was born in 1945 in Memphis, Tennessee, and grew up in a poor rural family. A scholarship student, he graduated first in his class from Brown University. Now a professor of English at Indiana University, he has written science fiction, folk tales, children's stories, essays, and novels. Among his many books are *Stone Country* (1985), about Indiana's limestone region; the novel *The Invisible Company* (1989); the picture books *Aurora Means Dawn* (1998) and *The Floating House* (1999); and the essay collection *The Force of Spirit* (2000). "The Men We Carry in Our Minds" appeared in his 1987 collection *The Paradise of Bombs*. Sanders writes here of his college years in the mid-1960s when, having grown up among working-class men, he was baffled by the vehemence of female classmates who argued that society favored all males over females and that men had "cornered the world's pleasures."

Background on men and women in higher education: In terms of men's higher educational and professional attainment, these women were correct. In 1970, female college undergraduates in the United States numbered some three million, while the figure for male undergraduates was about four million. More strikingly, women accounted for only 2.5 percent of law degrees, 8.4 percent of medical degrees, 3.6 percent of M.B.A.s, and 13 percent of Ph.D.s. By 2000, however, female undergraduates had surpassed male undergraduates by 1 million and are projected to increase that lead by almost 2.5 million by 2011. According to the most recent statistics, women now account for some 48 percent of law degrees, 45 percent of M.D.s, 45 percent of M.B.A.s, and 46.3 percent of Ph.D.s. Half of all managerial and professional positions are held by women, and close to 50 percent of U.S. businesses are female owned. Nevertheless, women have yet to hold executive positions in numbers similar to men, and they are still, on average, paid less than men who do comparable work.

The first men, besides my father, I remember seeing were black convicts and white guards, in the cottonfield across the road from our farm on the outskirts of Memphis. I must have been three or four. The prisoners wore dingy gray-and-black zebra suits, heavy as canvas, sodden with sweat. Hatless, stooped, they chopped weeds in the fierce heat, row after row, breathing the acrid dust of boll-weevil poison. The overseers wore dazzling white shirts and broad shadowy hats. The oiled barrels of their shotguns flashed in the sunlight. Their faces in memory are utterly blank. Of course those men, white and black, have become for me an emblem of racial hatred. But they have also come to stand for the twin poles of my early vision of manhood — the brute toiling animal and the boss.

When I was a boy, the men I knew labored with their bodies. They were   2
marginal farmers, just scraping by, or welders, steel workers, carpenters;
they swept floors, dug ditches, mined coal, or drove trucks, their forearms
ropy with muscle; they trained horses, stoked furnaces, built tires, stood on
assembly lines wrestling parts onto cars and refrigerators. They got up
before light, worked all day long whatever the weather, and when they
came home at night they looked as though somebody had been whipping
them. In the evenings and on weekends they worked on their own places,
tilling gardens that were lumpy with clay, fixing broken-down cars, hammering on houses that were always too drafty, too leaky, too small.

The bodies of the men I knew were twisted and maimed in ways visible   3
and invisible. The nails of their hands were black and split, the hands tat-
tooed with scars. Some had lost fingers. Heavy lifting had given many of
them finicky backs and guts weak from hernias. Racing against conveyor
belts had given them ulcers. Their ankles and knees ached from years of
standing on concrete. Anyone who had worked for long around machines
was hard of hearing. They squinted, and the skin of their faces was creased
like the leather of old work gloves. There were times, studying them, when
I dreaded growing up. Most of them coughed, from dust or cigarettes, and
most of them drank cheap wine or whiskey, so their eyes looked bloodshot
and bruised. The fathers of my friends always seemed older than the mothers. Men wore out sooner. Only women lived into old age.

As a boy I also knew another sort of men, who did not sweat and break   4
down like mules. They were soldiers, and so far as I could tell they scarcely
worked at all. During my early school years we lived on a military base, an
arsenal in Ohio, and every day I saw GIs in the guardshacks, on the stoops
of barracks, at the wheels of olive drab Chevrolets. The chief fact of their
lives was boredom. Long after I left the Arsenal I came to recognize the
sour smell the soldiers gave off as that of souls in limbo. They were all waiting — for wars, for transfers, for leaves, for promotions, for the end of their
hitch — like so many braves waiting for the hunt to begin. Unlike the warriors of older tribes, however, they would have no say about when the battle
would start or how it would be waged. Their waiting was broken only when
they practiced for war. They fired guns at targets, drove tanks across the
churned-up fields of the military reservation, set off bombs in the wrecks
of old fighter planes. I knew this was all play. But I also felt certain that
when the hour for killing arrived, they would kill. When the real shooting
started, many of them would die. This was what soldiers were *for*, just as a
hammer was for driving nails.

Warriors and toilers: those seemed, in my boyhood vision, to be the   5
chief destinies for men. They weren't the only destinies, as I learned from
having a few male teachers, from reading books, and from watching television. But the men on television — the politicians, the astronauts, the generals, the savvy lawyers, the philosophical doctors, the bosses who gave
orders to both soldiers and laborers — seemed as remote and unreal to me
as the figures in tapestries. I could no more imagine growing up to become

one of these cool, potent creatures than I could imagine becoming a prince.

A nearer and more hopeful example was that of my father, who had escaped from a red-dirt farm to a tire factory, and from the assembly line to the front office. Eventually he dressed in a white shirt and tie. He carried himself as if he had been born to work with his mind. But his body, remembering the earlier years of slogging work, began to give out on him in his fifties, and it quit on him entirely before he turned sixty-five. Even such a partial escape from man's fate as he had accomplished did not seem possible for most of the boys I knew. They joined the Army, stood in line for jobs in the smoky plants, helped build highways. They were bound to work as their fathers had worked, killing themselves or preparing to kill others.

6

A scholarship enabled me not only to attend college, a rare enough feat in my circle, but even to study in a university meant for the children of the rich. Here I met for the first time young men who had assumed from birth that they would lead lives of comfort and power. And for the first time I met women who told me that men were guilty of having kept all the joys and privileges of the earth for themselves. I was baffled. What privileges? What joys? I thought about the maimed, dismal lives of most of the men back home. What had they stolen from their wives and daughters? The right to go five days a week, twelve months a year, for thirty or forty years to a steel mill or a coal mine? The right to drop bombs and die in war? The right to feel every leak in the roof, every gap in the fence, every cough in the engine, as a wound they must mend? The right to feel, when the layoff comes or the plant shuts down, not only afraid but ashamed?

7

I was slow to understand the deep grievances of women. This was because, as a boy, I had envied them. Before college, the only people I had ever known who were interested in art or music or literature, the only ones who read books, the only ones who ever seemed to enjoy a sense of ease and grace were the mothers and daughters. Like the menfolk, they fretted about money, they scrimped and made-do. But, when the pay stopped coming in, they were not the ones who had failed. Nor did they have to go to war, and that seemed to me a blessed fact. By comparison with the narrow, ironclad days of fathers, there was an expansiveness, I thought, in the days of mothers. They went to see neighbors, to shop in town, to run errands at school, at the library, at church. No doubt, had I looked harder at their lives, I would have envied them less. It was not my fate to become a woman, so it was easier for me to see the graces. Few of them held jobs outside the home, and those who did filled thankless roles as clerks and waitresses. I didn't see, then, what a prison a house could be, since houses seemed to me brighter, handsomer places than any factory. I didn't realize—because such things were never spoken of—how often women suffered from men's bullying. I did learn about the wretchedness of abandoned wives, single mothers, widows; but I also learned about the wretchedness of lone men. Even then I could see how exhausting it was for

8

a mother to cater all day to the needs of young children. But if I had been asked, as a boy, to choose between tending a baby and tending a machine, I think I would have chosen the baby. (Having now tended both, I know I would choose the baby.)

So I was baffled when the women at college accused me and my sex of having cornered the world's pleasures. I think something like my bafflement has been felt by other boys (and by girls as well) who grew up in dirt-poor farm country, in mining country, in black ghettos, in Hispanic barrios, in the shadows of factories, in Third World nations — any place where the fate of men is as grim and bleak as the fate of women. Toilers and warriors. I realize now how ancient these identities are, how deep the tug they exert on men, the undertow of a thousand generations. The miseries I saw, as a boy, in the lives of nearly all men I continue to see in the lives of many — the body-breaking toil, the tedium, the call to be tough, the humiliating powerlessness, the battle for a living and for territory.

When the women I met at college thought about the joys and privileges of men, they did not carry in their minds the sort of men I had known in my childhood. They thought of their fathers, who were bankers, physicians, architects, stockbrokers, the big wheels of the big cities. These fathers rode the train to work or drove cars that cost more than any of my childhood houses. They were attended from morning to night by female helpers, wives and nurses and secretaries. They were never laid off, never short of cash at month's end, never lined up for welfare. These fathers made decisions that mattered. They ran the world.

The daughters of such men wanted to share in this power, this glory. So did I. They yearned for a say over their future, for jobs worthy of their abilities, for the right to live at peace, unmolested, whole. Yes, I thought, yes yes. The difference between me and these daughters was that they saw me, because of my sex, as destined from birth to become like their fathers, and therefore as an enemy to their desires. But I knew better. I wasn't an enemy, in fact or in feeling. I was an ally. If I had known, then, how to tell them so, would they have believed me? Would they now?

•   •   •

Comprehension

1. What does Sanders mean in paragraph 1 when he characterizes the black convicts and white guards as "an emblem of racial hatred"? In what sense do they represent "the twin poles of [his] early vision of manhood"?

2. When he was a child, what did Sanders expect to become when he grew up? Why? How did he escape this destiny?

3. What advantages did Sanders initially attribute to women? Why? What challenged his assumptions?

4. What kind of men did the women Sanders met in college carry in their minds? Why did the women see Sanders as "an enemy to their desires" (11)? How did he defend himself against their charges?

Purpose and Audience

1. What purpose do you think Sanders had in mind when he wrote this essay? Is his essay intended to be a personal memoir, or does he have another agenda? Explain.
2. What is the essay's thesis?
3. Is this essay directed primarily at workers like the ones Sanders observed when he was growing up or at the "children of the rich" (7)? At men or at women? On whom would you expect it to have the greatest impact? Why?

Style and Structure

1. What is Sanders categorizing in this essay? What categories does he name? What other, unnamed categories does he identify?
2. What principle of classification determines the categories Sanders discusses?
3. What, if anything, determines the order of Sanders's categories?
4. Is the treatment of the various categories in this essay balanced, or does Sanders give more attention to some than to others? If some categories are given more attention, does this weaken the essay? Explain.

Vocabulary Projects

1. Define each of the following words as it is used in this selection.

acrid (1)	finicky (3)	expansiveness (8)
boll weevil (1)	slogging (6)	undertow (9)
overseers (1)	fretted (8)	unmolested (11)
maimed (3)	ironclad (8)	

2. Invent descriptive titles for the categories Sanders discusses but does not name. Be sure to include categories that cover women's roles as well as men's, and be sure your categories do not overlap.

Journal Entry

Do you agree with Sanders when he suggests that many men have harder lives than women do? What is your reaction to his parenthetical comment at the end of paragraph 8?

Writing Workshop

1. Imagine the possible kinds of work available to you in the field you expect to study. Write a classification-and-division essay discussing several categories of possible future employment, arranging them from least to most desirable.

2. Consider the adult workers you know best—your relatives, friends' parents, employers, teachers—and other workers you come in contact with on a regular basis (store clerks, for example). Write a classification-and-division essay devising categories that distinguish different types of workers. Then, discuss these categories of workers in terms of how fortunate (or unfortunate) they are. Consider income level, job security, working conditions, prestige, and job satisfaction in your discussion of each category. In your essay's introduction and conclusion, consider how the employment categories you have devised are like or unlike Sanders's.

3. What kinds of jobs do you see as "dream jobs"? Why? List as many of these ideal jobs as you can, and group them into logical categories. Then, write an essay with a thesis statement that explains the value you see in these jobs.

Combining the Patterns

After he establishes his categories, Sanders uses **description** to characterize workers and distinguish them from one another. Identify and evaluate the descriptive passages that serve these two purposes. Is any category of worker identified but not described? Explain.

Thematic Connections

- "My Mother Never Worked" (page 108)
- "I Want a Wife" (page 524)
- "Stigmatic Uniforms" (page 544)
- "What Work Is" (page 550)

AMY TAN

Mother Tongue

Amy Tan was born in 1952 in Oakland, California, the daughter of recent Chinese immigrants. She studied linguistics at San Francisco State University and began a career as a corporate communications specialist. In 1984, Tan began to write stories as a sort of do-it-yourself therapy. At the same time, she began thinking about the contradictions she faced as a highly Americanized Chinese American who was also the daughter of immigrant parents. Three years later, she published *The Joy Luck Club* (1987), a best-selling novel about four immigrant Chinese women and their American-born daughters. Later works include the novels *The Hundred Secret Senses* (1995) and *The Bonesetter's Daughter* (2001), two children's books, and *The Opposite of Fate: A Book of Musings* (2003). In this 1990 essay, Tan considers her mother's heavily Chinese-influenced English, as well as the different "Englishes" she herself uses, especially in communicating with her mother. She then thinks about the potential limitations of growing up with immigrant parents who do not speak fluent English.

Background on Asian Americans and standardized tests: The children of Asian immigrants tend to be highly assimilated and are often outstanding students, in part because their parents expect them to work hard and do well. Most who were born in the United States speak and read English fluently. Yet on standardized tests, while they generally score much higher than average in math, their verbal scores are a bit lower than average. For example, average SAT scores for all student test-takers beginning college in 2004 were 528 on the verbal section and 531 on the math section; the average scores for Asian-American students were 507 on the verbal section and 577 on the math section. In some cases, this lower verbal score means that an Asian-American student's combined score may limit his or her college choices. Moreover, as Tan suggests, Asian-American students' performance on such standardized tests may lead teachers to discourage them from pursuing degrees in fields outside of math and science.

I am not a scholar of English or literature. I cannot give you much more than personal opinions on the English language and its variations in this country or others.

I am a writer. And by that definition, I am someone who has always loved language. I am fascinated by language in daily life. I spend a great deal of my time thinking about the power of language — the way it can evoke an emotion, a visual image, a complex idea, or a simple truth. Language is the tool of my trade. And I use them all — all the Englishes I grew up with.

Recently, I was made keenly aware of the different Englishes I do use. I was giving a talk to a large group of people, the same talk I had already given to half a dozen other groups. The nature of the talk was about my writing, my life, and my book, *The Joy Luck Club*. The talk was going along well enough, until I remembered one major difference that made the whole talk sound wrong. My mother was in the room. And it was perhaps the first time she had heard me give a lengthy speech, using the kind of English I have never used with her. I was saying things like, "The intersection of memory upon imagination" and "There is an aspect of my fiction that relates to thus-and-thus"—a speech filled with carefully wrought grammatical phrases, burdened, it suddenly seemed to me, with nominalized forms, past perfect tenses, conditional phrases, all the forms of standard English that I had learned in school and through books, the forms of English I did not use at home with my mother.

Just last week, I was walking down the street with my mother, and I again found myself conscious of the English I was using, and the English I do use with her. We were talking about the price of new and used furniture and I heard myself saying this: "Not waste money that way." My husband was with us as well, and he didn't notice any switch in my English. And then I realized why. It's because over the twenty years we've been together I've often used that same kind of English with him, and sometimes he even uses it with me. It has become our language of intimacy, a different sort of English that relates to family talk, the language I grew up with.

So you'll have some idea of what this family talk I heard sounds like, I'll quote what my mother said during a recent conversation which I videotaped and then transcribed. During this conversation my mother was talking about a political gangster in Shanghai who had the same last name as her family's, Du, and how the gangster in his early years wanted to be adopted by her family, which was rich by comparison. Later, the gangster became more powerful, far richer than my mother's family, and one day showed up at my mother's wedding to pay his respects. Here's what she said in part:

"Du Yusong having business like fruit stand. Like off the street kind. He is Du like Du Zong—but not Tsung-ming Island people. The local people call putong, the river east side, he belong to that side local people. The man want to ask Du Zong father take him in like become own family. Du Zong father wasn't looking down on him, but didn't take seriously, until that man big like become a mafia. Now important person very hard to inviting him. Chinese way, come only to show respect, don't stay for dinner. Respect for making big celebration, he shows up. Mean gives lots of respect. Chinese custom. Chinese social life that way. If too important won't have to stay too long. He come to my wedding. I didn't see. I heard it. I gone to boy's side, they have YMCA dinner. Chinese age I was nineteen."

You should know that my mother's expressive command of English belies how much she actually understands. She reads the *Forbes* report, listens to *Wall Street Week*, converses daily with her stockbroker, reads all of Shirley MacLaine's books with ease—all kinds of things I can't begin to understand. Yet some of my friends tell me they understand 50 percent of what my mother says. Some say they understand 80 to 90 percent. Some say they understand none of it, as if she were speaking pure Chinese. But to me, my mother's English is perfectly clear, perfectly natural. It's my mother's tongue. Her language, as I hear it, is vivid, direct, full of observation and imagery. This was the language that helped shape the way I saw things, expressed things, made sense of the world.

Lately, I've been giving more thought to the kind of English my mother speaks. Like others, I have described it to people as "broken" or "fractured" English. But I wince when I say that. It has always bothered me that I can think of no way to describe it other than "broken," as if it were damaged and needed to be fixed, as if it lacked a certain wholeness and soundness. I've heard other terms used, "limited English," for example. But they seem just as bad, as if everything is limited, including people's perceptions of the limited English speaker.

I know this for a fact, because when I was growing up, my mother's "limited" English limited *my* perception of her. I was ashamed of her English. I believed that her English reflected the quality of what she had to say. That is, because she expressed them imperfectly her thoughts were imperfect. And I had plenty of empirical evidence to support me: the fact that people in department stores, at banks, and at restaurants did not take her seriously, did not give her good service, pretended not to understand her, or even acted as if they did not hear her.

My mother has long realized the limitations of her English as well. When I was fifteen, she used to have me call people on the phone to pretend I was she. In this guise, I was forced to ask for information or even complain and yell at people who had been rude to her. One time it was a call to her stockbroker in New York. She had cashed out her small portfolio and it just so happened we were going to go to New York the next week, our very first trip outside California. I had to get on the phone and say in an adolescent voice that was not very convincing, "This is Mrs. Tan."

And my mother was standing in the back whispering loudly, "Why he don't send me check, already two weeks late. So mad he lie to me, losing me money."

And then I said in perfect English, "Yes, I'm getting rather concerned. You had agreed to send the check two weeks ago, but it hasn't arrived."

Then she began to talk more loudly. "What he want, I come to New York tell him front of his boss, you cheating me?" And I was trying to calm her down, make her be quiet, while telling the stockbroker, "I can't tolerate any more excuses. If I don't receive the check immediately I am going to have to speak to your manager when I'm in New York next week." And sure enough, the following week there we were in front of this astonished stockbroker, and I was sitting there red-faced and quiet, and my mother, the real Mrs. Tan, was shouting at his boss in her impeccable broken English.

We used a similar routine just five days ago, for a situation that was far less humorous. My mother had gone to the hospital for an appointment, to find out about a benign brain tumor a CAT scan had revealed a month ago. She said she had spoken very good English, her best English, no mistakes. Still, she said, the hospital did not apologize when they said they had lost the CAT scan and she had come for nothing. She said they did not seem to have any sympathy when she told them she was anxious to know the exact diagnosis, since her husband and son had both died of brain tumors. She said they would not give her any more information until the next time and she would have to make another appointment for that. So she said she would not leave until the doctor called her daughter. She wouldn't budge. And when the doctor finally called her daughter, me, who spoke in perfect English — lo and behold — we had assurances the CAT scan would be found, promises that a conference call on Monday would be held, and apologies for any suffering my mother had gone through for a most regrettable mistake.

I think my mother's English almost had an effect on limiting my possibilities in life as well. Sociologists and linguists probably will tell you that a person's developing language skills are more influenced by peers. But I do think that the language spoken in the family, especially in immigrant families which are more insular, plays a large role in shaping the language of the child. And I believe that it affected my results on achievement tests, IQ tests, and the SAT. While my English skills were never judged as poor, compared to math, English could not be considered my strong suit. In grade school I did moderately well, getting perhaps B's, sometimes B-pluses, in English and scoring perhaps in the sixtieth or seventieth percentile on achievement tests. But those scores were not good enough to override the opinion that my true abilities lay in math and science, because in those areas I achieved A's and scored in the ninetieth percentile or higher. 15

This was understandable. Math is precise; there is only one correct answer. Whereas, for me at least, the answers on English tests were always a judgment call, a matter of opinion and personal experience. Those tests were constructed around items like fill-in-the-blank sentence completion, such as "Even though Tom was _____, Mary thought he was _____." And the correct answer always seemed to be the most bland combinations of thoughts, for example, "Even though Tom was shy, Mary thought he was charming," with the grammatical structure "even though" limiting the correct answer to some sort of semantic opposites, so you wouldn't get answers like, "Even though Tom was foolish, Mary thought he was ridiculous." Well, according to my mother, there were very few limitations as to what Tom could have been and what Mary might have thought of him. So I never did well on tests like that. 16

The same was true with word analogies, pairs of words in which you were supposed to find some sort of logical, semantic relationship — for example, "*Sunset* is to *nightfall* as _____ is to _____." And here you would be presented with a list of four possible pairs, one of which showed the same kind of relationship: *red* is to *stoplight, bus* is to *arrival, chills* is to 17 *fever, yawn* is to *boring*. Well, I could never think that way. I knew what the tests were asking, but I could not block out of my mind the images already created by the first pair, "*sunset* is to *nightfall*" — and I would see a burst of colors against a darkening sky, the moon rising, the lowering of a curtain of stars. And all the other pairs of words — red, bus, stoplight, boring — just threw up a mass of confusing images, making it impossible for me to sort out something as logical as saying: "A sunset precedes nightfall" is the same as "a chill precedes a fever." The only way I would have gotten that answer right would have been to imagine an associative situation, for example, my being disobedient and staying out past sunset, catching a chill at night, which turns into feverish pneumonia as punishment, which indeed did happen to me.

I have been thinking about all this lately, about my mother's English, about achievement tests. Because lately I've been asked, as a writer, why there are not more Asian Americans represented in American literature. Why are there few Asian Americans enrolled in creative writing programs? Why do so many Chinese students go into engineering? Well, these are broad sociological questions I can't begin to answer. But I have noticed in surveys — in fact, just last week — that Asian students, as a whole, always do significantly better on math achievement tests than in English. And this makes me think that there are other Asian-American students whose English spoken in the home might also be described as "broken" or "limited." And perhaps they also have teachers who are steering them away from writing and into math and science, which is what happened to me. 18

Fortunately, I happen to be rebellious in nature and enjoy the challenge of disproving assumptions made about me. I became an English major my first year in college, after being enrolled as pre-med. I started writing nonfiction as a freelancer the week after I was told by my former boss that writing was my worst skill and I should hone my talents toward account management. 19

But it wasn't until 1985 that I finally began to write fiction. And at first I wrote using what I thought to be wittily crafted sentences, sentences that would finally prove I had mastery over the English language. Here's an example from the first draft of a story that later made its way into *The Joy Luck Club,* but without this line: "That was my mental quandary in its nascent state." A terrible line, which I can barely pronounce. 20

Fortunately, for reasons I won't get into today, I later decided I should envision a reader for the stories I would write. And the reader I decided upon was my mother because these were stories about mothers. So with this reader in mind — and in fact she did read my early drafts — I began to write stories using all the Englishes I grew up with: the English I spoke to my mother, which for lack of a better term might be described as "simple"; the English she used with me, which for lack of a better term might be described as "broken"; my translation of her Chinese, which could certainly 21 be described as "watered down"; and what I imagined to be her translation of her Chinese if she could speak in perfect English, her internal language, and for that I sought to preserve the essence, but neither an English nor a Chinese structure. I wanted to capture what language ability tests can never reveal: her intent, her passion, her imagery, the rhythms of her speech and the nature of her thoughts.

Apart from what any critic had to say about my writing, I knew I had   22
succeeded where it counted when my mother finished reading my book and gave me her verdict: "So easy to read."

•   •   •

Comprehension

1. What is Tan classifying in this essay? What individual categories does she identify?

2. Where does Tan identify the different categories she discusses in "Mother Tongue"? Should she have identified these categories earlier? Why, or why not?

3. Does Tan illustrate each category she identifies? Does she treat all categories equally? If she does not, do you see this as a problem? Explain.

4. In what specific situations does Tan say her mother's "limited English" was a handicap? In what other situations might Mrs. Tan face difficulties?

5. What effects have her mother's English had on Tan's life?

6. How does Tan account for the difficulty she had in answering questions on achievement tests, particularly word analogies? Do you think her problems in this area can be explained by the level of her family's language skills, or might other factors also be to blame? Explain.

7. In paragraph 18, Tan considers the possible reasons for the absence of Asian Americans in the fields of language and literature. What explanations does she offer? What other explanations can you think of?

Purpose and Audience

1. Why do you suppose Tan opens her essay by explaining her qualifications? Why, for example, does she tell her readers she is "not a scholar of English or literature" (1) but a writer who is "fascinated by language in daily life" (2)?

2. Do you think Tan expects most of her readers to be Asian American? To be familiar with Asian-American languages and culture? How can you tell?

3. Is Tan's primary focus in this essay on language or on her mother? Explain your conclusion.

Style and Structure

1. This essay's style is relatively informal. For example, Tan uses *I* to refer to herself and addresses her readers as *you*. Identify other features that characterize her style as informal. Do you think a more formal style would strengthen her credibility? Explain your reasoning.

2. In paragraph 6, Tan quotes a passage of her mother's speech. What purpose does Tan say she wants this quotation to serve? What impression does it give of her mother? Do you think this effect is what Tan intended? Explain.

3. In paragraphs 10 through 13, Tan juxtaposes her mother's English with her own. What point do these quoted passages make?

4. The expression used in Tan's title, "Mother Tongue," is also used in paragraph 7. What does this expression generally mean? What does it seem to mean in this essay?

5. In paragraph 20, Tan quotes a "terrible line" from an early draft of part of her novel *The Joy Luck Club*. Why do you suppose she quotes this line? How is it different from the style she uses in "Mother Tongue"?

Vocabulary Projects

1. Define each of the following words as it is used in this selection.

   nominalized (3)   guise (10)   semantic (16)
   belies (7)   impeccable (13)   quandary (20)
   empirical (9)   insular (15)   nascent (20)

2. In paragraph 8, Tan discusses the different words and phrases that might be used to describe her mother's spoken English. Which of these terms seems most accurate? Do you agree with Tan that these words are unsatisfactory? What other term for her mother's English would be both neutral and accurate?

Journal Entry

In paragraph 9, Tan says that when she was growing up she was sometimes ashamed of her mother because of her limited English proficiency. Have you ever felt ashamed of a parent (or a friend) because of his or her inability to "fit in" in some way? How do you feel now about your earlier reaction?

Writing Workshop

1. What different "Englishes" (or other languages) do you use in your day-to-day life as a student, employee, friend, and family member? Write a classification-and-division essay identifying, describing, and

illustrating each kind of language and explaining the purpose it serves.

2. What kinds of problems does a person whose English is as limited as Mrs. Tan's face today? Write a classification-and-division essay that identifies and explains the kinds of problems you might encounter if the level of your spoken English were comparable to hers.

3. Tan's essay focuses on spoken language, but people also use different kinds of *written* language in different situations. Write a classification-and-division essay that identifies and analyzes three different kinds of written English: one appropriate for your parents, one for a teacher or employer, and one for a friend. Illustrate each kind of language with a few sentences to each audience about your plans for your future. In your thesis statement, explain why you need all three kinds of language.

Combining the Patterns

Tan develops her essay with a series of anecdotes about her mother and about herself. How does this use of **narration** strengthen her essay? Could she have made her point about the use of different "Englishes" without these anecdotes? What other strategy could she have used?

Thematic Connections

- "Only Daughter" (page 96)
- "Words Left Unspoken" (page 168)
- "The Human Cost of an Illiterate Society" (page 252)
- "Chinese Space, American Space" (page 421)

STEPHANIE ERICSSON

The Ways We Lie

Stephanie Ericsson (b. 1953) grew up in San Francisco and began writing as a teenager. She has been a screenwriter and an advertising copywriter and has published several books based on her own life. *Shamefaced: The Road to Recovery* and *Women of AA: Recovering Together* (both 1985) focus on her experiences with addiction; *Companion through the Darkness: Inner Dialogues on Grief* (1993) deals with the sudden death of her husband; and *Companion into the Dawn: Inner Dialogues on Loving* (1994) is a collection of essays.

Background on lies in politics and business: The following piece origi-nally appeared as the cover article in the January 1993 issue of the *Utne Reader*, which was devoted to the theme of lies and lying. The subject had particular relevance after a year when the honesty of Bill Clinton—the newly elected U.S. president—had been questioned. (It also followed the furor surrounding the confirmation hearings of U.S. Supreme Court nominee Clarence Thomas, who denied allegations by attorney Anita Hill of workplace sexual harassment; here the question was who was telling the truth and who was not.) Six years later, President Clinton was accused of perjury and faced a Senate impeachment trial. More recently, lying was featured prominently in the news as executives at a number of major cor-porations were charged with falsifying records at the expense of employees and shareholders, and the Bush administration was accused of exaggerat-ing the danger of weapons of mass destruction in Iraq to justify going to war.

The bank called today and I told them my deposit was in the mail, even 1 though I hadn't written a check yet. It'd been a rough day. The baby I'm pregnant with decided to do aerobics on my lungs for two hours, our three-year-old daughter painted the living-room couch with lipstick, the IRS put me on hold for an hour, and I was late to a business meeting because I was tired.

I told my client the traffic had been bad. When my partner came home, 2 his haggard face told me his day hadn't gone any better than mine, so when he asked, "How was your day?" I said, "Oh, fine," knowing that one more straw might break his back. A friend called and wanted to take me to lunch. I said I was busy. Four lies in the course of a day, none of which I felt the least bit guilty about.

We lie. We all do. We exaggerate, we minimize, we avoid confrontation, 3 we spare people's feelings, we conveniently forget, we keep secrets, we jus-tify lying to the big-guy institutions. Like most people, I indulge in small falsehoods and still think of myself as an honest person. Sure I lie, but it doesn't hurt anything. Or does it?

I once tried going a whole week without telling a lie, and it was paralyzing. I discovered that telling the truth all the time is nearly impossible. It means living with some serious consequences: The bank charges me $60 in overdraft fees, my partner keels over when I tell him about my travails, my client fires me for telling her I didn't feel like being on time, and my friend takes it personally when I say I'm not hungry. There must be some merit to lying.

But if I justify lying, what makes me any different from slick politicians or the corporate robbers who raided the S&L industry? Saying it's okay to lie one way and not another is hedging. I cannot seem to escape the voice deep inside me that tells me: When someone lies, someone loses.

What far-reaching consequences will I, or others, pay as a result of my lie? Will someone's trust be destroyed? Will someone else pay *my* penance because I ducked out? We must consider the *meaning of our actions*. Deception, lies, capital crimes, and misdemeanors all carry meanings. *Webster's* definition of *lie* is specific:

1: a false statement or action especially made with the intent to deceive;
2: anything that gives or is meant to give a false impression.

A definition like this implies that there are many, many ways to tell a lie. Here are just a few.

The White Lie

> A man who won't lie to a woman has very little consideration for her feelings.
>
> – BERGEN EVANS

The white lie assumes that the truth will cause more damage than a simple, harmless untruth. Telling a friend he looks great when he looks like hell can be based on a decision that the friend needs a compliment more than a frank opinion. But, in effect, it is the liar deciding what is best for the lied to. Ultimately, it is a vote of no confidence. It is an act of subtle arrogance for anyone to decide what is best for someone else.

Yet not all circumstances are quite so cut-and-dried. Take, for instance, the sergeant in Vietnam who knew one of his men was killed in action but listed him as missing so that the man's family would receive indefinite compensation instead of the lump-sum pittance the military gives widows and children. His intent was honorable. Yet for twenty years this family kept their hopes alive, unable to move on to a new life.

Facades

> Et tu, Brute?
> – CAESAR*

We all put up facades to one degree or another. When I put on a suit to go to see a client, I feel as though I am putting on another face, obeying the

---

* EDS. NOTE — "And you, Brutus?" (Latin). In Shakespeare's play *Julius Caesar*, Caesar asks this question when he sees Brutus, whom he has believed to be his friend, among the conspirators who are stabbing him.

expectation that serious businesspeople wear suits rather than sweatpants. But I'm a writer. Normally, I get up, get the kid off to school, and sit at my computer in my pajamas until four in the afternoon. When I answer the phone, the caller thinks I'm wearing a suit (though the UPS man knows better).

But facades can be destructive because they are used to seduce others   11
into an illusion. For instance, I recently realized that a former friend was a liar. He presented himself with all the right looks and the right words and offered lots of new consciousness theories, fabulous books to read, and fascinating insights. Then I did some business with him, and the time came for him to pay me. He turned out to be all talk and no walk. I heard a plethora of reasonable excuses, including in-depth descriptions of the big break around the corner. In six months of work, I saw less than a hundred bucks. When I confronted him, he raised both eyebrows and tried to convince me that I'd heard him wrong, that he'd made no commitment to me. A simple investigation into his past revealed a crowded graveyard of disenchanted former friends.

Ignoring the Plain Facts

> Well, you must understand that Father Porter is only human. . . .
> – A MASSACHUSETTS PRIEST

In the '60s, the Catholic Church in Massachusetts began hearing com-   12
plaints that Father James Porter was sexually molesting children. Rather than relieving him of his duties, the ecclesiastical authorities simply moved him from one parish to another between 1960 and 1967, actually providing him with a fresh supply of unsuspecting families and innocent children to abuse. After treatment in 1967 for pedophilia, he went back to work, this time in Minnesota. The new diocese was aware of Father Porter's obsession with children, but they needed priests and recklessly believed treatment had cured him. More children were abused until he was relieved of his duties a year later. By his own admission, Porter may have abused as many as a hundred children.

Ignoring the facts may not in and of itself be a form of lying, but con-   13
sider the context of this situation. If a lie is *a false action done with the intent to deceive*, then the Catholic Church's conscious covering for Porter created irreparable consequences. The church became a co-perpetrator with Porter.

Deflecting

> When you have no basis for an argument, abuse the plaintiff.
> – CICERO

I've discovered that I can keep anyone from seeing the true me by being   14
selectively blatant. I set a precedent of being up-front about intimate issues, but I never bring up the things I truly want to hide; I just let people assume I'm revealing everything. It's an effective way of hiding.

Any good liar knows that the way to perpetuate an untruth is to de-   15
flect attention from it. When Clarence Thomas exploded with accusations

that the Senate hearings were a "high-tech lynching," he simply switched the focus from a highly charged subject to a radioactive subject. Rather than defending himself, he took the offensive and accused the country of racism. It was a brilliant maneuver. Racism is now politically incorrect in official circles — unlike sexual harassment, which still rewards those who can get away with it.

Some of the most skillful deflectors are passive-aggressive people who, 16 when accused of inappropriate behavior, refuse to respond to the accusations. This you-don't-exist stance infuriates the accuser, who, understandably, screams something obscene out of frustration. The trap is sprung and the act of deflection successful, because now the passive-aggressive person can indignantly say, "Who can talk to someone as unreasonable as you?" The real issue is forgotten and the sins of the original victim become the focus. Feeling guilty of name-calling, the victim is fully tamed and crawls into a hole, ashamed. I have watched this fighting technique work thousands of times in disputes between men and women, and what I've learned is that the real culprit is not necessarily the one who swears the loudest.

Omission

> The cruelest lies are often told in silence.
> – R. L. STEVENSON

Omission involves telling most of the truth minus one or two key facts 17 whose absence changes the story completely. You break a pair of glasses that are guaranteed under normal use and get a new pair, without mentioning that the first pair broke during a rowdy game of basketball. Who hasn't tried something like that? But what about omission of information that could make a difference in how a person lives his or her life?

For instance, one day I found out that rabbinical legends tell of 18 another woman in the Garden of Eden before Eve. I was stunned. The omission of the Sumerian goddess Lilith from Genesis — as well as her demonization by ancient misogynists as an embodiment of female evil — felt like spiritual robbery. I felt like I'd just found out my mother was really my stepmother. To take seriously the tradition that Adam was created out of the same mud as his equal counterpart, Lilith, redefines all of Judeo-Christian history.

Some renegade Catholic feminists introduced me to a view of Lilith 19 that had been suppressed during the many centuries when this strong goddess was seen only as a spirit of evil. Lilith was a proud goddess who defied Adam's need to control her, attempted negotiations, and when this failed, said adios and left the Garden of Eden.

This omission of Lilith from the Bible was a patriarchal strategy to 20 keep women weak. Omitting the strong-woman archetype of Lilith from Western religions and starting the story with Eve the Rib has helped keep Christian and Jewish women believing they were the lesser sex for thousands of years.

Stereotypes and Clichés

> Where opinion does not exist, the status quo becomes stereotyped
> and all originality is discouraged.
>
> – BERTRAND RUSSELL

Stereotype and cliché serve a purpose as a form of shorthand. Our   21
need for vast amounts of information in nanoseconds has made the stereotype vital to modern communication. Unfortunately, it often shuts down
original thinking, giving those hungry for the truth a candy bar of misinformation instead of a balanced meal. The stereotype explains a situation
with just enough truth to seem unquestionable.

All the "isms" — racism, sexism, ageism, et al. — are founded on and   22
fueled by the stereotype and the cliché, which are lies of exaggeration,
omission, and ignorance. They are always dangerous. They take a single
tree and make it a landscape. They destroy curiosity. They close minds and
separate people. The single mother on welfare is assumed to be cheating.
Any black male could tell you how much of his identity is obliterated daily
by stereotypes. Fat people, ugly people, beautiful people, old people, large-
breasted women, short men, the mentally ill, and the homeless all could
tell you how much more they are like us than we want to think. I once
admitted to a group of people that I had a mouth like a truck driver. Much
to my surprise, a man stood up and said, "I'm a truck driver, and I never
cuss." Needless to say, I was humbled.

Groupthink

> Who is more foolish, the child afraid of the dark, or the man afraid
> of the light?
>
> – MAURICE FREEHILL

Irving Janis, in *Victims of GroupThink*, defines this sort of lie as a psycho-   23
logical phenomenon within decision-making groups in which loyalty to
the group has become more important than any other value, with the
result that dissent and the appraisal of alternatives are suppressed. If
you've ever worked on a committee or in a corporation, you've encountered groupthink. It requires a combination of other forms of lying —
ignoring facts, selective memory, omission, and denial, to name a few.

The textbook example of groupthink came on December 7, 1941. From   24
as early as the fall of 1941, the warnings came in, one after another, that
Japan was preparing for a massive military operation. The Navy command
in Hawaii assumed Pearl Harbor was invulnerable — the Japanese weren't
stupid enough to attack the United States' most important base. On the
other hand, racist stereotypes said the Japanese weren't smart enough to
invent a torpedo effective in less than 60 feet of water (the fleet was docked
in 30 feet); after all, U.S. technology hadn't been able to do it.

On Friday, December 5, normal weekend leave was granted to all the   25
commanders at Pearl Harbor, even though the Japanese consulate in

Hawaii was busy burning papers. Within the tight, good-ole-boy cohesiveness of the U.S. command in Hawaii, the myth of invulnerability stayed well entrenched. No one in the group considered the alternatives. The rest is history.

Out-and-Out Lies

> The only form of lying that is beyond reproach is lying for its own sake.
>
> – OSCAR WILDE

Of all the ways to lie, I like this one the best, probably because I get   26
tired of trying to figure out the real meanings behind things. At least I can
trust the bald-faced lie. I once asked my five-year-old nephew, "Who broke
the fence?" (I had seen him do it.) He answered, "The murderers." Who
could argue?

At least when this sort of lie is told it can be easily confronted. As the   27
person who is lied to, I know where I stand. The bald-faced lie doesn't toy
with my perceptions — it argues with them. It doesn't try to refashion reality, it tries to refute it. *Read my lips*. . . . No sleight of hand. No guessing. If
this were the only form of lying, there would be no such thing as floating
anxiety or the adult-children of alcoholics movement.

Dismissal

> Pay no attention to that man behind the curtain! I am the
> Great Oz!
>
> – THE WIZARD OF OZ

Dismissal is perhaps the slipperiest of all lies. Dismissing feelings, per-   28
ceptions, or even the raw facts of a situation ranks as a kind of lie that can
do as much damage to a person as any other kind of lie.

The roots of many mental disorders can be traced back to the dis-   29
missal of reality. Imagine that a person is told from the time she is a tot
that her perceptions are inaccurate. *"Mommy, I'm scared."* "No, you're not,
darling." *"I don't like that man next door, he makes me feel icky."* "Johnny, that's
a terrible thing to say, of course you like him. You go over there right now
and be nice to him."

I've often mused over the idea that madness is actually a sane reaction   30
to an insane world. Psychologist R. D. Laing supports this hypothesis in
Sanity, Madness & the Family, an account of his investigations into families
of schizophrenics. The common thread that ran through all of the families
he studied was a deliberate, staunch dismissal of the patient's perceptions
from a very early age. Each of the patients started out with an accurate
grasp of reality, which, through meticulous and methodical dismissal, was
demolished until the only reality the patient could trust was catatonia.

Dismissal runs the gamut. Mild dismissal can be quite handy for for-   31
giving the foibles of others in our day-to-day lives. Toddlers who have just

learned to manipulate their parents' attention sometimes are dismissed out of necessity. Absolute attention from the parents would require so much energy that no one would get to eat dinner. But we must be careful and attentive about how far we take our "necessary" dismissals. Dismissal is a dangerous tool, because it's nothing less than a lie.

Delusion

> We lie loudest when we lie to ourselves.
> – ERIC HOFFER

I could write the book on this one. Delusion, a cousin of dismissal, is   32
the tendency to see excuses as facts. It's a powerful lying tool because it filters out information that contradicts what we want to believe. Alcoholics who believe that the problems in their lives are legitimate reasons for drinking rather than results of the drinking offer the classic example of deluded thinking. Delusion uses the mind's ability to see things in myriad ways to support what it wants to be the truth.

But delusion is also a survival mechanism we all use. If we were to fully   33
contemplate the consequences of our stockpiles of nuclear weapons or global warming, we could hardly function on a day-to-day level. We don't want to incorporate that much reality into our lives because to do so would be paralyzing.

Delusion acts as an adhesive to keep the status quo intact. It shame-   34
lessly employs dismissal, omission, and amnesia, among other sorts of lies. Its most cunning defense is that it cannot see itself.

> The liar's punishment . . . is that he cannot believe anyone else.
> – GEORGE BERNARD SHAW

These are only a few of the ways we lie. Or are lied to. As I said earlier,   35
it's not easy to entirely eliminate lies from our lives. No matter how pious we may try to be, we will still embellish, hedge, and omit to lubricate the daily machinery of living. But there is a world of difference between telling functional lies and living a lie. Martin Buber* once said, "The lie is the spirit committing treason against itself." Our acceptance of lies becomes a cultural cancer that eventually shrouds and reorders reality until moral garbage becomes as invisible to us as water is to a fish.

How much do we tolerate before we become sick and tired of being   36
sick and tired? When will we stand up and declare our *right* to trust? When do we stop accepting that the real truth is in the fine print? Whose lips do we read this year when we vote for president? When will we stop being so reticent about making judgments? When do we stop turning over our personal power and responsibility to liars?

---

* EDS. NOTE — Austrian-born Judaic philosopher (1878–1965).

Maybe if I don't tell the bank the check's in the mail I'll be less tolerant   37
of the lies told me every day. A country song I once heard said it all for me:
"You've got to stand for something or you'll fall for anything."

• • •

Comprehension

1. List and briefly define each of the ten kinds of lies Ericsson identifies.
2. Why, in Ericsson's view, is each kind of lie necessary?
3. According to Ericsson, what is the danger of each kind of lie?
4. Why does Ericsson like "out-and-out lies" (26–27) best?
5. Why is "dismissal" the "slipperiest of all lies" (28)?

Purpose and Audience

1. Is Ericsson's thesis simply that "there are many, many ways to tell a
   lie" (7)? Or is she defending — or attacking — the process of lying? Try
   to state her thesis in a single sentence.
2. Do you think Ericsson's choice of examples reveals a political bias? If
   so, do you think she expects her intended audience to share her views?
   Explain.

Style and Structure

1. Despite the seriousness of her subject matter, Ericsson's essay is informal; her opening paragraphs are especially personal and breezy. Why
   do you think she uses this kind of opening? Do you think her decision makes sense? Why, or why not?
2. Ericsson introduces each category of lie with a quotation. What function do these quotations serve? Would the essay be more or less effective without them? Explain your conclusion.
3. In addition to a heading and a quotation, what other elements does
   Ericsson include in her treatment of each kind of lie? Are all the discussions parallel — that is, does each include *all* the standard elements
   and *only* those elements? If not, do you think this lack of balance is a
   problem? Explain.
4. What, if anything, determines the order in which Ericsson arranges
   her categories? Should any category be relocated? Explain.
5. Throughout her essay, Ericsson uses **rhetorical questions**. Why do
   you suppose she uses this stylistic device?
6. Ericsson occasionally cites the views of experts. Why does she do so? If
   she wished to cite additional experts, what professional backgrounds
   or fields of study do you think they should represent? Why?
7. In paragraph 29, Ericsson says, "Imagine that a person is told from
   the time she is a tot. . . ." Does she use *she* in similar contexts else-

where in the essay? Do you find the feminine form of the personal pronoun appropriate or distracting? Explain.

8. Paragraphs 35–37 constitute Ericsson's conclusion. How does this conclusion parallel the essay's introduction in terms of style, structure, and content?

Vocabulary Projects

1. Define each of the following words as it is used in this selection.

travails (4)	deflectors (16)	staunch (30)
hedging (5)	passive-aggressive (16)	catatonia (30)
pittance (9)	misogynists (18)	gamut (31)
facades (10)	counterpart (18)	foibles (31)
plethora (11)	archetype (20)	reticent (36)
pedophilia (12)	nanoseconds (21)	
blatant (14)	obliterated (22)	

2. Ericsson uses many **colloquialisms** in this essay — for example, "I could write the book on this one" (32). Identify as many of these expressions as you can. Why do you think she uses colloquialisms instead of more formal expressions? Do they have a positive or negative effect on your reaction to her ideas? Explain.

Journal Entry

In paragraph 3, Ericsson says, "We lie. We all do." Later in the paragraph, she comments, "Sure I lie, but it doesn't hurt anything. Or does it?" Answer her question.

Writing Workshop

1. Choose three or four of Ericsson's categories, and write a classification-and-division essay called "The Ways I Lie." Base your essay on personal experience, and include an explicit thesis statement that defends these lies — or is sharply critical of their use.

2. In paragraph 22, Ericsson condemns stereotypes. Write a classification-and-division essay with the following thesis statement: "Stereotypes are usually inaccurate, often negative, and always dangerous." In your essay, consider the stereotypes applied to four of the following groups: people who are disabled, overweight, or elderly; teenagers; welfare recipients; housewives; and immigrants.

3. Using the thesis provided in question 2, write a classification-and-division essay that considers the stereotypes applied to four of the following occupations: police officers, librarians, used-car dealers, flight attendants, lawyers, construction workers, rock musicians, accountants, and telemarketers.

Combining the Patterns

A dictionary **definition** is a familiar — even tired — strategy for an essay's introduction. Would you advise Ericsson to delete the definition in paragraph 6 for this reason, or do you believe it is necessary? Explain.

Thematic Connections

- " 'What's in a Name?' " (page 5)
- "Thirty-Eight Who Saw Murder Didn't Call the Police" (page 120)
- "The Lottery" (page 317)
- "The Power of Words in Wartime" (page 377)

Five Ways to Kill a Man (Poetry)

Edwin Brock (1927–1997) was born in London, England. As a young man, he served in the Royal Navy for two years, and he later worked as a police officer. His first poetry collection, *An Attempt at Exorcism,* was published in 1959. He went on to work as an advertising copywriter while publishing more than a dozen poetry collections. He is also the author of the novel *The Little White God* (1962) and the memoir *Here, Now, Always* (1977).

Background on the poem: In the following 1963 poem, the first stanza refers to the crucifixion of Jesus, as described in the New Testament. Nailing a victim to a pole or cross was a form of capital punishment practiced in ancient times, especially by the Romans. The second stanza of the poem refers to the battling of knights suited in armor during the European Middle Ages. The third stanza refers to the trench warfare and mustard-gas bombs used by German and British forces during World War I. These bombs caused severe blistering, blindness, and respiratory failure, resulting in many casualties. The fourth stanza refers to the aerial bombing conducted during World War II — the German attacks on London, the Japanese attack on Pearl Harbor, and the U.S. atomic bombs dropped on Hiroshima and Nagasaki in Japan.

There are many cumbersome ways to kill a man:
you can make him carry a plank of wood
to the top of a hill and nail him to it. To do this
properly you require a crowd of people
wearing sandals, a cock that crows, a cloak   5
to dissect, a sponge, some vinegar and one
man to hammer the nails home.

Or you can take a length of steel,
shaped and chased in a traditional way,
and attempt to pierce the metal cage he wears.   10
But for this you need white horses,
English trees, men with bows and arrows,
at least two flags, a prince and a
castle to hold your banquet in.

Dispensing with nobility, you may, if the wind   15
allows, blow gas at him. But then you need
a mile of mud sliced through with ditches,
not to mention black boots, bomb craters,
more mud, a plague of rats, a dozen songs
and some round hats made of steel.   20

In an age of aeroplanes, you may fly
miles above your victim and dispose of him by
pressing one small switch. All you then
require is an ocean to separate you, two
systems of government, a nation's scientists,   25
several factories, a psychopath and
land that no one needs for several years.

These are, as I began, cumbersome ways
to kill a man. Simpler, direct, and much more neat
is to see that he is living somewhere in the middle   30
of the twentieth century, and leave him there.

• • •

Reading Literature

1. What five ways to kill a man does the poem's speaker identify?
2. What other examples can you give for each category?
3. When the speaker uses the word *you,* to whom is he referring?

Journal Entry

Why does the speaker see the first four methods of killing as "cumbersome" (1)? Why is the final method "Simpler, direct, and much more neat" (29)?

Thematic Connections

- "Thirty-Eight Who Saw Murder Didn't Call the Police" (page 120)
- "Ground Zero" (page 162)
- "Get It Right: Privatize Executions" (page 305)
- "The Lottery" (page 317)

WRITING ASSIGNMENTS FOR CLASSIFICATION AND DIVISION

1. Choose a film you have seen recently, and list all the elements you consider significant—plot, direction, acting, special effects, and so on. Then, further subdivide each category (for instance, listing each of the special effects). Using this list as an organizational guide, write a review of the film.

2. Write an essay classifying the teachers or bosses you have had into several distinct categories, and make a judgment about the relative effectiveness of the individuals in each group. Give each category a name, and be sure your essay has a thesis statement.

3. What fashion styles do you observe on your college campus? Establish four or five distinct categories, and write an essay classifying students on the basis of how they dress. Give each group a descriptive title.

4. Do some research to help you identify the subclasses of a large class of animals or plants. Write an essay enumerating and describing the subclasses in each class for an audience of elementary school students.

5. Many consider violence in sports a serious problem. Write an essay expressing your views on this problem. Use a classification-and-division structure, categorizing information according to sources of violence (such as the players, the nature of the game, and the fans).

6. Classify television shows according to type (reality show, crime drama, and so forth), audience (preschoolers, school-age children, adults, and so on), or any other logical principle. Write an essay based on your system of classification, making sure to include a thesis statement. For instance, you might assert that the relative popularity of one kind of program over others reveals something about television watchers or that one kind of program shows signs of becoming obsolete.

7. Write a lighthearted essay discussing kinds of snack foods, cartoons, pets, status symbols, toys, shoppers, vacations, weight-loss diets, hairstyles, or drivers.

8. Write an essay assessing the relative merits of several different politicians, news broadcasts, or academic majors.

9. What kinds of survival skills does a student need to get through college successfully? Write a classification-and-division essay identifying and discussing several kinds of skills and indicating why each category is important. If you like, you may write your essay in the form of a letter to a beginning college student.

10. After attending a party or concert, write an essay dividing the people you observe there into categories according to some logical principle. Include a thesis statement that indicates how different the various groups are.

COLLABORATIVE ACTIVITY FOR CLASSIFICATION AND DIVISION

Working in a group of four students, devise a classification system encompassing all the different kinds of popular music the members of your group favor. You may begin with general categories, such as country, pop, and rhythm and blues, but you should also include more specific categories, such as rap and heavy metal, in your classification system. After you decide on categories and subcategories that represent the tastes of all group members, fill in examples for each category. Then, devise several different options for arranging your categories into an essay.

INTERNET ASSIGNMENT FOR CLASSIFICATION AND DIVISION

Imagine you are a writer for *Beat* magazine and have been asked to write a feature article titled "American Music of the New Millennium." Referring to the following Web sites, use a classification-and-division structure to discuss the types of music you think represent the future of the music industry. Be sure to give each type of music a name and to describe its characteristics so as to give your audience a sense of the differences between the categories.

Spin Magazine
<spin.com>
Along with articles on bands and "pop life," this site contains audio and video clips of new music.

New Music Box
<newmusicbox.org>
This magazine from the American Music Center includes articles, interviews, a calendar, news sections, and sound and audio files.

Rolling Stone Magazine
<rollingstone.com>
This site offers up-to-date music news, reviews, and interviews with various popular music groups and artists of various genres.

13
Definition

What Is Definition?

A **definition** tells what a term means and how it differs from other terms in its class. In the following paragraph from "Altruistic Behavior," anthropologist Desmond Morris defines *altruism,* the key term of his essay:

Topic sentence	Altruism is the performance of an unselfish act. As a pattern of behavior, this act must have two properties: it must benefit someone else, and it must do so to the disadvantage of the benefactor. It is not merely a matter of being helpful; it is helpfulness at a cost to yourself.
Extended definition defines term by enumeration and negation	

Most people think of definition in terms of dictionaries, which give brief, succinct explanations—called **formal definitions**—of what words mean. But definition also includes explaining what something, or even someone, *is*—that is, its essential nature. Sometimes a definition requires a paragraph, an essay, or even a whole book. These longer, more complex definitions are called **extended definitions**.

Understanding Formal Definitions

Look at any dictionary, and you will notice that all definitions have a standard three-part structure. First, they present the *term* to be defined, then the general *class* it is a part of, and finally the *qualities that differentiate it* from the other terms in the same class.

TERM	CLASS	DIFFERENTIATION
behaviorism	a theory	that regards the objective facts of a subject's actions as the only valid basis for psychological study

cell	a unit of protoplasm	with a nucleus, cytoplasm, and an enclosing membrane
naturalism	a literary movement	whose original adherents believed that writers should treat life with scientific objectivity
mitosis	a process	of nuclear division of cells, consisting of prophase, metaphase, anaphase, and telophase
authority	a power	to command and require obedience

Understanding Extended Definitions

An extended definition includes the three basic parts of a formal definition — the term, its class, and its distinguishing characteristics. Beyond these essentials, an extended definition does not follow a set **pattern of development**. Instead, it uses whatever strategies best suit the term being defined and the writing situation. In fact, any one (or more than one) of the essay patterns illustrated in this book can be used to structure a definition essay.

Using Definition

Providing a formal definition of each term you use is seldom necessary or desirable. Readers will either know what a word means or be able to look it up. Sometimes, however, defining your terms is essential — for example, when a word has several meanings, each of which might fit your context, or when you want to use a word in a special way.

When taking an exam, of course, you are likely to encounter questions that require extended definitions. You might, for example, be asked to define *behaviorism;* tell what a *cell* is; explain the meaning of the literary term *naturalism;* include a comprehensive definition of *mitosis* in your answer; or define *authority*. Such exam questions cannot always be answered in one or two sentences. In fact, the definitions they call for often require several paragraphs.

Extended definitions are useful in many academic assignments besides exams. For example, definitions can explain abstractions such as *freedom,* controversial terms such as *right to life,* or **slang** terms (informal expressions whose meanings may vary from locale to locale or change as time passes). In a particular writing situation, a definition may be essential because a term has more than one meaning, because you are using it in an unusual way, or because you are fairly certain the term will be unfamiliar to your readers.

Many extended-definition essays include short formal definitions like those in dictionaries. In such an essay, a brief formal definition can introduce readers to the extended definition, or it can help to support the essay's thesis. In addition, essays with other dominant patterns of development often incorporate brief definitions to clarify points or explain basic information for the reader.

Planning a Definition Essay

You can organize a definition essay according to one or more of the patterns of development described in this book, or you can use other strategies. This section explains both approaches.

Using Patterns of Development

As you plan your essay and jot down your ideas about the term or subject you will define, you will see which other patterns are most useful. For example, the formal definitions of the five terms discussed on pages 509–10 could be expanded with five different patterns of development:

- **Exemplification**   To explain *behaviorism,* you could give **examples**. Carefully chosen cases could show how this theory of psychology applies to different situations. These examples could help readers see exactly how behaviorism works and what it can and cannot account for. Often, examples are the clearest way to explain something. Defining dreams as "the symbolic representation of mental states" might convey little to readers who do not know much about psychology, but a few examples would help you make your meaning clear. Many students have dreams about taking exams—perhaps dreaming that they are late for the test, that they remember nothing about the course, or that they are writing their answers in disappearing ink. You might explain the nature of dreams by interpreting these particular dreams, which may reflect anxiety about a course or about school in general.

- **Description**   You can explain the nature of something by **describing** it. For example, the concept of a *cell* is difficult to grasp from just a formal definition, but your readers would understand the concept more clearly if you were to describe what a cell looks like, possibly with the aid of a diagram or two. Concentrating on the cell membrane, cytoplasm, and nucleus, you could detail each structure's appearance and function. These descriptions would enable readers to visualize the whole cell and understand its workings. Of course, description involves more than the visual: a definition of a tsunami might describe the sounds and the appearance of this enormous ocean wave, and a definition of Parkinson's disease might include a description of how its symptoms affect a patient.

- **Comparison and contrast**   An extended definition of *naturalism* could use a **comparison-and-contrast** structure. Naturalism is one of several major movements in American literature, so its literary aims could be contrasted with those of other literary movements, such as romanticism or realism. Or you might compare and contrast the plots and characters of several naturalistic works with those of romantic or realistic works. Anytime you need to define something unfamiliar, you can compare it to something familiar to your readers. For example, your readers may never have heard of the Chinese dish sweet-and-sour cabbage, but you can help them imagine it by saying it tastes something like cole slaw. You can also define a thing by contrasting it with something unlike it, especially if the two have some qualities in common. For instance, one way to explain the British sport of rugby is by contrasting it with American football, which is not as violent.

• **Process**   Because mitosis is a process, an extended definition of *mitosis* should be organized as a **process explanation**. By tracing the process from stage to stage, you would clearly define this type of cell division for your readers. Process is also a suitable pattern for objects that must be defined in terms of what they do. For example, because a computer carries out certain processes, an extended definition of a computer would probably include a process explanation.

• **Classification and division**   You could define *authority* by using **classification and division**. Basing your extended definition on the model developed by the German sociologist Max Weber, you could divide the class *authority* into the subclasses *traditional authority, charismatic authority,* and *legal-bureaucratic authority*. By explaining each type of authority, you could clarify this very broad term for your readers. In both extended and formal definitions, classification and division can be very useful. By identifying the class something belongs to, you are explaining what kind of thing it is. For instance, *monetarism* is an economic theory; *The Adventures of Huckleberry Finn* is a novel; and *emphysema* is a disease. Likewise, by dividing a class into subclasses, you are defining something more specifically. Emphysema, for instance, is a disease of the lungs and can therefore be classified with tuberculosis but not with appendicitis.

Using Other Strategies

In addition to using various patterns of development, you can expand a definition by using any of the following strategies:

- You can define a term by using **synonyms** (words with similar meanings).
- You can define a term by using **negation** (telling what it is *not*).
- You can define a term by using **enumeration** (listing its characteristics).
- You can define a term by using **analogies** (comparisons identifying similarities between the term and something dissimilar).
- You can define a term by discussing its **origin and development** (the word's derivation, original meaning, and usages).

Phrasing Your Definition

Whatever form your definitions take, make certain that they clearly define your terms. Be sure to provide a true definition, not just a descriptive statement such as "Happiness is a four-day weekend." Also, remember that repetition is not definition, so don't include the term you are defining in your definition. For instance, the statement "abstract art is a school of artists whose works are abstract" clarifies nothing for your readers. Finally, define as precisely as possible. Name the class of the term you are defining — "mitosis is *a process* of cell division" — and define this class as narrowly and as accurately as you can. Be specific when you differentiate your term from other members of its class. Careful attention to the language and structure of your definition will help readers understand your meaning.

Structuring a Definition Essay

Like other essays, a definition essay should have an **introduction**, a **body**, and a **conclusion**. Although a formal definition strives for objectivity, an extended definition may not. Instead, it may define a term in a way that reflects your attitude toward the subject or your reason for defining it. For example, your extended-definition paper about literary *naturalism* might argue that the significance of this movement's major works has been underestimated by literary scholars. Similarly, your definition of *authority* might criticize its abuses. In such cases, the thesis statement provides a focus for a definition essay, telling readers *your* approach to the definition.

Suppose your assignment is to write a short paper for your introductory psychology course. You decide to examine *behaviorism*. First, you have to determine whether your topic is appropriate for a definition essay. If the topic suggests a response such as "The true nature of A is B" or "A means B," then it is a definition. Of course, you can define the word in one sentence, or possibly two. But to explain the *concept* of behaviorism and its status in the field of psychology, you must go beyond the dictionary.

Second, you have to decide what kinds of explanations are most suitable for your topic and for your intended audience. If you are trying to define *behaviorism* for readers who know very little about psychology, you might use comparisons that relate behaviorism to your readers' experiences, such as how they were raised or how they train their pets. You might also use examples, but the examples would relate not to psychological experiments or clinical treatment but to experiences in everyday life. If, however, you are directing your paper to your psychology instructor, who obviously already knows what behaviorism is, your purpose is to show that you know, too. One way to do this is to compare behaviorism to other psychological theories; another way is to give examples of how behaviorism works in practice; still another is to briefly summarize the background and history of the theory. (In a long paper, you might use all of these strategies.)

After considering your paper's scope and audience, you might decide that because behaviorism is somewhat controversial, your best strategy is to supplement a formal definition with examples showing how behaviorist assumptions and methods are applied in specific situations. These examples, drawn from your class notes and textbook, would support your thesis that behaviorism is a valid approach for treating certain psychological dysfunctions. Together, your examples would define *behaviorism* as it is understood today.

An informal outline for your essay might look like this:

Introduction:	Thesis statement — Contrary to its critics' objections, behaviorism is a valid approach for treating a wide variety of psychological dysfunctions.
Background:	Definition of behaviorism, including its origins and evolution
First example:	The use of behaviorism to help psychotics function in an institutional setting
Second example:	The use of behaviorism to treat neurotic behavior, such as chronic anxiety, a phobia, or a pattern of destructive acts
Third example:	The use of behaviorism to treat normal but antisocial or undesirable behavior, such as heavy smoking or overeating
Conclusion:	Restatement of thesis or review of key points

Notice how the three examples in this paper define behaviorism with the kind of complexity, detail, and breadth that a formal definition could not duplicate. This definition is more like a textbook explanation, and, in fact, textbook explanations are often written as extended definitions.

Revising a Definition Essay

When you revise a definition essay, consider the items on the revision checklist on page 54. In addition, pay special attention to the items on the following checklist, which apply specifically to revising definition essays.

✓ **REVISION CHECKLIST: Definition**

- Does your assignment call for definition?
- Does your essay include a clearly stated thesis that identifies the term you will define and communicates your approach to the definition?
- Have you included a formal definition of your subject? Of any additional key terms?

- Have you identified a pattern or patterns of development that you can use to expand your definition?
- Have you used other strategies—such as synonyms, negation, enumeration, or analogies—to expand your definition?
- Have you discussed the origin and development of the term you are defining?

Editing a Definition Essay

When you edit your definition essay, follow the guidelines on the editing checklists on pages 71, 73, and 76. In addition, focus on the grammar, mechanics, and punctuation issues that are particularly relevant to definition essays. One of these issues—avoiding the phrases *is when* and *is where* in formal definitions—is discussed here.

GRAMMAR IN CONTEXT: Avoiding *is when* and *is where*

Many extended definitions include one or more one-sentence formal definitions. As you have learned, each of these definitions must include the term you are defining, the class to which the term belongs, and the characteristics that distinguish the term from other terms in the same class.

Sometimes, however, when you are defining a term or concept, you may find yourself using the phrase *is when* or *is where*. If so, your definition is not complete because it omits the term's class. In fact, the use of *is when* or *is where* indicates that you are actually presenting an example of the term and not a definition. You can avoid this error by making certain that the form of the verb *be* in your definition is always followed by a noun.

INCORRECT:	As described in the essay "The Untouchable," *prejudice* is when someone forms an irrational bias or negative opinion of a person or group (Mahtab 516).
CORRECT:	As described in the essay "The Untouchable," *prejudice* is an irrational bias or negative opinion of a person or group (Mahtab 516).
INCORRECT:	According to Paul Fussell, an *honorific uniform* is where people get a neutral or positive impression (544).
CORRECT:	According to Paul Fussell, an *honorific uniform* is a uniform that conveys a neutral or positive impression (544).

For more practice in avoiding faulty constructions, visit Exercise Central at <bedfordstmartins.com/patterns/faultyconstructions>.

> ✓ **EDITING CHECKLIST: Definition**
>
> - Have you avoided using *is when* and *is where* in your formal definitions?
> - Have you used the present tense for your definition — even if you have used the past tense elsewhere in your essay?
> - If you have included a formal definition, have you italicized the term you are defining (or underlined to indicate italics) and placed the definition itself in quotation marks?

A STUDENT WRITER: Definition

The following student essay, written by Ajoy Mahtab for a composition course, defines the untouchables, members of a caste that is shunned in India. In his essay, Ajoy, who grew up in Calcutta, presents a thesis that is sharply critical of the practice of ostracizing untouchables.

The Untouchable

Introduction: background

A word that is extremely common in India yet uncommon to the point of incomprehension in the West is the word <u>untouchable</u>. It is a word that has had extremely sinister connotations throughout India's history. A rigorously worked-out caste system has traditionally existed in Indian society. At the top of the social ladder sat the Brahmins, the clan of the priesthood. These people had renounced the material world for a spiritual one. Below them came the Kshatriyas, or the warrior caste. This caste included the kings and all their nobles along with their armies. Third on the social ladder were the Vaishyas, who were the merchants of the land. Trade was their only form of livelihood. Last came the Shudras — the menials. Shudras were employed by the prosperous as sweepers and laborers. Originally a person's caste was determined only by his profession. Thus, if the son of a merchant joined the army, he automatically converted from a Vaishya to a Kshatriya. However, the system soon became hereditary and rigid. Whatever one's occupation, one's caste was determined from birth according to the caste of one's father.

1

Formal definition

Outside of this structure were a group of people, human beings treated worse than dogs and shunned far more than lepers, people who were not considered even human, people who defiled with their very touch. These were the Achhoots:

2

Fig. 1. Untouchable woman sweeping in front of her house in a village in Tamil Nadu, India (2003).

Historical background

the untouchables, one of whom is shown in Fig. 1. The word untouchable is commonly defined as "that which cannot or should not be touched." In India, however, it was taken to a far greater extreme. The untouchables of a village lived in a separate community downwind of the borders of the village. They had a separate water supply, for they would make the village water impure if they were to drink from it. When they walked, they were made to bang two sticks together continuously so that passersby could hear them coming and thus avoid an untouchable's shadow. Tied to their waists, trailing behind them, was a broom that would clean the ground they had walked on. The penalty for not following these or any other rules was death for the untouchable and, in many instances, for the entire untouchable community.

Present situation

One of the pioneers of the fight against untouchability was Mahatma Gandhi. Thanks to his efforts and those of many others, untouchability no longer presents anything

3

like the horrific picture painted earlier. In India today, in fact, recognition of untouchability is punishable by law. Theoretically, there is no such thing as untouchability anymore. But old traditions linger on, and such a deep-rooted fear passed down from generation to generation cannot disappear overnight. Even today, caste is an important factor in most marriages. Most Indian surnames reveal a person's caste immediately, so it is a difficult thing to hide. The shunning of the untouchable is more prevalent in South India, where people are much more devout, than in the North. Some people would rather starve than share food and water with an untouchable. This concept is very difficult to accept in the West, but it is true all the same.

Example

I remember an incident from my childhood. I could not have been more than eight or nine at the time. I was on a holiday staying at my family's house on the river Ganges. A festival was going on, and, as is customary, we were giving the servants small presents. I was handing them out when an old lady, bent with age, slowly hobbled into the room. She stood in the far corner of the room all alone, and no one so much as looked at her. When the entire line ended, she stepped hesitantly forward and stood in front of me, looking down at the ground. She then held a cloth stretched out in front of her. I was a little confused about how I was supposed to hand her her present, since both her hands were holding the cloth. Then, with the help of prompting from someone behind me, I learned that I was supposed to drop the gift into the cloth without touching the cloth itself. It was only later that I found out that she was an untouchable. This was the first time I had actually come face to face with such prejudice, and it felt like a slap in the face. That incident was burned into my memory, and I do not think I will ever forget it.

Conclusion begins

The word untouchable is not often used in the West, and when it is, it is generally used as a complimentary term. For example, an avid fan might say of an athlete, "He was absolutely untouchable. Nobody could even begin to compare with him." It seems rather ironic that a word could be so favorable in one culture and so negative in another. Why does a word that gives happiness in one part of the world cause pain in

4

5

another? Why does the same word have different meanings to different people around the globe? Why do certain words cause rifts and others forge bonds? I do not think anyone can tell me the answers to these questions.

Conclusion continues No actual parallel can be found today that compares to   6
the horrors of untouchability. For an untouchable, life itself was a crime. The day was spent just trying to stay alive. From the
Thesis statement misery of the untouchables, the world should learn a lesson: isolating and punishing any group of people is dehumanizing and immoral.

Points for Special Attention

Thesis Statement.   Ajoy Mahtab's assignment was to write an extended definition of a term he assumed would be unfamiliar to his audience. Because he had definite ideas about the unjust treatment of the untouchables, Ajoy wanted his essay to have a strong thesis that communicated his disapproval. Still, because he knew his American classmates would need a good deal of background information before they would understand the context for such a thesis, he decided not to present it in his introduction. Instead, he decided to lead up to his thesis gradually and state it at the end of his essay. When other students in the class reviewed his draft, this subtlety was one of the points they reacted to most favorably.

Structure.   Ajoy's introduction establishes the direction of his essay by introducing the word he will define; he then places this word in context by explaining India's rigid caste system. In paragraph 2, he gives the formal definition of the word *untouchable* and goes on to sketch the term's historical background. Paragraph 3 explains the status of the untouchables in present-day India, and paragraph 4 gives a vivid example of Ajoy's first encounter with an untouchable. As he begins his conclusion in paragraph 5, Ajoy brings his readers back to the word his essay defines. Here he uses two strategies to add interest: he contrasts a contemporary American usage of *untouchable* with its pejorative meaning in India, and he asks a series of **rhetorical questions** (questions asked for effect and not meant to be answered). In paragraph 6, Ajoy presents a summary of his position to lead into his thesis statement.

Patterns of Development.   This essay uses a number of strategies commonly encountered in extended definitions: it includes a formal definition, explains the term's origin, and explores some of the term's connotations. The essay also incorporates several familiar patterns of development.

For instance, paragraph 1 uses classification and division to explain India's caste system; paragraphs 2 and 3 use brief examples to illustrate the plight of the untouchable; and paragraph 4 presents a narrative. Each of these patterns enriches the definition. In addition, Ajoy includes a photograph of an untouchable to supplement his passages of description and to help his readers understand this unfamiliar concept.

Focus on Revision

Because the term Ajoy defined was so unfamiliar to his classmates, many of the peer editing worksheets his classmates filled in asked for more information. One suggestion in particular — that he draw an **analogy** between the unfamiliar term *untouchable* and a more familiar concept — appealed to Ajoy as he planned his revision. Another student suggested that Ajoy could compare untouchables to other groups who are shunned — for example, people with AIDS. Although Ajoy states in his conclusion that no parallel exists, an attempt to find common ground between untouchables and other groups could make his essay more meaningful to his readers — and bring home to them a distinctly alien idea. Such a connection could also make his conclusion especially powerful.

📄   **PEER EDITING WORKSHEET: Definition**

1. What term is the writer defining? Does the essay include a formal dictionary definition? If so, where? Does the phrasing of this definition avoid *is when* and *is where*? If no formal definition is included, should one be added?

2. Why is the writer defining the term? Does the essay include a thesis statement that makes this purpose clear?

3. What patterns does the writer use to develop the definition? What other patterns could be used? Would a visual be helpful?

4. Does the essay define the term appropriately for its audience? Does the definition help you understand the meaning of the term?

5. Does the writer use **synonyms** to develop the definition? If so, where? If not, where could synonyms be used to help communicate the term's meaning?

6. Does the writer use **negation** to develop the definition? If so, where? If not, could the writer strengthen the definition by explaining what the term is *not?*

7. Does the writer use **enumeration** to develop the definition? If so, where? If not, where might the term's special characteristics be listed?

8. Does the writer use **analogies** to develop the definition? If so, where? Do you find these analogies helpful? What additional analogies might help readers understand the term more fully?

9. Does the writer explain the term's linguistic origin and development? If so, where? If not, do you believe this information should be added?

10. Reread the essay's introduction. If the writer uses a formal definition as an opening strategy, try to suggest an alternative opening.

The selections that follow use exemplification, description, narration, and other methods of developing extended definitions. The first selection, a visual text, is followed by questions designed to illustrate how definition can operate in visual form.

U.S. Census 2000 Form (Questionnaire)

→ **NOTE: Please answer BOTH Questions 7 and 8.**

7. Is Person 1 Spanish/Hispanic/Latino? *Mark* ☒ *the* ***"No"*** *box if **not** Spanish/Hispanic/Latino.*

☐ **No,** not Spanish/Hispanic/Latino   ☐ Yes, Puerto Rican

☐ Yes, Mexican, Mexican Am., Chicano   ☐ Yes, Cuban

☐ Yes, other Spanish/Hispanic/Latino — *Print group.* ↙

| | | | | | | | | | | | | | | | | | | |

8. What is Person 1's race? *Mark* ☒ *one or more races* to indicate what this person considers himself/herself to be.

☐ White

☐ Black, African Am., or Negro

☐ American Indian or Alaska Native — *Print name of enrolled or principal tribe.* ↙

| | | | | | | | | | | | | | | | | | | |

☐ Asian Indian   ☐ Japanese   ☐ Native Hawaiian

☐ Chinese   ☐ Korean   ☐ Guamanian or Chamorro

☐ Filipino   ☐ Vietnamese   ☐ Samoan

☐ Other Asian — *Print race.* ↙   ☐ Other Pacific Islander — *Print race.* ↙

| | | | | | | | | | | | | | | | | | | |

☐ Some other race — *Print race.* ↙

| | | | | | | | | | | | | | | | | | | |

• • •

Reading Images

1. In a single complete sentence, define yourself in terms of your race, religion, or ethnicity (whatever is most important to you).

2. Look at the U.S. Census questions above. Which boxes would you mark? Do you see this choice as an accurate expression of what you consider yourself to be? Explain.

3. Only recently has the Census Bureau permitted respondents to mark "one or more races" to indicate their ethnic identity. Do you think this option is a good idea?

Journal Entry

Why do you think the government needs to know "what [a] person considers himself/herself to be"? Do you think it is important for the government to know how people define themselves, or do you consider this information an unwarranted violation of a person's privacy? Explain.

Thematic Connections

- "Only Daughter" (page 96)
- "Indian Education" (page 134)
- "The 'Black Table' Is Still There" (page 366)
- "Two Ways to Belong in America" (page 415)
- "Mother Tongue" (page 487)

JUDY BRADY

I Want a Wife

Judy Brady was born in San Francisco in 1937 and earned a B.F.A. in painting from the University of Iowa in 1962. She has raised two daughters, worked as a secretary, and published articles on many social issues. Diagnosed with breast cancer in 1980, she became active in the politics of cancer and has edited *Women and Cancer* (1990) and *One in Three: Women with Cancer Confront an Epidemic* (1991). She also helped found the Toxic Links Coalition, an organization devoted to lobbying for cancer and environmental issues.

Background on the status of women: Brady has been active in the women's movement since 1969, and "I Want a Wife" first appeared in the premiere issue of the feminist *Ms.* magazine in 1972. That year represented perhaps the height of the feminist movement in the United States. The National Organization for Women, established in 1966, had hundreds of chapters around the country. The Equal Rights Amendment, barring discrimination against women, passed in Congress (although it was ratified by only thirty-five of the necessary thirty-eight states), and Congress also passed Title IX of the Education Amendments Act, which required equal opportunity (in sports as well as academics) for all students in any school that receives federal funding. At that time, women accounted for just under 40 percent of the labor force (up from 23 percent in 1950), a number that has grown to almost 50 percent today. Of mothers with children under age eighteen, fewer than 40 percent were employed in 1970; today, three-quarters work, 38 percent of them full-time and year-round. As for stay-at-home fathers, their numbers have increased from virtually zero to more than three million.

I belong to that classification of people known as wives. I am A Wife. And, not altogether incidentally, I am a mother. 1

Not too long ago a male friend of mine appeared on the scene fresh from a recent divorce. He had one child, who is, of course, with his ex-wife. He is looking for another wife. As I thought about him while I was ironing one evening, it suddenly occurred to me that I, too, would like to have a wife. Why do I want a wife? 2

I would like to go back to school so that I can become economically independent, support myself, and, if need be, support those dependent upon me. I want a wife who will work and send me to school. And while I am going to school I want a wife to take care of my children. I want a wife to keep track of the children's doctor and dentist appointments. And to keep track of mine, too. I want a wife to make sure my children eat properly and are kept clean. I want a wife who will wash the children's clothes and keep them mended. I want a wife who is a good nurturant attendant to my 3 children, who arranges for their schooling, makes sure that they have an adequate social life with their peers, takes them to the park, the zoo, etc. I want a wife who takes care of the children when they are sick, a wife who arranges to be around when the children need special care, because, of course, I cannot miss classes at school. My wife must arrange to lose time at work and not lose the job. It may mean a small cut in my wife's income from time to time, but I guess I can tolerate that. Needless to say, my wife will arrange and pay for the care of the children while my wife is working.

I want a wife who will take care of *my* physical needs. I want a wife who 4 will keep my house clean. A wife who will pick up after my children, a wife who will pick up after me. I want a wife who will keep my clothes clean, ironed, mended, replaced when need be, and who will see to it that my personal things are kept in their proper place so that I can find what I need the minute I need it. I want a wife who cooks the meals, a wife who is a *good* cook. I want a wife who will plan the menus, do the necessary grocery shopping, prepare the meals, serve them pleasantly, and then do the cleaning up while I do my studying. I want a wife who will care for me when I am sick and sympathize with my pain and loss of time from school. I want a wife to go along when our family takes a vacation so that someone can continue to care for me and my children when I need a rest and change of scene.

I want a wife who will not bother me with rambling complaints about 5 a wife's duties. But I want a wife who will listen to me when I feel the need to explain a rather difficult point I have come across in my course of studies. And I want a wife who will type my papers for me when I have written them.

I want a wife who will take care of the details of my social life. When my 6 wife and I are invited out by my friends, I want a wife who will take care of the babysitting arrangements. When I meet people at school that I like and want to entertain, I want a wife who will have the house clean, will prepare a special meal, serve it to me and my friends, and not interrupt when I talk about things that interest me and my friends. I want a wife who will have arranged that the children are fed and ready for bed before my guests arrive so that the children do not bother us. I want a wife who takes care of the needs of my guests so that they feel comfortable, who makes sure that they have an ashtray, that they are passed the hors d'oeuvres, that they are offered a second helping of the food, that their wine glasses are replenished when necessary, that their coffee is served to them as they like it. And I want a wife who knows that sometimes I need a night out by myself.

I want a wife who is sensitive to my sexual needs, a wife who makes love 7 passionately and eagerly when I feel like it, a wife who makes sure that I am satisfied. And, of course, I want a wife who will not demand sexual attention when I am not in the mood for it. I want a wife who assumes the complete responsibility for birth control, because I do not want more children. I want a wife who will remain sexually faithful to me so that I do not have to clutter up my intellectual life with jealousies. And I want a wife who understands that *my* sexual needs may entail more than strict adherence to monogamy. I must, after all, be able to relate to people as fully as possible.

If, by chance, I find another person more suitable as a wife than the wife I already have, I want the liberty to replace my present wife with another one. Naturally, I will expect a fresh new life; my wife will take the children and be solely responsible for them so that I am left free.   8

When I am through with school and have a job, I want my wife to quit working and remain at home so that my wife can more fully and completely take care of a wife's duties.   9

My God, who *wouldn't* want a wife?   10

• • •

Comprehension

1. In one sentence, define what Brady means by *wife*. Does this ideal wife actually exist? Explain.
2. List some of the specific duties of the wife Brady describes. Into what five general categories does Brady arrange these duties?
3. What complaints does Brady apparently have about the life she actually leads? To what does she seem to attribute her problems?
4. Under what circumstances does Brady say she would consider leaving her wife? What would happen to the children if she left?

Purpose and Audience

1. This essay was first published in *Ms.* magazine. In what sense is it appropriate for the audience of this feminist publication? Where else can you imagine it appearing?
2. Does this essay have an explicitly stated thesis? If so, where is it? If the thesis is implied, paraphrase it.
3. Do you think Brady *really* wants the kind of wife she describes? Explain.

Style and Structure

1. Throughout the essay, Brady repeats the words "I want a wife." What is the effect of this repetition?
2. The first and last paragraphs of this essay are quite brief. Does this weaken the essay? Why, or why not?
3. In enumerating a wife's duties, Brady frequently uses the verb *arrange*. What other verbs does she use repeatedly? How do these verbs help her make her point?
4. Brady never uses the personal pronouns *he* or *she* to refer to the wife she defines. Why not?
5. Comment on Brady's use of phrases such as *of course* (2, 3, and 7), *needless to say* (3), *after all* (7), *by chance* (8), and *naturally* (8). What do these

expressions contribute to the sentences where they appear? To the essay as a whole?

Vocabulary Projects

1. Define each of the following words as it is used in this selection.

    nurturant (3)   adherence (7)
    replenished (6)   monogamy (7)

2. Going beyond the dictionary definitions, decide what Brady means to suggest by the following words. Is she using any of these words sarcastically? Explain.

    proper (4)   necessary (6)   suitable (8)
    pleasantly (4)   demand (7)   free (8)
    bother (6)   clutter up (7)

Journal Entry

Is Brady's 1972 characterization of a wife still accurate today? Which of the characteristics she describes have remained the same? Which have changed? Why?

Writing Workshop

1. Write an essay defining your ideal spouse.
2. Write an essay titled "I Want a Husband." Taking an **ironic** stance, use society's notions of the ideal husband to help you shape your definition.
3. Write a definition essay called "The Ideal Couple," in which you try to divide household chores and other responsibilities equitably between the two partners. Your essay can be serious or humorous. Develop your definition with examples.

Combining the Patterns

Like most definition essays, "I Want a Wife" uses several patterns of development. Which ones does it use? Which of these do you consider most important for supporting Brady's thesis? Why?

Thematic Connections

- "My Mother Never Worked" (page 108)
- "Sex, Lies, and Conversation" (page 440)
- "The Men We Carry in Our Minds" (page 481)
- Declaration of Sentiments and Resolutions (page 590)

Tortillas

José Antonio Burciaga (1940–1996) was born in El Chuco, Texas, and served in the U.S. Air Force from 1960 to 1964. He graduated from the University of Texas at El Paso in 1968 and attended the Corcoran School of Art and the San Francisco Art Institute. Burciaga was the founder of *Diseños Literarios,* a publishing company in California, as well as the comedy troupe Culture Clash. He contributed fiction, poetry, and articles to many anthologies, as well as to journals and newspapers. He also published several books of poems, drawings, and essays, including the poetry collection *Undocumented Love* (1992) and the essay collection *Drink Cultura* (1993). "Tortillas," originally titled "I Remember Masa," was first published in *Weedee Peepo* (1988), a collection of essays in Spanish and English.

Background on tortillas: Tortillas have been a staple of Mexican cooking for thousands of years. These thin, round griddlecakes made of cornmeal *(masa)* are often eaten with every meal, and the art of making them is still passed from generation to generation (although they now are widely available commercially as well). The earliest Mexican immigrants introduced them to the United States, and in the past twenty-five years tortillas, along with many other popular items of Mexican cuisine, have entered the country's culinary landscape (as, over the decades, has a wide variety of other "ethnic" foods, such as pizza, egg rolls, bagels, and gyros). Still, tortillas have special meaning for Mexican Americans, and in this essay Burciaga discusses the role of the tortilla within his family's culture.

1   My earliest memory of *tortillas* is my *Mamá* telling me not to play with them. I had bitten eyeholes in one and was wearing it as a mask at the dinner table.

2   As a child, I also used *tortillas* as hand warmers on cold days, and my family claims that I owe my career as an artist to my early experiments with *tortillas.* According to them, my clowning around helped me develop a strong artistic foundation. I'm not so sure, though. Sometimes I wore a *tortilla* on my head, like a *yarmulke,* and yet I never had any great urge to convert from Catholicism to Judaism. But who knows? They may be right.

3   For Mexicans over the centuries, the *tortilla* has served as the spoon and the fork, the plate and the napkin. *Tortillas* originated before the Mayan civilizations, perhaps predating Europe's wheat bread. According to Mayan mythology, the great god Quetzalcoatl, realizing that the red ants knew the secret of using maize as food, transformed himself into a black ant, infiltrated the colony of red ants, and absconded with a grain of corn. (Is it any wonder that to this day, black ants and red ants do not get along?) Quetzalcoatl then put maize on the lips of the first man and woman, Oxomoco and Cipactonal, so that they would become strong. Maize festivals are still celebrated by many Indian cultures of the Americas.

When I was growing up in El Paso, *tortillas* were part of my daily life. I used   4
to visit a *tortilla* factory in an ancient adobe building near the open *mercado* in
Ciudad Juárez. As I approached, I could hear the rhythmic slapping of the
masa as the skilled vendors outside the factory formed it into balls and patted
them into perfectly round corn cakes between the palms of their hands. The
wonderful aroma and the speed with which the women counted so many
dozens of *tortillas* out of warm wicker baskets still linger in my mind. Watching them at work convinced me that the most handsome and *deliciosas tortillas*
are handmade. Although machines are faster, they can never adequately
replace generation-to-generation experience. There's no place in the factory
assembly line for the tender slaps that give each *tortilla* character. The best
thing that can be said about mass-producing *tortillas* is that it makes it possible for many people to enjoy them.

In the *mercado* where my mother shopped, we frequently bought *taquitos*   5
de nopalitos, small tacos filled with diced cactus, onions, tomatoes, and
jalapeños. Our friend Don Toribio showed us how to make delicious, crunchy
taquitos with dried, salted pumpkin seeds. When you had no money for the
filling, a poor man's *taco* could be made by placing a warm *tortilla* on the left
palm, applying a sprinkle of salt, then rolling the *tortilla* up quickly with the
fingertips of the right hand. My own kids put peanut butter and jelly on *tortillas,* which I think is truly bicultural. And speaking of fast foods for kids,
nothing beats a *quesadilla,* a *tortilla* grilled-cheese sandwich.

Depending on what you intend to use them for, *tortillas* may be made   6
in various ways. Even a run-of-the-mill *tortilla* is more than a flat corn cake.
A skillfully cooked homemade *tortilla* has a bottom and a top; the top skin
forms a pocket in which you put the filling that folds your *tortilla* into a
taco. Paper-thin *tortillas* are used specifically for *flautas,* a type of taco that
is filled, rolled, and then fried until crisp. The name *flauta* means *flute,*
which probably refers to the Mayan bamboo flute; however, the only sound
that comes from an edible *flauta* is a delicious crunch that is music to the
palate. In México *flautas* are sometimes made as long as two feet and then
cut into manageable segments. The opposite of *flautas* is *gorditas,* meaning
little fat ones. These are very thick small *tortillas.*

The versatility of *tortillas* and corn does not end here. Besides being   7
tasty and nourishing, they have spiritual and artistic qualities as well. The
Tarahumara Indians of Chihuahua, for example, concocted a corn-based
beer called *tesgüino,* which their descendants still make today. And everyone
has read about the woman in New Mexico who was cooking her husband a
tortilla one morning when the image of Jesus Christ miraculously appeared
on it. Before they knew what was happening, the man's breakfast had
become a local shrine.

Then there is *tortilla* art. Various Chicano artists throughout the South-   8
west have, when short of materials or just in a whimsical mood, used a dry
tortilla as a small, round canvas. And a few years back, at the height of the
Chicano movement, a priest in Arizona got into trouble with the Church
after he was discovered celebrating mass using a *tortilla* as the host. All of

which only goes to show that while the *tortilla* may be a lowly corn cake, when the necessity arises, it can reach unexpected distinction.

•   •   •

Comprehension

1. What exactly is a tortilla?
2. List the functions — both practical and whimsical — that tortillas serve.
3. In paragraph 7, Burciaga cites the "spiritual and artistic qualities" of tortillas. Do you think he is being serious? Explain your reasoning.

Purpose and Audience

1. Burciaga states his thesis explicitly in his essay's final sentence. Paraphrase this thesis. Why do you think he does not state it sooner?
2. Do you think Burciaga expects most of his readers to be of Hispanic descent? To be familiar with tortillas? How can you tell?
3. Why do you think Burciaga uses humor in this essay? Is it consistent with his essay's purpose? Could the humor have a negative effect on his audience? Explain.
4. Why are tortillas so important to Burciaga? Is it just their versatility he admires, or do they represent something more to him?

Style and Structure

1. Where does Burciaga provide a formal definition of *tortilla*? Why does he locate this formal definition at this point in his essay?
2. Burciaga uses many Spanish words, but he defines only some of them — for example, *taquitos de nopalitos* and *quesadilla* in paragraph 5 and *flautas* and *gorditas* in paragraph 6. Why do you think he defines some Spanish terms but not others? Should he have defined them all?
3. Does Burciaga use **synonyms** or **negation** to define *tortilla*? Does he discuss the word's origin? If so, where? If not, do you think any of these strategies would improve his essay? Explain.

Vocabulary Projects

1. Define each of the following words as it is used in this selection.

yarmulke (2)	absconded (3)	concocted (7)
maize (3)	adobe (4)	

2. Look up each of the following words in a Spanish-English dictionary, and (if possible) supply its English equivalent.

mercado (4)	deliciosas (4)
masa (4)	jalapeños (5)

Journal Entry

Explore some additional uses — practical or frivolous — for tortillas that Burciaga does not discuss.

Writing Workshop

1. Write an essay defining a food that is important to your family, ethnic group, or circle of friends. Use several patterns of development, as Burciaga does. Assume your audience is not familiar with the food you define.
2. Relying primarily on description and exemplification, define a food that is sure to be familiar to all your readers. Do not name the food until your essay's last sentence.
3. Write an essay defining a food — but include a thesis statement that paints a very favorable portrait of a much-maligned food (for example, Spam or brussels sprouts) or a very negative picture of a popular food (for example, chocolate or ice cream).

Combining the Patterns

Burciaga uses several patterns of development in his extended definition. Where, for example, does he use **description**, **narration**, **process**, and **exemplification**? Does he use any other patterns? Explain.

Thematic Connections

- "Once More to the Lake" (page 186)
- "Innovation" (page 231)
- "The Park" (page 707)

GAYLE ROSENWALD SMITH

The Wife-Beater

Gayle Rosenwald Smith was born in 1951 in Philadelphia and received her bachelor's degree from the University of Pennsylvania. A graduate of the University of Miami School of Law, she currently practices family law. She has published articles in a variety of journals and periodicals and is coauthor of *What Every Woman Should Know about Divorce and Custody* (1998) and *Divorce and Money: Everything You Need to Know* (2004). The following essay appeared in the *Philadelphia Inquirer* in 2001.

Background on the "wife-beater" shirt: As Smith notes here, *wife-beater* is a slang term for a type of sleeveless undershirt that has in recent years become fashionable. An Internet search of the term found a number of businesses that, in fact, market such shirts as "wife-beaters." The corresponding shirts for women are often called "boy-beaters." A Texas-based firm offers adult-sized shirts emblazoned with the slogan, as well as "Lil' Wife Beater" shirts for babies. The firm's Web site — accompanied by the beat of a rap recording about "smashing" women — includes a background screen showing a woman being spanked and provides a link to a "Wife Beater Hall of Fame." It also offers to send a second shirt at half price to any customer convicted of domestic violence (proof of conviction required, photos not acceptable). Many Web sites have sprung up condemning this business, but one of the site's customers is a victim of domestic violence who hands out wife-beater shirts to police officers, judges, and others whose professional conduct she believes encourages domestic violence. In another twist, a feminist retail site offered a "Wife Beater Beater" shirt with a cartoon image of a woman kicking a man in the groin.

Everybody wears them. The Gap sells them. Fashion designers Dolce and Gabbana have lavished them with jewels. Their previous greatest resurgence occurred in the 1950s, when Marlon Brando's Stanley Kowalski wore one in Tennessee Williams' *A Streetcar Named Desire*. They are all the rage.

What are they called?

The name is the issue. For they are known as "wife-beaters."

A Web search shows that kids nationwide are wearing the skinny-ribbed white T-shirts that can be worn alone or under another shirt. Women have adopted them with the same gusto as men. A search of boutiques shows that these wearers include professionals who wear them, adorned with designer accessories, under their pricey suits. They are available in all colors, sizes and price ranges.

Wearers under 25 do not seem to be disturbed by the name. But I   5
sure am.

It's an odd name for an undershirt. And even though the ugly stereo-   6
types behind the name are both obvious and toxic, it appears to be cool to
say the name without fear of (or without caring about) hurting anyone.

That the name is fueled by stereotype is now an academically estab-   7
lished fact, although various sources disagree on exactly when shirt and
name came together. The *Oxford Dictionary* defines the term *wife-beater* as:

1. A man who physically abuses his wife and
2. Tank-style underwear shirts. Origin: based on the stereotype that
   physically abusive husbands wear that particular type of shirt.

The *World Book Dictionary* locates the origin of the term *wife-beater* in the   8
1970s, from the stereotype of the Midwestern male wearing an undershirt
while beating his wife. The shirts are said to have been popular in the 1980s
at all types of sporting events, especially ones at which one sits in the sun
and develops "wife-beater marks." The undershirts also attained popularity
at wet T-shirt contests, in which the wet, ribbed tees accentuated contes-
tants' breasts.

In an article in the style section of the *New York Times,* Jesse Scheidlower,   9
principal editor of the *Oxford English Dictionary*'s American office, says the
association of the undershirt and the term *wife-beater* arose in 1997 from
varied sources, including gay and gang subcultures and rap music.

In the article, some sources argued that the reference in the term was   10
not to spousal abuse per se but to popular-culture figures such as Ralph
Cramden and Tony Soprano. And what about Archie Bunker?

It's not just the name that worries me. Fashion headlines reveal that we   11
want to overthrow '90s grunge and return to shoulder pads and hardware-
studded suits. Am I reading too much into a fashion statement that the
return is also to male dominance where physical abuse is acceptable as a
means of control?

There has to be a better term. After all, it's a pretty rare piece of clothing   12
that can make both men and women look sexier. You'd expect a term connoting flattery — not violence.

Wearers under 25 may not want to hear this, but here it is. More than   13
4 million women are victims of severe assaults by boyfriends and husbands each year. By conservative estimate, family violence occurs in 2
million families each year in the United States. Average age of the bat-
terer: 31.

Possibly the last statistic is telling. Maybe youth today would rather   14
ignore the overtones of the term *wife-beater.* It is also true, however, that the
children of abusers often learn the behavior from their elders.

Therein lies perhaps the worst difficulty: that this name for this shirt   15
teaches the wrong thing about men. Some articles quote women who felt

the shirts looked great, especially on guys with great bodies. One woman stated that it even made guys look "manly."

So *manly* equals *violent*? Not by me, and I hope not by anyone on any   16
side of age 25.

· · ·

Comprehension

1. Why is Smith "disturbed" (5) by the name "wife-beater"?

2. In paragraph 3, Smith says, "The name is the issue"; in paragraph 11, she says "It's not just the name that worries me." What does she mean by each statement? Does she contradict herself?

3. What relationship does Smith see between the name of a sleeveless undershirt and the prevalence of family violence? Does she believe a causal connection does — or could — exist? If so, which is the cause, and which is the effect?

4. In paragraph 12, Smith acknowledges that the shirt "can make both men and women look sexier." Does this remark in any way undercut her credibility? Explain.

5. How, according to Smith, does calling a shirt a wife-beater teach women "the wrong thing about men" (15)?

Purpose and Audience

1. How do you think Smith expects her audience to react to her opening statement ("Everybody wears them")?

2. Why do you think Smith wrote this essay? Is her purpose to change the name of the T-shirt, or does she seem to have a more ambitious purpose? Explain.

3. Twice in her essay, Smith mentions a group she calls "wearers under 25" (5, 13). Does she seem to direct her remarks at these young adults or at older readers? At wearers of the shirts or at a more general audience?

4. Restate Smith's thesis in your words.

Style and Structure

1. Why do you think Smith begins her essay by explaining the popularity of sleeveless undershirts? Is this an effective opening strategy?

2. In paragraph 7, Smith reproduces a formal definition from the *Oxford Dictionary*. Why does she include this definition when she has already defined her term? What, if anything, does the formal definition add?

3. Where does Smith present information on the history of the wife-beater? Why does she include this kind of information?

4. Where does Smith quote statistics? Do you see this information as relevant or incidental to her argument?

Vocabulary Projects

1. Define each of the following words as it is used in this selection.

   resurgence (1)   accentuated (8)
   gusto (4)   per se (10)
   toxic (6)   connoting (12)

2. In paragraph 12, Smith says, "There has to be a better term." Can you think of a "better term" — one that does not suggest violence — for the shirt Smith describes?

Journal Entry

Do you agree with Smith that the casual use of terms like *wife-beater* is dangerous, or do you think she is exaggerating the problem?

Writing Workshop

1. Relying primarily on description and exemplification, define an article of clothing that is essential to your wardrobe. Begin by checking the Internet or an unabridged dictionary to learn the item's history and the origin of its name.

2. Using comparison and contrast to structure your essay, define what a particular item of clothing means to you — and what it means to one of your parents.

3. Do members of your religious or ethnic group wear an item of clothing that is not well known to others? Define the article of clothing, and explain its significance and its history in terms that outsiders can understand.

Combining the Patterns

Do you think Smith should have spent more time in this essay on developing the **cause-and-effect** relationship, if any, between the "wife-beater" shirt and family violence? What additional information would she have to provide?

Thematic Connections

- "My First Conk" (page 285)
- "A Peaceful Woman Explains Why She Carries a Gun" (page 371)
- "Stigmatic Uniforms" (page 544)
- "Violent Films Cry 'Fire' in Crowded Theaters" (page 691)

REBECCA BLOOD

What Is a Weblog?

Rebecca Blood has maintained her own weblog, Rebecca's Pocket, since 1999 and has published articles about the theory and practice of weblogs in journals such as the *Nieman Reports* and *Communications of the ACM* (Association for Computing Machinery). Her book *The Weblog Handbook: Practical Advice on Creating and Maintaining Your Blog* (2002) was listed as one of Amazon.com's ten best books of the year on digital culture and led to mentions in feature articles in the *New York Times, Newsweek, Time,* and other popular periodicals. The following selection is the opening chapter of her book.

Background on political weblogs: Blood's focus here is on weblogs used to express personal stories and thoughts or to connect users to other sites that individual bloggers find interesting. However, the most influential and well-known blogs are those devoted to political reporting and commentary. Widespread awareness of such outlets for news not always covered by the mainstream media can be traced to the mid-1990s and Matt Drudge's The Drudge Report. Although not technically a weblog, the site's exposé of rumors about a relationship between President Clinton and former White House intern Monica Lewinsky eventually found its way onto the nightly news and demonstrated the potential power of nontraditional forms of Web reporting. Since then, blogs such as Instapundit, Blogs for Bush, and Crooks and Liars have sprung up across the political spectrum. These partisan bloggers do not always hold themselves to the highest journalistic standards, but some continue to break important stories, such as the 2004 examination by the blog Little Green Footballs of flawed reporting about President Bush's National Guard service and AmericaBlog's 2005 revelations about a member of the White House press corps who was actually being paid by a conservative lobbyist.

A weblog is a coffeehouse conversation in text,
with references as required.

–REBECCA BLOOD

You may have seen them in your travels around the World Wide Web. Some provide succinct descriptions of judiciously selected links. Some contain wide swaths of commentary dotted sparingly with links to the news of the day. Others consist of an endless stream of blurts about the writer's day; links, if they exist, are to other, similar, personal sites. Some are political. Some are intellectual. Some are hilarious. Some are topic-driven. Some are off-the-wall. Most are noncommercial and all are impassioned about their subjects. They are the weblogs.

What they have in common is a format: a webpage with new entries placed at the top, updated frequently—sometimes several times a day. 1

2

Often at the side of the page is a list of links pointing to similar sites. Some sites consist only of a weblog. Others include the weblog as part of a larger site. More than a list of links and less than a full-blown zine, weblogs are hard to describe but easy to recognize.

Personal sites and lists of links have existed since the Web was born. Indeed, the ability to link from one document to any other that existed on the global network was the great novelty that drew early enthusiasts to the Web. Like a text version of ham radio, early enthusiasts published pages and eagerly perused the pages of others. It didn't matter what a page contained, just that it was accessible from any computer with a modem and a browser.

There has been spirited discussion in some quarters of the weblog community about when the first weblog appeared, but I think of Mosaic's What's New page, which ran from June 1993 to June 1996, as the progenitor of the format. Updated daily, it pointed Web surfers to sites they might enjoy seeing — and in those days Web surfers enjoyed looking at any page. Early adopters spent countless hours waiting for countless home pages featuring countless pictures of cats to download over their 1200 baud modems — and they liked it!

For a while, any webpage was an interesting addition to cyberspace, but then that space got crowded. Companies began advertising their products and services on the Web. More and more people put up pages about their lives and interests, and some of those interests were unimaginably arcane, esoteric, or just plain wacky. Newspapers and magazines published Web editions. The Web grew at an exponential rate and finding the "good stuff" became simultaneously more difficult and more time-consuming. But the good stuff was there, and enthusiasts enjoyed seeking it out.

And then an interesting thing happened. A few of these enthusiasts decided to put the links they collected daily onto a single webpage. Some of them had tired of spamming their friends with a constant barrage of email. Others had accumulated bookmark files that were bursting at the seams and sought a better way to organize the interesting things they found as they surfed. Whatever their reasons, for these folks it seemed the most natural thing in the world to put the record of their travels around the Web *on* the Web, and so a particular type of website was born. Enthusiastic surfers turned their home pages into a running list of links with descriptive text to inform their readers why they should click the link and wait for the page to download.

Steve Bogart created News, Pointers & Commentary (later called Now This) in February 1997, and Dave Winer launched Scripting News in April of that same year; Michael Sippey began The Obvious Filter (later Filtered for Purity) in May, and Jorn Barger's Robot Wisdom was created in December. And there were more, most of them completely unaware of the other sites that resembled theirs. Some called them "news sites" and some called them "filters," but most people didn't call them anything at all. "Links with commentary, with the new stuff on top" was the formula; for those who found them, these sites served as a welcome guide through the increasingly complex World Wide Web.

In November 1998 Jesse James Garrett, editor of Infosift, another of the original weblogs, collected a list of "sites like his" and sent them to Cameron Barrett, maintainer of Camworld. Adopting Jorn Barger's term "weblog" to describe the kind of site he maintained, Cam wrote an essay in January 1999 called "Anatomy of a Weblog," which detailed the elements of the form. He placed the list in a narrow column to the right of his weblog . . . and a movement was born. Maintainers of similar sites emailed their URLs for inclusion on Cam's list and readers suddenly had twelve, then twenty, then thirty and more weblogs to peruse in a day. No one liked the name very well, but with Cam's essay, "weblog" became the accepted term. Peter Merholz announced on his site that he was going to pronounce it "wee-blog" and it was only a matter of weeks before the abbreviation "blog" began appearing as an alternate term.

Most of the early weblog editors designed or maintained websites for a living. Even those who did not work directly on the Web knew HTML, the simple coding language used to create webpages. A few computer programmers designed systems to help them manage their sites, but most people updated their weblogs by hand.

Some Web designers created "arty" pages, but most weblogs were designed on the principle of simple functionality. A main area, wide enough for easy reading, was reserved for daily entries. Often a narrow side column echoed Cam's original list of "other weblogs" and this sidebar persists on many weblogs today. Jesse James Garrett added a link to his personal portal, a list of news sites, e-zines, and other weblogs. Partly convenience, partly an invitation to "see where I surf," in 2002 this convention persists even among webloggers who have never heard of Infosift.

Weblogs continued to spring up. Instead of being similar sites that had discovered a commonality, these weblogs were deliberately patterned after the weblogs listed on Camworld's sidebar. Many of them were created by Web developers who had coding skills and presumably spent their days in front of the computer. Unlike their coworkers, who sighed that the last thing they wanted to do when they got home was look at a computer, the webloggers were excited about the Web and passionate about its potential. They eagerly embraced the global network, looking first to the Web for news, information, and entertainment. It was natural that they would see their personal websites as extensions of their day-to-day lives.

Many of the first-wave weblogs updated throughout the day, providing a sort of real-time record of their maintainer's surfing patterns. They linked to general interest articles, to online games, and often to Web-related news. Camworld's sidebar continued to grow as these first-wave weblogs were added to his list of old-school sites.

One of these sites, Lemonyellow, was notable for being the first weblog to gain the attention of traditional media. The *New York Times* article about the site, published in July 1999, didn't say a word about weblogs, but it affirmed the notion that webloggers were on to something. Maintainer Heather Anne Halpert mixed links to interesting sites with esoteric entries about information architecture and notes on going to the theater. Her engaging style inspired open admiration. Literate, personal, and undeniably "thinky" in tone, Lemonyellow is, to my mind, the prototype of the notebook-style weblog. It ceased publication in April 2001.

In July 1999, Andrew Smales, maintainer of the popular weblog Be 14 Nice to Bears, created Pitas, a service that enabled anyone with access to a computer with a Web browser to create a weblog entry by typing into a blank box and then clicking a button on the computer screen. A month later, a startup called Pyra produced a similar product called Blogger. With the introduction of these two services and the others that appeared quickly on their heels, anyone who could type and had access to the World Wide Web could create a weblog, and the bandwagon that had been steadily gaining momentum through the summer shot through the gate.

And weblogs changed. Weblogs devoted to short personal entries 15 appeared, usually created with one of the simple new weblog tools. When these sites included links, if they did at all, they pointed mainly to other weblogs. In public and in private, webloggers engaged in vigorous discussions over the definition of the weblog. How often did it need to be updated? Every day? More than once a week? And most heatedly: Must it include links? In an attempt to organize the increasing mass of weblogs, weblogger Brigitte Eaton created a central weblog portal for the new community. Her criterion was simple: that a site consisted of dated entries. Since the Eatonweb portal was the most complete listing available, by default her inclusive definition won the day.

The weblog community spread to include sites that originated in 16 Canada, Australia, the United Kingdom, and beyond. Numerous weblogs popped up in the Netherlands, which was known, for a while at least, as having the highest number of weblogs per capita in the world. Non-English weblogs proliferated, though they remained largely separate from the original community (Americans being, overall, relentlessly monolingual).

Today there are hundreds of thousands of weblogs, and dozens of soft- 17 ware products designed specifically to make updating them easier. They have evolved to encompass any subject matter and they reflect worldviews that range from the private world of the writer to the public world of culture and current events, and everything in between. The appeal of each weblog is grounded thoroughly in the personality of its writer: his interests, his opinions, and his personal mix of links and commentary. These links point to anything and everything, from obscure articles about artists, to news analysis concerning current events, to the sites of his friends.

Each site is different—each writer decides each day what to write—but I 18 place weblogs into three very broad categories: blogs, notebooks, and filters.

Blogs: These sites resemble short-form journals. The writer's subject 19 is his daily life, with links subordinate to the text. Even when entries point the reader to a news or magazine article, linktext gives the feeling of a quick, spontaneous remark, perhaps of the type found in an instant message to a friend. Links, when included, seem to be almost an afterthought, pointers to friends' sites or perhaps to the definition of a word. Completely unheard of when Cameron wrote his essay, this type of site dominated the weblog universe by the middle of 2000, probably due to the proliferation of tools that made posting a quick thought so easy that the addition of a link became seen as an unnecessary and (relatively) time-consuming step.

Notebooks: Sometimes personal, sometimes focused on the outside world, notebooks are distinguished from blogs by their longer pieces of focused content. Personal entries are sometimes in the form of a story. Some notebooks are designed as a space for public contemplation: Entries may contain links to primary material, but the weblogger's ruminations are front and center. Shorter than an essay, longer than the blog-style blurt, these sites are noted for writing that seems more edited than that of the typical blog. Both blogs and notebooks tend to focus on the webloggers' inner worlds or their reactions to the world around them; the links themselves play strictly a supporting role. 20

I suppose I should take a moment to differentiate both blogs and notebooks from online journals, which predate the weblog movement by many years. It is impossible to make a strict delineation; superficially, journals often contain one longer entry per day, one per page. Perhaps a deeper difference lies in the intent of the maintainer. Online journals are analogous to paper journals, with the sole difference that they are published for the world to see. Online journalers may keep a record of events, explore their inner world, or do any of the things that journalers traditionally have done with pen and paper. 21

Blogs tend to consist of much shorter entries, many per day, the blogger seemingly striving for communication more than self-enlightenment. Notebooks, while they sometimes use the "one entry per day" format, tend to be less a record of external events than a record of ideas, and those that focus on the personal tend to do so nonchronologically, dipping into their entire catalogue of experience to select individual stories rather than recount their journey day by day. In the end, it is the maintainer of the site who labels his work and chooses the community with whom he most closely identifies. 22

Filters: When I think of the classic weblog, I don't think of a short-form diary or a series of stories or short think pieces. I think of the old-style site organized squarely around the link, maintained by an inveterate Web surfer, personal information strictly optional. These weblogs have one thing in common: the primacy of the link. Whether their editors write at length or not at all, filter editors want to show you around the Web. Some of these editors strive for pithiness, others for completeness, but even those who use links as a springboard to extended diatribes are focused primarily on the world outside their door. These sites may visually resemble the blog 23 or the notebook, but they reveal the weblogger's personality from the outside in. The self, when it appears on a filter-style weblog, is revealed obliquely, through its relation to the larger world.

Some filter-style weblogs focus on a particular subject. The aim of these subject-specific filters is to provide their readers with a continuous source for all the available news about a given topic. Sometimes maintained by enthusiasts, sometimes by businesses or professionals, these sites are often designed to build and enhance the reputation of their maintainers.   24

Collaborative weblogs, as their name indicates, are maintained by a group of people instead of an individual. Usually filters, most collaborative weblogs are indistinguishable from an individually produced weblog, except that entries list several individuals as contributors. Some don't make even this distinction, and can be recognized only by reading the site's "About" page. Some collaborative weblogs are also community weblogs. These range from sites on which any member can post and comment, to those on which the site owners post to the main page and members contribute in discussion forums.   25

Of course, most weblogs do not strictly follow the roles I've outlined above. Blogs sometimes link to news articles or online games, notebooks sometimes contain one-line links, and filters sometimes contain linkless personal observations. It is just this variety in content and approach that makes weblogs so irresistible to many of us. Each weblogger creates a personal version of the weblog format, dictated by purpose, interest, and whim. The weblog is infinitely malleable and may be adapted to almost any end. There are travel weblogs, photo weblogs, sex weblogs, business weblogs, wedding weblogs, historical weblogs, humor weblogs, and weblogs focused on U.S. military actions. The very best weblogs, in my opinion, are designed to accommodate unexpected turns, to allow for a little experimentation.   26

●　●　●

Comprehension

1. What exactly is a weblog? Write a one-sentence definition.
2. What features do all weblogs share? In what sense are they "hard to describe but easy to recognize" (2)?
3. What is the origin of the term *weblog*? What is the origin of the term *blog*?
4. How does Blood explain the fast growth and increasing popularity of weblogs? Can you offer any other explanations?
5. In paragraph 13, Blood discusses a weblog called Lemonyellow. What does this paragraph contribute to her definition?
6. What is the significance of Pitas, Pyra, and similar services?
7. How have weblogs changed since their inception?

8. How are notebooks different from blogs? How are online journals different from both blogs and notebooks? How are filters similar to and different from other kinds of weblogs?

9. According to Blood, what makes weblogs so "irresistible" (26)?

Purpose and Audience

1. Given its subject and its vocabulary, what kind of audience does this essay seem to address? For example, does Blood direct her remarks at students? At newcomers to the Internet?

2. This essay is introduced by the one-sentence definition, "A weblog is a coffeehouse conversation in text, with references as required." What does this sentence mean? Is this definition also the essay's thesis? What other thesis can you suggest? For example, could the essay's last sentence be its thesis?

Style and Structure

1. Beginning with paragraph 4, Blood introduces a narrative. What is the subject of this narrative? What transitional elements link its events? Where does the narrative end?

2. At the end of paragraph 16, Blood inserts a parenthetical comment. Why does she include this comment? How is it related to her discussion?

3. In paragraphs 18–23, Blood uses classification to define three basic categories of weblogs. Should she have included other categories in this classification scheme? For example, should she have added the categories *collaborative weblog* or *online journal*? Do any of her three categories overlap?

4. In paragraph 21, Blood interjects her own voice, beginning with "I suppose I should take a moment." Where else does she do this? Do you think this use of the first person is appropriate? Do you find it distracting?

5. Do you think the addition of visuals would make Blood's definition clearer? If so, what kinds of images would you suggest?

6. Do you think section headings would make this essay easier to follow? If so, what headings would you suggest? Where do you think they should be placed?

Vocabulary Projects

1. Define each of the following words as it is used in this selection.

succinct (1)	esoteric (5)	primacy (23)
swaths (1)	exponential (5)	pithiness (23)
perused (3)	proliferated (16)	diatribes (23)
progenitor (4)	ruminations (20)	malleable (26)
arcane (5)	inveterate (23)	

2. Although Blood defines some of the technical terms she uses, she also uses many terms related to computers without defining them. List these undefined terms. Do you think any of them should have been defined? If so, which ones? Why? Write a one-sentence definition for each term you think should be defined.

Journal Entry

If you were going to develop and maintain a weblog, what kind of content and features would you include?

Writing Workshop

1. Write your own definition of *weblog*, developing your essay primarily with description and exemplification. In your essay, characterize the kind of weblog you yourself would develop.

2. Write a definition of *weblog* suitable for an audience that is less computer literate than the one Blood addresses. Simplify the discussion, define terms you think would be unfamiliar to your audience, and use plenty of examples, including visuals.

3. Write an essay defining another term familiar to Internet users — for example, *listserv, email, instant messaging,* or *netiquette.* Use process and exemplification to develop your definition. Assume your audience is not computer literate.

Combining the Patterns

In addition to **narration** and **classification**, what other patterns of development does Blood use in this essay? For instance, where does she use **comparison and contrast**? Where does she use **exemplification**?

Thematic Connections

- "Playing by the Rules" (page 114)
- "Innovation" (page 231)
- "The Death of the Moth" (page 728)
- "Strange Tools" (page 743)

PAUL FUSSELL

Stigmatic Uniforms

Paul Fussell (b. 1924) grew up in California and, after serving in World War II, he attended Pomona College and Harvard University. He began his teaching career at Connecticut College and then later taught at Rutgers University and the University of Pennsylvania, where he is currently Professor Emeritus of English literature. A scholar of eighteenth-century literature with many important publications in the field, Fussell turned in the 1970s to writing about twentieth-century culture and history for a popular audience. His book *The Great War and Modern Memory* (1976), about World War I and its influences, was followed by *Class: A Guide through the American Status System* (1983); *Bad, Or the Dumbing of America* (1992); and *Doing Battle: The Making of a Skeptic* (1998), among many others. The following is a chapter from his most recent book, *Uniforms: Why We Are What We Wear* (2002).

Background on uniforms: Except in the military, professionals generally do not wear uniforms. (Some notable exceptions are police officers, firefighters, airline pilots, and ship captains.) Many types of jobs have limited their use of uniforms, and some are doing away with them altogether. The disappearance of the traditional nurse's uniform provides an unusual example of this trend. The starched white dress, white stockings and hospital shoes, and distinctive white peaked cap — for years a symbol of professionalism — began by the 1970s to be seen as an indicator of the lower status of a "female" occupation, compared to the street wear and lab coats worn by (mostly male) physicians. Today, nearly all hospital floor workers — whether residents, nurses, technicians or cleaning staff — wear scrubs; as a result, professional workers are essentially indistinguishable from non-professionals. Some argue that this "democratization" allows hospitals to disguise the fact that patients increasingly are not primarily under the care of a trained nurse. However, most nurses apparently prefer the comfort and convenience of scrubs — and, as one hospital administrator has suggested, the entry of men into the nursing field made a change in dress inevitable.

Uniforms divide into two rough categories: honorific and stigmatic. 1
Honorific: the attire of police, McDonald's fast-food servers, United States Marines, the clergy. Stigmatic: the orange coveralls worn by prisoners, widely familiarized by the dress of Timothy McVeigh* as depicted in a TV clip repeatedly shown after his arrest. Some county sheriffs have put their prisoners back into the old-fashioned broad stripes, and added the distinc-

---

* EDS. NOTE — McVeigh was convicted of and put to death for the 1995 bombing of a government building in Oklahoma City, which killed 168 people, including many children in an on-site day care center.

tion of colors to distinguish types of malefactors: minimum security convicts wear green on white stripes; medium security, black on white (as in old films about prison life); and red on white for maximum security. It is beginning to be understood that striped prison wear is superior to solid orange because of the risk that escapees may resemble highway workers or sanitation employees. Either way, it is the sheriff who benefits politically when television shows a newly imprisoned law breaker. As Thomas Vinciguerra, a journalist, explained, "One sheriff, Gerald Hege of Davidson County, N.C., notes that in 1994 he won election by 227 votes. Then he clad his inmates in stripes. At his next election, he won by 5,000 votes. 'The public loves them,' he said of the stripes."

Both the striped and the plain color uniforms have neither pockets   2
nor trouser cuffs, where prisoners might conceal weapons or drugs. Despite objections from the ACLU, etc., the state of Michigan has disallowed normal clothes as wear for inmates, requiring them to wear dark blue (the naval influence again?) two-piece cotton uniforms with a single large orange stripe running down each leg and arm. There are over 130,000 prisoners in Michigan, and there were budget objections to supplying each with two sets of the new uniform, together with three T-shirts, nine sets of underwear, two sets of thermal underwear, and one winter coat—all specially made without seams, pockets, or cuffs.

The upshot was inevitable. "Convicts at an Oregon state prison have   3
sold their own line of designer prison clothes since 1990." Who buys? asks the *Detroit News*. "What free person would want to look like an inmate? Young people. 'If it will upset us, they'll wear it,' says Robert Butterworth, a psychologist who focuses on adolescents. The current style of baggy, ill-fitting clothes started in prison. The reason: belts are taken away from inmates so they're not used as a weapon or to commit suicide. So low-riding pants are a prison tradition."

During World War II, German and Italian prisoners held by the Amer-   4
icans wore used U.S. Army fatigues with the letters PW enlarged in white on the back of the jacket. The seams and pockets were left intact, attempts at escape being very rare, because most of the prisoners were pleased to be alive and well and nicely fed for a change, or were discouraged from escape by the emphatic isolation of their camps.

The situation was distinctly different for many civilians in Germany   5
and countries controlled by the Reich. For one thing, Jews could be identified by their worn-out clothes, for they were forbidden to enter any store selling new clothing. This sorry situation dated from September 19, 1941, when the Nazis decided that all Jews over the age of six living in German-controlled territory would have to give notice of their loathsome proximity by wearing on their outer clothing a five-inch-wide yellow cloth Star of David bearing the word *Jude* in black pseudo-Hebrew letters. This was bad enough. But worse, and very Nazi, was the ruling that Jews would have to pay for these stars, as if they were honorific. Jews had to fork over ten pfennigs for each star. The Jews called it the David Star; the Nazis, the Jewish

Star. It was like a badge, and a badge of shame it was designed to be. If it was a badge, can it be classified as a uniform? Professor Peter Gay, formerly of Yale, who was there as a child, senses that the star constituted a uniform. "Jews," he recalls, "were to be identified by a special uniform." It was a uniform because it identified a visible group of people and set them off from others.

Before this time, Jewish property had been seized, and Jews were for-   6
bidden to practice professions, sit on benches in parks, or buy what they might need; a common shop sign read, "Foods in Short Supply Are Not Sold to Jews." Since by this time it was virtually impossible for Jews to flee, the object now was to humiliate them and make them feel "ashamed," as if they'd done something wrong. As Marion Kaplan wrote in *Between Dignity and Despair: Jewish Life in Nazi Germany,*

> The introduction of the star signaled a new stage in persecution. "This was the most difficult day in the twelve years of hell," according to Victor Klemperer. Every person wearing a star "carried his ghetto with him, like a snail its house." With the yellow star blazing from their coats Jews could be identified, vilified, and attacked with impunity. Those who had earlier dared to circumvent shopping rules, limitations on public transport, or restrictions on entertainment could no longer do so unless they removed their star. This was a severe crime; even a loose star could be cause for sending its wearer to a concentration camp.

One German army Einsatzgruppe,* scouring the roads of rural Russia   7
for Jews, reported, "During the check along the roads, 135 people, mostly Jews, were apprehended. The Jews were not wearing the Jewish badge. . . . 127 people were shot." They were out of uniform.

And in a concentration camp, what uniform was an incarcerated Jew   8
obliged to wear? One similar to that worn by the other prisoners, as if he had done something terribly wrong. Donald Watt, a British soldier cap-tured early in the war and confined to Auschwitz, where he survived by helping to stoke the fires beneath the cremation furnaces, described the Auschwitz uniform: trousers and jacket of pseudo-linen artificial material, with vertical faded blue stripes. Primo Levi remembered the long striped overcoats worn by some lucky long-term prisoners, inexplicably not yet gassed to death.

Sewn onto the common uniform were cloth badges, each identifying   9
the crime that had landed the wearer in the camp: green triangle with numbers, a civil criminal; red triangle, a political criminal; pink triangle, a homosexual; red triangle with yellow star, a Jew. The SS guards especially despised the so-called asocials, who had escaped once from a prison camp or had distinguished themselves as public loafers, unwilling to work for the nation. Their uniforms bore a black triangle, and the SS guards, unwilling to overlook the presumed insult to their black uniform, plied their whips, truncheons, rifle butts, and gallows with special enthusiasm.

---

* EDS. NOTE—A special military unit, charged with killing Jews and Gypsies, that accompanied regular forces.

The "uniform" was the same in summer and winter, in heat and terri-   10
ble cold, and lice always went with it. To add to the shame and the punishment, the prisoners were given no underclothes. Donald Watt spoke of
"scrounging an extra shirt which I turned into a pair of underpants by
tying the sleeves around my waist."

As we have seen, the Germans had a thing about buttons. The rules for   11
prisoners at Auschwitz prescribed that precisely five buttons must appear
on the front of the jacket. Prisoners were forbidden to leave their huts with
the jackets unbuttoned, and at the same time there was no way to sew buttons on, the possession of needle and thread being forbidden. A perfect
Catch-22. But at many of the extermination camps in Poland, the matter
of uniforms was moot. Prisoners had no time to don them, being stripped
naked and escorted to the gas chamber immediately upon arrival.

Not everyone was debased by uniform. Some specially privileged pris-   12
oners wore more civilized garb. For example, the women's orchestra at
Auschwitz, which supplied rhythm and melody for the work-commandos
as they marched out in the morning and marched back in the evening. The
female musicians wore navy blue skirts and white blouses, presumably out
of respect for the Germanic instrumental repertory—except, of course,
works by the Jew Felix Mendelssohn.

•   •   •

Comprehension

1. What is the difference between honorific and stigmatic uniforms?
   Define each in a single sentence.

2. What is Fussell's opinion of stigmatic uniforms? How can you tell?

3. Can you give additional examples of honorific uniforms? Of stigmatic
   uniforms? Can some uniforms be both stigmatic and honorific?
   Explain.

4. How does the psychologist quoted in paragraph 3 explain why young
   people adopt aspects of prison garb? Do you think there could be
   another explanation for this phenomenon? When this "uniform" is
   worn by young people, do you see it as honorific or stigmatic?

5. In what sense was the star that Nazis forced Jews to wear a uniform?
   How does Fussell define *uniform*?

6. In paragraph 11, Fussell describes a scenario he calls "A perfect
   Catch-22." What does he mean?

Purpose and Audience

1. In paragraph 6, Fussell introduces a long quotation from a book
   about Jews in Nazi Germany. What does this tell you about his purpose in "Stigmatic Uniforms"?

2. Does Fussell state his thesis? What is it?

3. Do you think Fussell expects his readers to be familiar with the World
   War II stigmatic uniforms he discusses?

Style and Structure

1. This selection, a chapter from Fussell's book *Uniforms,* has no formal introductory or concluding paragraph. If he were to add a brief introduction and a brief conclusion, what strategies might he use?
2. In addition to using various patterns of development, what other strategies does Fussell use to develop his definition? For example, does he use **negation**?
3. Why does Fussell place *uniform* in quotation marks in paragraph 10?
4. Although Fussell devotes a few paragraphs to discussing present-day prison uniforms, most of his essay focuses on World War II. Should he have discussed additional categories of stigmatic uniforms? Given the examples of honorific uniforms he mentions in his essay's opening lines, do you think he should have discussed them also? Should he have given additional examples of uniforms from both categories?

Vocabulary Projects

1. Define each of the following words as it is used in this selection.

   honorific (1)   stoke (8)   truncheons (9)
   stigmatic (1)   asocials (9)   debased (12)
   malefactors (1)   plied (9)   repertory (12)
   upshot (3)

2. What words does Fussell use as synonyms for *uniform*? Can you think of others? How do the connotations of these words differ?
3. What other names could you give for the two categories of uniforms Fussell identifies in this essay?

Journal Entry

According to Fussell's definition of *uniform* in paragraph 7, what "uniforms" do you and your friends wear? Do you see them as honorific or stigmatic?

Writing Workshop

1. Write an essay defining *stigmatic uniforms*. Support your thesis with examples of uniforms worn by janitorial staff, sanitation workers, and entry-level workers in fast-food restaurants, discount stores, and so on. (Note that Fussell classifies McDonald's uniforms as honorific.)
2. Write an essay defining *honorific uniforms*. Support your thesis with examples of uniforms worn by professionals in various high-status fields.
3. Write an essay defining a uniform that can be seen either as honorific or stigmatic. Support your definition with description, narration, and comparison and contrast.

Combining the Patterns

Which patterns of development does Fussell use in developing his definition? Would an extended **comparison and contrast** between honorific and stigmatic uniforms have strengthened his essay?

Thematic Connections

- "My First Conk" (page 285)
- "The Power of Words in Wartime" (page 377)
- "Five Ways to Kill a Man" (page 505)
- "The Wife-Beater" (page 532)

PHILIP LEVINE

What Work Is (Poetry)

Philip Levine (b. 1928) grew up in Detroit, Michigan, and received degrees from Wayne State University and the University of Iowa. From 1958 to 1992, he taught at California State University, Fresno, and he now teaches at New York University. Levine published his first volume of poetry, *On the Edge,* in 1961 and is the author of some fifteen more, including *Not This Pig* (1968); *Ashes: Poems New and Old* (1979), which received the National Book Critics' Circle Award; *What Work Is* (1991), which won the National Book Award; *The Simple Truth* (1994), which won the Pulitzer Prize; and, most recently, *Breath* (2004). He has also published a collection of essays, *The Bread of Time: Toward an Autobiography* (1994). A manual laborer during most of his early life, Levine eventually drew on those experiences for his poetry: "It's ironic that while I was a worker in Detroit, which I left when I was twenty-six, my sense was that the thing that's going to stop me from being a poet is the fact that I'm doing this crummy work. . . . The irony is, going to work every day became the subject of probably my best poetry. But I couldn't see that at the time. And it took me another ten years to wake up to it. That I had a body of experience that nobody else had."

Background on the poem: As Levine relates in a commentary on the poem, "What Work Is" was inspired by an experience from his youth. In need of a job and responding to an employment ad that required applicants to be at the plant at eight A.M. on a Monday morning, he arrived to find that the employment office didn't open until ten A.M. He stood in the rain with some two hundred others until employment personnel showed up at about twenty of ten to unlock the doors. "Then they locked them in our faces," Levine observes. "I realized that they had done this on purpose. They required a test of our docility. If we hadn't waited for two hours, we weren't right for this [crummy] job. It angered me. I carried that anger with me for many, many years." When he finally got to the front of the line, a man behind a desk asked Levine what kind of work he wanted. Levine replied, "I'd like your job," meaning, he says, "I'd like to dump on people the way you do." Levine continues: "He said, 'Next,' and that was the end of that. So my big mouth again." (The brother he refers to in "What Work Is," and who turns up in many of Levine's poems, is his twin.)

We stand in the rain in a long line
waiting at Ford Highland Park. For work.
You know what work is — if you're
old enough to read this you know what
work is, although you may not do it.   5
Forget you. This is about waiting,
shifting from one foot to another.
Feeling the light rain falling like mist

into your hair, blurring your vision
until you think you see your own brother   10
ahead of you, maybe ten places.
You rub your glasses with your fingers,
and of course it's someone else's brother,
narrower across the shoulders than
yours but with the same sad slouch, the grin   15
that does not hide the stubbornness,
the sad refusal to give in to
rain, to the hours wasted waiting,
to the knowledge that somewhere ahead
a man is waiting who will say, "No,   20
we're not hiring today," for any
reason he wants. You love your brother,
now suddenly you can hardly stand
the love flooding you for your brother,
who's not beside you or behind or   25
ahead because he's home trying to
sleep off a miserable night shift
at Cadillac so he can get up
before noon to study his German.
Works eight hours a night so he can sing   30
Wagner,* the opera you hate most,
the worst music ever invented.
How long has it been since you told him
you loved him, held his wide shoulders,
opened your eyes wide and said those words,   35
and maybe kissed his cheek? You've never
done something so simple, so obvious,
not because you're too young or too dumb,
not because you're jealous or even mean
or incapable of crying in   40
the presence of another man, no,
just because you don't know what work is.

• • •

Reading Literature

1. How does this poem define *work*? Does it really explain "what work
   is"? Explain.
2. Who is the poem's speaker? Where is he, and what is he doing? What
   do you think the speaker means when he says, "you think you see your

---

* EDS. NOTE—Richard Wagner (1813–1883), groundbreaking German composer
whose works many singers still find difficult.

own brother / ahead of you" (lines 10–11) but "of course it's someone else's brother" (line 13)?

3. How do you explain the poem's last few lines? How does the speaker's ignorance of what work is keep him from telling his brother he loves him? What is the connection?

Journal Entry

In lines 3–5, the speaker says, "You know what work is—if you're / old enough to read this you know what / work is, although you may not do it." Do you know "what work is"? Explain.

Thematic Connections

- "My Mother Never Worked" (page 108)
- "Midnight" (page 213)
- "The Peter Principle" (page 220)
- "Down and Out in Discount America" (page 659)

WRITING ASSIGNMENTS FOR DEFINITION

1. Choose a document or ritual that is a significant part of your religious or cultural heritage. Define it, using any pattern or combination of patterns you choose, but be sure to include a formal definition somewhere in your essay. Assume your readers are not familiar with the term you are defining.

2. Define an abstract term — for example, *stubbornness, security, courage,* or *fear* — by making it concrete. You can develop your definition with a series of brief examples or with an extended narrative that illustrates the characteristic you are defining.

3. The readings in this chapter define (among other things) a food, a family role, and an item of clothing. Write an essay using examples and description to define one of these topics — for instance, sushi (food), a stepmother (family role), or a chador (item of clothing).

4. Do some research to learn the meaning of one of these medical conditions: angina, migraine, Down syndrome, attention deficit disorder, schizophrenia, autism, osteoporosis, or Alzheimer's disease. Then, write an extended definition essay explaining the condition to an audience of high school students.

5. Use a series of examples to support a thesis in an essay that defines *racism, sexism,* or another type of bigoted behavior.

6. Choose a term that is central to one of your courses — for instance, *naturalism, behaviorism,* or *authority* — and write an essay defining the term. Assume your audience is made up of students who have not yet taken the course. You may begin with an overview of the term's origin if you believe this is appropriate. Then, develop your essay with examples and **analogies** that will facilitate your audience's understanding of the term.

7. Assume your audience is from a culture unfamiliar with modern American pastimes. Write a definition essay for this audience describing the form and function of a Frisbee, a Barbie doll, an action figure, a skateboard, or a video game.

8. Review any one of the following narrative essays from Chapter 6, and use it to help you develop an extended definition of one of the following terms.

    "Only Daughter" or "Finishing School" — prejudice

    "My Mother Never Worked" — work

    "Thirty-Eight Who Saw Murder Didn't Call the Police" — apathy

    "Shooting an Elephant" — power

9. What constitutes an education? Define the term *education* by identifying several different sources of knowledge, formal or informal, and explaining what each contributes. You might read — or reread — "Finishing School" (page 101), "Indian Education" (page 134), "The Human Cost of an Illiterate Society" (page 252), or "Strange Tools" (page 743).

10. What qualifies someone as a hero? Developing your essay with a series of examples, define the word *hero*. Include a formal definition, and try to incorporate at least one paragraph defining the term by explaining and illustrating what a hero is *not*.

COLLABORATIVE ACTIVITY FOR DEFINITION

Working as a group, choose one of the following words to define: *pride, hope, sacrifice,* or *justice*. Then, define the term with a series of extended examples drawn from films your group members have seen, with each of you developing an illustrative paragraph based on a different film. (Before beginning, your group may decide to focus on one particular genre of film.) When everyone in the group has read each paragraph, work together to formulate a thesis that asserts the vital importance of the quality your examples have defined. Finally, write suitable opening and closing paragraphs for the essay, and arrange the body paragraphs in a logical order, adding transitions where necessary.

INTERNET ASSIGNMENT FOR DEFINITION

After visiting the following Web sites, write an essay defining the term *Industrial Revolution*. To give your readers a better understanding of the effects of industrialization, develop your definition by considering changes it led to in any of these areas: art, science, technology, medicine, working conditions, and transportation.

IRWeb: The Industrial Revolution
<library.thinkquest.org/4132>
This educational site about the Industrial Revolution contains information, links to other sites, and games, including an Industrial Revolution quiz.

Internet Modern History Sourcebook: The Industrial Revolution
<fordham.edu/halsall/mod/modsbook14.html>
This site offers original texts written during the Industrial Revolution, including lectures and discussions about the process of industrialization and the revolution's social and political effects. It also features literary responses to the revolution.

The Industrial Revolution: A Trip to the Past
<members.aol.com/mhirotsu/kevin/trip2.html>
This site discusses advances in art, science, medicine, and transportation.

14
Argumentation

What Is Argumentation?

Argumentation is a process of reasoning that asserts the soundness of a debatable position, belief, or conclusion. Argumentation takes a stand — supported by evidence — and urges people to share the writer's perspective and insights. In the following paragraph from his essay "Holding Cell," Jerome Groopman argues that with its decision to limit therapeutic cloning, the President's Council on Bioethics has prevented scientists from carrying out important medical research that could possibly save lives:

Issue identified	The President's Council on Bioethics, chaired by Dr. Leon R. Kass, presented its long-awaited report on human cloning to the White House on July 10, 2002. The council unanimously advised against "cloning to produce children," commonly called "reproductive cloning." But on "cloning for biomedical research" — therapeutic cloning to produce stem cells to try to ameliorate disease — it split. Of the seventeen members, ten (including
Background presents both sides of issue	Kass) voted against it. They couched their rejection as a compromise since they called not for a permanent ban but for a four-year moratorium. This moratorium, according to the letter accompanying the report, would allow "a thorough federal review . . . to clarify the issues and foster a public consensus about how to proceed." It would also give researchers time to seek alternative ways to generate stem cells. But for scientists and, more importantly, for the millions of patients with incurable maladies, the compromise is a painful disappoint-
Topic sentence (take a stand)	ment. It shackles potentially lifesaving research and provides no clear framework to advance the ethical debate. What's more, the arguments deployed on its behalf don't withstand scrutiny.

Argumentation can be used to convince other people to accept (or at least acknowledge the validity of) your position; to defend your position, even if you cannot convince others to agree; or to question or refute a position you believe to be misguided, untrue, dangerous, or evil (without necessarily offering an alternative).

Understanding Argumentation and Persuasion

Although the terms *persuasion* and *argumentation* are frequently used interchangeably, they do not mean the same thing. **Persuasion** is a general term that refers to how a writer influences an audience to adopt a belief or follow a course of action. To persuade an audience, a writer relies on various appeals — to the emotions, to reason, or to ethics.

Argumentation is the appeal to reason. In an argument, a writer connects a series of statements so that they lead logically to a conclusion. Argumentation is different from persuasion in that it does not try to move an audience to action; its primary purpose is to demonstrate that certain ideas are valid and others are not. Moreover, unlike persuasion, argumentation has a formal structure: an argument makes points, supplies evidence, establishes a logical chain of reasoning, refutes opposing arguments, and accommodates the audience's views.

As the selections in this chapter demonstrate, however, most effective arguments combine two or more appeals: even though their primary appeal is to reason, they may also appeal to emotions. For example, you could use a combination of logical and emotional appeals to argue against lowering the drinking age in your state from twenty-one to eighteen. You could appeal to *reason* by constructing an argument leading to the conclusion that the state should not condone policies that have a high probability of injuring or killing citizens. You could support your conclusion by presenting statistics showing that alcohol-related traffic accidents kill more teenagers than disease does. You could also cite a study showing that when the drinking age was raised from eighteen to twenty-one, fatal accidents declined. In addition, you could include an appeal to the *emotions* by telling a particularly sad story about an eighteen-year-old alcoholic or by pointing out how an increased number of accidents involving drunk drivers would cost some innocent people their lives. These appeals to your audience's emotions could strengthen your argument by widening its appeal. Keep in mind, however, that in an effective argument emotion does not take the place of logic; it supports and reinforces it.

The appeals you choose and how you balance them depend in part on your purpose and your sense of your audience. As you consider what strategies to use, remember that some extremely effective appeals are unfair. Although most people would agree that lies, threats, misleading statements, and appeals to greed and prejudice are unacceptable ways of reaching an audience, such appeals are used frequently in daily conversation, political campaigns, and even international diplomacy. Nevertheless, in your college writing you should use only those appeals that most people would consider fair. To do otherwise will undercut your audience's belief in your trustworthiness and weaken your argument.

Planning an Argumentative Essay

Choosing a Topic

In an argumentative essay, as in all writing, choosing the right topic is important. Ideally, you should have an intellectual or emotional stake in your topic. Still, you should be open-minded and willing to consider all sides of a question. If the evidence goes against your position, you should be willing to change your thesis. You should also be able, from the outset, to consider your topic from other people's viewpoints; this will help you determine what their beliefs are and how they are likely to react. You can then use this knowledge to build your case and to refute opposing viewpoints. If you cannot be open-minded, you should choose another topic you can deal with more objectively.

Other factors should also influence your selection of a topic. First, you should be well informed about your topic. In addition, you should choose an issue narrow enough to be treated in the space available to you or be willing to confine your discussion to one aspect of a broad issue. It is also important to consider your **purpose** — what you expect your argument to accomplish and how you wish your audience to respond. If your topic is so far-reaching that you cannot identify what you want to convince readers to think, or if your purpose is so idealistic that your expectations of their response are impossible or unreasonable, your essay will suffer.

Taking a Stand

After you have chosen your topic, you are ready to **take a stand** — to state the position you will argue in the form of a thesis. Consider the following thesis statement:

> Education is the best way to address the problem of increased drug use among teenagers.

This thesis statement says that increased drug use is a problem among teenagers, that more than one possible solution to this problem exists, and that education is a better solution than any other. In your argument, you will have to support each of these three points logically and persuasively.

After stating your thesis, you should examine it to make sure it is **debatable**. Arguing a statement of fact or a point that most people accept as self-evident is useless. A good argumentative thesis presents a proposition that at least some people would object to. A good way to test the suitability of your thesis for an argumentative essay is to formulate an **antithesis**, a statement that asserts the opposite position. If you think that some people would support the antithesis, you can be certain your thesis is indeed debatable.

Thesis:	Because immigrants have contributed much to the development of the United States, immigration quotas should be relaxed.
Antithesis:	Even though immigrants have contributed much to the development of the United States, immigration quotas should not be relaxed.

Analyzing Your Audience

Before writing any essay, you should analyze the characteristics, values, and interests of your audience. In argumentation, it is especially important to consider what beliefs or opinions your readers are likely to have and whether your audience is likely to be friendly, neutral, or hostile to your thesis. It is probably best to assume that some, if not most, of your readers are at least skeptically neutral—that they are open to your ideas but need to be convinced. This assumption will keep you from making claims you cannot support. If your position is controversial, you should assume that an informed and determined opposition is looking for holes in your argument.

In an argumentative essay, you face a dual challenge. You must appeal to readers who are neutral or even hostile to your position, and you must influence those readers so that they are more receptive to your viewpoint. For example, it would be relatively easy to convince college students that tuition should be lowered or instructors that faculty salaries should be raised. You could be reasonably sure, in advance, that each group would agree with your position. But argument requires more than just telling people what they already believe. It would be much harder to convince college students that tuition should be raised to pay for an increase in instructors' salaries or to persuade instructors to forgo raises so that tuition can remain the same. Remember, your audience will not just take your word for the claims you make. You must provide evidence that will support your thesis and reasoning that will lead logically to your conclusion.

Gathering and Documenting Evidence

All the points you make in your paper must be supported. If they are not, your audience will dismiss them as unfounded, irrelevant, or unclear. Sometimes you can support a statement with appeals to emotion, but most of the time you support your argument's points by appealing to reason—by providing **evidence**, facts and opinions in support of your position.

As you gather evidence and assess its effectiveness, keep in mind that evidence in an argumentative essay never proves anything conclusively. If it did, there would be no debate—and hence no point in arguing. The best that evidence can do is convince your audience that an assertion is reasonable and worth considering.

Kinds of Evidence.   Evidence can be *fact* or *opinion*. **Facts** are statements that most people agree are true and that can be verified independently. Facts—including statistics—are the most commonly used type of evidence. It is a fact, for example, that fewer people per year were killed in automobile accidents in the 1990s than in the 1970s. Facts may be drawn from your own experience as well as from reading and observation. It may, for instance, be a fact you have had a serious automobile accident. Quite often, facts are more convincing when they are supplemented by **opinions**, or interpretations of facts. To connect your facts about automobile accidents to the assertion that the installation of side-impact airbags in all SUVs, as well as cars, could reduce deaths still further, you could cite the opinions of an expert—consumer advocate Ralph Nader, for example. His statements, along with the facts and statistics you have assembled and your own interpretations of those facts and statistics, could convince readers that your solution to the problem of highway deaths is reasonable.

Keep in mind that not all opinions are equally convincing. The opinions of experts are more convincing than are those of individuals who have limited knowledge of an issue. Your personal opinions can be excellent evidence (provided you are knowledgeable about your subject), but they are usually less convincing to your audience than expert opinion. In the final analysis, what is important is not just the quality of the evidence but also the credibility of the person offering it.

What kind of evidence might change readers' minds? That depends on the readers, the issue, and the facts at hand. Put yourself in the place of your readers, and ask what would make them receptive to your thesis. Why, for example, should a student agree to pay higher tuition? You might concede that tuition is high but point out that it has not been raised for three years while the college's costs have kept going up. The cost of heating and maintaining the buildings has increased, and professors' salaries have not, with the result that several excellent teachers have recently left the college for higher-paying jobs. Furthermore, cuts in federal and state funding have already caused a reduction in the number of courses offered. Similarly, how could you convince a professor to agree to accept no raise at all, especially in light of the fact that faculty salaries have not kept up with inflation? You could say that because cuts in government funding have already reduced course offerings and because the government has also reduced funds for student loans, any further rise in tuition to pay faculty salaries would cause some students to drop out — and that in turn would eventually cost some instructors their jobs. As you can see, the evidence you use in an argument depends to a great extent on whom you want to persuade and what you know about them.

Criteria for Evidence.   As you select and review material, choose your evidence with the following three criteria in mind:

1. Your evidence should be **relevant**. It should support your thesis and be pertinent to your argument. As you present evidence, be careful not to concentrate so much on a specific example that you lose sight of the point you are supporting. Such digressions may confuse your readers. For example, in arguing for mandatory HIV testing for all health-care workers, one student made the point that AIDS is at epidemic proportions. To illustrate this point, he offered a discussion of the bubonic plague in fourteenth-century Europe. Although interesting, this example was not relevant. To show its relevance, the student would have to link his discussion to his assertions about AIDS, possibly by comparing the spread of the bubonic plague in the fourteenth century to the spread of AIDS in Africa today.

2. Your evidence should be **representative**. It should represent the full range of opinions about your subject, not just one side. For example, in an essay arguing against the use of animals in medical experimentation, you would not just use information provided by animal rights activists. You would also use information supplied by medical researchers, pharmaceutical companies, and perhaps medical ethicists. In addition, the examples and expert opinions you include should be **typical**, not aberrant. Suppose you are writing an essay in support of building a trash-to-steam plant in your city. To support your thesis, you present the example of Baltimore, which has a successful trash-to-steam program. As you consider your evidence, ask yourself if Baltimore's experience with trash-to-steam is typical. Did other cities have less success? Take a close look at the opinions that disagree with the position you plan to take. If you understand your opposition, you can refute it effectively when you write your paper.

3. Your evidence should be **sufficient**. It should include enough facts, opinions, and examples to support your claims. The amount of evidence you need depends on the length of your paper, your audience, and your thesis. It stands to reason that you would use fewer examples in a two-page paper than in a ten-page research assignment. Similarly, an audience that is favorably disposed to your thesis might need only one or two examples to be convinced, whereas a skeptical audience would need many more. As you develop your thesis, think about the amount of support you will need

to write your paper. You may decide that a narrower, more limited thesis will be easier to support than a more inclusive one.

Documentation of Evidence.   As soon as you decide on a topic, you should begin to gather your evidence. Sometimes you can use your own ideas and observations to support your claims. Most of the time, however, you will have to use the print and electronic resources of the library or search the Internet to locate the information you need. Whenever you use such evidence in your paper, you have to **document** it by providing the source of the information. (When documenting sources, follow the documentation format recommended by the Modern Language Association, which is explained in the Appendix of this book.) If you don't document your sources, your readers are likely to dismiss your evidence, thinking that it may be inaccurate, unreliable, or simply false. **Documentation** gives readers the ability to evaluate the sources you cite and to consult them if they wish. When you document sources, you are telling your readers that you are honest and have nothing to hide.

Documentation also helps you avoid **plagiarism** — presenting the ideas or words of others as if they were your own. Certainly you don't have to document every idea you use in your paper. For example, **common knowledge** — information you could easily find in several reference sources — can be presented without documentation, and so can your own ideas. You must, however, document any use of a direct quotation and any ideas, statistics, charts, diagrams, or pictures that you obtain from your source.

Dealing with the Opposition

When gathering evidence, keep in mind that you cannot ignore arguments against your position. In fact, you should specifically address the most obvious — and sometimes the not-so-obvious — objections to your position. Try to anticipate the objections a reasonable person would have. By directly addressing these objections in your essay, you will help convince readers that your arguments are sound. This part of an argument, called **refutation**, is essential to making the strongest case possible.

You can **refute** opposing arguments by showing that they are unsound, unfair, or weak. Frequently, you will present evidence to show the weakness of your opponent's points and to reinforce your own case. Careful use of definition and cause-and-effect analysis may also prove effective. In the following passage from the classic essay "Politics and the English Language," George Orwell refutes an opponent's argument:

> I said earlier that the decadence of our language is probably curable. Those who deny this would argue, if they produced an argument at all, that language merely reflects existing social conditions, and that we cannot influence its development by any direct tinkering with words and

constructions. So far as the general tone or spirit of a language goes, this may be true, but it is not true in detail. Silly words and expressions have often disappeared, though not through any evolutionary process but owing to the conscious actions of a minority.

Orwell begins by stating the point he wants to make, goes on to define the argument against his position, and then identifies its weakness. Later in the essay, Orwell bolsters his argument by presenting examples that support his point.

When an opponent's argument is so compelling that it cannot be easily dismissed, you should concede its strength. By acknowledging that a point is well taken, you reinforce the impression that you are a fair-minded person. If possible, identify the shortcomings of the opposing position, and then move your argument to more solid ground. (Often an opponent's strong point addresses only *one* facet of a multifaceted problem.) Notice in the example above that Orwell concedes an opposing argument when he says, "So far as the general tone or spirit of a language goes, this may be true." Later in his discussion, he refutes this argument by pointing out its shortcomings.

When planning an argumentative essay, write down all possible arguments against your thesis that you can identify. Then, as you marshal your evidence, decide which points you will refute, keeping in mind that careful readers will expect you to refute the most compelling of your opponent's arguments. Take care, though, not to distort an opponent's argument by making it seem weaker than it actually is. This technique, called creating a **straw man**, can backfire and actually turn fair-minded readers against you.

Understanding Rogerian Argument

Psychologist Carl Rogers has written about how to argue without assuming an adversarial relationship. According to Rogers, traditional strategies of argument rely on **confrontation**—proving that an opponent's position is wrong. With this method of arguing, one person is "wrong" and one is "right." By attacking an opponent and repeatedly hammering home the message that his or her arguments are incorrect or misguided, a writer forces the opponent into a defensive position. The result is conflict, disagreement, and frequently ill will and hostility.

Rogers recommends that you think of those who disagree with you as colleagues, not adversaries. With this approach, now known as **Rogerian argument**, you enter into a cooperative relationship with opponents. Instead of aggressively refuting opposing arguments, you emphasize points of agreement. You thus collaborate to find mutually satisfying solutions. By adopting a conciliatory attitude, you demonstrate your respect for opposing viewpoints and your willingness to compromise and work toward a position that both you and those who disagree with you will find acceptable. To use a Rogerian strategy in your writing, follow the guidelines on page 563.

> ✓ **CHECKLIST: Guidelines for Using Rogerian Argument**
>
> - Begin by summarizing opposing viewpoints.
> - Carefully consider the position of those who disagree with you. What are their legitimate concerns? If you were in their place, how would you react?
> - Present opposing viewpoints accurately and fairly. Demonstrate your respect for the ideas of those who disagree with you.
> - Concede the strength of a compelling opposing argument.
> - Acknowledge the concerns you and your opposition share.
> - Point out to readers how they will benefit from the position you are defining.
> - Present the evidence that supports your viewpoint.

Using Deductive and Inductive Arguments

In an argument, you move from evidence to a conclusion in two ways. One method, called **deductive reasoning**, proceeds from a general premise or assumption to a specific conclusion. Deduction is what most people mean when they speak of logic. Using strict logical form, deduction holds that if all the statements in the argument are true, the conclusion must also be true. The other method of moving from evidence to conclusion is called **inductive reasoning**. Induction proceeds from individual observations to a more general conclusion and uses no strict form. It requires only that all the relevant evidence be stated and that the conclusion fit the evidence better than any other conclusion would. Most written arguments use a combination of deductive and inductive reasoning, but it is simpler to discuss and illustrate them separately.

Using Deductive Arguments

The basic form of a deductive argument is a **syllogism**. A syllogism consists of a **major premise**, which is a general statement; a **minor premise**, which is a related but more specific statement; and a **conclusion**, which is drawn from those premises. Consider the following example:

Major premise:	All Olympic runners are fast.
Minor premise:	Jesse Owens was an Olympic runner.
Conclusion:	Therefore, Jesse Owens was fast.

As you can see, if you grant both the major and minor premises, then you must also grant the conclusion. In fact, it is the only conclusion you can properly draw. You cannot conclude that Jesse Owens was slow because that conclusion contradicts the premises. Nor can you conclude (even if it is true) that Jesse Owens was tall because that conclusion goes beyond the premises.

Of course, this argument seems obvious, and it is much simpler than an argumentative essay would be. In fact, a deductive argument's premises can be fairly elaborate. The Declaration of Independence, which appears later in this chapter, has at its core a deductive argument that could be summarized in this way:

> Major premise: Tyrannical rulers deserve no loyalty.
>
> Minor premise: King George III is a tyrannical ruler.
>
> Conclusion: Therefore, King George III deserves no loyalty.

The major premise is a truth that the Declaration claims is **self-evident** — so obvious that it needs no proof. Much of the Declaration consists of evidence to support the minor premise that King George is a tyrannical ruler. The conclusion, because it is drawn from those premises, has the force of irrefutable logic: the king deserves no loyalty from his American subjects, who are therefore entitled to revolt against him.

When a conclusion follows logically from the major and minor premises, then the argument is said to be **valid**. But if the syllogism is not logical, the argument is not valid, and the conclusion is not sound. For example, the following syllogism is not logical:

> Major premise: All dogs are animals.
>
> Minor premise: All cats are animals.
>
> Conclusion: Therefore, all dogs are cats.

Of course, the conclusion is absurd. But how did we wind up with such a ridiculous conclusion when both premises are obviously true? The answer is that although both cats and dogs are animals, cats are not included in the major premise of the syllogism, which deals only with dogs. Therefore, the syllogism is defective, and the argument is invalid. Consider the following example of an invalid argument:

> Major premise: All dogs are animals.
>
> Minor premise: Ralph is an animal.
>
> Conclusion: Therefore, Ralph is a dog.

Here, an error in logic occurs because the minor premise refers to a term in the major premise that is **undistributed** — it covers only some of the items in the class it denotes. (To be valid, the minor premise must refer to the term in the major premise that is **distributed** — it covers *all* the items in the class it denotes.) In the major premise, *dogs* is the distributed term; it designates *all dogs*. The minor premise, however, refers to *animals,* which is undistributed because it refers only to animals that are dogs. As the minor premise establishes, Ralph is an animal, but it does not follow that he is a dog. He could be a cat, a horse, or even a human being.

Even if a syllogism is valid — that is, correct in its form — its conclusion will not necessarily be **true**. The following syllogism draws a false conclusion:

Major premise:	All dogs are brown.
Minor premise:	My poodle Toby is a dog.
Conclusion:	Therefore, Toby is brown.

As it happens, Toby is black. The conclusion is false because the major premise is false: many dogs are *not* brown. If Toby were actually brown, the conclusion would be correct, but only by chance, not by logic. To be **sound**, a syllogism must be both logical and true.

The advantage of a deductive argument is that if you convince your audience to accept your major and minor premises, the force of logic should bring them to accept your conclusion. Therefore, you should try to select premises that you know your audience accepts or that are self-evident — that is, premises that most people believe to be true. Do not assume, however, that "most people" refers only to your friends and acquaintances. Consider, too, those who may hold different views. If you think your premises are too controversial or difficult to establish firmly, you should use inductive reasoning.

Using Inductive Arguments

Inductive arguments move from specific examples or facts to a general conclusion. Unlike deduction, induction has no distinctive form, and its conclusions are less definitive than those of syllogisms. Still, much inductive thinking (and writing based on that thinking) tends to follow a particular process. First, you decide on a question to be answered — or, especially in the sciences, a tentative answer to such a question, called a **hypothesis**. Then, you gather the evidence that is relevant to the question and that may be important to finding the answer. Finally, you move from your evidence to your conclusion by making an **inference** — a statement about the unknown based on the known — that answers the question and takes the evidence into account. Here is a very simple example of the inductive process:

Question:	How did that living-room window get broken?
Evidence:	There is a baseball on the living-room floor.
	The baseball was not there this morning.
	Some children were playing baseball this afternoon.
	They were playing in the vacant lot across from the window.

> They stopped playing a little while ago.
> They aren't in the vacant lot now.

Conclusion: One of the children hit or threw the ball through the window; then, they all ran away.

The conclusion, because it takes all of the evidence into account, seems obvious. But if it turned out that the children had been playing volleyball, not baseball, that one additional piece of evidence would make the conclusion doubtful—and the true answer could not be inferred. Even if the conclusion is believable, you cannot necessarily assume it is true: after all, the window could have been broken in some other way. For example, perhaps a bird flew against it, and perhaps the baseball in the living room had gone unnoticed all day, making the second piece of "evidence" on the list not true.

Considering several possible conclusions is a good way to avoid reaching an unjustified or false conclusion. In the preceding example, a hypothesis like this one might follow the question:

Hypothesis: One of those children playing baseball broke the living-room window.

Many people stop reasoning at this point, without considering the evidence. But when the gap between your evidence and your conclusion is too great, you may reach a hasty conclusion or one that is not supported by the facts. This well-named error is called **jumping to a conclusion** because it amounts to a premature inductive leap. In induction, the hypothesis is merely the starting point. The rest of the inductive process continues as if the question were still to be answered—as in fact it is until all the evidence has been taken into account.

Because inductive arguments tend to be more complicated than the example on pages 565–66, it is not always easy to move from the evidence you have collected to a sound conclusion. Of course, the more information you gather, the smaller the gap between your evidence and your conclusion. Still, whether large or small, the crucial step from evidence to conclusion always involves what is called an **inductive leap**. For this reason, it is important to remember that inductive conclusions are not facts. **Facts** are verifiable statements, but inductive conclusions are inferences and opinions that, at best, are never certain, only highly probable.

Using Toulmin Logic

Another approach for structuring arguments has been advanced by philosopher Stephen Toulmin. Known as **Toulmin logic**, this method is an effort to describe argumentation as it actually occurs in everyday life. Toulmin puts forth a model that divides arguments into three parts: the *claim,* the *grounds,* and the *warrant.* The **claim** is the main point of the essay. Usually the claim is stated directly as the thesis, but in some arguments it may be implied. The **grounds**—the material a writer uses to support the claim—can be evidence (facts or expert opinion) or appeals to the emotions or values of the audience. The **warrant** is the inference that connects the claim to the grounds. It can be a belief that is taken for granted or an assumption that underlies the argument.

In its simplest form, an argument following Toulmin logic would look like this:

Claim:	Carol should be elected class president.
Grounds:	Carol is an honor student.
Warrant:	A person who is an honor student would make a good class president.

When you formulate an argument using Toulmin logic, you can still use inductive and deductive reasoning. You derive your claim inductively from facts and examples, and you connect the grounds and warrant to your claim deductively. For example, the deductive argument in the Declaration of Independence that was summarized on page 564 can be represented this way:

Claim:	King George III deserves no loyalty.
Grounds:	King George III is a tyrannical ruler.
Warrant:	Tyrannical rulers deserve no loyalty.

As Toulmin points out, the clearer your warrant, the more likely readers will be to agree with it. Notice that in the two preceding examples, the warrants are very explicit.

Recognizing Fallacies

Fallacies are illogical statements that may sound reasonable or true but are actually deceptive and dishonest. When careful readers detect them, such statements can turn even a sympathetic audience against your position. Here are some of the more common fallacies that you should avoid.

Begging the Question.   Begging the question is a logical fallacy that assumes in the premise what the arguer should be trying to prove in the conclusion. This tactic asks readers to agree that certain points are self-evident when in fact they are not.

The unfair and shortsighted legislation that limits free trade is a threat to the American economy.

Restrictions against free trade may or may not be unfair and shortsighted, but emotionally loaded language does not constitute proof. The statement begs the question because it assumes what it should be proving—that restrictive legislation is dangerous.

Argument from Analogy.   An **analogy** is a form of comparison that explains something unfamiliar by comparing it to something more familiar. Although analogies can explain abstract or unclear ideas, they do not constitute proof. An argument based on an analogy frequently ignores important dissimilarities between the two things being compared. When this occurs, the argument is fallacious.

> The overcrowded conditions in some parts of our city have forced people together like rats in a cage. Like rats, they will eventually turn on one another, fighting and killing until a balance is restored. It is therefore necessary that we vote to appropriate funds to build low-cost housing.

No evidence is offered to establish that people behave like rats under these or any other conditions. Just because two things have some characteristics in common, you should not assume they are alike in other respects.

Personal Attack (Argument *Ad Hominem*).   This fallacy tries to divert attention from the facts of an argument by attacking the motives or character of the person making the argument.

> The public should not take seriously Dr. Mason's plan for improving county health services. He is a former alcoholic whose wife recently divorced him.

This attack on Dr. Mason's character says nothing about the quality of his plan. Sometimes a connection exists between a person's private and public lives—for example, in a case of conflict of interest. However, no evidence of such a connection is presented here.

Hasty or Sweeping Generalization.   Sometimes called *jumping to a conclusion,* this fallacy occurs when a conclusion is reached on the basis of too little evidence.

> Because our son really benefited from nursery school, I am convinced that every child should go.

Perhaps other children would benefit from nursery school, and perhaps not, but no conclusion about children in general can be reached on the basis of just one child's experience.

False Dilemma (Either/Or Fallacy).   This fallacy occurs when a writer suggests that only two alternatives exist even though there may be others.

> We must choose between life and death, between intervention and geno-
> cide. No one can take a neutral position on this issue.

An argument like this oversimplifies an issue and forces people to choose
between extremes instead of exploring more moderate positions.

Equivocation.   This fallacy occurs when the meaning of a key term
changes at some point in an argument. Equivocation makes it seem as if a
conclusion follows from premises when it actually does not.

> As a human endeavor, computers are a praiseworthy and even remarkable
> accomplishment. But how human can we hope to be if we rely on comput-
> ers to make our decisions?

The use of *human* in the first sentence refers to the entire human race. In
the second sentence, *human* means "merciful" or "civilized." By subtly
shifting this term to refer to qualities characteristic of people as opposed
to machines, the writer makes the argument seem more sound than it is.

Red Herring.   This fallacy occurs when the focus of an argument is
shifted to divert the audience from the actual issue.

> The mayor has proposed building a new baseball-only sports stadium.
> How can he even consider allocating millions of dollars to this scheme
> when so many professional baseball players are being paid such high
> salaries?

The focus of this argument should be the merits of the sports stadium.
Instead, the writer shifts to the irrelevant issue of athletes' high salaries.

You Also (*Tu Quoque*).   This fallacy asserts that an opponent's argument has no value because the opponent does not follow his or her own
advice.

> How can that judge favor stronger penalties for convicted drug dealers?
> During his confirmation hearings, he admitted smoking marijuana when
> he was a student.

Appeal to Doubtful Authority.   Often people will attempt to bolster an argument with references to experts or famous people. These
appeals are valid when the person quoted or referred to is an expert in the
area being discussed. They are not valid, however, when the individuals
cited have no expertise on the issue.

> According to Ted Koppel, interest rates will remain low during the next
> fiscal year.

Although Ted Koppel is a respected journalist, he is not an expert in business or finance. Therefore, his pronouncements about interest rates are no more than a personal opinion or, at best, an educated guess.

Misleading Statistics.   Although statistics are a powerful form of factual evidence, they can be misrepresented or distorted in an attempt to influence an audience.

> Women will never be competent firefighters; after all, 50 percent of the women in the city's training program failed the exam.

Here, the writer has neglected to mention that there were only two women in the program. Because this statistic is not based on a large enough sample, it cannot be used as evidence to support the argument.

***Post Hoc, Ergo Propter Hoc* (After This, Therefore Because of This).** This fallacy, known as ***post hoc* reasoning**, assumes that because two events occur close together in time, the first must be the cause of the second.

> Every time a Republican is elected president, a recession follows. If we want to avoid another recession, we should elect a Democrat as our next president.

Even if it were true that recessions always occur during the tenure of Republican presidents, no causal connection has been established. (See pages 332–33.)

***Non Sequitur* (It Does Not Follow).**   This fallacy occurs when a statement does not logically follow from a previous statement.

> Disarmament weakened the United States after World War I. Disarmament also weakened the United States after the Vietnam War. For this reason, efforts to control guns will weaken the United States.

The historical effects of disarmament have nothing to do with current efforts to control the sale of guns. Therefore, the conclusion is a *non sequitur.*

Using Transitions

Transitional words and **phrases** are extremely important in argumentative essays. Without these words and phrases, readers will find it difficult to follow your logic and could very well lose track of your argument.

Argumentative essays use transitions to signal a shift in focus. For example, paragraphs that present the specific points in support of your argument can signal this purpose with transitions such as *first, second, third, in addition,* and *finally.* In the same way, paragraphs that refute opposing arguments can signal this purpose with transitions such as *still, nevertheless, however,* and *yet.* Transitional words and phrases — such as *therefore* and *for these reasons* — are also useful when you are presenting your argument's conclusions.

USEFUL TRANSITIONS FOR ARGUMENTATION

all in all	in conclusion
as a result	in other words
finally	in short
first, second, third	in summary
for example	nevertheless
for instance	on the one hand . . . on the other hand
for these reasons	still
however	therefore
in addition	thus
in brief	yet

A more complete list of transitions appears on page 43.

Structuring an Argumentative Essay

An argumentative essay, like other kinds of essays, has an **introduction**, a **body**, and a **conclusion**. However, an argumentative essay has its own special structure, one that ensures that ideas are presented logically and convincingly. The Declaration of Independence follows the typical structure of many classic arguments:

Introduction:	Introduces the issue States the thesis
Body:	Induction — offers evidence to support the thesis Deduction — uses syllogisms to support the thesis States the arguments against the thesis and refutes them
Conclusion:	Restates the thesis in different words Makes a forceful closing statement

Jefferson begins the Declaration by presenting the issue that the document addresses: the obligation of the people of the American colonies to tell the world why they must separate from Great Britain. Next, Jefferson states his thesis that because of the tyranny of the British king, the colonies must replace his rule with another form of government. In the body of the Declaration, he offers as evidence twenty-eight examples of injustice endured by the colonies. Following the evidence, Jefferson refutes counterarguments by explaining how again and again the colonists have appealed to the British for redress, but without result. In his concluding paragraph, he restates the thesis and reinforces it one final time. He ends with a flourish: speaking for the representatives of the United States, he explicitly dissolves all political connections between England and America.

Not all arguments, however, follow this pattern. Your material, your thesis, your purpose, your audience, the type of argument you are writing, and the limitations of your assignment all help you determine the strategies you use. If your thesis is especially novel or controversial, for example, the refutation of opposing arguments may come first. In this instance, opposing positions might even be mentioned in the introduction — provided they are discussed more fully later in the argument.

Suppose your journalism instructor gives you the following assignment:

> Select a controversial topic that interests you, and write a brief editorial about it. Direct your editorial to readers who do not share your views, and try to convince them that your position is reasonable. Be sure to acknowledge the view your audience holds and to refute possible criticisms of your argument.

You are well informed about one local issue because you have just read a series of articles on it. A citizens' group is lobbying for a local ordinance that would authorize government funding for parochial schools in your community. Since you have also recently studied the constitutional doctrine of separation of church and state in your American government class, you know you could argue fairly and strongly against the position taken by this group.

An informal outline of your essay might look like this:

Issue introduced:	Should public tax revenues be spent on aid to parochial schools?
Thesis statement:	Despite the pleas of citizen groups like Parochial School Parents United, using tax dollars to support church-affiliated schools violates the U.S. Constitution.
Evidence (deduction):	Explain general principle of separation of church and state in the Constitution.
Evidence (induction):	Present recent examples of court cases interpreting and applying this principle.
Evidence (deduction):	Explain how the Constitution and the court cases apply to your community's situation.
Opposition refuted:	Identify and respond to arguments used by Parochial School Parents United. Concede the

point that parochial schools educate many children who would otherwise have to be educated in public schools at taxpayers' expense.

Conclusion: Restate the thesis; end with a strong closing statement.

Revising an Argumentative Essay

When you revise an argumentative essay, consider the items on the revision checklist on page 54. In addition, pay special attention to the items on the following checklist, which apply specifically to argumentative essays.

✓**REVISION CHECKLIST: Argumentation**

- Does your assignment call for argumentation?
- Have you chosen a topic you can argue about effectively?
- Do you have a debatable thesis?
- Have you considered the beliefs and opinions of your audience?
- Is your evidence relevant, representative, and sufficient?
- Have you documented evidence you have gathered from sources?
- Have you made an effort to address your audience's possible objections to your position?
- Have you refuted opposing arguments?
- Have you used inductive or deductive reasoning (or a combination of the two) to move from your evidence to your conclusion?
- Have you avoided logical fallacies?
- Have you used appropriate transitional words and phrases?

Editing an Argumentative Essay

When you edit your argumentative essay, follow the guidelines on the editing checklists on pages 71, 73, and 76. In addition, focus on the grammar, mechanics, and punctuation issues that are particularly relevant to argumentative essays. One of these issues — using coordinating and subordinating conjunctions to link ideas — is discussed on the pages that follow.

GRAMMAR IN CONTEXT: Using Coordinating
and Subordinating Conjunctions

When you write an argumentative essay, you often have to use **con-junctions** — words that join other words or groups of words — to express the logical and sequential relationships between ideas in your sentences. Conjunctions are especially important because they help readers follow your logic so that they will be persuaded by your argument. For this reason, you should be certain that the conjunctions you select clearly and accurately communicate the connections between the ideas you are discussing.

Using Coordinating Conjunctions. A **compound sentence** is made up of two or more independent clauses (simple sentences) connected by a coordinating conjunction. **Coordinating conjunctions** join two independent clauses that express ideas of equal importance, and they also indicate how those ideas are related.

> *independent clause*   *independent clause*
> [People can disobey unjust laws], <u>or</u> [they can be oppressed by them].

COORDINATING CONJUNCTIONS

and (*indicates addition*)
but, yet (*indicate contrast or contradiction*)
or (*indicates alternatives*)
nor (*indicates an elimination of alternatives*)
so, for (*indicate a cause-and-effect connection*)

According to William Safire, a national ID card would give the police almost unlimited surveillance power, <u>and</u> it would give businesses unprecedented access to personal information (615).

"A national ID card would not prevent all threats of terrorism, <u>but</u> it would make it more difficult for potential terrorists to hide in open view" (Dershowitz 619).

Oliver Stone does not believe that his movie drove people to commit murder, <u>nor</u> does he believe that it should be banned (687–88).

When you use a coordinating conjunction to join two independent clauses, always place a comma before the coordinating conjunction.

Using Subordinating Conjunctions. A **complex sentence** is made up of one independent clause (simple sentence) and one or more dependent clauses. (A dependent clause cannot stand alone as a sentence.) Subordinating conjunctions link dependent and independent clauses that express ideas of unequal importance, and they also indicate how those ideas are related.

independent clause   dependent clause

[According to Michael Zimecki, film executives should be sued] [so that they will stop making violent movies] (693–94).

SUBORDINATING CONJUNCTIONS

SUBORDINATING CONJUNCTION	RELATIONSHIP BETWEEN CLAUSES
after, before, since, until, when, whenever, while	Time
as, because, since, in order that, so that	Cause or effect
even if, if, unless	Condition
although, even though, though	Contrast

"All segregation statutes are unjust because segregation distorts the soul and damages the personality" (King 601–2).

"If this war is truly worth fighting, then the burdens of doing so should fall on all Americans" (Broyles 640).

"Until there is more of a consensus on the best choice, we cannot take chances on a doubtful alternative when children's lives are concerned" (Adkins 627).

"If the AAP recommendations become law, they would likely apply not only to second-parent adoptions, but to other adoptions by gay couples or singles" (Birtha 631–32).

When you use a subordinating conjunction to join two clauses, place a comma after the dependent clause when it comes *before* the independent clause. Do not use a comma when the dependent clause comes *after* the independent clause.

When they signed the Declaration of Independence, Thomas Jefferson and the others knew they were committing treason. (*comma*)

Thomas Jefferson and the others knew they were committing treason when they signed the Declaration of Independence. (*no comma*)

For more practice in using coordinating and subordinating conjunctions, visit Exercise Central at <bedfordstmartins.com/patterns/conjunctions>.

> ✓ **EDITING CHECKLIST: Argumentation**
>
> - Have you used coordinating conjunctions correctly to connect two or more independent clauses?
> - Do the coordinating conjunctions accurately express the relationship between the ideas in the independent clauses?
> - Have you placed a comma before the coordinating conjunction?
> - Have you used subordinating conjunctions correctly to connect an independent clause and one or more dependent clauses?
> - Do the subordinating conjunctions accurately express the relationship between the ideas in the dependent and independent clauses?
> - Have you placed a comma after the dependent clause when it comes before the independent clause?
> - Have you remembered not to use a comma when the dependent clause comes after the independent clause?

A STUDENT WRITER: Argumentation

The following editorial, written by Matt Daniels for his college newspaper, illustrates the techniques discussed earlier in this chapter.

An Argument against the Anna Todd Jennings Scholarship

Introduction

Summary of controversy

Recently, a dispute has arisen over the "Caucasian-restricted" Anna Todd Jennings scholarship.* Anna Jennings died in 1955, and her will established a trust that granted a scholarship of up to $15,000 for a deserving student. Unfortunately, Jennings, who had certain racist views, limited her scholarship to "Caucasian students." After much debate with family and friends, I, a white, well-qualified, and definitely deserving student, have decided not to apply for the scholarship. It is my view that despite arguments to the contrary, applying for the Anna Todd Jennings scholarship furthers the racist ideas held by its founder.   1

Thesis statement

Argument (deductive)

Most people would agree that racism in any form is an evil that should be opposed. The Anna Todd Jennings scholarship is a subtle but nonetheless dangerous expression of   2

---

* EDS. NOTE — This essay discusses an actual situation, but the name of the scholarship has been changed here.

racism. It explicitly discriminates against African Americans, Asians, Latinos, Native Americans, and others. By providing a scholarship for whites only, Anna Jennings frustrates the aspirations of groups who until recently had been virtually kept out of the educational mainstream. On this basis alone, students should refuse to apply and should actively work to encourage the school to challenge the racist provisions of Anna Todd Jennings's will. Such challenges have been upheld by the courts: the striking down of a similar clause in the will of the eighteenth-century financier Stephen Girard is just one example.

Argument (inductive)

Evidence

The school itself must share some blame in this case. Students who applied for the Anna Todd Jennings scholarship were unaware of its restrictions. The director of the financial aid office has acknowledged that he knew about the racial restrictions of the scholarship but thought that students should have the right to apply anyway. The materials distributed by the financial aid office also gave no indication that the award was limited to Caucasians. Students were required to fill out forms, submit financial statements, and forward transcripts. In addition to this material, all students were told to attach a recent photograph to their application. Little did the applicants know that the sole purpose of this innocuous little picture was to distinguish whites from nonwhites. By keeping secret the scholarship's restrictions, the school has put students in the position of unwittingly endorsing Anna Jennings's racism. Thus, both the school and the unsuspecting students have been in collusion with the administrators of the Anna Todd Jennings trust.

3

Refutation of opposing argument

The question students face is this: What is the best way to deal with the generosity of a racist? A recent edition of the school paper contained several letters saying that students should accept Anna Jennings's scholarship money. One student said, "If we do not take that money and use our education to topple the barriers of prejudice, we are giving the money to those who will use the money in the opposite fashion." This argument, although attractive, is flawed. If an individual accepts a scholarship with racial restrictions, then he or she is actually endorsing the principles behind it. If a student does

4

not want to appear to endorse racism, then he or she should reject the scholarship, even if this action causes hardship or gives adversaries a momentary advantage. To do otherwise is to further the cause of the individual who set up the scholarship. The best way to register a protest is to work to change the requirement for the scholarship and to encourage others not to apply as long as the racial restrictions exist.

Refutation of opposing argument

Another letter to this newspaper made the point that a number of other restricted scholarships are available at the school and no one seems to question them. For example, one is for the children of veterans, another is for women, and yet another is earmarked for African Americans. Even though these scholarships have restrictions, to assume that all restrictions are the same is to make a hasty generalization. Women, African Americans, and the children of veterans are groups that many believe deserve special treatment. Both women and African Americans have been discriminated against for years, and, as a result, educational opportunities have been denied them. Earmarking scholarships for them is simply a means of restoring some measure of equality. The children of veterans have been singled out because their parents have performed an extraordinary service for their country. Whites, however, do not fall into either of these categories. Special treatment for them is based solely on race and has nothing to do with any objective standard of need or merit.

5

Conclusion

I hope that by refusing to apply for the Anna Todd Jennings scholarship, I have encouraged other students to think

Restatement of thesis

about the issues involved in their own decisions. All of us have a responsibility to ourselves and to society. If we truly believe that racism in all its forms is evil, then we have to make a

Concluding statement

choice between sacrifice and hypocrisy. Faced with these options, our decision should be clear: accept the loss of funds as an opportunity to explore your values and fight for your principles; if you do, this opportunity is worth far more than any scholarship.

6

Points for Special Attention

Gathering Evidence.   Because of his involvement with his subject, Matt Daniels could support his points with examples from his own experience and did not have to do much research. Still, Matt did have to spend a lot of time thinking about ideas and selecting evidence. He had to review the requirements for the scholarship and decide on the arguments he would make. In addition, he reviewed an article that appeared in the school newspaper and the letters students wrote in response to the article. He then chose material that would add authority to his arguments.

Certainly, statistics, studies, and expert testimony, if they exist, would strengthen Matt's argument. But even without such evidence, an argument such as this one, based on solid reasoning and personal experience, can be quite compelling.

Refuting Opposing Arguments.   Matt devotes two paragraphs to summarizing and refuting arguments made by those who believe qualified students should apply for the scholarship despite its racial restrictions. He begins this section by asking a **rhetorical question** — a question asked not to elicit an answer but to further the argument. He goes on to refute what he considers the two best arguments against his thesis — that students should take the money and work to fight racism and that other scholarships at the school have restrictions. Matt refutes these arguments by identifying a flaw in the logic of the first argument and by pointing to a fallacy, a hasty generalization, in the second.

Audience.   Because he wrote his essay as an editorial for his college newspaper, Matt assumed his audience would be familiar with the issue he was discussing. Letters to the editor of the paper convinced him that his position was controversial, so he decided that his readers, mostly students and instructors, would have to be persuaded that his points were valid. To achieve this purpose, he carefully presents himself as a reasonable person, explains issues he believes are central to his case, and avoids *ad hominem* attacks. In addition, he avoids sweeping generalizations and name-calling and includes many details to support his assertions and convince readers his points are worth considering.

Organization.   Matt uses several strategies discussed earlier in this chapter. He begins his essay by introducing the issue he is going to discuss and then states his thesis: "Applying for the Anna Todd Jennings scholarship furthers the racist ideas held by its founder."

Because Matt had given a good deal of thought to his subject, he was able to construct two fairly strong arguments to support his position. His first argument is deductive. He begins by stating a premise he believes is self-evident — racism should be opposed. The rest of this argument follows a straightforward deductive pattern:

Major premise:	Racism should be opposed.
Minor premise:	The Anna Todd Jennings scholarship is racist.
Conclusion:	Therefore, the Anna Todd Jennings scholarship should be opposed.

Matt ends his first argument with factual evidence that reinforces his conclusion: the successful challenge to the will of financier Stephen Girard, which limited admittance to Girard College in Philadelphia to white male orphans.

Matt's second argument is inductive, asserting that the school has put students in the position of unknowingly supporting racism. The argument begins with Matt's hypothesis and presents the fact that even though the school is aware of the racist restrictions of the scholarship, it has not made students aware of them. According to Matt, the school's knowledge (and tacit approval) of the situation leads to the conclusion that the school is in collusion with those who manage the scholarship.

In his fourth and fifth paragraphs, Matt refutes two opposing arguments. Although his conclusion is rather brief, it does effectively reinforce and support his main idea. Matt ends his essay by recommending a course of action to his fellow students.

Focus on Revision

Matt constructed a solid argument that addressed his central issue very effectively. However, some students on the newspaper's editorial board thought he should add a section giving more information about Anna Todd Jennings and her bequest. These students believed that such information would help them better understand the implications of accepting her money. As it now stands, the essay dismisses Anna Todd Jennings as a racist, but biographical material and excerpts from her will—both of which appeared in the school paper—would enable readers to grasp the extent of her prejudice. Matt decided to follow up on this advice and to strengthen his conclusion as well. He thought that including the exact words of Anna Todd Jennings would help him to reinforce his points forcefully and memorably.

📄 **PEER EDITING WORKSHEET: Argumentation**

1. Does the essay take a stand on an issue? What is it? At what point does the writer state his or her thesis? Is the thesis debatable?
2. What evidence does the writer include to support his or her position? What additional evidence could the writer supply?
3. Does the essay summarize and refute the opposing arguments? List these arguments.
4. How effective are the writer's refutations? Should the writer address any other arguments?

5. Does the essay use inductive reasoning? Deductive reasoning? Both? Provide an example of each type of reasoning used in the essay.

   Inductive reasoning:

   Deductive reasoning:

6. Does the essay include any logical fallacies? How would you correct these fallacies?

7. Do coordinating and subordinating conjunctions convey the logical and sequential connections between ideas?

8. How could the introduction be improved?

9. How could the conclusion be improved?

10. What would you add to make this essay more convincing?

The essays that follow represent a wide variety of topics, and the purpose of each essay is to support a controversial thesis. Each of the four debates pairs two essays that take opposing stands on the same issue. In the casebook, four essays on a single topic offer a greater variety of viewpoints. The first selection, a visual text, is followed by questions designed to illustrate how argumentation can operate in visual form.

THANKS TO MODERN SCIENCE
17 INNOCENT PEOPLE HAVE BEEN REMOVED FROM DEATH ROW.
THANKS TO MODERN POLITICS
23 INNOCENT PEOPLE HAVE BEEN REMOVED FROM THE LIVING.

On April 15, 1999, Ronald Keith Williamson walked away from Oklahoma State Prison a free man. An innocent man. He had spent the last eleven years behind bars. "I did not rape or kill Debra Sue Carter," he would shout day and night from his death row cell. His voice was so torn and raspy from his pleas for justice that he could barely speak. DNA evidence would eventually end his nightmare and prove his innocence. He came within five days of being put to death for a crime he did not commit.

Williamson's plight is not an isolated one. Nor is it even unusual.

Anthony Porter also came within days of being executed. The state of Illinois halted his execution as it questioned whether or not Porter was mentally competent. Porter has an I.Q. of fifty-one. As the state questioned his competence, a journalism class at Northwestern University questioned his guilt. With a small amount of investigating, they managed to produce the real killer. After sixteen years on death row, Anthony Porter would find his freedom. He was lucky. He escaped with his life. A fate not shared by twenty-three other innocent men.

The Chicago Tribune, in its five-part series "Death Row justice derailed," pronounced, "Capital punishment in Illinois is a system so riddled with faulty evidence, unscrupulous trial tactics, and legal incompetence that justice has been forsaken." The governor of Illinois recently declared a moratorium on the death penalty after the state had acquired the dubious honor of releasing more men from death row than it had executed.

The unfairness that plagues the Illinois system also plagues every other state as well: incompetent lawyers, racial bias, and lack of access to DNA testing all inevitably lead to gross miscarriages of justice. As Supreme Court Justice William J. Brennan, Jr., stated, "Perhaps the bleakest fact of all is that the death penalty is imposed not only in a freakish and discriminatory manner, but also in some cases upon defendants who are actually innocent."

Even those who support capital punishment are finding it increasingly more difficult to endorse it in its current form. Capital punishment is a system that is deeply flawed – a system that preys on the poor and executes the innocent. It is a system that is fundamentally unjust and unfair. Please support our efforts to have a moratorium on further executions declared now. Support the ACLU.

• • •

Reading Images

1. What points does the ad's headline make? Does the rest of the ad support these points?
2. How would you describe the picture that accompanies the text? How does the picture reinforce the message of the text?
3. Does this ad appeal primarily to logic, to emotions, or to both? Explain.
4. List the specific points the ad makes. Which points are supported by evidence? Which points should be supported by evidence but are not? How does this lack of support affect your response to the ad?

Journal Entry

Overall, do you find this ad convincing? Write an email to the ACLU presenting your position. Be sure to refer to specific parts of the ad to support your argument.

Thematic Connections

- "Thirty-Eight Who Saw Murder Didn't Call the Police" (page 120)
- "Get It Right: Privatize Executions" (page 305)
- "A Peaceful Woman Explains Why She Carries a Gun" (page 371)
- "Five Ways to Kill a Man" (page 505)

THOMAS JEFFERSON

The Declaration of Independence

Thomas Jefferson was born in 1743 in what is now Albemarle County, Virginia, and attended the College of William and Mary. A lawyer, he was elected to Virginia's colonial legislature in 1769 and began a distinguished political career that strongly influenced the early development of the United States. In addition to his participation in the Second Continental Congress of 1775–1776, which ratified the Declaration of Independence, he served as governor of Virginia; as minister to France; as secretary of state under President George Washington; as vice president under John Adams; and, finally, as president from 1801 to 1809. After his retirement, he founded the University of Virginia. He died on July 4, 1826.

Background on the struggle for American independence: By the early 1770s, many residents of the original thirteen American colonies had come to believe that King George III and his ministers, both in England and in the New World, wielded too much power over the colonists. In particular, they objected to a series of taxes imposed on them by the British Parliament, and, being without political representation, they asserted that "taxation without representation" amounted to tyranny. In response to a series of laws Parliament passed in 1774 to limit the political and geographic freedom of the colonists, representatives of each colony met at the Continental Congress of 1774 to draft a plan of reconciliation, but it was rejected.

As cries for independence increased, British soldiers and state militias began to engage in armed conflict, which by 1776 had become a full-fledged civil war. On June 11, 1776, the Second Continental Congress chose Jefferson, Benjamin Franklin, and several other delegates to draft a declaration of independence. The draft was written by Jefferson, with suggestions and revisions contributed by other commission members. Jefferson's Declaration of Independence challenges a basic assumption of its time — that the royal monarch ruled by divine right — and, in so doing, became one of the most important political documents in world history.

As you read, keep in mind that to the British, the Declaration of Independence was a call for open rebellion. For this reason, the Declaration's final sentence, in which the signatories pledge their lives, fortunes, and honor, is no mere rhetorical flourish. Had England defeated the colonists, everyone who signed the Declaration of Independence would have been arrested, charged with treason or sedition, stripped of his property, and probably hanged.

When in the course of human events, it becomes necessary for one people to dissolve the political bonds which have connected them with another, and to assume among the powers of the earth, the separate and equal station to which the Laws of Nature and of Nature's God entitle them, a decent respect to the opinions of mankind requires that they should declare the causes which impel them to the separation.

We hold these truths to be self-evident, that all men are created equal, that they are endowed by their Creator with certain unalienable rights, that among these are life, liberty and the pursuit of happiness. That to secure these rights, governments are instituted among men, deriving their just powers from the consent of the governed. That whenever any form of government becomes destructive to these ends, it is the right of the people to alter or to abolish it, and to institute new government, laying its foundation on such principles and organizing its powers in such form, as to them shall seem most likely to effect their safety and happiness. Prudence, indeed, will dictate that governments long established should not be changed for light and transient causes; and accordingly all experience hath shown, that mankind are more disposed to suffer, while evils are sufferable, than to right themselves by abolishing the forms to which they are accustomed. But when a long train of abuses and usurpations, pursuing invariably the same object, evinces a design to reduce them under absolute despotism, it is their right, it is their duty, to throw off such government, and to provide new guards for their future security. Such has been the patient sufferance of these Colonies; and such is now the necessity which constrains them to alter their former systems of government. This history of the present king of Great Britain is a history of repeated injuries and usurpations, all having in direct object the establishment of an absolute tyranny over these States. To prove this, let facts be submitted to a candid world.

He has refused his assent to laws, the most wholesome and necessary for the public good.

He has forbidden his Governors to pass laws of immediate and pressing importance, unless suspended in their operation till his assent should be obtained; and when so suspended, he has utterly neglected to attend to them.

He has refused to pass other laws for the accommodation of large districts of people, unless those people would relinquish the right of representation in the legislature, a right inestimable to them and formidable to tyrants only.

He has called together legislative bodies at places unusual, uncomfortable, and distant from the depository of their public records, for the sole purpose of fatiguing them into compliance with his measure.

He has dissolved representative houses repeatedly, for opposing with manly firmness his invasions on the rights of people.

He has refused for a long time, after such dissolutions, to cause others to be elected; whereby the legislative powers, incapable of annihilation, have returned to the people at large for their exercise; the State remaining in the meantime exposed to all the dangers of invasion from without, and convulsions within.

He has endeavoured to prevent the population of these states; for that 9
purpose obstructing the laws for naturalization of foreigners; refusing to
pass others to encourage their migration hither, and raising the conditions
of new appropriations of lands.

He has obstructed the administration of justice, by refusing his assent 10
to laws for establishing judiciary powers.

He has made judges dependent on his will alone, for the tenure of their 11
offices, and the amount and payment of their salaries.

He has erected a multitude of new offices, and sent hither swarms of 12
officers to harass our people, and eat out their substance.

He has kept among us, in times of peace, standing armies without the 13
consent of our legislatures.

He has affected to render the military independent of and superior to 14
the civil power.

He has combined with others to subject us to a jurisdiction foreign to 15
our constitution, and unacknowledged by our laws; giving his assent to
their acts of pretended legislation:

For quartering large bodies of troops among us: 16

For protecting them, by a mock trial, from punishment for any mur- 17
ders which they should commit on the inhabitants of these States:

For cutting off our trade with all parts of the world: 18

For imposing taxes on us without our consent: 19

For depriving us in many cases, of the benefits of trial by jury: 20

For transporting us beyond seas to be tried for pretended offences: 21

For abolishing the free system of English laws in a neighbouring 22
Province, establishing therein an arbitrary government, and enlarging its
boundaries so as to render it at once an example and fit instrument for
introducing the same absolute rule into these Colonies:

For taking away our Charters, abolishing our most valuable laws, and 23
altering fundamentally the forms of our governments:

For suspending our own legislatures, and declaring themselves 24
invested with power to legislate for us in all cases whatsoever.

He has abdicated government here, by declaring us out of his protec- 25
tion and waging war against us.

He has plundered our seas, ravaged our coasts, burnt our towns, and 26
destroyed the lives of our people.

He is at this time transporting large armies of foreign mercenaries to 27
complete the works of death, desolation and tyranny, already begun with
circumstances of cruelty and perfidy scarcely paralleled in the most bar-
barous ages, and totally unworthy the head of a civilized nation.

He has constrained our fellow citizens taken captive on the high seas 28
to bear arms against their country, to become the executioners of their
friends and brethren, or to fall themselves by their hands.

He has excited domestic insurrections amongst us, and has endeav- 29
oured to bring on the inhabitants of our frontiers, the merciless Indian

savages, whose known rule of warfare, is an undistinguished destruction of all ages, sexes and conditions.

In every stage of these oppressions we have petitioned for redress in the most humble terms: our repeated petitions have been answered only by repeated injury. A prince whose character is thus marked by every act which may define a tyrant, is unfit to be the ruler of a free people.   30

Nor have we been wanting in attentions to our British brethren. We have warned them from time to time of attempts by their legislature to extend an unwarrantable jurisdiction over us. We have reminded them of the circumstances of our emigration and settlement here. We have appealed to their native justice and magnanimity, and we have conjured them by the ties of our common kindred to disavow these usurpations, which, would inevitably interrupt our connections and correspondence. They too have been deaf to the voice of justice and of consanguinity. We must, therefore, acquiesce in the necessity, which denounces our separation, and hold them, as we hold the rest of mankind, enemies in war, in peace friends.   31

We, therefore, the Representatives of the United States of America, in General Congress, assembled, appealing to the Supreme Judge of the world for the rectitude of our intentions, do, in the name, and by authority of the good people of these Colonies, solemnly publish and declare, That these United Colonies are, and of right ought to be Free and Independent States; that they are absolved from all allegiance to the British Crown, and that all political connection between them and the state of Great Britain, is and ought to be totally dissolved; and that as Free and Independent States, they have full power to levy war, conclude peace, contract alliances, establish commerce, and to do all other acts and things which Independent States may of right do. And for the support of this declaration, with a firm reliance on the protection of divine Providence, we mutually pledge to each other our lives, our fortunes, and our sacred honor.   32

• • •

Comprehension

1. What "truths" does Jefferson assert are "self-evident"?
2. What does Jefferson say is the source from which governments derive their powers?
3. What reasons does Jefferson give to support his premise that the United States should break away from Great Britain?
4. What conclusions about the British crown does Jefferson draw from the evidence he presents?

Purpose and Audience

1. What is the major premise of Jefferson's argument? Should Jefferson have done more to establish the truth of this premise?

2. The Declaration of Independence was written during a period now referred to as the Age of Reason. In what ways has Jefferson tried to make his document appear reasonable?

3. For what audience (or audiences) was the document intended? Which groups of readers would have been most likely to accept it? Explain.

4. How effectively does Jefferson anticipate and refute the opposition?

5. In paragraph 31, following the list of grievances, why does Jefferson address his "British brethren"?

6. At what point does Jefferson state his thesis? Why does he state it where he does?

Style and Structure

1. Does the Declaration of Independence rely primarily on inductive or deductive reasoning? Identify examples of each.

2. What techniques does Jefferson use to create smooth and logical transitions from one paragraph to another?

3. Why does Jefferson list all of his twenty-eight grievances? Why doesn't he just summarize them or mention a few representative grievances?

4. Jefferson begins the last paragraph of the Declaration of Independence with "We, therefore." How effective is this conclusion? Explain.

Vocabulary Projects

1. Define each of the following words as it is used in this selection.

station (1)	evinces (2)	tenure (11)
impel (1)	despotism (2)	jurisdiction (15)
self-evident (2)	sufferance (2)	arbitrary (22)
endowed (2)	candid (2)	insurrections (29)
deriving (2)	depository (6)	disavow (31)
prudence (2)	dissolutions (8)	consanguinity (31)
transient (2)	annihilation (8)	rectitude (32)
usurpations (2)	appropriations (9)	levy (32)

2. Underline ten words that have negative connotations. How does Jefferson use these words to help him make his point? Do you think words with more neutral connotations would strengthen or weaken his case? Why?

3. What words does Jefferson use that are rarely used today? Would the Declaration of Independence be more meaningful to today's readers if it were updated, with more familiar words substituted? To help you formulate your response, try rewriting a paragraph or two, and assess your updated version.

Journal Entry

Do you think Jefferson is being fair to the king? Do you think he should be?

Writing Workshop

1. Following Jefferson's example, write a declaration of independence from your school, job, family, or any other institution with which you are associated.
2. Write an essay stating a grievance you share with other members of some group, and then argue for the best way to eliminate the grievance.
3. In an argumentative essay written from the viewpoint of King George III, try to convince the colonists that they should not break away from Great Britain. If you can, refute some of the points Jefferson makes in the Declaration.

Combining the Patterns

The middle section of the Declaration of Independence is developed by means of **exemplification**: it presents a series of examples to support Jefferson's assertion that the colonists have experienced "repeated injuries and usurpations" (2). Are these examples relevant? Representative? Sufficient? What other pattern of development could Jefferson have used to support his assertion?

Thematic Connections

- "The 'Black Table' Is Still There" (page 366)
- "The Power of Words in Wartime" (page 377)
- "Grant and Lee: A Study in Contrasts" (page 409)
- "Letter from Birmingham Jail" (page 597)

ELIZABETH CADY STANTON

Declaration of Sentiments and Resolutions, Seneca Falls Convention, 1848

Elizabeth Cady was born in Johnstown, New York, in 1815 and attended the Troy Female Seminary. At the age of twenty-five, she married the writer and abolitionist Henry Brewster Stanton, joining him in the struggle to end slavery. She also became active in the woman suffrage movement, lobbying for the right of women to vote. This movement had its beginnings in the United States at the first Woman's Rights Convention, which was organized by Stanton and other early petitioners for women's rights and held in Seneca Falls, New York, in July 1848. There, the following declaration was first presented, amended, and then unanimously adopted by the three hundred delegates. (All the resolutions were passed unanimously except for the one calling for women's right to vote, which was thought by some to be extreme enough to discredit the larger feminist movement.) Stanton went on to lead the National Woman Suffrage Movement from 1869 to 1890 and to coedit *Revolution,* a feminist periodical. A popular lecturer and skilled writer, she continued to work toward the goal of equality for women until her death in 1902.

Background on the women's suffrage movement: Conventional wisdom of the day held that women were, in general, far inferior to men in terms of intelligence and rationality, so the Founding Fathers' "all men are created equal" did not seem to apply to them. In fact, the idea for the Seneca Falls Convention was spurred by Stanton's experiences at the 1840 World Anti-Slavery Convention in London, which she attended with her husband and which refused to admit women delegates to the floor. When made public, the Declaration of Sentiments was universally derided by the press and by contemporary religious leaders — even Henry Stanton thought his wife had gone too far — and it had little practical effect. The Civil War interrupted the budding women's rights movement, but at its close, when emancipated African-American men were granted the right to vote, the movement picked up steam again. Its leaders lobbied for an amendment to the U.S. Constitution allowing women to vote and pressed state legislatures for voting rights as well. It was a long road, however. By 1913, only 12 states had extended voting rights to women, and not until the Nineteenth Amendment to the Constitution was ratified in 1920 did all American women achieve this right.

Declaration of Sentiments

When, in the course of human events, it becomes necessary for one portion of the family of man to assume among the people of the earth a position different from that which they have hitherto occupied, but one to which the laws of nature and of nature's God entitle them, a decent respect to the opinions of mankind requires that they should declare the causes that impel them to such a course.

We hold these truths to be self-evident: that all men and women are created equal; that they are endowed by their Creator with certain inalienable rights; that among these are life, liberty, and the pursuit of happiness; that to secure these rights governments are instituted, deriving their just powers from the consent of the governed. Whenever any form of government becomes destructive of these ends, it is the right of those who suffer from it to refuse allegiance to it, and to insist upon the institution of a new government, laying its foundation on such principles, and organizing its powers in such form, as to them shall seem most likely to effect their safety and happiness. Prudence, indeed, will dictate that governments long established should not be changed for light and transient causes; and accordingly all experience hath shown that mankind are more disposed to suffer, while evils are sufferable, than to right themselves by abolishing the forms to which they were accustomed. But when a long train of abuses and usurpations, pursuing invariably the same object, evinces a design to reduce them under absolute despotism, it is their duty to throw off such government, and to provide new guards for their future security. Such has been the patient sufferance of the women under this government, and such is now the necessity which constrains them to demand the equal station to which they are entitled. 2

The history of mankind is a history of repeated injuries and usurpations on the part of man toward woman, having in direct object the establishment of an absolute tyranny over her. To prove this, let facts be submitted to a candid world. 3

He has never permitted her to exercise her inalienable right to the elective franchise. 4

He has compelled her to submit to laws, in the formation of which she had no voice. 5

He has withheld from her rights which are given to the most ignorant and degraded men — both natives and foreigners. 6

Having deprived her of this first right of a citizen, the elective franchise, thereby leaving her without representation in the halls of legislation, he has oppressed her on all sides. 7

He has made her, if married, in the eye of the law, civilly dead. 8

He has taken from her all right in property, even to the wages she earns. 9

He has made her, morally, an irresponsible being, as she can commit many crimes with impunity, provided they be done in the presence of her husband. In the covenant of marriage, she is compelled to promise obedience to her husband, he becoming, to all intents and purposes, her master — the law giving him power to deprive her of her liberty, and to administer chastisement. 10

He has so framed the laws of divorce, as to what shall be the proper causes, and in case of separation, to whom the guardianship of the children shall be given, as to be wholly regardless of the happiness of women — 11 the law, in all cases, going upon the false supposition of the supremacy of man, and giving all power into his hands.

After depriving her of all rights as a married woman, if single, and the   12
owner of property, he has taxed her to support a government which recognizes her only when her property can be made profitable to it.

He has monopolized nearly all the profitable employments, and from   13
those she is permitted to follow, she receives but a scanty remuneration. He closes against her all the avenues to wealth and distinction which he considers most honorable to himself. As a teacher of theology, medicine, or law, she is not known.

He has denied her the facilities for obtaining a thorough education, all   14
colleges being closed against her.

He allows her in Church, as well as State, but a subordinate position,   15
claiming Apostolic authority for her exclusion from the ministry, and, with some exceptions, from any public participation in the affairs of the Church.

He has created a false public sentiment by giving to the world a differ-   16
ent code of morals for men and women, by which moral delinquencies which exclude women from society, are not only tolerated, but deemed of little account in man.

He has usurped the prerogative of Jehovah himself, claiming it as his   17
right to assign for her a sphere of action, when that belongs to her conscience and to her God.

He has endeavored, in every way that he could, to destroy her confi-   18
dence in her own powers, to lessen her self-respect, and to make her willing to lead a dependent and abject life.

Now, in view of this entire disenfranchisement of one-half the people   19
of this country, their social and religious degradation — in view of the unjust laws above mentioned, and because women do feel themselves aggrieved, oppressed, and fraudulently deprived of their most sacred rights, we insist that they have immediate admission to all the rights and privileges which belong to them as citizens of the United States.

In entering upon the great work before us, we anticipate no small   20
amount of misconception, misrepresentation, and ridicule; but we shall use every instrumentality within our power to effect our object. We shall employ agents, circulate tracts, petition the State and National legislatures, and endeavor to enlist the pulpit and the press in our behalf. We hope this Convention will be followed by a series of Conventions embracing every part of the country.

Resolutions

Whereas, The great precept of nature is conceded to be, that "man   21
shall pursue his own true and substantial happiness." Blackstone* in his

---

* EDS. NOTE — Sir William Blackstone (1723–80), English jurist. Many regard his *Commentaries* (1765–69) as the most thorough treatment of English law ever produced.

Commentaries remarks, that this law of Nature being coeval with mankind, and dictated by God himself, is of course superior in obligation to any other. It is binding over all the globe, in all countries and at all times; no human laws are of any validity if contrary to this, and such of them as are valid, derive all their force, and all their validity, and all their authority, mediately and immediately, from this original; therefore,

Resolved, That such laws as conflict, in any way, with the true and sub-   22
stantial happiness of woman, are contrary to the great precept of nature and of no validity, for this is "superior in obligation to any other."

Resolved, That all laws which prevent woman from occupying such a   23
station in society as her conscience shall dictate, or which place her in a position inferior to that of man, are contrary to the great precept of nature, and therefore of no force or authority.

Resolved, That woman is man's equal—was intended to be so by the   24
Creator, and the highest good of the race demands that she should be recognized as such.

Resolved, That the women of this country ought to be enlightened in   25
regard to the laws under which they live, that they may no longer publish their degradation by declaring themselves satisfied with their present position, nor their ignorance, by asserting that they have all the rights they want.

Resolved, That inasmuch as man, while claiming for himself intellec-   26
tual superiority, does accord to woman moral superiority, it is preeminently his duty to encourage her to speak and teach, as she has an opportunity, in all religious assemblies.

Resolved, That the same amount of virtue, delicacy, and refinement of   27
behavior that is required of woman in the social state, should also be required of man, and the same transgressions should be visited with equal severity on both man and woman.

Resolved, That the objection of indelicacy and impropriety, which is so   28
often brought against woman when she addresses a public audience, comes with a very ill-grace from those who encourage, by their attendance, her appearance on the stage, in the concert, or in feats of the circus.

Resolved, That woman has too long rested satisfied in the circum-   29
scribed limits which corrupt customs and a perverted application of the Scriptures have marked out for her, and that it is time she should move in the enlarged sphere which her great Creator has assigned her.

Resolved, That it is the duty of the women of this country to secure to   30
themselves their sacred right to the elective franchise.

Resolved, That the equality of human rights results necessarily from the   31
fact of the identity of the race in capabilities and responsibilities.

Resolved, therefore, That, being invested by the Creator with the same   32
capabilities, and the same consciousness of responsibility for their exercise, it is demonstrably the right and duty of woman, equally with man, to promote every righteous cause by every righteous means; and especially in regard to the great subjects of morals and religion, it is self-evidently her right to participate with her brother in teaching them, both in private and

in public, by writing and by speaking, by any instrumentalities proper to be used, and in any assemblies proper to be held; and this being a self-evident truth growing out of the divinely implanted principles of human nature, any custom or authority adverse to it, whether modern or wearing the hoary sanction of antiquity, is to be regarded as a self-evident falsehood, and at war with mankind.

Resolved, That the speedy success of our cause depends upon the zealous and untiring efforts of both men and women, for the overthrow of the monopoly of the pulpit, and for the securing to woman an equal participation with men in the various trades, professions, and commerce.* 33

• • •

Comprehension

1. According to Stanton, why is it necessary for women to declare their sentiments?
2. What truths does Stanton say are "self-evident" (2)?
3. What injuries does Stanton list? Which injuries seem most important?
4. What type of reception does Stanton expect the Declaration of Sentiments and Resolutions to receive? What does she propose to do about this reception?
5. What conclusion does Stanton draw? According to her, what self-evident right do women have? What does she believe should be regarded as "a self-evident falsehood" (32)?

Purpose and Audience

1. Is Stanton addressing men, women, or both? How can you tell? Does she consider one segment of her audience to be more receptive to her argument than another? Explain.
2. What strategies does Stanton use to present herself as a reasonable person? Do you think she is successful? Explain.
3. What is Stanton's thesis? At what point does she state it? Why do you think she states it when she does?
4. What is Stanton's purpose? Do you think she actually expects to change people's ideas and behavior, or does she have some other purpose in mind?

Style and Structure

1. Does Stanton present her argument inductively or deductively? Why do you think she chose this arrangement?

---

* EDS. NOTE — This last resolution was given by Lucretia Mott at the actual convention. All the previous resolutions were drafted earlier by Elizabeth Cady Stanton.

2. The Declaration of Sentiments and Resolutions imitates the tone, style, and, in some places, the wording of the Declaration of Independence. What are the advantages of this strategy? What are the disadvantages?

3. In paragraphs 2 and 32, Stanton mentions "self-evident" truths. Are these truths really self-evident? Should she have done more to establish the validity of these statements?

4. What are the major and minor premises of Stanton's argument? Do these premises lead logically to her conclusion?

5. How do transitional words and phrases help Stanton move readers from one section of her argument to another? Are the transitions effective?

6. Should Stanton have specifically refuted arguments against her position? Could she be accused of ignoring her opposition?

Vocabulary Projects

1. Define each of the following words as it is used in this selection.

hitherto (1)	station (2)	validity (21)
impel (1)	franchise (4)	transgressions (27)
inalienable (2)	degraded (6)	indelicacy (28)
allegiance (2)	impunity (10)	impropriety (28)
dictate (2)	chastisement (10)	circumscribed (29)
sufferable (2)	subordinate (15)	sphere (29)
invariably (2)	delinquencies (16)	antiquity (32)
sufferance (2)	abject (18)	zealous (33)
constrains (2)	disenfranchisement (19)	

2. Today, many people would consider the style of some of the passages in the Declaration of Sentiments and Resolutions stiff and overly formal. Find a paragraph that fits this description, and rewrite it using less formal diction. What is lost in your revision, and what is gained?

Journal Entry

Review Stanton's list of injuries to women. How many of these wrongs have been corrected? How many have yet to be addressed?

Writing Workshop

1. Choose an issue you care about, and write your own Declaration of Sentiments and Resolutions. Like Stanton, echo the phrasing of the Declaration of Independence in your essay.

2. Reread your journal entry, and select one of the injuries to women that has not yet been corrected. Write a letter to the editor of your school newspaper arguing that this issue needs to be resolved. In your letter, refer specifically to the Declaration of Sentiments and Resolutions.

3. When the Declaration of Sentiments and Resolutions was voted on at the Seneca Falls Convention in 1848, the only resolution not passed unanimously was the one that called for women to win the right to vote (30). Write a letter to the convention calling on the delegates to vote for this resolution. Make sure you refute the main argument against this resolution — that it would alienate so many people that it would discredit the entire feminist movement.

Combining the Patterns

Like the Declaration of Independence, the Declaration of Sentiments and Resolutions is partly developed by **exemplification**. A series of examples supports Stanton's assertion that women now "demand the equal station to which they are entitled" (2). How effective are these examples? Are they relevant? Representative? Sufficient?

Thematic Connections

- "My Mother Never Worked" (page 108)
- "A Peaceful Woman Explains Why She Carries a Gun" (page 371)
- "I Want a Wife" (page 524)
- The Declaration of Independence (page 584)

Letter from Birmingham Jail

Martin Luther King Jr. was born in Atlanta, Georgia, in 1929. He attended Morehouse College and Crozer Theological Seminary, and after receiving his doctorate in theology from Boston University in 1955, he became pastor of the Dexter Avenue Baptist Church in Montgomery, Alabama. There, he organized a 382-day bus boycott that led to the 1956 Supreme Court decision outlawing segregation on Alabama's buses. As leader of the Southern Christian Leadership Conference, he was instrumental in securing the civil rights of black Americans, using methods based on a philosophy of nonviolent protest. His books include *Stride towards Freedom* (1958) and *Why We Can't Wait* (1964). In 1964, he was awarded the Nobel Peace Prize. He was assassinated in 1968 in Memphis, Tennessee.

Background on racial segregation: In 1896, the Supreme Court ruled in *Plessy v. Ferguson* that "separate but equal" accommodations on railroad cars gave African Americans the equal protection guaranteed by the Fourteenth Amendment of the Constitution. This decision, with few challenges, was used to justify separate public facilities — including schools — for blacks and whites well into the twentieth century.

In the mid-1950s, long-standing state support for segregation of the races and discrimination against blacks had begun to be challenged from a variety of quarters. Supreme Court decisions in 1954 and 1955 declared segregation in public schools and other publicly financed venues unconstitutional, while blacks and whites alike were calling for an end to discrimination. Their actions took the form of marches, boycotts, and sit-ins (organized protests whose participants refuse to move from a public area). Many whites, however, particularly in the South, vehemently resisted any change in race relations.

By 1963, when King organized a campaign against segregation in Birmingham, Alabama, tensions ran deep. He and his followers met fierce opposition from the police, as well as from white moderates, who considered him an "outside agitator." During the demonstrations, King was arrested and jailed for eight days. He wrote his "Letter from Birmingham Jail" to white clergymen to explain his actions and answer those who urged him to call off the demonstrations.

April 16, 1963

My Dear Fellow Clergymen:

While confined here in the Birmingham city jail, I came across your recent statement calling my present activities "unwise and untimely." Seldom do I pause to answer criticism of my work and ideas. If I sought to answer all the criticisms that cross my desk, my secretaries would have little time for anything other than such correspondence in the course of the day, and I would have no time for constructive work. But since I feel that you are men of genuine good will and that your criticisms are sincerely set forth, I want to try to answer your statement in what I hope will be patient and reasonable terms.

I think I should indicate why I am here in Birmingham, since you have been influenced by the view which argues against "outsiders coming in." I have the honor of serving as president of the Southern Christian Leadership Conference, an organization operating in every southern state, with headquarters in Atlanta, Georgia. We have some eighty-five affiliated organizations across the South, and one of them is the Alabama Christian Movement for Human Rights. Frequently we share staff, educational, and financial resources with our affiliates. Several months ago the affiliate here in Birmingham asked us to be on call to engage in a nonviolent direct-action program if such were deemed necessary. We readily consented, and when the hour came we lived up to our promise. So I, along with several members of my staff, am here because I was invited here. I am here because I have organizational ties here.

But more basically, I am in Birmingham because injustice is here. Just as the prophets of the eighth century B.C. left their villages and carried their "thus saith the Lord" far beyond the boundaries of their home towns, and just as the Apostle Paul left his village of Tarsus and carried the gospel of Jesus Christ to the far corners of the Greco-Roman world, so am I compelled to carry the gospel of freedom beyond my own home town. Like Paul, I must constantly respond to the Macedonian call for aid.

Moreover, I am cognizant of the interrelatedness of all communities and states. I cannot sit idly by in Atlanta and not be concerned about what happens in Birmingham. Injustice anywhere is a threat to justice everywhere. We are caught in an inescapable network of mutuality, tied in a single garment of destiny. Whatever affects one directly, affects all indirectly. Never again can we afford to live with the narrow, provincial, "outside agitator" idea. Anyone who lives inside the United States can never be considered an outsider anywhere within its bounds.

You deplore the demonstrations taking place in Birmingham. But your statement, I am sorry to say, fails to express a similar concern for the conditions that brought about the demonstrations. I am sure that none of you would want to rest content with the superficial kind of social analysis that deals merely with effects and does not grapple with underlying causes. It is unfortunate that demonstrations are taking place in Birmingham, but it is even more unfortunate that the city's white power structure left the Negro community with no alternative.

In any nonviolent campaign there are four basic steps: collection of the facts to determine whether injustices exist; negotiation; self-purification; and direct action. We have gone through all these steps in Birmingham. There can be no gainsaying the fact that racial injustice engulfs this community. Birmingham is probably the most thoroughly segregated city in the United States. Its ugly record of brutality is widely known. Negroes have experienced grossly unjust treatment in courts. There have been more unsolved bombings of Negro homes and churches in Birmingham than in any other city in the nation. These are the hard, brutal facts of the case. On the basis of these conditions, Negro leaders sought to negotiate with the city fathers. But the latter consistently refused to engage in good-faith negotiation.

Then, last September, came the opportunity to talk with leaders of   7
Birmingham's economic community. In the course of the negotiations, certain promises were made by the merchants — for example, to remove the stores' humiliating racial signs. On the basis of these promises, the Reverend Fred Shuttlesworth and the leaders of the Alabama Christian Movement for Human Rights agreed to a moratorium on all demonstrations. As the weeks and months went by, we realized that we were the victims of a broken promise. A few signs, briefly removed, returned; the others remained.

As in so many past experiences, our hopes had been blasted, and the   8
shadow of deep disappointment settled upon us. We had no alternative except to prepare for direct action, whereby we would present our very bodies as means of laying our case before the conscience of the local and the national community. Mindful of the difficulties involved, we decided to undertake a process of self-purification. We began a series of workshops on nonviolence, and we repeatedly asked ourselves: "Are you able to accept blows without retaliating?" "Are you able to endure the ordeal of jail?" We decided to schedule our direct-action program for the Easter season, realizing that except for Christmas, this is the main shopping period of the year. Knowing that a strong economic-withdrawal program would be the byproduct of direct action, we felt that this would be the best time to bring pressure to bear on the merchants for the needed change.

Then it occurred to us that Birmingham's mayoral election was coming up in March, and we speedily decided to postpone action until after election day. When we discovered that the Commissioner of Public Safety, Eugene "Bull" Connor, had piled up enough votes to be in the run-off, we decided again to postpone action until the day after the run-off so that the demonstrations could not be used to cloud the issues. Like many others, we waited to see Mr. Connor defeated, and to this end we endured postponement after postponement. Having aided in this community need, we felt that our direct-action program could be delayed no longer.

You may well ask, "Why direct action? Why sit-ins, marches, and so   10
forth? Isn't negotiation a better path?" You are quite right in calling for negotiation. Indeed, this is the very purpose of direct action. Nonviolent direct action seeks to create such a crisis and foster such a tension that a community which has constantly refused to negotiate is forced to confront the issue. It seeks so to dramatize the issue that it can no longer be ignored. My citing the creation of tension as part of the work of the nonviolent-resistor may sound rather shocking. But I must confess that I am not afraid of the word "tension." I have earnestly opposed violent tension, but

there is a type of constructive, nonviolent tension which is necessary for growth. Just as Socrates felt that it was necessary to create a tension in the mind so that individuals could rise from the bondage of myths and half-truths to the unfettered realm of creative analysis and objective appraisal, so must we see the need for nonviolent gadflies to create the kind of tension in society that will help men rise from the dark depths of prejudice and racism to the majestic heights of understanding and brotherhood.

11   The purpose of our direct-action program is to create a situation so crisis-packed that it will inevitably open the door to negotiation. I therefore concur with you in your call for negotiation. Too long has our beloved Southland been bogged down in a tragic effort to live in monologue rather than dialogue.

12   One of the basic points in your statement is that the action that I and my associates have taken in Birmingham is untimely. Some have asked: "Why didn't you give the new city administration time to act?" The only answer that I can give to this query is that the new Birmingham administration must be prodded about as much as the outgoing one, before it will act. We are sadly mistaken if we feel that the election of Albert Boutwell as mayor will bring the millennium to Birmingham. While Mr. Boutwell is a much more gentle person than Mr. Connor, they are both segregationists, dedicated to maintenance of the status quo. I have hoped that Mr. Boutwell will be reasonable enough to see the futility of massive resistance to desegregation. But he will not see this without pressure from devotees of civil rights. My friends, I must say to you that we have not made a single gain in civil rights without determined legal and nonviolent pressure. Lamentably, it is an historical fact that privileged groups seldom give up their privileges voluntarily. Individuals may see the moral light and voluntarily give up their unjust posture; but, as Reinhold Niebuhr* has reminded us, groups tend to be more immoral than individuals.

13   We know through painful experience that freedom is never voluntarily given by the oppressor; it must be demanded by the oppressed. Frankly, I have yet to engage in a direct-action campaign that was "well timed" in the view of those who have not suffered unduly from the disease of segregation. For years now I have heard the word "Wait!" It rings in the ear of every Negro with piercing familiarity. This "Wait" has almost always meant "Never." We must come to see, with one of our distinguished jurists, that "justice too long delayed is justice denied."

14   We have waited for more than 340 years for our constitutional and God-given rights. The nations of Asia and Africa are moving with jetlike speed toward gaining political independence, but we still creep at horse-and-buggy pace toward gaining a cup of coffee at a lunch counter. Perhaps it is easy for those who have never felt the stinging darts of segregation to say, "Wait." But when you have seen vicious mobs lynch your mothers and fathers at will and drown your sisters and brothers at whim; when you have

---

* EDS. NOTE — American religious and social thinker (1892–1971).

seen hate-filled policemen curse, kick, and even kill your black brothers and sisters; when you see the vast majority of your twenty million Negro brothers smothering in an airtight cage of poverty in the midst of an affluent society; when you suddenly find your tongue twisted and your speech stammering as you seek to explain to your six-year-old daughter why she can't go to the public amusement park that has just been advertised on television, and see tears welling up in her eyes when she is told that Funtown is closed to colored children, and see ominous clouds of inferiority beginning to form in her little mental sky, and see her beginning to distort her personality by developing an unconscious bitterness toward white people; when you have to concoct an answer for a five-year-old son who is asking, "Daddy, why do white people treat colored people so mean?"; when you take a cross-country drive and find it necessary to sleep night after night in the uncomfortable corners of your automobile because no motel will accept you; when you are humiliated day in and day out by nagging signs reading "white" and "colored"; when your first name becomes "nigger," your middle name becomes "boy" (however old you are) and your last name becomes "John," and your wife and mother are never given the respected title "Mrs."; when you are harried by day and haunted at night by the fact that you are a Negro, living constantly at tiptoe stance, never quite knowing what to expect next, and are plagued with inner fears and outer resentments; when you are forever fighting a degenerating sense of "nobodiness"—then you will understand why we find it difficult to wait. There comes a time when the cup of endurance runs over, and men are no longer willing to be plunged into the abyss of despair. I hope, sirs, you can understand our legitimate and unavoidable impatience.

You express a great deal of anxiety over our willingness to break laws.   15
This is certainly a legitimate concern. Since we so diligently urge people to obey the Supreme Court's decision of 1954 outlawing segregation in the public schools, at first glance it may seem rather paradoxical for us consciously to break laws. One may well ask: "How can you advocate breaking some laws and obeying others?" The answer lies in the fact that there are two types of laws: just and unjust. I would be the first to advocate obeying just laws. One has not only a legal but a moral responsibility to obey just laws. Conversely, one has a moral responsibility to disobey unjust laws. I would agree with St. Augustine* that "an unjust law is no law at all."

Now, what is the difference between the two? How does one determine   16
whether a law is just or unjust? A just law is a man-made code that squares with the moral law or the law of God. An unjust law is a code that is out of harmony with the moral law. To put it in the terms of St. Thomas Aquinas:† An unjust law is a human law that is not rooted in eternal law and natural law. Any law that uplifts human personality is just. Any law that degrades human personality is unjust. All segregation statutes are

---

* Eds. note — Early church father and philosopher (354–430).
† Eds. note — Italian philosopher and theologian (1225–1274).

unjust because segregation distorts the soul and damages the personality. It gives the segregator a false sense of superiority and the segregated a false sense of inferiority. Segregation, to use the terminology of the Jewish philosopher Martin Buber, substitutes an "I-it" relationship for an "I-thou" relationship and ends up relegating persons to the status of things. Hence segregation is not only politically, economically, and sociologically unsound, it is morally wrong and sinful. Paul Tillich* has said that sin is separation. Is not segregation an existential expression of man's tragic separation, his awful estrangement, his terrible sinfulness? Thus it is that I can urge men to obey the 1954 decision of the Supreme Court, for it is morally right; and I can urge them to disobey segregation ordinances, for they are morally wrong.

Let us consider a more concrete example of just and unjust laws. An   17
unjust law is a code that a numerical or power majority group compels a minority group to obey but does not make binding on itself. This is *difference* made legal. By the same token, a just law is a code that a majority compels a minority to follow and that it is willing to follow itself. This is *sameness* made legal.

Let me give another explanation. A law is unjust if it is inflicted on a   18
minority that, as a result of being denied the right to vote, had no part in enacting or devising the law. Who can say that the legislature of Alabama which set up that state's segregation laws was democratically elected? Throughout Alabama all sorts of devious methods are used to prevent Negroes from becoming registered voters, and there are some counties in which, even though Negroes constitute a majority of the population, not a single Negro is registered. Can any law enacted under such circumstances be considered democratically structured?

Sometimes a law is just on its face and unjust in its application. For   19
instance, I have been arrested on a charge of parading without a permit. Now, there is nothing wrong in having an ordinance which requires a permit for a parade. But such an ordinance becomes unjust when it is used to maintain segregation and to deny citizens the First-Amendment privilege of peaceful assembly and protest.

I hope you are able to see the distinction I am trying to point out. In no   20
sense do I advocate evading or defying the law, as would the rabid segregationist. That would lead to anarchy. One who breaks an unjust law must do so openly, lovingly, and with a willingness to accept the penalty. I submit that an individual who breaks a law that conscience tells him is unjust, and who willingly accepts the penalty of imprisonment in order to arouse the conscience of the community over its injustice, is in reality expressing the highest respect for law.

Of course, there is nothing new about this kind of civil disobedience. It   21
was evidenced sublimely in the refusal of Shadrach, Meshach, and Abed-

---

* EDS. NOTE — American philosopher and theologian (1886–1965).

nego* to obey the laws of Nebuchadnezzar, on the ground that a higher moral law was at stake. It was practiced superbly by the early Christians, who were willing to face hungry lions and the excruciating pain of chopping blocks rather than submit to certain unjust laws of the Roman Empire. To a degree, academic freedom is a reality today because Socrates practiced civil disobedience. In our own nation, the Boston Tea Party represented a massive act of civil disobedience.

We should never forget that everything Adolph Hitler did in Germany   22
was "legal" and everything the Hungarian freedom fighters did in Hungary was "illegal." It was "illegal" to aid and comfort a Jew in Hitler's Germany. Even so, I am sure that, had I lived in Germany at the time, I would have aided and comforted my Jewish brothers. If today I lived in a Communist country where certain principles dear to the Christian faith are suppressed, I would openly advocate disobeying that country's anti-religious laws.

I must make two honest confessions to you, my Christian and Jewish   23
brothers. First, I must confess that over the past few years I have been gravely disappointed with the white moderate. I have almost reached the regrettable conclusion that the Negro's great stumbling block in his stride toward freedom is not the White Citizens Counciler or the Ku Klux Klanner, but the white moderate, who is more devoted to "order" than to justice; who prefers a negative peace which is the absence of tension to a positive peace which is the presence of justice; who constantly says, "I agree with you in the goal you seek, but I cannot agree with your methods of direct action"; who paternalistically believes he can set the timetable for another man's freedom; who lives by a mythical concept of time and who constantly advises the Negro to wait for a "more convenient season." Shallow understanding from people of good will is more frustrating than absolute misunderstanding from people of ill will. Lukewarm acceptance is much more bewildering than outright rejection.

I had hoped that the white moderate would understand that law and   24
order exist for the purpose of establishing justice and that when they fail in this purpose they become the dangerously structured dams that block the flow of social progress. I had hoped that the white moderate would understand that the present tension in the South is a necessary phase of the transition from an obnoxious negative peace, in which the Negro passively accepted his unjust plight, to a substantive and positive peace, in which all men will respect the dignity and worth of human personality. Actually, we who engage in nonviolent direct action are not the creators of tension. We merely bring to the surface the hidden tension that is already alive. We bring it out in the open, where it can be seen and dealt with. Like a boil that can never be cured so long as it is covered up but must be opened with

---

* Eds. note — In the Book of Daniel, three men who were thrown into a blazing fire for refusing to worship a golden statue.

all its ugliness to the natural medicines of air and light, injustice must be exposed, with all the tension its exposure creates, to the light of human conscience and the air of national opinion, before it can be cured.

In your statement you assert that our actions, even though peaceful, must be condemned because they precipitate violence. But is this a logical assertion? Isn't this like condemning a robbed man because his possession of money precipitated the evil act of robbery? Isn't this like condemning Socrates because his unswerving commitment to truth and his philosophical inquiries precipitated the act by the misguided populace in which they made him drink hemlock? Isn't this like condemning Jesus because his unique God-consciousness and never-ceasing devotion to God's will precipitated the evil act of crucifixion? We must come to see that, as the federal courts have consistently affirmed, it is wrong to urge an individual to cease his efforts to gain his basic constitutional rights because the quest may precipitate violence. Society must protect the robbed and punish the robber.

I had also hoped that the white moderate would reject the myth concerning time in relation to the struggle for freedom. I have just received a letter from a white brother in Texas. He writes: "All Christians know that the colored people will receive equal rights eventually, but it is possible that you are in too great a religious hurry. It has taken Christianity almost two thousand years to accomplish what it has. The teachings of Christ take time to come to earth." Such an attitude stems from a tragic misconception of time, from the strangely irrational notion that there is something in the very flow of time that will inevitably cure all ills. Actually, time itself is neutral; it can be used either destructively or constructively. More and more I feel that the people of ill will have used time much more effectively than have the people of good will. We will have to repent in this generation not merely for the hateful words and actions of the bad people, but for the appalling silence of the good people. Human progress never rolls in on wheels of inevitability; it comes through the tireless efforts of men willing to be co-workers with God, and without this hard work, time itself becomes an ally of the forces of social stagnation. We must use time creatively, in the knowledge that the time is always ripe to do right. Now is the time to make real the promise of democracy and transform our pending national elegy into a creative psalm of brotherhood. Now is the time to lift our national policy from the quicksand of racial injustice to the solid rock of human dignity.

You speak of our activity in Birmingham as extreme. At first I was rather disappointed that fellow clergymen would see my nonviolent efforts as those of an extremist. I began thinking about the fact that I stand in the middle of two opposing forces in the Negro community. One is a force of complacency, made up in part of Negroes who, as a result of long years of oppression, are so drained of self-respect and a sense of "somebodiness" that they have adjusted to segregation; and in part of a few middle-class Negroes who, because of a degree of academic and economic security and because in some ways they profit by segregation, have become insensitive to the problems of the masses. The other force is one of bitterness and hatred, and it comes perilously close to advocating violence. It is expressed in the various black nationalist groups that are springing up across the nation, the largest and best-known being Elijah Muhammad's Muslim movement. Nourished by the Negro's frustration over the continued existence of racial discrimination, this movement is made up of people who have lost faith in America, who have absolutely repudiated Christianity, and who have concluded that the white man is an incorrigible "devil."

I have tried to stand between these two forces, saying that we need emulate neither the "do-nothingism" of the complacent nor the hatred and despair of the black nationalist. For there is the more excellent way of love and nonviolent protest. I am grateful to God that, through the influence of the Negro church, the way of nonviolence became an integral part of our struggle.   28

If this philosophy had not emerged, by now many streets of the South would, I am convinced, be flowing with blood. And I am further convinced that if our white brothers dismiss as "rabble-rousers" and "outside agitators" those of us who employ nonviolent direct action, and if they refuse to support our nonviolent efforts, millions of Negroes will, out of frustration and despair, seek solace and security in black-nationalist ideologies — a development that would inevitably lead to a frightening racial nightmare.   29

Oppressed people cannot remain oppressed forever. The yearning for freedom eventually manifests itself, and that is what has happened to the American Negro. Something within has reminded him of his birthright of freedom, and something without has reminded him that it can be gained. Consciously or unconsciously, he has been caught up by the *Zeitgeist,* and with his black brothers of Africa and his brown and yellow brothers of Asia, South America, and the Caribbean, the United States Negro is moving with a sense of great urgency toward the promised land of racial justice. If one recognizes this vital urge that has engulfed the Negro community, one should readily understand why public demonstrations are taking place. The Negro has many pent-up resentments and latent frustrations, and he must release them. So let him march; let him make prayer pilgrimages to the city hall; let him go on freedom rides — and try to understand why he must do so. If his repressed emotions are not released in nonviolent ways, they will seek expression through violence; this is not a threat but a fact of history. So I have not said to my people, "Get rid of your discontent." Rather, I have tried to say that this normal and healthy discontent can be channeled into the creative outlet of nonviolent direct action. And now this approach is being termed extremist.   30

But though I was initially disappointed at being categorized as an extremist, as I continued to think about the matter I gradually gained a measure of satisfaction from the label. Was not Jesus an extremist for love: "Love your enemies, bless them that curse you, do good to them that hate you, and pray for them which despitefully use you, and persecute you." Was   31 not Amos an extremist for justice: "let justice roll down like waters and righteousness like an everflowing stream." Was not Paul an extremist for the Christian gospel: "I bear in my body the marks of the Lord Jesus." Was not Martin Luther an extremist: "Here I stand; I cannot do otherwise, so help me God." And John Bunyan: "I will stay in jail to the end of my days before I make a butchery of my conscience." And Abraham Lincoln: "This nation cannot survive half slave and half free." And Thomas Jefferson: "We hold these truths to be self-evident, that all men are created equal. . . ." So the question is not whether we will be extremists, but what kind of extremists we will be. Will we be extremists for hate or for love? Will we be extremists for the preservation of injustice or for the extension of justice? In that dramatic scene of Calvary's hill three men were crucified. We must never forget that all three were crucified for the same crime—the crime of extremism. Two were extremists for immorality, and thus fell below their environment. The other, Jesus Christ, was an extremist for love, truth, and goodness, and thereby rose above his environment. Perhaps the South, the nation, and the world are in dire need of creative extremists.

I hoped that the white moderate would see this need. Perhaps I was too **32** optimistic; perhaps I expected too much. I suppose I should have realized that few members of the oppressor race can understand the deep groans and passionate yearnings of the oppressed race, and still fewer have the vision to see that injustice must be rooted out by strong, persistent, and determined action. I am thankful, however, that some of our white brothers in the South have grasped the meaning of this social revolution and committed themselves to it. They are still all too few in quantity, but they are big in quality. Some—such as Ralph McGill, Lillian Smith, Harry Golden, James McBride Dabbs, Ann Braden, and Sarah Patton Boyle—have written about our struggle in eloquent and prophetic terms. Others have marched with us down nameless streets of the South. They have languished in filthy, roach-infested jails, suffering the abuse and brutality of policemen who view them as "dirty nigger-lovers." Unlike so many of their moderate brothers and sisters, they have recognized the urgency of the movement and sensed the need for powerful "action" antidotes to combat the disease of segregation.

Let me take note of my other major disappointment. I have been so **33** greatly disappointed with the white church and its leadership. Of course, there are some notable exceptions. I am not unmindful of the fact that each of you has taken some significant stands on this issue. I commend you, Reverend Stallings, for your Christian stand on this past Sunday, in welcoming Negroes to your worship service on a nonsegregated basis. I commend the Catholic leaders of this state for integrating Spring Hill College several years ago.

But despite these notable exceptions, I must honestly reiterate that I **34** have been disappointed with the church. I do not say this as one of those negative critics who can always find something wrong with the church. I say this as a minister of the gospel, who loves the church; who was nurtured in its bosom; who has been sustained by its spiritual blessings and who will remain true to it as long as the cord of life shall lengthen.

When I was suddenly catapulted into the leadership of the bus protest   35
in Montgomery, Alabama, a few years ago, I felt we would be supported by the white church. I felt that the white ministers, priests, and rabbis of the South would be among our strongest allies. Instead, some have been outright opponents, refusing to understand the freedom movement and misrepresenting its leaders; all too many others have been more cautious than courageous and have remained silent behind the anesthetizing security of stained-glass windows.

In spite of my shattered dreams, I came to Birmingham with the hope   36
that the white religious leadership of this community would see the justice of our cause and, with deep moral concern, would serve as the channel through which our just grievances could reach the power structure. I had hoped that each of you would understand. But again I have been disappointed.

There was a time when the church was very powerful — in the time   37
when the early Christians rejoiced at being deemed worthy to suffer for what they believed. In those days the church was not merely a thermometer that recorded the ideas and principles of popular opinion; it was a thermostat that transformed the mores of society. Whenever the early Christians entered a town, the people in power became disturbed and immediately sought to convict the Christians for being "disturbers of the peace" and "outside agitators." But the Christians pressed on, in the conviction that they were "a colony of heaven," called to obey God rather than man. Small in number, they were big in commitment. They were too God-intoxicated to be "astronomically intimidated." By their effort and example they brought an end to such ancient evils as infanticide and gladiatorial contests.

Things are different now. So often the contemporary church is a weak,   38
ineffectual voice with an uncertain sound. So often it is an archdefender of the status quo. Far from being disturbed by the presence of the church, the power structure of the average community is consoled by the church's silent — and often even vocal — sanction of things as they are.

But the judgment of God is upon the church as never before. If today's   39
church does not recapture the sacrificial spirit of the early church, it will lose its authenticity, forfeit the loyalty of millions, and be dismissed as an irrelevant social club with no meaning for the twentieth century. Every day I meet young people whose disappointment with the church has turned into outright disgust.

Perhaps I have once again been too optimistic. Is organized religion   40
too inextricably bound to the status quo to save our nation and the world? Perhaps I must turn my faith to the inner spiritual church, the church

within the church, as the true *ekklesia** and the hope of the world. But again I am thankful to God that some noble souls from the ranks of organized religion have broken loose from the paralyzing chains of conformity and joined us as active partners in the struggle for freedom. They have left their secure congregations and walked the streets of Albany, Georgia, with us. They have gone down the highways of the South on tortuous rides for freedom. Yes, they have gone to jail with us. Some have been dismissed from their churches, have lost the support of their bishops and fellow ministers. But they have acted in the faith that right defeated is stronger than evil triumphant. Their witness has been the spiritual salt that has preserved the true meaning of the gospel in these troubled times. They have carved a tunnel of hope through the dark mountain of disappointment.

I hope the church as a whole will meet the challenge of this decisive   41
hour. But even if the church does not come to the aid of justice, I have no despair about the future. I have no fear about the outcome of our struggle in Birmingham, even if our motives are at present misunderstood. We will reach the goal of freedom in Birmingham and all over the nation, because the goal of America is freedom. Abused and scorned though we may be, our destiny is tied up with America's destiny. Before the pilgrims landed at Plymouth, we were here. Before the pen of Jefferson etched the majestic words of the Declaration of Independence across the pages of history, we were here. For more than two centuries our forebears labored in this country without wages; they made cotton king; they built the homes of their masters while suffering gross injustice and shameful humiliation — and yet out of a bottomless vitality they continued to thrive and develop. If the inexpressible cruelties of slavery could not stop us, the opposition we now face will surely fail. We will win our freedom because the sacred heritage of our nation and the eternal will of God are embodied in our echoing demands.

Before closing I feel impelled to mention one other point in your state-   42
ment that has troubled me profoundly. You warmly commended the Birmingham police for keeping "order" and "preventing violence." I doubt that you would have so warmly commended the police force if you had seen its dogs sinking their teeth into unarmed, nonviolent Negroes. I doubt that you would so quickly commend the policemen if you were to observe their ugly and inhumane treatment of Negroes here in the city jail; if you were to watch them push and curse old Negro women and young Negro girls; if you were to see them slap and kick old Negro men and young boys; if you were to observe them, as they did on two occasions, refuse to give us food because we wanted to sing our grace together. I cannot join you in your praise of the Birmingham police department.

It is true that the police have exercised a degree of discipline in han-   43
dling the demonstrators. In this sense they have conducted themselves rather "nonviolently" in public. But for what purpose? To preserve the vile

---

* EDS. NOTE — Greek word for the early Christian church.

system of segregation. Over the past few years I have consistently preached that nonviolence demands that the means we use must be as pure as the ends we seek. I have tried to make clear that it is wrong to use immoral means to attain moral ends. But now I must affirm that it is just as wrong, or perhaps even more so, to use moral means to preserve immoral ends. Perhaps Mr. Connor and his policemen have been rather nonviolent in public, as was Chief Pritchett in Albany, Georgia, but they have used the moral means of nonviolence to maintain the immoral end of racial injustice. As T. S. Eliot has said, "The last temptation is the greatest treason: To do the right deed for the wrong reason."

I wish you had commended the Negro sit-inners and demonstrators of   44
Birmingham for their sublime courage, their willingness to suffer, and their amazing discipline in the midst of great provocation. One day the South will recognize its real heroes. They will be the James Merediths,* with the noble sense of purpose that enables them to face jeering and hostile mobs, and with the agonizing loneliness that characterizes the life of the pioneer. They will be old, oppressed, battered Negro women, symbolized in a seventy-two-year-old woman in Montgomery, Alabama, who rose up with a sense of dignity and with her people decided not to ride segregated buses, and who responded with ungrammatical profundity to one who inquired about her weariness: "My feets is tired, but my soul is at rest." They will be the young high school and college students, the young ministers of the gospel and a host of their elders, courageously and nonviolently sitting in at lunch counters and willingly going to jail for conscience's sake. One day the South will know that when these disinherited children of God sat down at lunch counters, they were in reality standing up for what is best in the American dream and for the most sacred values in our Judaeo-Christian heritage, thereby bringing our nation back to those great wells of democracy which were dug deeply by the founding fathers in their formulation of the Constitution and the Declaration of Independence.

Never before have I written so long a letter. I'm afraid it is much too   45
long to take your precious time. I can assure that it would have been much shorter if I had been writing from a comfortable desk, but what else can one do when he is alone in a narrow jail cell, other than write long letters, think long thoughts, and pray long prayers?

If I have said anything in this letter that overstates the truth and indi-   46
cates an unreasonable impatience, I beg you to forgive me. If I have said anything that understates the truth and indicates my having a patience that allows me to settle for anything less than brotherhood, I beg God to forgive me.

I hope this letter finds you strong in the faith. I also hope that circum-   47
stances will soon make it possible for me to meet each of you, not as an integrationist or a civil-rights leader but as a fellow clergyman and a

---

* EDS. NOTE — James Meredith was the first African American to enroll at the University of Mississippi.

Christian brother. Let us all hope that the dark clouds of racial prejudice will soon pass away and the deep fog of misunderstanding will be lifted from our fear-drenched communities, and in some not too distant tomorrow the radiant stars of love and brotherhood will shine over our great nation with all their scintillating beauty.

> Yours for the cause of Peace and Brotherhood,
> Martin Luther King Jr.

• • •

Comprehension

1. King says he seldom answers criticism. Why not? Why, then, does he decide to do so in this instance?
2. Why do the other clergymen consider King's activities to be "'unwise and untimely'" (1)?
3. What reasons does King give for the demonstrations? Why does he think it is too late for negotiations?
4. What does King say *wait* means to black people?
5. What are the two types of laws King defines? What is the difference between the two?
6. What does King find illogical about the claim that the actions of his followers precipitate violence?
7. Why is King disappointed in the white church?

Purpose and Audience

1. Why, in the first paragraph, does King establish his setting (the Birmingham city jail) and define his intended audience?
2. Why does King begin his letter with a reference to his audience as "men of genuine good will" (1)? Is this phrase **ironic** in light of his later criticism of them? Explain.
3. What indicates that King is writing his letter to an audience other than his fellow clergymen?
4. What is the thesis of this letter? Is it stated or implied?

Style and Structure

1. Where does King seek to establish that he is a reasonable person?
2. Where does King address the objections of his audience?
3. As in the Declaration of Independence, transitions are important in King's letter. Identify the transitional words and phrases that connect the different parts of his argument.

4. Why does King cite Jewish, Catholic, and Protestant philosophers to support his position?

5. King relies heavily on appeals to authority (Augustine, Aquinas, Buber, Tillich, and so forth). Why do you think he uses this strategy?

6. King uses both induction and deduction in his letter. Find an example of each, and explain how they function in his argument.

7. Throughout the body of his letter, King criticizes his audience of white moderates. In his conclusion, however, he seeks to reestablish a harmonious relationship with them. How does he do this? Is he successful?

Vocabulary Projects

1. Define each of the following words as it is used in this selection.

affiliate (2)	devotees (12)	reiterate (34)
cognizant (4)	estrangement (16)	intimidated (37)
mutuality (4)	ordinances (16)	infanticide (37)
provincial (4)	anarchy (20)	inextricably (40)
gainsaying (6)	elegy (26)	scintillating (47)
unfettered (10)	incorrigible (27)	
millennium (12)	emulate (28)	

2. Locate five **allusions** to the Bible in this essay. How do these allusions help King express his ideas?

3. In paragraph 14, King refers to his "cup of endurance." What is this a reference to? How is the original phrase worded?

Journal Entry

Do you believe King's remarks go too far? Do you believe they do not go far enough? Explain.

Writing Workshop

1. Write an argumentative essay supporting a deeply held belief of your own. Assume that your audience, like King's, is not openly hostile to your position.

2. Assume you are a militant political leader writing a letter to Martin Luther King Jr. Argue that King's methods do not go far enough. Be sure to address potential objections to your position. You might want to search the Internet or read some newspapers and magazines from the 1960s to help you prepare your argument. (Be sure to document all material you borrow from your sources. See the Appendix for information on documentation formats.)

3. Read your local newspaper for several days, collecting articles about a controversial subject that interests you. Using information from the

articles, take a position on the issue, and write an essay supporting it. (Be sure to document all material you borrow from your sources. See the Appendix for information on documentation formats.)

Combining the Patterns

In "Letter from Birmingham Jail," King includes several passages of **narration**. Find two of these passages, and discuss what use King makes of narration. Why do you think narration plays such an important part in King's argument?

Thematic Connections

- "Finishing School" (page 101)
- "The 'Black Table' Is Still There" (page 366)
- "Two Ways to Belong in America" (page 415)

DEBATE

Should U.S. Citizens Be Required to Carry National Identity Cards?

On the morning of September 11, 2001, two commercial passenger planes, hijacked by Al-Qaeda terrorists, slammed into the two towers of New York's World Trade Center. By 10:30 that morning, the two buildings lay in ruins, and more than 2,800 people were dead. As the towers burned, another hijacked passenger plane hit the Pentagon in Washington, D.C., killing almost 200 people, and a fourth plane, which was thought to be headed for either the Capitol building or the White House, was forced by passengers to crash in a field in Shanksville, Pennsylvania. Not since the Japanese attack on Pearl Harbor in 1941 had the United States been attacked on its own soil; never before had so many American civilians lost their lives in a single incident. The effects of these acts of terrorism were immediate: fighter jets patrolled the skies over many major cities in the United States, President George W. Bush declared a national state of emergency, and the armed forces were put on high alert.

In response to the events of September 11, the federal government instituted a number of programs designed to combat terrorism and increase national security. Although many of these policies met little or no resistance, some — such as instituting military tribunals and setting up a network of civilian informants — caused so much controversy that they were either scaled back or eliminated entirely. One proposed program — a system of national identity cards — has attracted a great deal of attention. Asserting that it goes too far, detractors claim that the plan is an unnecessary extension of governmental power that would deprive people of fundamental civil liberties. They point out that every time the country has curtailed civil liberties — for example, by confining Japanese Americans in internment camps during World War II — Americans later regretted it. Supporters of national ID cards say that they too are reluctant to undermine the principles the country was founded on. They argue, however, that the need to protect civil liberties must be balanced by the need to defend the country against the real security threats it faces. For them, national ID cards represent a middle ground between instituting extreme measures to ensure security and preserving individual liberties at all costs.

The two writers in this debate, writing soon after September 11, 2001, hold opposite opinions concerning national identity cards. In "The Threat of National ID," William Safire asserts that both the government and commercial marketers are exploiting the public's fears to "sell" them on the idea of national identity cards. In "Why Fear National ID Cards?" Alan M. Dershowitz argues that even though national identity cards do take away some measure of personal freedom, their advantages far outweigh their disadvantages.

WILLIAM SAFIRE

The Threat of National ID

Born in New York City in 1929, William Safire attended Syracuse University for two years before becoming a reporter for the *New York Herald Tribune*. He later became a television producer for WNBC in New York, worked in public relations, and in 1961 opened his own public relations firm. From 1968 to 1973, he served as speechwriter to President Richard Nixon and then joined the *New York Times* as a political columnist. His columns are widely syndicated, and he won a Pulitzer Prize for commentary in 1978. He is the author of more than twenty books on politics and language, as well as several novels.

Background on the Fourth Amendment: Safire bases his argument against a national identity card in part on the fact that "U.S. citizens [are] protected by the Fourth Amendment." The Fourth Amendment to the U.S. Constitution reads, "The right of the people to be secure in their persons, houses, papers, and effects, against unreasonable searches and seizures, shall not be violated, and no warrants shall issue but upon probable cause, supported by oath or affirmation, and particularly describing the place to be searched, and the persons or things to be seized." This amendment has been broadly interpreted as guaranteeing to U.S. citizens a right to privacy from government intrusion. For example, it provides the basis for the U.S. Supreme Court's 1973 *Roe v. Wade* ruling that struck down antiabortion statutes. Increasingly, however, the Supreme Court has tended to interpret the amendment more narrowly. For example, the Court has ruled that the Fourth Amendment does not prevent school districts from conducting drug testing of any student engaged in extracurricular activities, whether or not there is reasonable suspicion of drug use.

1   A device is now available to help pet owners find lost animals. It's a little chip implanted under the skin in the back of the neck; any animal shelter can quickly scan lost dogs or cats and pick up the address of the worried owner.

2   That's a good side of identification technology. There's a bad side: fear of terrorism has placed Americans in danger of trading our "right to be let alone" for the false sense of security of a national identification card.

3   All of us are willing to give up some of our personal privacy in return for greater safety. That's why we gladly suffer the pat-downs and "wanding" at airports, and show a local photo ID before boarding. Such precautions contribute to our peace of mind.

4   However, the fear of terror attack is being exploited by law enforcement sweeping for suspects as well as by commercial marketers seeking prospects. It has emboldened the zealots of intrusion to press for the holy grail of snoopery—a mandatory national ID.

Police unconcerned with the sanctity of an individual's home have   5
already developed heat sensors to let them look inside people's houses. The
federal "Carnivore" surveillance system feeds on your meatiest e-mail.
Think you can encrypt your way to privacy? The Justice Department is
proud of its new "Magic Lantern": all attempts by computer owners to
encode their messages can now be overwhelmed by an electronic bug the
F.B.I. can plant on your keyboard to read every stroke.

But in the dreams of Big Brother and his cousin, Big Marketing, noth-   6
ing can compare to forcing every person in the United States — under
penalty of law — to carry what the totalitarians used to call "papers."

The plastic card would not merely show a photograph, signature and   7
address, as driver's licenses do. That's only the beginning. In time, and
with exquisite refinements, the card would contain not only a fingerprint,
description of DNA, and the details of your eye's iris, but a host of other
information about you.

Hospitals would say: How about a chip providing a complete medical   8
history in case of emergencies? Merchants would add a chip for credit rating, bank accounts, and product preferences, while divorced spouses
would lobby for a rundown of net assets and yearly expenditures. Politicians would like to know voting records and political affiliation. Cops, of
course, would insist on a record of arrests, speeding tickets, E-Z pass auto
movements, and links to suspicious Web sites and associates.

All this information and more is being collected already. With a   9
national ID system, however, it can all be centered in a single dossier, even
pressed on a single card — with a copy of that card in a national databank,
supposedly confidential but available to any imaginative hacker.

What about us libertarian misfits who take the trouble to try to "opt   10
out"? We will not be able to travel, or buy on credit, or participate in
tomorrow's normal life. Soon enough, police as well as employers will consider those who resist full disclosure of their financial, academic, medical,
religious, social, and political affiliations to be suspect.

The universal use and likely abuse of the national ID — a discredit   11
card — will trigger questions like: When did you begin subscribing to these
publications, and why were you visiting that spicy or seditious Web site?
Why are you afraid to show us your papers on demand? Why are you paying cash? What do you have to hide?

Today's diatribe will be scorned as alarmist by the same security-   12
mongers who shrugged off our attorney general's attempt to abolish
habeas corpus (which libertarian protests and the Bush administration's
sober second thoughts seem to be aborting). But the lust to take advantage
of the public's fear of terrorist penetration by penetrating everyone's private lives — this time including the lives of U.S. citizens protected by the
Fourth Amendment — is gaining popularity.

Beware: It is not just an efficient little card to speed you through lines   13
faster or to buy you sure-fire protection from suicide bombers. A national
ID card would be a ticket to the loss of much of your personal freedom. Its

size could then be reduced for implantation under the skin in the back of your neck.

• • •

Comprehension

1. According to Safire, why are most people willing to give up their privacy? In what sense does he believe that law enforcement officials are already taking advantage of this situation?
2. What does Safire mean when he says that national ID cards give Americans a "false sense of security" (2)? Do you agree with him?
3. Why couldn't people choose not to carry national ID cards?
4. What does Safire mean in paragraph 6 when he says, "But in the dreams of Big Brother and his cousin, Big Marketing, nothing can compare to forcing every person in the United States — under penalty of law — to carry what the totalitarians used to call 'papers' "?
5. What are the advantages of national ID cards? What are the dangers of such cards?

Purpose and Audience

1. Does Safire see his readers as friendly, hostile, or neutral? How can you tell?
2. Is Safire's purpose primarily to change people's ideas or to change their behavior?
3. What preconceptions does Safire seem to think his readers have about his subject?

Style and Structure

1. Safire begins his essay with a discussion of lost animals. How effective is this strategy? Would another opening strategy have been more effective?
2. Is Safire's argument primarily inductive or deductive? Explain.
3. What evidence does Safire use to support his points? Do you think he includes enough support? Explain.
4. What opposing arguments does Safire refute? How effective are these refutations?
5. Throughout his essay, Safire uses **rhetorical questions** as a stylistic device to move his argument along. Find some examples of his use of rhetorical questions. How effective is this technique? Would another strategy — such as using direct statements or transitional words and phrases — be more effective?
6. What strategy does Safire use to conclude his essay? Is this a wise choice? Could he be accused of overstating his case?

Vocabulary Projects

1. Define each of the following words as it is used in this selection.

   implanted (1)   sanctity (5)   dossier (9)
   exploited (4)   encrypt (5)   seditious (11)
   emboldened (4)   totalitarians (6)   diatribe (12)
   mandatory (4)   exquisite (7)   habeas corpus (12)

2. In his conclusion, Safire uses **colloquialisms**. Do such informal expressions help him make his point more clearly, or do they undercut his credibility?

Journal Entry

Would you be willing to give up your personal privacy for more security? Or, do you believe that the benefits of increased surveillance are not worth the cost?

Writing Workshop

1. Do you agree or disagree with Safire? Do you think national ID cards are necessary for national security, or do you think they are an unjustified invasion of privacy? Be specific, and use information from your own experience and from "The Threat of National ID" to support your points.

2. Write an essay taking two of Safire's points and refuting them, either by questioning their accuracy or by demonstrating flaws in their logic.

3. What specific steps — other than national ID cards — do you think the national government could take to protect Americans from terrorism?

Combining the Patterns

In his essay, Safire includes several **exemplification** paragraphs. How do examples help him make his point? Should he have included more examples? Different kinds of examples? Why, or why not?

Thematic Connections

- "Ground Zero" (page 162)
- "A Peaceful Woman Explains Why She Carries a Gun" (page 371)
- "The Power of Words in Wartime" (page 377)

ALAN M. DERSHOWITZ

Why Fear National ID Cards?

Alan Dershowitz was born in Brooklyn, New York, in 1938. A graduate of Brooklyn College and the Yale School of Law, he was the youngest tenured professor in the history of Harvard Law School. He has long been an avid proponent of civil liberties, taking on many controversial cases—including the defenses of O. J. Simpson and Mike Tyson. In a recent article, he argued that suspected terrorists should be offered the best legal defense possible. Dershowitz's many books include *The Abuse Excuse* (1994), *Shouting Fire: Civil Liberties in a Turbulent Age* (2002), *Why Terrorism Works* (2002), and *Rights from Wrongs: A Secular Theory of the Origin of Rights* (2004). He has also published more than three hundred op-ed columns syndicated throughout the country and appeared on numerous television talk shows.

Background on national identity cards: National identity cards have long been associated with highly repressive governments. They were required under the Nazi regime in Germany, which used them to deny basic civil liberties to "undesirables." Communist dictators used national identity cards to control dissenters, and in South Africa the system of apartheid was enforced through national identity cards. In the United States today, some people—both liberal and conservative—oppose them because of their potential for governmental abuse. For example, they could be used to monitor almost every aspect of a person's life, required for check cashing, travel, and admission to public facilities such as airports and hospitals. Critics contend that with national identity cards, the government could easily compile a national database that would track the behavior of every man, woman, and child in the United States. In 2005, the U.S. House of Representatives passed the Real ID Act, which would strengthen identification requirements for state drivers' licenses and other official forms of identification but falls short of requiring a national identity card; as of this writing, the Senate has not yet acted on the bill.

At many bridges and tunnels across the country, drivers avoid long delays at the toll booths with an unobtrusive device that fits on a car's dashboard. Instead of fumbling for change, they drive right through; the device sends a radio signal that records their passage. They are billed later. It's a tradeoff between privacy and convenience: the toll-takers know more about you—when you entered and left Manhattan, for instance—but you save time and money.

An optional national identity card could be used in a similar way, offering a similar kind of tradeoff: a little less anonymity for a lot more security. Anyone who had the card could be allowed to pass through airports or building security more expeditiously, and anyone who opted out could be examined much more closely.

As a civil libertarian, I am instinctively skeptical of such tradeoffs. But   3
I support a national identity card with a chip that can match the holder's
fingerprint. It could be an effective tool for preventing terrorism, reducing
the need for other law-enforcement mechanisms — especially racial and
ethnic profiling — that pose even greater dangers to civil liberties.

I can hear the objections: What about the specter of Big Brother? What   4
about fears of identity cards leading to more intrusive measures? (The
National Rifle Association, for example, worries that a government that
registered people might also decide to register guns.) What about fears that
such cards would lead to increased deportation of illegal immigrants?

First, we already require photo IDs for many activities, including fly-   5
ing, driving, drinking, and check-cashing. And fingerprints differ from
photographs only in that they are harder to fake. The vast majority of
Americans routinely carry photo IDs in their wallets and pocketbooks.
These IDs are issued by state motor vehicle bureaus and other public and
private entities. A national card would be uniform and difficult to forge or
alter. It would reduce the likelihood that someone could, intentionally or
not, get lost in the cracks of multiple bureaucracies.

The fear of an intrusive government can be addressed by setting crite-   6
ria for any official who demands to see the card. Even without a national
card, people are always being asked to show identification. The existence of
a national card need not change the rules about when ID can properly be
demanded. It is true that the card would facilitate the deportation of illegal immigrants. But President Bush has proposed giving legal status to
many of the illegal immigrants now in this country. And legal immigrants
would actually benefit from a national ID card that could demonstrate
their status to government officials.

Finally, there is the question of the right to anonymity. I don't believe   7
we can afford to recognize such a right in this age of terrorism. No such
right is hinted at in the Constitution. And though the Supreme Court has
identified a right to privacy, privacy and anonymity are not the same.
American taxpayers, voters, and drivers long ago gave up any right of
anonymity without loss of our right to engage in lawful conduct within
zones of privacy. Rights are a function of experience, and our recent experiences teach that it is far too easy to be anonymous — even to create a false
identity — in this large and decentralized country. A national ID card
would not prevent all threats of terrorism, but it would make it more difficult for potential terrorists to hide in open view, as many of the September
11 hijackers apparently managed to do.

A national ID card could actually enhance civil liberties by reducing   8
the need for racial and ethnic stereotyping. There would be no excuse for
hassling someone merely because he belongs to a particular racial or ethnic
group if he presented a card that matched his print and that permitted his
name to be checked instantly against the kind of computerized criminal-
history retrieval systems that are already in use. (If there is too much personal information in the system, or if the information is being used

improperly, that is a separate issue. The only information the card need contain is name, address, photo, and print.)

From a civil liberties perspective, I prefer a system that takes a little bit   9 of freedom from all to one that takes a great deal of freedom and dignity from the few—especially since those few are usually from a racially or ethnically disfavored group. A national ID card would be much more effective in preventing terrorism than profiling millions of men simply because of their appearance.

•   •   •

Comprehension

1. In paragraphs 1 and 2, Dershowitz makes an **analogy** between a national ID card and an E-Z Pass transmitter on a car. How are they alike?

2. According to Dershowitz, why is the tradeoff between privacy and convenience acceptable?

3. What are some fears people have about national ID cards? Does Dershowitz believe these fears are justified?

4. According to Dershowitz, what could the government do to make sure national ID cards do not excessively curtail people's civil liberties?

5. What does Dershowitz mean in paragraph 7 when he says, "No such right [to anonymity] is hinted at in the Constitution"?

Purpose and Audience

1. What audience does Dershowitz seem to address—those who support national ID cards or those who oppose them? Explain.

2. In paragraph 3, Dershowitz attempts to establish his credentials as a civil libertarian. Why does he do this? How successful is he?

3. At what points in the essay does Dershowitz concede the legitimacy of opposing arguments? How effective is this strategy?

Style and Structure

1. In paragraphs 1 and 2, Dershowitz compares national ID cards and E-Z Pass transmitters. Why does he do this? What point is he trying to make?

2. What arguments against national ID cards does Dershowitz refute? Why does he devote so much of his essay—paragraphs 4 to 7—to refutation?

3. Dershowitz does not fully present his arguments in favor of national ID cards until paragraph 8. Should he have presented these arguments sooner? Why does he wait so long to make his case?

4. What evidence does Dershowitz use to support his position? Would other kinds of evidence strengthen his case? Explain.

5. How well does Dershowitz summarize his argument in his final paragraph? What new point does he introduce? Is this a wise strategy?

Vocabulary Projects

1. Define each of the following words as it is used in this selection.

   intrusive (4)   facilitate (6)
   bureaucracies (5)   perspective (9)

2. What does Dershowitz mean by the phrase *civil libertarian*? What connotations does this expression have?

Journal Entry

Do you agree with Dershowitz when he says that a national ID card could actually "enhance civil liberties by reducing the need for racial and ethnic stereotyping" (8)?

Writing Workshop

1. Who makes a better argument, Safire or Dershowitz? Write an essay summarizing the positions of both writers and then taking a stand in support of one or the other. Include your reasons for preferring one over the other, and use material from both essays to support your thesis.

2. How do you think Dershowitz would respond to Safire's argument? Assuming you are Dershowitz, write a letter to Safire that responds to the specific points Safire makes in his essay.

3. Write an essay responding to Dershowitz's statement, "From a civil liberties perspective, I prefer a system that takes a little bit of freedom from all to one that takes a great deal of freedom and dignity from the few — especially since those few are usually from a racially or ethnically disfavored group" (9). Use examples from personal experience (your own or someone else's) to support your thesis.

Combining the Patterns

In paragraph 7, Dershowitz uses **comparison and contrast** to discuss the terms *privacy* and *anonymity*. How clear is the distinction he makes between these two terms? Should he have provided **formal definitions** of both terms in his discussion? What would be the advantages and disadvantages of such a strategy?

Thematic Connections

- "Just Walk On By" (page 240)
- "Two Ways to Belong in America" (page 415)
- "Five Ways to Kill a Man" (page 505)
- The Declaration of Independence (page 584)

DEBATE

Should Gay and Lesbian Couples Be Allowed to Adopt?

Some studies have shown that more than 500,000 children are in foster care and that more than 100,000 of these children are waiting to be adopted. Unfortunately, each year only 20,000 qualified parents adopt such children. Many children in foster care are considered "unadoptable" because they are too old, have significant health problems, or are members of minority groups. Frequently, child welfare agencies place these "unwanted" children into foster-care homes, some of which are substandard. The lack of qualified adoptive parents has trapped thousands of children in a foster-care system stretched to its limits, and the results have been disastrous. For example, a child in foster care may have lived in as many as twenty homes by the time he or she is eighteen. In Florida, a child in the foster-care system was "lost" and never located. In Arkansas, the foster-care system was deemed so inefficient that it was placed under court supervision. Not surprisingly, children in foster care suffer from substance abuse, delinquency, and academic problems to a much greater degree than children raised with their birth parents in two-parent households.

In response to this situation, many states have liberalized their foster-care and adoption policies. To find suitable couples, welfare agencies have made the options of adoption and foster care available to a wider range of adults — many of whom would have been ineligible in the past — including single people, people with physical disabilities, and low-income families. Many gay and lesbian couples are attempting to join this group, but they are facing resistance. Supporters of gay and lesbian rights say that gay parents should be judged by the same standards heterosexual parents are: if they are stable, loving, and caring, they should be allowed to adopt or to serve as foster parents. In other words, a parent's sexual orientation should not be a criterion in determining adoption or foster-care eligibility. Many people — some of them well intentioned — strongly oppose this position. They claim that a family should consist of a mother and father who are married to each other. In addition, they say that children need both male and female role models. Finally, they say that gays and lesbians do not have stable relationships and for this reason would not be good parents.

The two writers in this debate hold opposite opinions concerning adoption by gay and lesbian couples. In "Traditional Mother and Father: Still the Best Choice for Children," Tom Adkins asserts that until compelling evidence demonstrates that children adopted by gay couples will not face irreparable harm, children should continue to be

623

placed solely with heterosexual couples. In "Laws Should Support Loving Households, Straight or Not," Becky Birtha states that the well-being of the children, not the prospective parents' sexual orientation, should be the only issue considered in adoption and foster-care cases.

TOM ADKINS

Traditional Mother and Father: Still the Best Choice for Children

Tom Adkins (b. 1958) grew up in Plymouth Meeting, Pennsylvania. He attended West Chester University and then toured the country as a rock artist until 1984, when he settled into a career in real estate. Disillusioned with the Clinton presidency, Adkins began to express his concerns in letters to the *Philadelphia Inquirer*, which published sixty of them over the course of two years and eventually invited him to write an op-ed article. This led to more op-ed articles (in the *Washington Times* and elsewhere) and eventually to national notoriety. Today, Adkins publishes a Web magazine, CommonConservative.com, and has appeared as a commentator on such television programs as *Hannity & Colmes, Beyond the News, Politically Incorrect,* and *It's Your Call with Lynn Doyle.*

Background on same-sex marriage: Adkins suggests in the following essay that gay and lesbian couples may be unsuitable as parents in part because they are relatively unstable, implying that their relationships tend to be shorter than those of heterosexual couples. Although many advocates for gay and lesbian rights question this assertion, particularly when compared to the relationships of unmarried heterosexual couples, they also argue that extending marriage rights to same-sex couples would lead to greater long-term stability. At this point, more than five thousand corporations, educational institutions, and municipalities in the United States extend "marriage" benefits to cohabitating same-sex partners by allowing gay and lesbian employees to register their domestic partnerships.

In a controversial 1999 decision, the Vermont Supreme Court ruled that same-sex couples could enter into civil unions that provide many of the legal benefits of marriage. In an even more controversial opinion, the Massachusetts Supreme Court ruled in 2003 that same-sex partners should be allowed to marry. In May 2004, gay and lesbian couples began to be issued marriage licenses in the state (although attempts are under way to amend the state constitution to define marriage as a union between a man and a woman). The 1996 federal Defense of Marriage Act denies federal recognition of same-sex marriage and gives states the right to refuse to recognize same-sex marriage licenses issued by other states. So far, legislation to amend the U.S. Constitution to prohibit same-sex marriage has failed to pass in Congress. Four states have pre-1996 laws that specifically ban marriages between men or between women; in November 2004, voters in eleven states overwhelmingly approved ballot initiatives that amended their state constitutions to ban same-sex marriage. Polls show that half of Americans oppose same-sex marriage but 46 percent support civil unions that grant same-sex couples some of the benefits of marriage.

There are all sorts of prizes in politics. The White House. The governor's mansion. A congressional seat. Since gays have left the closet and entered the political arena, those prizes have rightfully become available to them.

But political prizes come by the will of voters. Social prizes are different. A few motivated people in the right places can often coerce public policy. Now gays have their eyes set on a critical prize: children — more specifically, who has rights to adopt children.

On February 4, 2002, the American Academy of Pediatrics released a controversial policy statement on those rights, claiming that children could be brought up with equally good results by gay or by heterosexual parents. The AAP points to 31 published studies that "prove" its case. But these studies are far from airtight. Each one had already been thoroughly sliced and diced in the report *No Basis: What the Studies Don't Tell Us about Same Sex Parenting,* written by quantitative analysts Robert Lerner and Althea Nagai and published by the Ethics and Public Policy Center. Lerner and Nagai had debunked these studies as unsound, often politically motivated fiction. Lerner told me that "the studies are fatally flawed in methodology, technique, and analysis. Some didn't even have control groups."

The AAP authors told me that they'd never heard of the Lerner/Nagai study and that they had not been able to find much contrary evidence. Yet University of Southern California sociologists Judith Stacey and Timothy Biblarz reviewed studies showing that while "psychologically fine," daughters of lesbian couples are more likely to be sexually promiscuous and engage in lesbian experimentation (though Stacey believes that gay parents may be better parents than heterosexuals). In her recent book *Children as Trophies,* sociologist Patricia Morgan pored over 144 academic papers and concluded that same-sex parenting fosters homosexual behavior and confused gender roles, and that such children often suffer serious psychological problems later in life.

Stacey of USC points out that no one can get an accurate, broad-based sample "as long as you have a closet." And lead AAP author Ellen Perrin admits, "We need more longitudinal research to see effects of different kinds of family structures."

In other words, there are huge holes in the data, conflicting reports, and almost no review of contrary evidence. Yet everyone is taking sides. So why would an institution like the AAP make a sweeping, one-sided policy statement likely to be used in pediatric guidance and court cases? It appears the AAP has slipped into the trap of politics.

People generally expect a nonpartisan stance when an organization like AAP endorses a practice or social movement that affects children. Yet recently, the AAP has taken decidedly liberal stances on numerous issues — in favor of gun control, and against mandated parental disclosure for children seeking abortions. Once again, it appears the AAP has assumed a political stance. If so, that calls into question the credibility of any AAP policy statements. In this case, with incomplete and conflicting evidence, children may be exposed to irreparable harm. Yet the AAP is willing to use orphans as little trophies in the political wars.

To be fair, AAP chair Joseph Hagan points out that the AAP study 8 "concerns itself primarily with children who are already in the [gay] family. There are already special needs such as health insurance, health decisions, legal responsibilities, inheritance, and such." Quite true, and not necessarily a direct endorsement of gay adoption.

But the report's attitude is quite clear. Barbara Howard, a co-author of 9 the AAP statement, said, "Lesbian-parented daughters may experiment with lesbian sex more than a control group, but is this necessarily a problem?" Apparently, not for the AAP.

In the middle of all this lies the Gay Paradox: On one hand, gay people 10 demand we accept them as parental equals. On the other, popular gay culture seems preoccupied with emphasizing its unstable, dark side, frightening away those who seek a truly unvarnished inspection of this issue. Sorry, you can't have it both ways.

Most of us can't pick our parents. But those who take on this immense 11 responsibility for the less fortunate have rightly created a long, expensive, and complicated adoption process. Now, they must weed through supposedly objective organizations who make sweeping and conflicting declarations with little or no real evidence and disregard warning flags. Without real data on alternatives, society is forced to favor the sure thing: a loving, responsible mother and father. That is still the best certain choice—not grandpa, not same-sex parents, and not single mothers, the single most highly correlated poverty factor for children.

The real question is, should parentless children be given to loving gay 12 parents or loving heterosexual parents? Until there is more of a consensus on the best choice, we cannot take chances on a doubtful alternative when children's lives are concerned.

• • •

Comprehension

1. What does Adkins mean in paragraph 2 when he says, "Now gays have their eyes set on a critical prize: children"? Why does he see the right to adopt children as a "prize"?

2. What does the policy statement of the American Academy of Pediatrics (AAP) say about children brought up by gay parents? Why is this policy statement controversial?

3. What potential negative effects of gay parenting does Adkins mention?

4. In paragraph 5, Adkins quotes one of the authors of the AAP policy statement who says, "We need more longitudinal research to see effects of different kinds of family structures." If this is the case, why, according to Adkins, does the AAP endorse gay parenting?

5. In paragraph 8, Adkins concedes that the AAP policy statement focuses primarily on the "special needs" of children who are already in gay families. What does he mean when he says that acknowledging this fact is "not necessarily a direct endorsement of gay adoption" (8)?

6. According to Adkins, what responsibility do those who control the adoption process have to children?

Purpose and Audience

1. Does Adkins assume his readers are familiar with the issues involved in gay adoption? How can you tell?

2. What efforts does Adkins make to convince his readers he is being fair? Does he succeed?

3. What is Adkins's thesis? Why does he state it where he does?

4. Does Adkins reveal any of his own biases in his essay? Explain.

Style and Structure

1. Adkins begins his essay by discussing the difference between political prizes and social prizes. Is his distinction clear? Is this an effective opening strategy? Explain.

2. Adkins spends most of his essay refuting the AAP policy statement. What faults does he find with the report's methodology and with its conclusion?

3. In paragraph 7, Adkins accuses the AAP of playing politics. How fair is this accusation? Why, according to Adkins, does this challenge "the credibility of any AAP policy statements" (7)?

4. Does Adkins present a fair cross-section of opinion about gay parenting? Should he have made more of an effort to include (and refute) studies that supported gay adoption?

5. In paragraph 11, Adkins says, "Without real data on alternatives, society is forced to favor the sure thing: a loving, responsible mother and father." In other words, the burden is on gay advocates to prove that gay adoption causes no harm. Is this conclusion fair? Is it logical?

6. In paragraph 12, Adkins sums up his position with the statement, "The real question is, should parentless children be given to loving gay parents or loving heterosexual parents?" Is this statement accurate, or is it an example of a **false dilemma**?

Vocabulary Projects

1. Define each of the following words as it is used in this selection.

pediatrics (3)	longitudinal (5)	control group (9)
methodology (3)	nonpartisan (7)	declarations (11)
promiscuous (4)	credibility (7)	correlated (11)
fosters (4)	irreparable (7)	consensus (12)

2. In paragraph 3, Adkins uses the phrase *sliced and diced*. Is this language appropriate for this essay's purpose and subject? What is the effect of its use here? What other term could Adkins have used?

Journal Entry

Do you agree that gay adoption should wait until "there is more of a consensus on the best choice," or should parentless children be given to "loving gay parents" now (12)?

Writing Workshop

1. Assume you are the director of an adoption agency and you have received an adoption application from a gay couple. Write a letter to the couple either granting or denying their request to adopt. Be specific. If you wish, you may refer to Adkins's essay or the essay by Becky Birtha on page 630.
2. Write an essay expanding your journal entry. Make sure that you include a thesis statement and that you specifically refute the arguments against your position.
3. Write an essay setting your own criteria for adoptive parents. Explain why these specific criteria should govern adoptions, and be sure to refute the major objections to any of your criteria.

Combining the Patterns

Paragraphs 3 through 5 are developed primarily by **exemplification**. Does Adkins provide enough examples? How do these examples help him set up his argument in paragraphs 11 and 12?

Thematic Connections

- "Words Left Unspoken" (page 168)
- "The Lottery" (page 317)
- "A Modest Proposal" (page 733)

BECKY BIRTHA

Laws Should Support Loving Households, Straight or Not

Born in Hampton, Virginia, in 1948, Becky Birtha is of Irish, Cherokee, Catawba, and African ancestry and is named for a great-grandmother who began life as a slave. She grew up in Philadelphia and attended Case Western Reserve University and the State University of New York at Buffalo, where she earned a B.S. in children's studies. She also holds an M.F.A. in creative writing from Vermont College. Birtha has published several collections of poetry, including *The Forbidden Poems* (1991), as well as the short-story collections *For Nights Like This One* (1983) and *Lover's Choice* (1987). She is a lesbian adoptive parent as well as an adoption consultant.

Background on the status of gay and lesbian adoption: The American Academy of Pediatrics report mentioned here and in the previous essay by Tom Adkins recommends that in a same-sex relationship, children born to or adopted by one partner should be allowed to be adopted by the other partner. A larger question is whether same-sex couples should have the same right as heterosexual couples to adopt children neither are tied to biologically. In many states where single-parent foster care and adoption are allowed, gay and lesbian individuals have been allowed to serve as foster parents or to adopt because social services agencies wanted to reduce the number of hard-to-place children. This situation began to change as gay men and lesbians became more visible politically, bringing on a kind of backlash.

So far, only one state, Florida, totally bans gay adoption. Nine states — California, Massachusetts, New Jersey, New Mexico, New York, Ohio, Vermont, Washington, and Wisconsin — as well as the District of Columbia allow for openly gay and lesbian couples to adopt jointly. (It is more common for one partner to adopt and then for the other to apply as the second parent, or coparent. The courts in twenty-one states and the District of Columbia have granted second-parent adoptions.) Currently, six states (Arkansas, Idaho, Indiana, Oklahoma, Texas, and Utah) are considering or have recently considered bans on gay and lesbian adoption. These actions have led to cases such as the one brought to national attention in Florida, where five foster children with AIDS are threatened with losing the only parents they have known, a gay male couple, both nurses, who are not allowed to adopt them.

The American Academy of Pediatrics, 55,000 physicians strong, has 1 taken a giant step forward on behalf of 1 million to 9 million children who are growing up with gay or lesbian parents. The organization's policy statement, issued February 4, 2002, states that children born to or adopted by a parent in a same-sex couple have the right to be adopted by their nonlegal parent, entitling them to custody, visitation, and child support, as well as health benefits and inheritance rights from both parents.

The pediatricians say parents' sexual orientation alone cannot predict their ability to provide a supportive home environment for children. I wholeheartedly agree. Like race, gender, or being able-bodied, sexual orientation isn't linked to good or bad parenting. 2

Opponents of the policy suggest the data the AAP used to reach its conclusion are limited and flawed. However, 31 different research studies are cited in its technical report, gleaned from numerous books and scholarly journals and spanning a 20-year period from 1981 to 2001. 3

Others argue that legalizing gay adoption is a political issue, not a medical one. But the AAP's concern isn't really whether gays have the right to parent children; it's whether children of gays have the right to have parents. These pediatricians have seen gay parents unable to sign a medical consent for treatment of a child they have raised from birth and now view this as an issue of the health, safety, and well-being of children who didn't choose — but happen to have — same-gender parents. 4

Some question whether gay people are capable of making lasting commitments. Gay men, lesbians, and other sexual minorities don't just happen to become parents. Children, whether newborn, adopted, or from a former marriage or relationship, enter a gay couple's lives only after the couple have gone through much soul-searching, planning, and effort, whether through attempts at donor insemination, stringently screened home studies, or negotiated custody agreements. These are serious commitments. 5

Those who say it is wrong to deny a child two heterosexual parents miss the point. The children in question already have parents. They are not about to gain a parent of the opposite sex, whether their second parent's rights are legally recognized or not. Certainly, children should grow up with adult role models of both genders. As every single mother of sons knows, grandfathers and uncles can contribute here. Undoubtedly, each of us knows someone who was raised by a single parent and is a productive, responsible, and heterosexual adult. 6

Still, probably the greatest fear is that children raised by gays or lesbians will be homosexual themselves. And if they are? As one lesbian friend of mine commented, "There will be gay adults in the next generation, just as there have been gay people in every generation in history." Most of them won't come from gay-parented families. They never have. 7

One study found young adults with lesbian mothers slightly more likely to consider same-sex partners but not to identify themselves as homosexual. In another study, children of heterosexual parents are presented as more aggressive, bossy, negative, and domineering than other children. Apparently, there are also advantages to being raised by gay parents. 8

If the AAP recommendations become law, they would likely apply not only to second-parent adoptions, but to other adoptions by gay couples or 9 singles. I think of the 134,000* children in foster care in the United States who wait to be adopted. These kids are school-age or teenage. Some have learning and emotional problems, and many of them have been waiting for years. Maybe there would be a few more homes for them.

If anything, gay parenting and the AAP's encouragement of two-parent families can be seen as a move toward, not away from, traditional family values. Any gay parent hurrying to the day-care center at 6 P.M. can tell you that he has more in common with straight parents than his child-free gay friends do.   10

New Jersey has taken the lead in recognizing second-parent and joint adoptions, and other states would do well to follow. I applaud the AAP in its conviction that children should grow up in families in which parents are protective, caring, loving, and, regardless of sexual orientation, recognized as parents by the law.   11

• • •

Comprehension

1. What is the adoption policy recommended by the American Academy of Pediatrics?

2. What criticisms do the opponents of this policy put forward?

3. According to Birtha, what is the greatest fear people have about having children raised by gay or lesbian parents? How does she address these concerns?

4. According to Birtha, what would happen if the AAP recommendations became law?

5. How, according to Birtha, is gay parenting "a move toward, not away from, traditional family values" (10)? Do you agree? Explain.

Purpose and Audience

1. Birtha states her thesis in paragraph 2 of her essay, while Adkins (in the previous essay) waits until his conclusion to state his thesis. How do you account for this difference?

2. Does Birtha see her readers as hostile, receptive, or neutral toward her position? Explain.

3. What steps does Birtha take to calm the fears of readers who might oppose gay adoption? Are these strategies effective?

4. Birtha is an adoptive parent and an adoption professional. Should she have mentioned these facts in her essay?

---

* EDS. NOTE — Estimates vary widely.

Style and Structure

1. What strategy does Birtha use in her introduction? How effective do you think it is? Explain.

2. Birtha begins refuting arguments against her thesis in paragraph 3. Why do you think she addresses these arguments so soon?

3. Birtha introduces her refutations with the phrases "Opponents . . . suggest" (3), "Others argue" (4), and "Some question" (5). She also introduces evidence with phrases such as "One study found" (8) and "In another study" (8). Should Birtha have been more specific? Do such general references undercut her credibility? Explain.

4. List the arguments Birtha presents to support her thesis. How effective are these arguments?

5. In paragraph 4, Birtha says, "But the AAP's concern isn't really whether gays have the right to parent children; it's whether children of gays have the right to have parents." What distinction is Birtha making? Does this distinction make sense to you? Explain.

6. Birtha ends her essay by saying, "New Jersey has taken the lead in recognizing second-parent and joint adoptions" (11). Why does she introduce this piece of information in her conclusion? Do you believe this is an effective strategy?

7. What transitions does Birtha use to move her readers from one point to another? How successfully do these transitions guide readers through the argument?

Vocabulary Projects

1. Define each of the following words as it is used in this selection.

orientation (2)	scholarly (3)	stringently (5)
gleaned (3)	insemination (5)	domineering (8)

2. In paragraph 10, Birtha uses the term *family values*. What does this term mean? Should she have used a more precise term?

Journal Entry

Which of the two essays in this debate do you find more convincing? Why?

Writing Workshop

1. Do you think it is in society's interest to allow the children of a gay or lesbian parent to be adopted by the parent's partner? Write an essay presenting your view on this issue. Make sure that you include a thesis and that you refute the main arguments against your position.

2. Write an essay taking two of Birtha's points and refute them, either by questioning their accuracy or by identifying flaws in their logic.

3. Go on the Internet and research your state's policy toward gay adoption rights. Then, write a letter to your state representative arguing that the current policy is sound — or that it should be modified.

Combining the Patterns

Paragraph 8 is developed by means of **cause and effect**. What point is Birtha making in paragraph 8? Could she have made the same point by using another pattern of development — for example, comparison and contrast?

Thematic Connections

- "Why Boys Don't Play with Dolls" (page 361)
- "The Men We Carry in Our Minds" (page 481)

DEBATE:

Should the Draft Be Reinstated
in the United States?

The military draft (also known as conscription) has had a long history in the United States. Originally, it was used to recruit troops for short-term conflicts. During the American Revolution, for example, the new state governments used the draft to supply troops to their state militias and, in turn, to the new Continental Army. Although George Washington wanted the central government to have the authority to draft, his request was denied by the states. In 1789, however, the new Constitution gave Congress the power "to raise and support armies."

Throughout the first half of the nineteenth century, the Regular Army was composed of volunteers, with the draft used only occasionally, if at all. During the Civil War, however, the draft became commonplace. Even though most of the combatants were volunteers, both the South and the North used the draft to maintain a constant supply of troops. The general population, which saw the draft as a violation of their civil liberties, frequently opposed conscription — sometimes violently. For example, the 1863 antidraft riots in New York City destroyed property and took the lives of more than one hundred people.

Not until World War I did the United States rely on the draft to supply the majority of its troops. In the early years of World War II, Congress approved a draft in response to the fall of France in 1940. When the United States entered the war after the attack on Pearl Harbor, Congress widened the draft to include all men between the ages of eighteen and thirty-eight for the duration of the war. After the war ended, Congress extended the draft law to ensure that the armed forces could maintain an adequate supply of men during the cold war.

During the Vietnam War, opposition to the draft grew stronger as the war because increasingly unpopular. Although draftees made up only 16 percent of the armed forces, they made up the bulk of front-line units and ultimately accounted for half the army's combat deaths. In addition, because of the availability of student and occupational deferments, the draft affected a disproportionate number of poor people, both black and white. In 1969, in response to widespread protests, President Richard M. Nixon ended deferments and instituted a lottery system. After the American withdrawal from Vietnam, the United States switched to an all-volunteer fighting force. However, in 1980, President Jimmy Carter instituted compulsory draft registration in response to the Soviet invasion of Afghanistan. Currently, although there is no draft, young men must still register for selective service on their eighteenth birthday.

Although both writers in this debate oppose the war in Iraq, they hold distinctly different opinions concerning the advisability of reinstituting the draft. In "A War for Us, Fought by Them," William Broyles Jr. says that if Iraq is worth the sacrifice, then everyone, including the children of those legislators who support the war, should be involved in fighting it. According to Broyles, the only way to be certain this occurs is to make sure that everyone—both rich and poor—is subject to a draft. In "For Those Who Believe We Need a Draft," Rick Jahnkow maintains that a draft will not address the fact that our society is becoming increasingly militaristic. On the contrary, says Jahnkow, the way to eliminate America's tendency to rely on war to solve problems is to encourage people to question and challenge authority—especially governmental and military authority.

WILLIAM BROYLES JR. _Marine_ ~activist~

credentials

A War for Us, Fought by Them

William Broyles Jr. (b. 1948) grew up in Baytown, Texas, and attended Rice
University and then Oxford University in England as a Marshall scholar.
An activist in the civil rights movement, he later served as a marine
infantry lieutenant in Vietnam. Broyles was a founding editor of _Texas
Monthly_ magazine and also served as editor-in-chief at _California_ magazine
and _Newsweek_. In 1995 he published the book _Brothers in Arms: A Journey
from War to Peace,_ an account of his return to Vietnam to meet with the soldiers he had fought against. An accomplished screenwriter, Broyles was
cocreator of the television series _China Beach_ and has worked on screenplays for _Apollo 13_ (1995), for which he was nominated for an Academy
Award; _Entrapment_ (1998); _Cast Away_ (2000); _Planet of the Apes_ (2001); and
Unfaithful (2002). He is also a frequent lecturer on college campuses across
the country.

   Background on the current military draft: In January of 2003, as the
Bush administration prepared for a military strike on Iraq, Representative
Charles B. Rangel of New York's Harlem district introduced a bill in Congress that would have reinstated a military draft — in part to bring home
to Americans the ramifications of such a military strike, but also to ensure
"more equitable representation of people making sacrifices." His bill
would have applied to men and women aged eighteen to twenty-six, with
deferments only for high school students and for those physically unable
to serve, who would be required to perform community service instead.
The bill was rejected overwhelmingly by the House of Representatives just
prior to the 2004 presidential election. Still, with U.S. forces stretched thin
by the country's engagement in Iraq and elsewhere around the globe,
some believe that an all-volunteer military may not be able to continue to
meet its defensive needs. ~men & women~

deferment

   The longest love affair of my life began with a shotgun marriage. It was   1
the height of the Vietnam War and my student deferment had run out.
Desperate not to endanger myself or to interrupt my personal plans, I
wanted to avoid military service altogether. I didn't have the resourcefulness of Bill Clinton, so I couldn't figure out how to dodge the draft. I tried _allusions_
to escape into the National Guard, where I would be guaranteed not to be _war.
service (back)_
sent to war, but I lacked the connections of George W. Bush, so I couldn't
slip ahead of the long waiting list. My attitude was the same as Dick
Cheney's: I was special, I had "other priorities." Let other people do it.

   When my draft notice came in 1968, I was relieved in a way. Although I   2
had deep doubts about the war, I had become troubled about how I had
angled to avoid military service. My classmates from high school were in

angled to avoid

637

the war; my classmates from college were not—exactly the dynamic that exists today. But instead of reporting for service in the Army, on a whim I joined the Marine Corps, the last place on earth I thought I belonged.

My sacrifice turned out to be minimal. I survived a year as an infantry lieutenant in Vietnam. I was not wounded; nor did I struggle for years with post-traumatic stress disorder.* A long bout of survivor guilt† was the price I paid. Others suffered far more, particularly those who had to serve after the war had lost all sense of purpose for the men fighting it. I like to think that in spite of my being so unwilling at first, I did some small service to my country and to that enduring love of mine, the United States Marine Corps.

To my profound surprise, the Marines did a far greater service to me. In three years I learned more about standards, commitment and yes, life, than I did in six years of university. I also learned that I had had no idea of my own limits: when I was exhausted after humping up and down jungle mountains in 100-degree heat with a 75-pound pack, terrified out of my mind, wanting only to quit, convinced I couldn't take another step, I found that in fact I could keep going for miles. And my life was put in the hands of young men I would otherwise never have met, by and large high-school dropouts, who turned out to be among the finest people I have ever known.

I am now the father of a young man who has far more character than I ever had. I joined the Marines because I had to; he signed up after college because he felt he ought to. He volunteered for an elite unit and has served in both Afghanistan and Iraq. When I see images of Americans in the war zones, I think of my son and his friends, many of whom I have come to know and deeply respect. When I opened this newspaper yesterday and read the front-page headline, "9 G.I.'s Killed," I didn't think in abstractions. I thought very personally.

The problem is, I don't see the images of or read about any of the young men and women who, as Dick Cheney and I did, have "other priorities." There are no immediate family members of any of the prime civilian planners of this war serving in it—beginning with President Bush and extending deep into the Defense Department. Only one of the 535 members of Congress, Senator Tim Johnson of South Dakota, has a child in the war—and only half a dozen others have sons and daughters in the military.

The memorial service yesterday for Pat Tillman,‡ the football star killed in Afghanistan, further points out this contrast. He remains the only professional athlete of any sport who left his privileged life during this war

---

* Eds. note—A psychiatric illness following a traumatic event, particularly one involving the threat of injury or death.

† Eds. note—A deep feeling of guilt felt by some survivors of a tragedy that took the lives of many others.

‡ Eds. note—National Football League star who gave up a lucrative contract with the Arizona Cardinals to join the U.S. military after the terrorist attacks of September 2001 and was killed by friendly fire in Afghanistan in 2003.

and turned in his play uniform for a real one. With few exceptions, the only men and women in military service are the profoundly patriotic or the economically needy.

It was not always so. In other wars, the men and women in charge made sure their family members led the way. Since 9/11, the war on terrorism has often been compared to the generational challenge of Pearl Harbor; but Franklin D. Roosevelt's sons all enlisted soon after that attack, Both of Lyndon B. Johnson's sons-in-law served in Vietnam.

This is less a matter of politics than privilege. The Democratic elites have not responded more nobly than have the Republican; it's just that the Democrats' hypocrisy is less acute. Our president's own family illustrates the loss of the sense of responsibility that once went with privilege. In three generations the Bushes have gone from war hero in World War II, to war evader in Vietnam, to none of the extended family showing up in Iraq and Afghanistan.

Pat Tillman didn't want to be singled out for having done what other patriotic Americans his age should have done. The problem is, they aren't doing it. In spite of the president's insistence that our very civilization is at stake, the privileged aren't flocking to the flag. The war is being fought by Other People's Children. The war is impersonal for the very people to whom it should be most personal.

If the children of the nation's elites were facing enemy fire without body armor, riding through gantlets of bombs in unarmored Humvees, fighting desperately in an increasingly hostile environment because of arrogant and incompetent civilian leadership, then those problems might well find faster solutions.

The men and women on active duty today—and their companions in the National Guard and the reserves—have seen their willingness, and that of their families, to make sacrifices for their country stretched thin and finally abused. Thousands of soldiers promised a one-year tour of duty have seen that promise turned into a lie. When Eric Shinseki, then the Army chief of staff, told the president that winning the war and peace in Iraq would take hundreds of thousands more troops, Mr. Bush ended his career. As a result of this and other ill-advised decisions, the war is in danger of being lost, and my beloved military is being run into the ground.

This abuse of the voluntary military cannot continue. How to ensure adequate troop levels, with a diversity of backgrounds? How to require the privileged to shoulder their fair share? In other words, how to get today's equivalents of Bill Clinton, George W. Bush, Dick Cheney—and me—into the military, where their talents could strengthen and revive our fighting forces?

The only solution is to bring back the draft. Not since the nineteenth century has America fought a war that lasted longer than a week with an all-volunteer army; we can't do it now. It is simply not built for a protracted major conflict. The arguments against the draft—that a voluntary army is of higher quality, that the elites will still find a way to evade service—are bogus. In World War II we used a draft army to fight the Germans and Japanese—two of the most powerful military machines in history—and we won. The problems in the military toward the end of Vietnam were not caused by the draft; they were the result of young Americans being sent to fight and die in a war that had become a disaster.

One of the few good legacies of Vietnam is that after years of abuses we   15 finally learned how to run the draft fairly. A strictly impartial lottery, with no deferments, can ensure that the draft intake matches military needs. Chance, not connections or clever manipulation, would determine who serves.

If this war is truly worth fighting, then the burdens of doing so should   16 fall on all Americans. If you support this war, but assume that Pat Tillman and Other People's Children should fight it, then you are worse than a hypocrite. If it's not worth your family fighting it, then it's not worth it, period. The draft is the truest test of public support for the administration's handling of the war, which is perhaps why the administration is so dead set against bringing it back.

. . .

Comprehension

1. What was Broyles's attitude toward the Vietnam War? How did he try to evade the draft?

2. Why did Broyles decide to enlist? What does he mean when he calls this decision "a shotgun marriage" (1)?

3. What problem does Broyles have with politicians—both Republicans and Democrats—who help plan and fund the war in Iraq? What does he mean in paragraph 9 when he says, "This is less a matter of politics than privilege"?

4. Why does Broyles think the military is being abused? What is his solution to the abuses he lists in paragraph 12?

5. According to Broyles, why does the Bush administration oppose reinstituting the draft?

Purpose and Audience

1. Broyles does not state his thesis until paragraph 14 of his essay. Why does he wait so long? What does he try to establish before he presents his thesis?

2. Does Broyles expect his readers to be friendly, hostile, or neutral? How can you tell?

3. How would you describe the tone of this essay? Assured? Confident? Frustrated? Angry? Something else?

Style and Structure

1. Broyles begins his essay by telling how he came to enlist in the Marine Corps. What does he gain by beginning in this way?
2. What does Pat Tillman represent to Broyles? What function does Tillman serve in this essay?
3. What efforts does Broyles make to demonstrate that he is a fair, unbiased critic? Is he successful?
4. At what point in the essay does Broyles refute arguments against his thesis? How effective are his refutations of these opposing arguments?
5. Does Broyles present enough evidence to support his contention that "the privileged aren't flocking to the flag" (10)? Explain.
6. In paragraph 14, Broyles says that the draft is the "only solution" for the problems he sees with the volunteer fighting force. What support does he offer for this assertion? Can you think of any other solutions?

Vocabulary Projects

1. Define each of these words as it is used in this selection.

   profound (4)   protracted (14)
   priorities (6)   impartial (15)
   acute (9)   hypocrite (16)

2. What words and phrases reveal Broyles's attitude toward the war in Iraq? Toward the Bush administration? Toward those who would argue against the draft? Do you think this kind of language helps or hurts his case?

Journal Entry

Broyles concludes his essay by saying that a draft is "the truest test of public support" (16) for the war in Iraq. Do you believe Broyles is really arguing for a draft, or is he actually arguing for something else?

Writing Workshop

1. Write an essay agreeing or disagreeing with Broyles's assertion that if a "war is truly worth fighting, then the burdens of doing so should fall on all Americans" (16). Make sure you present evidence to support your claim.
2. According to Rick Jahnkow (page 646), instead of demanding that everyone be subject to a draft, "we should demand that NO one be drafted, and NO one be recruited to fight" (19). Write a letter from Broyles responding to Jahnkow's statement. Use material from both essays to support your points.

3. One issue Broyles does not consider is whether women should be included in a potential draft. How would the requirement that women be included in any renewed draft affect his argument? For example, could a draft that did not apply to women be described as a burden that would "fall on all Americans" (16)?

Combining the Patterns

Broyles begins his essay with a passage of **narration**. How effective is this introductory strategy? What other pattern of development could he have used here?

Thematic Connections

- "Ground Zero" (page 162)
- "Star-Spangled Stupidity" (page 246)
- "The Power of Words in Wartime" (page 377)

RICK JAHNKOW

For Those Who Believe We Need a Draft

Longtime San Diego–based peace activist Rick Jahnkow was born in Los Angeles in 1950. A graduate of the University of California, San Diego, he is currently program coordinator for the Project on Youth and Non-Military Opportunities (www.projectyano.org) and a member of the Committee Opposed to Militarism and the Draft. He also serves on the executive committee of the American Friends Service Committee for Peacebuilding and the steering committee of the National Network Opposing the Militarization of Youth. He has published articles in various print journals and online publications, including the *Progressive,* the *Utne Reader, Nonviolent Activist, Fellowship,* Truthout.org, and Zmag.com and is a regular contributor to Draft NOtices (www.comdsd.org), where the following essay originally appeared.

Background on protests of the Vietnam War: United States military personnel had been involved in the conflict between North and South Vietnam since the mid-1950s, and the early 1960s saw some limited protest against this involvement. However, not until the United States began sustained bombing of North Vietnam in 1965 did a true protest movement form. An organized march on Washington in April of that year drew 25,000 participants — more than anticipated — and across the country, college professors and students participated in "teach-ins" advocating opposition to the undeclared war.

In 1966, more than six thousand American servicemen were killed in Vietnam, a number that rose to eleven thousand in 1968. By then, half of all Americans no longer supported escalation of U.S. involvement. Protests turned violent: draft boards were raided and manufacturers of chemical weapons were targeted for sabotage. In November of 1968, at the National Democratic Convention in Chicago, tens of thousands of protesters were brutally contained by police. A 1969 march on Washington against the war drew over 500,000 people, and revelations later that year of the massacre of hundreds of unarmed Vietnamese civilians by U.S. soldiers at My Lai sparked even more antiwar sentiment. Then, in May of 1970, an outcry arose across the country when national guardsmen fired on student protesters at Ohio's Kent State University, killing four and wounding sixteen others. Still, not until 1973 did U.S. involvement in Vietnam effectively end.

Every now and then we hear people talk about wanting to bring back conscription. Sometimes it comes from conservatives and militarists who would like to see a larger military force so they can expand U.S. bases abroad and conduct warfare in more places simultaneously.

1

We also hear it from liberals, and even a few leftists, who are under the   2
impression that conscription would be doing a big favor for disadvantaged
youths or would lessen the chances of war by spreading the burden for
maintaining our bloated military establishment and overly aggressive foreign policy to more middle-class people. They even make the argument,
sometimes, that we need a draft to keep us from drifting toward Prussian
militarism* and a Hitler-type dictatorship.†

These aren't new arguments. Some of them were used to successfully   3
convince people to keep the draft that was begun during WWII, even though
the people of this country had historically been suspicious of conscription
and previously had only allowed drafts briefly during the Civil War and
WWI. Many of these arguments were also used in the early 1970s to try to
keep the draft going as we began to pull out of the war in Southeast Asia. By
then, however, Vietnam had brought back the traditional understanding
that conscription exploits those who are politically and economically disadvantaged and makes it easier for governments to wage illegitimate wars.

Unfortunately, the memory of this lesson is not as fresh as it once was,   4
and there are both liberals and conservatives who are now taking advantage of the post-9/11 climate of fear to make people think that a draft
would be good for the nation.

Right now, our military doesn't really require conscription to maintain   5
its current force levels, and the Pentagon has found that using its well-
funded recruiting campaign and expanded outreach to schools can influence young people in a way that would be impossible with a draft
(threatening people with jail if they don't enter the military is hardly an
effective way to win the hearts and minds of younger generations). However, if the war hawks in this country continue to have their way, there will
be more pressure to enlarge the armed forces beyond what can be supported with voluntary enlistments, and the voices calling for conscription
will get much louder than they presently are. This is a good time, therefore,
to review some of the key issues that should be considered:

1. There are those who claim that conscription is needed for national   6
   defense. However, it takes months to move people through the draft
   classification system, the induction process and military training,
   so it has no usefulness for meeting short-term emergencies. (The
   Reserves and National Guard are designed to play that role.) The
   draft's main military value is to provide a steady stream of draftees
   for a long, drawn-out war or when the size of military commitments
   is so large that the force level can't be maintained with only enlistments. With a draft, the government doesn't have to rely on people
   voluntarily stepping forward to fill the military's ranks, so it can

---

* EDS. NOTE — Referring to aggressive military campaigns led by the German state of
Prussia in the nineteenth century.

† EDS. NOTE — Adolf Hitler, all-powerful leader of Germany from 1934 to 1945,
whose aggressive military policies and campaign against Jews prompted World War II.

maintain a larger force size and pursue the kind of unpopular military adventurism that led to more than 10 years of U.S. warfare in Southeast Asia. Not having a draft doesn't guarantee the U.S. won't wage illegitimate wars, but it creates more pressure on the government to justify its actions than if we gave the president the blank check he would have with conscription. Imagine what that would be like with a commander-in-chief like George Bush II.

2. Conscription is an unfair tax. Any government can provide staffing   7
   for public services two basic ways: it can pay people to do the necessary work, or confiscate their labor and order them to do it. A draft is confiscation that forces individuals to give up their freedom and some of the higher civilian income they could have earned while in the military. Because of the higher turnover of drafted military personnel, training becomes more expensive and the government is forced to set wages low for both draftees and professional volunteers, so all military members—but especially the draftees—pay a severe personal tax, and the true cost of the military is not shared equally by all.

3. Contrary to some people's claim, a draft would not protect us from   8
   the dangerous influence of a professional military class. By nature, the military is not a democratic organization, and with or without conscription it is the officer corps and politicians who set and control policy, not the lower ranks. Lower-ranking military members take a great risk in defying orders; even merely questioning them can bring reprisals that have much greater consequences than those faced by employees with civilian jobs.

   If the draft were a protection from totalitarianism and dictator-   9
   ship, then conscription would not have been relied upon as it was by past totalitarian governments in Spain, Russia, China, various Latin American countries, Prussia/Germany and Japan.

4. The argument that a draft will keep us out of illegitimate wars   10
   because draftees would be more likely to resist them is often heard, but it ignores some important facts:
   • Draftees are picked young and have the least understanding of   11
     the political policies for which their lives may be sacrificed.
   • They are the most obedient of troops because, above all, they want   12
     to get out of the military, and they know that if they stay out of trouble, they only have to wait a couple of years. Volunteers, on the other hand, are in for a longer term and have much more at stake.
   • A historical fact that has been forgotten even by many liberals is   13
     that most of the organized resistance to the Vietnam War within the armed forces—like the Concerned Officers Movement and Movement for a Democratic Military—came largely from volunteers, not draftees.
   • A draft was in place prior to the Vietnam War, yet it took more   14
     than 10 years of body bags coming home before resistance and general opposition grew strong enough to finally force an end to the war. If the draft was supposed to be an obstacle to illegitimate war, it didn't do a very good job with that conflict.

5. Some people believe that the problem with the Vietnam draft was 15
   that it disproportionately affected non-white and low-income
   people. They say a draft that includes more middle-class, white
   people would be more just and would cause greater reluctance to go
   to war. There are several problems with this argument:
   - Once a U.S. president sends people into combat and body bags 16
     start coming home, it becomes very difficult, politically, to
     retreat; those who are intent on making war know that no politi-
     cian will ever want to be the one who says that U.S. soldiers died
     in vain. This means that if a president wants to launch military
     action, he can do so with confidence that both Congress and the
     public will back him, at least initially. Draftees would not provide
     a braking effect until after there are great losses and probably
     years of stalemate (Vietnam is a prime example).
   - The U.S. government has learned that the key to avoiding the 17
     kind of civilian and military resistance that occurred with
     Vietnam is to keep the U.S. casualty count, length of battle,
     and media coverage down to a minimum. That's why the
     Pentagon has shifted to fighting wars more with massive air
     bombardment, missile attacks and native client forces on the
     ground. Having conscription would not be a reason to change
     this strategy, so spreading the burden of war with a draft would
     still not create the potential opposition that some people
     predict.
   - We will always have a ground combat force that is disproportion- 18
     ately poorer and non-white. Even with a draft, people with privi-
     lege would be more able to get the medical deferments and
     conscientious objector status that would keep them out of uni-
     form, and if they failed to stay out of the military, their education
     would put them disproportionately into noncombat jobs. The
     most important thing that we can do today to address racial and
     class imbalance in the military is to demand a more equitable
     economy and an improved, demilitarized educational system,
     while also working to shrink the war budget.
   - The logic that we need a draft so that more members of a particular 19
     group can be killed or placed at risk in order to bring home to the
     public that war is wrong has serious ethical implications. Aside
     from being a form of hostage-taking, it's like saying people should
     become drug users to learn about the harmful consequences of
     using drugs, or that we should support another nuclear arms race,
     because more people would feel the threat of annihilation and that
     would then lead to the elimination of war — or at least nuclear
     weapons (though that clearly didn't happen after the 1980s nuclear
     arms race). If the U.S. government had the power to send EVERYONE
     off to kill and/or be killed in its wars of intervention, it would be a
     form of equality — but it would be equality of the *grave*. Instead, we
     should demand that NO one be drafted, and NO one be recruited to
     fight for the economic and political exploitation of the rest of the
     world by the U.S.

We have wars because people have been brought up with a predomi-   20
nant value system that encourages people to solve disagreements with violence. The general population is indoctrinated in this value system from an
early age, and our culture and governmental institutions reinforce it.
Military training is the extreme form of pro-war indoctrination, which
is why people like Napoleon, Hitler and the militarists of today have
wanted to universally subject young people to conscription. The draft is a
quick and effective way to indoctrinate more people and then send them
back to civilian society to spread the authoritarian value system they have
learned.

The Pentagon was forced to give up the draft at the end of Vietnam,   21
but it has been increasingly insinuating itself in institutions of socialization to continue the process of militarization. If we brought back the draft,
it wouldn't remove the military from our schools or culture, it would just
make it easier to put more people through the militarization process. We'd
end up repeating the post–WWII cycle that led to decades of reactionary
politics and an obedient population that was willing to give the Pentagon
anything it wanted.

Practicing effective self-government and democracy requires that we   22
instill in individuals a propensity for critical, creative thinking and a willingness to challenge the "chain of command" when institutions are not
serving their needs. Bringing back the draft is the opposite of what we
should do to achieve those goals.

• • •

Comprehension

1. According to Jahnkow, why is it so important to review some of the
   key issues concerning the draft?
2. Exactly what key issues does Jahnkow think people should consider?
3. Why does Jahnkow think the United States engages in wars? Why,
   according to him, does the general population comply with the government's actions?
4. What role does Jahnkow think the Pentagon plays in "the process of
   militarization" (21)?
5. What is the solution to the problem of militarization? Why, according
   to Jahnkow, is bringing back the draft the opposite of what we should
   be doing? What does Jahnkow think we should be doing instead?

Purpose and Audience

1. At what point does Jahnkow state his thesis? What is his thesis?
2. What does Jahnkow hope to achieve with his essay? Do you think he
   succeeds?

3. What preconceived ideas about the United States government does Jahnkow have? What preconceptions does he have about the Pentagon? What does he think about the American population? Does he assume his readers share his assumptions? How do you know?

4. How would you characterize the tone of this essay? Would a different tone have better suited Jahnkow's purpose?

Style and Structure

1. Why does Jahnkow begin his essay by summing up the arguments people make in favor of the draft? Can you think of another way he could have opened his essay?

2. Jahnkow develops his argument primarily by refutation. What opposing arguments does he refute? How effective are his refutations?

3. What points does Jahnkow concede? Should he have conceded others? Should he have made more of an effort to assure readers he is both fair and reasonable?

4. In paragraph 20, Jahnkow says, "The draft is a quick and effective way to indoctrinate more people and then send them back to civilian society to spread the authoritarian value system they have learned." Is this statement self-evident, or should Jahnkow have offered evidence to support it?

5. In his conclusion, Jahnkow introduces the idea of being willing "to challenge the 'chain of command'" (22). Should he have discussed this idea sooner and in more depth? What other way could he have ended his essay?

Vocabulary Projects

1. Define each of these words as it is used in this selection.

conscription (1)	reluctance (15)	exploitation (19)
militarists (1)	stalemate (16)	predominant (20)
bloated (2)	disproportionately (18)	indoctrinate (20)
exploits (3)	conscientious (18)	insinuating (21)
illegitimate (3)	annihilation (19)	reactionary (21)
adventurism (6)	intervention (19)	propensity (22)
obstacle (14)		

2. **Hyperbole** is deliberate exaggeration used for emphasis or for humorous effect. Find one or two examples of hyperbole in this essay. How do these uses of hyperbole help Jahnkow achieve his purpose? Do you think they weaken his argument in any way?

Journal Entry

Do you, like Jahnkow, believe that reinstituting the draft would harm the United States, or do you believe that the merits of a draft outweigh any problems such an action would create?

Writing Workshop

1. How would Jahnkow respond to Broyles's contention that the only way to ensure that the privileged assume their fair share of the military burden is to bring back the draft? Make sure you refer specifically to both essays to support your points.

2. Jahnkow's essay appeared on a Web site opposed to both militarism and the draft. Assume you are the editor of a magazine that appeals to a more middle-of-the-road readership and that Jahnkow has submitted his essay for possible publication. Write a letter to him suggesting changes he would have to make before his essay could be published. Remember, you are not telling Jahnkow to change his position against the draft; you are telling him how to best appeal to your readership. Let him know what you think he should change, but be respectful and encouraging.

3. Expand your journal entry into an essay. If you wish, you can gather some specific information about this topic from the Internet, but be sure to document all ideas you get from your sources. (See the Appendix for information on MLA documentation format.)

Combining the Patterns

Paragraphs 6 through 16 are largely developed by means of **cause and effect**. How does this strategy help Jahnkow advance his argument?

Thematic Connections

- "Shooting an Elephant" (page 125)
- "The Lottery" (page 317)
- "Two Ways to Belong in America" (page 415)
- "Five Ways to Kill a Man" (page 505)

DEBATE

Is Wal-Mart Good for America?

Not only is Wal-Mart the largest retailer in the United States, but it is also the largest retailer in the world, with stores in Canada, Mexico, South and Central America, Europe, the United Kingdom, China, and Korea. In the United States, more than 100 million people shop at Wal-Mart every week. In 2000, Wal-Mart opened a new store almost every two days, and in 2004, it began opening a new store almost every day. (This does not include Wal-Mart discount stores and SAM'S Clubs.) Most Wal-Mart stores are "megastores," measuring more than 200,000 square feet, and include groceries, pharmacies, and hardware and garden supply areas. With 1.2 million employees and 3,600 stores, Wal-Mart is the largest employer in the United States after the federal government. Given the size and scope of Wal-Mart, the humble beginnings of Sam Walton, the founder of the Wal-Mart empire, come as something of a surprise.

Sam Walton began his career in 1940 at J. C. Penney as a management trainee at a salary of seventy-five dollars a month. After serving in the military during World War II, Walton borrowed twenty thousand dollars from his father-in-law and opened a variety store. The store was a success, largely because Walton stocked his shelves with low-priced merchandise and experimented with buying directly from wholesalers and passing the saving on to his customers. After selling the variety store, Walton bought a 5 & 10 cent store. By 1962, he, his father-in-law, and his brother had opened sixteen other stores, including several larger stores called Walton's Family Centers. In these stores, Walton instituted a number of innovations, such as special promotions, profit sharing for employees, and limited partnerships for managers.

In 1962, Walton and his brother opened the first Wal-Mart—a discount store that sold name brands at low prices. Soon, Wal-Marts had sprung up all across rural America. Walton believed that the reason for Wal-Mart's success was its hometown identity. He also believed that each store should reflect the values of both its customers and the community it served. Walton actively managed his company, overseeing its expansion until his death in 1992.

Because of its size and its dominance of the discount market, it is not surprising that Wal-Mart has attracted its share of controversy. Critics point out, for example, that given its large sales volume, Wal-Mart does not contribute enough to charity. (Walton's own position on this matter was that the company already "gives something back" because it keeps prices low.) Another criticism is that despite a "Made in the USA" advertising campaign, the majority of products Wal-Mart sells are made overseas, often in sweatshops in developing nations. In addition, critics assert that Wal-Mart keeps its prices down and its profits up by paying low wages and by not providing health care for many of its workers. They point to the fact that even though Wal-Mart's starting salary is the same as that of other discount retailers, salaries are significantly lower than its competitors' at the end of an employee's second year. Critics also condemn many of Wal-Mart's other employment practices. At this point, Wal-Mart has lost a class-action sex-discrimination lawsuit, and has also been fined by the government for employing illegal aliens and for not allowing some workers to take mandated meal breaks. Finally, it has doggedly opposed unions whenever they have attempted to organize workers.

The writers in this debate hold very different opinions about Wal-Mart. In "The Case for Wal-Mart," Karen De Coster and Brad Edmonds attempt to refute many of the criticisms leveled at Wal-Mart. According to them, by enabling low-income people to buy a host of products at very low prices, Wal-Mart performs a service to the low-wage communities it serves. In "Down and Out in Discount America," Liza Featherstone disagrees with this assessment, pointing out that Sam Walton's business model requires a large number of low-wage customers. For this reason, says Featherstone, it is in Wal-Mart's best interest to keep the wages of its employees low so that they, too, will have to shop at Wal-Mart and further increase its customer base.

KAREN DE COSTER AND BRAD EDMONDS

The Case for Wal-Mart

Karen De Coster is a Michigan-based certified public accountant, a graduate student in economics at Walsh College, and a member of the Mackinac
Center for Public Policy Board of Scholars. As a freelance writer, she
has contributed articles and essays to the libertarian Web sites
LewRockwell.com and Mises.org as well as to publications such as *The Free
Market, Liberty,* the *Washington Times,* and a number of Michigan newspapers. Brad Edmonds, an Alabama-based banker, holds a master's degree in
industrial psychology and a doctorate in musical arts. He is also a frequent contributor to LewRockwell.com as well as to Patriotist.com.

Background on big-box retailing: Large discount department stores as
we know them today had their beginnings in the five-and-dime variety-
store chains popular in small-town America beginning in the early part of
the twentieth century. The first discount department stores can be traced
to 1962, when the F. W. Woolworth corporation opened its first Woolco
(now defunct), the S. S. Kresge corporation opened its first Kmart, the
Dayton Hudson corporation opened its first Target, and Sam Walton
opened the first Wal-Mart. Kmart grew most rapidly, opening 250 locations by 1967; Wal-Mart, by contrast, had only 18 locations by that year. By
the early 1970s, Kmart had become a major competitor of mainstream
department stores, such as Sears.

The 1980s saw the introduction nationwide of specialty "big-box"
retailers: Lowe's hardware supplies, which had begun as a chain of regular-
sized hardware stores in the 1950s, began to expand its retail space in new
locations to as much as 160,000 square feet; Home Depot, a new venture
in 1979, similarly opened huge hardware and building supply showrooms;
Barnes and Noble, a New York book-selling institution since the 1800s,
began expanding its market with the opening of mega-bookstores in free-
standing malls; and Toys "Я" Us started its chain of "full-scale toy-store
extravaganzas" (in the words of its Web site). Many others followed. By the
late 1990s, Wal-Mart had eclipsed them all, becoming the country's
largest retailer—due, in part, to the introduction of the massive SAM'S
Clubs, originally geared toward small businesses, and Wal-Mart Supercenters, combined department and grocery stores almost twice as large as
previous Wal-Marts. While some communities have fought the development of such big-box chains, in much of the United States they have
become a ubiquitous part of the landscape.

The accusations against Wal-Mart are numerous, and they include: 1
paying overseas workers too little; not paying benefits to part-time workers; refusing to sell items that don't fall within its criteria for being "family-
oriented"; not giving enough back to the community; and discriminating
against women.

All the accusations leveled against Wal-Mart can be applied to just   2
about any large corporation in America, as frequently is the case. For example, Kathie Lee Gifford was almost run out of the country for indirectly
giving jobs to otherwise unemployable, Third World workers.

In addition, most retail and service sector employees still do not get   3
paid full job benefits, so what makes Wal-Mart so distinctive in that case?
What's more, Wal-Mart management has indeed made decisions to refrain
from selling certain items that did not live up to its moral standards —
including certain music CDs and a brand of barbecue sauce sold by a man
who promoted his Confederate heritage — but what's wrong with a private
company exercising its own moral discretion according to its stated values?
Accordingly, the marvelous ways of the free market allow us to move on
elsewhere for our purchases when we are dissatisfied with what we perceive
as corporate nonsense.

Wal-Mart is an employer that pays relatively low wages compared to   4
most jobs or careers, and that engenders a sense of loathing from people
getting paid those wages. But Wal-Mart is not unlike any other retailer in
the respect that it, for the most part, provides jobs and not careers. Other
gigantic corporations such as General Electric or General Motors, on the
other hand, employ executives, college graduates, and skilled laborers, so
they avoid much of the wage-related scrutiny given to retail employers. Add
to that the labor union organizers' inability to unionize Wal-Mart and you
have the perfect recipe for resentment and scorn.

The overriding charges one comes across amid the many Wal-Mart   5
rants are "too large" and "too powerful." Thus it's just more anti-industry,
anti-free market claptrap. Along with that are the hoots and hollers about
this great chain "destroying small towns" by way of buying property in rural
areas and opening its doors to townsfolk so they have access to convenient,
one-stop shopping, an ample supply of products, and unbeatable prices.

However, there is one prevailing phenomenon that makes Wal-Mart a   6
unique target for contempt and that is its "bigness." Americans, generally
speaking, like to attack bigness. There are things associated with bigness
that Americans aren't keen on, like clout and domination.

In fact, the favorite indictment of Wal-Mart is that they dominate the   7
market wherever they go and sell goods at prices that are too low (gasp!).
This in turn — say the naysayers — drives small, local competitors out of
business because they can't compete with Wal-Mart's pricing or product
selection.

Suppose it's true that Wal-Mart went around opening giant stores in   8
small towns, pricing goods below their own cost long enough to drive local
stores out of business. Even if this were correct, Wal-Mart would only be
selling its own property. Suppose you want to sell a house you inherited,
and quickly. Should you not be allowed to set the price as low as you want?

The theory goes that Wal-Mart could then set prices high, and make   9
monopoly profits. How plausible is this, really? First, Wal-Mart executives

would have to be able to see the future — they'd have to know about how long it would take to drive everyone out of business in advance, and know whether they could afford to price goods below cost for long enough to corner the market. Then, through trial and error, they'd have to find the point at which they could set prices low enough to keep customers from driving to another town, but high enough to recoup the losses from the earlier below-cost pricing.

It gets less plausible the more you think about it: The smaller the town, the easier it would be to drive competitors out of business. Then again, a town small enough for this would be small enough to have bitter memories of the pricing strategy and small enough to boycott Wal-Mart before the strategy succeeded. And a very small town would not support a giant Wal-Mart anyway. The larger the town, the less feasible it would be to drive others out of business in that town — Wal-Mart would have to drive their prices far below those of large grocery and department stores, which would be much more difficult.

Further, where is there evidence of Wal-Mart ever driving up prices after becoming established in a market? Wal-Mart has indeed set prices low enough to drive mom and pop stores out of business all over the country and kept the prices that low forever. Yet a journalist for the *Cleveland Scene* said about Wal-Mart's pricing policy: "That's 100 million shoppers a week lured by 'Always Low Prices.'" Lured — as if consumers really don't want low prices; they are just tricked into thinking they do!

In a free market, large suppliers of nearly everything will drive most small suppliers out of business. The only people who can afford to do business on a small scale are people at the top of their fields or in a niche: McDonald's has to keep prices low, and economies of scale do this, while Brennan's restaurant in New Orleans can keep prices high. People who produce house paint and wallpaper must compete on price with other suppliers, while famous artists can keep their prices high. General Motors must keep prices low, while Rolls-Royce doesn't have to.

Nobody complains that there aren't family auto manufacturers, but the powerful farmers' political lobby makes sure we pay inflated prices to keep inefficient farmers in business. Of course, giant agribusinesses don't complain that their weaker competition is kept in the market, because the giant agribusinesses enjoy the inflated prices just as do the family farmers, some of whom are paid to leave their fields fallow.

Nobody complains that there aren't family pharmaceutical manufacturers, but people complain when Wal-Mart drives a corner drug store out of business. Yet if the corner drug store owners had the same political lobbying power farmers have, you can bet we'd be paying $20 for Q-tips.

If the truth be told, Wal-Mart improves the lives of people in rural areas because it gives them access to a lifestyle that they otherwise would not have — a gigantic store showcasing the world's greatest choice of products from groceries to music to automotive products. When it comes to prices and service, try finding 70 percent off clearances at your local mom-

and-pop store or try going to that same store and returning shoes you've worn for three months for a full-price refund with no questions asked.

On the whole, if one doesn't like Wal-Mart and finds it to be of greater utility to support their local mom-and-pop stores for an assortment of cultural and non-economic reasons, then they may do so. If consumers wish to obstruct the development of a Wal-Mart store in their small town, they have scores of non-bullying options to pick from in order to try and persuade their fellow townsfolk that a new Wal-Mart is not the best option.   16

Still, it is not always easy to convince folks to eschew ultra-convenience for the sake of undefined, moral purposes. Consumers most often shop with their wallet, not with political precepts. For that reason, the anti–Wal-Mart crowd uses political coercion and an assortment of anti-private property decrees — such as zoning manipulation — in order to stave off the construction of a new Wal-Mart store in their town.   17

Hating Wal-Mart is the equivalent of hating Bill Gates.* Sam Walton had a grandiose vision for himself, and sought to realize that vision by providing something people want — low prices. He has done every bit as much for your lifestyle as Bill Gates.   18

Families who shop carefully at Wal-Mart can actually budget more for investing, children's college funds, or entertainment. And unlike other giant corporations, Wal-Mart stores around the country make an attempt to provide a friendly atmosphere by spending money to hire greeters, who are often people who would have difficulty finding any other job. This is a friendly, partial solution to shoplifting problems; the solution K-mart applied ("Hey, what's in that bag?") didn't work as well.   19

It's interesting to observe that the consumers who denounce Wal-Mart are often the same folks who take great joy in reaping the rewards of corporate bigness, such as saving money with sales, clearances, and coupons, being able to engage in comparative shopping, and taking advantage of generous return policies.   20

When all's said and done, Wal-Mart employs lots of people; provides heaps of things you need in one place at the lowest prices you'll find; and gives millions to charities every year. Add up the charitable giving of all the mom and pop stores in the country and it probably won't equal that of one giant corporation.   21

To be sure, if Americans didn't love Wal-Mart so much it wouldn't be sitting at the top of the 2002 Fortune 500† with $219 billion in revenues. And we do love Wal-Mart. We love it because it gives us variety and abundance. We love it because it saves us time and wrangling. And we love it because no matter where we are, it's always there when we need it.   22

• • •

---

* Eds. note — Multibillionaire chairman and chief software architect of Microsoft Corporation.

† Eds. note — *Fortune* magazine's yearly list of the country's five hundred most profitable companies.

Comprehension

1. What are the major accusations against Wal-Mart? According to De Coster and Edmonds, how does Wal-Mart compare to other large American corporations?

2. What is the difference between a corporation that provides a job and one that provides a career? Which type of corporation is Wal-Mart? How does this fact explain the relatively low wages Wal-Mart pays to its workers?

3. According to Wal-Mart's critics, what problems does Wal-Mart create by being "'too large' and 'too powerful'" (5)? How do De Coster and Edmonds respond to this charge?

4. How, according to De Coster and Edmonds, does Wal-Mart improve the lives of people in rural areas? How does Wal-Mart help families save money?

5. What do De Coster and Edmonds mean when they say, "Hating Wal-Mart is the equivalent of hating Bill Gates" (18)?

Purpose and Audience

1. Do De Coster and Edmonds expect readers to be familiar with Wal-Mart? How can you tell?

2. What was De Coster's and Edmonds's purpose in writing this essay?

3. The title of this essay leaves no doubt about the writers' position. Was this choice a good idea? Should they have used a title that was not so explicit? Explain.

4. What is De Coster's and Edmonds's attitude toward Wal-Mart's critics? What words and phrases convey their attitude?

Style and Structure

1. De Coster and Edmonds introduce their essay by listing the accusations against Wal-Mart. Why do they begin this way? Is this a good strategy?

2. In paragraph 2, De Coster and Edmonds say, "All the accusations leveled against Wal-Mart can be applied to just about any large corporation in America." Does this response adequately deal with the issue? Does it constitute a logical fallacy? Explain.

3. What arguments against Wal-Mart do De Coster and Edmonds address? How convincingly do they refute them?

4. In paragraph 20, De Coster and Edmonds say, "It's interesting to observe that the consumers who denounce Wal-Mart are often the same folks who take great joy in reaping the rewards of corporate bigness." Is this statement a logical fallacy? Explain.

5. Are there any places where you think De Coster and Edmonds overstate their case? If so, how do you react to these overstatements?

6. De Coster and Edmonds end their essay by saying, "if Americans didn't love Wal-Mart so much it wouldn't be sitting at the top of the 2002 Fortune 500 with $219 billion in revenues." Is this a reasonable conclusion? Can Wal-Mart's financial success be explained in any other way?

Vocabulary Projects

1. Define each of these words as it is used in this selection.

   accusations (1)   agribusinesses (13)
   distinctive (3)   utility (16)
   scrutiny (4)   eschew (17)
   claptrap (5)   precepts (17)
   indictment (7)   grandiose (18)
   feasible (10)

2. In paragraph 22, De Coster and Edmonds repeat the word *love* five times. What is the meaning of this word as it is used here?

Journal Entry

What do you think of Wal-Mart? Do you love it, as De Coster and Edmonds say Americans do, or do you have another opinion of it?

Writing Workshop

1. Write an essay agreeing or disagreeing with De Coster's and Edmonds's statement, "If the truth be told, Wal-Mart improves the lives of people in rural areas because it gives them access to a lifestyle that they otherwise would not have" (15). Make sure you present evidence to support your points.

2. Assume you are the regional manager of a Wal-Mart attempting to open a store in a small town. To do so, you must get approval from the local zoning board. Write a letter to the zoning board discussing the benefits the store would bring to the community. In your discussion, acknowledge some of the problems that might result, but make sure you make your case that, on the whole, Wal-Mart would be good for the local economy. Use material from "The Case for Wal-Mart" to support your points.

3. In her essay "Down and Out in Discount America" (page 659), Liza Featherstone says that organized labor should oppose Wal-Mart "not just because Wal-Mart is a grave threat to unionized workers' jobs (which it is) but because it threatens all American ideals that are at odds with profit — ideals such as justice, equality and fairness" (28). Write a response from De Coster and Edmonds to Featherstone's statement. Use material from both essays to support your points.

Combining the Patterns

Paragraphs 9 through 11 are developed by means of **cause and effect**. How does this strategy help De Coster and Edmonds support their argument?

Thematic Connections

- "My Mother Never Worked" (page 108)
- "The Peter Principle" (page 220)
- "Innovation" (page 231)

LIZA FEATHERSTONE

Down and Out in Discount America

Journalist Liza Featherstone was born in the Boston area in 1969. A graduate of the University of Michigan, she has written frequently about student and youth activism for such periodicals as the *Nation, Lingua Franca,* San Francisco's *Bay Guardian, Left Business Observer, Dissent,* and the *Columbia Journalism Review.* Featherstone has also published articles in *Ms., Salon, Nerve, US,* and *Rolling Stone,* among others, and is the coauthor of *Students against Sweatshops: The Making of a Movement* (2002) and author of *Selling Women Short: The Landmark Battle for Workers' Rights at Wal-Mart* (2004). The following essay appeared in the *Nation.*

Background on efforts to unionize Wal-Mart: Labor unions have a long history in the United States. These official organizations of workers within an industry grant their elected officials the power to negotiate matters of salaries, benefits, and working conditions with employers, backed up by the threat of strikes. They are largely responsible for the significant improvement in working conditions for union members for the first half of the twentieth century. Critics argue, however, that by driving up salaries and the cost of medical benefits, unions place companies at a disadvantage, discourage employment nationally, and contribute to the cost of goods for consumers.

In response to union membership's decline (from close to half the workforce in the 1940s to less than 12.5 percent in 2004), efforts at unionizing have been stepped up in recent years. As the largest private employer in the United States, Wal-Mart has been a prime target of these efforts — and Wal-Mart has fought back vigorously. Handbooks for managers are full of antiunion advice, and potential employees are screened to exclude those who have been members of unions or whose personality type suggests they might be open to union membership. While Wal-Mart officials deny the charges, critics claim that the corporation has illegally barred efforts by employees to promote a union in stores, forced employees to sign forms stating that they will not support union efforts, and fired employees sympathetic to unions. (Such actions violate federal law, which permits workers to lobby other workers in their workplace to form a labor union.) When meat cutters in a Texas Wal-Mart Supercenter voted to form a union in their department, the company eliminated their jobs by switching to selling precut and packaged meat. And, when a Canadian Wal-Mart store voted to unionize, the company promptly closed the store down.

On the day after Thanksgiving, the biggest shopping day of the year, Wal-Mart's many progressive critics — not to mention its business competitors — finally enjoyed a bit of schadenfreude* when the retailer had to

---

* EDS. NOTE — Taking pleasure in the misfortune of others.

admit to "disappointing" sales. The problem was quickly revealed: Wal-Mart hadn't been discounting aggressively enough. Without low prices, Wal-Mart just isn't Wal-Mart.

That's not a mistake the big-box behemoth is likely to make again. Wal-Mart knows its customers, and it knows how badly they need the discounts. Like Wal-Mart's workers, its customers are overwhelmingly female, and struggling to make ends meet. Betty Dukes, the lead plaintiff in Dukes v. Wal-Mart,* the landmark sex-discrimination case against the company, points out that Wal-Mart takes out ads in her local paper the same day the community's poorest citizens collect their welfare checks. "They are promoting themselves to low-income people," she says. "That's who they lure. They don't lure the rich. . . . They understand the economy of America. They know the haves and have-nots. They don't put Wal-Mart in Piedmonts. They don't put Wal-Mart in those high-end parts of the community. They plant themselves right in the middle of Poorville."

Betty Dukes is right. A 2000 study by Andrew Franklin, then an economist at the University of Connecticut, showed that Wal-Mart operated primarily in poor and working-class communities, finding, in the bone-dry language of his discipline, "a significant negative relationship between median household income and Wal-Mart's presence in the market." Although fancy retailers noted with chagrin during the 2001 recession that absolutely everybody shops at Wal-Mart — "Even people with $100,000 incomes now shop at Wal-Mart," a PR flack for one upscale mall fumed — the Bloomingdale's set is not the discounter's primary market, and probably never will be. Only 6 percent of Wal-Mart shoppers have annual family incomes of more than $100,000. A 2003 study found that 23 percent of Wal-Mart Supercenter customers live on incomes of less than $25,000 a year. More than 20 percent of Wal-Mart shoppers have no bank account, long considered a sign of dire poverty. And while almost half of Wal-Mart Supercenter customers are blue-collar workers and their families, 20 percent are unemployed or elderly.

Al Zack, who until his retirement in 2004 was the United Food and Commercial Workers' vice president for strategic programs, observes that appealing to the poor was "Sam Walton's real genius. He figured out how to make money off of poverty. He located his first stores in poor rural areas and discovered a real market. The only problem with the business model is that it really needs to create more poverty to grow." That problem is cleverly solved by creating more bad jobs worldwide. In a chilling reversal of Henry Ford's strategy, which was to pay his workers amply so they could buy Ford cars, Wal-Mart's stingy compensation policies — workers make, on average, just over $8 an hour, and if they want health insurance, they

---

* EDS. NOTE — Case of seven California women — current and former Wal-Mart employees — charging the company with systematic sex discrimination in promotions, assignments, training, and pay.

must pay more than a third of the premium — contribute to an economy in which, increasingly, workers can only afford to shop at Wal-Mart.

To make this model work, Wal-Mart must keep labor costs down. It   5
does this by making corporate crime an integral part of its business strategy. Wal-Mart routinely violates laws protecting workers' organizing rights (workers have even been fired for union activity). It is a repeat offender on overtime laws; in more than thirty states, workers have brought wage-and-hour class-action suits against the retailer. In some cases, workers say, managers encouraged them to clock out and keep working; in others, managers locked the doors and would not let employees go home at the end of their shifts. And it's often women who suffer most from Wal-Mart's labor practices. Dukes v. Wal-Mart, which is the largest civil rights class-action suit in history, charges the company with systematically discriminating against women in pay and promotions.

Solidarity across the Checkout Counter

Given the poverty they have in common, it makes sense that Wal-   6
Mart's workers often express a strong feeling of solidarity with the shoppers. Wal-Mart workers tend to be aware that the customers' circumstances are similar to their own, and to identify with them. Some complain about rude customers, but most seem to genuinely enjoy the shoppers.

One longtime department manager in Ohio cheerfully recalls her suc-   7
cessful job interview at Wal-Mart. Because of her weight, she told her interviewers, she'd be better able to help the customer. "I told them I wanted to work in the ladies department because I'm a heavy girl." She understands the frustrations of the large shopper, she told them: "'You know, you go into Lane Bryant and some skinny girl is trying to sell you clothes.' They laughed at that and said, 'You get a second interview!'"

One plaintiff in the Dukes lawsuit, Cleo Page, who no longer works at   8
Wal-Mart, says she was a great customer service manager because "I knew how people feel when they shop, so I was really empathetic."

Many Wal-Mart workers say they began working at their local Wal-   9
Mart because they shopped there. "I was practically born in Wal-Mart," says Alyssa Warrick, a former employee now attending Truman State University in Missouri. "My mom is obsessed with shopping. . . . I thought it would be pretty easy since I knew where most of the stuff was." Most assumed they would love working at Wal-Mart. "I always loved shopping there," enthuses Dukes plaintiff Dee Gunter. "That's why I wanted to work for 'em."

Shopping is traditionally a world of intense female communication   10
and bonding, and women have long excelled in retail sales in part because of the identification between clerk and shopper. Page, who still shops at Wal-Mart, is now a lingerie saleswoman at Mervyn's (owned by Target). "I do enjoy retail," she says. "I like feeling needed and I like helping people, especially women."

Betty Dukes says, "I strive to give Wal-Mart customers one hundred   11
percent of my abilities." This sentiment was repeated by numerous other
Wal-Mart workers, always with heartfelt sincerity. Betty Hamilton, a 61-
year-old clerk in a Las Vegas Sam's Club, won her store's customer service
award last year. She is very knowledgeable about jewelry, her favorite
department, and proud of it. Hamilton resents her employer—she complains about sexual harassment and discrimination, and feels she has been
penalized on the job for her union sympathies—but remains deeply
devoted to her customers. She enjoys imparting her knowledge to shoppers
so "they can walk out of there and feel like they know something." Like
Page, Hamilton feels she is helping people. "It makes me so happy when I
sell something that I know is an extraordinarily good buy," she says. "I feel
like I've done somebody a really good favor."

The enthusiasm of these women for their jobs, despite the workplace   12
indignities many of them have faced, should not assure anybody that the
company's abuses don't matter. In fact, it should underscore the tremendous debt Wal-Mart owes women: This company has built its vast profits
not only on women's drudgery but also on their joy, creativity and genuine
care for the customer.

Why Boycotts Don't Always Work

Will consumers return that solidarity and punish Wal-Mart for dis-   13
criminating against women? Do customers care about workers as much as
workers care about them? Some women's groups, like the National Organization for Women and Code Pink, have been hoping that they do, and
have encouraged the public not to shop at Wal-Mart. While this tactic
could be fruitful in some community battles, it's unlikely to catch on
nationwide. A customer saves 20–25 percent by buying groceries at Wal-
Mart rather than from a competitor, according to retail analysts, and poor
women need those savings more than anyone.

That's why many women welcome the new Wal-Marts in their commu-   14
nities. The *Winona* (Minnesota) *Post* extensively covered a controversy over
whether to allow a Wal-Mart Supercenter into the small town; the letters to
the editor in response offer a window into the female customer's loyalty to
Wal-Mart. Though the paper devoted substantial space to the sex discrimination case, the readers who most vehemently defended the retailer were
female. From the nearby town of Rollingstone, Cindy Kay wrote that she
needed the new Wal-Mart because the local stores didn't carry large-
enough sizes. She denounced the local anti-Wal-Mart campaign as a plot
by rich and thin elites: "I'm glad those people can fit into and afford such
clothes. I can barely afford Shopko and Target!"

A week later, Carolyn Goree, a preschool teacher also hoping for a   15
Winona Wal-Mart, wrote in a letter to the *Post* editor that when she shops
at most stores, $200 fills only a bag or two, but at Wal-Mart, "I come out
with a cart full top and bottom. How great that feels." Lacking a local Wal-

Mart, Goree drives over the Wisconsin border to get her fix. She was incensed by an earlier article's lament that some workers make only $15,000 yearly. "Come on!" Goree objected. "Is $15,000 really that bad of a yearly income? I'm a single mom and when working out of my home, I made $12,000 tops and that was with child support. I too work, pay for a mortgage, lights, food, everything to live. Everything in life is a choice. . . . I am for the little man/woman — I'm one of them. So I say stand up and get a Wal-Mart."

Sara Jennings, a disabled Winona reader living on a total of $8,000, heartily concurred. After paying her rent, phone, electric and cable bills, Jennings can barely afford to treat herself to McDonald's. Of a recent trip to the LaCrosse, Wisconsin, Wal-Mart, she raved, "Oh boy, what a great treat. Lower prices and a good quality of clothes to choose from. It was like heaven for me." She, too, strongly defended the workers' $15,000 yearly income: "Boy, now that is a lot of money. I could live with that." She closed with a plea to the readers: "I'm sure you all make a lot more than I. And I'm sure I speak for a lot of seniors and very-low-income people. We need this Wal-Mart. There's nothing downtown." 16

From Consumers to Workers and Citizens

It is crucial that Wal-Mart's liberal and progressive critics make use of the growing public indignation at the company over sex discrimination, low pay and other workers' rights issues, but it is equally crucial to do this in ways that remind people that their power does not stop at their shopping dollars. It's admirable to drive across town and pay more for toilet paper to avoid shopping at Wal-Mart, but such a gesture is, unfortunately, not enough. As long as people identify themselves as consumers and nothing more, Wal-Mart wins. 17

The invention of the "consumer" identity has been an important part of a long process of eroding workers' power, and it's one reason working people now have so little power against business. According to the social historian Stuart Ewen, in the early years of mass production, the late nineteenth and early twentieth centuries, modernizing capitalism sought to turn people who thought of themselves primarily as "workers" into "consumers." Business elites wanted people to dream not of satisfying work and egalitarian societies — as many did at that time — but of the beautiful things they could buy with their paychecks. 18

Business was quite successful in this project, which influenced much early advertising and continued throughout the twentieth century. In addition to replacing the "worker," the "consumer" has also effectively displaced the citizen. That's why, when most Americans hear about the Wal-Mart's worker-rights abuses, their first reaction is to feel guilty about shopping at the store. A tiny minority will respond by shopping elsewhere — and only a handful will take any further action. A worker might call her union and organize a picket. A citizen might write to her congressman 19 or local newspaper, or galvanize her church and knitting circle to visit local management. A consumer makes an isolated, politically slight decision: to shop or not to shop. Most of the time, Wal-Mart has her exactly where it wants her, because the intelligent choice for anyone thinking as a consumer is not to make a political statement but to seek the best bargain and the greatest convenience.

To effectively battle corporate criminals like Wal-Mart, the public   20
must be engaged as citizens, not merely as shoppers. What kind of politics could encourage that? It's not clear that our present political parties are up to the job. Unlike so many horrible things, Wal-Mart cannot be blamed on George W. Bush. The Arkansas-based company prospered under the state's native son Bill Clinton when he was governor and President. Sam Walton and his wife, Helen, were close to the Clintons, and for several years Hillary Clinton, whose law firm represented Wal-Mart, served on the company's board of directors. Bill Clinton's "welfare reform" has provided Wal-Mart with a ready workforce of women who have no choice but to accept its poverty wages and discriminatory policies.

Still, a handful of Democratic politicians stood up to the retailer. Cali-   21
fornia Assemblywoman Sally Lieber, who represents the 22nd Assembly District and is a former mayor of Mountain View, was outraged when she learned about the sex discrimination charges in Dukes v. Wal-Mart, and she smelled blood when, tipped off by dissatisfied workers, her office discovered that Wal-Mart was encouraging its workers to apply for public assistance, "in the middle of the worst state budget crisis in history!" California had a $38 billion deficit at the time, and Lieber was enraged that taxpayers would be subsidizing Wal-Mart's low wages, bringing new meaning to the term "corporate welfare."

Lieber was angry, too, that Wal-Mart's welfare dependence made it   22
nearly impossible for responsible employers to compete with the retail giant. It was as if taxpayers were unknowingly funding a massive plunge to the bottom in wages and benefits — quite possibly their own. She held a press conference in July 2003, to expose Wal-Mart's welfare scam. The Wal-Mart documents — instructions explaining how to apply for food stamps, Medi-Cal (the state's healthcare assistance program) and other forms of welfare — were blown up on posterboard and displayed. The morning of the press conference, a Wal-Mart worker who wouldn't give her name for fear of being fired snuck into Lieber's office. "I just wanted to say, right on!" she told the assemblywoman.

Wal-Mart spokespeople have denied that the company encourages   23
employees to collect public assistance, but the documents speak for themselves. They bear the Wal-Mart logo, and one is labeled "Wal-Mart: Instructions for Associates." Both documents instruct employees in procedures for applying to "Social Service Agencies." Most Wal-Mart workers I've interviewed had co-workers who worked full time for the company and received public assistance, and some had been in that situation themselves. Public assistance is very clearly part of the retailer's cost-cutting strategy.

(It's ironic that a company so dependent on the public dole supports so many right-wing politicians who'd like to dismantle the welfare state.)

Lieber, a strong supporter of the social safety net who is now assistant   24
speaker pro tempore of the California Assembly, last year passed a bill that would require large and mid-sized corporations that fail to provide decent, affordable health insurance to reimburse local governments for the cost of providing public assistance for those workers. When the bill passed, its opponents decided to kill it by bringing it to a statewide referendum. Wal-Mart, which just began opening Supercenters in California this year, mobilized its resources to revoke the law on election day this November, even while executives denied that any of their employees depended on public assistance.

Citizens should pressure other politicians to speak out against Wal-   25
Mart's abuses and craft policy solutions. But the complicity of both parties in Wal-Mart's power over workers points to the need for a politics that squarely challenges corporate greed and takes the side of ordinary people. That kind of politics seems, at present, strongest at the local level.

Earlier this year, labor and community groups in Chicago prevented   26
Wal-Mart from opening a store on the city's South Side, in part by pushing through an ordinance that would have forced the retailer to pay Chicago workers a living wage. In Hartford, Connecticut, labor and community advocates just won passage of an ordinance protecting their free speech rights on the grounds of the new Wal-Mart Supercenter, which is being built on city property. Similar battles are raging nationwide, but Wal-Mart's opponents don't usually act with as much coordination as Wal-Mart does, and they lack the retail behemoth's deep pockets.

With this in mind, SEIU* president Andy Stern has recently been call-   27
ing attention to the need for better coordination—and funding—of labor and community anti-Wal-Mart efforts. Stern has proposed that the AFL-CIO allocate $25 million of its royalties from purchases on its Union Plus credit card toward fighting Wal-Mart and the "Wal-Martization" of American jobs.

Such efforts are essential not just because Wal-Mart is a grave threat to   28
unionized workers' jobs (which it is) but because it threatens all American ideals that are at odds with profit—ideals such as justice, equality and fairness. Wal-Mart would not have so much power if we had stronger labor laws, and if we required employers to pay a living wage. The company knows that, and it hires lobbyists in Washington to vigorously fight any effort at such reforms—indeed, Wal-Mart has recently beefed up this political infrastructure substantially, and it's likely that its presence in Washington will only grow more conspicuous.

The situation won't change until a movement comes together and   29
builds the kind of social and political power for workers and citizens that can balance that of Wal-Mart. This is not impossible: In Germany, unions

---

* EDS. NOTE—Service Employees International Union.

are powerful enough to force Wal-Mart to play by their rules. American citizens will have to ask themselves what kind of world they want to live in. That's what prompted Gretchen Adams, a former Wal-Mart manager, to join the effort to unionize Wal-Mart. She's deeply troubled by the company's effect on the economy as a whole and the example it sets for other employers. "What about our working-class people?" she asks. "I don't want to live in a Third World country." Working people, she says, should be able to afford "a new car, a house. You shouldn't have to leave the car on the lawn because you can't afford that $45 part."

● ● ●

Comprehension

1. What are Featherstone's major complaints against Wal-Mart? How does Betty Dukes epitomize Wal-Mart's abuses?

2. What does Al Zack mean when he says that Sam Walton's genius was to discover "how to make money off of poverty" (4). How is Walton's strategy different from that of Henry Ford?

3. What do Wal-Mart shoppers and employees have in common? What, according to Featherstone, is the "tremendous debt Wal-Mart owes women" (12)?

4. Why does Featherstone think boycotting Wal-Mart will not work? What strategy does she think people should use to punish Wal-Mart?

5. Why does Featherstone single out Assemblywoman Sally Lieber for praise?

6. According to Featherstone, how is Wal-Mart a threat to American ideals? What does she think should be done to change the situation? How is Germany a model for action against Wal-Mart?

Purpose and Audience

1. What is Featherstone's purpose in writing this essay? To change readers' ideas? To move people to action? Something else? Explain.

2. Does Featherstone consider her readers friendly, hostile, or neutral? What political leanings does she expect her readers to have? How can you tell?

3. Where does Featherstone state her thesis? Should she have used a more explicit thesis statement?

4. In paragraph 20, Featherstone calls Wal-Mart a corporate criminal. Does this strategy help her case, hurt it, or have no effect at all?

Style and Structure

1. Featherstone introduces her essay by describing a sex-discrimination lawsuit brought by an employee. Why does she begin this way? Is this a successful opening strategy?

2. Featherstone supports her points with a number of quotations from women who work or shop at Wal-Mart. How effective are these quotations as support? Should she have used a greater variety of evidence — such as the statistics she introduces in paragraph 3 — to support her points? If so, what evidence should she have used?

3. In paragraph 4, Featherstone uses deductive reasoning to reach the conclusion that "Wal-Mart's stingy compensation policies . . . contribute to an economy in which, increasingly, workers can only afford to shop at Wal-Mart." Examine the logic of this paragraph — perhaps creating a **syllogism** — and determine whether or not Featherstone's conclusion is logical.

4. How clearly does Featherstone lay out the case against Wal-Mart? What points, if any, need further explanation or illustration?

5. In paragraph 28, Featherstone says that Wal-Mart "threatens all American ideals that are at odds with profit — ideals such as justice, equality and fairness." How is profit at odds with "justice, equality and fairness"? Does she need to present evidence to support this statement, or is it self-evident?

6. While acknowledging Wal-Mart's low prices, Featherstone does not concede any other points. Should she have? Would further concessions have strengthened her argument?

Vocabulary Projects

1. Define each of these words as it is used in this selection.

behemoth (2)	bonding (10)	deficit (21)
median (3)	indignities (12)	subsidizing (21)
chagrin (3)	drudgery (12)	dismantle (23)
recession (3)	fruitful (13)	referendum (24)
dire (3)	indignation (17)	revoke (24)
stingy (4)	elites (18)	infrastructure (28)
integral (5)	displaced (19)	

2. In paragraph 2 of her essay, Featherstone quotes Betty Dukes, plaintiff in a sexual-discrimination lawsuit against Wal-Mart: "'They are promoting themselves to low-income people,' she says. 'That's who they lure. They don't lure the rich.'" What is the **denotation** — literal meaning — of *lure*? What are its **connotations**? In what sense could Wal-Mart be said to "lure" people? Do you think the use of the word *lure* here is accurate?

Journal Entry

Do you think Featherstone makes a strong case against Wal-Mart?

Writing Workshop

1. Do you, like Featherstone, believe that Wal-Mart does a great deal of damage to low-income people? Or, do you believe that the inexpensive goods and services Wal-Mart provides outweigh any problems the company might create? Write a short essay presenting your ideas.

2. Assume you own a small business in a town where Wal-Mart is trying to open. Before they can open, however, they have to get approval from the local zoning board. Write a letter to the zoning board saying why Wal-Mart should not be allowed to come to your town. In your essay, concede some of the benefits Wal-Mart would bring, but make the point that, on the whole, the store would do more harm than good. Be specific, and talk about the effect Wal-Mart would have on local business. Use material in "Down and Out in Discount America" to support your points.

3. In "The Case for Wal-Mart" (p. 652), De Coster and Edmonds say, "If the truth be told, Wal-Mart improves the lives of people in rural areas because it gives them access to a lifestyle that they otherwise would not have" (15). Write an essay considering how Featherstone would respond to this statement. Use ideas from both essays to support your points.

Combining the Patterns

Paragraphs 18 and 19 are developed by **definition**. What words is Featherstone defining? How do these definitions help her further her argument?

Thematic Connections

- "Innovation" (page 231)
- "Swollen Expectations" (page 425)
- "What Work Is" (page 550)

CASEBOOK
Does Media Violence Cause Societal Violence?

Violence is a disturbing and sometimes frightening undercurrent of life in the United States. In any given year, more murders occur in any one of our major cities than in all of the British Isles combined. This fact has not been lost on lawmakers, especially those running for reelection. Violent behavior (and how to curb it) has been a frequent issue in elections. Although the causes of violent crime are complex, some people look for a single cause that will point to a quick fix for the problem. In the 1950s, for example, parents and educators blamed graphically violent comic books for an increase in "juvenile delinquency." In the 1970s, pressure from Congress caused Hollywood to institute a rating system so that parents could judge the suitability of movies. More recently, lawmakers mandated that a V-chip, enabling parents to block violent or sexually explicit programs, be built into all new television sets.

The debate about the connection between media violence and violent behavior heats up whenever a particularly horrible crime is linked to a movie. In one case, for example, two teenagers, Sarah Edmondson and Ben Darras, went on a murder spree and at their murder trial tried unsuccessfully to blame their actions on Oliver Stone's 1994 movie *Natural Born Killers.* One of the murder victims, Bill Savage, was an acquaintance of the best-selling writer John Grisham. In response to the murder, Grisham wrote "Unnatural Killers," an essay arguing that Hollywood has the responsibility to stop glamorizing and glorifying murder and mayhem. According to Grisham, the public has two ways to curtail the gratuitous violence that has become a staple of many Hollywood movies. The first, Grisham says, is to send a message to producers such as Oliver Stone by boycotting movies that encourage violence. The second is to sue. To Grisham, it is inconceivable that the makers of movies do not know the effects of the steady diet of violence they feed the American public, and, for this reason, Grisham believes they should be held legally accountable for the damage their products cause:

> It will take only one large verdict against the likes of Oliver Stone, and his production company, and perhaps the screenwriter, and the studio itself, and the party will be over. The verdict will come from the heartland, far away from Southern California, in some small courtroom with no cameras. A jury will finally say enough is enough; that the demons placed in Sarah Edmondson's mind were not solely of her making.

In 1996, a civil lawsuit was filed by Patsy Byers, a paralyzed victim of Sarah and Ben's crime spree, against Oliver Stone and Warner Brothers, who produced the film, as well as against the two assailants and their families' insurance companies. After several appeals, the suit was dismissed in 2001.

The judge in the case ruled that the plaintiffs had not presented any evidence that Stone or the studios had intended to incite violence, and he rejected the argument that the movie was not protected by the First Amendment.

The four essays in this casebook examine the issue of media violence. In "Sizing Up the Effects," Sissela Bok discusses the effects of media violence on television viewers — especially children. She warns that the situation is getting worse and calls for reduced levels of media violence as well as increased parental awareness of its effects. In "Violent Media Is Good For Kids," comic-book author Gerard Jones disagrees with those who condemn violence in the media. He argues that explicitly violent video games, gun-celebrating gangsta rap, and other forms of "creative violence" help children master the frustration they experience as they grow up. In "Memo to John Grisham: What's Next — 'A Movie Made Me Do It'?" the movie director Oliver Stone responds to author John Grisham's editorial attacking his film *Natural Born Killers*. According to Stone, Grisham singled out his film for blame and ignored the more direct causes of the crimes committed by some who saw his movie. Finally, in "Violent Films Cry 'Fire' in Crowded Theaters," attorney Michael Zimecki argues that legal precedents exist for finding filmmakers negligent when they make movies that glorify violence.

Sizing Up the Effects

Born in Stockholm, Sweden, in 1934, Sissela Bok attended the Sorbonne in Paris and received a Ph.D in philosophy from Harvard University in 1970. Formerly a professor of philosophy at Brandeis University, she is currently a Distinguished Fellow at the Harvard Center for Population and Development Studies. Bok writes frequently about ethical issues in government and media, in books such as *Lying: Moral Choice in Public and Private Life* (1978), *On the Ethics of Concealment and Revelation* (1982), and *Common Values* (1996). She is also the author of *Alva Myrdal: A Daughter's Memoir* (1991). The following is a chapter from her 1998 book, *Mayhem: Violence as Public Entertainment*.

Background on children and violence in the media: The National Television Violence Study of the Center for Communication and Social Policy at the University of California, Santa Barbara, reported in 1998 that 66 percent of children's television programming included some kind of violence. It was estimated that in four hours of prime-time television viewing, one could view thirty instances of murder and forty of beatings. A survey by the Kaiser Family Foundation in 2003 showed that 47 percent of parents of children four to six years old reported that their children had imitated aggressive behavior that they had seen on television. Another study reports that children who play violent video games are more likely than others to be aggressive, and a survey of five hundred college students found that listening to violent music lyrics led to an increase in aggressive thoughts and hostile feelings. Most alarming, a study published in 2005 suggested the possibility that prolonged exposure to violent media images may negatively affect brain function in some children. While some critics question the methodology of such studies, violence is unquestionably a problem among young people: 55 percent of those arrested for murder in the United States are under twenty-five years old, and people under twenty-one commit one-third of all violent crimes.

A great deal of research has been conducted to sort out the kinds and amounts of violence in the media and to learn how exposure to media violence affects viewers, and especially children. There have also been many meta-analyses, or studies *of* existing studies.[1] Focusing primarily on television, they all confirm the commonsense observation that the screen is a powerful teaching medium, for good and for ill, when it comes to violent as to all other material.

There is general agreement that children ought neither to be insulated from gradual acquaintance with the treatment of violence in art and in the media nor assaulted by material they cannot handle. The *"catharsis* theory" put forth in the 1960s and 1970s, to the effect that violent material can help young people live out their aggressive impulses vicariously so that their day-to-day conduct becomes less aggressive, has been abandoned by almost all scholars in the field today. The debate suffers, however, from the fact that different studies concern persons of different ages with different levels of understanding of the nature of violence and of distinctions between real and fictitious events. It seems reasonable to suppose that screen violence offers some viewers a chance for strictly vicarious role-playing and an outlet for aggressive fantasies, just as others are more easily frightened or mesmerized or incited by what they view. But scholars increasingly dismiss as unfounded any categorical claims that the average heavy viewer of media violence is somehow less likely to be aggressive than someone without such exposure.

Instead, the vast majority of the studies now concur that media vio-   3
lence can have both short-term and long-term debilitating effects. In 1993, the American Psychological Association published a report by a commission appointed to survey and review existing studies. According to this report,

> There is absolutely no doubt that higher levels of viewing violence on television are correlated with increased acceptance of aggressive attitudes and increased aggressive behavior. . . . Children's exposure to violence in the mass media, particularly at young ages, can have harmful lifelong consequences. Aggressive habits learned early in life are the foundation for later behavior. Aggressive children who have trouble in school and in relating to peers tend to watch more television; the violence they see there, in turn, reinforces their tendency toward aggression, compounding their academic and social failure. These effects are both short-term and long-lasting: A longitudinal study of boys found a significant relation between exposure to television violence at 8 years of life and anti-social acts — including serious violent criminal offenses and spouse abuse — 22 years later. . . . In addition to increasing violent behaviors toward others, viewing violence on television changes attitudes and behaviors toward violence in significant ways. Even those who do not themselves increase their violent behaviors are significantly affected by their viewing of violence in three [further] ways:
>
> • Viewing violence increases fear of becoming a victim of violence, with a resultant increase in self-protective behaviors and increased mistrust of others;
>
> • Viewing violence increases desensitization to violence, resulting in calloused attitudes toward violence directed at others and a decreased likelihood to take action on behalf of the victim when violence occurs (behavioral apathy); and
>
> • Viewing violence increases viewers' appetites for becoming involved with violence or exposing themselves to violence.[2]

The report, like most of the research it surveys, speaks of viewing vio-   4
lence as correlated with effects rather than as directly causing them. And it specifies a number of risk factors capable of contributing to the first of

these effects — increasing aggression. Among these risk factors, some, such as access to firearms, substance abuse, and experience of abuse as a child, doubtless play a larger role than media violence.[3] But it is on the screen that, as in no earlier generation, today's children, including those not subject to the other risk factors, become familiar with them all and with graphic depictions of every form of mayhem.

Commentators have spoken of the four effects specified in the report   5
as increased aggression, fear, desensitization, and appetite.[4] Psychologist Ronald Slaby, a member of the APA commission, has named them "the aggressor effect, the victim effect, the bystander effect, and the appetite effect."[5] Not all of these effects, he suggests, occur for all viewers; much depends on how they identify themselves in relation to the violence they see and on their ability to evaluate programs critically.

Without taking such variations into account, it is natural to ask, as   6
does critic John Leonard, "How, anyway, does TV manage somehow to *desensitize* but also *exacerbate*, to *sedate* but also *incite?*"[6] As with other stimuli, individuals react to media violence in different ways. While many people experience the quite natural reactions of fear and numbing when exposed to repeated depictions of assault, homicide, or rape, fewer will ever come close to feeling incited by them, much less to engaging in such acts. But among those who do cross that line, the combination of a surge of aggression and numb pitilessness is surely not unusual. Psychiatrist James Gilligan, in a study of homicidally violent men, takes it as a precondition for their being able to engage in violent behavior that ordinary human responses are absent: "What is most startling about the most violent people is how incapable they are, at least at the time they commit their violence, of feeling love, guilt, or fear."[7] In such a state, Macbeth's words are anything but incongruous:

> I am in blood
> Stepp'd in so far that, should I wade no more,
> Returning were as tedious as go o'er.[8]

As research evidence accumulates about the effects linked to media   7
violence, it reinforces the commonsense view that violent programming influences viewers at least as much as the advertising directed at them for the express purpose of arousing their desire for candy and toys. Both types of exposure affect children most strongly to the degree that they are more suggestible and less critical of what is placed before them, and have more time to watch than most. The American Academy of Pediatrics, the American Medical Association, and the National PTA are among the many organizations signaling such effects and calling for reduced levels of television violence and greater parental involvement with children's viewing.

In the early 1990s, researchers frequently mentioned the estimate that   8
the average child leaving elementary school has watched 8,000 murders and more than 100,000 acts of violence.[9] Because network television was for decades the primary source for screen violence in most homes, its role

has been especially carefully charted in this regard. In recent years, growing access to numerous cable channels has brought in considerably more violent fare and made it available at all hours. By now, the vast assortment of slasher and gore films on video contribute to a climate of media violence different from that studied over the past four decades. So does the proliferation of video games offering players the chance to engage in vicarious carnage of every sort. These sources bring into homes depictions of graphic violence, often sexual in nature, never available to children and young people in the past. Because videos and interactive games also provide opportunities to play sequences over and over, they add greatly to the amount of violence to which viewers now have access. As a result, it may well be necessary to revise the earlier figures sharply upward.

Although most of the public's concern has been directed primarily toward the first of the four effects noted by researchers — increased levels of aggression — the other three may have a more widespread and debilitating impact on adults as well as children. After all, even in a high-crime society such as ours, the vast majority of citizens will never commit violent crimes; but many are still affected to the extent that the prominence of violence in news and entertainment programs brings an intensified fear of crime, greater callousness toward suffering, and a greater craving for ever more realistic entertainment violence.

9

1. See Jeffrey Cole, *The UCLA Television Monitoring Report* (Los Angeles: UCLA Center for Communications Policy, 1995).

2. American Psychological Association Commission on Youth and Violence, *Violence and Youth, Psychology's Response,* Washington, DC: The American Psychological Association, 1993.

3. For efforts to chart the different risk factors, see Mark L. Rosenberg and Mary Ann Fenley, *Violence in America: A Public Health Approach* (Oxford: Oxford University Press, 1991), pp. 24–33, and National Research Council, *Understanding and Preventing Violence* (Washington, D.C.: National Academy Press, 1995), p. 20.

4. Some have stressed three of these effects. The 1996 National Television Violence Study proposes three substantial risks from viewing television violence: "learning to behave violently, becoming more desensitized to the harmful consequences of violence, and becoming more fearful of being attacked." Levine sees most of the research to date as attempting to answer three questions: "Does media violence encourage children to act more aggressively? Does media violence cultivate attitudes that are excessively distorted, frightening, and pessimistic? Does media violence desensitize children to violence?" in *Viewing Violence,* pp. 16–17.

5. Ronald G. Slaby, "Combating Television Violence," *Chronicle of Higher Education,* vol. 40, no. 18 (January 5, 1994), pp. B1–2.

6. John Leonard, *Smoke and Mirrors: Violence, Television, and Other American Cultures* (New York: Free Press, 1997).

7. James Gilligan, *Violence: Our Deadly Epidemic and Its Causes* (New York: G. P. Putnam's Sons, 1996), p. 113.

8. William Shakespeare, *Macbeth,* III, 4. For commentary linking this passage to desensitization in media violence and in real life, see Martin Amis, "Blown Away," in Karl French, ed., *Screen Violence* (London: Bloomsbury, 1996), p. 13.

9. David Hamburg, *Today's Children* (New York: Times Books, 1992), p. 192.

• • •

Comprehension

1. What is the "catharsis theory" of media violence (2)? What do current scholars think about this theory?

2. What do researchers now believe about the effects of media violence? How does this view of media violence differ from the previous view?

3. What does the APA commission's report cite as the four effects of media violence? What accounts for the fact that media violence affects people differently?

4. According to Bok, as evidence accumulates, it becomes clear that "violent programming influences viewers at least as much as the advertising directed at them . . . " (7). How is media violence like television advertising? Why are children especially vulnerable to violent programming and to advertising? What can be done about this situation?

5. Why does Bok believe that the current situation concerning media violence is worse than it was in the early 1990s? What are the implications of this growing problem?

Purpose and Audience

1. What is Bok's purpose in writing this essay? Does she achieve her purpose?

2. How would you describe the tone of this essay? Is it appropriate for Bok's purpose?

3. At what point does Bok state her thesis? Why does she state it where she does?

Style and Structure

1. What strategy does Bok use to introduce her essay? Considering her purpose, is this an effective strategy?

2. Why does Bok discuss "catharsis theory" in paragraph 2? How does this discussion help her develop her argument?

3. In paragraph 3, Bok includes a long quotation from a report. Should she have summarized this material? What does she gain (or lose) by quoting her source so fully?

4. At what point in the essay does Bok address arguments against her position? How effectively does she refute these arguments?

5. What evidence does Bok use to support her points? What other kinds of evidence could she have used? Would this have made her argument more convincing? Explain.

6. At the end of the essay, Bok provides a list of endnotes. What purpose does this documentation serve? How does it enhance Bok's argument?

Vocabulary

1. Define each of the following words as it is used in this selection.

medium (1)

desensitization (3)

depictions (6)

fictitious (2)

calloused (3)

incongruous (6)

vicarious (2)

mayhem (4)

suggestible (7)

categorical (2)

bystander (5)

proliferation (8)

concur (3)

exacerbate (6)

prominence (9)

debilitating (3)

sedate (6)

craving (9)

correlated (3)

incite (6)

2. In paragraphs 1 and 7, Bok speaks of a "commonsense observation" and a "commonsense view." What does the word *commonsense* mean? What idea is Bok trying to convey by using this term?

Journal Entry

How convincing is Bok's argument that media violence can have "both short-term and long-term debilitating effects" (3)?

Writing Workshop

1. Write a letter from Bok to Gerard Jones arguing that he should not write comic books that glorify violence. Use material from Bok's essay to support your argument. Before you begin, read Jones's essay "Violent Media Is Good for Kids" (page 678). You might also want to look at some of Jones's work at a comic-book store or on the Internet.

2. Assume you are a lawyer defending a client charged with assault because he tried to hit a coworker during a disagreement. During your meetings with your client, you discover he is a heavy viewer of violent films and television programs, and you are convinced the violent programming is largely responsible for your client's aggressive behavior. With the help of Bok's essay, write an opening statement to deliver to the jury. You should admit your client did something he should not have, but you should explain how the violence he watched caused him to overreact.

3. Rent a violent action film. After viewing it, write an editorial for your college newspaper discussing the movie's violent content. Do you agree with Gerard Jones, who says that violent media help children come to terms with their own emotional and developmental needs? Or do you agree with Bok, who says that the levels of violence in the media are affecting children and should be drastically reduced?

Combining the Patterns

Although this essay's primary pattern of development is **cause and effect**, it is also an argument. What specific components of this essay make it an argument? Explain.

Thematic Connections

- "Thirty-Eight Who Saw Murder Didn't Call the Police" (page 120)
- "Just Walk on By" (page 240)
- "A Peaceful Woman Explains Why She Carries a Gun" (page 371)

GERARD JONES

Violent Media Is Good for Kids

Gerard Jones, born in 1955 in Ann Arbor, Michigan, has written for the *Green Lantern, Batman, Incredible Hulk,* and *Spiderman* comic-book series and has created the original series *The Trouble with Girls.* He has also adapted a number of comic-book Pokémon adventures from the original Japanese. Jones is the author of *Honey, I'm Home: Sitcoms — Selling the American Dream* (1992); *Killing Monsters: Why Children Need Fantasy, Super Heroes, and Make-Believe* (2003); *Men of Tomorrow: Geeks, Gangsters, and the Birth of the Comic Book* (2004); and the novel *Ginny Good* (2003). He has developed the Art & Story Workshop to help children express their creativity. This essay appeared in *Mother Jones* magazine in 2000.

Background on childhood development: Psychologist Erik Erikson (1902–1994) postulated a theory of human personality development in the 1950s that continues to influence psychology practice today. He enumerated eight stages of development, five of them pertaining to childhood and adolescence. In the first stage, which encompasses the first two years of a child's life, the main issue is dependency. If a child's needs are met by parents and other caregivers, he or she learns to trust; if a child is not adequately nurtured, the result is mistrust. During the early childhood stage, through age four or so, the healthy child develops a sense of self-assurance and pride; in a negative environment, a child learns to feel shame. The third stage, which Erikson called the "play age," lasts until formal schooling begins. Here, in a positive and productive environment, a child learns to get along with peers — to lead as well as to follow — and develops a rich world of imagination and fantasy. Otherwise, he or she experiences a marked dependency on adults and exhibits an inability to socialize with others. The early school age, roughly through junior high, is the fourth stage, a period of developing competency in learning and in rule-based play or, if not adequately negotiated, of feeling inferior and defeated. During the fifth stage, from age fourteen to twenty, the healthy personality develops a functioning identity, a comfortable knowledge of who one is within the larger world. The opposite result is a dysfunctional identity: unthinkingly rebellious of the larger world, self-doubting, and unable to grow. Jones sees fantasy violence as a positive influence on development during stages three through five.

At 13 I was alone and afraid. Taught by my well-meaning, progressive, English-teacher parents that violence was wrong, that rage was something to be overcome and cooperation was always better than conflict, I suffocated my deepest fears and desires under a nice-boy persona. Placed in a small, experimental school that was wrong for me, afraid to join my peers in their bumptious rush into adolescent boyhood, I withdrew into passivity and loneliness. My parents, not trusting the violent world of the late 1960s, built a wall between me and the crudest elements of American pop culture.

Then the Incredible Hulk smashed through it.   2

One of my mother's students convinced her that Marvel Comics,   3
despite their apparent juvenility and violence, were in fact devoted to lofty messages of pacifism and tolerance. My mother borrowed some, thinking they'd be good for me. And so they were. But not because they preached lofty messages of benevolence. They were good for me because they were juvenile. And violent.

The character who caught me, and freed me, was the Hulk: overgen-   4
dered and undersocialized, half-naked and half-witted, raging against a frightened world that misunderstood and persecuted him. Suddenly I had

A scene from Gerard Jones and Gene Ha's comic book "Oktane."

a fantasy self to carry my stifled rage and buried desire for power. I had a fantasy self who was a self: unafraid of his desires and the world's disapproval, unhesitating and effective in action. "Puny boy follow Hulk!" roared my fantasy self, and I followed.

I followed him to new friends—other sensitive geeks chasing their own inner brutes—and I followed him to the arrogant, self-exposing, self-assertive, superheroic decision to become a writer. Eventually, I left him behind, followed more sophisticated heroes, and finally my own lead along a twisting path to a career and an identity. In my 30s, I found myself writing action movies and comic books. I wrote some Hulk stories, and met the geek-geniuses who created him. I saw my own creations turned into action figures, cartoons, and computer games. I talked to the kids who read my stories. Across generations, genders, and ethnicities I kept seeing the same story: people pulling themselves out of emotional traps by immersing themselves in violent stories. People integrating the scariest, most fervently denied fragments of their psyches into fuller senses of selfhood through fantasies of superhuman combat and destruction.

I have watched my son living the same story—transforming himself into a bloodthirsty dinosaur to embolden himself for the plunge into preschool, a Power Ranger to muscle through a social competition in kindergarten. In the first grade, his friends started climbing a tree at school. But he was afraid: of falling, of the centipedes crawling on the trunk, of sharp branches, of his friends' derision. I took my cue from his own fantasies and read him old Tarzan comics, rich in combat and bright with flashing knives. For two weeks he lived in them. Then he put them aside. And he climbed the tree.

But all the while, especially in the wake of the recent burst of school shootings, I heard pop psychologists insisting that violent stories are harmful to kids, heard teachers begging parents to keep their kids away from "junk culture," heard a guilt-stricken friend with a son who loved Pokémon lament, "I've turned into the bad mom who lets her kid eat sugary cereal and watch cartoons!"

That's when I started the research.

"Fear, greed, power-hunger, rage: these are aspects of our selves that we try not to experience in our lives but often want, even need, to experience vicariously through stories of others," writes Melanie Moore, Ph.D., a psychologist who works with urban teens. "Children need violent entertainment in order to explore the inescapable feelings that they've been taught to deny, and to reintegrate those feelings into a more whole, more complex, more resilient selfhood."

Moore consults to public schools and local governments, and is also raising a daughter. For the past three years she and I have been studying the ways in which children use violent stories to meet their emotional and developmental needs—and the ways in which adults can help them use those stories healthily. With her help I developed Power Play, a program for helping young people improve their self-knowledge and sense of potency through heroic, combative storytelling.

We've found that every aspect of even the trashiest pop-culture story   11 can have its own developmental function. Pretending to have superhuman powers helps children conquer the feelings of powerlessness that inevitably come with being so young and small. The dual-identity concept at the heart of many superhero stories helps kids negotiate the conflicts between the inner self and the public self as they work through the early stages of socialization. Identification with a rebellious, even destructive, hero helps children learn to push back against a modern culture that cultivates fear and teaches dependency.

At its most fundamental level, what we call "creative violence" — head-   12 bonking cartoons, bloody videogames, playground karate, toy guns — gives children a tool to master their rage. Children will feel rage. Even the sweetest and most civilized of them, even those whose parents read the better class of literary magazines, will feel rage. The world is uncontrollable and incomprehensible; mastering it is a terrifying, enraging task. Rage can be an energizing emotion, a shot of courage to push us to resist greater threats, take more control, than we ever thought we could. But rage is also the emotion our culture distrusts the most. Most of us are taught early on to fear our own. Through immersion in imaginary combat and identification with a violent protagonist, children engage the rage they've stifled, come to fear it less, and become more capable of utilizing it against life's challenges.

I knew one little girl who went around exploding with fantasies so vio-   13 lent that other moms would draw her mother aside to whisper, "I think you should know something about Emily. . . ." Her parents were separating, and she was small, an only child, a tomboy at an age when her classmates were dividing sharply along gender lines. On the playground she acted out "Sailor Moon" fights, and in the classroom she wrote stories about people being stabbed with knives. The more adults tried to control her stories, the more she acted out the roles of her angry heroes: breaking rules, testing limits, roaring threats.

Then her mother and I started helping her tell her stories. She wrote   14 them, performed them, drew them like comics: sometimes bloody, sometimes tender, always blending the images of pop culture with her own most private fantasies. She came out of it just as fiery and strong, but more self-controlled and socially competent: a leader among her peers, the one student in her class who could truly pull boys and girls together.

I worked with an older girl, a middle-class "nice girl," who held herself   15 together through a chaotic family situation and a tumultuous adolescence with gangsta rap. In the mythologized street violence of Ice T, the rage and strutting of his music and lyrics, she found a theater of the mind in which she could be powerful, ruthless, invulnerable. She avoided the heavy drug use that sank many of her peers, and flowered in college as a writer and political activist.

I'm not going to argue that violent entertainment is harmless. I think   16
it has helped inspire some people to real-life violence. I am going to argue that it's helped hundreds of people for every one it's hurt, and that it can help far more if we learn to use it well. I am going to argue that our fear of "youth violence" isn't well-founded on reality, and that the fear can do more harm than the reality. We act as though our highest priority is to prevent our children from growing up into murderous thugs — but modern kids are far more likely to grow up too passive, too distrustful of themselves, too easily manipulated.

We send the message to our children in a hundred ways that their   17
craving for imaginary gun battles and symbolic killings is wrong, or at least dangerous. Even when we don't call for censorship or forbid "Mortal Kombat," we moan to other parents within our kids' earshot about the "awful violence" in the entertainment they love. We tell our kids that it isn't nice to play-fight, or we steer them from some monstrous action figure to a pro-social doll. Even in the most progressive households, where we make such a point of letting children feel what they feel, we rush to substitute an enlightened discussion for the raw material of rageful fantasy. In the process, we risk confusing them about their natural aggression in the same way the Victorians confused their children about their sexuality. When we try to protect our children from their own feelings and fantasies, we shelter them not against violence but against power and selfhood.

The title character of "Oktane" gets nasty.

• • •

Comprehension

1. How did the Incredible Hulk free Jones? What did he free him from? Why did Jones eventually leave him behind?
2. What is the "dual-identity concept" (11) that is central to many super-hero stories? Why are children drawn to this type of hero? How does this figure help them "push back against a modern culture that cultivates fear and teaches dependency" (11)?
3. What is "creative violence" (12)? How does it help children deal with the challenges of life?
4. Why does Jones support violent entertainment even though he acknowledges that it can "inspire some people to real-life violence" (16)?
5. According to Jones, what problems arise when well-meaning parents send the message to children that violent entertainment is wrong?

Purpose and Audience

1. What is Jones's purpose in writing this essay?
2. Where does Jones state his thesis? Why does he state it where he does?
3. Does Jones expect his audience to agree with him about violence or to be skeptical? How do you know?
4. Jones tells readers that he writes action movies and comic books. Why does he offer this information?

Style and Structure

1. Why does Jones begin his essay with an anecdote about the difficulty of growing up? How does this narrative help him construct his argument?
2. Paragraphs 2 and 8 are single sentences. What does Jones hope to accomplish with these short paragraphs? Is he successful?
3. What evidence does Jones provide to support his points? Should he have supplied more evidence? Explain.
4. Jones includes pictures in his essay. Are they a distraction, or do they help to support his argument?
5. At what point does Jones refute the major argument against his position? How effective is his refutation?
6. Jones makes a number of points in his conclusion. Do these points flow naturally out of his essay, or are they new issues that need further discussion? Explain.

Vocabulary Projects

1. Define each of the following words as it is used in this selection.

progressive (1)	immersing (5)	dependency (11)
bumptious (1)	vicariously (9)	protagonist (12)
passivity (1)	reintegrate (9)	competent (14)
pacifism (3)	resilient (9)	tumultuous (15)
benevolence (3)	selfhood (9)	mythologized (15)
stifled (4)	negotiate (11)	enlightened (17)
sophisticated (5)	cultivates (11)	

2. In paragraph 8, Jones says, "That's when I started the research." What does he mean by *research*? What information does Jones provide to clarify his use of this term? Should he have provided more information so that readers could be certain of his meaning?

Journal Entry

Do you believe, as Jones does, that bloody video games, gun-glorifying gangsta rap, and other forms of "creative violence" help more children than they hurt?

Writing Workshop

1. Do you agree or disagree with Jones on children's need for "creative violence"? Write a letter to Jones stating your position. Be sure to define *creative violence* and to address the specific points that Jones makes in his essay.

2. Do your own survey of violent entertainment. Observe some violent games at a video arcade, or read a few superhero comic books. Then, write an essay arguing for or against Jones's thesis. For example, on the basis of your observations, do you think some video games or comic books are so violent that they cannot serve the purpose Jones describes?

3. Some studies suggest a link between violent entertainment and aggressive behavior in children, but no studies have demonstrated conclusively that a link exists between viewing violent media and violent behavior. Even so, do you believe some kind of censorship is called for? Write an essay taking a stand on this issue. Use material from Jones's essay as well as from Sissela Bok's "Sizing Up the Effects" (page 671).

Combining the Patterns

Paragraph 12 is developed by means of **definition**. What is the function of this paragraph? How does it help Jones develop his argument?

Thematic Connections

- "Playing by the Rules" (page 114)
- "Who Killed Benny Paret?" (page 346)
- "Why Boys Don't Play with Dolls" (page 361)

OLIVER STONE

Memo to John Grisham: What's Next— "A Movie Made Me Do It"?

Controversial filmmaker Oliver Stone was born in New York City in 1946 and educated at Yale. After serving in the Vietnam War, he studied film at New York University and in the following years wrote screenplays for violent but well-received films such as *Midnight Express* (1978) and *Scarface* (1983). His directorial debut came with *Salvador* (1986), about the revolution then taking place in El Salvador; it was followed that same year by *Platoon,* a drama set during the Vietnam War, which won the Academy Award for best picture and earned Stone the award for best director. His films *JFK* (1991) and *Nixon* (1995) sparked considerable debate about the fictionalization of film biography. His most recent film is *Alexander* (2004).

Background on *Natural Born Killers*: Stone's most controversial film is *Natural Born Killers* (1994), about a young couple who go on a crime spree, killing fifty-two people and becoming media stars in the process. Condemned for its apparent glorification of casual murder, the movie, according to Stone, was intended as a satire of the media's obsession with violence. While not a box-office hit, the film found a cult audience after it was released on videotape. In 1995, however, two teenagers went on a crime spree that was allegedly influenced by Stone's film. One of the murder victims was a friend of best-selling author John Grisham; consequently, Grisham wrote an essay, "Unnatural Killers," in response to the murders. Here he argues that filmmakers and film studios need to either stop glamorizing violence or be held legally responsible for crime sprees like the one he describes. In the following essay, commissioned by *LA Weekly* as a response to "Unnatural Killers," Stone argues that his film had no influence on the couple who killed Grisham's friend and that Grisham's advocacy of "silencing artists" is only a small step from taking away freedom of speech altogether. Other copycat crimes associated with *Natural Born Killers* include the 1994 decapitation of a thirteen-year-old Texas girl by a fourteen-year-old boy who told police he "wanted to be famous like the natural born killers" and the 1995 murder of a Georgia truck driver by four people in their twenties after they had watched the movie nineteen times.

The hunt for witches to explain society's ills is ancient in our blood, but unholy for that nonetheless. The difference is that now we do not blame the village hag and her black cat, but the writer and the photographer and the filmmaker. Increasingly indicted by art and fearful of technology, our society scours them for scapegoats, in the process ignoring Shakespeare, who reminds us that artists do not invent nature but merely hold up to it a mirror. That the mirror now is electronic or widescreen or cyberspace is all the more intimidating to the unschooled, and the more tempting to the lawyers.

John Grisham predictably draws upon the superstition about the magical power of pictures to conjure up the undead specter of censorship. Too sophisticated to clamor for government intervention, he calls instead for civil action. Victims of crimes should, he declares, rise up against the purveyors of culture high and low and demand retribution, thereby "sending a message" about the mood of the popular mind. And so we arrive at yet another, more modern, more typically American superstition: that the lawsuit is the answer to everything. Fall victim to a crime acted out in the movies and all you have to do is haul the director into court. Has your father been brutalized? Sue Oedipus and call Hamlet as a witness. Do you hate your mother? Blame Medea and Joan Crawford.* And has your lawyer-husband been unfaithful? Why, then slap a summons on John Grisham, since, after all, he wrote *The Firm*.

Grisham is at pains to insist that before seeing my film *Natural Born Killers,* accused murderers Ben Darras (18) and Sarah Edmondson (19) had "never hurt anyone." But, even by his own admission, Ben and Sarah are deeply disturbed youths with histories of drug and/or alcohol abuse and psychiatric treatment. Ben's alcoholic father divorced his mother twice, then committed suicide. Grisham mentions as if it is insignificant that Sarah carried a gun because she feared that Ben would attack her. Far from never having hurt anyone, it seems Ben and Sarah had for years been hurting themselves and their families, and it was only a matter of time until they externalized their anger.

It is likely that, whether they had seen *Natural Born Killers* or *The Green Berets* or a *Tom and Jerry* cartoon the night before their first crime, Ben and Sarah would have behaved in exactly the way they did. And it is equally clear that the specific identity of the victim was entirely irrelevant. "Ben was quite anxious to kill someone," Grisham states, and Sarah was ready to help. And at the crucial moment when the carefully twisted springs of their psyches finally uncoiled, as they were bound to do, not I nor Newt Gingrich nor Father Sullivan of Boys Town could or did influence them.[†]

Did *Natural Born Killers* have an impact on members of its audience? Undoubtedly. Did it move some to a heightened sensitivity toward violence? It did, some. Does it reveal a truth about the media's obsession with the senseless sensational? Ask O. J. Simpson. But did it drive Ben and Sarah to commit two murders? No. If they are guilty, perhaps a negligent or abusive upbringing, combined with defects in their psyches, *did*. Parents, school,

2

3

4

5

---

* EDS. NOTE — Oedipus, Hamlet, and Medea are tragic figures of classical drama. Former Hollywood star Joan Crawford was accused of child abuse by her adopted daughter in a best-selling memoir.

† EDS. NOTE — Gingrich, former speaker of the U.S. House of Representatives, recommended homes like Boys Town as refuges for youths from troubled families.

and peers shape children from their earliest days, not films. And, once grown and gone horribly wrong, those children must answer for their actions — not Hollywood directors. An elementary principle of our civilization is that people are responsible for their own actions. If Dan White, the killer of San Francisco Supervisor Harvey Milk and Mayor George Moscone, could claim that "Twinkies made me do it," what's next—"A movie made me do it"?

A recent study showed that the average teenager spends 1,500 hours a year watching television, compared with 1,100 hours a year in school. According to the study, most programs contain violence, and fully half of these violent acts do not depict the victim's injuries or pain. Astonishingly, only 16 percent of all programs show the long-term effects of violence, while three-quarters of the time, perpetrators of violence on television go unpunished. Is it just possible that these 1,500 hours of mostly violent TV programming might have had slightly more effect on these two youngsters than two hours of *Natural Born Killers*?

Grisham points to "at least several" anonymous youths who claim to have committed crimes under the influence "to some degree" of my film. Leaving aside the self-serving vagueness of this statement, we might ask: How many thousands of murders have been committed under the influence of alcohol? Yet Grisham does not call for the breweries and distilleries to be shut down by lawsuits. How many homicidal lunatics have purchased guns? Yet he mounts no campaign to close the weapons factories. Even if we admit, for the sake of argument, that Ben and Sarah were influenced by a film, only a lawyer in search of a client could see in this an indictment of the entertainment industry and not of the teenage killers and those who reared them.

Grisham disparages the First Amendment (which also protects the films that have sprung from Grisham's own brainless works of fiction) and those who believe in it. He has nothing to say, however, about the Second Amendment, which permits gun-toting crazies to litter the American landscape with bodies. To my mind, his priorities are severely distorted. But then, the First Amendment protects even the views of those who don't believe in it. In America, we call that freedom of speech.

It gives me a shiver of fear when an influential lawyer and writer argues, as Grisham does, that a particular work of art *should never have been allowed to be made*. Strangle art in its infancy, he suggests, and society will be a better place. One might more persuasively argue that cold-blooded murderers should be strangled in their infancy. Yet as with human infants, we can never know the outcome of nascent art, and so both must be protected and nurtured, precisely for society's sake. For it is only a small step from silencing art to silencing artists, and then to silencing those who support them, and so on, until, while we may one day live in a lawyer's paradise, we will surely find ourselves in a human hell.

• • •

Comprehension

1. In paragraph 1, Stone says that the function of an artist is to hold a mirror up to nature. What does he mean? How does this statement help explain why he made a movie as violent as *Natural Born Killers*?

2. In paragraph 1, Stone suggests that Grisham's attack against *Natural Born Killers* is a witch hunt. What does he mean? Do you agree?

3. In criticizing Grisham's article, Stone implies that Grisham is engaging in *post hoc* reasoning. At what point in his essay does Stone suggest this? Do you agree that Grisham's article is flawed by *post hoc* reasoning?

4. According to Stone, what impact does *Natural Born Killers* have on audiences? What impact does he say television has on viewers?

5. In paragraphs 7 and 8, Stone says that Grisham targets his movie while ignoring other possible causes of violence. What other causes can you identify? How persuasive is Stone's line of reasoning?

Purpose and Audience

1. What preconceptions does Stone have about movie violence? Does he expect his readers to share his ideas? How do you know?

2. Do you think Stone respects his readers' intelligence, or does he talk down to his audience? Explain.

3. Why do you think Stone wrote this essay? What is his purpose?

4. Is Stone's argument likely to appeal to those who already think television and movies are too violent? Does he make any attempt to appeal to readers who are hostile to his position? If so, where?

Style and Structure

1. Stone begins his essay by comparing Grisham's attack against *Natural Born Killers* to a witch hunt. Is this a good strategy? Is it likely to alienate some of his readers? Why, or why not?

2. Where does Stone attempt to refute Grisham's major points? How successful is he in doing so?

3. In paragraph 5, Stone concedes some points to his opposition. Is this a good strategy, or should he have denied any connection between movie violence and societal violence?

4. In paragraph 8, Stone asks why those who want to censor him don't consider the implications of the Second Amendment, "which permits gun-toting crazies to litter the American landscape with bodies." What effect does the phrase *gun-toting crazies* have on you? Is Stone overstating his case?

5. How effective is Stone's conclusion? Does it adequately restate his position? Is his point about lawyers valid, or is it an *ad hominem* attack? Explain.

Vocabulary Projects

1. Define each of the following words as it is used in this selection.

scapegoats (1)   retribution (2)
cyberspace (1)   perpetrators (6)
specter (2)   nascent (9)

2. At times, Stone's feelings come through. Underline words and phrases in the essay that show his attitude toward Grisham. How would you describe his tone?

Journal Entry

Do you believe a link exists between movie violence and societal violence? Do you think that seeing a movie such as *Natural Born Killers* can cause someone to do something he or she would not normally do?

Writing Workshop

1. Do you believe, as Stone does, that filmmakers should not be legally responsible for the consequences of their films? Or, do you agree with Michael Zimecki (page 691), who says that filmmakers should be held liable for damages caused by their products? Write an essay arguing for one side or the other.
2. Stone says that people like Grisham are creating a society of people who no longer have to take responsibility for their actions. Do you agree with Stone? Write an essay arguing for or against this position. Use your own experiences as well as examples from the news to support your points.
3. Assume you are either Ben Darras or Sarah Edmondson. Write a letter to Stone arguing that he is responsible for the crime you committed. Use the facts of the case as presented in Stone's essay to support your argument.

Combining the Patterns

Stone includes several paragraphs organized according to a **cause-and-effect** pattern. Find two of these paragraphs, and determine how they help Stone support his thesis.

Thematic Connections

- "Thirty-Eight Who Saw Murder Didn't Call the Police" (page 120)
- "Who Killed Benny Paret?" (page 346)
- "The Power of Words in Wartime" (page 377)

MICHAEL ZIMECKI

Violent Films Cry "Fire" in Crowded Theaters

Michael Zimecki was born in Detroit in 1950 and received degrees from the University of Pittsburgh and Carnegie Mellon. For many years, he was a medical writer affiliated with the University of Pittsburgh Medical School. After receiving a law degree from Duquesne University, he established a private practice in Pittsburgh.

Background on Hollywood and copycat crimes: Zimecki contributed the following essay to the *National Law Journal* in 1996 in the aftermath of the torching of a New York City subway token booth attendant, a crime similar to a scene depicted in the movie *The Money Train*. The following year, a Kentucky teenager killed three girls after firing on a prayer group; this crime was allegedly influenced by a dream sequence in *The Basketball Diaries* in which Leonardo DiCaprio played a student who gunned down his classmates. Up through the 1960s, Hollywood adhered to a production code that stringently limited onscreen violence. This code included the provision that "methods of crime shall not be explicitly presented." Its purpose was, in part, to ensure that movie violence would not lead viewers to copycat crimes. That code was extensively revised in 1966, however, opening the door to the graphic depictions of violence that prevail today. In this essay, Zimecki argues that such violent images in the media undoubtedly contribute to real-life violence.

1   The late Richard Weaver, professor of rhetoric at the University of Chicago, was fond of reminding his students that "ideas have consequences."

2   Bad ideas can have abominable consequences. Nevertheless, U.S. courts have permitted moviemakers, magazine publishers, and other members of the mass media to represent some of the most odious and repulsive scenes imaginable, "on the confidence," as Circuit Judge Alvin B. Run once said, "that the benefits society reaps from the free flow and exchange of ideas outweigh the costs society endures by receiving reprehensible or dangerous ideas." *Herceg v. Hustler Magazine Inc.,* 814 F.2d 1017 (1987).

3   In 1995, a few days after Thanksgiving, a group of five young men torched a subway token booth in Brooklyn, N.Y., trapping the toll clerk inside. He died of his burns within the week. The act that caused his death bore an eerie resemblance to two scenes from the recently released Columbia Pictures movie *Money Train*. In the movie, a pyromaniac sets token booths on fire by squirting a flammable liquid through the token slots and throwing in a lighted match.

Senate Majority Leader Bob Dole, the *Wall Street Journal,* the head of the New York Transit Authority and New York's police commissioners were quick to blame the movie for sparking a copycat crime. As it turned out, the movie may not have been responsible. Shortly after his arrest, the youth accused of squirting the flammable liquid denied that the movie had any connection to the incident. In a letter to the *New York Times,* Jack Valenti, President and CEO of the Motion Picture Association of America, could scarcely contain his glee. 4

For its part, Columbia Pictures steadfastly maintained that it was merely holding a mirror up to life, noting that its film was based on a series of attacks in New York subway stations in 1988. 5

It may be premature to conclude that *Money Train* did or did not play a part in the 1995 Thanksgiving incident: As of this writing, police have declined to say whether any of the men in custody saw the movie. Moreover, two suspects remain at large, and the match-thrower, who could face a capital murder charge, has not been identified. 6

One thing is certain: Life and art exert a strong tug on each other. 7

Money Train was not the only such example. In 1993, a Pennsylvania youth died after he attempted to duplicate a scene from *The Program.* In a peculiar display of male bravado, he lay down on the center line of a highway and was run over by a car. 8

In an earlier era, the perpetrators of the 1974 Hi-Fi Murders in Ogden, Utah, forced their victims to drink liquid Drano after watching a similar scene in the Clint Eastwood picture *Magnum Force.* 9

That same year, a 9-year-old girl was raped with a bottle by a group of juveniles at a San Francisco beach — just days after the nationwide telecast of the film *Born Innocent,* which showed a young girl being sexually assaulted with a plunger. The parents of the San Francisco girl subsequently sued NBC for her physical and emotional injuries, alleging that they were attributable to the broadcaster's negligence and recklessness in airing the film. *Olivia N. v. National Broadcasting Co. Inc.,* 178 Cal. Rptr. 888, 126 Cal. App. 3d 488 (1982). Although the suit proved to be unsuccessful, it was nonetheless a signal attempt to expand tort liability for speech outside the area of defamation. 10

Courts Support Filmmakers

U.S. courts have routinely rejected attempts to hold filmmakers liable in tort for the harm they cause. Plaintiffs' attorneys seeking recovery on a theory of strict products liability have encountered some of the same difficulties that have impeded anti-gun and anti-tobacco litigation: Movies are meant to be seen, just as guns are meant to be fired and cigarettes to be smoked, and there is nothing defective about a product that accomplishes its purpose all too well. In fact, brutally violent films are especially popular box-office fare. 11

The biggest obstacle to plaintiffs' attorneys, however, isn't the courts'   12
rejection of claims based on negligence, nuisance, or products liability. It's
the courts' narrow interpretation of "incitement."

Speech that advocates violence but that does not incite imminent   13
harm is protected by the First Amendment under the U.S. Supreme
Court's holding in *Brandenburg v. Ohio,* 396 U.S. 444, 23 L.Ed.2d 430, 89
S.Ct. 1827 (1969).

In *Brandenburg,* the high court overturned the conviction of a Klans-   14
man under Ohio's criminal syndicalism statute for saying that "there
might have to be some revengence [sic] taken," if "our President, our Congress, our Supreme Court continues to suppress the white, Caucasian
race." The finding of the court was that the mere advocacy of violence is
not enough.

As Justice William O. Douglas wrote in his concurring opinion, the   15
line between what is permissible and what is not is "the line between ideas
and overt acts." The Klansman was on the constitutionally protected side
of the line because he was not advocating violent deeds now, in the temporal present; his message had an abstract, rather than an urgent, quality. By
contrast, someone who falsely shouts "fire" in a crowded theater has
impermissibly crossed the line because his speech is "brigaded with
action."

But what about a film that shouts "fire" in that same, proverbially   16
crowded theater? Film industry executives maintain that movies portray
violence but do not advocate it; to the contrary, industry spokespeople
claim, the perpetrators of movie violence typically get their comeuppance
by film's end.

Unfortunately, filmmakers say one thing while showing another. As   17
social psychologist Albert Bandura observed more than 20 years ago, the
message of most violent films is not that "crime does not pay," but rather
that the wages of violent sin are pretty good except for an occasional
mishap.

Indifferent to the anti-social repercussions of their cinematic special   18
effects, violent movies such as *Money Train* advocate violence implicitly, if not
explicitly. Violence is as much a product of external reinforcement as internal pathology. By modeling, legitimizing, and sanctioning violence, movies
do not just loosen restraints on those who are already predisposed to violence. Violent movies actively promote aggressive behavior as a social norm.

Legally Flawed Definition

By any definition other than the legal one, this would constitute   19
"incitement." The rub, of course, is that harm delayed is no harm at all
under the *Brandenburg* standard, which distinguishes violence that takes to
the streets from violence that erupts in the theater. While fine in theory,
the *Brandenburg* concept of "speech brigaded with action" gets reduced in

practice to "Take it outside, boys!" — which is poor advice to a schoolchild and hardly more sagacious as a constitutional principle.

The difference between a risk of eventual harm and immediate bodily injury has been minimized of late in the toxic torts arena, where medical monitoring awards embrace the principle that a polluter should not be allowed to escape responsibility for his actions simply because environmentally induced cancers are late-developing. Violence, too, can fester for years. 20

Unfortunately, constitutional law has been slow to appreciate the toxic power of words, slow to recognize that exposure to cruel and degrading images is like exposure to a carcinogen, slower still to understand that speech and act occupy a continuum of cause and effect. 21

The premiere of *Money Train* may not have been a substantial factor in bringing about the death of subway token clerk Harry Kaufman. But movies are a significant cause of the violence that has become so prevalent in our society. Film-inspired violence may not be "imminent" in the constitutional sense, but the constitutional difference between "I will kill you now" and "I will kill you later" is cold comfort to the victims of movie-modeled murder. 22

The problem is that we, as a society, are becoming increasingly deadened and desensitized to violence through repeated exposure to its display. Under *Brandenburg,* the onslaught continues. But film industry executives should take heed: Violence is now so imminent in our society that a wrong look can get you shot on many street corners. The hour has come at last, and the rough beast that the poet William Butler Yeats warned about is already born.* As we continue to split hairs, failing to address the need for legislation, we can take comfort in the cliché, "Enjoy yourself. It's later than you think." 23

* * *

Comprehension

1. According to Zimecki, why have courts in the United States allowed moviemakers and magazine publishers to "represent some of the most odious and repulsive scenes imaginable" (2)?

2. In paragraph 7, Zimecki says, "Life and art exert a strong tug on each other." What does he mean? What examples does he offer to support this statement?

3. Why have courts routinely rejected attempts to hold filmmakers liable on the theory of product liability? How has the narrow interpretation of *incitement* created an obstacle for plaintiffs?

---

* EDS. NOTE — "And what rough beast, its hour come round at last, / Slouches toward Bethlehem to be born?" (from "The Second Coming" by William Butler Yeats).

4. According to Zimecki, how do certain types of film shout "fire" in a crowded theater?

5. What does Zimecki mean when he says, "Unfortunately, constitutional law has been slow to appreciate the toxic power of words" (21)?

Purpose and Audience

1. At what point does Zimecki state his thesis? Why does he wait as long as he does?

2. Is this essay aimed at an audience of lawyers or at a more general audience? How do you know?

3. What is Zimecki's purpose in writing this essay? Is it to change attitudes? To bring about legislation? To change policy? Explain.

Style and Structure

1. Zimecki begins his essay with a quotation by Richard Weaver. Why do you think he chose this quotation? What other strategies could he have used to introduce his essay?

2. This essay appeared in the *National Law Journal*. If Zimecki were to rewrite the essay for *People* magazine, what kinds of changes would he need to make? What additional information would he need to provide? Explain.

3. Do you think Zimecki undercuts his case by conceding the point that "*Money Train* may not have been a substantial factor in bringing about the death of subway token clerk Harry Kaufman" (22)? Explain.

4. What evidence does Zimecki use to support his assertions? Why do you think he chose this type of support?

5. Zimecki concludes his essay with a quotation that he admits is a **cliché**. How effective is this strategy? Would another quotation be more effective? Explain your reasoning.

Vocabulary Projects

1. Define each of the following words as it is used in this selection.

repulsive (2)	negligence (10)	brigaded (15)
reaps (2)	defamation (10)	repercussions (18)
endures (2)	tort (11)	pathology (18)
reprehensible (2)	liability (11)	norm (18)
pyromaniac (3)	incitement (12)	sagacious (19)
capital (6)	advocacy (14)	toxic (21)
attributable (10)	impermissibly (15)	carcinogen (21)

2. What is the dictionary definition of *incitement*? What additional meanings does Zimecki say the word has acquired?

Journal Entry

Do you believe the courts should hold filmmakers responsible for the effects of their movies? What might be the possible effects on movies of such a change in policy?

Writing Workshop

1. Write an essay arguing that moviemakers should not be held responsible for the consequences of their films. Consider the effect on free expression of holding moviemakers liable years after their movies are released. Make sure you refute Zimecki's arguments against your position.

2. Using as evidence several violent movies you have seen, write an essay arguing that by glorifying violence, certain films encourage violent behavior.

3. How do you think Zimecki would respond to Stone's essay? Choose a section of Stone's essay, and refute it using any of Zimecki's points that are relevant to the issue.

Combining the Patterns

In paragraph 15, Zimecki uses **comparison and contrast** to make his point. What point is he making? Would a paragraph of cause and effect be just as effective here? Why, or why not?

Thematic Connections

- "Thirty-Eight Who Saw Murder Didn't Call the Police" (page 120)
- "A Peaceful Woman Explains Why She Carries a Gun" (page 371)
- "The Wife-Beater" (page 532)

WRITING ASSIGNMENTS FOR ARGUMENTATION

1. Write an essay discussing whether parents have a right to spank their children. If your position is that they do, under what circumstances? What limitations should exist? If your position is that they do not, how should parents discipline children? How should they deal with inappropriate behavior?

2. Assume that a library in your town has decided that certain books are objectionable and has removed them from the shelves. Write a letter to your local paper arguing for or against the library's actions. Make a list of the major arguments that might be advanced against your position, and try to refute some of them in your letter. Remember to respect the views of your audience and to address them in a respectful manner.

3. In Great Britain, cities began installing video surveillance systems in public areas in the 1970s. Police departments claim that these cameras help them do their jobs more efficiently. For example, such cameras enabled police to identify and capture terrorists who bombed the London subway in 2005. Opponents of the cameras say that the police are creating a society that severely compromises the right of personal privacy. How do you feel about this issue? Assume that the police department in your city is proposing to install cameras in the downtown and other pedestrian areas. Write an editorial for your local paper presenting your views on the topic.

4. Write an essay discussing under what circumstances, if any, animals should be used for scientific experimentation.

5. Write an essay arguing for or against the proposition that women soldiers should be able to serve in combat situations.

6. Research some criminal cases that resulted in the death penalty. Write an essay using these accounts to support your arguments either for or against the death penalty. Be sure to give credit to your sources. (See the Appendix for information about documentation.)

7. Write an argumentative essay discussing whether any situations exist when a nation has an obligation to go (or not to go) to war.

8. Since the events of September 11, 2001, the idea of arming pilots of commercial passenger planes has been debated. Those opposed to arming pilots claim that the risks — that a gun will fall into the hands of hijackers or that a passenger will be accidentally shot — outweigh any benefits. Those who support the idea say that the pilot is the last line of defense and must be able to defend the cockpit from terrorists. Due to public pressure in favor of arming pilots, a small trial program has been instituted. Do you think all pilots of commercial airplanes should be armed? Write an essay presenting your views on this subject.

9. In the Declaration of Independence, Jefferson says that all individuals are entitled to "life, liberty and the pursuit of happiness." Write an essay arguing that these rights are not absolute.

10. Write an argumentative essay on one of these topics: Should high school students be required to recite the Pledge of Allegiance at the start of each school day? Should college students be required to do community

service? Should public school teachers be required to pass periodic competency tests? Should the legal drinking age be raised (or lowered)? Should states be required to educate the children of illegal immigrants?

COLLABORATIVE ACTIVITY FOR ARGUMENTATION

Working with three other students, select a controversial topic—one not covered in any of the debates in this chapter—that interests all of you. (You can review the previous Writing Assignments for Argumentation to get ideas.) State your topic the way a topic is stated in a formal debate:

Resolved: The United States should ban all human cloning.

Then, divide into two two-member teams, and decide which team will take the pro position and which will take the con. Each team should list the arguments on its side of the issue and then write two or three paragraphs summarizing its position. Finally, each team should stage a ten-minute debate—five minutes for each side—in front of the class. (The pro side presents its argument first.) At the end of each debate, the class should discuss which team has presented the stronger arguments.

INTERNET ASSIGNMENT FOR ARGUMENTATION: SHOULD U.S. CITIZENS BE REQUIRED TO CARRY NATIONAL IDENTITY CARDS?

Write an essay arguing for or against the implementation of national identity cards in the United States. Use the following Web sites to explore the two viewpoints and their implications.

American Association of Motor Vehicles Administrators
<aamva.net/IDSecurity>
The American Association of Motor Vehicles Administrators (AAMVA) site offers additional resources on legislation, statistical information, and press releases regarding the national ID debate and the AAMVA's plan to convert the states' driver's license programs into an effective national ID system.

Electronic Privacy Information Center
<epic.org/privacy/id_cards>
This national-ID-cards Web page, sponsored by the Electronic Privacy Information Center, gives links to several articles and current news features regarding the use of national ID cards all over the world and several resources for additional information.

CATO Institute
<cato.org/tech/tk/010928-tk.html>
This site, sponsored by the CATO Institute's department of telecommunications and technology, features an article by Adam Thierer that discusses problems that might arise with implementing a national ID card.

Computer Professionals for Social Responsibility
<cpsr.org/program/natlID/natlIDfaq.html>

Sponsored by Computer Professionals for Social Responsibility, this site includes a helpful FAQ list about plans for national ID implementation and its relation to terrorism. The site also specifically addresses how certain systems might and might not work.

Smart Cards
<opinionjournal.com/extra/?id=95001336>
In this article for *Opinion Journal,* Larry Ellison, CEO of Oracle Corp., writes in support of a unified national ID system and offers ways of forming one based on the security and ID systems already in place.

INTERNET ASSIGNMENT FOR ARGUMENTATION: SHOULD GAY AND LESBIAN COUPLES BE ALLOWED TO ADOPT?

Focusing on one of the following three issues — the prejudice experienced by children of gay and lesbian parents, the example that homosexual parents set for their children, and the influence that homosexual parents have on a child's sexual orientation — write an essay that argues for or against adoption rights for gays and lesbians. Use the following Web sites for additional background information to support your argument.

American Civil Liberties Union
<aclu.org/LesbianGayRights/LesbianGayRightsMain.cfm>
This American Civil Liberties Union page for lesbian and gay rights includes ACLU press releases, legal documents, and other resources regarding parenting and adoption issues.

Same-Sex Parenting: Are Lesbians and Gays Good Parents?
<religioustolerance.org/hom_pare.htm>
This site includes research on the effectiveness of parenting and child development in homosexual households, as well as an overview of the legal status of same-sex adoptions in various states and countries.

Technical Report: Coparent or Second-Parent Adoption
by Same-Sex Parents
<aap.org/policy/020008t.html>
From the American Academy of Pediatrics, this report discusses the current legal situation of homosexual parents, options for homosexuals who want children, and the development of children who grow up in households headed by homosexuals.

Family Research Council
<frc.org/get/cu02c2.cfm>
This site includes several feature articles sponsored by the Family Research Council that provide arguments against allowing homosexual men and women to adopt.

INTERNET ASSIGNMENT FOR ARGUMENTATION: SHOULD THE DRAFT BE REINSTATED IN THE UNITED STATES?

Although no draft exists today, young men must nonetheless register on their eighteenth birthday for selective service. If Congress were to reinstate compulsory conscription, all young men registered for selective service would be drafted. Imagine that Congress was, in fact, planning to pass such a bill. Then, write an essay to your representative explaining why you think the bill should be supported or defeated. Visit the following Web sites to find additional information to support your argument.

Selective Service System
<sss.gov>
This site provides history, information, and answers to frequently asked questions about the Selective Service System—a system requiring American men between the ages of eighteen and twenty-five to register in a "peacetime draft" so that they can be called for military service in the event of an emergency.

Why We Need the Draft Back
<washingtonpost.com/wp-dyn/articles/A19322-2004Jun30.html>
In this column, former Nixon speechwriter Noel Koch (who volunteered for the army in 1957) discusses the various (and not so obvious) merits of a draft.

Central Committee for Conscientious Objectors (CCCO)
The Central Committee for Conscientious Objectors "supports and promotes individual and collective resistance to war and preparations for war." A particularly interesting article on the site is "Should There Be a Draft?" which considers among other topics why some typically "anti-war people are speaking for a draft."

The Cato Institute: Conscription
<cato.org/defense-studies/conscription.html>
The Web site for the Cato Institute, a libertarian think tank, includes articles about the history and future of the draft in America. Economist Walter Oi provides a particularly thoughtful analysis in his article, "The Virtue of the All-Volunteer Force."

INTERNET ASSIGNMENT FOR ARGUMENTATION: IS WAL-MART GOOD FOR AMERICA?

Wal-Mart employs 1.2 million workers at its 3,600 stores, making it the largest employer in the United States after the federal government. However, it has also sent countless manufacturing jobs overseas, where labor is cheap. This is just one of the reasons Wal-Mart has lately come under attack. Using the following Internet resources, write an essay demonstrating how Wal-Mart has helped—or harmed—American workers, the American public, or the U.S. economy.

Wal-Mart
<walmart.com>
Browse Wal-Mart's online store for news about the store. Under the "Wal-Mart Facts" section of the site, you can read "Wal-Mart Sets the Record Straight," where the store differentiates between the myths and truths about its employment practices.

Is Wal-Mart Good for America?
<pbs.org/wgbh/pages/frontline/shows/walmart/>
This *Frontline* piece provides extensive history, fact sheets and perspectives on Wal-Mart, including interviews with former and current employees and executives and links to other resources, such as the *Los Angeles Times*'s Pulitzer Prize–winning reports on the company.

The Wal-Mart You Don't Know
<fastcompany.com/magazine/77/walmart.html>
This article, published in *Fast Company* magazine, discusses the flip side to Wal-Mart's commitment to low prices: namely, the pressure Wal-Mart puts on its suppliers.

Time 100: Sam Walton
<time.com/time/time100/builder/profile/walton.html>
Wal-Mart founder Sam Walton is profiled in this article from *Time Magazine*'s "100 Most Important People of the Century" issue.

INTERNET ASSIGNMENT FOR ARGUMENTATION: DOES MEDIA VIOLENCE CAUSE SOCIETAL VIOLENCE?

Write an essay arguing for or against holding the television and movie industries responsible for violence in our society. Use the following Web sites to explore the two viewpoints and their implications.

Media Violence
<media-awareness.ca/english/issues/violence/index.cfm>
This site, sponsored by the Media Awareness Network, includes feature articles, statistics, and legislation on media violence.

Culture Shock
<pbs.org/wgbh/cultureshock/index_1.html>
This companion site to the PBS series *Culture Shock* deals with art, cultural values, and freedom of expression in the arts.

MediaWise
<mediafamily.org/index.shtml>
This site, dedicated to education and research, focuses on "the positive and harmful effects of media on children and youth." It is sponsored by the National Institute on Media and the Family.

15
Combining the Patterns

Most paragraphs combine several patterns of development. In the following paragraph, for example, Paul Hoffman uses narration, exemplification, and cause and effect to explain why we tend to see numbers as more than "instruments of enumeration":

Topic sentence

Narration

Exemplification

Cause and effect

The idea that numbers are not mere instruments of enumeration but are sacred, perfect, friendly, lucky, or evil goes back to antiquity. In the sixth century B.C. Pythagoras, whom schoolchildren associate with the famous theorem that in a right triangle the square of the hypotenuse always equals the sum of the squares of its sides, not only performed brilliant mathematics but made a religion out of numbers. In numerology, the number 12 has always represented completeness, as in the 12 months of the year, the 12 signs of the zodiac, the 12 hours of the day, the 12 gods of Olympus, the 12 labors of Hercules, the 12 tribes of Israel, the 12 apostles of Jesus, the 12 days of Christmas, and, more recently perhaps, the 12 eggs in an egg carton. Since 13 exceeds 12 by only one, the number lies just beyond completeness and, hence, is restless to the point of being evil.

Like paragraphs, essays do not usually follow a single pattern of development; in fact, nearly every essay, including those in this text, combines a variety of patterns. Even though an essay may be organized primarily as, say, a comparison and contrast, it is still likely to include paragraphs, and even groups of paragraphs, shaped by other patterns of development. In fact, combining various patterns in a single essay gives writers the flexibility to express their ideas most effectively. For this reason, each essay in Chapters 6 through 14 of this text is followed by Combining the Patterns questions that focus on how the essay uses (or might use) other patterns of development along with its dominant pattern.

Structuring an Essay by Combining the Patterns

Essays that combine various patterns of development, like essays structured primarily by a single pattern, include an **introduction**, several **body paragraphs**, and a **conclusion**. The introduction typically ends with the thesis statement that gives the essay its focus, and the conclusion often restates that thesis or summarizes the essay's main points. Each body paragraph (or group of paragraphs) is structured according to the pattern of development that best suits the material it develops.

Suppose you are planning your answer to the following question on a take-home essay exam for a sociology of religion course:

> What factors attract people to cults? For what reasons do they join? Support your answer with specific examples that illustrate how cults recruit and retain members.

The wording of this exam question clearly suggests both **cause and effect** ("for what reasons") and **exemplification** ("specific examples"); in addition, you may decide to develop your response with **definition** and **process**.

An informal outline for your essay might look like this:

Introduction:	Definition of *cult* (defined by negation — telling what it is *not* — and by comparison and contrast with *religion*). Thesis statement: Using aggressive recruitment tactics and isolating potential members from their families and past lives, cults appeal to new recruits by offering them a highly structured environment.
Cause and effect:	Why people join cults
Process:	How cults recruit new members
Exemplification:	Tactics various cults use to retain members (series of brief examples)
Conclusion:	Restatement of thesis or review of key points

This essay will supply all the information the exam question asks for, with material organized and developed clearly and logically.

Combining the Patterns: Revising and Editing

When you revise an essay that combines several patterns of development, consider the items on the revision checklist on page 54, as well as any of the more specific revision checklists in Chapers 6 through 14 that apply to the patterns in your essay. As you edit your essay, refer to the editing checklists on pages 71, 73, and 76, and to the individual editing checklists in Chapters 6 through 14. You may also wish to consult the Grammar in Context sections that appear throughout the book, as well as the one that follows.

GRAMMAR IN CONTEXT: Agreement with Indefinite Pronouns

A **pronoun** is a word that takes the place of a noun or another pronoun in a sentence. Unlike most pronouns, an **indefinite pronoun** (*anyone, either, each,* and so on) does not refer to a specific person or thing.

Subject-Verb Agreement.   Pronoun subjects must agree in number with their verbs: singular pronouns (*I, he, she, it,* and so on) take singular verbs, and plural pronouns (*we, they,* and so on) take plural verbs.

"I have learned much as a scavenger" (Eighner 713).

"We were free like comets in the heavens" (Truong 708).

Indefinite pronoun subjects also must agree in number with their verbs: singular indefinite pronouns take singular verbs, and plural indefinite pronouns take plural verbs. Most indefinite pronouns are singular, but some are plural.

SUBJECT–VERB AGREEMENT WITH INDEFINITE PRONOUN SUBJECTS

SINGULAR INDEFINITE PRONOUNS

another	anyone	everyone	one	each
either	neither	anything	everything	

"Everyone was darker or lighter than we were" (Truong 709).

"Everything seems to stink" (Eighner 718).

PLURAL INDEFINITE PRONOUNS

both	many	few	several	others

"Many are discarded for minor imperfections that can be pared away" (Eighner 715).

Note: A few indefinite pronouns — *some, all, any, more, most,* and *none* — may be either singular or plural, depending on their meaning in the sentence.

SINGULAR: Some of the moth's suffering is difficult for Woolf to witness. (*Some* refers to *suffering,* so the verb is singular.)

(continued on next page)

(continued from previous page)

PLURAL: <u>Some</u> of the moths Woolf has seen in the past <u>were</u> creatures of the night, but the moth that captures her attention in "The Death of the Moth" appears in the daytime. (*Some* refers to *moths*, so the verb is plural.)

Pronoun-Antecedent Agreement. An **antecedent** is the noun or pronoun a pronoun refers to in a sentence. Pronouns must agree in number with their antecedents.

Use a singular pronoun to refer to a singular indefinite pronoun antecedent.

<u>Each</u> day has <u>its</u> surprises for Lars Eighner and his dog Lizbeth.

Use a plural pronoun to refer to a plural indefinite pronoun antecedent.

<u>Many</u> of the people who pass Eighner and Lizbeth avert <u>their</u> eyes.

Note: Although the indefinite pronoun *everyone* is singular, it is often used with a plural pronoun in everyday speech and informal writing.

INFORMAL: <u>Everyone</u> turns <u>their</u> heads when Eighner and Lizbeth walk by.

This usage is generally acceptable in informal situations, but college writing requires correct pronoun-antecedent agreement.

CORRECT: <u>Everyone</u> turns <u>his or her</u> head when Eighner and Lizbeth walk by.

CORRECT: <u>People</u> turn <u>their</u> heads when Eighner and Lizbeth walk by.

For more practice in avoiding agreement problems with indefinite pronouns, visit Exercise Central at <bedfordsmartins.com/patterns/indefinitepronouns>.

The essays in this chapter illustrate how different patterns of development work together in a single piece of writing. The first two essays — "The Park" by Michael Huu Truong, a student, and "On Dumpster Diving" by Lars Eighner — include annotations that identify the various patterns these writers use. Truong's essay relies primarily on narration, description, and exemplification to express his memories of childhood. Eighner's combines sections of definition, exemplification, classification and division, cause and effect, comparison and contrast, and process; at the same time, he tells the story (narration) and provides vivid details (description) of his life as a homeless person. Following these annotated essays are three additional selections that combine patterns: Virginia Woolf's classic essay "The Death of the Moth," Jonathan Swift's satire "A Modest Proposal," and

Richard Rodriguez's autobiographical essay "Strange Tools." Each of the essays in this chapter is followed by the same types of questions that accompany the other reading selections in the text.

A STUDENT WRITER: Combining the Patterns

This essay was written by Michael Huu Truong for a first-year composition course in response to the assignment "Write an essay about the person and/or place that defined your childhood."

The Park

Background

My childhood did not really begin until I came to this country from the jungle of Vietnam. I can't really remember much from this period, and the things I do remember are vague images that I have no desire or intention to discuss. However, my childhood in the States was a lot different, especially after I met my friend James. While it lasted, it was paradise.

Thesis statement

Narrative begins

It was a cold wintry day in February after a big snowstorm — the first I'd ever seen. My lips were chapped, my hands were frozen stiff, and my cheeks were burning from the biting wind, and yet I loved it. I especially loved the snow. I had come from a country where the closest things to snow were white paint and cotton balls. But now I was in America. On that frosty afternoon, I was determined to build a snowman. I had seen them in books, and I had heard they could talk. I knew they could come alive, and I couldn't wait.

Description: effects of cold

Comparison and contrast: U.S. vs. Vietnam

"Eyryui roeow ierog," said a voice that came out of nowhere. I turned around, and right in my face was a short, red-faced (probably from the cold wind) Korean kid with a dirty, runny nose. I responded, "Wtefkjkr ruyjft gsdfr" in my own tongue. We understood each other perfectly, and we expressed our understanding with a smile. Together, we built our first snowman. We were disappointed that evening when the snowman just stood there; however, I was happy because I had made my first friend.

Description: James

Narration: the first day

Ever since then we've been a team like Abbott and Costello (or, when my cousin joined us, The Three Stooges). The two of us were inseparable. We could've made the greatest Krazy Glue commercial ever.

Analogies

1

2

3

4

Narration: what they did that summer

The summer that followed the big snowstorm, from what   5
I can recall, was awesome. We were free like comets in the
heavens, and we did whatever our hearts wanted. For the most
part, our desires were fulfilled in a little park across the street.
This park was ours; it was like our own planet guarded by our
own robot army (disguised as trees). Together we fought against
the bigger people who always tried to invade and take over our
world. The enemy could never conquer our fortress because they
would have to destroy our robots, penetrate our force field, and
then defeat us; this last feat would be impossible.

Narrative continues

Examples: what they banished

This park was our fantasy land where everything we   6
wished for came true and everything we hated was banished
forever. We banished vegetables, cheese, bigger people, and —
of course — girls. The land was enchanted, and we could be
whatever we felt like. We were super ninjas one day and
millionaires the next; we became the heroes we idolized and

Examples: superhero fantasies

lived the lives we dreamed about. I had the strength of Bruce
Lee and Superman; James possessed the power of Clint
Eastwood and the Bionic Man. My weapons were the skills of
Bruce and a cape. James, however, needed a real weapon for
Clint, and the weapon he made was awesome. The Death Ray
could destroy a building with one blast, and it even had a shield
so that James was always protected. Even with all his mighty
weapons and gadgets, though, he was still no match for
Superman and Bruce Lee. Every day, we fought until death (or
until our parents called us for dinner).

Narrative continues

When we became bored with our super powers, the park   7
became a giant spaceship. We traveled all over the Universe,
conquering and exploring strange new worlds and mysterious
planets. Our ship was a top-secret indestructible space warship

Examples: new worlds and planets

called the X–007. We went to Mars, Venus, Pluto, and other
alien planets, destroying all the monsters we could find. When
necessary, our spacecraft was transformed into a submarine for
deep-sea adventures. We found lost cities, unearthed treasures,
and saved Earth by destroying all the sea monsters that were
plotting against us. We became heroes — just like Superman,
Bruce Lee, the Bionic Man, and Clint Eastwood.

Cause and effect: prospect of school leads to problems

James and I had the time of our lives in the park that   8
summer. It was great — until we heard about the horror of
starting school. Shocked and terrified, we ran to our fortress to

escape. For some reason, though, our magic kingdom had lost its powers. We fought hard that evening, trying to keep the bigger people out of our planet, but the battle was soon lost. Bruce Lee, Superman, the Bionic Man, and Clint Eastwood had all lost their special powers.

Narrative continues

School wasn't as bad as we'd thought it would be. The 9 first day, James and I sat there with our hands folded. We didn't talk or move, and we didn't dare look at each other (we would've cracked up because we always made these goofy faces). Even though we had pens that could be transformed into weapons, we were still scared.

Description: school

Everyone was darker or lighter than we were, and the 10 teacher was speaking a strange language (English). James and I giggled as she talked. We giggled softly when everyone else talked, and they laughed out loud when it was our turn to speak.

Narrative continues

The day dragged on, and all we wanted to do was go home 11 and rebuild our fortress. Finally, after an eternity, it was almost three o'clock. James and I sat at the edge of our seats as we counted under our breath: "10, 9, 8, 7, 6, 5, 4, 3, 2, 1." At last, the bell sounded. We dashed for the door and raced home and across the street — and then we stopped. We stood still in the middle of the street with our hearts pounding like the beats of a drum. The cool September wind began to pick up, and everything

Description: the fence

became silent. We stood there and watched the metal of the fence reflect the beautiful colors of the sun. It was beautiful, and yet we hated everything about it. The new metal fence separated us from our fortress, our planet, our spaceship, our submarine — and, most important of all, from our heroes and our dreams.

We stood there for a long time. As the sun slowly turned 12 red and sank beneath the ground, so did our dreams, heroes, and hearts. Darkness soon devoured the park, and after a while we walked home with only the memories of the summer that came after the big snowstorm.

Points for Special Attention

Writing a Personal Experience Essay. Michael's instructor specified that he was to write an essay about a person or place to help his readers — other students — understand what his childhood was like. Because it was a personal experience essay, Michael was free to use the first-person pronouns *I* and *we,* as well as contractions, although neither would be acceptable in a more formal essay.

Thesis Statement.   Because Michael's primary purpose in this essay was to communicate personal feelings and impressions, an argumentative thesis statement (such as "If every television in the United States disappeared, more people would have childhoods like mine") would have been inappropriate. Still, Michael states his thesis explicitly in order to unify his essay around the dominant impression he wants to convey: "While it lasted, it was paradise."

Combining the Patterns.   Michael also had more specific purposes, and these determined the patterns that shape his essay. His essay's dominant pattern is *narration,* but to help students visualize the person (James) and the place (the park) he discusses, he includes sections that *describe* and give concrete, specific *examples* as well as summarize his daily routine. These patterns work together to create an essay that *defines* the nature of his childhood.

Transitions.   The transitions between the individual sentences and paragraphs of Michael's essay—"now," "Ever since," "The summer that followed the big snowstorm"—serve primarily to move readers through time. This is appropriate because narration is the dominant pattern governing his essay's overall structure.

Detail.   Michael's essay is full of specific detail—for example, quoted bits of dialogue in paragraph 3 and names of his heroes and of particular games (and related equipment and weapons) elsewhere. The descriptive details that re-create the physical scenes—in particular, the snow, cold, frost, and wind of winter and the sun reflected in the fence—are vivid enough to help readers visualize the places Michael writes about.

Figures of Speech.   Michael's essay describes a time when his imagination wandered without the restraints of adulthood. Appropriately, he uses **simile**, **metaphor**, and **personification**—"We were free like comets in the heavens"; "The park became a giant spaceship"; "We found lost cities, unearthed treasures, and saved Earth"; "darkness soon devoured the park"—to evoke the time and place he describes.

Focus on Revision

Michael's assignment asked him to write about his childhood, and he chose to focus on his early years in the United States. When his peer editing group discussed his essay, however, a number of students were curious about his life in Vietnam. Some of them thought he should add a paragraph summarizing the "vague images" he remembered of his earlier child-hood, perhaps contrasting it with his life in the United States, as he does in passing in paragraph 2. An alternate suggestion, made by one classmate, was that Michael consider deleting the sentence in paragraph 1 that states he has "no desire or intention to discuss" this part of his life, since it raises issues his essay does not address. After thinking about these ideas, Michael decided to delete this sentence and to add a brief paragraph about his life in Vietnam, contrasting the park and his friendship with James with some of his earlier memories.

📄 **PEER EDITING WORKSHEET: Combining the Patterns**

1. Using the annotations for "The Park" (page 707) or "On Dumpster Diving" (page 712) as a guide, annotate the essay to identify the patterns of development it uses.

2. What is the essay's thesis? If it is not explicitly stated, state it in your own words. What pattern or patterns of development are suggested by the wording of the thesis statement?

3. What pattern of development determines the essay's overall structure? Could the writer use a different pattern for this purpose? Which one?

4. What patterns does the writer use to develop the body paragraphs of the essay? Explain why each pattern is used in a particular paragraph or group of paragraphs.

5. What patterns are *not* used? Where, if anywhere, might one of these patterns serve the writer's purpose?

6. Review the essay's topic sentences. Is the wording of each topic sentence consistent with the particular pattern it introduces? If not, suggest possible ways some of the topic sentences might be reworded.

Each of the following essays combines several patterns, blending strategies to achieve the writer's purpose.

LARS EIGHNER

On Dumpster Diving

Lars Eighner (b. 1948) dropped out of the University of Texas at Austin after his third year and took a job at a state mental hospital. After leaving his job over a policy dispute in 1988 and falling behind in his rent payments, Eighner became homeless. For three years, he traveled between Austin and Los Angeles with his dog, Lizbeth, earning what money he could from writing stories for magazines. Eighner's memories of his experiences living on the street, *Travels with Lizbeth* (1993), was written on a computer he found in a Dumpster. The following chapter from that book details the practical dangers as well as the many possibilities he discovered in his "Dumpster diving." Eighner now lives in Austin and works as a freelance writer and writing coach.

Background on the homeless: Although the number of homeless people is difficult to measure accurately, homelessness has become a highly visible issue in the past two decades. It is estimated, for example, that as many as ten million people experienced homelessness in this country in the late 1980s alone. A number of causes have been attributed to this surge in homelessness. Perhaps most important, a booming real estate market led to a significant drop in affordable housing in many areas of the country. In several cities, single-room-occupancy hotels, which had long provided cheap lodging, were demolished or converted into luxury apartments. At the same time, new technologies left many unskilled workers jobless. Government policies against detaining the nondangerous mentally ill against their will also played a significant role. (About a quarter of all homeless people are thought to be mentally ill.) Currently, the U.S. Department of Health and Human Services estimates that homelessness affects two to three million Americans each year.

This chapter was composed while the author was homeless. The present tense has been preserved.

Definition: Dumpster

Long before I began Dumpster diving I was impressed with Dumpsters, enough so that I wrote the Merriam-Webster research service to discover what I could about the word *Dumpster*. I learned from them that it is a proprietary word belonging to the Dempsey Dumpster company. Since then I have dutifully capitalized the word, although it was lowercased in almost all the citations Merriam-Webster photocopied for me. Dempsey's word is too apt. I have never heard these things called anything but Dumpsters. I do not know anyone who knows the generic name for these objects.

1

From time to time I have heard a wino or hobo give some corrupted credit to the original and call them Dipsy Dumpsters.

Narration: Eighner's story begins

I began Dumpster diving about a year before I became homeless.   2

Definition: Dumpster diving

I prefer the word *scavenging* and use the word   3
scrounging when I mean to be obscure. I have heard people, evidently meaning to be polite, use the word *foraging,* but I prefer to reserve that word for gathering nuts and berries and such, which I do also according to the season and the opportunity. *Dumpster diving* seems to me to be a little too cute and, in my case, inaccurate because I lack the athletic ability to lower myself into the Dumpsters as the true divers do, much to their increased profit.

I like the frankness of the word *scavenging,* which I   4
can hardly think of without picturing a big black snail on an aquarium wall. I live from the refuse of others. I am a scavenger. I think it a sound and honorable niche, although if I could I would naturally prefer to live the comfortable consumer life, perhaps — and only perhaps — as a slightly less wasteful consumer, owing to what I have learned as a scavenger.

*Narration:
story continues*

While Lizbeth and I were still living in the shack on   5
Avenue B as my savings ran out, I put almost all my sporadic income into rent. The necessities of daily life I began to extract from Dumpsters. Yes, we ate from

Exemplification: things found in Dumpsters

them. Except for jeans, all my clothes came from Dumpsters. Boom boxes, candles, bedding, toilet paper, a virgin male love doll, medicine, books, a typewriter, dishes, furnishings, and change, sometimes amounting to many dollars — I acquired many things from Dumpsters.

Thesis statement

I have learned much as a scavenger. I mean to put   6
some of what I have learned down here, beginning with the practical art of Dumpster diving and proceeding to the abstract.

What is safe to eat?   7

After all, the finding of objects is becoming some-   8
thing of an urban art. Even respectable employed people will sometimes find something tempting sticking out of a Dumpster or standing beside one. Quite a number of people, not all of them of the bohemian type, are willing to brag that they found this or that piece of trash. But eating from Dumpsters is what separates the dilettanti

from the professionals. Eating safely from the Dumpsters involves three principles: using the senses and common sense to evaluate the condition of the found materials, knowing the Dumpsters of a given area and checking them regularly, and seeking always to answer the question "Why was this discarded?"

Comparison and contrast: Dumpster divers vs. others

Perhaps everyone who has a kitchen and a regular supply of groceries has, at one time or another, made a sandwich and eaten half of it before discovering mold on the bread or got a mouthful of milk before realizing the milk had turned. Nothing of the sort is likely to happen to a Dumpster diver because he is constantly reminded that most food is discarded for a reason. Yet a lot of perfectly good food can be found in Dumpsters.   9

Classification and division: different kinds of food found in Dumpsters and their relative safety

Canned goods, for example, turn up fairly often in the Dumpsters I frequent. All except the most phobic people will be willing to eat from a can, even if it came from a Dumpster. Canned goods are among the safest foods to be found in Dumpsters but are not utterly foolproof.   10

Although very rare with modern canning methods, botulism is a possibility. Most other forms of food poisoning seldom do lasting harm to a healthy person, but botulism is almost certainly fatal and often the first symptom is death. Except for carbonated beverages, all canned goods should contain a slight vacuum and suck air when first punctured. Bulging, rusty, and dented cans and cans that spew when punctured should be avoided, especially when the contents are not very acidic or syrupy.   11

Heat can break down the botulin, but this requires much more cooking than most people do to canned goods. To the extent that botulism occurs at all, of course, it can occur in cans on pantry shelves as well as in cans from Dumpsters. Need I say that home-canned goods are simply too risky to be recommended.   12

From time to time one of my companions, aware of the source of my provisions, will ask, "Do you think these crackers are really safe to eat?" For some reason it is most often the crackers they ask about.   13

This question has always made me angry. Of course I would not offer my companion anything I had doubts about. But more than that, I wonder why he cannot evaluate the condition of the crackers for himself. I have no special knowledge and I have been wrong   14 before. Since he knows where the food comes from, it seems to me he ought to assume some of the responsibility for deciding what he will put in his mouth. For myself I have few qualms about dry foods such as crackers, cookies, cereal, chips, and pasta if they are free of visible contaminates and still dry and crisp. Most often such things are found in the original packaging, which is not so much a positive sign as it is the absence of a negative one.

Raw fruits and vegetables with intact skins seem   15
perfectly safe to me, excluding of course the obviously rotten. Many are discarded for minor imperfections that can be pared away. Leafy vegetables, grapes, cauliflower, broccoli, and similar things may be contaminated by liquids and may be impractical to wash.

Candy, especially hard candy, is usually safe if it has   16
not drawn ants. Chocolate is often discarded only because it has become discolored as the cocoa butter de-emulsified. Candying, after all, is one method of food preservation because pathogens do not like very sugary substances.

All of these foods might be found in any Dumpster   17
and can be evaluated with some confidence largely on the basis of appearance. Beyond these are foods that cannot be correctly evaluated without additional information.

I began scavenging by pulling pizzas out of the   18
Dumpster behind a pizza delivery shop. In general, prepared food requires caution, but in this case I knew when the shop closed and went to the Dumpster as soon as the last of the help left.

Such shops often get prank orders; both the orders   19
and the products made to fill them are called *bogus*. Because help seldom stays long at these places, pizzas are often made with the wrong topping, refused on delivery for being cold, or baked incorrectly. The products to be discarded are boxed up because inventory is kept by counting boxes: A boxed pizza can be written off; an unboxed pizza does not exist.

I never placed a bogus order to increase the supply   20
of pizzas and I believe no one else was scavenging in this Dumpster. But the people in the shop became suspicious and began to retain their garbage in the shop overnight. While it lasted I had a steady supply of fresh, sometimes warm pizza. Because I knew the Dumpster I

knew the source of the pizza, and because I visited the Dumpster regularly I knew what was fresh and what was yesterday's.

Cause and effect: why Eighner visits certain Dumpsters; why students throw out food

The area I frequent is inhabited by many affluent college students. I am not here by chance; the Dumpsters in this area are very rich. Students throw out many good things, including food. In particular they tend to throw everything out when they move at the end of a semester, before and after breaks, and around midterm, when many of them despair of college. So I find it advantageous to keep an eye on the academic calendar.   21

Students throw food away around breaks because they do not know whether it has spoiled or will spoil before they return. A typical discard is a half jar of peanut butter. In fact, nonorganic peanut butter does not require refrigeration and is unlikely to spoil in any reasonable time. The student does not know that, and since it is Daddy's money, the student decides not to take a chance. Opened containers require caution and some attention to the question "Why was this discarded?" But in the case of discards from student apartments, the answer may be that the item was thrown out through carelessness, ignorance, or wastefulness. This can sometimes be deduced when the item is found with many others, including some that are obviously perfectly good.   22

Some students, and others, approach defrosting a freezer by chucking out the whole lot. Not only do the circumstances of such a find tell the story, but also the mass of frozen goods stays cold for a long time and items may be found still frozen or freshly thawed.   23

Yogurt, cheese, and sour cream are items that are often thrown out while they are still good. Occasionally I find cheese with a spot of mold, which of course I just pare off, and because it is obvious why such a cheese was discarded, I treat it with less suspicion than an apparently perfect cheese found in similar circumstances. Yogurt is often discarded, still sealed, only because the expiration date on the carton had passed. This is one of my favorite finds because yogurt will keep for several days, even in warm weather.   24

Students throw out canned goods and staples at the end of semesters and when they give up college at midterm. Drugs, pornography, spirits, and the like are often discarded when parents are expected—Dad's Day,   25 for example. And spirits also turn up after big party weekends, presumably discarded by the newly reformed. Wine and spirits, of course, keep perfectly well even once opened, but the same cannot be said of beer.

My test for carbonated soft drinks is whether they 26 still fizz vigorously. Many juices or other beverages are too acidic or too syrupy to cause much concern, provided they are not visibly contaminated. I have discovered nasty molds in the vegetable juices, even when the product was found under its original seal; I recommend that such products be decanted slowly into a clear glass. Liquids always require some care. One hot day I found a large jug of Pat O'Brien's Hurricane mix. The jug had been opened but was still ice cold. I drank three large glasses before it became apparent to me that someone had added rum to the mix, and not a little rum. I never tasted the rum, and by the time I began to feel the effects I had already ingested a very large quantity of the beverage. Some divers would have considered this a boon, but being suddenly intoxicated in a public place in the early afternoon is not my idea of a good time.

Examples: liquids that require care

I have heard of people maliciously contaminating 27 discarded food and even handouts, but mostly I have heard of this from people with vivid imaginations who have had no experience with Dumpsters themselves. Just before the pizza shop stopped discarding its garbage at night, jalapeños began showing up on most of the thrown-out pizzas. If indeed this was meant to discourage me, it was a wasted effort because I am a native Texan.

For myself, I avoid game, poultry, pork, and egg- 28 based foods, whether I find them raw or cooked. I seldom have the means to cook what I find, but when I do I avail myself of plentiful supplies of beef, which is often in very good condition. I suppose fish becomes disagreeable before it becomes dangerous. Lizbeth is happy to have any such thing that is past its prime and, in fact, does not recognize fish as food until it is quite strong.

Home leftovers, as opposed to surpluses from 29 restaurants, are very often bad. Evidently, especially among students, there is a common type of personality that carefully wraps up even the smallest leftover and shoves it into the back of the refrigerator for six months or so before discarding it. Characteristic of this type are the reused jars and margarine tubs to which the remains are committed. I avoid ethnic foods I am unfamiliar with. If I do not know what it is supposed to look like when it is good, I cannot be certain I will be able to tell if it is bad.

No matter how careful I am I still get dysentery at least once a month, oftener in warmer weather. I do not want to paint too romantic a picture. Dumpster diving has serious drawbacks as a way of life. 30

Process: how to scavenge

I learned to scavenge gradually, on my own. Since then I have initiated several companions into the trade. I have learned that there is a predictable series of stages a person goes through in learning to scavenge. 31

At first the new scavenger is filled with disgust and self-loathing. He is ashamed of being seen and may lurk around, trying to duck behind things, or he may try to dive at night. (In fact, most people instinctively look away from a scavenger. By skulking around, the novice calls attention to himself and arouses suspicion. Diving at night is ineffective and needlessly messy.) 32

Every grain of rice seems to be a maggot. Everything seems to stink. He can wipe the egg yolk off the found can, but he cannot erase from his mind the stigma of eating garbage. 33

That stage passes with experience. The scavenger finds a pair of running shoes that fit and look and smell brand-new. He finds a pocket calculator in perfect working order. He finds pristine ice cream, still frozen, more than he can eat or keep. He begins to understand: People throw away perfectly good stuff, a lot of perfectly good stuff. 34

At this stage, Dumpster shyness begins to dissipate. The diver, after all, has the last laugh. He is finding all manner of good things that are his for the taking. Those who disparage his profession are the fools, not he. 35

He may begin to hang on to some perfectly good things for which he has neither a use nor a market. Then he begins to take note of the things that are not perfectly good but are nearly so. He mates a Walkman with broken earphones and one that is missing a battery cover. He picks up things that he can repair. 36

At this stage he may become lost and never recover. Dumpsters are full of things of some potential value to 37 someone and also of things that never have much intrinsic value but are interesting. All the Dumpster divers I have known come to the point of trying to acquire everything they touch. Why not take it, they reason, since it is all free? This is, of course, hopeless. Most divers come to realize that they must restrict themselves to items of relatively immediate utility. But in some cases the diver simply cannot control himself. I have met several of these pack-rat types. Their ideas of the values of various pieces of junk verge on the psychotic. Every bit of glass may be a diamond, they think, and all that glisters,* gold.

Cause and effect: why Eighner gains weight when he scavenges

I tend to gain weight when I am scavenging. Partly   38
this is because I always find far more pizza and doughnuts than water-packed tuna, nonfat yogurt, and fresh vegetables. Also I have not developed much faith in the reliability of Dumpsters as a food source, although it has been proven to me many times. I tend to eat as if I have no idea where my next meal is coming from. But mostly I just hate to see food go to waste and so I eat much more than I should. Something like this drives the obsession to collect junk.

As for collecting objects, I usually restrict myself to   39
collecting one kind of small object at a time, such as pocket calculators, sunglasses, or campaign buttons.

Cause and effect: why Eighner saves items

To live on the street I must anticipate my needs to a certain extent: I must pick up and save warm bedding I find in August because it will not be found in Dumpsters in November. As I have no access to health care, I often hoard essential drugs, such as antibiotics and antihistamines. (This course can be recommended only to those with some grounding in pharmacology. Antibiotics, for example, even when indicated are worse than useless if taken in insufficient amounts.) But even if I had a home with extensive storage space, I could not save everything that might be valuable in some contingency.

Comparison and contrast: Dumpsters in rich and poorer areas

I have proprietary feelings about my Dumpsters. As   40
I have mentioned, it is no accident that I scavenge from ones where good finds are common. But my limited experience with Dumpsters in other areas suggests to me that even in poorer areas, Dumpsters, if attended with sufficient diligence, can be made to yield a livelihood.

---

* EDS. NOTE — Glitters.

The rich students discard perfectly good kiwi fruit; poorer people discard perfectly good apples. Slacks and Polo shirts are found in one place; jeans and T-shirts in the other. The population of competitors rather than the affluence of the dumpers most affects the feasibility of survival by scavenging. The large number of competitors is what puts me off the idea of trying to scavenge in places like Los Angeles.

Curiously, I do not mind my direct competition, other scavengers, so much as I hate the can scroungers.   41

Cause and effect: why people scrounge cans

People scrounge cans because they have to have a little cash. I have tried scrounging cans with an able-bodied companion. Afoot a can scrounger simply cannot make more than a few dollars in a day. One can extract the necessities of life from the Dumpsters directly with far less effort than would be required to accumulate the equivalent value in cans. (These observations may not hold in places with container redemption laws.)   42

Can scroungers, then, are people who must have small amounts of cash. These are drug addicts and winos, mostly the latter because the amounts of cash are so small. Spirits and drugs do, like all other commodities, turn up in Dumpsters and the scavenger will from time to time have a half bottle of a rather good wine with his dinner. But the wino cannot survive on these occasional finds; he must have his daily dose to stave off the DTs. All the cans he can carry will buy about three bottles of Wild Irish Rose.   43

Comparison and contrast: can scroungers vs. true scavengers

I do not begrudge them the cans, but can scroungers tend to tear up the Dumpsters, mixing the contents and littering the area. They become so specialized that they can see only cans. They earn my contempt by passing up change, canned goods, and readily hockable items.   44

There are precious few courtesies among scavengers. But it is common practice to set aside surplus items: pairs of shoes, clothing, canned goods, and such. A true scavenger hates to see good stuff go to waste, and what he cannot use he leaves in good condition in plain sight.   45

Can scroungers lay waste to everything in their path and will stir one of a pair of good shoes to the bottom of a Dumpster, to be lost or ruined in the muck. Can scroungers will even go through individual garbage cans, something I have never seen a scavenger do.   46

Individual garbage cans are set out on the public 47
easement only on garbage days. On the other days going
through them requires trespassing close to a dwelling.

*Cause and effect: why
scavengers do not go
through individual
garbage cans*
Going through individual garbage cans without scat-
tering litter is almost impossible. Litter is likely to
reduce the public's tolerance of scavenging. Individual
cans are simply not as productive as Dumpsters; people
in houses and duplexes do not move so often and for
some reason do not tend to discard as much useful
material. Moreover, the time required to go through
one garbage can that serves one household is not much
less than the time required to go through a Dumpster
that contains the refuse of twenty apartments.

But my strongest reservation about going through 48
individual garbage cans is that this seems to me a very
personal kind of invasion to which I would object if I
were a householder. Although many things in Dumpsters are obviously meant never to come to light, a
Dumpster is somehow less personal.

I avoid trying to draw conclusions about the 49
people who dump in the Dumpsters I frequent. I think
it would be unethical to do so, although I know many
people will find the idea of scavenger ethics too funny
for words.

*Examples: things
found in Dumpsters*
Dumpsters contain bank statements, correspon- 50
dence, and other documents, just as anyone might
expect. But there are also less obvious sources of information. Pill bottles, for example. The labels bear the
name of the patient, the name of the doctor, and the
name of the drug. AIDS drugs and antipsychotic medicines, to name but two groups, are specific and are seldom prescribed for any other disorders. The plastic
compacts for birth-control pills usually have complete
label information.

Despite all of this sensitive information, I have had 51
only one apartment resident object to my going
through the Dumpster. In that case it turned out the
resident was a university athlete who was taking bets
and who was afraid I would turn up his wager slips.

Occasionally a find tells a story. I once found a small 52
paper bag containing some unused condoms, several
partial tubes of flavored sexual lubricants, a partially
used compact of birth-control pills, and the torn pieces
of a picture of a young man. Clearly she was through
with him and planning to give up sex altogether.

Dumpster things are often sad — abandoned teddy   53
bears, shredded wedding books, despaired-of sales kits.
I find many pets lying in state in Dumpsters. Although
I hope to get off the streets so that Lizbeth can have a
long and comfortable old age, I know this hope is not
very realistic. So I suppose when her time comes she
too will go into a Dumpster. I will have no better place
for her. And after all, it is fitting, since for most of her
life her livelihood has come from the Dumpster. When
she finds something I think is safe that has been spilled
from a Dumpster, I let her have it. She already knows
the route around the best ones. I like to think that if
she survives me she will have a chance of evading the
dog catcher and of finding her sustenance on the route.

Silly vanities also come to rest in the Dumpsters. I   54
am a rather accomplished needleworker. I get a lot of
material from the Dumpsters. Evidently sorority girls,
hoping to impress someone, perhaps themselves, with
their mastery of a womanly art, buy a lot of embroider-
by-number kits, work a few stitches horribly, and eventually discard the whole mess. I pull out their stitches,
turn the canvas over, and work an original design. Do
not think I refrain from chuckling as I make gifts from
these kits.

I find diaries and journals. I have often thought of   55
compiling a book of literary found objects. And perhaps I will one day. But what I find is hopelessly commonplace and bad without being, even unconsciously,
camp. College students also discard their papers. I am
horrified to discover the kind of paper that now merits
an A in an undergraduate course. I am grateful, however, for the number of good books and magazines the
students throw out.

In the area I know best I have never discovered ver-   56
min in the Dumpster, but there are two kinds of kitty
surprise. One is alley cats whom I meet as they leap,
claws first, out of Dumpsters. This is especially
thrilling when I have Lizbeth in tow. The other kind of
kitty surprise is a plastic garbage bag filled with some
ponderous, amorphous mass. This always proves to be
used cat litter.

City bees harvest doughnut glaze and this makes   57
the Dumpster at the doughnut shop more interesting.
My faith in the instinctive wisdom of animals is always
shaken whenever I see Lizbeth attempt to catch a bee in
her mouth, which she does whenever bees are present.

Evidently some birds find Dumpsters profitable, for birdie surprise is almost as common as kitty surprise of the first kind. In hunting season all kinds of small game turn up in Dumpsters, some of it, sadly, not entirely dead. Curiously, summer and winter, maggots are uncommon.

The worst of the living and near-living hazards of the Dumpsters are the fire ants. The food they claim is not much of a loss, but they are vicious and aggressive. It is very easy to brush against some surface of the Dumpster and pick up half a dozen or more fire ants, usually in some sensitive area such as the underarm. One advantage of bringing Lizbeth along as I make Dumpster rounds is that, for obvious reasons, she is very alert to ground-based fire ants. When Lizbeth recognizes a fire-ant infestation around our feet, she does the Dance of the Zillion Fire Ants. I have learned not to ignore this warning from Lizbeth, whether I perceive the tiny ants or not, but to remove ourselves at Lizbeth's first *pas de bourée.** All the more so because the ants are the worst in the summer months when I wear flip-flops if I have them. (Perhaps someone will misunderstand this. Lizbeth does the Dance of the Zillion Fire Ants when she recognizes more fire ants than she cares to eat, not when she is being bitten. Since I have learned to react promptly, she does not get bitten at all. It is the isolated patrol of fire ants that falls in Lizbeth's range that deserves pity. She finds them quite tasty.) 58

Process: how to go through a Dumpster

By far the best way to go through a Dumpster is to lower yourself into it. Most of the good stuff tends to settle at the bottom because it is usually weightier than the rubbish. My more athletic companions have often demonstrated to me that they can extract much good material from a Dumpster I have already been over. 59

To those psychologically or physically unprepared to enter a Dumpster, I recommend a stout stick, preferably with some barb or hook at one end. The hook can be used to grab plastic garbage bags. When I find canned goods or other objects loose at the bottom of a Dumpster, I lower a bag into it, roll the desired object into the bag, and then hoist the bag out — a procedure more easily described than executed. Much Dumpster diving is a matter of experience for which nothing will do except practice. 60

---

* EDS. NOTE — A ballet step.

Dumpster diving is outdoor work, often surpris- 61
ingly pleasant. It is not entirely predictable; things of
interest turn up every day and some days there are
finds of great value. I am always very pleased when I can
turn up exactly the thing I most wanted to find. Yet in
spite of the element of chance, scavenging more than
most other pursuits tends to yield returns in some pro-
portion to the effort and intelligence brought to bear.
It is very sweet to turn up a few dollars in change from a
Dumpster that has just been gone over by a wino.

The land is now covered with cities. The cities are 62
full of Dumpsters. If a member of the canine race is
ever able to know what it is doing, then Lizbeth knows
that when we go around to the Dumpsters, we are
hunting. I think of scavenging as a modern form of
self-reliance. In any event, after having survived nearly
ten years of government service, where everything is
geared to the lowest common denominator, I find it
refreshing to have work that rewards initiative and
effort. Certainly I would be happy to have a sinecure
again, but I am no longer heartbroken that I left one.

Cause and effect: results I find from the experience of scavenging two rather 63
of Eighner's experiences deep lessons. The first is to take what you can use and
as a scavenger let the rest go by. I have come to think that there is no
value in the abstract. A thing I cannot use or make use-
ful, perhaps by trading, has no value however rare or
fine it may be. I mean useful in some broad sense —
some art I would find useful and some otherwise.

I was shocked to realize that some things are not 64
worth acquiring, but now I think it is so. Some material
things are white elephants that eat up the possessor's
substance. The second lesson is the transience of material being. This has not quite converted me to a dual-
ist,* but it has made some headway in that direction. I
do not suppose that ideas are immortal, but certainly
mental things are longer lived than other material
things.

Once I was the sort of person who invests objects 65
with sentimental value. Now I no longer have those
objects, but I have the sentiments yet.

Many times in our travels I have lost everything but 66
the clothes I was wearing and Lizbeth. The things I find
in Dumpsters, the love letters and rag dolls of so many

---

* EDS. NOTE — Someone who believes that the world consists of two opposing forces,
such as mind and matter.

lives, remind me of this lesson. Now I hardly pick up a thing without envisioning the time I will cast it aside. This I think is a healthy state of mind. Almost everything I have now has already been cast out at least once, proving that what I own is valueless to someone.

Anyway, I find my desire to grab for the gaudy bauble has been largely sated. I think this is an attitude I share with the very wealthy—we both know there is plenty more where what we have came from. Between us are the rat-race millions who nightly scavenge the cable channels looking for they know not what. 67

I am sorry for them. 68

• • •

Comprehension

1. In your own words, give a one-sentence definition of *Dumpster diving*.

2. List some of Eighner's answers to the question, "Why was this discarded?" (8). What additional reasons can you think of?

3. What foods does Eighner take particular care to avoid? Why?

4. In paragraph 30, Eighner comments, "Dumpster diving has serious drawbacks as a way of life." What drawbacks does he cite in his essay? What additional drawbacks are implied? Can you think of others?

5. Summarize the stages in the process of learning to scavenge.

6. In addition to food, what else does Eighner scavenge for? Into what general categories do these items fall?

7. Why does Eighner hate can scroungers?

8. What lessons has Eighner learned as a Dumpster diver?

Purpose and Audience

1. In paragraph 6, Eighner states his purpose: to record what he has learned as a Dumpster diver. What additional purposes do you think he had in setting his ideas down on paper?

2. Do you think most readers are apt to respond to Eighner's essay with sympathy? Pity? Impatience? Contempt? Disgust? How do you react? Why?

3. Why do you think Eighner chose not to provide much background about his life—his upbringing, education, or work history—before he became homeless? Do you think this decision was a wise one? How might such information (for example, any of the details in the headnote that precedes the essay) have changed readers' reactions to his discussion?

4. In paragraph 8, Eighner presents three principles one must follow to eat safely from a Dumpster; in paragraphs 59–60 he explains how to

go through a Dumpster; and throughout the essay he includes many cautions and warnings. Clearly, he does not expect his audience to take up Dumpster diving. What, then, is his purpose in including such detailed explanations?

5. When Eighner begins paragraph 9 with "Perhaps everyone who has a kitchen," he encourages readers to identify with him. Where else does he make efforts to help readers imagine themselves in his place? Are these efforts successful? Explain.

6. What effect do you think the essay's last sentence is calculated to have on readers? What effect does it have on you?

Style and Structure

1. Eighner opens his essay with a fairly conventional strategy: extended definitions of *Dumpster* and *Dumpster diving*. What techniques does he use in paragraphs 1 through 3 to develop these definitions? Is beginning with definitions the best strategy for this essay? Explain.

2. This long essay contains three one-sentence paragraphs. Why do you think Eighner isolates these sentences? Do you think any of them should be combined with an adjacent paragraph? Explain your reasoning.

3. As the introductory note explains, Eighner chose to retain the present tense even though he was no longer homeless when the essay was published. Why do you think he decided to preserve the present tense? Was this a good decision?

4. Eighner's essay includes a number of lists that catalog items he came across (for example, in paragraphs 5 and 50). Identify as many of these lists as you can. Why do you think Eighner includes such extensive lists?

Vocabulary Projects

1. Define each of the following words as it is used in this selection.

proprietary (1)	decanted (26)	contingency (39)
niche (4)	ingested (26)	feasibility (40)
sporadic (5)	avail (28)	stave (43)
bohemian (8)	skulking (32)	commonplace (55)
dilettanti (8)	stigma (33)	vermin (56)
phobic (10)	pristine (34)	sinecure (62)
pared (15)	dissipate (35)	transience (64)
de-emulsified (16)	disparage (35)	gaudy (67)
pathogens (16)	intrinsic (37)	bauble (67)
staples (25)		

2. In paragraph 3, Eighner suggests several alternative words for *diving* as he uses it in his essay. Consult a dictionary to determine the connotations of each of his alternatives. What are the pros and cons of substi-

tuting one of these words for *diving* in Eighner's title and throughout the essay?

Journal Entry

In paragraphs 21–25, Eighner discusses the discarding of food by college students. Does your own experience support his observations? Do you think he is being too hard on students, or does his characterization seem accurate?

Writing Workshop

1. Write an essay about a homeless person you have seen in your community. Use any patterns you like to structure your paper. When you have finished, annotate your essay to identify the patterns you have used.

2. Write a memo to your school's dean of students recommending steps that can be taken on your campus to redirect discarded (but edible) food to the homeless. Use process and exemplification to structure your memo.

3. Taking Eighner's point of view and using information from his essay, write an argumentative essay with a thesis statement that takes a strong stand against homelessness and recommends government or private measures to end it. If you like, you may write your essay in the form of a statement by Eighner to a congressional committee.

Combining the Patterns

Review the annotations that identify each pattern of development used in this essay. Which patterns seem to be most effective in helping you understand and empathize with the life of a homeless person? Why?

Thematic Connections

- "The Human Cost of an Illiterate Society" (page 252)
- "The Power of Words in Wartime" (page 377)
- "The Untouchable" (page 516)
- The Declaration of Independence (page 584)

VIRGINIA WOOLF

The Death of the Moth

Virginia Woolf was born in 1882 into a London literary family and educated at home by her father. Her early life was marked by tragedy: her mother died when she was barely in her teens, and her father and beloved brother died before her twenty-fifth birthday, pushing her toward a mental breakdown. Despite her unhappiness, in 1905 she began publishing essays and reviews, which eventually numbered more than five hundred. Her first novel, *The Voyage Out*, appeared in 1915; later novels, including *Mrs. Dalloway* (1925), *To the Lighthouse* (1927), and *The Waves* (1931), exhibit an experimental modernist style that is particularly effective in revealing the female experience. With her husband, Leonard Woolf, she began the Hogarth Press, publishing a number of twentieth-century masterpieces by other writers. She was a central figure of the Bloomsbury Group (named after the London neighborhood where she lived), a circle of leading writers and artists who exerted a broad cultural influence, and was one of the most acclaimed writers of her day. Still, she remained plagued by personal demons, and in 1941, she took her own life.

Background on writers and suicide: "I have a feeling I shall go mad," Virginia Woolf wrote in her final note to her husband. "I cannot go on longer in these terrible times. I hear voices and cannot concentrate on my work. I have fought against it but cannot fight any longer. I owe all my happiness to you but cannot go on and spoil your life." Woolf then filled her pockets with stones and drowned herself in a river near their country home. Woolf is not alone among successful writers in committing suicide. Novelist Ernest Hemingway, for example, died of a self-inflicted gunshot wound. Researchers estimate that writers in general are ten to twenty times more likely to suffer depression or manic depression than others and that poets, in particular, are eighteen times as likely to commit suicide—a fate that befell Randall Jarrell (who slit his wrists before being hit by a car on a dark street), John Berryman (who threw himself from a bridge), Anne Sexton (who sat in a garage in a running car and died of carbon monoxide poisoning), and Sylvia Plath (who gassed herself in an unlit oven). In its reflection on one creature's struggle between life and death, "The Death of the Moth" may well represent the artist's often conflicted state of mind.

Moths that fly by day are not properly to be called moths; they do not   1
excite that pleasant sense of dark autumn nights and ivy-blossom which the commonest yellow-underwing asleep in the shadow of the curtain never fails to rouse in us. They are hybrid creatures, neither gay like butterflies nor somber like their own species. Nevertheless the present specimen, with his narrow hay-colored wings, fringed with a tassel of the same color, seemed to be content with life. It was a pleasant morning, mid-September,

mild, benignant, yet with a keener breath than that of the summer months. The plough was already scoring the field opposite the window, and where the share had been, the earth was pressed flat and gleamed with moisture. Such vigor came rolling in from the fields and the down beyond that it was difficult to keep the eyes strictly turned upon the book. The rooks too were keeping one of their annual festivities; soaring round the tree tops until it looked as if a vast net with thousands of black knots in it had been cast up into the air; which, after a few moments sank slowly down upon the trees until every twig seemed to have a knot at the end of it. Then, suddenly, the net would be thrown into the air again in a wider circle this time, with the utmost clamor and vociferation, as though to be thrown into the air and settle slowly down upon the tree tops were a tremendously exciting experience.

The same energy which inspired the rooks, the ploughmen, the horses, and even, it seemed, the lean bare-backed downs, sent the moth fluttering from side to side of his square of the windowpane. One could not help watching him. One was, indeed, conscious of a queer feeling of pity for him. The possibilities of pleasure seemed that morning so enormous and so various that to have only a moth's part in life, and a day moth's at that, appeared a hard fate, and his zest in enjoying his meager opportunities to the full, pathetic. He flew vigorously to one corner of his compartment, and after waiting there a second, flew across to the other. What remained for him but to fly to a third corner and then to a fourth? That was all he could do, in spite of the size of the downs, the width of the sky, the far-off smoke of houses, and the romantic voice, now and then, of a steamer out at sea. What he could do he did. Watching him, it seemed as if a fiber, very thin but pure, of the enormous energy of the world had been thrust into his frail and diminutive body. As often as he crossed the pane, I could fancy that a thread of vital light became visible. He was little or nothing but life.

Yet, because he was so small, and so simple a form of the energy that was rolling in at the open window and driving its way through so many narrow and intricate corridors in my own brain and in those of other human beings, there was something marvelous as well as pathetic about him. It was as if someone had taken a tiny bead of pure life and decking it as lightly as possible with down and feathers, had set it dancing and zigzagging to show us the true nature of life. Thus displayed one could not get over the strangeness of it. One is apt to forget all about life, seeing it humped and bossed and garnished and cumbered so that it has to move with the greatest circumspection and dignity. Again, the thought of all that life might have been had he been born in any other shape caused one to view his simple activities with a kind of pity.

After a time, tired by his dancing apparently, he settled on the window ledge in the sun, and, the queer spectacle being at an end, I forgot about him. Then, looking up, my eye was caught by him. He was trying to resume his dancing, but seemed either so stiff or so awkward that he could only flutter to the bottom of the windowpane; and when he tried to fly across it he failed. Being intent on other matters I watched these futile attempts for a time without thinking, unconsciously waiting for him to resume his flight, as one waits for a machine, that has stopped momentarily, to start again without considering the reason of its failure. After perhaps a seventh attempt he slipped from the wooden ledge and fell, fluttering his wings, on to his back on the windowsill. The helplessness of his attitude roused me. It flashed upon me that he was in difficulties; he could no longer raise himself; his legs struggled vainly. But, as I stretched out a pencil, meaning to help him to right himself, it came over me that the failure and awkwardness were the approach of death. I laid the pencil down again.

The legs agitated themselves once more. I looked as if for the enemy   5
against which he struggled. I looked out of doors. What had happened there? Presumably it was midday, and work in the fields had stopped. Stillness and quiet had replaced the previous animation. The birds had taken themselves off to feed in the brooks. The horses stood still. Yet the power was there all the same, massed outside, indifferent, impersonal, not attending to anything in particular. Somehow it was opposed to the little hay-colored moth. It was useless to try to do anything. One could only watch the extraordinary efforts made by those tiny legs against an oncoming doom which could, had it chosen, have submerged an entire city, not merely a city, but masses of human beings; nothing, I knew had any chance against death. Nevertheless after a pause of exhaustion the legs fluttered again. It was superb this last protest, and so frantic that he succeeded at last in righting himself. One's sympathies, of course, were all on the side of life. Also, when there was nobody to care or to know, this gigantic effort on the part of an insignificant little moth, against a power of such magnitude, to retain what no one else valued or desired to keep, moved one strangely. Again, somehow, one saw life, a pure bead. I lifted the pencil again, useless though I knew it to be. But even as I did so, the unmistakable tokens of death showed themselves. The body relaxed, and instantly grew stiff. The struggle was over. The insignificant little creature now knew death. As I looked at the dead moth, this minute wayside triumph of so great a force over so mean an antagonist filled me with wonder. Just as life had been strange a few minutes before, so death was now as strange. The moth having righted himself now lay most decently and uncomplainingly composed. O yes, he seemed to say, death is stronger than I am.

• • •

Comprehension

1. What is Woolf doing when she begins watching the moth? What is going on in the background?
2. Why does Woolf notice the moth? Why do you think she continues to watch it?
3. What feelings does Woolf express for the moth? What feelings does she imagine the moth has?

4. What human qualities does Woolf see in the moth?

5. In paragraph 2, Woolf says of the moth, "He was little or nothing but life." What does she mean? Why is this statement important to the essay?

6. What antagonist does the moth struggle against? Why does Woolf believe it is "useless" to try to save it (5)?

7. Do you think Woolf exaggerates the moth's importance? Explain.

8. What do you think this essay is really about?

Purpose and Audience

1. What is the main point of Woolf's essay? State this main idea as a one-sentence thesis. Which sentence in the essay comes closest to the sentence you wrote?

2. What do you think Woolf wants her audience to feel when they read this essay? What do you think she wants them to learn?

Style and Structure

1. Study Woolf's use of the pronoun *one* in this essay. (For example, in paragraph 2, she says, "One was, indeed, conscious of a queer feeling of pity" for the moth.) To whom does this pronoun refer? What pronoun could she use instead? Why do you suppose she uses *one*?

2. Where does Woolf use **personification**? What does it add to her essay?

3. In paragraph 4, Woolf uses passive voice ("my eye was caught by him"). Can you locate other examples of passive voice in this essay? Why does Woolf use the passive voice? How would her essay be different if she had used the active voice?

4. List the adjectives Woolf uses to describe the moth. Which of these provide **objective description**? Which provide **subjective description**?

5. In paragraph 4, Woolf uses an **analogy**, saying she is waiting for the moth "to resume his flight, as one waits for a machine, that has stopped momentarily, to start again. . . ." What purpose does this analogy serve? Is it effective? Can you identify other analogies?

6. Woolf uses a very distant, detached tone in this essay. For instance, in paragraph 5, she says that the moth's effort "moved one strangely." Is this kind of tone appropriate here?

7. Although this essay's paragraphs are very long, Woolf frequently uses short sentences. For example, in paragraph 2, she says, "What he could do he did." Identify as many of these short sentences as you can. What is the effect of these sentences on readers? Do they all serve the same purpose?

8. In addition to its literal meaning in this essay, could you also see the moth as a **symbol**? If so, what might it symbolize?

Vocabulary Projects

1. Define each of the following words as it is used in this selection.

   hybrid (1)   downs (2)
   benignant (1)   fancy (2)
   rooks (1)   decking (3)
   vociferation (1)   wayside (5)
   ploughmen (2)   righted (5)

2. In paragraph 3, Woolf says, "One is apt to forget all about life, seeing it humped and bossed and garnished and cumbered so that it has to move with the greatest circumspection and dignity." Use an unabridged dictionary to help you define the unfamiliar words in this sentence. Then, explain what Woolf means.

Journal Entry

What do you think Woolf finds so fascinating about the moth? In what sense, if any, do you think she identifies with it?

Writing Workshop

1. Study an animal in motion (in person or on a television nature program), and write a detailed description of its movements. Also describe the animal's interaction with its environment. Use narrative, description, process, and cause and effect to develop your essay.

2. Study a photograph or painting of an insect, and then observe the actual insect in motion. Use comparison and contrast, description, and exemplification to discuss the two subjects.

3. Write a detailed description of a scene in nature. Then, imagine an event taking place against the backdrop you have described, and write a narrative tracing that event. Finally, add a thesis statement that observes the relationship between the event and its setting, and expand your essay with other patterns of development.

Combining the Patterns

What patterns of development does Woolf use? Annotate the essay to identify each pattern. Use the annotations accompanying "On Dumpster Diving" (page 712) as a guide.

Thematic Connections

- "Shooting an Elephant" (page 125)
- "The Amazon Queen" (page 173)
- "Once More to the Lake" (page 186)

JONATHAN SWIFT

A Modest Proposal

Jonathan Swift (1667–1745) was born in Dublin, Ireland, and spent much of his life journeying between his homeland, where he had a modest income as an Anglican priest, and England, where he wished to be part of the literary establishment. The author of many satires and political pamphlets, he is best known today for *Gulliver's Travels* (1726), a sharp satire that, except among academics, is now read primarily as a fantasy for children.

Background on the English-Irish conflict: At the time Swift wrote "A Modest Proposal," Ireland had been essentially under British rule since 1171, with the British often brutally suppressing rebellions by the Irish people. When Henry VIII of England declared a Protestant Church of Ireland, many of the Irish remained fiercely Roman Catholic, and this led to even greater contention. By the early 1700s, the English-controlled Irish Parliament had passed laws that severely limited the rights of Irish Catholics, and British trade policies had begun to seriously depress the Irish economy. A fierce advocate for the Irish people in their struggle under British rule, Swift published several works supporting the Irish cause. The following sharply ironic essay was written during the height of a terrible famine in Ireland, when the British were proposing a devastating tax on the impoverished Irish citizenry. Note that Swift does not write in his own voice here but adopts the persona of one who does not recognize the barbarity of his "solution."

It is a melancholy object to those who walk through this great town* or travel in the country, when they see the streets, the roads, and cabin doors, crowded with beggars of the female sex, followed by three, four, or six children, all in rags and importuning every passenger for an alms. These mothers, instead of being able to work for their honest livelihood, are forced to employ all their time in strolling to beg sustenance for their helpless infants, who, as they grow up, either turn thieves for want of work, or leave their dear native country to fight for the Pretender in Spain, or sell themselves to the Barbadoes.†

I think it is agreed by all parties that this prodigious number of children in the arms, or on the backs, or at the heels of their mothers, and frequently of their fathers, is in the present deplorable state of the kingdom a very great additional grievance; and therefore whoever could find out a fair, cheap, and easy method of making these children sound, useful

1

2

---

* EDS. NOTE — Dublin.

† EDS. NOTE — Many young Irishmen left their country to fight as mercenaries in Spain's civil war or to work as indentured servants in the West Indies.

members of the commonwealth would deserve so well of the public as to have his statue set up for a preserver of the nation.

But my intention is very far from being confined to provide only for 3 the children of professed beggars; it is of a much greater extent, and shall take in the whole number of infants at a certain age who are born of parents in effect as little able to support them as those who demand our charity in the streets.

As to my own part, having turned my thoughts for many years upon 4 this important subject, and maturely weighed the several schemes of the other projectors, I have always found them grossly mistaken in their computation. It is true, a child just dropped from its dam may be supported by her milk for a solar year, with little other nourishment; at most not above the value of two shillings, which the mother may certainly get, or the value in scraps, by her lawful occupation of begging; and it is exactly at one year old that I propose to provide for them in such a manner as instead of being a charge upon their parents or the parish, or wanting food and raiment for the rest of their lives, they shall on the contrary contribute to the feeding, and partly to the clothing, of many thousands.

There is likewise another great advantage in my scheme, that it will 5 prevent those involuntary abortions, and that horrid practice of women murdering their bastard children, alas, too frequent among us, sacrificing the poor innocent babies, I doubt, more to avoid the expense than the shame, which would move tears and pity in the most savage and inhuman breast.

The number of souls in this kingdom being usually reckoned one mil- 6 lion and a half, of these I calculate there may be about two hundred thousand couples whose wives are breeders, from which number I subtract thirty thousand couples who are able to maintain their own children, although I apprehend there cannot be so many under the present distress of the kingdom; but this being granted, there will remain an hundred and seventy thousand breeders. I again subtract fifty thousand for those women who miscarry, or whose children die by accident or disease within the year. There only remain an hundred and twenty thousand children of poor parents annually born. The question therefore is, how this number shall be reared and provided for, which, as I have already said, under the present situation of affairs, is utterly impossible by all the methods hitherto proposed. For we can neither employ them in handicraft nor agriculture; we neither build houses (I mean in the country) nor cultivate land. They can very seldom pick up livelihood by stealing till they arrive at six years old, except where they are of towardly parts,* although I confess they learn the rudiments much earlier, during which time they can however be looked upon only as probationers, as I have been informed by a principal gentleman in the country of Cavan, who protested to me that he never

---

* EDS. NOTE — Precocious.

knew above one or two instances under the age of six, even in a part of the kingdom so renowned for the quickest proficiency in that art.

I am assured by our merchants that a boy or a girl before twelve years old is no salable commodity; and even when they come to this age, they will not yield above three pounds, or three pounds and half a crown at most on the Exchange; which cannot turn to account either to the parents or the kingdom, the charge of nutriment and rags having been at least four times that value. 7

I shall now therefore humbly propose my own thoughts, which I hope will not be liable to the least objection. 8

I have been assured by a very knowing American of my acquaintance in London, that a young healthy child well nursed is at a year old a most delicious, nourishing, and wholesome food, whether stewed, roasted, baked, or boiled; and I make no doubt that it will equally serve in fricasee or a ragout. 9

I do therefore humbly offer it to public consideration that of the hundred and twenty thousand children, already computed, twenty thousand may be reserved for breed, whereof only one fourth part to be males, which is more than we allow to sheep, black cattle, or swine; and my reason is that these children are seldom the fruits of marriage, a circumstance not much regarded by our savages, therefore one male will be sufficient to serve four females. That the remaining hundred thousand may at a year old be offered in sale to the persons of quality and fortune through the kingdom, always advising the mother to let them suck plentifully in the last month, so as to render them plump and fat for a good table. A child will make two dishes at an entertainment for friends; and when the family dines alone, the fore or hind quarter will make a reasonable dish, and seasoned with a little pepper or salt, will be very good boiled on the fourth day, especially in winter. 10

I have reckoned upon a medium that a child just born will weigh twelve pounds, and in a solar year if tolerably nursed increaseth to twenty-eight pounds. 11

I grant this food will be somewhat dear, and therefore very proper for landlords, who, as they have already devoured most of the parents, seem to have the best title to the children. 12

Infant's flesh will be in season throughout the year, but more plentiful in March, and a little before and after. For we are told by a grave author, an eminent French physician,* that fish being a prolific diet, there are more children born in Roman Catholic countries about nine months after Lent, than at any other season; therefore, reckoning a year after Lent, the markets will be more glutted than usual, because the number of popish infants is at least three to one in this kingdom; and therefore it will have one other collateral advantage, by lessening the number of Papists† among us. 13

---

* Eds. note — François Rabelais, a sixteenth-century satirical writer.
† Eds. note — Roman Catholics.

I have already computed the charge of nursing a beggar's child (in 14 which list I reckon all cottagers, laborers, and four fifths of the farmers) to be about two shillings per annum, rags included; and I believe no gentleman would repine to give ten shillings for the carcass of a good fat child, which, as I have said, will make four dishes of excellent nutritive meat, when he hath only some particular friend or his own family to dine with him. Thus the squire will learn to be a good landlord, and grow popular among the tenants; the mother will have eight shillings net profit, and be fit for work till she produces another child.

Those who are more thrifty (as I must confess the times require) may 15 flay the carcass; the skin of which artificially* dressed will make admirable gloves for ladies, and summer boots for fine gentlemen.

As to our city of Dublin, shambles† may be appointed for this purpose 16 in the most convenient parts of it, and butchers we may be assured will not be wanting; although I rather recommend buying the children alive, and dressing them hot from the knife as we do roasting pigs.

A very worthy person, a true lover of his country, and whose virtues I 17 highly esteem, was lately pleased in discoursing on this matter to offer a refinement upon my scheme. He said that many gentlemen of his kingdom, having of late destroyed their deer, he conceived that the want of venison might be well supplied by the bodies of young lads and maidens, not exceeding fourteen years of age nor under twelve, so great a number of both sexes in every county being now ready to starve for want of work and service; and these to be disposed of by their parents, if alive, or otherwise by their nearest relations. But with due deference to so excellent a friend and so deserving a patriot I cannot be altogether in his sentiments; for as to the males, my American acquaintance assured me from frequent experience that their flesh was generally tough and lean, like that of our schoolboys, by continual exercise, and their taste disagreeable; and to fatten them would not answer the charge. Then as to the females, it would, I think with humble submission, be a loss to the public, because they soon would become breeders themselves; and besides, it is not improbable that some scrupulous people might be apt to censure such a practice (although indeed very unjustly) as a little bordering upon cruelty; which, I confess, hath always been with me the strongest objection against any project, how well soever intended.

But in order to justify my friend, he confessed that this expedient was 18 put into his head by the famous Psalmanazar,‡ a native of the island Formosa, who came from thence to London above twenty years ago, and in conversation told my friend that in his country when any young person happened to be put to death, the executioner sold the carcass to the

---

* EDS. NOTE — Skillfully.

† EDS. NOTE — A slaughterhouse or meat market.

‡ EDS. NOTE — Frenchman who passed himself off as a native of Formosa (present-day Taiwan).

persons of quality as a prime dainty; and that in his time the body of a plump girl of fifteen, who was crucified for an attempt to poison the emperor, was sold to the Imperial Majesty's prime minister of state, and other great mandarins of the court, in joints from the gibbet, at four hundred crowns. Neither indeed can I deny that if the same use were made of several plump young girls in this town, who without one single groat to their fortunes cannot stir abroad without a chair,* and appear at the playhouse and assemblies in foreign fineries which they never will pay for, the kingdom would not be the worse.

Some persons of a desponding spirit are in great concern about the vast number of poor people who are aged, diseased, or maimed, and I have been desired to employ my thoughts what course may be taken to ease the nation of so grievous an encumbrance. But I am not in the least pain upon that matter, because it is very well known that they are every day dying and rotting by cold and famine, and filth and vermin, as fast as can be reasonably expected. And as to the younger laborers, they are now in almost as hopeful a condition. They cannot get work, and consequently pine away for want of nourishment to a degree that if any time they are accidentally hired to common labor, they have not strength to perform it; and thus the country and themselves are happily delivered from the evils to come. 19

I have too long digressed, and therefore shall return to my subject. I think the advantages by the proposal which I have made are obvious and many, as well as of the highest importance. 20

For first, as I have already observed, it would greatly lessen the number of Papists, with whom we are yearly overrun, being the principal breeders of the nation as well as our most dangerous enemies; and who stay at home on purpose to deliver the kingdom to the Pretender, hoping to take their advantage by the absence of so many good Protestants, who have chosen rather to leave their country than to stay at home and pay tithes against their conscience to an Episcopal curate. 21

Secondly, the poorer tenants will have something valuable of their own, which by law may be made liable to distress,† and help to pay their landlord's rent, their corn and cattle being already seized and money a thing unknown. 22

Thirdly, whereas the maintenance of an hundred thousand children, from two years old and upwards, cannot be computed at less than ten shillings a piece per annum, the nation's stock will be thereby increased fifty thousand pounds per annum, besides the profit of a new dish introduced to the tables of all gentlemen of fortune in the kingdom who have any refinement in taste. And the money will circulate among ourselves, the goods being entirely of our own growth and manufacture. 23

---

* EDS. NOTE—A sedan chair; that is, a portable covered chair designed to seat one person and then to be carried by two men.
† EDS. NOTE—Property could be seized by creditors.

Fourthly, the constant breeders, besides the gain of eight shillings sterling per annum by the sale of their children, will be rid of the charge for maintaining them after the first year.   24

Fifthly, this food would likewise bring great custom to taverns, where the vintners will certainly be so prudent as to procure the best receipts* for dressing it to perfection, and consequently have their houses frequented by all the fine gentlemen, who justly value themselves upon their knowledge in good eating; and a skillful cook, who understands how to oblige his guests, will contrive to make it as expensive as they please.   25

Sixthly, this would be a great inducement to marriage, after which all wise nations have either encouraged by rewards or enforced by laws and penalties. It would increase the care and tenderness of mothers toward their children, when they were sure of a settlement for life to the poor babes, provided in some sort by the public, to their annual profit instead of expense. We should see an honest emulation among the married women, which of them could bring the fattest child to the market. Men would become as fond of their wives during the time of pregnancy as they are now of their mares in foal, their cows in calf, or sows when they are ready to farrow; nor offer to beat or kick them (as is too frequent a practice) for fear of miscarriage.   26

Many other advantages might be enumerated. For instance, the addition of some thousand carcasses in our exportation of barreled beef, the propagation of swine's flesh, and improvements in the art of making good bacon, so much wanted among us by the great destruction of pigs, too frequent at our tables, which are no way comparable in taste or magnificence to a well-grown, fat, yearling child, which roasted whole will make a considerable figure at a lord mayor's feast or other public entertainment. But this and many others I omit, being studious of brevity.   27

Supposing that one thousand families in this city would be constant customers for infants' flesh, besides others who might have it at merry meetings, particularly weddings and christenings, I compute that Dublin would take off annually about twenty thousand carcasses, and the rest of the kingdom (where probably they will be sold somewhat cheaper) the remaining eighty thousand.   28

I can think of no one objection that will possibly be raised against this proposal, unless it should be urged that the number of people will be thereby much lessened in the kingdom. This I freely own, and it was indeed one principal design in offering it to the world. I desire the reader will observe; that I calculate my remedy for this one individual kingdom of Ireland and for no other that ever was, is, or I think ever can be upon earth. Therefore, let no man talk to me of other expedients: of taxing our absentees at five shillings a pound: of using neither clothes nor household furniture except what is of our own growth and manufacture: of utterly rejecting the materials and instruments that promote foreign luxury: of   29

---

* EDS. NOTE — Recipes.

curing the expensiveness of pride, vanity, idleness, and gaming in our women: of introducing a vein of parsimony, prudence, and temperance: of learning to love our country, in the want of which we differ even from Low-landers and the inhabitants of Topinamboo:* of quitting our animosities and factions, nor acting any longer like the Jews,† who were murdering one another at the very moment their city was taken: of being a little cautious not to sell our country and conscience for nothing: of teaching landlords to have at least one degree of mercy toward their tenants: lastly, of putting a spirit of honesty, industry, and skill into our shopkeepers; who, if a reso-lution could now be taken to buy only our native goods, would immedi-ately unite to cheat and exact upon us in the price, the measure, and the goodness, nor could ever yet be brought to make one fair proposal of just dealing, though often and earnestly invited to it.

Therefore, I repeat, let no man talk to me of these and the like expedi-   30
ents, till he hath at least some glimpse of hope that there will ever be some hearty and sincere attempt to put them in practice.‡

But as to myself, having been wearied out for many years with offering   31
vain, idle, visionary thoughts, and at length utterly despairing of success, I fortunately fell upon this proposal, which, as it is wholly new, so it hath something solid and real, of no expense and little trouble, full in our own power, and whereby we can incur no danger in disobliging England. For this kind of commodity will not bear exploration, the flesh being of too tender a consistence to admit a long continuance in salt, although perhaps I could name a country which would be glad to eat up our whole nation without it.

After all, I am not so violently bent upon my own opinion as to reject   32
any offer proposed by wise men, which shall be found equally innocent, cheap, easy, and effectual. But before something of that kind shall be advanced in contradiction to my scheme, and offering a better, I desire the author or authors will be pleased maturely to consider two points. First, as things now stand, how they will be able to find food and raiment for an hundred thousand useless mouths and backs. And secondly, there being a round million of creatures in human figure throughout this kingdom, whose sole subsistence put into a common stock would leave them in debt two million of pounds sterling, adding those who are beggars by profes-sion to the bulk of farmers, cottagers, and laborers, with their wives and children who are beggars in effect; I desire those politicians who dislike my overture, and may perhaps be so bold to attempt an answer, that they will first ask the parents of these mortals whether they would not at this day think it a great happiness to have been sold for food at a year old in this manner I prescribe, and thereby have avoided such a perpetual scene of

---

* EDS. NOTE — A place in the Brazilian jungle.

† EDS. NOTE — In the first century B.C., the Roman general Pompey could conquer Jerusalem in part because the citizenry was divided among rival factions.

‡ EDS. NOTE — Note that these measures represent Swift's true proposal.

misfortunes as they have since gone through by the oppression of land-lords, the impossibility of paying rent without money or trade, the want of common sustenance, with neither house nor clothes to cover them from the inclemencies of the weather, and the most inevitable prospect of entailing the like or greater miseries upon their breed forever.

I profess, in the sincerity of my heart, that I have not the least personal interest in endeavoring to promote this necessary work, having no other motive than the public good of my country, by advancing our trade, providing for infants, relieving the poor, and giving some pleasure to the rich. I have no children by which I can propose to get a single penny; the youngest being nine years old, and my wife past childbearing.　　33

● ● ●

Comprehension

1. What problem does Swift identify? What general solution does he recommend?
2. What advantages does Swift see in his plan?
3. What does he see as the alternative to his plan?
4. What clues indicate that Swift is not serious about his proposal?
5. In paragraph 29, Swift lists and rejects a number of "other expedients." What are they? Why do you think he presents and rejects these ideas?

Purpose and Audience

1. Swift's target here is the British government, in particular its poor treatment of the Irish. How would you expect British government officials to respond to his proposal? How would you expect Irish readers to react?
2. What do you think Swift hoped to accomplish in this essay? Was his purpose simply to amuse and shock, or did he want to change people's minds — or even inspire them to take some kind of action? Explain.
3. In paragraphs 6, 14, 23, and elsewhere, Swift presents a series of mathematical calculations. What effect do you think he expected these computations to have on his readers?
4. Explain why each of the following groups might have been offended by this essay: women, Catholics, butchers, and the poor.
5. How do you think Swift expected the appeal in his conclusion to affect his audience?

Style and Structure

1. In paragraph 6, Swift uses the word *breeders* to refer to fertile women. What connotations does this word have? Why does he use this word rather than a more neutral alternative?

2. What purpose does paragraph 8 serve in the essay? Do the other short paragraphs have the same function? Explain.

3. Swift's remarks are presented as an argument. Where, if anywhere, does he anticipate and refute his readers' objections?

4. Swift applies to infants many words usually applied to animals who are slaughtered to be eaten — for example, *fore or hind quarter* (10) and *carcass* (15). Identify as many examples of this kind of usage as you can. Why do you think Swift uses such words?

5. Throughout his essay, Swift cites the comments of others — "our merchants" (7), "a very knowing American of my acquaintance" (9), and "an eminent French physician" (13), for example. Cite additional examples. What, if anything, does he accomplish by referring to these people?

6. A **satire** is a piece of writing that uses wit, **irony**, and ridicule to attack foolishness, incompetence, or evil. How does "A Modest Proposal" fit this definition of satire?

7. Evaluate the strategy Swift uses to introduce each advantage he cites in paragraphs 21 through 26.

8. Swift uses a number of parenthetical comments in his essay — for example, in paragraphs 14, 17, and 26. Identify all of his parenthetical comments, and consider what they contribute to the essay.

9. Swift begins paragraph 20 with the words, "I have too long digressed, and therefore shall return to my subject." Has he in fact been digressing? Explain.

Vocabulary Projects

1. Define each of the following words as it is used in this selection.

importuning (1)	rudiments (6)	encumbrance (19)
alms (1)	nutriment (7)	tithes (21)
prodigious (2)	repine (14)	vintners (25)
professed (3)	flay (15)	expedients (29)
dam (4)	scrupulous (17)	parsimony (29)
reckoned (6)	censure (17)	temperance (29)
apprehend (6)	desponding (19)	raiment (32)

2. The title states that Swift's proposal is a "modest" one; elsewhere he says he proposes his ideas "humbly" (8). Why do you think he chooses these words? Does he really mean to present himself as modest and humble?

Journal Entry

What is your emotional reaction to this essay? Do you find it amusing or offensive? Why?

Writing Workshop

1. Write a "modest proposal," either straightforward or satirical, for solving a problem in your school or community.
2. Write a "modest proposal" for achieving one of these national goals:
   - Making health care more affordable
   - Improving gun safety
   - Eliminating binge drinking on college campuses
   - Improving public education
   - Reducing children's consumption of unhealthy foods
   - Eliminating teenage pregnancy
   - Reducing the use of illegal drugs
3. Write a letter to an executive of the tobacco industry, a television network, or an industry that threatens the environment. In your letter, set forth a "modest proposal" for making the industry more responsible.

Combining the Patterns

What patterns of development does Swift use in his argument? Annotate the essay to identify each pattern. Use the annotations accompanying "On Dumpster Diving" (page 712) as a guide.

Thematic Connections

- "The Embalming of Mr. Jones" (page 310)
- "The Irish Famine, 1845–1849" (page 338)
- "I Want a Wife" (page 524)
- The Declaration of Independence (page 584)

Strange Tools

The son of working-class immigrants from Mexico, Richard Rodriguez (b. 1944) grew up in Sacramento, California, and received an undergraduate degree from Stanford University and a doctorate in English Renaissance literature from the University of California at Berkeley. He initially sought a career as a college educator but abandoned that pursuit to become a full-time writer. His first book, the highly praised *Hunger of Memory* (1981), was a series of essays tracing the story of his education and its influence on his relationship with his parents. His later books include *Days of Obligation: An Argument with My Mexican Father* (1992) and *Brown: The Last Discovery of America* (2002), a meditation on personal identity at cultural borderlines. A regular essayist on *NewsHour with Jim Lehrer* on public television, Rodriguez is also a frequent commentator on National Public Radio, a correspondent with the Pacific News Service, and contributing editor to a number of periodicals.

Background on the concept of the "scholarship boy": Earlier in *Hunger of Memory,* the source of the following selection, Rodriguez describes discovering as a graduate student the book *The Uses of Literacy* by Richard Hoggart. In this book, Hoggart defines a certain kind of student as a "scholarship boy," a child of uneducated working-class parents who himself strives desperately for academic achievement, "who has to be more and more alone if he is going to 'get on.' " Such a child's gradual mental and emotional separation from his family, his growing allegiance to the classroom, his wrenching sense of personal loss, his anxiety even as he succeeds at school—all these qualities Rodriguez recognized immediately as markers of his own childhood, exacerbated by his parents' limited English skills. As Rodriguez concludes, "If, because of my schooling, I had grown culturally separated from my parents, my education finally had given me ways of speaking and caring about that fact."

From an early age I knew that my mother and father could read and write both Spanish and English. I had observed my father making his way through what, I now suppose, must have been income tax forms. On other occasions I waited apprehensively while my mother read onion-paper letters airmailed from Mexico with news of a relative's illness or death. For both my parents, however, reading was something done out of necessity and as quickly as possible. Never did I see either of them read an entire book. Nor did I see them read for pleasure. Their reading consisted of work manuals, prayer books, newspapers, recipes.

Richard Hoggart imagines how, at home,

   . . . [The scholarship boy] sees strewn around, and reads regularly himself, magazines which are never mentioned at school, which seem not to belong to the world to which the school introduces him; at school he hears about and reads books never mentioned at home. When he brings those books into the house they do not take their place with other books which the family are reading, for often there are none or almost none; his books look, rather, like strange tools.

In our house each school year would begin with my mother's careful instruction: "Don't write in your books so we can sell them at the end of the year." The remark was echoed in public by my teachers, but only in part: "Boys and girls, don't write in your books. You must learn to treat them with great care and respect."

OPEN THE DOORS OF YOUR MIND WITH BOOKS, read the red and white   3
poster over the nun's desk in early September. It soon was apparent to me that reading was the classroom's central activity. Each course had its own book. And the information gathered from a book was unquestioned. READ TO LEARN, the sign on the wall advised in December. I privately wondered: What was the connection between reading and learning? Did one learn something only by reading it? Was an idea only an idea if it could be written down? In June, CONSIDER BOOKS YOUR BEST FRIENDS. Friends? Reading was, at best, only a chore. I needed to look up whole paragraphs of words in a dictionary. Lines of type were dizzying, the eye having to move slowly across the page, then down, and across. . . . The sentences of the first books I read were coolly impersonal. Toned hard. What most bothered me, however, was the isolation reading required. To console myself for the loneliness I'd feel when I read, I tried reading in a very soft voice. Until: "Who is doing all that talking to his neighbor?" Shortly after, remedial reading classes were arranged for me with a very old nun.

At the end of each school day, for nearly six months, I would meet with   4
her in the tiny room that served as the school's library but was actually only a storeroom for used textbooks and a vast collection of *National Geographics.* Everything about our sessions pleased me: the smallness of the room; the noise of the janitor's broom hitting the edge of the long hallway outside the door; the green of the sun, lighting the wall; and the old woman's face blurred white with a beard. Most of the time we took turns. I began with my elementary text. Sentences of astonishing simplicity seemed to me lifeless and drab: "The boys ran from the rain . . . She wanted to sing . . . The kite rose in the blue." Then the old nun would read from her favorite books, usually biographies of early American presidents. Playfully she ran through complex sentences, calling the words alive with her voice, making it seem that the author somehow was speaking directly to me. I smiled just to listen to her. I sat there and sensed for the very first time some possibility of fellowship between a reader and a writer, a communication, never *intimate* like that I heard spoken words at home convey, but one nonetheless *personal.*

One day the nun concluded a session by asking me why I was so reluc-   5
tant to read by myself. I tried to explain; said something about the way written words made me feel all alone — almost, I wanted to add but didn't,

as when I spoke to myself in a room just emptied of furniture. She studied my face as I spoke; she seemed to be watching more than listening. In an uneventful voice she replied that I had nothing to fear. Didn't I realize that reading would open up whole new worlds? A book could open doors for me. It could introduce me to people and show me places I never imagined existed. She gestured toward the bookshelves. (Bare-breasted African women danced, and the shiny hubcaps of automobiles on the back covers of the *Geographic* gleamed in my mind.) I listened with respect. But her words were not very influential. I was thinking then of another consequence of literacy, one I was too shy to admit but nonetheless trusted. Books were going to make me "educated." *That* confidence enabled me, several months later, to overcome my fear of the silence.

In fourth grade I embarked upon a grandiose reading program. "Give me the names of important books," I would say to startled teachers. They soon found out that I had in mind "adult books." I ignored their suggestion of anything I suspected was written for children. (Not until I was in college, as a result, did I read *Huckleberry Finn* or *Alice's Adventures in Wonderland.*) Instead, I read *The Scarlet Letter* and Franklin's *Autobiography.* And whatever I read I read for extra credit. Each time I finished a book, I reported the achievement to a teacher and basked in the praise my effort earned. Despite my best efforts, however, there seemed to be more and more books I needed to read. At the library I would literally tremble as I came upon whole shelves of books I hadn't read. So I read and I read and I read: *Great Expectations;* all the short stories of Kipling; *The Babe Ruth Story;* the entire first volume of the *Encyclopaedia Britannica* (A–ANSTEY); the *Iliad; Moby Dick; Gone with the Wind; The Good Earth; Ramona; Forever Amber; The Lives of the Saints; Crime and Punishment; The Pearl.* . . . Librarians who initially frowned when I checked out the maximum ten books at a time started saving books they thought I might like. Teachers would say to the rest of the class, "I only wish the rest of you took reading as seriously as Richard obviously does."

But at home I would hear my mother wondering, "What do you see in your books?" (Was reading a hobby like her knitting? Was so much reading even healthy for a boy? Was it the sign of "brains"? Or was it just a convenient excuse for not helping around the house on Saturday mornings?) Always, "What do you see . . . ?"

What *did* I see in my books? I had the idea that they were crucial for my academic success, though I couldn't have said exactly how or why. In the sixth grade I simply concluded that what gave a book its value was some major idea or theme it contained. If that core essence could be mined and memorized, I would become learned like my teachers. I decided to record in a notebook the themes of the books that I read. After reading *Robinson Crusoe,* I wrote that its theme was "the value of learning to live by oneself." When I completed *Wuthering Heights,* I noted the danger of "letting emotions get out of control." Rereading these brief moralistic appraisals usually left me disheartened. I couldn't believe that they were really the source of reading's value. But for many more years, they constituted the only means I had of describing to myself the educational value of books.

In spite of my earnestness, I found reading a pleasurable activity. I   9
came to enjoy the lonely good company of books. Early on weekday mornings, I'd read in my bed. I'd feel a mysterious comfort then, reading in the dawn quiet — the bluegray silence interrupted by the occasional churning of the refrigerator motor a few rooms away or the more distant sounds of a city bus beginning its run. On weekends I'd go to the public library to read, surrounded by old men and women. Or, if the weather was fine, I would take my books to the park and read in the shade of a tree. A warm summer evening was my favorite reading time. Neighbors would leave for vacation and I would water their lawns. I would sit through the twilight on the front porches or in backyards, reading to the cool, whirling sounds of the sprinklers.

I also had favorite writers. But often those writers I enjoyed most I was   10
least able to value. When I read William Saroyan's *The Human Comedy,* I was immediately pleased by the narrator's warmth and the charm of his story. But as quickly I became suspicious. A book so enjoyable to read couldn't be very "important." Another summer I determined to read all the novels of Dickens. Reading his fat novels, I loved the feeling I got — after the first hundred pages — of being at home in a fictional world where I knew the names of the characters and cared about what was going to happen to them. And it bothered me that I was forced away at the conclusion, when the fiction closed tight, like a fortune-teller's fist — the futures of all the major characters neatly resolved. I never knew how to take such feelings seriously, however. Nor did I suspect that these experiences could be part of a novel's meaning. Still, there were pleasures to sustain me after I'd finish my books. Carrying a volume back to the library, I would be pleased by its weight. I'd run my fingers along the edge of the pages and marvel at the breadth of my achievement. Around my room, growing stacks of paperback books reenforced my assurance.

I entered high school having read hundreds of books. My habit of   11
reading made me a confident speaker and writer of English. Reading also enabled me to sense something of the shape, the major concerns, of Western thought. (I was able to say something about Dante and Descartes and Engels and James Baldwin in my high school term papers.) In these various ways, books brought me academic success as I hoped that they would. But I was not a good reader. Merely bookish, I lacked a point of view when I read. Rather, I read in order to acquire a point of view. I vacuumed books for epigrams, scraps of information, ideas, themes — anything to fill the hollow within me and make me feel educated. When one of my teachers suggested to his drowsy tenth-grade English class that a person could not have a "complicated idea" until he had read at least two thousand books, I heard the remark without detecting either its irony or its very complicated truth. I merely determined to compile a list of all the books I had ever read. Harsh with myself, I included only once a title I might have read several

times. (How, after all, could one read a book more than once?) And I included only those books over a hundred pages in length. (Could anything shorter be a book?)

There was yet another high school list I compiled. One day I came   12 across a newspaper article about the retirement of an English professor at a nearby state college. The article was accompanied by a list of the "hundred most important books of Western Civilization." "More than anything else in my life," the professor told the reporter with finality, "these books have made me all that I am." That was the kind of remark I couldn't ignore. I clipped out the list and kept it for the several months it took me to read all of the titles. Most books, of course, I barely understood. While reading Plato's *Republic,* for instance, I needed to keep looking at the book jacket comments to remind myself what the text was about. Nevertheless, with the special patience and superstition of a scholarship boy, I looked at every word of the text. And by the time I reached the last word, relieved, I convinced myself that I had read *The Republic.* In a ceremony of great pride, I solemnly crossed Plato off my list.

•   •   •

Comprehension

1. What do Rodriguez's parents read, and for what purpose? What is their attitude toward books?

2. How is Rodriguez's home like the home of the "scholarship boy" (2) described by Richard Hoggart?

3. What attitude toward books is communicated to Rodriguez at school?

4. Why does Rodriguez have to take remedial reading classes? What does he learn in his sessions with the elderly nun? How do her ideas about the purpose of reading differ from his?

5. How does Rodriguez finally "overcome [his] fear of the silence" (5)?

6. What motivates Rodriguez to begin his "grandiose reading program" (6)? How does his mother react to his reading?

7. Why does Rodriguez write down the theme of each book he reads?

8. What benefits does Rodriguez derive from his reading?

Purpose and Audience

1. In paragraph 11, speaking of his high school years, Rodriguez says, "But I was not a good reader. Merely bookish, I lacked a point of view when I read. Rather, I read in order to acquire a point of view." What does he mean? Does Rodriguez's essay illustrate that he has now acquired a point of view? Explain.

2. Do you think Rodriguez's purpose here is to promote the importance of reading? To analyze his own misguided efforts to educate himself? To reveal something about his upbringing or about his education? Might he have several different purposes?

3. Rodriguez grew up in a bilingual household. Do you think his essay has relevance only for those from bilingual families, or do you think his comments apply just as well to a broader audience? Explain.

Style and Structure

1. Throughout this essay, Rodriguez lists specific titles of books he has read. Why? Are these lists essential, or could he have omitted them? Explain.

2. Paragraph 7 is much shorter than the other paragraphs in this essay. Why? What purpose does this paragraph serve?

3. In paragraph 9, Rodriguez paints a picture of the "dawn quiet" during which he reads each day. What does this passage reveal about him?

4. In paragraph 10, Rodriguez compares the conclusion of a book to a "fortune-teller's fist." What does he mean?

Vocabulary Projects

1. Define each of the following words as it is used in this selection.

   fellowship (4)   earnestness (9)
   grandiose (6)   sustain (10)
   basked (6)

2. What does Rodriguez mean in paragraph 11 when he says he "vacuumed books"? What other expression could you substitute for this phrase?

Journal Entry

In paragraph 3, Rodriguez gives three examples of slogans that appeared on posters in his classroom. Create several new slogans designed to promote reading in the elementary school classroom, and briefly describe how each poster might be illustrated.

Writing Workshop

1. Write an essay discussing the role books played in the household you grew up in. What did your parents read, and for what purpose? What did you learn from their reading habits and attitudes? How are your own reading habits and attitudes like and unlike theirs? Use narration, exemplification, cause and effect, and comparison and contrast to structure your essay.

2. Clearly, books changed Rodriguez's life. What activity had a similar impact on you? Write an essay explaining how the activity you pursued shaped your character and personality. Although the dominant pattern of your essay will be cause and effect, you may use other patterns as well.

3. Make a list of five or six childhood books you remember with affection, and then write a combined book review trying to explain why these books are memorable. Include brief plot summaries (in present tense) and evaluations as well as a thesis statement that ties the books together and communicates their importance. Label your paragraphs to indicate the patterns of development you use.

Combining the Patterns

What patterns of development does Rodriguez use? Annotate the essay to identify each pattern. Use the annotations accompanying "On Dumpster Diving" (page 712) as a guide.

Thematic Connections

- "Only Daughter" (page 96)
- "The Human Cost of an Illiterate Society" (page 252)
- "Television: The Plug-In Drug" (page 351)
- "Mother Tongue" (page 487)

WRITING ASSIGNMENTS FOR COMBINING THE PATTERNS

1. Reread Michael Huu Truong's essay at the beginning of this chapter. Responding to the same assignment he was given ("Write an essay about the person and/or place that defined your childhood"), use several different patterns to communicate to readers what your childhood was like.

2. Write an essay about the political, social, or economic events that you believe have dominated and defined your life or a stage in your life. Use cause and effect and any other patterns you think are appropriate to explain and illustrate why these events were important to you and how they affected you.

3. Develop a thesis statement that draws a general conclusion about the nature, quality, or effectiveness of advertising in print media (in newspapers or magazines or on billboards). Write an essay that supports this thesis statement with a series of very specific paragraphs. Use the patterns of development that best help you to characterize particular advertisements.

4. Exactly what do you think it means to be an American? Write a definition essay that answers this question, developing your definition with whatever patterns best serve your purpose.

5. Many of the essays in this text recount the writers' personal experiences. Identify one essay that describes experiences that are either similar to your own or in sharp contrast to your own. Then, write a comparison-and-contrast essay *either* comparing *or* contrasting your experiences with those of the writer. Use several different patterns to develop your essay.

COLLABORATIVE ACTIVITY FOR COMBINING THE PATTERNS

Working in pairs, choose an essay from Chapters 6 through 14 of this text. Then, working individually, identify the various patterns of development used in the essay. When you have finished, compare notes with your classmate. Have both of you identified the same patterns in the essay? If not, try to reach a consensus. Working together, write a paragraph summarizing why each pattern is used and explaining how the various patterns combine to support the essay's thesis.

INTERNET ASSIGNMENT FOR COMBINING THE PATTERNS

Write an essay considering the moral and ethical implications of new breakthroughs in cloning. Use several different patterns to support your thesis and to illustrate the potential benefits and dangers of cloning. Visit the following Web sites to learn more about the process of cloning and the future possibilities it suggests.

Time Newsfile: Cloning
<time.com/time/newsfiles/cloning>
This site sponsored by *Time* magazine offers information about the cloning process, futurist scenarios, and a discussion of the ethics of cloning.

Actionbioscience.org
<actionbioscience.org/biotech>
This site, sponsored by BioScience Productions, Inc., an organization promoting bioscience literacy, includes links to articles on cloning and the ethical issues surrounding cloning technology, as well as links to other sites on the cloning debate.

Human Cloning Foundation
<humancloning.org>
This nonprofit group's site links to interviews, frequently asked questions, essays about the benefits of human cloning, and lists of books and movies that address human cloning issues.

Using Research in Your Writing

In some essays, you can use your own ideas to support your points. In other essays — such as argumentative essays — you may have to supplement your own ideas with **research**: material from books, articles, television programs, the Internet, and electronic databases. As you research and write, remember what you have learned about the writing process, and keep in mind that your main task is to present ideas clearly and convincingly. You will have an easier time writing a research paper if you follow an orderly process:

1. Choose a topic.
2. Test your topic.
3. Do research.
4. Take notes.
5. Watch out for plagiarism.
6. Draft a thesis statement.
7. Make an outline.
8. Write your essay.
9. Document your sources.

Step 1: Choosing a Topic

The first step in writing an essay that calls for research is finding a topic to write about. Before you decide on a topic, ask yourself the following questions:

- What is my page limit?
- When is my paper due?
- How many sources am I expected to use?

The answers to these questions can help you make sure your topic is neither too broad nor too narrow.

Caitlin Byrne, a student in a college composition course, was asked to write a three- to five-page paper that was due in five weeks and that required research. She knew she wanted to write about what could have been done to prevent the terrorist violence that occurred on September 11, 2001. Caitlin was interested in airport security — especially since an hour-long delay at a security checkpoint had recently caused her to miss a flight. She realized, however, that the general topic "airport security" would be too broad for a short paper and that a topic such as "my long delay at the airport" would be much too narrow. "What can be done to improve airport security?" however, might work well: she could discuss the topic in the required number of pages and complete her paper within the time limit.

Caitlin knew from her instructor's guidelines that the purpose of her paper should be either to *present information* (for example, to discuss what was being done around the country to increase airport security) or to *make a point* (for example, that some form of national ID card could speed up airport security checks as well as eliminate racial profiling). Caitlin decided on the second option.

Step 2: Testing Your Topic

Before you choose a topic, you should **test** it to see if it will work — in other words, if you can find enough to write about. You begin testing your topic by going to the Internet and doing a keyword search. You should also survey the resources of your library. (Before you do this, arrange a meeting with a college librarian, who can answer questions, give you suggestions, and point you toward helpful resources.)

In the library, begin by looking at the *subject catalog* or the *online central information system* to see what books and articles about your topic are listed there. (Frequently, the online central information system contains the library's catalog as well as a number of databases you can search.) For example, under the general topic "airport security," Caitlin discovered a number of books and articles that focused on this topic. Several of these articles dealt with racial profiling — searching people solely on the basis of their race — and the title of one suggested that the government could eliminate racial profiling by creating a national identity card that each citizen could carry.

Step 3: Doing Research

Finding Information in the Library

The best place to start your research is in your college library. It contains resources you cannot find anywhere else — including on the Internet. For the best results, you should do your library research systematically:

begin by looking at reference works; then, search the library's catalog and periodical indexes; and, finally, look for any additional facts or statistics you need to support your ideas.

GUIDELINES FOR USING LIBRARY RESOURCES

Reference Works   Begin your research in the reference section of the library. There you can consult works that will give you an overview of your topic as well as key facts, dates, and names to use in your paper. **General encyclopedias**—like the *New Encyclopaedia Britannica*—contain articles on a wide variety of topics. **Specialized encyclopedias** contain articles that give you detailed information about a specific field—psychology or sociology, for example. Other reference works—such as *Who's Who in America*—provide information about people's lives.

The Library's Catalog   Once you get a general sense of your topic, you can consult the library's catalog. Most libraries have replaced print catalogs with **online catalogs** that enable you to use a computer to search all the resources held by the library. By typing in words or phrases related to your topic on computer terminals located around the library, you can find books, periodicals, and other materials to use in your paper. If you know exactly what you are looking for, you can find it by typing in the title of a book or the name of its author.

Periodical Indexes   After consulting the online catalog, you may want to look at the periodical indexes your library subscribes to. **Periodical indexes** are databases that access information from newspapers, magazines, and journals. Some indexes list just citations, while others provide the full text of articles. You can usually search the periodical indexes on the same computer terminals you use to search the library's online catalog. Many college libraries have classes that teach you how to access articles in periodical indexes.

Sources for Facts and Statistics   As you write your paper, you may find that you need certain facts or statistics to support particular points. Reference works such as *Facts on File,* the *Information Please Almanac,* and the *Statistical Abstract of the United States* can help you get such information. These resources are available in the reference section of your college library, where a librarian can help you find sources of factual and statistical information specific to your topic. (They are also available online.)

Remember, once you find information in the library, you still have to **evaluate** it—that is, you need to determine its usefulness and reliability. For example, an article in a respected periodical such as the *New York Times* or the *Wall Street Journal* is more trustworthy and believable than one in a tabloid such as the *National Enquirer* or the *Sun.* You should also check the date of publication to see if the book or article is up-to-date. Finally, look at the author's biographical information. Is he or she an expert? Does the author's background suggest a particular viewpoint (or bias)? Your instructor or college librarian can help you select appropriate and reliable sources.

Finding Information on the Internet

The Internet can give you access to a great deal of information that you can use to help you support the points you make. To use the Internet, you need an Internet **browser**, a tool that enables you to access and display Web pages. The most popular browsers are Netscape Navigator and Microsoft Internet Explorer. Once you are online, you need to connect to a **search engine**, a program that enables you to sort through the millions of documents available on the Internet. Among the popular search engines are Google, AltaVista, and Yahoo.

There are three ways to use a search engine to find information.

1. *You can enter a Web site's URL.* All search engines have a box in which you can enter a Web site's electronic address, or **URL** (uniform resource locator). When you click on the URL—or hit your computer's Enter or Return key—the search engine connects you to the Web site. For example, to find information about family members who entered the United States through Ellis Island, you would type in the URL www.ellisislandrecords.com.

2. *You can do a keyword search.* All search engines enable you to do a **keyword search**. You type a term into a box, and then the search engine looks for documents that contain the term. If you type a broad term like *civil war,* you might get hundreds of thousands of hits—far too many to consider. If this occurs, narrow your search by using a more specific term—*Battle of Gettysburg,* for example. You can focus your term even further by putting quotation marks around the term ("*Battle of Gettysburg*"). When you do this, the search engine will search only for documents that contain this specific phrase.

3. *You can do a subject search.* Many search engines, such as Yahoo, let you do a subject search. First, you click on a broad subject from a list of subjects: *The Humanities, The Arts, Entertainment, Business,* and so on. Each of these general subjects leads you to a list of more specific subjects, until, eventually, you get to the subtopic you want. For example, you could start your search by clicking on the general topic *Entertainment.* Clicking on this would lead you to *Movies* and then to *Movie Reviews.* Finally, you would get to a list of movie reviews that might link to the specific movie you were interested in.

Remember, not every Internet site you access will be a valuable source of information. Because anyone can put information on the Internet, you need to be skeptical when you approach Internet sites. Just as you would with a print source, you should evaluate each electronic source—determine whether the information it contains is believable and useful.

When Caitlin searched the periodical index in her college library for the terms *airport security* and *racial profiling*, she found an article on racial profiling published in the *Atlantic Monthly*. Her instructor told her that this publication was well respected and usually reliable so she could be sure the writer was someone who knew a lot about his subject.

Step 4: Taking Notes

Once you have gathered the material you will need, read it carefully, writing down any information you think you can use in your essay. As you take notes, record relevant information in a computer file you set up for your paper.

When you use information from a source in your paper, you do not always *quote* the exact words of your source. In fact, most often you *paraphrase* or *summarize* a source, putting its ideas into your own words. For this reason, most of your notes should be in the form of paraphrase or summary.

Paraphrasing

When you **paraphrase**, you use your own words to present the main ideas of a source, but you keep the order and emphasis of the original. You paraphrase when you want to use detailed information from the source but not the author's exact words. Paraphrasing is useful when you want to make a difficult discussion easier to understand while still conveying an accurate sense of the original.

Begin by reading the source until you are sure you understand it. As you write, go through the source sentence by sentence, writing down ideas in the order in which they occur. Include only the author's ideas; keep your own opinions to yourself. As you write, follow your source closely. Be sure to present only the passage's main idea and key supporting points, eliminating examples and asides that are not essential to meaning. Remember, *because a paraphrase expresses the original ideas of the source's author, it must be documented.*

GUIDELINES FOR WRITING A PARAPHRASE

1. Read the passage you intend to paraphrase until you understand it.
2. Jot down the main idea of the passage, and list all supporting points.
3. As you write, follow the order and emphasis of the original.
4. When you revise, make sure you have used your own words and phrases, not the words or sentence structure of the original.
5. Document your source.

Here is a passage from "Why Fear National ID Cards?" by Alan M. Dershowitz (page 618), an article Caitlin uses in her paper, followed by her paraphrase.

Original

Finally, there is the question of the right to anonymity. I don't believe we can afford to recognize such a right in this age of terrorism. No such right is hinted at in the Constitution. And though the Supreme Court has identified a right to privacy, privacy and anonymity are not the same. American taxpayers, voters, and drivers long ago gave up any right of anonymity without loss of our right to engage in lawful conduct within zones of privacy. Rights are a function of experience, and our recent experiences teach that it is far too easy to be anonymous — even to create a false identity — in this large and decentralized country. A national ID card would not prevent all threats of terrorism, but it would make it more difficult for potential terrorists to hide in open view, as many of the September 11 hijackers apparently managed to do.

Paraphrase

According to Alan Dershowitz, a right to anonymity would undercut the country's ability to deal with terrorism. The right to anonymity is not recognized by the United States Constitution, and a clear difference exists between anonymity and privacy, a right that the Constitution does acknowledge. As anyone who files a tax return or registers to vote knows, many daily activities require people to give up a certain degree of anonymity. In many other areas of our lives, however, we have a great deal of personal privacy. A national ID card would make it harder for terrorists to use this privacy to live among us and to travel freely. At the same time, it would give people the security of knowing that hijackers could not carry out their plans as easily as they did on September 11 (619).

Summarizing

Unlike a paraphrase, which restates the ideas of a source in detail, a **summary** is a general restatement, in your own words, of a passage's main idea. Because it is so general, a summary is always much shorter than the original. Unlike a paraphrase, a summary does not follow the order or emphasis of the original.

Before you begin to write, make sure you understand the passage you want to summarize. Read it several times, identifying the writer's main idea. As you write, use your own words, not those of your source. Keep in mind that a summary can be one sentence or several sentences in length, depending on the complexity of the ideas in the original passage. As you revise, make sure your summary expresses just the main idea of your source, not your own opinions or conclusions. Remember, *because a summary expresses the original ideas of the source's author, it must be documented.*

> **GUIDELINES FOR WRITING A SUMMARY**
>
> 1. Read the passage you intend to summarize until you understand it.
> 2. Jot down the main idea of the passage.
> 3. As you write, make sure you use your own words, not those of your source.
> 4. When you revise, make sure your summary contains only the ideas of the source.
> 5. Document your source.

Here is Caitlin's summary of the passage from Dershowitz's article reproduced on the previous page.

Summary

According to Alan Dershowitz, a national ID card would require every citizen to give up a certain degree of anonymity, but it would also make it difficult for people to move anonymously around the country and engage in terrorist activities.

Quoting

When you quote, you use the author's exact words as they appear in the source, including all punctuation, capitalization, and spelling. Enclose all words from your source in quotation marks — *followed by appropriate documentation.* Because quotations distract readers, use them only when you think the author's exact words will add something to your discussion. As a rule, unless you have a definite reason to quote a source, you should paraphrase or summarize it.

> **GUIDELINES FOR QUOTING SOURCES**
>
> 1. Quote when the original language is so memorable that paraphrasing would lessen the impact of the writer's ideas.
> 2. Quote when a paraphrase or summary would change the meaning of the original.
> 3. Quote when the original language adds authority to your discussion. The exact words of an expert on your topic can help you make your point convincingly.

Introduce paraphrases, summaries, and quotations with a phrase that identifies the source or its author. You can place this identifying phrase at various points in a sentence. Instead of always using the same words to introduce source material — *says* or *states,* for example — try using different words and phrases — *points out, observes, comments, notes, remarks,* and *concludes.*

Identifying Phrase at the Beginning

In the article "Why Fear National ID Cards?" <u>Alan Dershowitz notes</u>, "A national ID card would not prevent all threats of terrorism, but it would make it more difficult for potential terrorists to hide in open view, as many of the September 11 hijackers apparently managed to do" (619).

Identifying Phrase at the End

"A national ID card would not prevent all threats of terrorism, but it would make it more difficult for potential terrorists to hide in open view, as many of the September 11 hijackers apparently managed to do," <u>Alan Dershowitz claims</u> (619).

Identifying Phrase in the Middle

"A national ID card would not prevent all threats of terrorism," <u>constitutional law expert Alan Dershowitz observes</u>, "but it would make it more difficult for potential terrorists to hide in open view, as many of the September 11 hijackers apparently managed to do" (619).

Step 5: Watching Out for Plagiarism

As a rule, **document** (provide source information for) all words, ideas, pictures, or statistics from an outside source. (It is not necessary, however, to document **common knowledge** — information most readers will probably know or factual information widely available in reference works.) When you present information from another source as if it were your own (whether intentionally or unintentionally), you are committing **plagiarism** — and plagiarism is theft. You can avoid plagiarism by understanding what you must document and what you do not have to document.

GUIDELINES FOR AVOIDING PLAGIARISM

YOU MUST DOCUMENT

- All word-for-word quotations from a source
- All summaries and paraphrases of material from a source
- All ideas — opinions, judgments, and insights — that are not your own
- All tables, graphs, charts, and statistics you get from a source

YOU DO NOT NEED TO DOCUMENT

- Your own ideas
- Common knowledge
- Familiar quotations

Avoiding Common Errors That Lead to Plagiarism

The following paragraph from "The Threat of National ID" (page 614), an essay by William Safire, and the four rules listed after it will help you understand and avoid the most common causes of plagiarism.

Original

Today's diatribe will be scorned as alarmist by the same security-mongers who shrugged off our attorney general's attempt to abolish habeas corpus (which libertarian protests and the Bush administration's sober second thoughts seem to be aborting). But the lust to take advantage of the public's fear of terrorist penetration by penetrating everyone's private lives — this time including the lives of U.S. citizens protected by the Fourth Amendment — is gaining popularity. (Safire, William. "The Threat of National ID." *Patterns for College Writing*. 10th ed. Ed. Laurie G. Kirszner and Stephen R. Mandell. New York: Bedford, 2007. 614–16.)

1. Identify Your Source

Plagiarism

Even though the government has pulled back from its most extreme plans to defeat terrorists, a danger still exists that the government will undermine our Fourth Amendment rights.

The writer does not quote Safire directly, but she still must identify him as the source of her paraphrased material. She can do this by adding an identifying phrase and parenthetical documentation.

Correct

According to William Safire, even though the government has pulled back from its most extreme plans to defeat terrorists, a danger still exists that the government will undermine our Fourth Amendment rights (615).

2. Place Borrowed Words in Quotation Marks

Plagiarism

According to William Safire, the government, as well as big business, is increasingly willing to take advantage of the public's fear of terrorist penetration by penetrating everyone's private lives (615).

Although the writer cites Safire as her source, the passage incorrectly uses Safire's exact words without quoting them. The writer must either place the borrowed words in quotation marks or paraphrase them.

Correct (Borrowed Words in Quotation Marks)

According to William Safire, the government, as well as big business, is increasingly willing to "take advantage of the public's fear of terrorist penetration by penetrating everyone's private lives" (615).

Correct (Borrowed Words Paraphrased)

According to William Safire, the government, as well as big business, is increasingly willing to use the excuse of terrorism to extend the scope of its surveillance power (615).

3. Use Your Own Wording

Plagiarism

Those who criticize plans for a national ID card will be dismissed as excessive by the same people who had no problem when the attorney general attempted to do away with habeas corpus protection. (Thankfully, the administration seems to have decided to abandon these plans.) Even so, the drive to exploit people's fear of terrorism by intruding into their private affairs — thus violating the Fourth Amendment — is becoming increasingly popular (Safire 615).

Even though the writer acknowledges Safire as her source and provides parenthetical documentation, and even though she does not use Safire's exact words, her passage closely follows the order, emphasis, syntax, and phrasing of the original. In the following passage, the writer uses her own wording, quoting one distinctive phrase from her source.

Correct

Unfortunately, many people have no problem with the government's plan for a national ID card. According to William Safire, these people do not realize the danger of the government's "lust to take advantage of the public's fear of terrorist penetration" (615). As Safire makes clear, this intrusion into people's private lives clearly violates the Fourth Amendment (615).

4. Distinguish Your Own Ideas from Your Source's Ideas

Plagiarism

Unfortunately, many people have no problem with the government's plan for a national ID card. These people are afraid and want to be protected, and they do not realize that government is more than willing to take advantage of their fears. Its attempt to institute a national ID card is simply another unwarranted (and dangerous) incursion into "the lives of U.S. citizens protected by the Fourth Amendment" (Safire 615).

In the preceding passage, it appears that only the quotation in the last sentence is borrowed from Safire's article. In fact, the ideas in the second sentence are also Safire's. The writer should use an identifying phrase (such as

"According to Safire") to acknowledge the borrowed material in this sentence and to indicate where it begins.

Correct

Unfortunately, many people have no problem with the government's plan for a national ID card. According to William Safire, these people are afraid and want to be protected, and they do not realize that government is more than willing to take advantage of their fears (615). Its attempt to institute a national ID card is simply another unwarranted (and dangerous) incursion into "the lives of U.S. citizens protected by the Fourth Amendment" (615).

Avoiding Plagiarism with Online Sources

Most students know that using long passages (or entire articles) from a print source without documenting the source is plagiarism. Unfortunately, many students assume that borrowing material found on a Web site or elsewhere online without documentation is acceptable. However, such borrowing is also plagiarism. Perhaps these students feel differently about online borrowing because it is so easy to cut and paste from an online source into a text document. They may also see copying online material as acceptable because—with authors often unidentified online—no one appears to take credit for the source. No matter what the explanation is for this casual treatment of online sources, instructors consider the use of undocumented words or ideas from online sources to be as serious as the same kind of plagiarism from a print source. Therefore, just as you do for print sources, you must document words or ideas you get from online sources.

Note: It goes without saying that downloading entire papers from Web sites and turning them in as your own work is plagiarism. Such conduct is unfair to you, your instructor, and your fellow students, and it undercuts the learning process.

Step 6: Drafting a Thesis Statement

After you have taken notes, review the information you have gathered, and draft a **thesis statement**—a single sentence that states the main idea of your paper and tells readers what to expect.

After completing her research, Caitlin Byrne came up with the following tentative thesis statement for her paper on airport security.

If every U.S. citizen had a national ID card or a Safe Traveler Card, airports could screen for terrorists more effectively than they do now and avoid procedures that single out individuals solely on the basis of race.

Step 7: Making an Outline

Once you have drafted a thesis statement, you are ready to make an outline from your notes. Your outline, which covers just the body paragraphs of your paper, can be either a *topic outline* (each idea is expressed in a word or short phrase) or a *sentence outline* (each idea is expressed in a complete sentence). When it is finished, your outline will be your guide as you write your paper.

After reviewing her notes, Caitlin Byrne constructed the following sentence outline for her paper. Notice that she uses roman numerals for first-level headings, capital letters for second-level headings, and arabic numerals for third-level headings.

If every U.S. citizen had a national ID card or a Safe Traveler Card, airports could screen for terrorists more effectively than they do now and avoid procedures that single out individuals solely on the basis of race.

I. To avoid charges of harassing people of Middle Eastern descent, many airports have instituted a policy of searching passengers at random.
   A. Random searches have advantages.
      1. Random searches occasionally detect people who would not be detected by racial profiling.
      2. Random searches encourage security personnel to scrutinize all passengers.
   B. Random searches also have disadvantages.
      1. Random searches waste time and resources on people who pose no threat.
      2. Security personnel focus on passengers randomly selected by a computer and not on specific passengers.
II. Other strategies are more effective for screening airline passengers, but they also have disadvantages.
   A. Routine preflight security checks for all passengers are effective.
      1. They are time consuming.
      2. They are expensive.
   B. New developments in airport security could alleviate problems.
      1. They have not been perfected.
      2. They are expensive.
III. The cheapest and most efficient airport security method is some type of Safe Traveler Card or national ID card.
   A. These cards have many advantages.
      1. They would be small and cost little to produce.
      2. They would be like E-Z Pass devices and simple to use.
      3. Airport officials would be able to scan the cards.
      4. Airport officials would be able to obtain background information from government databases.
   B. These cards have drawbacks.
      1. They work only for travelers who do not mind volunteering personal information to obtain a card.

    2. They would not prevent passengers with "clean" backgrounds from bringing weapons or explosives on board.

    3. Some people believe that these cards would deprive people of their privacy.

IV. Syndicated columnist William Safire and constitutional law expert Alan Dershowitz have different positions concerning national ID cards.

  A. According to Safire, both the government and law-enforcement agencies could exploit national ID cards.

    1. Businesses could discover people's credit rating, bank accounts, and product preferences.

    2. The advantages of ID cards would undermine people's right to privacy.

  B. Dershowitz believes that the advantages of national ID cards outweigh their disadvantages.

    1. The national ID card would be only a little more intrusive than a photo ID or a voter registration card.

    2. It would reduce or eliminate the need for racial profiling.

    3. Airport security officials could do instant background checks on everyone.

    4. The personal information in the system would stay in the system and never be made public.

V. Even though Safe Traveler Cards and national ID cards have drawbacks, the alternatives are also problematic.

  A. Racial profiling could once more be used to screen passengers.

    1. Racial profiling would have identified the September 11 terrorists as they passed through airports.

    2. Racial profiling is discriminatory.

  B. Religion could be used as a criterion to screen passengers.

    1. Religious profiling would have identified the September 11 terrorists.

    2. Religious profiling presents the same problems as racial profiling.

  C. Age and gender could also be considered.

    1. Most September 11 terrorists were males between ages eighteen and forty.

    2. Profiling on the basis of age or gender can lead to discrimination.

  D. Behavioral characteristics could be used to screen passengers.

    1. Behavioral profiling would have identified the September 11 terrorists.

    2. Behavioral profiling would not work with passengers who knew what behavior security officials were looking for.

Step 8: Writing Your Essay

Once you have decided on a thesis and written an outline, you are ready to write a draft of your essay. Start by arranging your notes in the order in which you will use them. Follow your outline as you write, but don't be afraid to depart from it if new ideas occur to you.

Begin your essay with an **introduction** that includes your thesis statement. Usually your introduction will be a single paragraph, but sometimes it will be longer.

In the **body** of your essay, you support your thesis statement, with each body paragraph developing a single idea. Support your points with summaries, paraphrases, and quotations from your sources as well as with your own ideas and opinions. Your body paragraphs should have clear topic sentences so that your readers will know exactly what points you are making, and you should use transitional words and phrases to help readers follow the progression of your ideas.

Finally, your **conclusion** should give readers a sense of completion. Like your introduction, your conclusion is usually a single paragraph, but it can be longer. It should reinforce your thesis statement and your paper's main ideas and should end with a sentence that will stay with readers.

Once you have drafted your essay, you should consider adding **visuals** — photographs, charts, graphs, and so on. Because they have such an immediate impact on readers, visuals can make your essay more memorable and more persuasive. But to be effective, they must clearly relate to the points you are making. Used effectively, visuals are another type of evidence that can support your thesis statement; used ineffectively, however, visuals can distract readers.

You can get visuals online, from print documents that you can scan, from digital cameras, and from commercially available software packages. Remember, however, that not all visuals will be suitable for (or effective in) your essay. Depending on your purpose and audience, some visuals could actually undermine your argument. You must evaluate the appropriateness of the visuals you intend to use, just as you would with a print source. And, of course, you must include full documentation for any visual you use.

Once you select a visual, you have to decide how to use it in your essay. The following guidelines should make this task easier for you.

GUIDELINES FOR USING VISUALS

- *Use a sentence to introduce the visual.* Visuals should never be carelessly dropped into your paper. Make sure that the relationship between the visual and the discussion is clear.

- *When you introduce the visual, refer to it parenthetically in the text.* Example: "Random searches encourage security personnel to scrutinize all passengers, not some of them (see fig. 1)."

- *Place the visual as close as possible to the relevant portion of the discussion.* Ideally, you want to insert the visual at the point where you discuss it. If that is not possible (because, for example, the visual is too large to fit on the page), put it at the top of the following page.

- *Document the visual.* Remember, you must provide source information for all visual material that you get from a source.

Keep in mind that you will probably write several drafts of your essay before you submit it. You can use the revision checklist on page 54 to help you revise and edit your paper.

Caitlin Byrne's completed essay on airport security appears on page 778.

Step 9: Documenting Your Sources

When you **document** a source, you tell readers where you have found the information you have used in your essay. The Modern Language Association (MLA) recommends the following documentation style for essays that use research.* This format consists of *parenthetical references* in the body of the paper that refer to a *works-cited* list at the end of the paper.

Parenthetical References in the Text

A parenthetical reference should include just enough information to guide readers to a specific entry in your works-cited list. A typical parenthetical reference consists of the author's last name and the page number: (Safire 2). If you use more than one work by the same author, include a shortened form of the title in the parenthetical reference: (Safire, "National ID" 4). Notice that the entry has no comma and no p. before the page number.

Whenever possible, introduce information with a phrase that includes the author's name. (If you do this, include only the page number in parentheses.)

> According to Alan Dershowitz, the national ID card would be only a little
> more intrusive than a photo ID card or a voter registration card (619).

Place documentation so that it does not interrupt the flow of your ideas, preferably at the end of a sentence.

The format for parenthetical references departs from these guidelines in the following special situations:

WHEN YOU ARE CITING A WORK BY TWO AUTHORS

> Ever since the Bush administration suggested national ID cards, civil
> libertarians have attacked the idea (Kladstrup and Walker 27).

WHEN YOU ARE CITING A WORK WITHOUT A LISTED AUTHOR

> After screeners at airports were made federal employees, the government
> upgraded their training ("Airport Screeners" 54).

---

* For further information, see the sixth edition of the *MLA Handbook for Writers of Research Papers* (New York: Mod. Lang. Assn., 2003) or the MLA Web site at mla.org.

WHEN YOU ARE CITING AN INDIRECT SOURCE

If you use a statement by one author that is quoted in the work of another author, indicate this by including the abbreviation qtd. in ("quoted in").

> When speaking about racial profiling, William Bryson says, "The effects of such actions on the rights that Americans take for granted is devastating" (qtd. in Seidman 45).

WHEN YOU ARE CITING AN ELECTRONIC SOURCE

Sources from the Internet or from library databases frequently do not contain page numbers. If the electronic source uses paragraph, section, or screen numbers, use the abbreviation par., sec., or the full word screen, followed by the corresponding number, in your documentation. If the citation includes an author name, place a comma after the name.

> Random searches are not only time consuming, but they are also highly inefficient (Richmond, par. 16).

If the electronic source has no page numbers or markers of any kind, include just the name(s) of the author(s). Readers can tell that the citation refers to an electronic source when they consult the works-cited list.

> The problem with random searching is that security personnel focus on a list of passengers randomly selected by a computer and not on specific passengers (Cambanis and Daniel).

GUIDELINES FOR FORMATTING QUOTATIONS

SHORT QUOTATIONS.   Quotations of no more than four typed lines are run in with the text of your paper. End punctuation comes after the parenthetical reference (which follows the quotation marks).

> According to two constitutional law experts, when one group is singled out for scrutiny, "agents are more likely to miss dangerous persons who take care not to fit the profile" (Cole and Dempsey 170).

LONG QUOTATIONS.   Quotations of more than four lines are set off from the text of your paper. Indent a long quotation ten spaces (or one inch) from the left-hand margin, and do not enclose the passage in quotation marks. The first line of a long quotation is not indented even if it is the beginning of a paragraph. If a quoted passage has more than one paragraph, indent the first line of each paragraph after the first one three additional spaces (or one-quarter inch). Introduce a long quotation with a colon, and place the parenthetical reference one space *after* the end punctuation.

According to David Cole and James Dempsey, September 11 caused the American public to become more concerned about national security and less concerned about the personal liberties of those they considered to be possible terrorists:

> Before September 11, about 80 percent of the American public considered racial profiling wrong. . . . After September 11, however, polls reported the fact that 60 percent of the American public favored racial profiling, at least as long as it was directed at Arabs and Muslims. (168)

Note: Ellipsis points indicate that the student has deleted words from the quotation.

The Works-Cited List

The works-cited list includes all the works you cite (refer to) in your paper. Use the following guidelines to help you prepare your list.

GUIDELINES FOR PREPARING THE WORKS CITED LIST

- Begin the works-cited list on a new page after the last page of your paper.
- Number the works-cited page as the next page of the paper.
- Center the heading Works Cited one inch from the top of the page; do not underline the heading or put it in quotation marks.
- Double-space the list.
- List entries alphabetically according to the author's last name.
- Alphabetize unsigned articles according to the first major word of the title.
- Begin each entry flush with the left-hand margin.
- Indent second and subsequent lines one-half inch (or five spaces).
- Separate each division of the entry—author, title, and publication information—by a period and one space.

The following sample works-cited entries cover the situations you will encounter most often. Follow the formats exactly as they appear here.

Books

BOOKS BY ONE AUTHOR

List the author with last name first. Underline the title. Include the city of publication and a shortened form of the publisher's name—for example, *Prentice* for *Prentice Hall* or *Bedford* for *Bedford/St. Martin's*. Use the abbreviation *UP* for *University Press*, as in *Princeton UP* and *U of Chicago P*. End with a date of publication.

Goldsmith, Martin. The Beatles Come to America. Hoboken: Wiley, 2004.

BOOKS BY TWO OR THREE AUTHORS

List authors in the order in which they are listed on the book's title page. List second and subsequent authors with first names first.

Bigelow, Fran, and Helene Siegel. Pure Chocolate. New York: Broadway, 2004.

BOOK BY MORE THAN THREE AUTHORS

List only the first author, followed by the abbreviation *et al.* ("and others").

Ordeman, John T., et al. Artists of the North American Wilderness: George and Belmore Browne. New York: Warwick, 2004.

TWO OR MORE BOOKS BY THE SAME AUTHOR

List two or more books by the same author in alphabetical order according to title. In each entry after the first, use three unspaced hyphens (followed by a period) instead of the author's name.

Angelou, Maya. Hallelujah! The Welcome Table: A Lifetime of Memories with Recipes. New York: Random, 2004.

---. I Know Why the Caged Bird Sings. New York: Bantam, 1985.

EDITED BOOK

Whitman, Walt. The Portable Walt Whitman. Ed. Michael Warner. New York: Penguin, 2004.

TRANSLATION

García Márquez, Gabriel. Living to Tell the Tale. Trans. Edith Grossman. New York: Knopf, 2004.

REVISED EDITION

Bjelajac, David. American Art: A Cultural History. 2nd ed. New York: Prentice, 2004.

ANTHOLOGY

Kirszner, Laurie G., and Stephen R. Mandell, eds. Patterns for College Writing: A Rhetorical Reader and Guide. 10th ed. New York: Bedford, 2007.

ESSAY IN AN ANTHOLOGY

Zimecki, Michael. "Violent Films Cry 'Fire' in Crowded Theaters." Patterns
     for College Writing: A Rhetorical Reader and Guide. 10th ed. Ed. Laurie
     G. Kirszner and Stephen R. Mandell. New York: Bedford, 2007. 691-94.

MORE THAN ONE ESSAY IN THE SAME ANTHOLOGY

List each essay separately with a cross-reference to the entire anthology.

Kirszner, Laurie G., and Stephen R. Mandell, eds. Patterns for College
     Writing: A Rhetorical Reader and Guide. 10th ed. New York: Bedford,
     2007.

Stone, Oliver. "Memo to John Grisham: What's Next — 'A Movie Made Me Do
     It'?" Kirszner and Mandell 686-88.

Zimecki, Michael. "Violent Films Cry 'Fire' in Crowded Theaters." Kirszner
     and Mandell 691-94.

SECTION OR CHAPTER OF A BOOK

Gordimer, Nadine. "Loot." "Loot" and Other Stories. New York: Farrar, 2004.
     1-6.

INTRODUCTION, PREFACE, FOREWORD, OR AFTERWORD

Ingham, Patricia. Introduction. Martin Chuzzlewit. By Charles Dickens.
     London: Penguin, 1999. x-xxxii.

MULTIVOLUME WORK

Malory, Thomas. Le Morte D'Arthur. Ed. Janet Cowen. 2 vols. London:
     Penguin, 1986.

ARTICLE IN A REFERENCE WORK

For familiar reference works that publish new editions regularly,
include only the edition (if given) and the year of publication.

"Civil Rights." The World Book Encyclopedia. 2006 ed.

For less familiar reference works, provide a full citation.

Wagle, Greta. "Geisel, Theodor [Seuss]." The Encyclopedia of American
     Literature. Ed. Steven R. Serafin. New York: Continuum, 1999.

Periodicals

Journals.   A **journal** is a publication aimed at readers who know a
lot about a particular subject — English or history, for example.

ARTICLE IN A JOURNAL WITH CONTINUOUS PAGINATION THROUGHOUT AN ANNUAL VOLUME

Some scholarly journals have continuous pagination; that is, one issue might end on page 234, and the next would then begin with page 235. In this case, the volume number is followed by the date of publication in parentheses.

> Markley, Robert. "Gulliver and the Japanese: The Limits of the Postcolonial Past." Modern Language Quarterly 65 (2004): 457-80.

ARTICLE IN A JOURNAL WITH SEPARATE PAGINATION IN EACH ISSUE

For a journal with each issue beginning on page 1, the volume number is followed by a period and the issue number and then by the date. Leave no space after the period between the volume and issue numbers.

> Rushdie, Salman. "The Ministry of False Alarms." Virginia Quarterly Review 80.4 (2004): 7-23.

Magazines.   A **magazine** is a publication aimed at general readers. For this reason, it contains articles that are easier to understand than those in journals.

ARTICLE IN A MONTHLY OR BIMONTHLY MAGAZINE

Frequently, an article in a magazine does not appear on consecutive pages—for example, it might begin on page 43, skip to page 47, and continue on page 49. If this is the case, include only the first page, followed by a plus sign.

> Edwards, Owen. "Kilroy Was Here." Smithsonian Oct. 2004: 40+.

ARTICLE IN A WEEKLY OR BIWEEKLY MAGAZINE (SIGNED OR UNSIGNED)

> Schley, Jim. "Laid Off, and Working Harder than Ever." Newsweek 20 Sept. 2004: 16.

> "Real Reform Post-Enron." The Nation 4 Mar. 2002: 3.

ARTICLE IN A NEWSPAPER

> Bykowicz, Julie. "Man Faces Identity Theft Counts; College Worker Accused of Taking Students' Data." Sun 18 Sept. 2004: 2B.

EDITORIAL OR LETTER TO THE EDITOR

> "An Un-American Way to Campaign." Editorial. New York Times 25 Sept. 2004, late ed.: A14.

REVIEW IN A NEWSPAPER

Scott, A. O. "Forever Obsessing about Obsession." Rev. of Adaptation, dir. Spike Jonze. New York Times 6 Dec. 2002: F1+.

REVIEW IN A WEEKLY OR BIWEEKLY MAGAZINE

Urquhart, Brian. "The Prospect of War." Rev. of The Threatening Storm: The Case for Invading Iraq, by Kenneth M. Pollack. New York Review of Books 19 Dec. 2002: 16-22.

REVIEW IN A MONTHLY MAGAZINE

Jones, Kent. "The Lay of the Land." Rev. of Sunshine State, dir. John Sayles. Film Commentary May/June 2002: 22-24.

Internet Sources

Full source information is not always available for Internet sources. When citing Internet sources appearing on the World Wide Web, include whatever information you can find: the title of the Internet site (underlined), the date of electronic publication (if available), and the date you accessed the source. (Some of the following examples include only the date of access; this indicates that the date of publication was not available.) Always include the electronic address (URL), enclosed in angle brackets.

ENTIRE INTERNET SITE (SCHOLARLY PROJECT, INFORMATION DATABASE, JOURNAL, OR PROFESSIONAL WEB SITE)

International Dialects of English Archive. 2004. Dept. of Theatre and Film, U of Kansas. 4 Dec. 2005 <http://www.ku.edu/~idea/>.

The Dickens Project. Ed. Jon Michael Varese. 2004. U of California, Santa Cruz. 2 Dec. 2005 <http://humwww.ucsc.edu/dickens>.

Words of the Year. 2004. American Dialect Society. 18 Feb. 2004 <http://www.americandialect.org/woty.html>.

DOCUMENT WITHIN A WEB SITE

"Child and Adolescent Violence Research at the NIMH." National Institute of Mental Health Web Site. 2005. 2 April 2005 <http://www.nimh.nih.gov/publicat/violenceresfact.cfm>.

PERSONAL WEB SITE

Lynch, Jack. Home page. 2 Jan. 2005 <http://andromeda.rutgers.edu/~jlynch>.

ENTIRE ONLINE BOOK

Fielding, Henry. The History of Tom Jones, a Foundling. Ed. William Allan
    Nielson. New York: Collier, 1917. Bartleby.com: Great Books Online. Ed.
    Steven van Leeuwen. Sept. 2000. 29 Nov. 2003 <http://www.bartleby.com/301>.

Austen, Jane. Pride and Prejudice. 1813. 30 Nov. 2004 <http://
    www.online-literature.com/austen/prideprejudice>.

PART OF AN ONLINE BOOK

Radford, Dollie. "At Night." Poems. London, 1910. Victorian Women Writers
    Project. Ed. Perry Willett. Nov. 1995. Indiana U. 17 Mar. 2003
    <http://www.indiana.edu/~letrs/vwwp/radford/radpoems.html#p29>.

ARTICLE IN AN ONLINE SCHOLARLY JOURNAL

Condie, Kent C., and Jane Silverstone. "The Crust of the Colorado Plateau:
    New Views of an Old Arc." Journal of Geology 107.4 (1999). 9 Aug.
    2004 <http://www.journals.uchicago.edu/JG/journal/issues/v107n4/
    990034/990034.html>.

ARTICLE IN AN ONLINE REFERENCE BOOK OR ENCYCLOPEDIA

"Croatia." The World Factbook 2004. 30 Mar. 2004. Central Intelligence
    Agency. 30 Dec. 2004 <http://www.odci.gov/cia/publications/factbook/
    country-frame.html>.

ARTICLE IN AN ONLINE NEWSPAPER

Krim, Jonathan. "FCC Preparing to Overhaul Telecom, Media Rules."
    Washington Post 3 Jan. 2003. 6 Jan. 2003 <http://
    www.washingtonpost.com/wp-dyn/articles/A3541-2003Jan2.html>.

ONLINE EDITORIAL

"Ersatz Eve." Editorial. New York Times on the Web 28 Dec. 2002. 5 Jan.
    2003 <http://www.nytimes.com/2002/12/28/opinion/28SAT2.html>.

ARTICLE IN AN ONLINE MAGAZINE

Press, Eyal, and Jennifer Washburn. "The At-Risk-Youth Industry." Atlantic
    Online Dec. 2002. 3 Jan. 2003 <http://www.theatlantic.com/
    issues/2002/12/press.htm>

REVIEW IN AN ONLINE PERIODICAL

Chocano, Carina. "Sympathy for the Misanthrope." Rev. of Curb Your
Enthusiasm, dir. Robert Weide, prod. Larry David. Salon 17 Sept.
2002. 4 Dec. 2002 <http://www.salon.com/ent/tv/diary/2002/09/17/
curb/index.html>.

WORK FROM A LIBRARY'S PERIODICAL INDEX

Prince, Stephen. "Why Do Film Scholars Ignore Media Violence?" Chronicle
of Higher Education. 10 Aug. 2001: B18. Academic Research Premier.
EBSCO. City U of New York, City College Lib. 14 Feb. 2003
<http://www.epnet.com/>.

POSTING TO A DISCUSSION LIST

Thune, W. Scott. "Emotion and Rationality in Argument." Online
posting. 23 Mar. 1997. CCCC/97 Online. 11 Nov. 1997
<http://www.missouri.edu/HyperNews/get/cccc98/proplink/12.html>.

Other Internet Sources

A PAINTING ON THE INTERNET

O'Keeffe, Georgia. Evening Star, III. 1917. Museum of Mod. Art, New York.
9 Nov. 2005 <http://www.moma.org/collection/depts./drawings/blowups/
draw_011.html>.

A PHOTOGRAPH ON THE INTERNET

Cartier-Bresson, Henri. William Faulkner, 1947. Nat. Portrait Gallery.
Portraits by Henri Cartier-Bresson. 8 Oct. 2005 <http://npg.si.edu/exh/
cb/index-int2.htm>.

A CARTOON ON THE INTERNET

Trudeau, Garry. "Doonesbury." Comic strip. Washingtonpost.com 7 Apr.
2005. 5 May 2005 <http://www.washingtonpost.com/wp-srv/style/comics/
king.htm?name=doonsbury>.

A MAP OR CHART ON THE INTERNET

"Fort Worth, Texas." Map. U.S. Gazetteer. US Census Bureau. 26 Oct. 2004
<http://factfinder.census.gov.serviet/
ReferenceMapFramesetServiet?_lang=en>.

MATERIAL ACCESSED ON A CD-ROM, DVD, DISKETTE, OR MAGNETIC TAPE

In addition to the publication information, include the medium (CD-ROM, for example) and the distribution vendor, if relevant (UMI-Proquest, for example).

> Aristotle. "Poetics." The Complete Works of Aristotle. Ed. Jonathan Barnes.
> 2 vols. Princeton: Princeton UP, 1984. CD-ROM. Clayton: InteLex,
> 1994.

> "Feminism." The Oxford English Dictionary. 2nd ed. DVD. New York: Oxford
> UP, 1992.

EMAIL

> De Roo, Mikola. "Re: Headnotes." E-mail to Laurie G. Kirszner. 13 Dec.
> 2002.

SYNCHRONOUS COMMUNICATION

When citing from a synchronous communication, such as a MOO or MUD, you should include the name of the speaker, a description of the event, the date of the event, and the name of the forum.

> Harris, Lee. "Titles." Online lecture. 14 Nov. 2004. Diversity University
> MOO. 16 Nov. 2004 <telnet://moo.du.org>.

DOWNLOADED SOFTWARE

> CryptoHeaven. Vers. 2.1.3. 30 Nov. 2002 <http://
> linux-ny.tucows.webusenet.com/internet/adnload/231445_94803.html>.

MATERIAL ACCESSED THROUGH AN ONLINE SERVICE

Frequently, online services like America Online and Lexis-Nexis enable you to access material without providing a URL. If you access such material by using a keyword, provide the keyword (following the date of access) at the end of the entry.

> "Kafka, Franz." Compton's Encyclopedia Online. Vers. 2.0. 2003. America
> Online. 8 June 2003. Keyword: Compton's.

If, instead of using a keyword, you follow a series of paths, list the paths separated by semicolons.

> "Elizabeth Adams." History Resources. 11 Nov. 2004. America Online. 28
> June 2004. Path: Research: Biography; Women in Science;
> Biographies.

Other Nonprint Sources

TELEVISION OR RADIO PROGRAM

"Prime Suspect 3." Writ. Lynda La Plante. <u>Mystery!</u> PBS. WNET, New York.
28 Apr. 1994.

VIDEOTAPE, MOVIE, RECORD, OR SLIDE PROGRAM

Murray, Donald, perf. <u>Interview with John Updike</u>. Dir. Bruce Schwartz.
Videocassette. Harcourt, 1997.

PERSONAL INTERVIEW

Garcetti, Gilbert. Personal interview. 7 May 2000.

Sample Student Research Essay in MLA Style

Caitlin Byrne's final essay on the topic of airport security appears on
page 778. The essay follows MLA documentation style.

Byrne 1

Caitlin Byrne
Professor Hernandez
HUM 101
9 Apr. 2006

Airport Insecurity

Introduction

After the September 11, 2001, terrorist attacks on New York's World Trade Towers and the Pentagon, the debate surrounding racial profiling in airports intensified. Many people believed that profiling was the best way to identify possible terrorists, but many others worried about violations of civil liberties. While some airports began to target passengers because they were Middle Eastern, others instituted random searches of all passengers. Neither of these strategies, however, is likely to eliminate terrorism. Now, many experts in security are recommending the use of a national ID card or a Safe

Thesis statement

Traveler Card. If every U.S. citizen had such a card, airlines could screen for terrorists while avoiding procedures that single out individuals solely on their national origin or race.

Paragraph combines Caitlin's own ideas, a paraphrase and quotation from Cambanis and Daniel, and a paraphrase and quotation from Cole and Dempsey

The events of September 11 dramatically revealed the shortcomings of airport security in the United States. Clearly, what was needed was a way to identify terrorists before they got on airplanes. In an attempt to avoid charges of racial profiling, many airlines decided that they would search passengers at random. Although random searches are highly inefficient, they do occasionally detect people who would not have been identified by racial profiling. For example, benign-looking passengers have been caught smuggling drugs and even explosives. In one case, agents stopped a pregnant woman trying to board a flight "with a bomb hidden in her luggage by her boyfriend" (Cambanis and Daniel). In addition, random searches force security personnel to scrutinize all passengers, not just some of them. According to two constitutional law experts, when one group is singled out for scrutiny, "agents are more likely to miss dangerous persons who take care not to fit the profile" (Cole and Dempsey 170).

Byrne 2

Paragraph contains a paraphrase from the Cambanis and Daniel article

Although random searches may have some limited success, they are less likely to detect terrorists than are searches based on racial profiling. Many critics of random searches believe that airports are wasting their time searching children or elderly people who pose no legitimate threat (see Fig. 1). The problem with random searching is that security personnel focus on a list of passengers randomly selected by a computer and not on specific passengers (Cambanis and Daniel). Passengers whose names are not on the list can usually board a plane without much difficulty.

Fig. 1. Four-year-old boy goes through security screening at Denver International Airport (2002).

Paragraph combines Caitlin's ideas with a paraphrase from the Easterbrook article

A routine preflight security check for all passengers is another strategy for detecting potential terrorists. Although they are more effective than random searches, they can be expensive and time consuming, requiring passengers to come to the airport two to three hours early. According to Gregg Easterbrook, new developments in airport security — such as full-body X-ray systems and mechanized bomb detectors — may alleviate these problems, but they are still a long way from being perfected. And even if they were available, their cost would be beyond the reach of most airports (179).

Paragraph uses material from the Dershowitz and Safire articles to support Caitlin's own conclusions

Perhaps the cheapest and most efficient security method is a Safe Traveler Card or a national ID card. This card would be about the size of a credit card, contain a computer chip, and cost little to produce. In some ways, these cards are like the E-Z Pass devices that enable people to drive without having to stop and pay tolls (Dershowitz 618). By scanning the card, airport security officials would obtain background information from government databases for every passenger (Safire 615). It is easy to see how such a card could expedite security checks at airports. One swipe of the card, and security officials could tell at a glance whether a person should be searched or let through.

Paragraph contains a paraphrase from the Easterbrook article

As attractive as Safe Traveler Cards or national ID cards are, they are not without drawbacks. For one thing, as Easterbrook notes, these cards would expedite security procedures only for travelers who volunteer such information to obtain a card. Moreover, they would not prevent passengers with "clean" backgrounds from bringing weapons or explosives on board. Perhaps the biggest drawback is that some people believe that the disadvantages of these cards outweigh their advantages because they would deprive people of their privacy (168).

Paragraph contains quotation and summary of ideas in the Safire article

According to syndicated columnist William Safire, both the government and law-enforcement agencies could exploit national ID cards. By tapping into the computer databases, these agencies could obtain a great deal of personal data about an individual. For example, they could tell what magazines people subscribed to, what Web sites they visited, and what their political affiliations were. In addition, businesses could

Byrne 4

discover people's "credit rating, bank accounts, and product preferences" (Safire 615). Safire acknowledges the advantages of such cards but concludes that they would compromise people's right to privacy guaranteed by the Fourth Amendment (Safire 615).

Paragraph contains quotations and a summary from the Dershowitz article

Constitutional law expert Alan Dershowitz dismisses Safire's fears. Although he concedes that national ID cards would lessen a person's anonymity, he believes that this small loss would be offset by a great increase in personal security. To Dershowitz—a self-proclaimed civil libertarian—the national ID card would be only a little more intrusive than a photo ID or voter registration card. In addition, it would reduce or eliminate the need for racial profiling: "Anyone who had the [national ID] card could be allowed to pass through airports or building security more expeditiously, and anyone who opted out could be examined much more closely" (618). Such cards would enable airport security officials to do instant background checks on everyone. The personal information in the system would stay in the system and never be made public. The only information on the card would be a person's "name, address, photo, and [finger]print" (Dershowitz 620).

Paragraph contains Caitlin's own ideas as well as a long quotation from the Cole and Dempsey article

Even though Safe Traveler Cards or national ID cards have drawbacks, the alternatives are even more problematic. One alternative—racial profiling—is discriminatory. Nevertheless, the Transportation Security Administration—which was established in February 2002 to federalize airport security— has recently been rethinking its ban on racial profiling. One reason for this reversal is that the government policy against racial profiling probably kept authorities from questioning the September 11 terrorists as they passed through airports. Another reason is that since the attacks, the American public has changed its opinion regarding racial profiling—at least in airports. According to David Cole and James X. Dempsey, September 11 caused the American public to become more concerned about national security and less concerned about the personal liberties of those they considered to be possible terrorists:

Byrne 5

Before September 11, about 80 percent of the
American public considered racial profiling
wrong. . . . After September 11, however, polls
reported the fact that 60 percent of the American
public favored racial profiling, at least as long as it
was directed at Arabs and Muslims. (168)

Those who favor racial profiling believe that security personnel
should focus on people who would be likely to be involved in
terrorism rather than waste time and money on random
searches of innocent people.

Paragraph uses two examples from the CNN article to support Caitlin's own conclusion

Even though racial profiling may be effective, it raises
disturbing questions about personal liberties and civil rights.
One example of the problems that can occur with racial
profiling is the case of the Arab software developer who
was removed from his flight simply because the pilot felt
uncomfortable flying with him. This action was taken despite
the fact the passenger was a United States citizen who
purchased his ticket through a corporate travel agency
("Airlines"). Another case of racial profiling involved a
passenger who refused to sit next to another passenger because
she thought he looked suspicious. This "suspicious" passenger
was also escorted off the plane and, after questioning, was
asked to board a different flight. In both these situations, a
national ID card or Safe Traveler Card could easily have spared
the passengers embarrassment and enabled them to continue
their flights ("Airlines").

Paragraph contains a quotation from Taylor and statistics from Mooney

One way to avoid racial profiling would be to use some
characteristic (or characteristics) other than race to screen
passengers. One possible criterion could be religion. For
example, the knowledge that all "of the people who have
hijacked airliners for the purpose of murdering Americans have
been Arab men" (Taylor) who practice a form of radical Islam
could lead to the scrutiny of Islamic Arab men — but not of all
Arab men. In this case, most Arab Americans would be
eliminated from suspicion because only 23 percent of Arab

Byrne 6

Americans are Muslim, while 77 percent are Christians (Mooney).

Age and gender could also be considered when screening terrorists. Most of those who committed the acts of September 11 were men between the ages of eighteen and forty (Mooney 2). It would therefore make sense to concentrate on Arab men who are between these ages and who practice some form of radical Islam. However, both these criteria single out individuals on the basis of a single characteristic, and for many people, this is disturbing. Using religion, age, or gender as a basis for questioning leads to discrimination — much like the racial discrimination that results from racial profiling.

Paragraph contains a paraphrase from the Easterbrook article followed by Caitlin's own conclusions

Another way to avoid racial profiling would be to use behavior to screen people. For example, terrorists tend to be males who travel alone, pay cash, buy one-way tickets, and do not have luggage. Other warning signs include people who are traveling alone but seem to be communicating with others on the airplane, who are adjusting items underneath their clothes, or who seem overwrought or nervous (Easterbrook 140). However, even using behavior patterns to identify potential terrorists is not without problems. After all, passengers involved in terrorism would probably know the behavior that airport security would be looking for and would most likely try to control their actions.

Conclusion

It is clear then that the best way of ensuring the safety of airline passengers is to begin issuing Safe Traveler Cards or national ID cards to United States citizens. These cards would screen out those who are unlikely to be terrorists and would also eliminate the delays that currently plague air travel. Most important, they would prevent terrorists from hijacking American planes. At the same time, by making racial profiling unnecessary, these cards would protect our personal and civil liberties. Only by instituting a national ID card system can we make certain that the terrorists who attacked the United States did not also hijack the liberties that are so precious to us.

Paragraph needs no documentation because it contains Caitlin's own ideas

Byrne 7
Works Cited

"Airlines, Passengers Confront Racial Profiling." CNN.com. 3 Oct. 2001.
    Cable News Network. 26 Mar. 2006 <http://www.cnn.com/2001/
    TRAVEL/NEWS/10/03/rec.airlines.profiling/index.html>.

Cambanis, Thanassis, and Mac Daniel. "Air Security under Fire: Travelers
    Irate over Aggressive Airport Searches." Boston Globe 17 Mar.
    2002. 21 Mar. 2006 <http://freerepublic.com/focus/news/
    648367/posts>.

Cole, David, and James X. Dempsey. Terrorism and the Constitution:
    Sacrificing Civil Liberties in the Name of National Security. 2nd ed.
    New York: New Press, 2002.

Dershowitz, Alan M. "Why Fear National ID Cards?" Kirszner and Mandell
    618-20.

Easterbrook, Gregg. "The All-Too-Friendly Skies: Security as an
    Afterthought." How Did This Happen? Terrorism and the New War.
    Ed. James F. Hoge Jr. and Gideon Rose. New York: Public Affairs,
    2001. 163-82.

Kirszner, Laurie G., and Stephen R. Mandell, eds. Patterns for College
    Writing. 10th ed. New York: Bedford, 2007.

Mooney, Chris. "Smart — and Stupid — Profiling." American Prospect
    Online 23 Oct. 2001. 26 Jul. 2002 <http://www.prospect.org/
    webfeatures/2001/10/mooney-c-10-23.html>.

Safire, William. "The Threat of National ID." Kirszner and Mandell 614-16.

Taylor, Stuart Jr. "The Case for Using Racial Profiling at Airports." Atlantic
    Online 25 Sep. 2001. 21 Mar. 2006 <http://www.theatlantic.com/
    politics/nj/taylor2001-09-25.htm>.

Glossary

Abstract/Concrete language   Abstract language names concepts or qualities that cannot be directly seen or touched: *love, emotion, evil, anguish*. Concrete language denotes objects or qualities that the senses can perceive: *fountain pen, leaky, shouting, rancid*. Abstract words are sometimes needed to express ideas, but they are very vague unless used with concrete supporting detail. The abstract phrase "The speaker was overcome with emotion" could mean almost anything, but the addition of concrete language clarifies the meaning: "He clenched his fist and shook it at the crowd" (anger).

Allusion   A brief reference to literature, history, the Bible, mythology, popular culture, and so on that readers are expected to recognize. An allusion evokes a vivid impression in very few words. "The gardener opened the gate, and suddenly we found ourselves in Eden" suggests in one word (*Eden*) the stunning beauty of the garden.

Analogy   A form of comparison that explains an unfamiliar element by comparing it to another that is more familiar. Analogies also enable writers to put abstract or technical information in simpler, more concrete terms: "The effect of pollution on the environment is like that of cancer on the body."

Annotating   The technique of recording one's responses to a reading selection by writing notes in the margins of the text. Annotating a text might involve asking questions, suggesting possible parallels with other selections or with the reader's own experience, arguing with the writer's points, commenting on the writer's style, or defining unfamiliar terms or concepts.

Antithesis   A viewpoint opposite to one expressed in a *thesis*. In an argumentative essay, the thesis must be debatable. If no antithesis exists, the writer's thesis is not debatable. (See also **Thesis**.)

Antonym   A word opposite in meaning to another word. *Beautiful* is the antonym of *ugly*. *Synonym* is the antonym of *antonym*.

Argumentation   The form of writing that takes a stand on an issue and attempts to convince readers by presenting a logical sequence of points supported by evidence. Unlike *persuasion*, which uses a number of different appeals, argumentation is primarily an appeal to reason. (See Chapter 14.)

Audience   The people "listening" to a writer's words. Writers who are sensitive to their audience will carefully choose a tone, examples, and allusions that their readers will understand and respond to. For instance, an effective article attempting to persuade high school students not to drink alcohol would use examples and allusions pertinent to a teenager's life. Different examples would be chosen if the writer were addressing middle-aged members of Alcoholics Anonymous.

Basis for comparison   A fundamental similarity between two or more things that enables a writer to compare them. In a comparison of how two towns react to immigrants, the basis of comparison might be that both towns have a rapidly expanding immigrant population. (If one of the towns did not have any immigrants, this comparison would be illogical.)

Body paragraphs   The paragraphs that develop and support an essay's thesis.

Brainstorming   An invention technique that can be done individually or in a group. When writers brainstorm on their own, they jot down every fact or idea that relates to a particular topic. When they brainstorm in a group, they discuss a topic with others and write down the useful ideas that come up.

Causal chain   A sequence of events when one event causes another event, which in turn causes yet another event.

Cause and effect   The pattern of development that discusses either the reasons for an occurrence or the observed or predicted consequence of an occurrence. Often both causes and effects are discussed in the same essay. (See Chapter 10.)

Causes   The reasons for an event, situation, or phenomenon. An *immediate cause* is an obvious one; a *remote cause* is less easily perceived. The *main cause* is the most important cause, whether it is immediate or remote. Other, less important causes that nevertheless encourage the effect in some way (for instance, by speeding it up or providing favorable circumstances for it) are called *contributory causes.*

Chronological order   The time sequence of events. Chronological order is often used to organize a narrative; it is also used to structure a process essay.

Claim   In Toulmin logic, the thesis or main point of an essay. Usually the claim is stated directly, but sometimes it is implied. (See also **Toulmin logic**.)

Classification and division   The pattern of development that uses these two related methods of organizing information. *Classification* involves searching for common characteristics among various items and grouping them accordingly, thereby imposing order on randomly organized information. *Division* breaks up an entity into smaller groups or elements. Classification generalizes; division specifies. (See Chapter 12.)

Cliché   An overused expression, such as *beauty is in the eye of the beholder, the good die young,* or *a picture is worth a thousand words.*

Clustering   A method of invention whereby a writer groups ideas visually by listing the main topic in the center of a page, circling it, and surrounding it with words or phrases that identify the major points to be addressed. The writer then circles these words or phrases, creating new clusters or ideas for each of them.

Coherence   The tight relationship between all the parts of an effective piece of writing. Such a relationship ensures that the writing will make sense to readers. For a piece of writing to be coherent, it must be logical and orderly, with effective *transitions* making the movement between sentences and paragraphs clear. Within and between paragraphs, coherence may also be enhanced by the repetition of key words and ideas, by the use of pronouns to refer to nouns mentioned previously, and by the use of parallel sentence structure.

Colloquialisms Expressions that are generally appropriate for conversation and informal writing but not usually acceptable for the writing you do in college, business, or professional settings. Examples of colloquial language include contractions; clipped forms (*dorm* for *dormitory, exam* for *examination*); vague expressions such as *kind of* and *sort of;* conversation fillers such as *you know;* and other informal words and expressions, such as *get across* for *communicate* and *kids* for *children.*

Common knowledge Factual information that is widely available in reference sources. Writers do not need to document common knowledge.

Comparison and contrast The pattern of development that focuses on similarities and differences between two or more subjects. In a general sense, *comparison* shows how two or more subjects are alike; *contrast* shows how they are different. (See Chapter 11.) (See also **Point-by-point comparison**; **Subject-by-subject comparison**.)

Conclusion The group of sentences or paragraphs that brings an essay to a close. To *conclude* means not only "to end" but also "to resolve." Although a conclusion does not resolve all the issues in an essay, the conclusion is the place to show that they *have* been resolved. An effective conclusion indicates that the writer is committed to what has been expressed, and it is the writer's last chance to leave an impression or idea with readers.

Concrete language See **Abstract/Concrete language**.

Connotation The associations, meanings, or feelings a word suggests beyond its literal meaning. Literally, the word *home* means one's place of residence, but *home* also connotes warmth and a sense of belonging. (See also **Denotation.**)

Contributory cause See **Causes**.

Deductive reasoning The method of reasoning that moves from a general premise to a specific conclusion. Deductive reasoning is the opposite of *inductive reasoning.* (See also **Syllogism.**)

Definition An explanation of a word's meaning; the pattern of development in which a writer explains what something or someone is. (See Chapter 13.) (See also **Extended definition; Formal definition**.)

Denotation The literal meaning of a word. The denotation of *home* is "one's place of residence." (See also **Connotation**.)

Description The pattern of development that presents a word picture of a thing, a person, a situation, or a series of events. (See Chapter 7; see also **Objective description**; **Subjective description**.)

Digression A remark or series of remarks that wanders from the main point of a discussion. In a personal narrative, a digression may be entertaining because of its irrelevance, but in other kinds of writing it is likely to distract and confuse readers.

Division See **Classification and division**.

Documentation The formal way of giving credit to the sources a writer borrows words or ideas from. Documentation allows readers to evaluate a writer's sources and to consult them if they wish. Papers written for literature and writing classes use the documentation style recommended by the Modern Language Association (MLA). (See Appendix.)

Dominant impression The mood or quality that is central to a piece of writing.

Essay A short work of nonfiction writing on a single topic that usually expresses the author's impressions or opinions. An essay may be organized around one of the patterns of development presented in Chapters 6 through 14 of this book, or it may combine several of these patterns.

Euphemism A polite term for an unpleasant concept. (*Passed on* is a euphemism for *died.*)

Evidence Facts and opinions used to support a statement, position, or idea. *Facts,* which may include statistics, may be drawn from research or personal experience; *opinions* may represent the conclusions of experts or the writer's own ideas.

Example A concrete illustration of a general point.

Exemplification The pattern of development that uses a single extended *example* or a series of shorter examples to support a thesis. (See Chapter 8.)

Extended definition A paragraph-, essay-, or book-length definition developed by means of one or more of the rhetorical strategies discussed in this book.

Fallacy A statement that resembles a logical argument but is actually flawed. Logical fallacies are often persuasive, but they unfairly manipulate readers to win agreement. Fallacies include begging the question; argument from analogy; personal (*ad hominem*) attacks; hasty or sweeping generalizations; false dilemmas (the either/or fallacy); equivocation; red herrings; you also (*tu quoque*); appeals to doubtful authority; distorting statistics; *post hoc* reasoning; and *non sequiturs.*

Figures of speech (also known as *figurative language*) Imaginative language used to suggest a special meaning or create a special effect. Three of the most common figures of speech are *similes, metaphors,* and *personification.*

Formal definition A brief explanation of a word's meaning as it appears in the dictionary.

Freewriting A method of invention that involves writing without stopping for a fixed period—perhaps five or ten minutes—without paying attention to spelling, grammar, or punctuation. The goal of freewriting is to let ideas flow and get them down on paper.

Grounds In Toulmin logic, the material that a writer uses to support a claim. Grounds may be evidence (facts or expert opinions) or appeals to the emotions or values of an audience. (See also **Toulmin logic.**)

Highlighting   A technique used by a reader to record responses to a reading selection by marking the text with symbols. Highlighting a text might involve underlining important ideas, boxing key terms, numbering a series of related points, circling unfamiliar words (or placing question marks next to them), drawing vertical lines next to an interesting or important passage, drawing arrows to connect related points, or placing asterisks next to discussions of the selection's central issues or themes.

Hyperbole   Deliberate exaggeration for emphasis or humorous effect: "I froze to death out in the storm"; "She has hundreds of boyfriends"; "Senior year passed by in a second." The opposite of hyperbole is *understatement.*

Imagery   A set of verbal pictures of sensory experiences. These pictures, conveyed through concrete details, make a description vivid and immediate to the reader. Some images are literal ("The cows were so white they almost glowed in the dark"); others are more figurative ("The black and white cows looked like maps, with the continents in black and the seas in white"). A pattern of imagery (repeated images of, for example, shadows, forests, or fire) may run through a piece of writing.

Immediate cause   See **Causes**.

Inductive reasoning   The method of reasoning that moves from specific evidence to a general conclusion based on this evidence. Inductive reasoning is the opposite of *deductive reasoning.*

Instructions   A kind of process essay whose purpose is to enable readers to *perform* a process. Instructions use the present tense and speak directly to readers: "Walk at a moderate pace for twenty minutes."

Introduction   An essay's opening. Depending on the length of an essay, the introduction may be one paragraph or several paragraphs. In an introduction, a writer tries to encourage the audience to read the essay that follows. Therefore, the writer must choose tone and diction carefully, indicate what the paper is about, and suggest to readers what direction it will take.

Invention (also known as *prewriting*)   The stage of writing when a writer explores the writing assignment, focuses ideas, and ultimately decides on a thesis for an essay. A writer might begin by thinking through the requirements of the assignment—the essay's purpose, length, and audience. Then, using one or more methods of invention—such as *freewriting, questions for probing, brainstorming, clustering,* and *journal writing*—the writer can formulate a tentative thesis and begin to write the essay.

Irony   Language that points to a discrepancy between two different levels of meaning. *Verbal irony* is characterized by a gap between what is stated and what is really meant, which often has the opposite meaning—for instance, "his humble abode" (referring to a millionaire's estate). *Situational irony* points to a discrepancy between what actually happens and what readers expect will happen. This kind of irony is present, for instance, when a character, trying to frighten a rival, ends up frightening himself. *Dramatic irony* occurs when the reader understands more about what is happening in a story than the character who is telling the story does. For example, a narrator might tell an anecdote that he intends to illustrate how clever he is, while it is obvious to the reader from the story's events that the narrator has made a fool of himself because of his gullibility. (See also **Sarcasm**.)

Jargon   The specialized vocabulary of a profession or academic field. Although the jargon of a particular profession is an efficient means of communication within that field, it may not be clear or meaningful to readers outside that profession.

Journal writing   A method of invention that involves recording ideas that emerge from reading or other experiences and then exploring them in writing.

Looping   A method of invention that involves isolating one idea from a piece of freewriting and using this idea as a focus for a new piece of freewriting.

Main cause   See **Causes**.

Metaphor   A comparison of two dissimilar things that does not use the words *like* or *as* ("Not yet would they veer southward to the caldron of the land that lay below" — N. Scott Momaday).

Narration   The pattern of development that tells a story. (See Chapter 6.)

Objective description   A detached, factual picture presented in plain and direct manner. Although pure objectivity is impossible to achieve, writers of science papers, technical reports, and news articles, among others, strive for precise language that is free of value judgments.

Paradox   A statement that seems self-contradictory or absurd but is nonetheless true.

Paragraph   The basic unit of an essay. A paragraph is composed of related sentences that together express a single idea. This main idea is often stated in a single *topic sentence*. Paragraphs are also graphic symbols on the page, mapping the progress of the ideas in the essay and providing visual breaks for readers.

Parallelism   The use of similar grammatical elements within a sentence or sentences. "I like hiking, skiing, and to cook" is not parallel because *hiking* and *skiing* are gerund forms (*-ing*) while *to cook* is an infinitive form. Revised for parallelism, the sentence could read either "I like hiking, skiing, and cooking" or "I like to hike, to ski, and to cook." As a stylistic technique, parallelism can provide emphasis through repetition — for example, "Walk groundly, talk profoundly, drink roundly, sleep soundly" (William Hazlitt). Parallelism is also a powerful oratorical technique: "Until justice is blind to color, until education is unaware of race, until opportunity is unconcerned with the color of men's skins, emancipation will be a proclamation but not a fact" (Lyndon B. Johnson). Finally, parallelism can increase *coherence* within a paragraph or an essay.

Paraphrase   The restatement of another person's words in one's own words, following the order and emphasis of the original. Paraphrase is frequently used in source-based papers, where the purpose is to use information gathered during research to support the ideas in the paper. For example, Jonathan Kozol's "Illiterates cannot travel freely. When they attempt to do so, they encounter risks that few of us can dream of" (page 256) might be paraphrased like this: "According to Jonathan Kozol, people who cannot read find travel extremely dangerous."

Personification   Describing concepts or objects as if they were human ("the chair slouched"; "the wind sighed outside the window").

Persuasion   The method a writer uses to move an audience to adopt a belief or follow a course of action. To persuade an audience, a writer relies on the various appeals — to the emotions, to reason, or to ethics. Persuasion is different from *argumentation,* which appeals primarily to reason.

Plagiarism   Presenting the words or ideas of someone else as if they were one's own (whether intentionally or unintentionally). Plagiarism should always be avoided.

Point-by-point comparison   A comparison in which the writer first makes a point about one subject and then follows it with a comparable point about the other subject. (See also **Subject-by-subject comparison**.)

***Post hoc* reasoning**   A logical fallacy that involves looking back at two events that occurred in chronological sequence and wrongly assuming that the first event caused the second. For example, just because a car will not start after a thunderstorm, one cannot automatically assume that the storm caused the problem.

Prewriting   See **Invention**.

Principle of classification   In a classification-and-division essay, the quality the items have in common. For example, if a writer were classifying automobiles, one principle of classification might be "repair records."

Process   The pattern of development that presents a series of steps in a procedure in chronological order and shows how this sequence of steps leads to a particular result. (See Chapter 9.)

Process explanation   A kind of process essay whose purpose is to enable readers to understand a process rather than perform it.

Purpose   A writer's reason for writing. A writer's purpose may, for example, be to entertain readers with an amusing story, to inform them about a dangerous disease, to move them to action by enraging them with an example of injustice, or to change their perspective by revealing a hidden dimension of a person or situation.

Quotation   The exact words of a source, enclosed in quotation marks. A quotation should be used only to present a particularly memorable statement or to avoid a paraphrase that would change the meaning of the original.

Refutation   The attempt to counter an opposing argument by revealing its weaknesses. Three of the most common weaknesses are logical flaws in the argument, inadequate evidence, and irrelevance. Refutation greatly strengthens an argument by showing that the writer is aware of the complexity of the issue and has considered opposing viewpoints.

Remote cause   See **Causes**.

Rhetorical question   A question asked for effect and not meant to be answered.

Rogerian argument   A strategy put forth by psychologist Carl Rogers that rejects the adversarial approach that characterizes many arguments. Rather than attacking the opposition, Rogers suggests acknowledging the validity of opposing positions. By finding areas of agreement, a Rogerian argument reduces conflict and increases the chance that the final position will satisfy all parties.

Sarcasm   Deliberately insincere and biting irony — for example, "That's okay — I love it when you borrow things and don't return them."

Satire   Writing that uses wit, irony, and ridicule to attack foolishness, incompetence, or evil in a person or idea. Satire has a different purpose from comedy, which usually intends simply to entertain. For a classic example of satire, see Jonathan Swift's "A Modest Proposal," page 733.

Sexist language   Language that stereotypes people according to gender. Writers often use plural constructions to avoid sexist language. For example, *the doctors . . . they* can be used instead of *the doctor . . . he.* Words such as *police officer* and *firefighter* can be used instead of *policeman* and *fireman.*

Simile   A comparison of two dissimilar things using the words *like* or *as* ("Hills Like White Elephants" — Ernest Hemingway).

Slang   Informal words whose meanings vary from locale to locale or change as time passes. Slang is frequently associated with a particular group of people — for example, bikers, musicians, or urban youth. Slang is inappropriate in college writing.

Subject-by-subject comparison   A comparison that discusses one subject in full and then goes on to discuss the next subject. (See also **Point-by-point comparison**.)

Subjective description   A description that contains value judgments (*a saintly person,* for example). Whereas objective language is distanced from an event or object, *subjective language* is involved. A subjective description focuses on the author's reaction to the event, conveying not just a factual record of details but also their significance. Subjective language may include poetic or colorful words that impart a judgment or an emotional response (*stride, limp, meander, hobble, stroll, plod,* or *shuffle* instead of *walk*). Subjective descriptions often include *figures of speech.*

Summary   The ideas of a source as presented in one's own words. Unlike a paraphrase, a summary conveys only a general sense of a passage, without following the order and emphasis of the original.

Syllogism   A basic form of deductive reasoning. Every syllogism includes three parts: a major premise that makes a general statement ("Confinement is physically and psychologically damaging"); a minor premise that makes a related but more specific statement ("Zoos confine animals"); and a conclusion drawn from these two premises ("Therefore, zoos are physically and psychologically damaging to animals").

Symbol   A person, event, or object that stands for something more than its literal meaning.

Synonym   A word with the same basic meaning as another word. A synonym for *loud* is *noisy.* Most words in the English language have several synonyms, but each word has unique nuances or *connotations.*

Thesis   An essay's main idea; the idea that all the points in the body of the essay support. A thesis may be implied, but it is usually stated explicitly in the form of a *thesis statement*. In addition to conveying the essay's main idea, the thesis statement may indicate the writer's approach to the subject and the writer's purpose. It may also indicate the pattern of development that will structure the essay.

Topic sentence   A sentence stating the main idea of a paragraph. Often, but not always, the topic sentence opens the paragraph.

Toulmin logic   A method of structuring an argument according to the way arguments occur in everyday life. Developed by philosopher Stephen Toulmin, Toulmin logic divides an argument into three parts: the *claim*, the *grounds*, and the *warrant*.

Transitions   Words or expressions that link ideas in a piece of writing. Long essays frequently contain *transitional paragraphs* that connect one part of the essay to another. Writers use a variety of transitional expressions, such as *afterward, because, consequently, for instance, furthermore, however,* and *likewise*. See the list of transitions on page 43.

Understatement   Deliberate deemphasis for effect: "The people who live near the Mississippi River are not exactly looking forward to more flooding"; "Emily was a little upset about failing math." The opposite of understatement is *hyperbole*.

Unity   The desirable attribute of a paragraph in which every sentence relates directly to the paragraph's main idea. This main idea is often stated in a *topic sentence*.

Warrant   In Toulmin logic, the inference that connects the claim to the grounds. The warrant can be a belief that is taken for granted or an assumption that underlies the argument. (See also **Toulmin logic**.)

Writing process   The sequence of tasks a writer undertakes when writing an essay. During *invention*, or *prewriting*, the writer gathers information and ideas and develops a thesis. During the *arrangement* stage, the writer organizes material into a logical sequence. During *drafting and revision*, the essay is actually written and then rewritten. Finally, during *editing*, the writer puts the finishing touches on the essay by correcting misspellings, checking punctuation, searching for grammatical inaccuracies, and so on. These stages occur in no fixed order; many effective writers move back and forth among them. (See Chapter 2.)

Acknowledgments

Tom Adkins. "Traditional Mother, Father Still Best Choice for Children." From *The Philadelphia Inquirer*, March 4, 2002. Copyright © 2002 by Tom Adkins. Reprinted by permission of the author.

Sherman Alexie. "Indian Education." From *The Lone Ranger and Tonto Fistfight in Heaven* by Sherman Alexie. Copyright © 1993 by Sherman Alexie. Used by permission of Grove/Atlantic, Inc.

Isabel Allende. "The Amazon Queen." From *Wanderlust* on Salon.com. © Isabel Allende, 1997. Reprinted with permission of the author.

Maya Angelou. "Finishing School." From *I Know Why the Caged Bird Sings* by Maya Angelou. Copyright © 1969 and renewed 1997 by Maya Angelou. Used by permission of Random House, Inc.

Suzanne Berne. "Where Nothing Says Everything." From *The New York Times*, December 24, 2001. Copyright © 2001 by The New York Times Company. Reprinted by permission.

David J. Birnbaum. "The Catbird Seat." From *The New York Times*, December 6, 1998. Copyright © 1998 by David J. Birnbaum. Reprinted by permission of the author.

Becky Birtha. "Laws Should Support Loving Households, Straight or Not." Originally published in *The Philadelphia Inquirer*, Monday, March 4, 2002, p. A11. Copyright © 2002. Reprinted by permission of the author.

Rebecca Blood. "What Is a Weblog?" From *The Weblog Handbook* by Rebecca Blood. Copyright © 2002 by Rebecca Blood. Reprinted by permission of Perseus Books PLC, a member of Perseus Books, LLC.

Sissela Bok. "Sizing Up the Effects." From *Mayhem: Violence as Public Entertainment* by Sissela Bok. Copyright © 1998 by Sissela Bok. Reprinted by permission of Perseus Books PLC, a member of Perseus Books LLC.

Judy Brady. "I Want a Wife." From *Ms.* Magazine, 1972. Copyright © 1970 by Judy Syfers. Reprinted by permission.

Edwin Brock. "Five Ways to Kill a Man." Copyright © Edwin Brock. Reprinted by permission.

Gwendolyn Brooks. "Sadie and Maud." From *Blacks* by Gwendolyn Brooks. Copyright © 1991. Reprinted by Consent of Brooks Permissions.

William Broyles Jr. "A War for Us, Fought by Them." From *The New York Times* Op-Ed, Tuesday, May 4, 2004. Copyright © 2004 by The New York Times Company. Reprinted by permission.

José Antonio Burciaga. "Tortillas." Originally titled "I Remember Masa" by José Antonio Burciaga. From *Weedee Peepo* by José Antonio Burciaga. Published by Pan American University Press, Edinburgh, Texas. Reprinted by permission of the author.

Bruce Catton. "Grant and Lee: A Study in Contrasts." From *The American Story* edited by Earl Schneck Miers. Copyright © U.S. Capitol Historical Society. All rights reserved. Reprinted by permission of the U.S. Capitol Historical Society.

Kate Chopin. "The Storm." From *The Complete Works of Kate Chopin*, edited by Per Seyersted. Copyright © 1969, 1997 by Louisiana State University Press.

Sandra Cisneros. "Only Daughter." Copyright © 1990 by Sandra Cisneros. First published in *Glamour*, November 1990. Reprinted by permission of Susan Bergholz Literary Services, New York. All rights reserved.

Leah Hager Cohen. "Words Left Unspoken." From *Train Go Sorry* by Leah Cohen. Copyright © 1994 by Leah Hager Cohen. Reprinted by permission of Houghton Mifflin Company. All rights reserved.

Norman Cousins. "Who Killed Benny Paret?" From *Present Tense*, a collection of editorials by Norman Cousins. Copyright © 1967 by Norman Cousins. Reprinted by permission of Eleanor Cousins.

Karen De Coster and Brad Edmonds. "The Case for Wal-Mart." From www.mises.org. Daily Articles Archive. Reprinted by permission.

John De Graaf, David Wann, and Thomas H. Naylor. "Swollen Expectations." From *Affluenza: The All-Consuming Epidemic* by John De Graaf, David Wann, and Thomas H. Naylor. Copyright

© 2001 by John De Graaf, David Wann, and Thomas H. Naylor. Berrett-Koehler Publishers, Inc., San Francisco, CA. All rights reserved. www.bkconnection.com.

Alan M. Dershowitz. "Why Fear National ID Cards?" From *The New York Times*, October 31, 2001. Copyright © 2001 by the New York Times Company. Reprinted by permission.

Lars Eighner. "On Dumpster Diving." From *Travels with Lizbeth* by Lars Eighner. Copyright © 1993 by Lars Eighner. Reprinted by permission of St. Martin's Press, LLC.

Stephanie Ericsson. "The Ways We Lie." Originally published in the November/December 1992 issue of *The Utne Reader*. Copyright © 1992 by Stephanie Ericsson. This essay also appeared in *Companion into Dawn: Inner Dialogues on Loving* by Stephanie Ericsson. Reprinted by permission of Dunham Literary as agents for the author.

Liza Featherstone. "Down and Out in Discount America." From the December 18, 2004 issue of *The Nation*. Copyright © 2004. Reprinted by permission of The Nation.

Ian Frazier. "Dearly Disconnected." From *Mother Jones Magazine* (January/February 2000). Copyright © 2000 The Foundation for National Progress.

Paul Fussell. "Stigmatic Uniforms." From *Uniforms: Why We Are What We Wear* by Paul Fussell. Copyright © 2002 Paul Fussell. Reprinted by permission of Houghton Mifflin Company. All rights reserved.

Martin Gansberg. "Thirty-Eight Who Saw Murder." From *The New York Times*, January 1, 1964. Copyright © 1964 by The New York Times Company. Reprinted by permission.

Henry Louis Gates Jr. "What's in a Name?" Copyright © 1989 by Henry Louis Gates, Jr. Originally published in *Dissent*. Reprinted by permission of the author.

Lawrence Otis Graham. "The 'Black Table' Is Still There." From *The New York Times*, February 3, 1991. Copyright © 1991 by The New York Times Company. Reprinted by permission.

Daniel Gross. "Playing by the Rules." From *Attaché Archives*, November 2004. Reprinted by permission of the author.

Linda M. Hasselstrom. "A Peaceful Woman Explains Why She Carries a Gun." From *Land Circle*. Copyright © Linda M. Hasselstrom. Reprinted by permission of Fulcrum Publishing Inc.

Shirley Jackson. "The Lottery." From *The Lottery and Other Stories* by Shirley Jackson. Copyright © 1948, 1949 by Shirley Jackson. Copyright renewed 1976, 1977 by Laurence Hyman, Barry Hyman, Mrs. Sarah Webster, and Mrs. Joanne Schmurer. Reprinted by permission of Farrar, Straus & Giroux, LLC.

Rick Jahnkow. "For Those Who Believe We Need a Draft." From *Draft Notices*, September-October 2002. Copyright © 2002. Published by the Committee Opposed to Militarism and the Draft, San Diego, CA. www.comdsd.org. Reprinted by permission of Rick Jahnkow.

Gerard Jones. "Violent Media is Good for Kids." From www.motherjones.com. June 28, 2000. Copyright © 2000 The Foundation for National Progress.

Martin Luther King Jr. "Letter from Birmingham Jail." Reprinted by arrangement with the Estate of Martin Luther King, Jr., c/o Writer's House as agent for the proprietor, New York, NY. Copyright 1963 Dr. Martin Luther King Jr. Copyright renewed 1991 Coretta Scott King.

Jonathan Kozol. "The Human Cost of an Illiterate Society." From *Illiterate America* by Jonathan Kozol. Copyright © 1985 by Jonathan Kozol. Used by permission of Doubleday, a division of Random House, Inc.

Robin Tolmach Lakoff. "The Power of Words in Wartime." From *The New York Times*, May 18, 2004. Copyright © 2004 by The New York Times Company. Reprinted with permission.

Philip Levine. Excerpt from *What Work Is* by Philip Levine. Copyright © 1992 by Philip Levine. Used by permission of Alfred A. Knopf, a division of Random House, Inc.

Malcolm X. "My First Conk." From *The Autobiography of Malcolm X* by Malcolm X and Alex Haley. Copyright © 1964 by Alex Haley and Malcolm X. Copyright © 1965 by Alex Haley and Betty Shabazz. Used by permission of Random House, Inc.

Arthur Miller. "Get It Right: Privatize Executions." Originally published in *The New York Times,* May 8, 1992. Copyright © 1992 Arthur Miller. Reprinted by permission of International Creative Management, Inc.

Janice Mirikitani. "Suicide Note." From *Shedding Silence* by Janice Mirikitani. Copyright © 1987 by Janice Mirikitani. Reprinted by permission of Celestial Arts, P.O. Box 7123, Berkeley, CA 94707. www.tenspeed.com.

Jessica Mitford. "The Embalming of Mr. Jones." From *The American Way of Death* by Jessica Mitford. Copyright © 1963, 1978 by Jessica Mitford. Reprinted by permission of the Estate of Jessica Mitford. All rights reserved.

N. Scott Momaday. "The Way to Rainy Mountain." From *The Reporter*, January 26, 1997. Copyright © 1997 by N. Scott Momaday. Reprinted by permission of the University of New Mexico Press.

Bharati Mukherjee. "Two Ways to Belong in America." From *The New York Times*, September 22, 1996. Copyright © 1996 by The New York Times Company. Reprinted by permission.

Marcia Muller. "Creating a Female Sleuth." From *The Writer*, October 1978. Copyright © 1978 by Marcia Muller. Reprinted by permission of the author.

George Orwell. "Shooting an Elephant." From *Shooting an Elephant and Other Essays* by George Orwell. Copyright © 1950 by Sonia Brownell Orwell and renewed 1978 by Sonia Brownell Orwell. Reprinted with permission of Harcourt, Inc. and A.M. Heath.

Grace Paley. "Samuel." From *Enormous Changes at the Last Minute* by Grace Paley. Copyright © 1971, 1974 by Grace Paley. Reprinted by permission of Farrar, Straus & Giroux, LLC.

Phil Patton. "Innovation." From *50/50, The 50 Biggest Changes in the Last 50 Years*. Copyright © 2004 by Phil Patton. Published by American Heritage, 2004. Reprinted by permission of the author.

Laurence J. Peter and Raymond Hull. Excerpt from *The Peter Principle* by Laurence J. Peter and Raymond Hull. Copyright © 1969 by William Morrow & Company, Inc. Reprinted by permission of HarperCollins Publishers.

Joshua Piven, David Borgenicht, and Jennifer Worick. "How to Escape from a Bad Date." From *Worst Case Scenario Survival Handbook: Dating & Sex* by Joshua Piven, David Borgenicht and Jennifer Worick. Copyright © 2001 by Quirk Productions, Inc. Published by Chronicle Books, LLC., San Francisco. Used with permission. www.worstcasescenarios.com.

Katha Pollitt. "Why Boys Don't Play with Dolls." From *The New York Times*, October 8, 1995. Copyright © 1995 by the New York Times. Reprinted by permission.

Richard Rodriguez. "Strange Tools." From *The Hunger of Memory* by Richard Rodriguez. Copyright © 1982 by Richard Rodriguez. Reprinted by permission of David R. Godine Publisher, Inc.

William Safire. "The Threat of National ID." From *The New York Times*, December 24, 2001. Copyright © 2001 by The New York Times Company. Reprinted by permission.

Scott Russell Sanders. "The Men We Carry in Our Minds." From *The Paradise of Bombs* by Scott Russell Sanders. Copyright © 1984 by Scott Russell Sanders. Originally published in *Milkweed Chronicle*. Reprinted by permission of the author and the author's agent, Virginia Kidd, Literary Agent.

Carolyn Foster Segal. "The Dog Ate My Disk and Other Tales of Woe." From *The Chronicle of Higher Education*, August 11, 2000. Copyright © 2000 by Carolyn Foster Segal. Reprinted by permission of the author.

Gayle Rosenwald Smith. "T-shirts' Violent Nickname Is an Ugly Fashion Statement." From *The Philadelphia Inquirer*, July 2, 2001. Copyright © 2001. Reprinted by permission.

Bonnie Smith-Yackel. "My Mother Never Worked." Reprinted by permission of the author.

Brent Staples. "Just Walk On By: A Black Man Ponders His Power to Alter Public Space." From *Harper's*, December 1986. Reprinted with the permission of the author.

Oliver Stone. "Memo to John Grisham—What's Next—'A Movie Made Me Do It?'" From the *LA Weekly*, March 29-April 4, 1996, p. 39. Reprinted by permission of the author.

Amy Tan. "Mother Tongue." Copyright © 1990 by Amy Tan. First appeared in *The Threepenny Review*. Reprinted by permission of the author and the Sandra Dijkstra Literary Agency.

Deborah Tannen. "Sex, Lies, and Conversation." From *You Just Don't Understand* by Deborah Tannen. Copyright © 1990 by Deborah Tannen. Reprinted by permission of HarperCollins Publishers.

Dick Teresi. "Star-Spangled Stupidity." From *The Wall Street Journal* (Eastern edition), July 2, 2004 by Dick Teresi. Copyright © 2004 by Dow Jones & Co., Inc. Reproduced with permission of Dow Jones & Co., Inc. in the formal Textbook via Copyright Clearance Center.

Yi-Fu Tuan. "Chinese Space, American Space." From *The Sundance Reader*, 4th edition, April 2005.

E. B. White. "Once More to the Lake." From *One Man's Meat*, text copyright © 1941 by E. B. White. Copyright renewed. Reprinted by permission of Tilbury House, Publishers, Gardiner, Maine.

Marie Winn. "Family Life." From *The Plug-In Drug,* Revised and Updated 25th Anniversary Edition by Marie Winn. Copyright © 1977, 1985, 2002 by Marie Winn Miller. Used by permission of Viking Penguin, a division of Penguin Putnam, Inc.

Virginia Woolf. "The Death of the Moth." From *The Death of the Moth and Other Essays* by Virginia Woolf. Copyright © 1942 by Harcourt, Inc. and renewed 1970 by Marjorie T. Parsons, Executrix. Reprinted by permission of the publisher.

Michael Zimecki. "Violent Films Cry 'Fire' in Crowded Theaters." From *The National Law Journal*, February 19, 1996. Michael Zimecki is an attorney in Pittsburgh, PA. Reprinted by permission of the author.

William Zinsser. "College Pressures." From *Blair & Ketchum's Country Journal*, Vol. VI, No. 4, April 1979. Copyright © 1979 by William K. Zinsser. Reprinted by permission of the author.

Picture Credits

4, Alex Williams; **94,** ™ & © 2003, Marvel Characters Inc. Used with permission; **146,** from *Shakespeare: Six Plays and the Sonnets* by Thomas Marc Parrott and Edward Hubler, Charles Scribner's Sons, 1956; **160,** Vincent Laforet/The New York Times; **218** (clockwise from top left): Alex Williams; Joel Gordon; Charles Gatewood/Stock Boston; Bob Daemmrich/Stock Boston; **283,** from *Wordless Diagrams,* © Nigel Holmes; **299, 301,** from *The Worst-Case Scenario Survival Handbook: Dating and Sex* by Joshua Piven, David Borgenicht, and Jennifer Worick, © 2001 by Quirk Productions, Inc. Published by Chronicle Books, LLC, San Francisco. Used with permission. www.worstcasescenarios.com; **344,** AP Photo/Louis Requena; **402,** National Institute of Mental Health; **403,** Eli Lilly and Company; **407,** Musée Rodin, Paris, France; The Bridgeman Art Library; **408,** © Jon Burbank/The Image Works; **464, 465,** Office of the Public Health Service Historian; **517,** © Sean Sprague/The Image Works; **522,** courtesy of U.S. Dept. of Commerce/Bureau of the Census; **582,** DeVito/Verdi Advertising, New York; **679, 682,** © TM Gerard Jones & Gene Ha; **779,** © Steve Liss/Corbis.

Index

abstract language, 785
active reading, 2
active voice, 250–51
addition, transitional words and
    phrases for, 43
ad hominem argument (personal
    attack), 568
Adkins, Tom, "Traditional Mother and
    Father: Still the Best Choice for
    Children," 625–29
affect, effect, 337–38
agreement, 705–6
"Airport Insecurity" (student essay),
    777–84
Alexie, Sherman, "Indian Education,"
    134–41
Allende, Isabel, "The Amazon Queen,"
    173–79
allusions, 148, 611, 785
"Amazon Queen, The" (Allende),
    173–79
American Civil Liberties Union, *Thanks
    to Modern Science...,* 582–83
analogies, 387–88, 785
    argument from, 568
    defining a term by using, 494,
        501–2, 512
    effectiveness of, 731
    validity of, 308, 359
anecdotes, 39
Angelou, Maya, "Finishing School,"
    101–7
annotating, 3–4, 785
antecedents, 706
antithesis, 558, 785
antonyms, 785

appeals, 530–31
    to doubtful authority, 542–43
"Argument against the Anna Todd
    Jennings Scholarship, An"
    (student essay), 576–80
argumentation (argumentative essays),
    555–57, 785
    assignments for, 697–701
    "Declaration of Sentiments and Res-
        olutions, Seneca Falls Conven-
        tion, 1848" (Stanton), 590–96
    editing, 573–76
    image: *Thanks to Modern Science...,*
        582–83
    planning, 557–63
    in process essays, 309
    readings
        "Argument against the Anna Todd
            Jennings Scholarship, An" (stu-
            dent essay), 576–80
        "Case for Wal-Mart, The" (De
            Coster and Edmonds), 652–58
        "Declaration of Independence,
            The" (Jefferson), 584–89
        "Down and Out in Discount
            America" (Featherstone), 659–68
        "For Those Who Believe We Need
            a Draft" (Jahnkow), 643–49
        "Laws Should Support Loving
            Households, Straight or Not"
            (Birtha), 630–34
        "Letter from Birmingham Jail"
            (King), 597–612
        "Memo to John Grisham: What's
            Next — 'A Movie Made Me Do
            It'?" (Stone), 686–90

argumentation (cont.)
    "Sizing Up the Effects" (Bok),
       671–77
    "Threat of National ID, The"
       (Safire), 614–17
    "Traditional Mother and Father:
       Still the Best Choice for Chil-
       dren" (Adkins), 625–29
    "Violent Films Cry 'Fire' in
       Crowded Theaters" (Zimecki),
       691–96
    "Violent Media Is Good for Kids"
       (Jones), 678–85
    "War for Us, Fought by Them, A"
       (Broyles), 637–42
    "Why Fear National ID Cards?"
       (Dershowitz), 618–22
  revising, 573, 580–81
  structuring, 571–74
  student essay, 576–80
  transitional words and phrases for,
    570–71
argument from analogy, 568
arrangement, 13. See also organization,
    methods of
assignments. See also under specific pat-
    terns of development
  understanding, 15
audience, 17–18, 785–86
  argumentative essays, 558, 579
  process essays, 269
authority, appeals to, 569–70
awkward phrasing, 74–75

background information, in introduc-
    tion, 39
basis for comparison, 389–90, 399, 786
because, 337
begging the question, 567–68
Berne, Suzanne, "Ground Zero," 162–67
Birnbaum, David J., "The Catbird
    Seat," 227–30
Birtha, Becky, "Laws Should Support
    Loving Households, Straight or
    Not," 630–34
"'Black Table' Is Still There, The"
    (Graham), 366–70
Blood, Rebecca, "What Is a Weblog?,"
    536–43
Bobnak, Laura, "The Price of Silence"

final draft, 62–65
first draft, 57–59
second draft, 59–62
body (body paragraphs), 41–46, 786
  argumentative essays, 571–73
  classification and division essays,
    455
  comparison and contrast essays,
    391–93
  definition essays, 513–14
  descriptive essays, 150
  and drafting process, 766
  exemplification essays, 207
  narrative essays, 86
  process essays, 270
  revising, 54, 59, 61–62
  See also paragraphs
Bok, Sissela, "Sizing Up the Effects,"
    671–77
books, citing (MLA style), 769–71
Brady, Judy, "I Want a Wife," 524–27
brainstorming, 25–27, 786
"Brains versus Brawn" (student essay),
    396–401
Bredin, Kristy, letter of application,
    210–12
Brock, Edwin, "Five Ways to Kill a
    Man," 505–6
Brooks, Gwendolyn, "Sadie and
    Maud," 447–48
browsers, 756
Broyles, William, Jr., "A War for Us,
    Fought by Them," 637–42
"Building and Learning" (student
    essay), 153–56
Burciaga, José Antonio, "Tortillas,"
    528–31
Byrne, Caitlin, "Airport Insecurity,"
    778–84

capitalization, 77
"Case for Wal-Mart, The" (De Coster
    and Edmonds), 652–58
"Catbird Seat, The" (Birnbaum), 227–30
categories, 453–54
  transitional words and phrases for,
    454–55, 461–62
Catton, Bruce, "Grant and Lee: A
    Study in Contrasts," 409–14
causal chains, 331–32, 334, 341, 786

cause and effect (cause-and-effect essays), 327–28, 786
 assignments for, 385–86
 and combined patterns of development, 704
  argument essays, 634, 649, 658, 677, 690
  comparison and contrast essays, 420, 424
  exemplification essays, 239, 245
  process essays, 304
 editing, 337–38
 image: *Major League Baseball Brawl*, 344–45
 planning, 333–34
 readings
  "'Black Table' Is Still There, The" (Graham), 366–70
  "Irish Famine, 1845–1849, The" (student essay), 338–43
  "Peaceful Woman Explains Why She Carries a Gun, A"(Hasselstrom), 371–76
  "Power of Words in Wartime, The" (Lakoff), 377–81
  "Suicide Note" (Mirikitani), 382–84
  "Television: The Plug-In Drug" (Winn), 351–60
  "Who Killed Benny Paret?" (Cousins), 346–50
  "Why Boys Don't Play with Dolls" (Pollitt), 361–65
 recognizing, 38
 revising, 336–37
 structuring, 335–36
 student essay, 338–43
 transitional words and phrases for, 43, 334, 341
 using, 328–33
causes, 329–30, 334, 341, 535, 786–87
"Chinese Space, American Space" (Tuan), 421–24
choosing a topic. *See* topic selection
Chopin, Kate, "The Storm," 194–99
chronological organization, 786
 in cause-and-effect essays, 334
 in exemplification essays, 208
 in narrative essays, 85–87
Cisneros, Sandra, "Only Daughter," 96–100

citation style (MLA). *See* MLA citation style
claims (Toulmin logic), 567, 786
classification and division (classification and division essays), 451–52, 786
 assignments for, 507–8
 and combined patterns of development
  cause-and-effect essays, 370
  definition essays, 512, 542
 editing, 457–58
 images
  Eye Exam Administered to Immigrants, Ellis Island, 1910, 465
  Key to Chalk Marks Designating Medical Conditions of Immigrants, Ellis Island, 464
 planning, 453–55
 readings
  "College Pressures" (Zinsser), 466–74
  "Dog Ate My Disk, and Other Tales of Woe, The" (Segal), 475–80
  "Five Ways to Kill a Man" (Brock), 505–6
  "Men We Carry in Our Minds, The" (Sanders), 481–86
  "Mother Tongue" (Tan), 487–94
  "Ways We Lie, The" (Ericsson), 495–504
  "What I Learned (and Didn't Learn) in College" (student essay), 458–63
 recognizing, 38
 revising, 456–57
 structuring, 455–56
 student essay, 458–63
 using, 452–53
clauses, 72
clichés, 76, 93, 786
clustering, 28, 786
Cohen, Leah Hager, "Words Left Unspoken," 168–72
coherence, 42, 786–87
"College Pressures" (Zinsser), 466–74
colloquialisms, 27, 503, 617, 787
colons, 73, 457
combining patterns of development, 703–4
 assignments for, 750–51

combining patterns of development
    (cont.)
  readings
    "Death of the Moth, The" (Woolf),
        728–32
    "Modest Proposal, A" (Swift),
        733–42
    "On Dumpster Diving" (Eigner),
        712–27
    "Park, The" (student essay), 707–11
    "Strange Tools" (Rodriguez),
        743–49
  revising and editing, 704–6, 710–11
  student essay, 707–11
commas
  and clauses, 71–72
  and coordinating conjunctions, 88
  and series, 209–10, 457–58
comma splices, 69, 88
common knowledge, 561, 760, 787
commonly confused words, 76–77
comparison and contrast (comparison
        and contrast essays), 387–88, 787
  assignments for, 449–50
  and combined patterns of develop-
        ment
    argumentative essays, 621, 696
    cause-and-effect essays, 365
    definition essays, 511–12, 543, 549
    descriptive essays, 167
    exemplification essays, 239, 251
  editing, 394–95
  images
    Kiss, The, 407–8
    LOVE sculpture, 408
  planning, 388–91
  readings
    "Brains versus Brawn" (student
        essay), 396–401
    "Chinese Space, American Space"
        (Tuan), 421–24
    "Comparison of Two Web Sites on
        Attention Deficit Disorder, A"
        (student essay), 401–6
    "Dearly Disconnected" (Frazier),
        434–39
    "Grant and Lee: A Study in Con-
        trasts" (Catton), 409–14
    "Sadie and Maud" (Brooks),
        447–48
    "Sex, Lies, and Conversation"
        (Tannen), 440–46
    "Swollen Expectations" (De Graaf,
        Wann, and Naylor), 425–33
    "Two Ways to Belong in America"
        (Mukherjee), 415–20
  recognizing, 38
  revising, 393–94
  structuring, 391–93
  student essays, 395–406
  transitional words and phrases for,
        43, 393, 399–400, 405
  using, 388
"Comparison of Two Web Sites on
        Attention Deficit Disorder, A"
        (student essay), 401–6
complexity, organization by, 208
complex sentences, 75
compound sentences, 75
conciseness, 75
conclusions, 46–47, 787
  and drafting process, 766
  jumping to, 566, 568
  and patterns of development
    argumentative essays, 571–73
    classification and division essays,
        455
    definition essays, 513–14
    descriptive essays, 150
    exemplification essays, 207
    narrative essays, 86
    process essays, 270
  for research papers, 766
  revising, 54, 59
  and syllogisms, 563–65
  transitional words and phrases for,
        43
concrete language, 785
conjunctions, 72, 574–75
  coordinating, 88
  correlative, 395
  subordinating, 89
connotations, 147, 667, 787
contradiction, 40
contributory causes, 329–30, 334, 786,
        787
coordinating conjunctions, 72, 88, 574
correlative conjunctions, 395
Cotharn, Mark, "Brains versus Brawn,"
        396–401

Cousins, Norman, "Who Killed Benny Paret?," 346–50
"Creating a Female Sleuth" (Muller), 290–96

dangling modifiers, 70, 152
Daniels, Matt, "An Argument against the Anna Todd Jennings Scholarship," 576–80
dashes, 73
"Dearly Disconnected" (Frazier), 434–39
"Death of the Moth, The" (Woolf), 728–32
debatability, 558
"Declaration of Independence, The" (Jefferson), 584–89
"Declaration of Sentiments and Resolutions, Seneca Falls Convention, 1848" (Stanton), 590–96
De Coster, Karen, "The Case for Wal-Mart" (with Edmonds), 652–58
deductive reasoning, 563–65, 787
definition (definition essays), 509–10, 787
   assignments for, 553–54
   and combined patterns of development, 519–20, 704
      argumentative essays, 668, 684
      cause-and-effect essays, 360
   editing, 515–16
   image: *U.S. Census 2000 Form,* 522–23
   planning, 511–13
   readings
      "I Want a Wife" (Brady), 524–27
      "Stigmatic Uniforms" (Fussell), 544–49
      "Tortillas" (Burciaga), 528–31
      "Untouchable, The" (student essay), 516–21
      "What Is a Weblog?" (Blood), 536–43
      "What Work Is" (Levine), 550–52
      "Wife-Beater, The" (Smith), 532–35
   recognizing, 38
   revising, 514–15
   structuring, 513
   student essay, 516–21
   using, 510–11
definitions, 289

extended and formal, 509–10, 621, 788
in introductions, 39, 504
De Graaf, John, "Swollen Expectations" (with Wann and Naylor), 425–33
denotations, 147, 667, 787
dependent clauses, 71
Dershowitz, Alan M., "Why Fear National ID Cards?," 618–22
description (descriptive essays), 143–44, 787
   assignments for, 200–201
   and combined patterns of development
      classification and division essays, 486
      definition essays, 511, 531
      process essays, 296
   editing, 151–53
   image: *Girls in Front of 9/11 Mural,* 160
   planning, 149
   readings
      "Amazon Queen, The" (Allende), 173–79
      "Building and Learning" (student essay), 153–56
      "Ground Zero" (Berne), 162–67
      "Once More to the Lake" (White), 186–93
      "Storm, The" (Chopin), 194–99
      "Valley of Windmills, The" (student essay), 156–59
      "Way to Rainy Mountain, The" (Momaday), 180–85
      "Words Left Unspoken" (Cohen), 168–72
   recognizing, 38
   revising, 150–51
   structuring, 150
   student essays, 153–59
   transitional words and phrases for, 149
   using, 144–49
detail
   and combining patterns of development, 710
   in descriptive essays, 148–49, 156
   in narrative essays, 84–85, 92
   in process essays, 281

digression, 787–88
distributed terms, 564
division, 786. *See also* classification and division essays
documentation, 44, 561
  defined, 788
  MLA (Modern Language Association) style
    parenthetical references in the text, 767–69
    Works Cited list, 769–77
  what to document, 760–63
"Dog Ate My Disk, and Other Tales of Woe, The" (Segal), 475–80
dominant impression, 788
  in descriptive essays, 144
"Down and Out in Discount America" (Featherstone), 659–68
drafting, 13, 51–53, 765–67

editing, 13. *See also* proofreading
  for grammar, 67–71
  and patterns of development
    argumentative essays, 573–76
    cause-and-effect essays, 337–38
    classification and division essays, 457–58
    combined patterns, 704–6
    comparison and contrast essays, 394–95
    definition essays, 515–16
    descriptive essays, 151–3
    exemplification essays, 209-10
    narrative essays, 87–89
    process essays, 271–74
  for punctuation, 71–74
  for sentence style and word choice, 74–76
effect, affect, 337–38
Eigner, Lars, "On Dumpster Diving," 712–27
either/or fallacy (false dilemma), 568–69
electronic sources, citing (MLA style), 768
"Embalming of Mr. Jones, The" (Mitford), 310–16
encyclopedias, 755
enumeration, 512
equivocation, 569

Ericsson, Stephanie, "The Ways We Lie," 495–504
essay
  defined, 788
  parts of, 39–46
euphemisms, 788
evaluation of sources, 754, 755, 756
evidence, 558–61, 578–79, 788
examples, 788
  transitional words and phrases for, 43, 207
exemplification (exemplification essays), 203
  and combined patterns of development, 704
    classification and division essays, 474
    argumentative essays, 589, 596, 617, 629
    cause-and-effect essays, 360, 381
    comparison and contrast essays, 413–14, 433, 439
    definition essays, 511, 531, 543
  defined, 788
  editing, 209–13
  image: *Four Tattoos,* 218–19
  planning, 206–7
  readings
    "Catbird Seat, The" (Birnbaum), 227–30
    "Human Cost of an Illiterate Society, The" (Kozol), 252–61
    "Innovation" (Patton), 231–39
    "Just Walk On By: A Black Man Ponders His Power to Alter Public Space" (Staples), 240–45
    letter of application (student essay), 210–12
    "Midnight" (student essay), 213–16
    "Peter Principle, The" (Peter and Hull), 220–26
    "Samuel" (Paley), 262–66
    "Star-Spangled Stupidity" (Teresi), 246–51
  recognizing, 38
  revising, 208–9
  structuring, 207–8
  student essays, 210–16
  using, 204–6
expressive writing, 16

and thesis statements, 32
extended definitions, 509–10, 788
*Eye Exam Administered to Immigrants,
Ellis Island, 1910* (image), 465

facts, 559
    in introductions, 40
    vs. inductive conclusions, 566
fallacies, 567–70, 788
false dilemma (either/or fallacy),
    568–69, 628
Featherstone, Liza, "Down and Out in
    Discount America," 659–68
feedback, 53, 55–57
figures of speech, 147, 710, 788
"Finishing School" (Angelou), 101–7
first drafts. *See* drafting
"Five Ways to Kill a Man" (Brock),
    505–6
flashbacks, 85
formal definitions, 509–10, 621, 788
Forte, Tiffany, "My Field of Dreams,"
    89–93
"For Those Who Believe We Need a
    Draft" (Jahnkow), 643–49
Four Tattoos (images), 218
Frazier, Ian, "Dearly Disconnected,"
    434–39
freewriting, 23–25, 788
fused sentences, 69, 88
Fussell, Paul, "Stigmatic Uniforms,"
    544–49

Gansberg, Martin, "Thirty-Eight Who
    Saw Murder Didn't Call the
    Police," 120–24
Gates, Henry Louis, Jr., "What's in a
    Name?," 5–12
generalizations, hasty, 566, 568
generating ideas, 25–27
"Get It Right: Privatize Executions"
    (Miller), 305–9
Girls in Front of 9/11 Mural (Laforet),
    160
Graham, Lawrence Otis, "The 'Black
    Table' Is Still There," 366–70
"Grant and Lee: A Study in Contrasts"
    (Catton), 409–14
Greggs, James, "Building and Learn-
    ing," 153–56

Gross, Daniel, "Playing by the Rules,"
    114–19
grounds (Toulmin logic), 567, 788
"Ground Zero" (Berne), 162–67
grouping ideas, 28–29

Hasselstrom, Linda M., "A Peaceful
    Woman Explains Why She
    Carries a Gun," 371–76
hasty generalizations, 566, 568
headnotes, 2, 3
highlighting, 3–4, 789
Holmes, Nigel, *How to Cover Scratches on
    Furniture,* 283
How to Cover Scratches on Furniture
    (Holmes), 283
"How to Escape from a Bad Date"
    (Piven, Borgenicht, and
    Worick), 297–304
"Human Cost of an Illiterate Society,
    The" (Kozol), 252–61
Hunt, Melany, "Medium Ash Brown,"
    279–82
hyperbole, 648, 789
hypothesis, in inductive arguments, 565

imagery, 789
images
    *Eye Exam Administered to Immigrants,
        Ellis Island, 1910* (Office of the
        Public Health Service Historian),
        465
    Four Tattoos, 218
    Girls in Front of 9/11 Mural (Laforet),
        160
    How to Cover Scratches on Furniture
        (Holmes), 283
    *Key to Chalk Marks Designating
        Medical Conditions of Immigrants*
        (Ellis Island Immigration
        Museum/NPS), 464
    Kiss, The (Rodin), 407–8
    LOVE sculpture (Indiana), 408
    Major League Baseball Brawl
        (Requena), 344–5
    from *Spider-Man* (Marvel Comics),
        94–95
    Thanks to Modern Science... (Ameri-
        can Civil Liberties Union),
        582–83

images *(cont.)*
    U.S. Census 2000 Form (U.S. Census
        Bureau), 522–23
immediate causes, 330, 341, 786
implied thesis, 33
importance, organization by, 208
indefinite pronouns, 705–6
indenting, 78
independent clauses, 71–72
Indiana, Robert, *LOVE* sculpture, 408
"Indian Education" (Alexie), 134–41
inductive reasoning, 563, 565–66, 789
inferences, 565–66
informative writing, 16
    and thesis statements, 32
"Innovation" (Patton), 231–39
instructions, 268, 789
Internet
    citing sources from (MLA style), 768,
        773–77
    and plagiarism, 763
    as research tool, 756
introduction, 39–41
    and drafting process, 766
    and patterns of development
        argumentative essays, 571
        classification and division essays,
            455
        definition essays, 513–14
        descriptive essays, 150
        exemplification essays, 207
        narrative essays, 86
        process essays, 270, 277
    revising, 54, 58–59, 61
invention (prewriting), 13, 789
    generating ideas, 25–27
    grouping ideas, 28–29
    setting limits, 16–20
    and thesis statements, 30–35
    topic selection, 20–25
    understanding the assignment, 15
"Irish Famine, 1845–1849, The"
    (student essay), 338–43
irony, 198, 527, 741, 789–90
italics, 77
"I Want a Wife" (Brady), 524–27

Jackson, Shirley, "The Lottery," 317–24
Jahnkow, Rick, "For Those Who Believe
    We Need a Draft," 643–49

jargon, 446, 780
Jefferson, Thomas, "The Declaration of
    Independence," 584–89
Jones, Gerard, "Violent Media Is Good
    for Kids," 678–85
journal writing, 27, 790
jumping to conclusions, 566, 568
"Just Walk On By: A Black Man Pon-
    ders His Power to Alter Public
    Space" (Staples), 240–45

*Key to Chalk Marks Designating Medical
    Conditions of Immigrants* (image),
    464
keyword searches, 756
key words (in body paragraphs), 42
King, Martin Luther, Jr., "Letter
    from Birmingham Jail,"
    597–612
Kiss, The (Rodin), 407–8
knowledge of subject, 18
Kozol, Jonathan, "The Human Cost of
    an Illiterate Society," 252–61
Ku, Grace, "Midnight," 213–15

Laforet, Vincent, *Girls in Front of 9/11
    Mural,* 160
Lakoff, Robin Tolmach, "The Power of
    Words in Wartime," 377–81
"Laws Should Support Loving House-
    holds, Straight or Not" (Birtha),
    630–34
length of essays, 16
"Letter from Birmingham Jail" (King),
    597–612
letter of application (student essay),
    211–12
Levine, Philip, "What Work Is," 550–52
library research, 754–56
Lim, Mary, "The Valley of Windmills,"
    156–59
line spacing, 78
logic, 563–70
looping, 790
"Lottery, The" (Jackson), 317–24
LOVE sculpture (Indiana), 408

Mahtab, Ajoy, "The Untouchable,"
    516–21
main causes, 329–30, 334, 786

Major League Baseball Brawl (Requena), 344–45

major premise, 563–65

Malcolm X, "My First Conk," 285–89

manuscript format, 78–79

Martinez, Josie, "What I Learned (and Didn't Learn) in College," 458–63

Marvel Comics, *Spider-Man,* 94–95

McGlade, Eric, "The Search," 274–79

"Medium Ash Brown" (student essay), 279–82

"Memo to John Grisham: What's Next — 'A Movie Made Me Do It'?" (Stone), 686–90

"Men We Carry in Our Minds, The" (Sanders), 481–86

metaphors, 147, 710, 790

"Midnight" (student essay), 213–15

Miller, Arthur, "Get It Right: Privatize Executions," 305–9

minor premise, 563–65

Mirikitani, Janice, "Suicide Note," 382–84

misplaced modifiers, 70, 151–52

misspellings, 77–78

Mitford, Jessica, "The Embalming of Mr. Jones," 310–16

MLA (Modern Language Association) citation style
  parenthetical references in text, 767–69
  sample paper, 777–84
  Works Cited list, 769–77

"Modest Proposal, A" (Swift), 733–42

modifiers, 70, 151–53

Momaday, N. Scott, "The Way to Rainy Mountain," 180–85

mood, avoiding shifts in, 273

"Mother Tongue" (Tan), 487–94

Mukherjee, Bharati, "Two Ways to Belong in America," 415–20

Muller, Marcia, "Creating a Female Sleuth," 290–96

"My Field of Dreams" (student essay), 89–93

"My First Conk" (Malcolm X), 285–89

"My Mother Never Worked" (Smith-Yackel), 108–13

narration (narrative essays), 83, 790
  and combined patterns of development
    argumentative essays, 612, 642
    cause-and-effect essays, 349, 360, 376
    classification and division essays, 480, 494
    comparison and contrast essays, 446
    definition essays, 531, 542
    descriptive essays, 172
    exemplification essays, 226, 261
  editing, 87–93
  image: from *Spider-Man,* 94–95
  planning, 84–86
  readings
    "Finishing School" (Angelou), 101–7
    "Indian Education" (Alexie), 134–41
    "My Field of Dreams" (student essay), 89–93
    "My Mother Never Worked" (Smith-Yackel), 108–13
    "Only Daughter" (Cisneros), 96–100
    "Playing by the Rules" (Gross), 114–19
    "Shooting an Elephant" (Orwell), 125–33
    "Thirty-Eight Who Saw Murder Didn't Call the Police" (Gansberg), 120–24
  recognizing, 38
  structuring and revising, 86–87
  student essay, 89–93
  using, 83–84

negation, 512, 530, 548

nonrestrictive clauses, 72

non sequitur fallacy (it does not follow), 570

note taking, 757–60

objective description, 144–45, 155, 731, 790

occasions for writing, 18

"Once More to the Lake" (White), 186–93

"On Dumpster Diving" (Eigner), 712–27

online library catalog, 755

online sources. *See* Internet
"Only Daughter" (Cisneros), 96–100
opinions, 559
order of events, transitional words and
     phrases for, 43, 86, 92, 270, 278,
     281, 710
organization, methods of, 208, 212,
     215, 334, 341, 399
   argumentative essays, 571–73,
     579–80
   classification and division essays,
     461
   and combined patterns of develop-
     ment, 704
   comparison and contrast essays,
     404–5
   definition essays, 519
   descriptive essays, 155, 158
   process essays, 277–78, 280–81
origin and development (of terms), 512
Orwell, George, "Shooting an Ele-
     phant," 125–33
outlines, 29, 47–49
   and research process, 764–65
   revising with, 55

Paley, Grace, "Samuel," 262–66
paradox, 364, 790
paragraphs
   defined, 790 (*See also* body)
   development and support, 42–45
   indenting, 78
   transitional, 393, 399–400
parallelism
   in comparison and contrast essays,
     394–95
   defined, 70, 790
   and series, 210, 458
paraphrasing, 757–58, 761–62,
     790–91
"Park, The" (student essay), 707–11
parts of essay, 39–46
patterns of development
   combining (*See* combining patterns
     of development)
   recognizing, 37–38
Patton, Phil, "Innovation," 231–39
"Peaceful Woman Explains Why She
     Carries a Gun, A" (Hassel-
     strom), 371–76

peer critiques, 55–56
peer editing worksheets, 57–58
   argumentative essays, 580–81
   cause-and-effect essays, 342–43
   classification and division essays,
     462–63
   combined patterns of development,
     711
   comparison and contrast essays, 406
   definition essays, 520–21
   descriptive essays, 159
   exemplification essays, 216–17
   narrative essays, 93
   process essays, 282
Pellicane, Evelyn, "The Irish Famine,
     1845–1849," 338–43
periodical indexes, 755
periodicals, citing (MLA style), 771–73
periods, 88
person, avoiding shifts in, 272–73
personal attack argument (*ad
     hominem*), 568
personal experience essay, 709–10
personification, 147, 710, 731, 791
persuasion, 16, 791
   and exemplification, 205, 213
   and thesis statements, 33
   vs. argumentation, 556
Peter, Laurence J., "The Peter Principle"
     (with Hull), 220–26
"Peter Principle, The" (Peter and Hull),
     220–26
Piven, Joshua, "How to Escape from a
     Bad Date" (with Borgenicht and
     Worick), 297–304
plagiarism, 44, 561, 760–63, 791
"Playing by the Rules" (Gross), 114–19
point-by-point comparison, 392–93,
     399, 404–5, 791
Pollitt, Katha, "Why Boys Don't Play
     with Dolls," 361–65
post hoc reasoning, 332–33, 334, 570, 791
"Power of Words in Wartime, The"
     (Lakoff), 377–81
predictions, 47
premises (of syllogisms), 563–65
prewriting. *See* invention
"Price of Silence, The" (student essay)
   final draft, 62–65
   first draft, 57–59

second draft, 59–62
principle of classification, 453, 791
process (process essays), 267–68, 791
  assignments for, 325–26
  and combined patterns of develop-
    ment, 704
    definition essays, 512, 531
  editing, 271–74
  image: *How to Cover Scratches on Fur-
    niture*, 283
  planning, 269–70
  readings
    "Creating a Female Sleuth"
      (Muller), 290–96
    "Embalming of Mr. Jones, The"
      (Mitford), 310–16
    "Get It Right: Privatize Execu-
      tions" (Miller), 305–9
    "How to Escape from a Bad Date"
      (Piven, Borgenicht, and
      Worick), 297–304
    "Lottery, The" (Jackson), 317–24
    "Medium Ash Brown" (student
      essay), 279–82
    "My First Conk" (Malcolm X),
      285–89
    "Search, The" (student essay),
      274–79
  recognizing, 38
  structuring and revising, 270–71
  student essays, 274–82
  using, 269
pronoun-antecedent agreement, 68–69
pronouns, 705–6
  and coherence, 42
proofreading, 67, 76–78
punctuation, 69–74
purpose of essays, 16–17, 791

questions
  in introduction, 39
  for probing, 21–23
  rhetorical, 369, 502, 519, 616, 791
quotation marks, 72–73
quotations
  citation format, 768–69
  in conclusions, 47
  defined, 791
  in introduction, 39
  in research papers, 759–60, 761

range of examples, 206–7, 215
reading strategies, 1–4
"reason is because," 337
reasoning, 563–70
red herring fallacy, 569
reference works, 755
refutation, 561–62, 579, 791
relevance of evidence, 560
remote causes, 330, 341, 786
representativeness of evidence, 560
Requena, Louis, *Major League Baseball
  Brawl*, 344–5
research papers, 753
  documenting sources (MLA style)
    parenthetical references in text,
      767–69
      Works Cited list, 769–77
  drafting the essay, 765–67
  Internet resources, 756
  library resources, 754–56
  outlining, 764–65
  and plagiarism, 760–63
  sample student essay, 777–84
  taking notes, 757–60
  thesis statements, 763
  topic selection, 753–54
restrictive clauses, 72
revising, 53–58
  argumentative essays, 573, 580–81
  cause-and-effect essays, 336–37, 342
  classification and division essays,
    456–57, 462–63
  and combined patterns of develop-
    ment, 704–6, 710–11
  comparison and contrast essays,
    393–94, 400–401, 405–6
  definition essays, 514–15, 520
  descriptive essays, 156, 158
  exemplification essays, 208–9
  final draft, 62–65
  first draft, 58–61
  narrative essays, 87
  process essays, 271, 278–79, 281–82
rhetorical questions, 369, 502, 519, 616,
  791
Rodin, Auguste, *The Kiss,* 407–8
Rodriguez, Richard, "Strange Tools,"
  743–49
Rogerian argument, 562–63, 792
run-on sentences, 69, 88

"Sadie and Maud" (Brooks), 447–48
Safire, William, "The Threat of National ID," 614–17
"Samuel" (Paley), 262–66
Sanders, Scott Russell, "The Men We Carry in Our Minds," 481–86
sarcasm, 479
satire, 741, 792
"Search, The" (student essay), 274–79
search engines, 756
second drafts, 59–62
Segal, Carolyn Foster, "The Dog Ate My Disk, and Other Tales of Woe," 475–80
semicolons, 72, 88
sentence fragments, 69
sentences
    fused, 69, 88
    punctuation of, 69
    revising, 54
    style of, 74–75
sentence structure
    errors in, 88–89
    varying, 75, 85
"Sex, Lies, and Conversation" (Tannen), 440–46
sexist language, 792
shifts, avoiding unnecessary, 272–73
"Shooting an Elephant" (Orwell), 125–33
similes, 147, 710, 792
simple sentences, 75
situational irony, 789
"Sizing Up the Effects" (Bok), 671–77
slang, 27, 510, 792
Smith, Gayle Rosenwald, "The Wife-Beater," 532–35
Smith-Yackel, Bonnie, "My Mother Never Worked," 108–13
soundness (of arguments), 565
"Speaking Out" (student essay). See "Price of Silence, The"
spell checks, 78
Spider-Man (Marvel Comics), 94–95
stand, taking a, 557–58
Stanton, Elizabeth Cady, "Declaration of Sentiments and Resolutions, Seneca Falls, 1848," 590–96
Staples, Brent, "Just Walk On By: A Black Man Ponders His Power to Alter Public Space," 240–45

"Star-Spangled Stupidity" (Teresi), 246–51
statistics
    in introduction, 40
    misleading, 570
    sources for, 755
"Stigmatic Uniforms" (Fussell), 544–49
Stone, Oliver, "Memo to John Grisham: What's Next — 'A Movie Made Me Do It'?," 686–90
"Storm, The" (Chopin), 194–99
"Strange Tools" (Rodriguez), 743–49
straw man, creating a, 562
structure. See organization, methods of
student essays
    "Airport Insecurity" (research essay), 777–84
    "Argument against the Anna Todd Jennings Scholarship, An" (argument), 576–80
    "Brains versus Brawn" (comparison and contrast), 396–401
    "Building and Learning" (description), 153–56
    "Comparison of Two Web Sites on Attention Deficit Disorder, A" (comparison and contrast), 401–6
    "Irish Famine, 1845–1849, The" (cause-and-effect), 338–43
    letter of application (exemplification), 210–12
    "Medium Ash Brown" (process), 279–82
    "Midnight" (exemplification), 213–16
    "My Field of Dreams" (narration), 89–93
    "Park, The" (combined patterns), 707–11
    "Price of Silence, The" (drafting and revision example), 59–65
    "Search, The" (process), 274–79
    "Untouchable, The" (definition), 516–21
    "Valley of Windmills, The" (description), 156–59
    "What I Learned (and Didn't Learn) in College" (classification and division), 458–63

subject-by-subject comparison, 391–92, 399, 405, 792
subjective description, 146–48, 157–58, 731, 792
subject searches, 756
subject-verb agreement, 67–68, 705–6
subordinating conjunctions, 89, 574–75
sufficient evidence, 560–61
"Suicide Note" (Mirikitani), 382–84
summaries, 758–59, 792
    transitional words and phrases for, 43
support, 42–45
surprising statements, 40
sweeping generalizations, 566, 568
Swift, Jonathan, "A Modest Proposal," 733–42
"Swollen Expectations" (De Graaf, Wann, and Naylor), 425–33
syllogisms, 563–65, 667, 792
symbols, 792
synonyms, 413, 512, 530, 792

Tan, Amy, "Mother Tongue," 487–94
Tannen, Deborah, "Sex, Lies, and Conversation," 440–46
Tecson, Maria, "A Comparison of Two Web Sites on Attention Deficit Disorder," 401–6
"Television: The Plug-In Drug" (Winn), 351–60
tense (verb tense), 68
Teresi, Dick, "Star-Spangled Stupidity," 246–51
Thanks to Modern Science… (American Civil Liberties Union), 582–83
thesis statements, 793
    and invention (prewriting), 30–35
    patterns of development
        argumentative essays, 557–58
        cause-and-effect essays, 334, 335–36
        classification and division essays, 454, 461
        combined patterns, 710
        comparison and contrast essays, 390–91
        definition essays, 519
        descriptive essays, 150
        exemplification essays, 205–6, 207

narrative essays, 86
and research process, 763
revising, 54
"Thirty-Eight Who Saw Murder Didn't Call the Police" (Gansberg), 120–24
"Threat of National ID, The" (Safire), 614–17
time, transitional words and phrases for, 43, 86, 92, 270, 278, 281, 710
title, 54–55
    revising, 62
topic selection, 20–25, 753–54
    argumentative essays, 557
topic sentences, 793
    comparison and contrast essays, 400, 405
"Tortillas" (Burciaga), 528–31
Toulmin logic, 566–67, 793
"Traditional Mother and Father: Still the Best Choice for Children" (Adkins), 625–29
transitional paragraphs, 393, 399–400
transitional words and phrases, 42–43, 88, 793
    for argumentation, 570–71
    between categories, 454–55, 461–62
    for causes and effects, 334, 341
    for comparison and contrast, 393, 399–400, 405
    for examples, 207
    for spatial description, 149
    for time and order of events, 86, 92, 270, 278, 281, 710
Truong, Michael Huu, "The Park," 707–11
truth value (of arguments), 565
Tuan, Yi-Fu, "Chinese Space, American Space," 421–24
tu quoque fallacy (you also), 569
"Two Ways to Belong in America" (Mukherjee), 415–20
type size, 78
typographical errors, 77–78

underlining, 77
understatement, 793
undistributed terms, 564
unity, 793
    of body paragraphs, 41

unnecessary shifts, avoiding, 272–73
"Untouchable, The" (student essay),
     516–21
URLs (uniform resource locators), 756
U.S. Census 2000 Form (U.S. Census Bu-
     reau), 522–23

valid arguments, 564
"Valley of Windmills, The" (student
     essay), 156–59
verbs
  subject-verb agreement, 67–68
  voice and mood, 273
verb tense, 68, 85–86
  in narrative essays, 92
  shifts in, 272
"Violent Films Cry 'Fire' in Crowded
     Theaters" (Zimecki), 691–96
"Violent Media Is Good for Kids"
     (Jones), 678–85
visuals, 4, 78, 766
  and objective description, 145
voice, avoiding shifts in, 273

"War for Us, Fought by Them, A"
     (Broyles), 637–42
warrant (Toulmin logic), 567, 793
"Ways We Lie, The" (Ericsson),
     495–504
"Way to Rainy Mountain, The"
     (Momaday), 180–85
"What I Learned (and Didn't Learn) in
     College" (student essay), 458–63

"What Is a Weblog?" (Blood),
     536–43
"What's in a Name?" (Gates), 5–12
"What Work Is" (Levine), 550–52
White, E. B., "Once More to the Lake,"
     186–93
"Who Killed Benny Paret?" (Cousins),
     346–50
"Why Boys Don't Play with Dolls"
     (Pollitt), 361–65
"Why Fear National ID Cards?"
     (Dershowitz), 618–22
"Wife-Beater, The" (Smith),
     532–35
Winn, Marie, "Television: The Plug-In
     Drug," 351–60
Woolf, Virginia, "The Death of the
     Moth," 728–32
word choice, 76
"Words Left Unspoken" (Cohen),
     168–72

X, Malcolm, "My First Conk,"
     285–89

you also fallacy *(tu quoque)*, 569

Zimecki, Michael, "Violent Films Cry
     'Fire' in Crowded Theaters,"
     691–96
Zinsser, William, "College Pressures,"
     466–74

Grammar in Context Boxes

Each rhetorical chapter introduction contains a Grammar in Context box that offers advice about a common grammar, punctuation, or mechanics issue—one often associated with the pattern discussed in the chapter. Refer to the list below to find Grammar in Context boxes throughout *Patterns*.

Avoiding Run-On Sentences   88

Avoiding Misplaced and Dangling Modifiers   151

Using Commas in a Series   209

Avoiding Unnecessary Shifts   272

Avoiding "The reason is because"; Using *Affect* and *Effect* Correctly   337

Using Parallelism   394

Using a Colon to Introduce Your Categories   457

Avoiding *is when* and *is where*   515

Using Coordinating and Subordinating Conjunctions   574

Agreement with Indefinite Pronouns   705

Want to see what else *Patterns for College Writing* has to offer?

Visit our companion Web site

bedfordstmartins.com/patterns

The companion Web site for *Patterns for College Writing* is designed to help you get more out of the book, especially when it comes time to write papers.

- **TopLinks** is a database of links to reliable Web sites related to the readings and topics in the book. Each link has a brief annotation.

- **Author Research** offers access to annotated links for further research on authors whose writing appears in *Patterns*.

- **Reading Quizzes** for each essay in the book test comprehension skills. You can see your scores immediately.

- **Debate Topics** offers a list of annotated links for further research on debates that appear in current and past editions of *Patterns*; **Internet Assignments** from the end of each chapter conveniently appear online as well.

- **Peer Editing Worksheets** and **Grammar in Context boxes** are downloadable from the Web site.

- **Exercise Central**, the largest online collection of free editing exercises available, helps you to improve your grammar and usage skills; you can see your scores immediately.